Business in the Canadian Environment

Seventh Edition

Peter H. Fuhrman

Open University
Burnaby, British Columbia

Prentice
Hall

Toronto

Canadian Cataloguing in Publication Data

Fuhrman, Peter H. (Peter Harry), 1942–

7th ed.
Includes index.
ISBN 0-13-089773-6

1. Business enterprises.   2. Industrial management.   3. Business enterprises – Canada.   I. Title.

HF3224.F83 2001   338.7   C00-932064-4

0-13-089773-6

Vice President, Editorial Director: Michael Young
Acquisitions Editor: Samantha Scully
Marketing Manager: James Buchanan
Associate Editor: Pamela Voves
Production Editor: Marisa D'Andrea
Copy Editor: Dianne Broad
Production Coordinator: Deborah Starks
Page Layout: Debbie Kumpf and Anne Mac Innis
Photo Research: Susan Wallace-Cox
Art Director: Mary Opper
Interior Design: Alex Li
Cover Design: Alex Li
Cover Image: PhotoDisc Photography

1 2 3 4 5   05 04 03 02 01

Printed and bound in Canada.

To my mother and to the memory of my father.

P.H.F.

Table of Contents

PREFACE   XV

PART ONE

The Foundations of Business   1

CHAPTER 1
The Canadian Business System   2

OUR WAY OF LIFE   3
   Standard of Living and Production   4
   Factors of Production   5
   Raising the Standard of Living   7

BUSINESS   9
   Article: Overview of the Economy   9
   Business and Economics   10
   Business Cycles   10

ECONOMIC SYSTEMS   11
   How Economic Systems Differ   12
   The Historical Roots of Capitalism and Socialism   12
   Capitalism, Communism and Democratic Socialism:
      An Overview   14

DEVELOPMENT OF THE CANADIAN
   BUSINESS SYSTEM   16
   The National Policy   16
   The Golden Age of Canadian Growth   17
   From the Depression to the End of World War II   17
   Government Intervenes in the Economy   18
   A New Government Philosophy   19
   Keynes and the New Economics   19

CAPITALISM IN CANADA   20
   Private Property   20
   Freedom of Choice   20
   Freedom of Competition   21
   Freedom from Government Interference   21

PROFIT, COMPETITION AND THE MARKET   22
   What is Profit?   22
   Profit as an Incentive   22

Profit as a Measure of Efficiency and Effectiveness   23
Profit for Expansion and Capital Formation   23
Profit as a Return to Investors   23
Profits as a Contribution to Society   23
Why Are Profits High?   24
How Canadians View Profits   24
Do Businesses Attempt to Maximize Profits?   25

COMPETITION AND THE MARKET   25
   Effective and Responsible Competition   27
   Types of Competition   27

WHY STUDY BUSINESS?   29

CHAPTER SUMMARY   30

KEY TERMS   32

REVIEW QUESTIONS   32

DISCUSSION QUESTIONS   33

CASE 1-1 WORLD POPULATION AND THE STANDARD
   OF LIVING   34

CASE 1-2 PROFIT AND TAXATION   36

CHAPTER 2
Starting and Operating a Small Business   37

CANADA TODAY   38

SMALL BUSINESS IN CANADA   38

PROBLEMS FACED BY SMALL BUSINESS OWNERS   41
   Lack of Management Skills   41
   Inadequate Financing   41
   Government Regulations   42
   Taxes   42
   Mismanagement Main Cause of
      New Ventures Failure   43
   Requirements of Business Success   43
   Acquiring a Business Education   44
   Careful Planning   44
   Careful Money Management   44
   Keeping Accurate Records   44
   Effective Marketing   44

Time Management   45
Acquiring Human Resources   45
Growing with the Business   45

GOING INTO BUSINESS FOR YOURSELF   46
How Do You Avoid Failure?   46
Evaluating Business Opportunities   47
Availability of Existing Businesses   47
Buying an Established Business   48
Starting a New Business   50
Franchising   50
Article: Buying a Franchise or Starting Your Own
   Business   52
Factors to Consider When Buying a Franchise   52
Article: Is Franchising Really a Safe Bet?   54

THE HOME BUSINESS   54
Setting Up the Home Office   55
Canada Customs and Revenue Agency   56
Renovating the Home Office   56
Financing   57
Office Equipment   57
Communications   58
Insurance and Security   59
Motivation and Discipline   60

THE BUSINESS PLAN   61
Establishing Your Business's Objectives   61
Planning the Market Approach   61
Selecting the Location   62
Determining the Physical Facilities   62
Planning for the Financing   62
Human-Resource Planning   62
Legal Requirements   63
Setting Up the Business Plan   64

FINANCING A NEW BUSINESS   64
Determine What You Need   64
Types of Capital   64
Sources of Equity Financing   65
Sources of Debt Financing   65
Business Development Bank   66

CHAPTER SUMMARY   66

KEY TERMS   68

REVIEW QUESTIONS   68

DISCUSSION QUESTIONS   69

CASE 2-1 BUYING A VIDEO FRANCHISE   70

COMPREHENSIVE CASES 2-2
   SOMERSET OPTICAL   72

CHAPTER 3
Forms of Business Ownership   74

FORMS OF PRIVATE BUSINESS OWNERSHIP   75
Sole Proprietorship   75
Partnership   78
Article: How Important is a Partnership
   Agreement?   80
The Corporation   80
Article: Should You Incorporate Yourself?   84
Article: General Information Required
   for Incorporation   88
Article: How Corporate Governance Is Changing   92

FACTORS TO CONSIDER WHEN CHOOSING A FORM OF
   BUSINESS OWNERSHIP   95
The Need for Limited Liability   96
Availability of Financial Resources   96
The Need for a Variety of Management Skills   96
Other Considerations   97

MEMBER OWNERSHIP: THE COOPERATIVE   97

CHAPTER SUMMARY   99

KEY TERMS   100

REVIEW QUESTIONS   100

DISCUSSION QUESTIONS   101

CASE 3-1 DECIDING ON A FORM OF BUSINESS
   OWNERSHIP   102

COMPREHENSIVE CASE 3-2 SOMERSET OPTICAL   104

VIDEO CASE—PART 1: BEER MITTS   105   CBC ◉

PART TWO

Business and Management   106

CHAPTER 4
Management, Planning and Controlling   107

WHAT IS MANAGEMENT?   108
The Importance of Management   108
The Functions of Management   109
Levels of Management   111
Managerial Skills   112

What Is a Manager's Job? An Alternative View   114
Managers and Decision Making   115

PLANNING AND MANAGEMENT   115
Article: A New Manifesto for Management   116
The Need for Planning   116
Flexibility in Planning   116
Types of Plans   117
Long- and Short-Range Planning   117
Elements of Planning   118
Article: Canadian Pacific Railway: A Company That
    Redefined Its Mission   119
Article: How Wisconsin Central Is Practising
    Its Mission Statement   120
The Planning Process   123
Article: Strategic Planning and Small Business   124
Article: Strategic Management   126
Article: Hickson Moves into a Recovery Strategy   127

PLANNING AND CONTROLLING   127
The Process of Control   127
Article: Total Quality Management—
    Does It Work?   128
Control Techniques   129
Management Information Systems (MIS)   131

COMPUTERS IN BUSINESS   131
Data Gathering and Information Processing   132
Mainframes, Minicomputers and
    Microcomputers   133
How Managers Can Use Computers   134
Choosing Software, Hardware and Vendors   138
Article: What Is the Internet?   139

CHAPTER SUMMARY   140

KEY TERMS   141

REVIEW QUESTIONS   142

DISCUSSION QUESTIONS   143

CASE 4-1 PLANNING—WHO NEEDS IT?   144

CASE 4-2 TYLLER GORMAN & SONS MOVING
    AND STORAGE   146

COMPREHENSIVE CASE 4-3 SOMERSET OPTICAL   147

CHAPTER 5
Organizing for Management   149

THE FORMAL ORGANIZATION   150
Organization Charts   150
The Informal Organization   151

The Importance of Organizing   151
The Relationship Between Planning
    and Organizing   153

BUILDING AN ORGANIZATIONAL STRUCTURE   154
The Organizing Function of Managers   156
The Organizing Process   156

HORIZONTAL DIVISION OF LABOUR:
    DEPARTMENTATION   157
Functional Departmentation   158
Product and Geographic Departmentation   158
Project and Matrix Structures   159
Other Types of Departmentation   161
Combining Methods of Departmentation   163

VERTICAL DIVISION OF LABOUR: ESTABLISHING
    AUTHORITY RELATIONSHIPS   163
Influence, Authority and Power   164
Types of Authority   165
Delegation   168
Article: Whistle-blowing and Organizational
    Structure   170
Chain of Command   171
Span of Control   171
Decentralization and Centralization   173

COMMITTEES   173

Article: Two Radical Steps Can Save Hours of
    Time Spent in Meetings   175

THE NEXT EVOLUTIONARY STEP   176

THE VIRTUAL ORGANIZATION...
    TO BE OR NOT TO BE?   177

CHAPTER SUMMARY   178

KEY TERMS   179

REVIEW QUESTIONS   179

DISCUSSION QUESTIONS   180

CASE 5-1 THE GREENPEACE FOUNDATION
    AT 20   181

CASE 5-2 SURPRISE, SURPRISE!   183

COMPREHENSIVE CASE 5-3 SOMERSET OPTICAL   184

CHAPTER 6
Managing People   186

MOTIVATION   187
How to Motivate People   187

Classical Theory of Motivation 187
Human Relations and Elton Mayo 188
Maslow's Need Hierarchy 189
Article: Goals and Needs 191
Herzberg's Motivation-Hygiene Theory 192
McGregor's Theory X and Theory Y 194
Issue: Money, Recognition and Other Rewards 195

LEADERSHIP 196
Theories of Leadership 196
Matching the Leadership Style with the Situation 201
Article: Visionary Leadership 202
Criteria for Choosing Leaders 202
Japanese Management Techniques 203

COMMUNICATION 204
Problems with Communication 204
Overcoming Barriers to Effective Communication 205
Improving Listening Skills 206
E-mail and Communicating in the 21st Century 206

MORALE 207
Article: Getting the Message: How to Make Sure
You're Understood 208
Morale, Job Satisfaction and Productivity 209
Article: Building Morale in Tough Times 210

REDESIGNING WORK 211
Article: Weyerhauser's Intranet System Opens the Door
to Profits 211

MANAGEMENT BY OBJECTIVES 211
The MBO Process 212
Article: MBO: Is It Yesterday's News? 213
Benefits of MBO 213
Problems with MBO 213

CHAPTER SUMMARY 213

KEY TERMS 215

REVIEW QUESTIONS 215

DISCUSSION QUESTIONS 216

CASE 6-1 THE DEVIL WOULD KNOW! 217

CASE 6-2 THE PAINTED MEANING OF LIFE 218

COMPREHENSIVE CASE 6-3 SOMERSET OPTICAL 219

PART THREE

The Business Functions 221

CHAPTER 7
Production and Operations Management 223

THE PRODUCTION FUNCTION 224
Mass Production and Technology 225
Custom Production 226
The Job Shop 227

ORGANIZATION OF THE PRODUCTION
DEPARTMENT 227

DESIGNING PRODUCTION/OPERATIONS
SYSTEMS 229
Product/Service Planning and Design 229
Production Processes 229
Capacity Planning 230
Plant Location 231
Plant Layout 233
Work System Design 236

OPERATING PRODUCTION DECISIONS 237
Demand Forecasting 237
Inventory Management 238
Distribution Planning 245
Production Planning and Control 246
Article: Just-in-Time Inventory 250
Purchasing 253
Quality Control 254
Maintenance 256
Project Management 256

COMPUTERS IN PRODUCTION 257
Computers and Automation 259
CAD/CAM, Robots and the Automated Factory 259

CHAPTER SUMMARY 263

KEY TERMS 265

REVIEW QUESTIONS 266

DISCUSSION QUESTIONS 267

CASE 7-1 MARTIN'S QUICK OIL
CHANGE LIMITED 267

CASE 7-2 PACIFIC BOAT WORKS 268

COMPREHENSIVE CASE 7-3 SOMERSET OPTICAL 270

CHAPTER 8
Marketing Management 272

THE IMPORTANCE OF MARKETING   273

THE FUNCTIONS OF MARKETING   273

THE MARKETING CONCEPT   275
Marketing Research   275
Marketing Strategy   276
Article: The Four P's of Marketing   278
Consumer and Industrial Markets   278
Article: Segmenting the Market for a Video
Disc Player   279
Article: Differences Getting Too Much Attention   282

CREATING THE PRODUCT   283
Product Mix and Product Line   283
Product Planning and Development   283
Branding, Packaging and Labelling   286

PRICING THE PRODUCT   288
Pricing Strategies   288
Pricing Approaches   289

PROMOTING THE PRODUCT   292
Promotional Mix   292
Advertising   293
Marketing on the Net   294
Personal Selling   296
Sales Promotion   297
Publicity   298

DISTRIBUTING THE PRODUCT   298
Channels of Distribution for Consumer Goods   299
Channels of Distribution for Industrial Goods   300
Wholesalers   300
Retailers   301
Article: Big Box Store Growth Will Continue   305
Physical Distribution   305

CHAPTER SUMMARY   305

KEY TERMS   307

REVIEW QUESTIONS   307

DISCUSSION QUESTIONS   308

CASE 8-1 DIGITAL VIDEO DISC:
SUCCESS FINALLY   309

CASE 8-2 THE BOTTOMFEEDER   310

COMPREHENSIVE CASE 8-3 SOMERSET OPTICAL   311

CHAPTER 9
Accounting and Financial Management 313

THE FUNCTION OF THE FINANCE DEPARTMENT   314

ENSURING FINANCIAL SOLVENCY   314
Working Capital and the Cash Budget   315
Short-Term Borrowing   316
Sources of Short-Term Funds   316
Loans from Chartered Banks and Other Financial
Institutions   319
Acquiring Funds through Factoring   321
Loans from Finance Companies   321
Loans from Investors and Other Businesses   322
Sources of Funds from the Federal Government   322

CONTROLLING FINANCIAL OPERATIONS   322
Accounting and Bookkeeping   323
Financial Accounting   323
The Accounting Process   323
Accounting Statements   323
Financial Analysis   330
Forecasting and Budgeting   336
Break-Even Analysis   340

ACQUIRING LONG-TERM FUNDS   342
Types of Corporate Securities   343
Article: What Is a Dividend Tax Credit?   347
Choosing the Type of Security to Issue   348
Marketing Corporate Securities   350
The Securities Markets   351
Article: Trading Stocks on the Internet   354

CHAPTER SUMMARY   355

KEY TERMS   356

REVIEW QUESTIONS   357

DISCUSSION QUESTIONS   358

CASE 9-1 RAISING MONEY FOR PUBLISHING   358

CASE 9-2 PRAIRIE INDUSTRIAL CORPORATION   360

COMPREHENSIVE CASE 9-3 SOMERSET OPTICAL   362

CHAPTER 10
Human Resource Management 364

HUMAN RESOURCE MANAGEMENT   365
Human Resources: A Staff Department   365
Human Resource Planning   367

Job Analysis, Job Specification and
Job Description   368

ACQUIRING AND TRAINING HUMAN RESOURCES   370
Article: How Do RODs Affect Organizations?   370
Recruiting Job Candidates   373
Selecting the New Employee   375
Human-Rights Legislation and Employment
Discrimination   375
Article: The Defensive Approach to Hiring   377
Employee Orientation   379
Article: Do's and Don'ts at the Job Interview   380
Employee Training and Development   381
Article: Training Supervisors—On and
Off the Job   384

WAGE AND SALARY ADMINISTRATION   384
Establishing Wages and Salaries   384
Methods of Compensation   386
Article: Setting Wage Rates—A Problem for Small
Business   387
Article: Profit-Sharing, Productivity and More   389
Employee Benefits   390

HEALTH AND SAFETY   392
Article: What is the True Cost of an Employee?   393
Organizations Concerned with Health and Safety   395

EMPLOYEE EVALUATION   395

CAREER DEVELOPMENT   396

PROMOTION, TRANSFER AND SEPARATION   396
Promotion   396
Transfer   397
Separation   397

CHAPTER SUMMARY   398

KEY TERMS   400

REVIEW QUESTIONS   400

DISCUSSION QUESTIONS   401

CASE 10-1 TREES AND LEAVES   402

CASE 10-2 TEMGLOW   403

COMPREHENSIVE CASE 10-3 SOMERSET
OPTICAL   404

VIDEO CASE—PART 3: OVERBRANDING   405 **CBC** ⊕

PART FOUR

Business and Its Environment   406

CHAPTER 11
Business and Labour   407

AIMS OF MANAGEMENT AND LABOUR   408
Aims of Management   408
Aims of Labour   409

WHAT IS A LABOUR UNION?   409

LOOKING BACK: THE CANADIAN LABOUR
MOVEMENT   409
Article: The Winnipeg General Strike   413
The Canadian Labour Congress   413
Major Labour Legislation in Canada   415
Federal Labour Legislation   415

THE UNION PROCESS   416
Certification   417
Negotiation: Collective Bargaining   417
Conciliation and Mediation   419
Arbitration   420
Grievances   421

WHEN ALL ELSE FAILS   421
Weapons of Labour   422
Weapons of Management   423

BASIC ISSUES IN COLLECTIVE BARGAINING   423
Union Security   423
Wages and Employee Benefits   424
Hours of Work   424
Job Security and Promotion   425

LABOUR UNIONS IN CANADA TODAY   425

LABOUR-MANAGEMENT RELATIONS—SOME
CRITICAL ISSUES   427
The Adversarial Nature of Collective Bargaining   427
The Effectiveness of the Strike   428
Labour Disputes in Canada   428
Compulsory Arbitration   428
Labour in the Boardroom   428
Sharing Information and Management Credibility   429

CHAPTER SUMMARY   430

KEY TERMS   432

REVIEW QUESTIONS   432

DISCUSSION QUESTIONS   433

CASE 11-1 STRESSES AND STRAINS ON THE WAY TO
   GLORY   434

CASE 11-2 SHOULD GOVERNMENT EMPLOYEES
   BE ALLOWED TO STRIKE?   435

COMPREHENSIVE CASE 11-3 SOMERSET
   OPTICAL   437

CHAPTER 12
Business and Government   439

GOVERNMENT INVOLVEMENT IN THE CANADIAN
   ECONOMY: A HISTORICAL PERSPECTIVE   440

GOVERNMENT PROMOTION OF BUSINESS   441
   Protection from Foreign Competition   441
   Federal Industrial Development Incentives   443
   Article: How to Get Government Money   444
   Provincial Industrial Incentive Programs   444
   Agriculture and Natural Resource Development
      Incentives   444
   Other Federal Government Assistance   444
   Article: Other Federal Industrial Assistance
      Programs   445

GOVERNMENT CONTROL OF BUSINESS   447
   Regulation of Competition   448
   Issue: What Does Business Want—Competition
      Legislation or Government Regulation?   450
   Control of Retailing and Consumer Protection   450
   Control of Transportation   450
   The Canada Transportation Act   451
   Control of Communications   452
   Control of Public Utilities   454
   Government Ownership   454
   Control of Foreign Investment   456
   Article: Privatization   457

HOW GOVERNMENT IS FINANCED   458
   Types of Taxes   458
   Fiscal Policy   461
   Article: Taxation in Canada   462
   Monetary Policy and Its Effect on the Economy   464
   Article: Bank of Canada Services   466

GROWTH OF GOVERNMENT   468
   Financing Government Programs   469
   Government Rules and Regulations   472
   Article: Coming to Grips with Canada's
      National Debt   473

   What Should Government's Role Be?   474
      Article: An Industrial Strategy for Canada?   475

CHAPTER SUMMARY   476

KEY TERMS   477

REVIEW QUESTIONS   478

DISCUSSION QUESTIONS   478

CASE 12-1 CANADA POST REPORT DOESN'T
   DELIVER   479

COMPREHENSIVE CASE 12-2 SOMERSET
   OPTICAL   481

CHAPTER 13
International Business   482

WHY COUNTRIES TRADE WITH EACH OTHER   483
   Absolute and Comparative Advantage   484
   Canadian Foreign Trade   484

BARRIERS TO INTERNATIONAL TRADE   488
   Economic, Social and Cultural Barriers   489
   Legal and Political Barriers   490
   Tariff and Trade Restrictions   491

EFFORTS TO FACILITATE INTERNATIONAL TRADE   491
   International Agreements and Agencies   492
   Article: The Free Trade Debate   496
   Key Facts About the North American Free Trade
      Agreement   497
   Article: Interprovincial Trade Barriers   502
   Article: A European Free Trade Bloc   504
   Canadian Government Services and Programs   505
   Article: The IMF and the World Bank: How Do They
      Differ?   506

INTERNATIONAL FINANCE   509
   Balance of Trade   509
   Balance of Payments   510
   Currency Exchange   510

THE MULTINATIONAL CORPORATION (MNC)   513
   Characteristics of Multinational Corporations   515
   Evolution of the Multinational Corporation   515
   Managing the Multinational Corporation   515
   Advantages of Multinational Corporations   516
   Disadvantages of Multinational Corporations   517
   Foreign Investment in Canada   518
   Canadian Investment Abroad   522

CHAPTER SUMMARY   524

KEY TERMS   525

REVIEW QUESTIONS   526

DISCUSSION QUESTIONS   526

CASE 13-1 CANADA-U.S. CROSS-BORDER TRADE   527

CASE 13-2 THE CANADIAN DOLLAR'S ROLLER-COASTER RIDE   528

COMPREHENSIVE CASE 13-3 SOMERSET OPTICAL   529

CHAPTER 14
Social Responsibility and Business   530

WHAT IS SOCIAL RESPONSIBILITY?   531

LAWS, MORALS AND ETHICS   532

BUSINESS ETHICS   532

DOES BUSINESS HAVE A SOCIAL RESPONSIBILITY?   533
   The Case for Business Assuming Social Responsibility   533
   The Case Against Business Assuming Social Responsibility   534

SOCIAL OR PUBLIC ISSUES   535
   Business and Shareholders   535
   Business and Employees   536
   Business and Consumers   537
   Business and the Community   538
   Article: Joint Effort Only Way to Win   542
   Conservation of Energy and Resources   544
   Article: Types of Pollution   544
   Responsibility to Education and the Arts   545

ETHICAL ISSUES   545
   Employment Discrimination   545
   Relations with Labour Unions   546
   Acceptance of Voluntary Government Restraints   546
   Responsibility to Developing Countries   546
   Article: A Study in Ethics—The Body Shop International   547
   Article: A New View of Ethics   547

MANAGEMENT PHILOSOPHY   548

MEASURING SOCIAL RESPONSIBILITY   549
   Parameters of Social Behaviour   549

The Social and Environmental Audit   549
   Article: New Auditors Monitor Firms' Environmental Liability   550

WHERE DO BUSINESS AND SOCIETY STAND TODAY?   551

CHAPTER SUMMARY   551

KEY TERMS   552

REVIEW QUESTIONS   553

DISCUSSION QUESTIONS   553

CASE 14-1 WAGHORNER PHOTOGRAPHIC PROCESSORS INC.   554

CASE 14-2 THE SMELL OF OLD FISH   554

COMPREHENSIVE CASE 14-3 SOMERSET OPTICAL   556

PART FIVE

Business in Canada: The Future   557

CHAPTER 15
Business, the Future and Your Career   559

A WORD ABOUT PREDICTING THE FUTURE   560
   Change, Change, Change   560
   Methods of Predicting the Future   560

MAJOR CHANGES BASED ON CURRENT TRENDS   561
   Article: Canada in 2030—The Sustainable Scenario   561
   Article: Demographic—How Does It Rate as a Forecasting Tool?   562
   Population Changes   563
   Lifestyle Changes   564
   Article: Grim Projections for Canada's Population   565
   Article: Lifestyle of the Future— Some Projections   566
   Economic Changes   567
   Technological Changes   568

OUR FUTURE CANADIAN BUSINESS SYSTEM   569

THE MANAGER OF THE FUTURE   570

YOUR CAREER IN BUSINESS   572
   Going into Business for Yourself   572
   Joining a Small Company   572
   Joining a Large Company   573
   Choosing a Career   573
   Knowing What You Want to Do   574
   Finding Your Job: Beginning a Career Plan   575
   The Job Search Process   575
   Article: The Tailored Résumé   580
   Article: Résumé Checklist   580
   Article: Tips on Interview Dress and Behaviour   582
   Finding Your Job on the Internet   583

CHAPTER SUMMARY   583

KEY TERMS   584

REVIEW QUESTIONS   584

DISCUSSION QUESTIONS   585

CASE 15-1 THE AGING NATION   586

CASE 15-2 MAKING AN IMPACT IN YOUR FIRST JOB   586

COMPREHENSIVE CASE 15-3 SOMERSET OPTICAL   588

VIDEO CASE—PART 5: NORTEL VS CISCO; EMG   589   **CBC** ⊕

NOTES   590

INDEX   595

PHOTO CREDITS   603

Preface

Perhaps the most significant technological innovation affecting us at the beginning of the 21st century is the Internet. You have undoubtedly heard stories of individuals who, with nothing more than an Internet domain name, became multimillionaires virtually overnight. Share prices sometimes rose tenfold in a single day as people, fearful of missing out on huge capital gains, bought the newly-issued stock of a dot-com company at any price. But when expected sales and profits of the e-business didn't materialize, reason began to prevail and the subsequent drop in the share prices of these Internet companies resulted in the loss of billions of dollars. This experience shows us that a business must be established on a sound financial basis and managed in a proper manner for it to succeed.

Undoubtedly, the Internet and other technological changes will continue to impact business, and our lifestyle, in the foreseeable future. Those companies and individuals that use the Internet as a tool to promote and sell products, and gather information for their businesses, will surely reap great rewards. Nevertheless, proper management of people and resources is just as important as it was in the pre-Internet age.

Today, Canada remains a land of opportunity, in part because of its rich natural resources and educated population. But just as a business must be managed properly, so must a country. In retrospect, many now believe that during the three decades prior to the turn of the century, the federal and provincial governments made some serious mistakes in governing Canada. Their "borrow and spend" philosophies resulted in high inflation that eroded the purchasing power of Canadians and created a huge national debt, which now swallows 40 per cent of government revenues per year. It has also devalued the Canadian currency, allowing the purchase of Canadian assets at fire-sale prices.

As global competition increases, Canadian companies become less efficient—it is primarily the low value of the Canadian dollar that allows many Canadian companies to sell in the world market. Although high inflation was finally brought under control and yearly deficits were turned into surpluses, the "brain drain" phenomenon and our high levels of taxation are now of great concern. Many skilled Canadians are lured to the U.S. by lower levels of taxation and the promise of high salaries. This is particularly critical to Canada's healthcare system which, along with limited funding, is threatening to collapse at a time when Canada's aging population depends on it most.

The aforementioned are only some of the issues facing Canadians. *Business in the Canadian Environment*, Seventh Edition, presents the basics of business and management in a stimulating way. At the same time, it illustrates the issues that managers face vis-a-vis labour unions, government, the international environment and society as a whole. Starting and/or managing a profitable business in such an environment can be a daunting experience.

Suggestions received from previous users of *Business in the Canadian Environment* have been incorporated into this edition; the material has been updated, but still retains the structure of the previous editions. Video cases pertinent to each part of the book have also been updated.

Organization

Although this text is an introduction to business, its aim is to be a useful reference that can be kept on the shelf and consulted time and time again. An overriding concern has always been to ensure that readers get a good overview, are guided logically, and are ultimately led to understand the principles and concepts that underlie the subject. To this end, *Business in the Canadian Environment*, Seventh Edition, is organized to present the various aspects of business in a logical manner, as outlined by the Plan of this Book diagram.

Chapter 1 in Part One, "Foundations of Business," examines how the Canadian business system works and how it compares to other economic systems in the world. Chapter 2 looks at small business in some detail, specifically the requirements for starting and operating a business and the factors that contribute to its success. Particular emphasis is placed on the start-up and operation of a home business. In Chapter 3, the forms of business ownership, how to incorporate, and how corporations are governed once they grow large are examined.

Part Two, "Business and Management," examines the role of managers and their importance in the effective operation of any organization. The three chapters in this section provide a comprehensive picture of the functions of management—planning, controlling, organizing and leading people in order to achieve organizational goals. The use of computers by managers in their daily decision making is also discussed.

Part Three, "The Business Functions," looks at the four functional areas of business: operations management, marketing, finance and human resources. Each chapter in this section focuses on one of these basic functions, along with the major responsibilities of managers and the problems they are most likely to encounter. As it is essential to understand the interdependence of these functions, emphasis is placed on the cooperation between production and marketing in producing goods and services with the aid of financial and human resources.

Part Four, "Business and Its Environment," examines the relationship between business organizations and other groups in society. Since one-third of all Canadian workers belong to labour unions, the relationship between unions and business is discussed. This section also examines the relationship between business and government—how government regulates business on the one hand, and how it provides financial incentives and services to encourage business growth and economic expansion on the other. Since almost one-quarter of everything Canadians produce is sold to people living in other countries, international business, and in particular the various trade agreements, both external and internal, are discussed. The last chapter in Part Four looks at the responsibility of business to society, with a major focus on business ethics and the new environmental consciousness. Why is it near the end of the book? In the author's opinion, those studying the book have a better appreciation of the meaning of business' responsibility to society after they have gained a thorough understanding of the forces acting on managers in their daily tasks, as they attempt to run profitable businesses.

Finally, Part Five, "Business in Canada: The Future," takes a brief look at the influences responsible for our rapidly changing world. The more accurately management can forecast changes to the environment and the quicker it can respond to these changes, the more assured it will be of survival. The last section in Chapter 15 provides an important overview of career planning, particularly for people entering the job market from a college or university program. It also provides practical advice on how to search for a job.

Special Features

The emphasis of *Business in the Canadian Environment*, Seventh Edition, is on providing a thorough overview of how business operates, as well as how it interacts with society and other nations. Students are introduced to business vocabulary and the basic principles and practices involved in the management of any organization. To clarify difficult concepts, illustrations are used wherever possible. Other important features of the text include:

- Objectives: Each chapter begins with Learning Objectives—the concepts and ideas students should know and explain. The summary at the end of the chapter is tied to these objectives.

- Key Terms: Wherever an essential term is introduced in the text, it is printed in boldface and defined in the margin. To assist review, a list of Key Terms with page references appears at the end of every chapter. In the Index, boldface is used to identify the page on which a Key Term is defined.

- Issues: Short sections under the heading "Issues" are interspersed throughout the text. These sections raise topics for class discussion, encouraging students' awareness of the complexities involved in the topic and the need for careful examination of all sides in any debate.

- Internet resources: In order to help students take advantage of the dynamic resources available on the Internet, Weblinks for key sites appear in the margins of the text.

- Chapter-ending materials: Chapter Summary, Key Terms, Review Questions, and Discussion Questions are among the pedagogical features included at the end of each chapter.

- Case Studies: Two short case studies are positioned at the end of most chapters. These cases have been updated to reflect the latest issues in business.

- Comprehensive Case Study: The Somerset Optical case study, in units located at the ends of Chapters 2 through 15, enables readers to follow the activities of a single business enterprise as it confronts the various issues and problems presented in each of the chapters.

- CBC Video Cases: The textbook contains three video cases based on segments from the CBC's highly-acclaimed business series *Venture*. Each video case includes questions to generate class discussion or individual analysis.

Supplements

The purpose of this textbook is to make the study of business interesting for the student. This aim, in turn, makes it easier for the instructor. In addition, the following supplements are offered to support instructors in their preparation, classroom presentations, and testing.

- **Instructor's Resource Manual with Video Guide**: The Instructor's Resource Manual is based on the text's learning objectives and helps to focus the instructor's lecture. The manual provides course goals and a suggested course outline for a 15-week course. Each chapter contains an outline of the headings and learning objectives, teaching suggestions, lecture notes, and answer material. The teaching suggestions are primarily designed for instructors new to this course and suggest how to use the figures and tables shown in the text and how to present cases, articles, and issues to make lectures interesting and meaningful. The lecture notes are based on the learning objectives and provide extensive detail on the topics discussed. The answer section includes answers to review questions, comments on discussion questions, and suggested answers to the cases and CBC video cases. (ISBN 0-13-090144-X)

- **Test Item File**: This comprehensive test bank contains over 2300 questions, including true/false, multiple choice, fill-in-the-blank, short answer and essay questions. Answers and suggested answers are included. (ISBN 0-13-090145-8)

- **WIN PEC Custom Test**: Pearson Education Canada's computerized Test Item File uses a state-of-the-art software program that provides fast, simple, and error-free test generation in a Windows format. Entire tests can be previewed on-screen before printing. PEC Custom Test can print multiple variations of the same test, scrambling the order of questions and multiple-choice answers. Tests can be saved to ASCII format and revised in the instructor's word-processing system. (ISBN 0-13-090146-6)

CBC ⊛

- **CBC/Pearson Education Canada Video Library**: In an exclusive partnership, the CBC and Pearson Education Canada have worked together to develop the best and most comprehensive Canadian video package available in the college market. Seven segments from the prestigious series *Venture* provide students with the opportunity to apply the concepts they learn in the text to real-world issues and challenges. The video clips are an average of seven minutes long. (Please contact your Pearson Education Canada sales representative for details. These videos are subject to availability and terms negotiated upon adoption of the text.)(ISBN 0-13-090142-3)

- **Transparency Resource Package**: The Electronic Transparencies supplement enhances classroom presentation by providing key figures, tables and charts from the text in PowerPoint format. (ISBN 0-13-090147-4)

Acknowledgments

I am indebted to colleagues and students who have helped in the continuing development of this book. Particular thanks go to the reviewers who provided comments and suggestions for this edition, including: Victoria Digby, Fanshawe College; Glenn D. Coltman, Acadia University; David Parker, George Brown College; and Drew Evans, Red River College.

I would also like to thank Shirley Rose, Mount Royal University, for helping me to update seven chapters of the book. Her careful reading of the chapters and insertion of new material where necessary will enhance the learning experience for students.

Finally, I would also like to thank the many people at Pearson Education Canada who have contributed their time and skills to this book, especially Samantha Scully, Lisa Marshall, Marisa D'Andrea and Dianne Broad. Their help and attention to detail are very much appreciated.

Peter H. Fuhrman
bce@dccnet.com
www.businessincanada.com

The Plan of this Book

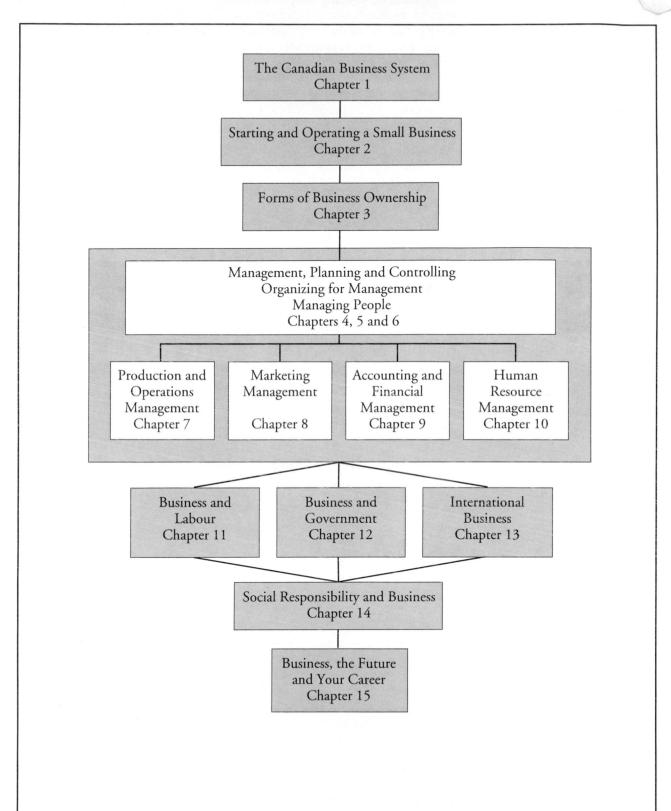

The Foundations of Business

Human beings are generally industrious and most strive to improve their lot in life. Unfortunately, many people lack the ability or the knowledge to convert resources into useful goods for production or consumption. In many countries, people do not have the freedom to do as they please. For some, living conditions are so fragile that a natural disaster, such as a flood or drought, is enough to destroy not only the few possessions they manage to acquire but also their means to feed themselves. Living at the subsistence level is the fate of millions of people on this earth, and their opportunity to improve their way of life is virtually hopeless.

Production is the key to prosperity. But the goods and services that are produced must be useful and must meet the needs of consumers. Basically, choices must be made in determining what to produce, how to produce it and how to distribute the goods and services among the people. To make these decisions, different countries have adopted different systems.

In Chapter 1, we examine how a country's economic system attempts to meet the requirements of its population for goods and services. We look at some key concepts—capital, profit, competition, the market system—and how they affect Canada's economic system. We also consider the role of business organizations in economic systems. In the Appendix we trace the development of business and the Canadian economy over the past 150 years.

In Chapter 2, we look at how to start a new business, and purchasing an existing business. We also consider the advantages and disadvantages of purchasing a franchise or, alternatively, starting a home-based business. Finally, we look at financing and business plans.

In Chapter 3, we consider the characteristics, advantages and disadvantages of each of the three private forms of business ownership and how to incorporate a business. A brief look at cooperatives ends the chapter.

1

The Canadian Business System

Learning Objectives

After reading this chapter, you will be able to

1 Explain how the standard of living in a given country is affected by the total population and the amount of goods and services it can produce.

2 List the five factors of production and indicate how they contribute to the gross national product.

3 Identify what business organizations are, and how they contribute to the production of goods and services.

4 Discuss the three basic functions of an economic system.

5 Name the three major economic systems and describe the differences between them.

6 Identify the principles underlying capitalism.

7 Explain how capitalism in Canada differs from pure capitalism.

8 Explain the role of profit and competition in the capitalistic business system in Canada.

9 Explain how profit and competition act as regulators to ensure that consumers receive the best possible product at the lowest possible price.

10 Recognize why it is important to know how business in general—and the Canadian business system in particular—operates.

Our Way of Life

Canadians cannot possibly imagine the poverty that still exists in underdeveloped countries. For example, in Calcutta, one of India's largest cities, an estimated 600 000 people live in the streets, drink contaminated water and depend for their food on the roughly 2000 tonnes of garbage that litter the streets. More than 70% of the city's people live at or below the poverty line, calculated as an income of less than $8 a month. The average earnings of a family of five are $34 per month. For at least 200 000 people, begging is the only source of income.[1] Similar conditions exist in many Asian and South American countries where tar-paper shacks and lean-tos are part of the suburban landscape of many large cities. And how can Canadians really understand that more than two billion people live in a continual state of hunger? In excess of 3.5 million people worldwide die of starvation each year.

There is no equivalent to Calcutta on this continent. Granted, even in Canada and the United States there are people who have no homes and go hungry most of the time. However, government programs exist to look after these people if they choose to take advantage of them. In 1997, the average Canadian family had an income of $57 146 per year. The family lives in a six-room suburban house, with most modern conveniences, and owns a fairly well-equipped car. Although that income does not allow for extravagant spending, the average Canadian family does have all the necessities and the time for leisure activities.

In Canada we define low-income families as those whose basic expenditures for food, clothing and shelter amount to 55% of their income. In 1997, this low-income cutoff (LICO) for a family of four in Canada was approximately $31 430. Of course, what we class as a low-or poverty-income in Canada would be considered undreamed-of luxury by many people in other parts of the world. Few Canadians die of starvation; private and government agencies ensure that those in need are provided with at least the basic necessities of life. Simple diseases are routinely cured and we generally live to old age.

< More than 70% of the people living in Calcutta, India, live at or below the poverty line

Standard of Living and Production

To understand why life is so much better in Canada than in many other countries, we must examine a country's ability to produce goods and services. We can express the relationship between the **standard of living** and what a country can produce by the following equation:

$$\text{Standard of living} = \frac{\text{Production}}{\text{Population}}$$

Standard of living (per capita GNP) depends directly on the amount of goods and services produced and the number of people that must share them.

Gross national product (GNP) is the final value of all the goods and services produced in a country over a given period.

Per capita GNP is equal to the gross national product divided by the population.

Gross national income (GNI) is calculated by adding the income of the various economic sectors in Canada.

Gross domestic product (GDP) is calculated by adding to GNP the investment income paid to non-residents and deducting the investment income received from non-residents.

The total value of production, also known as **gross national product (GNP)**, is determined by adding up the final value of all the goods and services produced in a country over a given period, such as one year. When the GNP is divided by the total population, the result is a **per-capita GNP**, or standard of living, which represents the average productive capability of a person in a particular country.

To make the calculation of the GNP easier we can take advantage of the fact that GNP is equal to gross national income. They are equal because everything produced in the country represents income to someone in the form of wages, rent, interest or profit. Since both businesses and individuals must file tax returns, it is not difficult to determine the **gross national income (GNI)**.

Table 1.1 shows how this calculation is performed in Canada. In the top half of the table, **gross domestic product (GDP)** at market prices is calculated by adding the income of the various economic sectors in Canada. But gross domestic product can also be arrived at on the basis of expenditures—that is, who purchased the goods that were produced. You can see that the various levels of government accounted for almost 25% of total direct expenditures for investment and for goods and services produced by the economy.

What does the per-capita GNP tell us? It basically lets us compare in a crude manner the productivity in different countries. But any comparison depends on the accuracy of the GNP calculated. In many developing countries, most people earn little in wages, and usually work from dawn to dusk simply to provide enough food, clothing and shelter for their families. Since barter is often used, no actual money changes hands and therefore it is not recorded. Non-existent or inaccurate business records further distort GNP. Finally, getting an accurate population count may also be a problem because of illiteracy and non-existent addresses for many people. Therefore, a standard-of-living figure is at best an educated guess.

But even an accurate per-capita GNP figure may provide no information as to how income is distributed among people or how readily goods and services are available to the average person. For example, a high GNP could mean that the top 40% of the population lives very well while the bottom 60% lives in extreme poverty.

Nevertheless, the per-capita GNP is the best measure we have and does allow some comparison of productivity in different countries (see Figure 1.1). Generally, individuals in countries with a low per-capita GNP are not as productive as their counterparts in countries with a high per-capita GNP. This does not mean that the former individuals do not work as hard as the latter, but rather that the latter get more out of a given amount of effort. In industrialized countries, workers have available large quantities of machines and equipment that greatly increase their capacity to produce.

A basic view of how money flows in an economy is shown in Figure 1.2. Of the total gross national income, some goes to private savings, and some is taken as taxes that become government revenue. What remains is personal disposable income, some of which goes to savings. However, the largest part is for personal consumption

Calculation of Canada's gross national product, income- and expenditure-based, 1998 and 1999 (millions of $) seasonally adjusted at annual rates.

 TABLE 1.1

Income-Based	1998 3rd Quarter	1999 3rd Quarter
Gross domestic product at market prices	**893 688**	**952 688**
Wages, salaries and supplementary labour income	471 744	492 708
Corporation profits before tax	80 312	101 120
Interest and investment income	43 900	45 632
Accrued net farm income	1 920	2 072
Unincorporated business income	56 708	59 336
Inventory valuation adjustment	-3 252	3 996
Net domestic income at factor cost	658 524	704 640
Indirect taxes less subsidies	120 072	124 796
Capital consumption allowance	114 784	120 084
Statistical discrepancy	308	3 168

Expenditure-Based

	1998 3rd Quarter	1999 3rd Quarter
Gross domestic product at market prices	**893 688**	**952 688**
Personal expenditures on consumer goods and services	533 960	558 504
Net government current expenditure on goods and services	177 108	179 808
Government gross fixed capital formation	18 708	19 500
Government inventories	24	24
Business gross fixed capital formation	151 852	163 084
Residential	44 060	49 148
Non-residential	43 032	46 024
Machinery and equipment	64 760	67 912
Business investment in inventories	4 596	3 440
Non farm	-3 800	3 208
Farm	796	232
Exports of goods and services	372 448	418 452
Deduct:: Imports of goods and services	355 460	386 912
Statistical discrepancy	308	3 164
Final domestic demand	881 628	920 896

Note: Gross national product at market prices is derived by adding investment income received from non-residents to gross domestic product and deducting investment income paid to non-residents.

SOURCE: Data adapted from Statistics Canada, CANSIM matrix 6520.
Http://www.statcan.ca/english/econoind/gdprev.htm

expenditures for goods and services from businesses, Crown corporations, government service departments and non-profit organizations. These organizations receive some of their revenue from the government, which purchases goods and services. Businesses also withdraw money from their savings for reinvestment in capital goods.

Factors of Production

Before considering how a nation's standard of living could be raised, we must examine more closely the meaning of the term **production**.

Production in the economic sense is the final value of all the goods and services produced in a country over a given period.

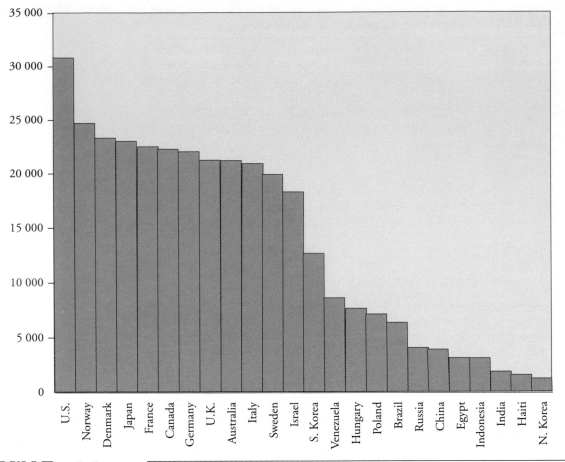

Source: World Fact Book, Central Intelligence Agency, Office of Public Affairs , Washington, DC 20505
http://www.odci.gov/cia/publications/factbook/concopy.html

FIGURE 1.1

Per capita GNP, 1998
selected countries
(U.S. dollars)

Factors of production—land, labour, capital, technology and the entrepreneur—are the basic components of the production system.

Land includes all natural resources.

Labour, both mental and physical, is the human resource required for producing goods and services.

Capital refers to the equipment used in the production of goods and services.

Technology is the practical application of scientific knowledge to the production and distribution of goods and services.

Goods and services are produced by combining human effort, raw materials and various equipment and machines. Economists call these factors land, labour and capital respectively, and they represent three of the five **factors of production**. **Land** means natural resources such as oil, iron ore and forests. **Labour** refers not only to human beings able to work, but also to the human effort, both mental and physical, required in the production process. The third factor of production, **capital**, refers to the equipment used in the production and distribution of goods and services, and includes simple tools as well as complex equipment such as oil refineries, assembly lines, railways, computers and steel plants.

Technology, a fourth factor of production, is the practical application of scientific knowledge to the production and distribution of goods and services. Technological advances can increase the productivity of individual workers, result in greater output and reduce manufacturing costs (and consequently prices). Henry Ford's invention of the assembly line, for example, significantly reduced the cost of producing automobiles, which in turn resulted in lower prices and allowed more people to purchase cars. The development of computers allowed automation of many production processes, increasing efficiency and leading to the development of many new products. As more products become available and as consumer prices drop due to more efficient production processes, the standard of living rises.

Technological development is the direct result of research and development programs established by government, industry, universities and private foundations. As they strive to earn a profit, firms must offer consumers a better product, better service or a lower price than the competition. Thus, they must develop better manufacturing processes or better products or both. Education is the foundation of research and development. As more people are educated and as the level of education per person rises, more consumer and industrial products are developed. At the same time, a highly educated population is needed to use the complex products that an industrialized society produces.

The **entrepreneur**, the fifth factor of production, is a risk-taker who, with effort and financial resources, brings together all the other factors of production—land, labour, capital and technology. If the venture proves successful, the entrepreneur reaps great financial rewards as well as prestige in the community. Failure, on the other hand, can mean a loss of the entire investment. The entrepreneur may be an individual, the government or an existing business firm.

Entrepreneur—a risk-taker who provides the financial resources to start and operate a business, and who brings together all the other factors of production in the hope of making a profit.

Raising the Standard of Living

Countries that have a low standard of living usually have a huge, largely unskilled and poorly educated population that continues to grow rapidly. Moreover, many of these people are engaged in agricultural activities designed to feed their own families. The little extra they can produce through various means is used to buy non-agricultural necessities. Any small increase in the country's productive capacity is cancelled out by the rise in population, and therefore the standard of living does not rise. There is little modern industrial machinery; when complex modern machinery is provided through foreign aid, few of the people have the training required to use it.

Bearing in mind that solutions to such vast problems are easier to suggest than to implement, some of the essential steps are clear. The rate of population growth must be reduced and the level of education raised. Then the country's resources must be developed and channelled into the production of capital goods. If all these steps can be accomplished, then the standard of living may slowly start to rise.

An agricultural lifestyle means something completely different for a Canadian farmer than the family working in the rice paddies

V

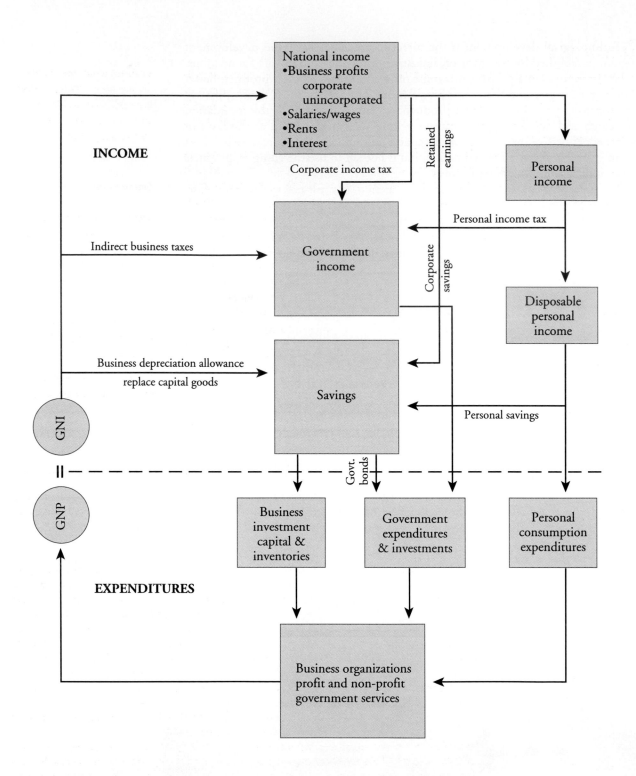

SOURCE: Adapted from Harold Koontz and Robert M. Fullmer, A Practical Introduction to Business (Homewood, Ill.: Richard D. Irwin, 1981).

FIGURE   1.2

The financial flow of a
private enterprise economy

Business

Business organizations exist in every country. They bring together the factors of production to produce goods and services in order to satisfy the needs and wants of the population. Private businesses are established to make a profit by selling goods or services. Profit is the money left over after expenses have been deducted from the money received from sales.

There are also businesses that provide a variety of services but do not make a profit. Charities, for example, depend on donations to carry on their work, while a business such as an automobile association is primarily interested in providing the motorist with a variety of services. These organizations may periodically have a surplus of revenue over expenditures, but they are basically **non-profit organizations**.

While some businesses produce only **consumer goods and services** such as food, clothing, television repairs and medical services, others create capital goods such as agricultural equipment, machines, assembly lines, trucks, locomotives, computers and so on. **Capital goods** are intended not for the final consumer, but rather to help in the production and distribution of consumer goods and services.

Not all businesses are privately owned. The federal government and the various provincial governments own businesses called Crown corporations. Canada Post and Canadian National Railways are examples of Crown corporations. Ontario Power Generation is a provincial Crown corporation. Water works, sewage and garbage disposal plants and the fire and police departments are often municipal corporations or departments. Some of these government functions, such as the fire and police departments, are entirely supported by taxpayers, while Crown corporations charge for their services. However, if the revenue is not enough to cover costs, the government must make up the difference from tax revenue.

> **Business organizations** bring together the factors of production to produce goods and services in order to satisfy the needs and wants of the population.
>
> **Non-profit organizations** provide a variety of services but are not established to make a profit, even though they may occasionally have a revenue surplus.
>
> **Consumer goods and services** are produced for the final consumer.
>
> **Capital goods** are used in the production and distribution of consumer goods and services.

Overview of the Economy

Figure 1.2 represents a simplified view of the economy. Gross national income minus business depreciation allowance (to replace worn-out capital goods) and indirect business taxes (sales taxes, customs duties and excise taxes) becomes national income. It consists of business profits from both incorporated and unincorporated companies, net income of farm operators, rents, interest income and salaries and wages.

National income minus corporate savings (retained earnings, funds that have not been paid out to shareholders) and minus corporate income taxes becomes personal income.

Personal income minus personal income tax becomes disposable personal income.

Individuals save some of their disposable income. The remainder goes for personal consumption expenditures to business organizations that include all profit and non-profit organizations as well as government departments that charge for goods and services to consumers.

Government income consists of indirect business taxes, corporate taxes and personal income tax.

Savings consist of business depreciation allowance, corporate savings known as retained earnings (both are discussed in more detail in Chapter 9) and the savings of private individuals.

A large chunk of government income is paid out to private business organizations for purchases of goods and services and for the salaries and wages of government employees. When government spends more than it takes in, it must approach private individuals, either in Canada or in other countries, to borrow money. It issues government bonds, treasury bills and Canada Savings Bonds to meet its need for additional funds.

A large part of what businesses and private individuals save is used by business organizations for investment in plants and equipment. However, savings are also used by private individuals for mortgages and personal loans.

This simplified view of the economy does not take into account the money government distributes to individuals in the form of pensions, veterans' allowances, employment insurance and so on. Nor does it take into account government subsidies to businesses. Furthermore, all international transactions are left out.

Business and Economics

Business revolves around the practical matters of producing goods and services. Business managers are concerned about the efficient combination of workers, machines and raw materials to ensure that a firm is profitable. They concentrate on the internal workings of the firm, developing new products and improving existing ones, motivating employees toward better performance, controlling expenses and so on. While they may be deeply concerned about society and its problems, their primary objective must always be profit.

Economics, on the other hand, sees business units as basic particles of the economic world. Economists are interested in the behaviour of these units and their interaction with each other; they are not concerned with what goes on inside individual firms. If the price of gasoline goes up, the economist will attempt to analyze how the price increase affects the consumer demand for gasoline and for cars. Economists are interested in such matters as the distribution of income, trends in prices and wages, total national income and business cycles.

Business Cycles

Business cycles are the fluctuations in economic activity over time. When the economy is in an expansionary phase of the cycle, business looks forward to increased production and greater profits. For individuals, it means greater employment. A typical expansionary phase can be as long as four years. During a contractionary phase, economic activity declines, resulting in decreasing sales and business profits and increasing unemployment. A severe contractionary period—the Great Depression—occurred during the 1930s. Since World War II, most contractionary periods have lasted about a year.

Business cycles—variations in the rate of economic growth—are a fundamental problem in the capitalistic system, and it is virtually impossible to eliminate them completely. The rate of growth is affected by the collective mental attitude of business leaders and consumers as well as by the occurrence of economic and political events in a particular country or in the world.

Any event can affect economic growth positively or negatively. When particular events make the economic outlook appear promising, businesses expand production, hire employees and provide money for new investment in plants and equipment. Inevitably, something happens to shake business confidence, or businesspeople collectively begin to believe that a downturn is inevitable. For example, a severe stock-market drop can shake business and consumer confidence so much that the subsequent drop in business investment and consumer spending can usher in a recession. Sometimes overproduction of goods increases inventory levels to the point that firms place fewer orders, resulting in some layoffs in the affected industries. This is often a trigger that causes a chain reaction of layoffs and reduced investment in plant and inventory. As workers are laid off and other news about a potential economic slowdown begins to spread, the mood of consumers changes. Consumers, particularly those most vulnerable to unemployment, stop making major purchases. This in turn has a detrimental effect on production, which in turn results in more layoffs and a further drop in consumer spending.

This economic downturn also affects the capital expenditures of business firms, because managers expect lower profits or even losses. With a drop in consumer expenditures and business investment, the economy can easily go into a recession. A **recession** is a decline in economic activity that is relatively small and short-lived. (The

---

Business revolves around the practical matters of producing goods and services.

Economics sees business units as basic particles of the economic world. It is concerned with the behaviour of these units and their interaction with each other.

Business cycles are the fluctuations in economic activity over time.

**MacLean's
Economic Policy Page**

www.geocities.com/WallStreet/8691/

Recession is a relatively small and short-lived decline in economic activity.

FIGURE 1.3
The business cycle

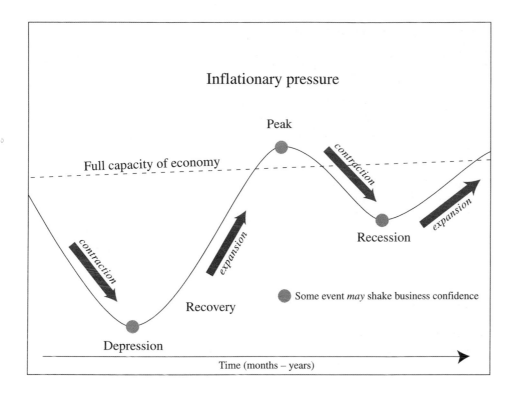

term **depression** refers to a much more severe drop in economic activity, with large-scale unemployment, high business failures and large declines in profit.)

Eventually, however, business inventories become so depleted that some new orders must be placed. Furthermore, business leaders and consumers become more optimistic about the economy. Employment begins gradually to increase, consumers start purchasing needed items and eventually the economic doom and gloom dissipates. At this point, the economy is once again in the early phases of recovery.

Economists study both the causes of these cycles and their effects on national income, unemployment and inflation. Through **economic forecasts** economists can help business managers to predict cyclical swings in business and thus help to prevent firms from incurring large losses. Government too uses economic forecasts to design economic policies that will help to smooth out the income inequalities and lessen the impact of business cycles.

Depression is a severe drop in economic activity that may last for several years, resulting in high unemployment and many business failures.

Economic forecasts attempt to predict the future level of economic activity.

Economic Systems

An **economic system** is a mechanism to help make the following decisions:

1. what goods and services are to be produced;

2. how they are to be produced;

3. how they are to be distributed among the people.

First, the economic system determines what should be produced, and what proportions of the basic factors of production—land, labour and capital—should be allocated to manufacturing consumer products and capital goods. In countries such as Canada, the choice is left to business owners who are motivated to make a profit

Economic system—determines what goods and services are to be produced how they are to be produced and how they are to be distributed.

by producing goods and services that consumers are willing to buy. But the decision can also be left to the state, in which case the government decides on the type, quantity and quality of goods to be produced.

The second decision can also be left to either private firms or government planners. In either case, decisions must be made regarding plant location, the type of equipment and machines to use, and the degree of automation. If private firms make these decisions, the results are likely to be quite different from the results of decisions made by government planners, because the objectives of the two sectors are different. Businesses are concerned with profit, while government is more concerned with the needs of society and employment.

The third problem that an economic system must resolve is the equitable distribution of goods and services among the nation's people. This is generally accomplished by allowing consumers to purchase whatever goods and services they require with their monetary income—the greater their income, the more they can buy.

How Economic Systems Differ

Even though all economic systems perform the same functions, as Figure 1.4 indicates, no two countries have an identical system. In fact, many countries have vastly different systems. Essentially the difference lies in the proportion of economic decisions made by government as opposed to private individuals—in other words, who controls the three tasks that all economic systems must resolve.

An economic system under private control is called capitalism, while one under government or state control is called socialism. To better understand these two major systems, we must examine their development. See also Table 1.2 for a comparison of economic systems.

The Historical Roots of Capitalism and Socialism

Capitalism is an economic philosophy that emphasizes the right of individuals to pursue their own self-interest. Underlying capitalism is the principle that private ownership of the means of production—implying the profit motive and competition among producers in the absence of government controls—is the most effective method of allocating the factors of production to provide people with the goods and services they want.

Capitalism evolved from the feudal system in England and Europe, and was later transplanted to the North American continent. The capitalist system developed because of social and economic changes that occurred during the 16th and 17th centuries and these changes laid the foundations for the Industrial Revolution in the 18th century. One major change was the monetization of many aspects of life—

Capitalism is an economic philosophy that emphasizes the right of private individuals to own property and establish businesses for the pursuit of profit.

FIGURE 1.4

Control of economic systems

A comparison of economic systems

TABLE 1.2

Modified Capitalism/Mixed Economy

- Means of production are mostly privately owned, except for some basic public services owned by government.
- Resources are allocated according to market forces of supply and demand.

Results

- Provides maximum incentive for private business to produce the goods and services wanted by consumers.
- Individual freedom to buy, work and invest.
- Business fluctuations can cause boom or bust periods leading to periods of inflation and unemployment.
- Pronounced gap between rich and poor, but the great majority of people usually live comfortably.

Democratic Socialism

- Industries essential to the country's economy are often owned by government.
- Considerable centralized economic planning involving government, labour and business. Within this planning framework, market forces operate to allocate resources for production of consumer goods and services.

Results

- Less pronounced business fluctuations, lower unemployment and extensive social welfare services, which work to eliminate poverty through income assistance of various kinds.
- Reduced incentive for individuals to work because of social welfare programs that look after everyone; extensive government rules and regulations reduce efficiency of private business; high taxation to pay for maintaining social welfare system means lower private investment, which tends to result in economic stagnation; government policies and programs often result in high government debt.

Communism

- Virtually all means of production are owned by government.
- Resources are allocated for the production of consumer and capital goods through centralized government planning.

Results

- Because of the dictatorial powers that leaders of communist countries have, the living conditions of people in poor countries can often be quickly improved and the population can be educated. Social welfare programs are also established to provide basic health care.
- Resources can be channelled into the build-up of capital goods; ability to better regulate economic growth.
- Unemployment is virtually eliminated because everyone is forced to work.
- Not suited for the production of consumer goods in the quantity and quality desired because of the absence of market forces and competition.
- Individuals lack freedom of choice.
- Little incentive to increase productivity of workers or plants.

money was used to buy goods and services, and labour was bought and sold in the marketplace. Goods and services were no longer exchanged in kind. Another major factor was the change in the religious climate in England and Europe. The new Protestant religions diffused the power of the Catholic Church and made the pursuit of commercial activities honourable and legitimate, an attitude that the Catholic Church strongly disapproved of during the feudal era.[2]

The new social climate allowed ambitious entrepreneurs to become industrial giants through the invention of new machinery or manufacturing processes that greatly increased the production of existing goods. The ownership of private property, together with the freedom to compete in the marketplace in any way they deemed necessary to sell their products, gave the early industrialists the incentive to build and

Laissez-faire capitalism is a lack of government intervention in the economy.

expand their factories and to accumulate wealth. Government did not interfere in business, or protect the consumer or worker, because the prevailing philosophy held that the individual was best able to make decisions on matters affecting his or her daily life. Lack of government intervention in the economy is also termed **laissez-faire**, which means "Let [people] do [as they please]."

While initially most goods produced in England were exported to other countries, particularly to the "New World," a growing English middle class increased the demand for new and existing goods and services. The Industrial Revolution raised living standards to levels unlike any the world had known before.[3]

However, during the late 18th and early 19th centuries, living and working conditions for most people were terrible. One individual who observed the misery of the working class was Karl Marx, who, together with Friedrich Engels, wrote *The Communist Manifesto* in 1848. On the basis of their observation of the English industrial system, Marx and Engels held the private ownership of property and the profit motive accountable for this misery; the working classes, they maintained, were being exploited by capitalists (industrialists) for monetary gain. In Marx's view, abolishing private ownership of property and substituting the state as owner would permit all members of society to live in peace and to channel all of their efforts into improving their society.

Marx anticipated a revolution in which the hereditary nobility and wealthy industrialists would be overthrown. A temporary regime known as the "dictatorship of the proletariat" would be established to govern during the transition from capitalism to **socialism**. Then a planned socialist economy would emerge. In this new state, goods and services would be produced on a voluntary basis, through the cooperation of all citizens. Since all would be equally and adequately rewarded for their work, society as a whole would be free for more humanistic pursuits.

Socialism is an economic system characterized by centralized planning and government ownership of business enterprises.

The economic systems that exist today are a mixture of these two philosophies—complete state ownership of the means of production on the one hand, and complete private ownership on the other. Needless to say, no nation operates under a pure form of either system. Countries with capitalistic economic systems—also known as free enterprise, private enterprise or mixed economies—all experience considerable government intervention. The purpose of intervention is to eliminate the most undesirable aspects of the capitalistic system and to provide a more stable economic environment.

All forms of socialism share two basic tenets: (1) a belief that if the means of production remain in private hands, the worker will be exploited and (2) a belief in egalitarianism (the conviction that all individuals should enjoy political and social equality).

Capitalism, Communism and Democratic Socialism: An Overview

Capitalism

Capitalism is the economic system of United States, Canada, Great Britain and Germany, to name only a few countries. Under this economic system, the productive capacity of the country is basically privately owned. Businesses compete with one another to produce goods and services on the basis of consumer needs and wants. Private business firms decide in the main how raw materials, labour and capital are to be used to produce both consumer and capital goods. Individuals may work where they choose; they may establish their own businesses and compete with others to produce and sell their goods to consumers. Individual income may be derived from any of a number of sources, including wages and salaries, rent, interest or business profits. After paying income taxes to the various levels of government, individuals may spend their remaining income as they wish on consumer goods and services; they may save it, or they may reinvest it in business.

Communism

Marxism-Leninism, commonly known as communism, began with the Russian Revolution in 1917 under Lenin and spread over the next 70 years to other countries. In 1991, the Communist Party in the USSR was disbanded, and, by the end of 1991, the USSR itself was dissolved, with individual republics forming a new commonwealth. But communism to a greater or lesser extent remains the dominant political ideology in China, Mongolia, North Korea and Cuba. Under this system, government (the state) owns all of the country's productive capacity. Government officials decide how the factors of production will be combined to produce both consumer and capital goods, as well as the types of products and services to be produced. Since property is state-owned, virtually all income is derived from wages and salaries that are largely determined by the state. The individual has few choices as to how to allocate his or her limited income among the limited goods and services available.

At one time communism's primary objective was to establish a classless society by abolishing private property and nationalizing the means of production. However, it soon became apparent that with no incentive, the state-owned enterprises could seldom produce enough of basic goods and services to satisfy consumers' requirements. Over time some private production was allowed in most of the communist countries except those where the leaders had a strong ideological attachment to communist principles. But political power remains concentrated in a tightly structured party, whose leaders direct most economic and social activities. Whatever form of communism exists, it is repressive and allows its citizens little freedom.

> **Marxism-Leninism,** or communism, is a political ideology that aims to abolish private property, nationalize all means of production and establish a classless society.
>
> **Communism** is an economic system where the government (the state) owns all of the country's productive capacity, and through centralized planning government officials allocate the factors of production to achieve the economic and social objectives of the state.

Democratic Socialism

Instead of resorting to revolutionary means to achieve a classless society as communists do, social democrats believe in achieving their socialist goals gradually and peacefully. They concentrate more on rectifying the hardships brought on by capitalist economies, such as unemployment, poverty and wage and salary inequities. Countries ruled by social democrats are generally mixed economies: they have state ownership or direction of key industries, but they also retain many elements of private enterprise competition.

Social democrats work within a multi-party system. Most European countries have had social democrats in power during this century. For example, Sweden's social democrats were in power for 53 years except for a brief six-year period from 1976 until 1982; they were again defeated in 1991.

Under this system, government generally owns basic industries—mines, utilities, sometimes major industrial complexes—that are important to the development of the country's economy or that employ a large number of people. Most other production is carried out by privately owned firms. The governments in general do not aim to eliminate private ownership of business or property. They are concerned with the collective welfare of the people. Philosophic aims of the government may include equal opportunity of employment and education, stable economic growth and high employment, reduction of poverty, social housing and a strong welfare system. To ensure

> **Democratic socialism** is an economic system in which the democratically elected government engages in centralized planning and some government ownership of key industries to achieve its economic and social objectives.

stable economic growth, government, industry and labour together determine overall economic goals for the nation and plan on how to achieve them. Government may therefore set overall wage and price guidelines, but producers and consumers interact in the marketplace to determine the type and quality of consumer goods to be produced. Individuals have the freedom to choose their occupations and the way in which they acquire their income. Citizens also elect their government in the hope that it will exercise the degree of control over economic matters that they desire.

Development of the Canadian Business System

The capitalistic economic system and its underlying principles were ideal for the development of North America. Here was a vast, relatively unexplored territory where an individual could easily acquire land or establish a business. As more settlers came to North America and the population increased, formerly small businesses also grew. As transportation systems developed, the market for many products expanded further still, contributing all the more to industrial growth.

Economic considerations played a major role in the Confederation of 1867. Although the new nation would still depend primarily on the production and export of staple goods, increased production and economic expansion were among the most important benefits expected. The anticipated increase in immigration, particularly to the West, would lead to a greater internal demand for manufactured goods. The growing population in the West would likely increase production of wheat and other staple products for export to Britain and Europe. At the same time, it would reduce the threat of U.S. expansion into the Prairies. As a side benefit, it was also expected that greater industrial activity and western expansion would mean better utilization of the newly built transportation system in the St. Lawrence and Great Lakes regions. This in turn would increase revenues and ensure payment of the debt incurred in building the system.[4]

Another major benefit from economic union for the various provinces was regional and national economic stability because of their complementary resources. Further benefits would come from growth in internal trade as well as from increased trade with the rest of the world as Canada gained prominence and the ability to bargain for more trading privileges with other nations. Finally, Confederation was expected to improve Canada's world credit position, ensuring new loans for both public and private development.

The National Policy

National Policy —a policy designed to help increase the export of staple commodities and settle the West; to increase the manufacturing of finished goods within Canada by imposing of high tariffs on American goods; to build a transportation link—the CPR—between East and West in order to move staple commodities from the West to the East for export and ship manufactured goods to the western settlers.

Shortly after Confederation, the first federal government introduced a program known as the **National Policy**. It had three major objectives:

1. To help increase the export of staple commodities, especially wheat; it was also hoped that the consequent settlement of the West would thwart an American invasion of the Prairies.

2. To increase the manufacturing of finished goods within Canada by imposing high tariffs on American goods.

3. To build a transportation link between East and West in order to move staple commodities from the West to the East for export and ship manufactured goods to the western settlers. The link was to be accomplished through the building of the Canadian Pacific Railway, which required heavy public financing.

To make the National Policy succeed, the north-south trade relations already established between the Canadian West and the United States would have to be severed. The western settlers would have to be compelled to buy their goods from Canadian manufacturers. Thus, the tariff policy of 1879 was instituted. This policy imposed high tariffs on imported goods. The tariff for finished consumer goods, for example, was 30%. For fully manufactured industrial machinery and equipment, the tariff was 25%, while for the bulk of miscellaneous manufactured products, semi-finished goods and industrial materials it ranged from 10 to 20%. The textile industry already established in eastern Canada received high tariff protection, since large quantities of textiles were imported, and tariffs were also imposed on agricultural products, even though Canada was primarily an exporter in this area. These tariffs remained basically unchanged until 1930.[5]

The Golden Age of Canadian Growth

A turning point in world economic conditions in 1896 brought new prosperity for Canada as exports began to rise again, and all sectors of the Canadian economy began to experience growth in investment and capital formation, and in manufacturing. Eventually the standard of living for the average Canadian improved as foreign investment flowed into Canada, primarily from the United States, for the development of manufacturing industries. This investment was stimulated by huge population growth that increased domestic demand for manufactured consumer goods. Between 1900 and 1910, one million immigrants poured into the West between the Lakehead and the Rockies. Although World War I reduced the flow somewhat, by the 1920s the population in this region had increased from 400 000 to 2 000 000. The increased demand for manufactured goods helped Canada's manufacturing industry to expand through foreign investment, and eventually the prices of consumer goods decreased.

Unfortunately, this great increase in prosperity came to an end on October 24, 1929. On that date—also known as Black Thursday—the New York stock market collapsed. While Canadian investors fared somewhat better in the market than their American counterparts, the economic consequences were deeply felt throughout the world.

From the Depression to the End of World War II

Although the stock-market crash itself did not cause the **Great Depression**, it did affect business confidence. Business investment dropped, and industries produced less, resulting in fewer jobs and loss of consumer purchasing power. And as fewer goods were bought, industrial output was further curtailed, resulting in more unemployment. Five years later, nearly one-quarter of the population was unemployed.

Hardest hit were Canada's primary industries. The price of wheat dropped from $1.60 per bushel in 1929 to 38 cents in 1932. Exports generally fell by 25%. Fishing, mining, lumber, and pulp and paper suffered similar declines, causing a chain reaction in other industries that depended on these commodities for their own prosperity. The CPR and CNR suffered losses as transportation volume dropped drastically. Manufacturers of farm machinery closed plants and laid off workers as demand for their products fell. By the end of 1932, 600 000 of Canada's 10 000 000 people were out of work, and, in 1933, 23% of the labour force was unemployed. By 1935, 10% of the population was receiving public relief.

In the West, it was the wheat farmers who suffered the most. Many had invested everything they had in their farms, only to be wiped out as demand and

Great Depression —a severe drop in the level of economic activity between 1929 and 1933. Ultimately, it resulted in 25% of the population being out of work.

During the Great Depression, the Scott Institute (Mission) provided food daily to 1000 or more people

prices for their products fell. Along with economic problems came natural disasters. For several years, a severe drought parched the topsoil, which was then carried away by exceptionally strong prairie winds in terrible dust storms. Plagues of grasshoppers followed, destroying anything that had managed to survive the drought.

Government Intervenes in the Economy

New Deal—a U.S. government initiative to finance public works in order to lessen the impact of the Great Depression. Money was loaned to railroads, construction companies, banks and farmers. Similar measures were later undertaken by the Canadian government.

In the United States, the government intervened in the economy to introduce a series of measures known as the **New Deal**. The government financed public works and loaned money to railways, construction companies, banks and farmers. By 1935, these policies had gradually lifted the United States out of the worst of the Depression. In Canada, Prime Minister R. B. Bennett offered his own version of the New Deal through unemployment insurance programs, social insurance acts and other measures, including the imposition of limits on the hours of work. His programs horrified many businesspeople and were often tested in court for their constitutionality. Nevertheless, the Unemployment Insurance Act was passed in 1940, paving the way for the health, welfare and social security services we enjoy today.

The last half of the 1930s saw Canada's economy climb out of the Depression. Government intervention, the fact that the Depression had apparently run its natural course and the beginning of World War II all contributed to the recovery. As industry readied itself to produce weapons, guns, warships and airplanes, unemployment decreased, while relief, soup kitchens and bread lines virtually disappeared.

A New Government Philosophy

What did not disappear was government intervention in the economy. The Great Depression had marked the end of old-style capitalism and ushered in what many called the "welfare state." The principle of individual self-sufficiency could no longer be accepted given that the Depression had caused so much suffering for people with very little influence on the system. Since the government was elected to represent all Canadians—not simply to support business and commercial interests—it had an obligation to minimize economic hardship for all.

The belief that national income should be more evenly distributed, on both an individual basis and a regional one, was gaining acceptance. Provincial governments in poorer regions of Canada received more money from federal tax revenues, and various social services—including unemployment insurance, family allowances, pensions, veterans' allowances, hospital insurance and disability allowances—were established.

Keynes and the New Economics

Until the Great Depression of the 1930s, Adam Smith's theory of economics was generally accepted. But the world of 1930 was very different from the world of 1776. More than 150 years had passed, during which business had grown immensely and the economic structure of many countries had changed. Particularly in North America, once-small businesses had grown into giant corporations, often with monopolistic powers. Labour unions (which did not even exist in Smith's day) had become established and presented a powerful opposing force to management. Government had been involved in the regulation of business for the past 40 years and by the 1930s was ready to take a major role in regulating business activities and managing the economy as a whole. As the Depression worsened, there was no hint that the market mechanism would lead the major world economies back to prosperity. Classical economic theory was not working as it should.

Why did it fail? Mainly because classical economics had always assumed full employment. According to the traditional view, depression and unemployment resulted from interference with the market mechanism that normally ensured the efficient allocation of human and material resources. That interference could come either from government or other forces, such as big business organizations and labour unions, with the power to monopolize resources. Thus, the classical economists preached that the Depression could be resolved only by returning to a laissez-faire system; by the early 20th century, such a return was virtually impossible.

In 1936 **John Maynard Keynes** published *The General Theory of Employment, Interest and Money*. Although the economic world held Keynes in great esteem and his book had been eagerly awaited, its revolutionary economic concepts were at first highly controversial.

The principles that Keynes expounded were not new, but he was the first to present them in logical fashion. He isolated the factors that had contributed to large-scale unemployment in the past. He strongly disagreed with the popular notion that decreasing wages would increase employment. Under this assumption, wages are considered only as production costs to the manufacturer, not as purchasing power for the consuming public that constitutes such a large part of the total demand for goods and services.

To maintain individual purchasing power during times of heavy unemployment, Keynes recommended that the government intervene to stimulate economic activity through government spending and appropriate use of the income tax system. Proper use of these two major fiscal tools would maintain the economy in a healthy

John Maynard Keynes was the author of *General Theory of Employment, Interest and Money*. To maintain individual purchasing power during times of heavy unemployment, Keynes recommended that government intervene to stimulate economic activity through government spending and appropriate use of the income tax system.

state. Government spending during times of recession and increasing unemployment would offset decreased investment on the part of the private sector and keep the capital-goods-producing sector alive. In addition, the progressive income tax structure would automatically ensure that the lower the consumer's income, the less tax would be taken by government, thus allowing individuals to spend as they saw fit and thereby maintain demand for goods and services. Programs such as unemployment insurance, which both Canada and the United States instituted in the late 1930s, would give those who were out of work the ability to purchase basic necessities, thus assuring ongoing demand for these products.

There is no doubt that Keynes has deeply affected business thought; it is to him that government intervention in the economy may be largely attributed. However, perhaps politicians misinterpreted Keynes. Although he supported heavy government spending during periods of depression, Keynes did not advocate socialism. Nor did he recommend excessive government spending in times of full employment, since that would contribute to inflation. Unfortunately, that is exactly what has happened. Almost half of Canada's national income originates with government, from employment, social programs, government support programs of various kinds to business and private institutions, purchase of supplies and services, and so on. **Deficit spending**—where government expenditures exceed tax revenues—contributed to high inflation in the 1970s and has resulted in a great increase in the national debt to finance it. The interest payments alone on this debt take one-third of government revenues. Trying to reduce the yearly deficit has become a major problem for the federal government.

> **Deficit spending** happens when the federal or provincial government has yearly expenditures that exceed yearly tax revenues.

Capitalism in Canada

Capitalism rests on four basic principles: private ownership of property, freedom of choice, free competition in the market and freedom from government interference. Neither Canada nor any other country in the world today operates according to pure capitalistic principles. In most modern nations, government is actively involved in ownership of economic enterprises and in managing the economy to protect individuals from the severe swings in business cycles and other undesirable aspects of capitalism. These modified capitalistic systems are known as **mixed economies**. Let's briefly look at these four principles.

> **Mixed economies** are modified capitalist social systems in which there is both private and government ownership of business with varying degrees of government planning and intervention designed to smooth out business cycles and lessen their effects on individuals.

Private Property

In North America particularly, individual ownership of property is considered almost sacred. The government cannot take away private property without due process of law. The possibility of ownership provides an incentive for individuals to work hard and save money to acquire property. Ownership becomes a source of pride that helps to ensure that property is well maintained and creates respect for the property of others. Private ownership of property extends to the ownership of business and underlies the profit motive, which encourages business owners and managers to strive to provide new products and services to consumers. Often profits are reinvested in a firm to ensure its growth.

Freedom of Choice

The right to own property goes hand in hand with the right to do as one pleases with that property as long as one does not harm others. Owners of land, resources and capital have the right to sell, rent, trade or even give those things away. Similarly, individuals are free to use their skills and talents as they see fit. Any individual is relatively free to open a business and to produce and sell whatever he or she believes will earn a profit. People may change jobs or occupations whenever they wish; they may choose to work or not to work. They are free to spend what they earn, or they may save, invest or otherwise dispose of it.

Freedom of Competition

Competition among businesses that provide similar goods and services ensures that consumers receive the best possible product at the lowest possible price. Competition also provides an incentive for businesses to produce superior products at an affordable price, since higher sales revenues usually mean higher profits, and ultimately, business success.

Freedom from Government Interference

According to pure capitalism, government has a limited role: ensuring the existence of free competition and free trade, and providing services (such as national defense, police and fire protection) that private industry would be unlikely to provide because of low or non-existent profits. Government is not to interfere in the economy by regulating businesses or influencing economic activity in any way. Nor should government provide social welfare to its citizens, since all individuals are expected to look after themselves.

Managing a Market Economy

Government clearly plays a major role in **economic management** and in shaping social policy. Government took on these tasks because the capitalistic system, although highly efficient in allocating resources and capable of providing an abundance of goods and services, rewarded only those who were industrious and gifted; those who were physically challenged or unemployed suffered extreme hardship, as was evident during the Great Depression. Programs such as unemployment insurance, old age pensions, social welfare and low-cost medical insurance are designed to help individuals who experience hardships. Government also protects the consumer through various agencies that monitor the quality of products and protect individuals from dangerous products that might inadvertently turn up in the marketplace.

Economic management is the attempt by government to control business cycles so as to reduce large fluctuations in GNP, unemployment and inflation.

One of the major tasks of government is to ensure that the economy is stable. **Stability** in economic terms means that prices of goods, interest rates and personal income do not vary too greatly over time. A stable economy allows people to plan for the future, and save for retirement or major purchases. However, when the prices of goods and services increase substantially over a short period of time we have **inflation,** which means basically that there are too many dollars chasing too few goods. Inflation happens because there is too much money in circulation that was not earned and is usually due to government programs that spend borrowed money. When inflation occurs, the Bank of Canada must institute monetary policies to curb the amount of money in circulation. As a result, interest rates rise, sometimes dramatically, which curbs business investment and consumer purchases. The result could be the beginning of a recession.

Stability means that prices of goods, interest rates, and personal income does not vary too greatly over time.

Inflation is a rise in the prices of all goods resulting from excessive demand for limited goods and services.

Too much government involvement, however, can interfere with individual freedom of choice, reduce the incentive to work and invest and make citizens more dependent on the state. The more services, subsidies and regulations that private individuals request, the more personal income the government must take in the form of taxes. Tremendous power has become concentrated in government, which is now both the largest employer and the largest purchaser of goods and services in Canada. The danger is that government might exert pressure on those that depend on it for their livelihood to conform to or support its policies.

There has been considerable debate over the size and influence of the public sector in Canada. Issues centre on the efficiency of government in managing tax revenue, allocating resources and providing necessary services. In private firms, the profit motive controls the firm's objectives and influences the performance of its managers. Those who operate government enterprises and provide services, however, often do not have to make a profit, and political objectives may therefore dominate. In addition, as government deepens its social involvement it requires more detailed information about its citizens. Another major issue, then, is the amount of personal information that must be revealed to government officials. We examine the government sector and its relationship to business and private individuals in Chapter 12.

Profit, Competition and the Market

The Importance of Profit

Underlying any capitalistic business system or market-based economy are two important factors—profit and competition. Both of these factors regulate the business activities that take place in the so-called marketplace where buyers and sellers are free to exchange their goods and services. Let's examine both factors now.

It sometimes seems that the term "profit" has become a dirty word. Many individuals, including some politicians, equate profit with profiteering—that is, making excessive profits by charging exorbitant prices for products or services. Of course, profiteering does occur. Some businesses are set up precisely to sell a shoddy product or service at high prices for a short time, then close shop and move on. But most businesses do not operate in that manner. Their owners establish them with permanency in mind—to produce and sell goods and services expecting to earn a profit.

What Is Profit?

Profit is a surplus of revenues over expenditures. It is what remains after all expenses associated with operating the business have been deducted from the revenue received from customers.

A **profit** is a surplus of revenues over expenditures. It is what remains after all expenses associated with operating the business have been deducted from the revenue received from customers. However, a consistent surplus (profit) is by no means guaranteed. Each business has costs associated with making and/or selling a product or service, and the prices it receives are usually dictated by what consumers are willing to pay and what competitors are charging for their goods or services. Therefore, a firm's profit may rise or fall depending on how it can manage its costs and on the actions of its competitors. A firm's profit may also be dictated by the seasonal nature of its business and/or by the swings of business cycles.

Profit as an Incentive

Profit is the major incentive for establishing a business. Profitable small businesses can provide their owners with a good income and prestige in the community, while allowing them independence. Many of the benefits that apply to owners of small businesses also apply to professional managers whose careers and income depend on the corporation's success and survival. Because managers gain personal benefit from a successful business, they strive for growth and compete with other firms for sales and profits. In this process, they develop and produce new, often better, products and services, thereby benefiting consumers. Above all, entrepreneurs create new job opportunities. This is especially true for small businesses, which provide the greatest number of new jobs in an economy.

Profit as a Measure of Efficiency and Effectiveness

Profit helps to measure the efficiency and effectiveness of a business. **Efficiency** refers to the relationship between input and output. Greater efficiency means that a greater output can be achieved from the same amount of input. If, for example, two firms produce the same product but one firm is more profitable than the other, the more profitable firm is probably the more efficient of the two firms. Efficiency may result from better equipment, better-trained production workers, better management or a better sales force. Ultimately, the more efficient firm will likely survive, whereas the less efficient one will disappear.

Aside from helping to gauge the efficiency of a business, profit also gauges its **effectiveness.** A profitable firm produces what buyers want; it is an indication that resources have been allocated to the proper business activities.

> **Efficiency** refers to the relationship between input and output.

> **Effectiveness** refers to the proper use of resources to produce the goods and services that people want.

Profit for Expansion and Capital Formation

To remain effective and efficient, firms must constantly strive to offer consumers a better product, better service or a lower price than the competition. To remain ahead of the competition and remain profitable, they must develop better manufacturing processes, or better products, or both. Therefore a large part of business profit is used to replace manufacturing plants and equipment that have become obsolete or worn out, increase the existing machines and equipment to expand production, and often conduct basic research to improve existing products and processes or develop new ones.

Profit as a Return to Investors

Capital investment often requires substantially more funds than a firm itself can generate. These additional funds can be acquired either by selling shares of the business to new investors or by borrowing from a financial institution such as a bank. A portion of a business's profits must therefore be used to pay shareholders and lenders. When profit is available, shareholders receive a per-share-based payment called a dividend. Furthermore, potential investors may also benefit from an increase in the price of their shares as other investors buy the shares of a profitable company and thereby bid up their price. A well-managed firm with a consistent dividend payment record attracts shareholders, who in turn make it easier for the firm to acquire funds for new investment. People invest in a business because they hope that the potential return—dividends plus appreciation of the firm's share prices—will be greater than the return they would get by, for example, putting their money in a savings account or buying Canada Savings Bonds.

Profits as a Contribution to Society

A business's drive for profit is not harmful to society—it is an effective method of allocating society's resources. The profit motive ensures that businesses are effective in what they do and efficient in the way they allocate the factors of production.

Reinvesting profits in new capital goods and in research and development increases productivity, which benefits society through an overall rise in the standard of living. In addition, almost half of all business profits are paid in the form of taxes to the federal, provincial and municipal governments. Tax revenue is used to finance social programs or to produce goods and services that might otherwise not be produced by private firms because there is little chance of making a profit.

Thus, profit stimulates the private sector of our economy, increasing output and employment, and at the same time helps to keep that sector in check. A similar control mechanism for non-profit organizations and government operations would serve to measure their effectiveness and efficiency.

Why Are Profits High?

Firms that report a high profit are often criticized or charged with gouging consumers. While profiteering should be exposed of course, in most instances there are valid reasons for a firm showing extraordinarily high profits in a given year. For example, it may be the first time that profits earned by a newly purchased subsidiary firm have been included with those of the parent company. High profits might also reflect the sale of a piece of real estate that has appreciated significantly. Sometimes firms earn high profits simply because they have the right product at the right time. A firm may struggle for years before a sudden change in consumer tastes puts its product in demand and makes the business profitable. At other times, a firm may profit because it is quick to perceive a new market and take advantage of the situation by providing a needed product or service. Usually in both of these instances, excess profits are soon eliminated as new firms offer similar or even improved products to the consumer, often at lower prices. Perhaps the major reason businesses show a high profit during particular years is that business cycles can cause substantial fluctuations in profits over time. During a recession, many firms actually lose money, sometimes for several years. Losses incurred during the bad years must be recovered with higher profits during the good years.

How Canadians View Profits

In a survey conducted in the 1970s, Canadians generally estimated profits to be much higher than they actually were, and most Canadians believed profits were excessive. Some Canadians believed that profits ran as high as 40 cents on the sales dollar.[6] Whether or not these views are still widely held is difficult to say. However, the concept of profit is generally not well understood, and the public is often unaware of the general level of profits and how and why they fluctuate.

In general, actual profits for manufacturing industries fluctuate between 7 cents and 11 cents per dollar on average. For individual industries, profit margins range from 2.5 cents per dollar for food processors, for example, to 13.5 cents per dollar for communications and pipe manufacturing. In any event, actual profits are well below the level estimated by the general public; in fact, they are less than what the public believes a fair profit for manufacturers would be.

A major reason for public confusion about profits is that whenever profits are cited in newspaper or magazine headlines or quoted by politicians, no clear distinction is made between profit as a proportion of revenue (or assets) and growth in profits. Because both are expressed as percentages, a person is left with the impression that a 50% increase in profit is no different from a 50% profit. The fact that profits may have grown from an 8% return on investment to 12% to make that 50% increase is, at best, buried deep down in the newspaper column.

Do Businesses Attempt to Maximize Profits?

Every business owner and manager sees profit as the major objective but it is almost impossible for businesses to get the most out of every sales dollar. Managers do not have complete knowledge of the future or of how the environment might affect the firm. Planning is an attempt to minimize the risks of future uncertainty, but even the most carefully laid plans may fall short as conditions change from day to day. The best managers can do is to plan for a profit that will satisfy investors and the firm's need for capital replacement and long-term growth. If firms plan for steady earnings in the long run, the inevitable short-term profit fluctuations are less likely to damage their operation.

Instead of attempting to maximize profits in the short run, which is almost impossible, firms will try to make satisfactory long-term profits. To do so, they attempt to become permanently established, to become good corporate citizens and to contribute to the community in which they operate. They also want loyal, well-trained employees working in pleasant surroundings. They are concerned about their image and reputation; they want to produce quality products and be innovators in their industry. Although the realization of all of these objectives increases the cost of doing business and reduces profit, it also helps to ensure a firm's long-term survival.

Competition and the Market

Under a capitalistic economic system, the market is the mechanism that regulates what goods are produced, how the factors of production are allocated, and how goods are distributed. The operation of a country's **market system** is not readily apparent, but the public market where sellers and buyers gather to exchange money for produce, fish and meat provides an illustration.

Although public market prices are usually marked on the goods, sellers are not inflexible. If large quantities of a perishable product are left as the day draws to a close, the seller is likely to lower the price to induce people to buy. On the other hand, when a particular commodity is in short supply, it is likely to be sold quickly. The seller has no need to reduce prices, and may even increase it as long as the buyers are willing to pay.

Market system refers to the mechanism in a capitalist economy whereby the supply of and demand for goods and services determine their price, and the quantities producers are willing to sell at that price.

< In a public market, buyers and sellers interact to determine the prices at which existing goods are sold

What happens in a public market happens in a market economy. Buyers and sellers interact to determine the prices at which existing goods are sold. If a particular product is in demand, producers will raise their prices for the existing quantities if they believe that consumers will buy the product. If possible, producers will attempt to bring greater quantities of the product to market to take advantage of the rising prices and the potentially greater profit. If this greater supply satisfies the consumer demand, then the price will stabilize at the new level. If producers flood the market, then prices will drop as supply exceeds demand.

Figure 1.5 shows this interaction between buyers and sellers by a supply and demand schedule. The schedule shows the various quantities that will be demanded depending on the price charged. If the price of peaches is low, for example, then people will buy more than if the price is high. Different individuals have different wants, so each person has a unique demand schedule, but the total demand schedule for a particular product is an average for all consumers. The supply schedule, on the other hand, shows the opposite. When prices are high, producers would be happy to produce and supply larger quantities as opposed to when prices are low.

When these two schedules are superimposed on each other, the point at which they cross—the **equilibrium point**—indicates the quantity that will be bought at the given price. Both consumer and producer are satisfied with the product price indicated at the equilibrium point. Keep in mind that there are always some people who are able to pay a high price for any product, while others are unable to pay even a very low price.

The market system works well when there are many producers. With only one or a few producers, however, the orderly working of the system is disrupted, since a few producers can easily control the amount of product supplied to consumers and keep prices artificially high. You can see from the supply and demand schedule that if less product is supplied (the supply line in Figure 1.5 would shift upward to the left), the price per unit would be higher. This kind of control over supply and price can be detrimental to consumers, particularly if the product or service is a necessity. In this case, the consumer must accept what the producer offers, regardless of quality or price.

Equilibrium point refers to the point at which the demand schedule and the supply schedule cross. This point indicates the quantity that will be bought at the given price.

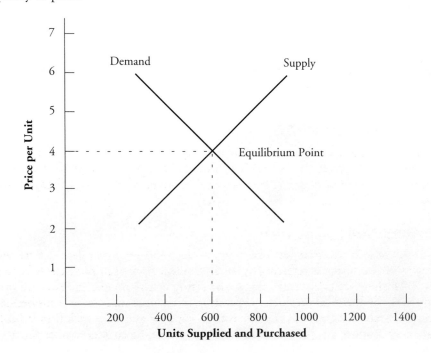

FIGURE 1.5

Product supply and demand

The market system, then, requires **competition** between producer and consumer in order to function properly. Without competition as a counter force, the drive for profits could be detrimental to individual consumers and to society as a whole. Imagine a situation in which there was only one producer in each industry. Consumers would be compelled to purchase what each produced, regardless of price or quality. Chances are that there would be little product variety, while the producer would have no particular incentive for innovation in product design or increased efficiency in the production process. Consumers would have only one alternative: to refuse to purchase the product.

> **Competition** occurs when several firms vie with each other to provide better products at lower prices in order to increase sales and make a profit.

Effective and Responsible Competition

Effective competition exists when many small firms compete with each other to provide the best products at the lowest possible cost. Under this system, one seller's gain is another seller's loss. Everyone is actively striving to gain a greater share of customers.

> **Effective competition** exists when many small firms compete with each other to provide the best products at the lowest possible cost.

Unfortunately, effective competition is not often present in the private enterprise system. A few giant firms produce steel, automobiles and electrical products, while there is frequently only one producer for such services as electricity, water and telephone. In addition, groups such as marketing boards and producers' co-operatives can reduce competition by setting prices and limiting quantities. Labour unions and employers' associations also impede the competitive forces of the market system.

Responsible competition should be practised by firms that compete among themselves. Competition should not be so aggressive as to destroy viable businesses through dishonest advertising and the discrediting of competitors. Unfair methods of competition may damage a firm's reputation to the point of bankruptcy or border on criminal acts that society cannot condone.

> **Responsible competition** means that firms should compete among themselves but refrain from using unfair methods that could damage a firm's reputation to the point of bankruptcy.

In an attempt to maintain effective and responsible competition, the federal government introduced legislation early in the century under the Combines Investigations Act. This legislation allows the government to press charges should violations occur with respect to mergers, agreements, monopolies, price discrimination, false and misleading advertising or price maintenance. Where monopolies are necessary because competition would mean higher prices and possibly poorer service, the government regulates prices, quality of service and various other aspects of operation. We will examine competition legislation in more detail in Chapter 12.

Types of Competition

We can classify competition under four main types depending on the number of firms that exist in an industry and how they behave toward other firms. These categories are perfect or pure competition, monopolistic competition, oligopoly and monopoly (see Table 1.3).

Perfect or Pure Competition

Although economists distinguish between perfect and pure competition, we will consider the two terms as referring to the same idea. **Perfect** or **pure competition** exists when there are many small firms competing in a particular industry, all producing virtually identical products. There are a substantial number of firms because the cost of establishing a small business is relatively low; and since each firm is small, it can never produce a sufficient quantity to influence the current market price.

> **Perfect** or **pure competition** means that there are many small firms in a particular industry. Each produces a virtually identical product, and no firm can influence the price charged.

The agricultural industry is a good example. Products are identical and no single producer has the power to influence the price of the product in the marketplace by withholding production. As prices of commodities are established in the market, producers enter or leave the industry depending on their ability to operate. High beef prices, for example, induce people to raise beef cattle, while low prices cause a drop in beef prices.

Since the 1970s, however, the federal and provincial governments have allowed various segments of this industry to establish marketing boards to which all producers of a particular product must belong. The objective is to protect individual producers from excessive competition and fluctuations in demand for the product, while ensuring orderly distribution for a particular commodity. Although marketing boards may guarantee steadier earnings for the producer, they have been accused of artificially restricting output and raising consumer product prices. They may also cause problems in other facets of the agricultural industry.

Monopolistic Competition

Monopolistic Competition

http://barney.sbe.csuhayward.edu/ ~acassuto/econ3552/summary/ chapter11.html

Monopolistic competition means that a large number of relatively small firms produce a product or provide a service that is slightly different. Each firm exerts some influence on the prices charged.

Under **monopolistic competition**, a large number of relatively small firms produce a product or provide a service that is slightly different, or at least perceived as such by the consumer. As a result, each firm exerts some influence on the prices charged. Retail operations such as service stations are a good example. The different gasoline and automotive products sold by each company, along with the various services each provides, serve to distinguish one company from another. Again, access to the industry is relatively easy.

Oligopoly

Oligopoly is a market situation in which a small number of firms produce a similar product, but each firm has control over prices charged.

Under an **oligopoly**, there are only a small number of producers. Whether the product is different, as in the case of automobiles, or similar, as in steel, entry into these industries is virtually impossible because of the great amounts of investment capital required. While the producers have considerable control over prices, they all stand to lose if price competition is intense, since, if one firm were to reduce prices, all the others would soon be forced to follow.

To attract customers away from other firms, businesses use non-price methods of competition such as advertising, consistent upgrading of existing products or offering new products and better customer service. In the case of automobile companies, for example, each tries to gain customers by offering extended warranties, quality construction and constant product changes, whether technical or simply cosmetic.

Monopoly

Monopoly exists when there is only one seller or producer.

When there is only one seller or producer, the situation is known as a **monopoly**. A monopoly may exist if the total market is too small for more than one producer to operate profitably. Even when a monopoly does exist, however, consumers usually have a choice as to whether they will buy the product. If the only beef producer in the area charges too much, for example, consumers can always switch to chicken or pork. Where there is no substitute available, such as telephone, utility or transportation services, the government regulates product quality, price and service.

Monopsony is the term for a monopoly on the buyer's side.

A **monopsony** is a monopoly on the buyer's side. Examples are giant supermarket chains that buy from small suppliers, or small manufacturers that depend on government contracts. These small companies are virtually at the mercy of the buyer and have little power to demand higher prices for their products. Often their only alternative is to refuse the order, which usually means severe hardship or bankruptcy.

Summary of the four main types of competition

 **TABLE 1.3**

Perfect or Pure Competition

Many firms in the industry.
Easy to establish a business because of low capital requirements.
Product is identical or very similar to that of other firms.
Individual firms have little control over prices.
Typical products: eggs and wheat.

Monopolistic Competition

Many firms in the industry.
Easy to establish a business because of low capital requirements.
Differences between products are slight and often due only to branding.
Individual firms set prices which may vary slightly over narrow range.
Typical products: the various brands of tires and gasoline.

Oligopoly

A few large firms make up the industry.
Difficult for a new firm to establish because of large capital requirements.
Products may be identical, similar or different.
Individual firms can have considerable control over prices charged for their products.
Typical products: steel, automobiles and aircraft.

Monopoly

Industry consists of one firm only.
Entry into the industry is virtually impossible because of small markets, existing government regulations or large capital requirements.
Prices charged for products or services are usually regulated by government.
Typical products: telephone service, waterworks and electricity.

Why Study Business?

At the beginning of this chapter, we saw how well the average Canadian lives. Since then, we have seen how the high standard of living in a capitalistic system depends on efficient and effective use of the factors of production by organizations. If our standard of living—indeed, our entire way of life—depends on our business system, it makes sense that we should understand how it works.

To understand how a business system operates, we must examine business organizations and the way they function in the economic system as a whole. We must understand how a firm produces goods and services, how it raises the money required to build manufacturing plants and purchase machinery and equipment, and how it recruits and pays people for their work. If we study the marketing function of a business, we will be better equipped to understand the importance of advertising, as well as the roles of the wholesaler and the retailer. At the same time, we must examine the function of managers: how they coordinate raw materials, labour, capital and technology for the efficient production of goods and services.

While the study of business is generally recommended, it is particularly important for those who intend to go into management in a large Canadian corporation or to open their own small business. The principles of business and management remain the same regardless of a company's size, although the method of operation may be different. Large corporations tend to have highly formalized organizational structures, with many specialists to perform the tasks that owners of small businesses must do themselves. It is therefore necessary that anyone intending to operate a small business acquire a more general business education and then hire specialists when appropriate, while those planning to enter large corporations should acquire more specialized training and education in their field of interest.

Finally, understanding our business system enables us to better evaluate the effectiveness of existing as well as proposed government policies. The 1993 federal election was a good example of how difficult it is to make sense of opposing claims by the various political parties. The Liberal Party claimed that job creation was the key to solving Canada's unemployment problems and that its proposed $6 billion infrastructure rebuilding program would get Canada back on track. Both the Conservative and the Reform Party argued that deficit reduction and the national debt were the key issues. The New Democratic Party claimed that the Canada-U.S. free trade agreement was the cause of Canada's unemployment problem and that it should be scrapped; the NDP also insisted that government must continue to intervene in the economy to create jobs. Other parties had still different ideas as to how to solve Canada's economic problems.

Which party does, indeed, have the correct policies? It is necessary to have a basic understanding of economics, business operation, international trade and so on in order to grasp the problems faced by Canada and to evaluate the claims made by businesspeople, politicians, government officials and labour leaders as to the appropriate remedies. People educated in business and economics will be able to analyze in a more critical manner the policies proposed by politicians and political parties.

Chapter Summary

1. A country's standard of living depends on the production of goods and services by the business organizations that are basic entities of its economic system.

2. An economic system is a mechanism that regulates the production and distribution of goods and services in a country by helping to make three basic decisions—what goods and services are to be produced, how to produce them and how to distribute the product among the people.

3. The Canadian economic system is basically capitalistic; but the principles underlying pure capitalism—freedom of choice, private property, freedom of competition and freedom from government intervention—have been influenced in varying degrees by the actions of government or other social institutions.

4. Socialist economic systems range from communism, in which government directs all economic and most social matters, to democratic socialism, in which government intervenes extensively in the nation's economic affairs, but holds power only as long as it is elected by the people.

5. Capitalism, because of the market system, is particularly well suited to the production of capital goods and a wide range of consumer goods and services. However, capitalist systems are subject to business cycles that can hurt economic activity and cause large-scale unemployment. While most industrialized

capitalist countries can protect their people from the ups and downs of the market system through comprehensive social welfare systems, people in less wealthy capitalist countries may suffer.

6. In a communist system, government controls the factors of production and can therefore channel resources into the production of goods or services deemed necessary. As a result, business cycles are eliminated and unemployment and inflation closely controlled. Communism can quickly improve subsistence living conditions that exist in third world countries, educate the population relatively quickly and provide basic social welfare services, housing and medical care. However, the system is unable to increase living standards substantially, because market forces are not allowed to allocate resources on the basis of consumer demand. Since private individuals generally cannot go into business, there is no competition and little incentive to provide consumers with the goods and services they need and want. Most important, as communist systems are basically one-party dictatorships, the political and economic freedom of the people is drastically curtailed.

7. Social democratic countries are a blend of the two extremes. Major industries are usually owned by government while most businesses that produce consumer goods are privately owned. However, economic freedom is often restricted through high taxation and government regulations, which discourage private incentive. Extensive social welfare services also tend to reduce the incentive to work, contributing to low productivity and slow economic growth.

8. Profit is a surplus of revenue over expenses. Profit ensures that firms are effective and efficient in their use of the factors of production, and is necessary for the replacement of worn-out capital goods and the development of new, more efficient machines and production processes. Profits also provide the funds to pay the owners of the firm for their investment. A significant portion (sometimes half) of all business profits are taken by government in the form of taxes. These funds are used to provide necessary services for the population as a whole that private firms might not provide due to their not being profitable. Thus, profits contribute significantly to society in general. For various reasons, including business cycles, profits can fluctuate from year to year, and many firms experience losses for several years in a row during a recession. These losses must be recouped during better economic times.

9. Under a capitalistic economic system, the market is the mechanism that regulates what goods are produced, how the factors of production are allocated and how goods are distributed. Buyers and sellers interact to determine the prices at which existing goods are sold. Greater demand for a particular product tends to cause the price to rise, unless a greater supply is readily available. Similarly if demand drops for a particular product, the price also tends to drop.

10. Competition among firms ensures that prices are kept as low as possible, and the quality of products as high as possible. Competition must be effective and responsible to ensure maximum benefit to society. Unfortunately, effective competition often does not exist. There is a natural tendency for successful firms to buy out their less successful rivals.

11. As both consumers and workers, it is important for us to understand the Canadian business system in order to make better-informed judgments about government policies that will influence Canada's future.

KEY TERMS

Standard of living 4
Gross national product (GNP) 4
Per capita GNP 4
Gross national income (GNI) 4
Gross domestic product (GDP) 4
Production 5
Factors of production 6
Land 6
Labour 6
Capital 6
Technology 6
Entrepreneur 7
Business organizations 9
Non-profit organizations 9
Consumer goods and services 9
Capital goods 9
Business 10
Economics 10

Business cycles 10
Recession 10
Depression 11
Economic forecasts 11
Economic system 11
Capitalism 12
Laissez-faire 14
Socialism 14
Democratic socialism 15
Communism 15
Marxism-Leninism 15
National Policy 16
Great Depression 17
New Deal 18
John Maynard Keynes 19
Deficit Spending 20
Mixed economies 20
Economic management 21

Stability 21
Inflation 21
Profit 22
Efficiency 23
Effectiveness 23
Market system 25
Equilibrium point 26
Competition 27
Effective competition 27
Responsible competition 27
Perfect or pure competition 27
Monopolistic competition 28
Oligopoly 28
Monopoly 28
Monopsony 28

REVIEW QUESTIONS

1 How is the standard of living determined? What does it indicate about the material well-being of people in a particular country?

2 What problems might be encountered in comparing the standard of living of people in countries with different industrialization levels?

3 Explain how each of the five factors of production can help to increase the standard of living.

4 What is the difference between business and economics?

5 What is an economic system?

6 What is the relationship between a country's economic and political systems?

7 Outline the basic differences between capitalism, democratic socialism and communism.

8 What four basic principles underlie pure capitalism? How does Canada's economic system differ from it?

9 Why is private property so central to capitalism?

10 Why has communism failed, where capitalism has succeeded, in improving the standard of living for citizens beyond meeting their basic needs?

11 Canada has an extensive social welfare system. Why is it then classified as a capitalistic country and not a social democracy?

12 What is profit? What are the benefits of profit to a business?

13 Why is profit called a regulator? Distinguish between effectiveness and efficiency.

14 How do business profits contribute to the welfare of society?

15 Why is it virtually impossible for businesses to maximize their profit?

16 What is the relationship between profit, competition and the market?

17 Distinguish between effective and responsible competition.

18 Distinguish between the four types of competition.

19 How can competition between firms be limited?

20 Why should every citizen have some knowledge of the Canadian business system?

DISCUSSION QUESTIONS

1 Faced with a huge and rapidly growing population, and an underdeveloped economy with a high illiteracy rate, what economic system would you implement if given the chance? Why?

2 Government intervention in our economic system has helped to make individuals' lives more secure, but it means more regulation of the activities of individuals and businesses; as well, government requires more information about its citizens. What are your views on this type of government intervention?

3 Keeping in mind the four principles of capitalism, why is political freedom so important to the survival of the entrepreneurial spirit? Discuss.

4 How might the concept of profit be applied to government and non-profit organizations, to ensure these services or products are provided effectively and efficiently?

5 Describe the competition that exists between auto manufacturers, Canada's cable television companies and airlines in Canada. Does effective competition exist in these industries? Why or why not?

CASE

1-1

World Population and the Standard of Living

Sometime during the summer of 1999, the earth's population reached six billion people, more than double the number there were in 1950 and two billion more than in 1974. Each day, 200 000 people are added to the world's population, with 90% of that growth occurring in the developing countries. These countries do not have the resources to offer their people a rising standard of education and living.

In recent years, the slow rate of population growth in Europe and North America has also occurred in countries in East Asia (primarily China and Japan, but also such newly industrialized countries as Taiwan and South Korea). Africa has the highest population growth rate. If present trends continue, Nigeria, for example, will have as many people by the year 2040 as the whole of Africa today. The population of Kenya is growing faster still and is expected to double by the year 2004; this growth rate is challenged only by Zimbabwe and Mozambique.

How does this population growth affect economic growth? For example, if West Germany's GDP (gross domestic product) continues to grow at 2% per year, GDP per capita will be 40% higher in 2004. For Kenya's per-capita GDP to be 40% higher in 2004, its growth rate would have to be 6.2% per year over the next 17 years. But the last time Kenya's growth rate exceeded 6% was in 1978.

On the other hand, countries with low growth rates have their problems too. There are fears in the West of mushrooming numbers of elderly who will have to be supported by a shrinking workforce. For example, the International Labour Organization projects that by 2020, Holland will have 756 people aged over 60 for every 1000 workers, compared to 364 in 1985. In comparison, Nigeria, which had 44 people aged over 60 for every 1000 workers in 1985, is expected to have only 74 aged over 60 in 2020, largely because the number of productive workers will continue to increase rapidly over the intervening years.

Unfortunately, the elderly are not the only dependants; the young are too. In Nigeria, for example, for every 1000 workers there are 1170 children under the age of 15. In Nigeria, in 2020, there will still be more dependants (1275, old and young) than there will be in Holland (1140). One of the most damaging effects of rapid population growth is that it reduces the amount of schooling available to each child, and with it the child's capacity to create more wealth than his or her parents.

The short-term probability that developing economies will grow fast enough to keep up with their population is not great. They are faced with two major problems: commodity dependence and huge external debts. Most of the world's poorest countries depend on the selling of commodities into a world market for their export earnings. These markets are not free or fair, with many of the advanced countries supporting schemes for price support and subsidies that have led to artificially swollen farm output in industrial countries. Between 1950 and 1985, the output of kilos of grain per head in Western Europe more than doubled from 234 to 501 kilograms, while output in Africa dropped from 157 to 150 during the same period. European surpluses depress the world prices available to Africans. External debts are also a problem, because money leaves the country and is therefore no longer available for investment—investment that can increase future growth and consequently produce >>

greater wealth creation from within. Although Latin American countries are in the limelight in terms of their foreign debts, African countries are experiencing a much greater problem. For example, Mexico's and Brazil's external debts at the end of 1998 amounted to 18% and 24% of their 1998 GDPs respectively, while those of Sudan and Zaire came to 65% and 42%.[7]

Questions

1 Under what circumstances would it be possible for a country such as Kenya to increase its GDP without increasing its standard of living? Look at the standard-of-living equation to answer this question.

2 How can education, or the lack of it, affect a country's standard of living?

3 Indicate how each of the following might affect the standard of living:

   (a) a large population growth rate, as in Kenya and Nigeria

   (b) when the number of active workers is exceeded by retired ones, as will be the case in Holland and some other European countries in the next century

   (c) illiteracy

   (d) overdependence on commodities

   (e) huge external debts

4 Many developing countries with a large population growth have a relatively high number of people (sometimes 60% to 75%) engaged in agriculture. Why might this be so? How does this factor affect the standard of living?

5 Define the five factors of production, and briefly explain how each factor can contribute to raising the standard of living for a country's citizens.

Profit and Taxation

On a recent radio talk show, during which a politician reviewed the state of the economy, the discussion turned to corporate profits. A listener phoned in and read an article from a newspaper that stated that one of Canada's large banks had announced its earnings were up 26% in the three months ended July 31. He also cited other companies that had claimed profit increases of 75% to 200% from the previous year. When he finished, he asked the talk-show host if it was fair that corporations be allowed to have such high profits. "Obviously, these companies must be taking advantage of the consumer when they rack up such a profit," he stated. Another caller offered her solution, which was to tax away all profits over a certain amount. A third caller went even further, suggesting that government tax away all corporate profits.

Many other callers phoned in to leave their comments. Among them were the following: "profits are excessive"; "many corporations pay little, if any, income tax"; "if corporations paid their employees properly, there wouldn't be any profits"; "all profits should be taxed away by government"; "profits go into the pockets of the rich."

Questions

1 Discuss the above comments made by the callers.

2 What are some basic misconceptions about profits brought out in the case? Why might companies show large profit increases in some years, particularly after a recession?

3 What problems would corporations face if all profits above a certain amount were taxed away?

4 If government taxed away all corporate profits, what potential effect might this have on investment? On employment? On government revenue? On potential entrepreneurs? On a country's standard of living?

2

Starting and Operating a Small Business

Learning Objectives

After reading this chapter, you will be able to

1. Recognize the importance of small business to the Canadian economy.

2. Explain the major problems faced by small business owners.

3. Identify the management practices that make a small business successful.

4. Describe the rewards of going into business, but also know how to avoid failure.

5. Identify the factors to consider in either buying an existing business or starting a new one.

6. Explain the advantages and disadvantages of franchises.

7. Discuss what factors to consider before buying a franchise.

8. Identify the key concerns about setting up a home-based business.

9. Explain the importance of a business plan and identify major items that must be addressed in such a plan.

10. Recognize the importance of adequate financing and explain the difference between debt and equity capital.

Canada Today

In Canada today, most businesses are very small. Ninety-seven per cent of all businesses have fewer than 50 employees. Firms with fewer than five employees represent 78.2% of all businesses. Firms with 5-19 employees represent 15.4%, firms with 20-49 employees represent 3.9%, firms with 50-499 employees represent 2.3% and firms with over 500 employees represent only 0.2% of all businesses in Canada.

A healthy small business sector is crucial to a healthy economy. Small businesses often develop new goods and services, provide innovative ideas and create jobs as they expand. Unfortunately, it is not easy to start a new business and even more difficult to keep it going. Few survive, but those that do may develop into large corporations. Large firms, on the other hand, have the resources to install the newest and most productive manufacturing equipment and thereby make production more efficient. Furthermore, costs such as executive salaries and insurance can be spread over large production volumes, reducing the cost per unit and resulting in lower prices for consumers.

Small Business in Canada

Canadian Federation of Independent Business
www.cfib.ca

Although large corporations provide employment to thousands of people, it is the small business sector that creates new jobs, and many bring to market innovative products or services. In the first eight years of the 1990s, self-employment expanded by an average of 4.1% per year, generating more than three out of four of the new jobs created in the economy. As of December 1998, 18% of the Canadian workforce were self-employed, representing almost 2.6 million workers, an increase of 120 000 from the previous year.[1] From 1991 to 1996 the number of self-employed women in Canada grew 44.3% compared to a 20% growth in self-employed men. This represents 190 780 new self-employed women and 211 265 self-employed men.

Canada leads all industrial nations in the percentage of women comprising the unincorporated workforce. Women are entering business areas such as architecture, engineering, and law, which had been predominately male-dominated in the past. See Figure 2.1 for a presentation of self-employed women by industry.

Women turn to self-employment for a variety of reasons, most of which are similar to the reasons men move toward self-employment. Reasons include independence, an existing family business and lack of suitable employment. However, women's reasons also include the opportunity to work from home and flexible schedules. Needless to say, the availability of reasonably priced technology has also been a major contributing factor to the increase in working from the home. From 1991 to 1996, the percentage of self-employed women working from home increased by 40.9% compared to an increase of only 1.0% in the number of self-employed men working from home. A point of interest to note here is that the increase in the number of immigrant businesswomen for the same period was 42.6%, keeping pace with the 44.3% increase in the number of self-employed women overall.

The educational level of the female entrepreneur is significantly different from the male, with an increase of 70% of businesswomen having a university education compared to an increase of 33.9% of men during the period from 1991 to 1996.

The age of women entrepreneurs also tends to be younger, with four out of five newly self-employed people under age 30 being women. Much has been written on female entrepreneurship recently. A good overview of this topic from a government perspective is found in the publication *Shattering the Glass Box, Women Entrepreneurs and the Knowledge-based Economy*, which is available from Industry Canada.[2]

FIGURE **2.1**

Self-employed women by industry, 1999

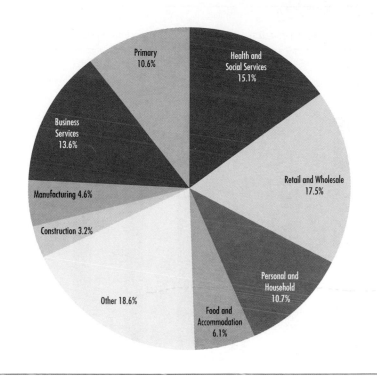

SOURCE: *Small Business Quarterly*, Winter 1999; www.strategis.qc.ca/SSG/mi0670ie.html

Small businesses are classified as having fewer than 100 employees in manufacturing and fewer than 50 employees in all other sectors, and less than $5 million in annual revenues.

Needless to say, a healthy small business sector is crucial to a healthy economy. Small businesses often develop new goods and services, provide innovative ideas and create jobs as they expand. Unfortunately, it is not easy to start a new business and even more difficult to sustain it. Only half of all new businesses survive the first three years of operation, and only one in five is still in operation after five years. A small percentage become medium-sized corporations and a much smaller number develop into large corporations.

Just how bad is the small business failure rate? It seems things are improving. In the third quarter of 1998, business bankruptcies in Canada declined by 8.4%, from 2715 in the second quarter to 2486. This number is down significantly from the third quarter of 1996, when the number reached 3260. Figure 2.2 shows a comparison of business bankruptcies from 1992 to 1998.

Obviously the bankruptcy rate will vary by industry. Which industries represent a decrease in the percentage of bankruptcies? In the fishing and trapping industries a 34% decline in the number of bankruptcies was reported; in transportation and storage, a 31% decline; in wholesale trade, a 26% decline; in logging and forestry, a 17% decline; and in finance and insurance, a 15% decline. Meanwhile, who is in trouble? In the mining, quarrying and oil exploration industries, a 39% increase was reported in the number of bankruptcies.[3]

Small business is defined by Statistics Canada as a business with revenues of between $10 000 and $2 million. In Canada, 97% of businesses are classed as small.

Business bankruptcies for the first and third quarters, 1992–1998

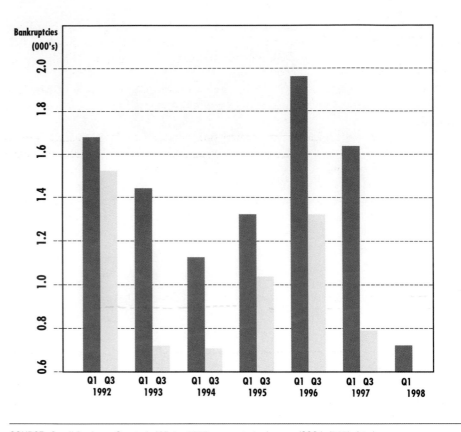

SOURCE: *Small Business Quarterly*, Winter 1999; www.strategis.qc.ca/SSG/mi067ie.html

A word of caution here—just what is the definition of *failure*? According to Dun and Bradstreet, a firm fails if the firm is involved in court proceedings or voluntary actions concerning losses to creditors. However, statistics bandied about with respect to small business *failures* include many other situations, such as discontinued ownership and discontinued businesses. Perhaps the owners felt they were unable to attain their personal financial goals, perhaps they were simply tired of working 100 hours per week, or perhaps the responsibility was too stressful. Yet, does this really mean that the small business owner has *failed*?[4]

If we examine the reasons for the failures rather than the numbers, the picture is interesting but still somewhat confusing. Studies contradict each other concerning what led to the failure of the business. Some of the most common variables examined in an attempt to create a prediction model for business failure include availability of capital, industry experience, management experience, education, staffing, partner(s), family-owned, marketing skills, record keeping, financial control, professional advisor and business plan. It has been suggested that some variables are more appropriate than others depending on the type of industry. For example, the existence of financial control, record keeping and planning are of major importance in predicting success in the retail sector.[5] In another study by the same author, planning, professional advice, education and staffing emerge as predictors of success or failure.[6] Another author suggests that understanding how to sell is even more important to the success of a new business than raising capital.[7] Other research suggests that young firms are more likely to fail than older, more established firms. Also, very young firms must exhibit growth at the outset within a short period of time to increase their chance of survival. This study also indicates that larger firms are more likely to succeed than smaller ones.[8]

Where does all this lead? Back to a business education. One must learn the fundamentals of planning, controlling, selling, marketing, record keeping (accounting) and leading.

A retail or service business is the easiest type of small business to start. This is evident in the many shoe, stationery, florist, drug and convenience stores that exist in shopping centres and downtown areas across Canada. Many businesses are established to provide services for large business firms or to supply parts and sub-assemblies for more complex products manufactured by them. Many businesses are started by individuals with expertise in an area of high technology. Some start their operation in modest quarters such as a garage, as was the case with Apple Computer, or in an old service station, as was the case with Ben and Jerry's Ice Cream.

Problems Faced by Small Business Owners

Many entrepreneurs strike out on their own because they are unable to develop a new idea with their former companies. But innovative ideas or expertise in one particular area are only part of a successful business. The new entrepreneur faces several problems. Some of the most difficult are lack of management skills, inadequate financing and government regulations.

Lack of Management Skills

Many factors can account for the high failure rate of new businesses, including poor sales, poor financing, problems of inventory, high operating costs, labour problems, poor location and so on. But in the final analysis, the failure often comes down to poor management or a lack of management skills. A business usually fails because of a series of mistakes made by its manager. Experience and perseverance pay off, however. Many entrepreneurs who fail in their first venture are successful the second or third time.

Inadequate Financing

Inadequate financing is often included under poor management as a major cause of small business failure. Many new entrepreneurs start a business without sufficient cash to carry them through the initial period of a year or more, when sales are low and expenses high. One common source of funds is a personal loan from a family member or friend. Money can also be borrowed from one of the chartered banks or from the Business Development Bank (BDB). These sources, however, require either collateral or a personal guarantee to secure the loan as well as detailed forecasts of sales, profits and cash flow. Getting funds is, therefore, not always easy. One solution is to find partners who will invest money and offer complementary business experience. Another solution is to incorporate and raise money through the sale of shares and/or to bring in venture capitalists. We will discuss these various options later in this chapter and also in Chapter 9.

Government Regulations

Complying with government regulations costs business time and money. Large companies have the resources to hire employees to fill out forms and supply the various levels of government with operating statistics. However, many small businesses cannot afford to hire additional employees, and owners often do the paperwork after hours. Thus, many small business owners consider the time and money involved in complying with government regulations a major problem. A major survey conducted by the Canadian Federation of Independent Business indicated that 34% of respondents found the employment-related paper burden an impediment to hiring.

Taxes

The Canadian Federation of Independent Business (CFIB) notes that 78.2% of all firms in Canada employ fewer than five people. Businesses must pay a variety of taxes including payroll taxes, property taxes, goods and services taxes, provincial sales taxes and income taxes. The proportion of these taxes that are payable irrespective of profitability have increased significantly over the last four decades. That is, taxes that are not dependent on the firm's profit, such as property taxes, have become a larger percentage of total taxes paid.

In the first half of 1998, over 75% of CFIB members reported total tax burdens to be an item of major concern. Approximately 50% favoured reductions of payroll and personal taxes in order to help their business. See Figure 2.3.

FIGURE 2.3

Comparison of top concerns for SMEs (1998–1999)

Concern	% Response		Ranking	
	1998	**1999**	**1998**	**1999**
Total tax burden	75.2	78.9	1	1
Employment insurance	52.6	60.9	4	2
Government regulations	56.3	58.6	3	3
Government debt/deficit	65.6	57.1	2	4
Workers' compensation	49.0	44.5	5	5
Cost of local government	43.1	41.7	6	6
Labour shortage	30.6	33.1	7	7
Provincial labour laws	24.9	26.6	9	8
Availability of financing	29.4		8	

SOURCE: Canadian Federation of Independent Business, Small Business Primer; www.cfib.ca/research/reports/primer98; www.cfib.ca/research/reports/primer99.

Why do 70% to 80% of all new businesses fail within their first five years?

Although many of those owner-managers who fail attribute their bankruptcy to adverse business conditions, beyond the control of the entrepreneur, statistics indicate that this is true for only a tiny number of bankruptcies. For example, consider several Toronto retailers that went bankrupt because of subway construction that made them inaccessible to customers.

A major reason is mismanagement. The entrepreneur or owner-manager often enters the market with extremely high expectations, but cannot manage the firm's finances. Without proper foresight, and proper operational decision making, a business can't survive. On the other hand, good management will bring the business through good times and bad, the vast majority of the time.

A common problem faced by small-business managers is that they want to do everything themselves. They refuse to delegate responsibility to subordinates, and as a result details are overlooked, the product suffers, and ultimately the business goes downhill. But sometimes even when responsibilities are successfully delegated, rapid growth can place owner-managers in jeopardy.

Another major problem involves heavy borrowing to finance capital expenditures and higher operating costs that can far exceed revenues needed to pay creditors. As a result, there is a cash squeeze. If this cash squeeze becomes too great, the enterprise could founder. And even if the inflow of money barely matches the outflow, bankers or creditors could become nervous as the original line of credit increases from $50 000 to $250 000, despite the fact that the business remains viable.

Another issue is undercapitalization, in which a business is unable to take off due to a shortage of operating cash. For example, a manufacturer may have used all start-up capital to invest in machinery and equipment, or a retailer has tied up the cash in leasehold improvements and inventories. A cash shortage accompanying a growth phase leaves little room to manoeuvre and can also jeopardize a new business if the economic climate sours. With no cash reserves, the business has nothing to fall back on during lean times. This was the situation facing many businesses during 1981 and 1982, when interest rates were more than 20%.

A related problem involves the lack of proper financial planning. Once financing has been obtained, many entrepreneurs discard the carefully prepared business plan and its associated budget. Although a budget isn't totally inflexible, nevertheless, the basic structure should be followed. Otherwise, there might be problems getting more money when it is needed for business expansion.

Managing customer credit is also a major challenge. By not offering credit to customers, the entrepreneur could lose business, yet if the credit policy is too liberal, it could mean loss of control of receivables. Once an outstanding account ages beyond a certain point, attention must be paid to the account. Instead, many inexperienced business owners simply continue to extend credit, and ultimately end up with huge losses.

Another common cause of small-business failure is a reluctance to spend the money required to draft a proper marketing strategy and put it in place. Many entrepreneurs believe that advertising is a discretionary expense and they can get by with an amateurish, low budget effort that misses the target clientele or doesn't hit it hard enough.

In the final analysis there is no sector where businesses are more or less vulnerable to bankruptcy. It all comes down to proper management and sufficient working capital.[9]

Mismanagement Main Cause of New Ventures Failure

Requirements for Business Success

Since lack of management skills such as planning, controlling, staffing, and record keeping (accounting) appears to be the main reason for small business failure, eliminating this problem is crucial to the success of any new venture. The new entrepreneur needs to acquire the basic management skills and continue to develop management potential through business education and his or her own hard work, creativity and self-discipline. Successful small business management depends on the following factors.

Acquiring a Business Education

There are many stories of successful entrepreneurs who never had formal business training or education. Some appear to have an inborn talent for starting and managing a business. Others are simply fortunate to have survived. For most, starting and operating a new business is an arduous process of trial and error, and learning from previous experience. The learning process can be accelerated through formal education at colleges and universities and by participation in courses. The entrepreneur needs to know about accounting, pricing, advertising, budgeting and handling people, and cannot rely on his or her own particular area of expertise. A good engineer or salesperson, for example, is not necessarily a good manager. If the entrepreneur is weak in any area, partners can often supply the necessary expertise.

Careful Planning

A major function of management is to plan for the future by establishing objectives and determining ways of achieving them. Although the future cannot be controlled and no plan can prevent future events from affecting the business, careful planning can minimize the risks by forecasting future problems and setting up contingency plans. Finding and training a reliable successor, for example, can prevent serious setbacks when an owner dies or cannot continue to manage the firm. Looking to the future can also help to identify business opportunities that might otherwise go unnoticed.

Careful Money Management

Money is the lifeblood of a business. Many profitable companies have gone bankrupt because they could not pay bills. Often, too much money is tied up in inventory or plant and equipment. Once there is a real possibility of bankruptcy, it is difficult, if not impossible, to secure a loan from a bank or other financial institution. Financial planning and cash budgeting can prevent serious money shortages. By projecting cash inflow and outflow for six months to a year, a business can match revenues with expenses, forecast shortages and take appropriate action. Careful money management also means control of a firm's inventory, purchases, payroll, accounts receivable, suppliers' discounts and customer services. All of these topics will be discussed in more detail in Chapter 9.

Keeping Accurate Records

Accurate records indicate how the firm is progressing from day to day, month to month and year to year. They can indicate trends in sales, inventory and accounts receivable, for example, allowing the owner to reverse dangerous trends early. Business records are required by tax department auditors and by bankers or investors if the owner needs to borrow money. Moreover, the owner must know where he or she stands financially. An accurate record system is the cornerstone of a good control system.

Effective Marketing

Marketing essentially means getting the right product to the right customer at the right time and at the right place. Marketing includes making a product that people need and want, and packaging, pricing and promoting it appropriately. It means launching the right sales effort in terms of advertising, merchandising and distribution, and keeping a check on the location to ensure that it continues to provide good access to customers. Finally, marketing means providing customer services such as delivery, maintenance, repair and service follow-up. All of these points must be considered before the business is started as well as during its operation. A new competitor, for example, could upset plans unless met head-on with an appropriate marketing strategy. A discussion of marketing management will be presented in Chapter 8.

Time Management

Most owner-managers will attest that a 70- or 80-hour workweek is commonplace. Unless the owner-manager practises time management by scheduling and prioritizing tasks on a daily, weekly and monthly basis, he or she will neglect work crucial to success. Time management also involves delegation. Delegation means assigning responsibility and authority to others in the organization. Many new owners and inexperienced managers are unwilling to delegate because they believe they can do the job better themselves. But without delegation, an owner-manager is soon preoccupied with minor details while important problems are not given necessary attention. With careful training and supervision, employees can learn to manage their responsibilities effectively. Delegation is not abdication of responsibility on the part of the owner-manager, but rather the key to success and growth.

Acquiring Human Resources

Incompetent and unmotivated employees can mean financial ruin for a small business. Salaries usually represent the greatest expense for businesses, and owners cannot afford employees who do not do their jobs effectively. Incompetent employees make mistakes that cost the firm money and cause poor customer relations.

Unless funds are available to employ an outside personnel agency to recruit new employees, the owner-manager must learn the basic personnel skills of recruiting and selecting employees. He or she will need to know where to look for employees, how to extract critical information about the job skills and interests during the interview, how to test for necessary employee skills and how to check on past employment habits. Once chosen, the new employee must be properly introduced to the firm and trained for the job. Later, new employees must be critically evaluated on their performance.

To recruit and keep good employees, a firm must pay appropriate salaries, benefits and incentives. A profit-sharing plan may be an excellent way to reward effort and ensure loyalty. In addition, most people want regular evaluations of their performance so they know where they stand and have the opportunity to advance in the firm through promotions. Making employees part of a team is an important and ongoing process for the owner-manager. In Chapter 6, we discuss managing people in detail; other aspects of personnel are addressed in Chapter 10.

Growing with the Business

Many entrepreneurs begin their business with the intention of making it grow well beyond the start-up size.

Growth can happen in many ways, but there are some general strategies that successful firms have used. One method is to expand the firm's market either domestically or internationally. Another method is to focus on a niche market—offering the best product or service for a narrow application suited to a narrow market. A third strategy is to sell the rights of a product, process or service to other individuals or companies. This approach can mean the establishment of distributors, licensees or franchisees who share in the profits. Companies have used these approaches singly or in combination. Regardless of the course of action chosen, it should match a firm's situation, resources and needs.

In the event of success, the owner-manager must decide how large the firm should become. The transition from a small to medium operation, and then to a large corporation, presents many new problems. Many owners prefer to remain small, particularly if they are making an adequate living and have achieved a high status in the community. However, if the business grows, the owner must be prepared for changes. In a large corporation, for example, he or she will be concerned mainly with planning and controlling products and finances.

Going into Business for Yourself

Guide to Government Services and Support for Small Businesses

strategis.ic.gc.ca/engdoc/main.html

Canada Business Service Centres

www.cbsc.org/english/

Going into business for yourself is not difficult. The problem lies in operating your business on an ongoing basis and getting an adequate return for your investment in both time and money.

What are the rewards? The advantages of operating your own business are many. You may know people in your own community who are well known and active in many areas. Owning a successful small business means that you are your own boss, and that you can achieve job security and have a good income (perhaps even a substantial one). Chances are that you will be well recognized in your community and have the ability to influence its development. You can meet and work with a great variety of people and experience a wide range of challenges. If the business grows and becomes an established company, you can eventually pass it on to your children. In short, owning a successful small business can fulfill most of your personal needs.

How Do You Avoid Failure?

How do you avoid joining the ranks of failed businesses? First, recognize that success generally comes only through hard work. Establishing and operating your business, at least for the first few years, requires many hours of work.

Second, determine whether your personal qualities match those required by a small business owner. Complete a rating form presented in many small business handbooks to identify your standing in each of the areas discussed there. Some of the personal questions you might ask yourself already are: Are you ambitious? Do you desire independence? Are you willing to take a calculated risk? Are you innovative and do you welcome a challenge? Are you a self-starter? Are you in good health? Are you self-confident? Do you have energy and persistence?

Some other questions that you should also consider carefully are: Would you be comfortable dealing with the uncertainties of income? Are you willing to take a substantial cut in income? Are you willing to put up your house as collateral for a bank loan? Do you need relatively stable hours? Does your family require you to spend time with them? Do you have your family's support for working long hours? Are you willing to live a lower lifestyle? Do you enjoy hobbies that require a lot of your time, and are you willing to sacrifice them if required by your business? Do you have the ability to take risks?

Keep in mind that starting your own business will take a considerable amount of sacrifice on your part and on the part of your family. There is no guarantee of success even if you invest a significant portion of your savings or borrowings in the business. In fact, there is a good chance you could lose it all. Above all, except in rare instances, you can expect it to take some time before your investment and hard work begins to pay off. Even then you may not earn any more than you made in your job and you may not have the non-wage benefits you had as an employee.

The key to reducing your risk in your own business is to plan ahead. Take the various tests and evaluation techniques available to determine if you have the qualities and skills that are required to be in business for yourself. Be sure to involve your family in these discussions because you will need their support. Then carefully identify what business you may want to get into. Your previous job and experience should be a determining factor.

Finally, carefully research the kind of business you would like to operate and then decide on whether to start it from scratch, buy an existing business or buy a franchise. Obviously, careful analysis and planning are critical for future success in your business.

Evaluating Business Opportunities

Perhaps you already know that the product or service you want to offer requires that you start a business from scratch. If that is the case, then your course is clear. However, if you are simply interested in going into a business that will give you a reasonable return, you will have to decide between buying an existing business or starting one from scratch. There are advantages and disadvantages to both options. Let's examine some of the critical factors you should keep in mind before deciding on one course or the other. We will look at franchises a little later in this chapter.

Availability of Existing Businesses

First, you must determine if there are businesses available to purchase, and, if so, whether they are suitable for you. A business may meet both criteria but be beyond your financial capabilities.

Amount of Capital Available

Generally, it costs more to buy an existing business than to start one from scratch. If you establish your own business, you can start small on the basis of your available capital and expand as your business becomes more profitable and you gain experience. Second, the seller of a business will often ask more money for an established business than it costs to start the same kind of business. In some cases, the higher price is justified by the customer base or by the reputation the business has acquired; this is known as goodwill. In some instances, a seller may want to get out of the business and sell at a bargain price—whether for health reasons, because of the need for cash or because the seller does not know the true value of the business. You may even be able to acquire an existing business at lower cost than if you built that business from scratch, especially if fixtures and equipment are required. The existing equipment, provided it is in good condition, can probably be purchased for a lower cost than comparable equipment that is new.

Risk

Generally speaking, purchasing an existing business is less risky than starting a new one. As discussed earlier in the chapter, most businesses do not last more than five years. If an existing business has lasted for some time and is profitable, you may be able to avoid many of the problems that new businesses experience and thus avoid premature failure.

However, certain risks are associated with buying even an established business. Past success does not assure future success. You should look at the business and determine whether the product or service that you are offering will still be required a few years down the road. In addition, there may be external changes to your surroundings that may cause your business to lose sales, such as a new road that takes your traffic away. Furthermore, the equipment and fixtures may be too old and inefficient or the existing inventory overvalued and/or outdated.

Time

Buying an established business is usually the quickest way to start your own business since everything—the equipment, inventory, employees, accounting system—is already in place. However, buying a business be a lengthy process depending on how long it takes to verify the soundness of the business, negotiate the purchase price and so on.

Location and Facilities

For retail businesses in particular, a prime location is a major advantage. If location is extremely important for a particular business, it may be wise to purchase the business for this factor alone.

Reputation

If an existing business has an excellent reputation, it may be worthwhile to purchase the business. If you start your own business, it may take a considerable period of time to acquire a similar reputation.

Assistance

If you purchase an existing business, you may also be able to negotiate for continued advice from the previous owner. You will also in all likelihood retain most of the employees, who have considerable experience and knowledge about the business. In exchange you are accepting an established way of doing things. If you later decide that some actions or procedures need to be changed, you may encounter resistance from existing employees.

As we have seen, there are several advantages to buying an established business. You have an established clientele, a building, fixtures and a stock of merchandise. You are familiar with your suppliers and need only establish credit with them to continue receiving merchandise or raw materials. You may also be able to retain the previous employees and consult the original owner until you know the intricacies of the business and are fully established. But it is important to ensure that the business is a sound venture. Ask yourself why the current owner wants to sell. Remember, the owner is not obligated to voluntarily point out any of the problems facing the business. If you ask, however, and he or she provides you with false information, you are likely to have grounds for legal recourse.

Buying an Established Business

Before actually buying an existing business, you should make a list of the types of businesses in which you are interested. Then determine the criteria you will use to evaluate each type of business. You may want to ask questions pertaining to maximum price, geographic area, existing profitability, size of established clientele, and willingness of present management to stay on, at least during the transition period.

Once you are clear about your criteria, then make an active search for the business. Talk to people who hear about businesses that are for sale (wholesalers, suppliers or retailers depending on the type of business you are interested in purchasing). Local newspapers and business publications are other sources of information. You may also want to talk with real estate agents who may have businesses for sale that are not advertised. Getting the word out that you are interested in purchasing a business may also provide some leads. Finally, if you know of an existing business that you would like, approach the owner to see if he or she is willing to sell it.

Once you have located a business that fits your criteria, you must investigate it thoroughly. Begin by inspecting the facilities and location, and by talking with employees, management, customers and suppliers. Ensure that the facilities and equipment are in good shape, and that the staff and management are well trained and competent. Try to find out why the owner wants to sell the business, and whether the selling price and other terms are reasonable.

If everything checks out up to this point, your next step is a complete financial analysis of the business. You will need financial statements for as many years back as possible (at least five years, unless the business has been in existence for a shorter period of time).

You may find that some owners are unwilling to hand over these financial statements. Perhaps they are not convinced that you are a legitimate buyer and are reluctant to give out confidential information. You must convince them that you are sincere. Show them your own financial statements or tax returns and provide some proof that you have the financial wherewithal to buy the business. If they are seriously interested in selling, at some point they must give you the financial statements. If they do not, they probably have something to hide, and you should look for a new opportunity. On the other hand, the financial condition of the business may be of less interest to you than the customer list, equipment, location or other tangible assets.

If you do get the financial statements, a preliminary look at the accounts receivable, accounts payable, existing assets and inventory, sales and profit and/or loss will give you a quick overview of how the business is performing. If everything looks satisfactory and there are no obvious problems, then a more thorough investigation is advisable. An accountant can provide you with a thorough analysis of the balance sheet and income statement, sales and expenses, assets and liabilities. This analysis will establish the value of plant equipment, machinery and inventory, and help you determine a realistic offer. An accountant will also verify that the financial statements have been audited to ensure that everything as stated is accurate. Remember that an unprofitable business can be made to look profitable on paper.

A lawyer must confirm the legal title of the company and find out if there are taxes owing or liens on any of the business's assets. The lawyer will also inquire into legal aspects of the existing business and identify if, for example, you are buying the shares of the company or its assets. In the former case, you may find yourself saddled with liabilities that put a severe strain on your financial situation. The local municipal office can tell you if the business is violating any local regulations. You should also analyze the industry to see whether the firm's products are viable. Statistics Canada can provide the data, and the Federal Business Development Bank has counsellors who will evaluate any company and help draw up a final offer.

In terms of your total investment, you have to be sure that your new business promises a return greater than what you might earn from a bank or from investing in government bonds. Keep in mind that you are risking your own money and there is always a chance, no matter how thorough you are in checking out the company, that you may go bankrupt. Your potential income has to be enough to offset the risk.

Starting a New Business

Starting a new business involves more work than buying an established business. It may be the only way, however, to profit from your skills or to get a new product on the market. Above all, everything can be tailored to your particular needs and wants. You can choose the location, facilities, fixtures and equipment. You can also develop your own operating and information systems. You can choose your suppliers, and if you need inventory, you can purchase it new. You can also select and train your own employees. Nor do you have to pay for goodwill—the payment that often must be made to a previous owner for establishing a good business reputation.

Franchising

Since starting a new business is a big undertaking for an inexperienced individual, franchising has become extremely popular. A **franchise** is a licence to either manufacture or sell (or both) a well-known product or service developed by the **franchiser**. The **franchisee** signs a contract that gives him or her the right to sell the franchiser's products or service and use the franchiser's name, trademark or other commercial symbols. The contract also stipulates how to operate the business on

Franchise—a licence either to manufacture or to sell, or both, a well-known product or service developed by the franchiser.

Franchiser—the person or company selling a franchise operation.

Franchisee—the person buying the franchise and operating it according to the franchiser's policies.

Franchise outlets   >

the basis of the franchiser's established methods. The right to this franchise usually lasts for a specified period of time and is usually limited to a particular territory.

More and more new businesses are started as franchises. Some of the best-known ones are McDonald's, Burger King and Midas Muffler. There are thousands of franchise opportunities and many of the newer ones can be purchased for as little as $5000. But beware: not all franchises mean instant riches. While some have been known to reward their owners handsomely, many others barely produce a nominal income, and some have gone bankrupt.

Franchises are particularly popular when it comes to small retail outlets such as specialty clothing stores, shoe stores and convenience stores. They combine the advantages of large chain-store retailers (e.g., centralized buying of merchandise, supplies and equipment) with the advantages of the small independent retailer, in particular the ability to make independent decisions about the operation of the business.

Advantages of Franchises

There are many advantages to owning a franchise. You start with a proven product or service and receive the accompanying marketing expertise and standardized operating methods. In addition, you have the benefit of the franchiser's name and goodwill, centralized research on the product or service and group purchasing power. The franchiser usually helps to set up the new business and find a location. If a building is required, plans and building expertise are available; any equipment required is furnished quickly by suppliers who are aware of the necessary specifications. Help is also available when it comes to setting up an advertising campaign and inventory control system. Indeed, many franchises are established as turn-key operations in which the future operator simply unlocks the door on the first day and is ready for business.

Training provided by the franchiser eliminates one of the major problems small businesses experience: failure due to lack of experience and poor management skills. Fewer than 10% of the 25 000 franchise outlets across Canada fail within the first year. Nevertheless, some franchises have failed, together with the franchisees; risk is never entirely eliminated from any business operation.

The major benefit to the franchiser is the rapid expansion of the franchiser's market without investment of great amounts of capital, and exposure of the products and/or service. The franchisees are motivated because they have a personal and often substantial investment in the business.

Disadvantages of Franchises

A franchise also has drawbacks. The initial investment may be high, especially if the franchise is well known and successful. For example, the franchise fee for A&W is $20 000, which seems fairly modest; however, the capital requirements are "net worth of $300 000 with $75 000 to invest." The franchise fee for McDonald's is $300 000 to $350 000. See www.mcdonalds.com/corporate/franchise/outside/require/index.html. The franchisee is also required to adhere strictly to policies regarding hours of operation, number of staff, methods of operation and so on. The franchisee usually also pays a monthly royalty based on percentage of sales.

The same care should be taken in buying a franchise as in buying any established small business. Many franchises are new and have not proven themselves for any length of time. New franchises may not give the owner many advantages in starting the business, and franchisers often inflate their projected earnings in order to sell their franchises.

Franchise handbook.com
www.franchisehandbook.com/featured.aw1

Buying a Franchise or Starting Your Own Business

Buying a Franchise

- Operational training usually provided by franchiser.

- Right to use a known trade name or trademark. Franchise operation completely identified with franchiser.

- Able to sell a proven product or service with established public acceptance.

- Buying a package, so ready to start full operation sooner.

- Less working capital may be required because of tighter controls and franchiser's terms of merchandise supply.

- Profit and loss forecasts may be more accurate since they are based on proven similar operations.

- Greater chance of initial success.

- Sales territory defined by franchiser.

- Benefit from standard national and local advertising of prices, products and service.

- Franchiser is often sole source for merchandise.

Starting Your Own Business

- Management ability based on your own expertise.

- Time required to establish name, but more identification of owner of business.

- Time required to establish name, products and/or service.

- May have to start slowly. Longer time to realize full potential.

- Risk of mistakes and longer time to start can mean greater financing needs. May be difficult to establish terms with suppliers.

- Risk of errors in estimating expenses, sales and profits, especially for an unproven venture.

- Greater chance of failure due to time required for establishment, and possibility of mistakes, especially in regard to marketing and planning.

- No restrictions on expanding territory. No risk that expanded territory already has identical operation to yours.

- Freedom to advertise when you want (and can afford to) and to set your own specials or discounts to meet competition.

- Can buy from any supplier in order to get best prices and terms.

SOURCE: *Buying a Franchise*, Pamphlet #20, Management Series, Federal Business Development Bank.

Factors to Consider When Buying a Franchise

The adage "Before you invest, investigate" holds true for a franchise as well. Some of the major factors that a potential buyer should investigate are listed below.

1. *Investigate the franchiser.* Since you are relying on the franchiser for expertise in selling or manufacturing a particular product or service, it should have an operating history. Is the franchise a large national company or a relatively unproven small company?

2. *Closely scrutinize the franchise itself.* What are you buying? Is it a product, process or trade name? How long has the franchise been in existence and operating? Is it well established, growing or stable? Try to find out how many franchises are currently operating and some names and addresses of owners.

3. *Find out how much the franchise generates in sales and profit on average.* You should be able to obtain forecasts of both sales and expenses over the next few years. At the same time, do your own market study; the franchiser might be too optimistic in his or her forecasts.

4. *Investigate the location and premises' requirements.* Who decides on the location? You or the franchiser? Do the premises have to meet certain standards, such as size or street frontage? Can you adapt existing premises or is a new building required?

5. *Investigate requirements for equipment, fixtures and layout.* Does the franchise agreement require you to purchase specific equipment and fixtures in order to maintain a uniform appearance? If so, do you have to buy them from a specific source or can you try to find the best deal? If you have to buy them from a particular source, find out if you can get comfortable repayment terms.

6. *Consider the franchise territory.* Has the territory been clearly defined? For how long is this territory exclusively yours? Has the franchiser guaranteed that no other franchises will be sold for a given period of time, or that you have the right to first refusal in your territory? Check to ensure that you do not have to buy more franchise operations in order to retain exclusive territory. Can the size of your territory be reduced at any time by the franchiser? Can you expand your territory? If you have a choice of initial location, examine each one carefully (preferably with an advisor) and study the potential of each location in terms of sales.

7. *Consider the purchase costs of the franchise.* Is there a franchise fee? If so, how much is it? What does the franchise package include? Is it just the use of a name or trademark, or are you also buying initial inventory, equipment and fixtures? Are there also service charges such as royalty fees?

8. *Find out about training offered.* Does the franchiser provide training for you and your staff? Is it only a one-time affair or is it ongoing? Does the training consist of management skills, product or service skills, operational skills or a combination of all three? How much do you have to pay for this service?

9. *Ask about prices and sales.* Are you able to adjust prices or are they set by the franchiser? Can you offer sales specials on your own? Are there sales quotas and, if so, are they realistic?

10. *Ask about products and supplies.* Does the contract specify what products you must carry? Can you stock product lines other than those of the franchiser? Are the sources for your products specified or can you shop around for the best deal? What are the payment terms? Are there minimums specified for order size?

11. *Find out about business controls.* Does the franchiser specify how the franchisee must operate the business? Although this may seem like a curtailment of freedom, it is also the only way of ensuring that the franchises operate in a uniform manner. These controls usually include advertising policies, hours and conduct of business, accounting procedures, reports from franchisee to franchiser, and even access to the franchisee's records. It may also stipulate that the franchisee must operate the business personally and that the franchiser has the final word in any disagreements between the two parties.

12. *Understand the franchise contract.* You must understand every clause of the contract and make sure that all obligations and freedoms are specified. Especially important are clauses pertaining to termination, bankruptcy, transfer, renewal and sale of the franchise. Under what conditions can the franchiser revoke the franchise agreement?

Many franchisers will prepare a package that includes general information about the franchise and forecasts of financial statements, including cash flow and projections

Is Franchising Really a Safe Bet?

In a discussion of small business failure rates in the United States and the United Kingdom, authors Stanworth, Purdy, Price and Zafiris have concluded that franchising appears to be more risky than conventional business enterprises in the early years. However, after four or five years the failure rate is relatively low. Once again a clear definition of what constitutes failure is not readily available. If a franchisee decides, for personal reasons, to close the franchise, is this "failure"? The authors reviewed many prior studies on franchising and found that several factors emerged to explain franchise failures. These factors include poor selection criteria for choosing franchisees, which can lead to franchiser/franchisee conflict and can also contribute to ineffective decision making on the part of the franchisee. Also a second factor is the problem of market saturation due to multiple franchise outlets in the same market area.[10]

Researchers Fenwick and Strombom identified the same two factors as being of utmost importance. They noted that the location, once chosen, is extremely difficult to change in most cases, and therefore location selection must be carefully examined. Also, the selection of a suitable franchisee is critical to the success of the operation. The researchers conducted a study of a New Zealand retail sporting-goods franchise operation to determine the importance of owner-managers' characteristics and store location on the performance of various outlets. The study found that entrepreneurial franchisees and those with previous management experience in a similar role performed poorly due to preconceived notions of how things should be done and the tendency to "rock the boat." Such behaviour often led to franchisee/franchiser conflict. Therefore, at least in this study, it was suggested that applicants with little or no management experience (those more readily accepting of franchise rules, regulations. policies and procedures), may be a better choice as a franchisee. As Fenwick and Strombom conclude, "The three keys to franchisee success appear to be location, location and the franchisee."[11]

of future income. An accountant can help uncover potential problems that may not be easily detected by a cursory examination and that require an in-depth financial analysis. For example, you may find that the franchise will be profitable if you can capture a large market, but this may take considerable time.

Finally, check on the franchise company with all available sources, including credit agencies, banks and the Better Business Bureau. If the franchiser has had financial problems or customer complaints about the service, these sources will have the information available. Remember, the better the franchise (i.e., the longer it has proven itself in the marketplace), the higher its cost.

The Home Business

The 1990s were probably best known for corporate downsizing—reducing the number of employees to reduce costs and become more efficient. The federal and provincial governments, faced with huge deficits and debts, were also forced to reduce the number of employees and new hiring. With few job prospects but often great skills, many of these individuals began to sell their skills to whomever required them. Often employees who were laid off by a company were hired back on a contract basis to do some of the same work they were doing before as employees. Others learned new skills and performed these out of their home.

One of the major advantages of operating a business out of your own home is the low overhead. In other words, the costs of operating the business are low because no expensive office space must be rented and often no renovations must be performed. A spare room is often all that is required as an office. Other operating costs such as telephone, heat and light are also minimal. Since commuting is often no longer required, automobile operating costs are reduced, as is the time spent on the road. But perhaps most important of all, whatever expenses are incurred can be deducted from revenues earned. For example, part of the total heating bill for the home can be classed as a business expense, as can property tax, telephone and cleaning. Any equipment purchased to carry on business, such as computers, fax machine, copier, desk and chairs, and all supplies, are also an expense and can be deducted from income before taxes are paid on it. A **home business** therefore can minimize one of the major problems in starting a business—adequate financing. And since a skill exists that is being sold, the risk in starting and operating a new business is also reduced.

A profound impact on the home office is the Internet. Not only is it an excellent method for communication via e-mail, but its potential uses for selling and advertising are tremendous. Through the World Wide Web, you can advertise your services, allow potential customers to download catalogues or advertising brochures and sell your product on-line. Statistics Canada reported that 4.3 million households used computer communication in 1998, up 24.6% from the 3.4 million users in 1997. It is important to note that Internet use increases with income and educational level. For example, 50.4% of the highest-income households reported a regular Internet user, whereas only 4.1% of the lowest-income group reported a regular user. Also, 68.1% of households in which the head of the household had a university education were connected, while only 12.6% of those households where the head did not complete high school were connected. Of the first group (university educated), 46.7% used the Internet at home and only 6.6% of the second group (less than high school) used the Internet at home. This type of demographic information is essential for entrepreneurs planning to advertise, market or sell a product via the Internet.

Setting Up the Home Office

A home office can be a spare room with a desk and chair or an elaborate office with all the latest office gadgets. It depends on the money that you have available to furnish it and the requirements of your business. If you do not have clients visiting your office, then anything that you can afford or that makes you comfortable goes.

> **Home business**— a small business operated out of the home, usually established because the person who starts it has a skill that can be performed at home. A home business has a number of cost advantages for the owner..

Working from Home

www.homeworks.com

< Jim Carroll, co-author of the best-selling *Canadian Internet Handbook*, works from a home office

If clients are involved, then a certain decor is required to make them feel comfortable and to inspire confidence in your services. Above all, one important consideration is to make your office acceptable to Canada Customs and Revenue Agency, since you will want to be able to deduct your office expenses from your revenues before you pay your taxes. Let's look at some of these requirements.

Canada Customs and Revenue Agency

Are you really a legitimate self-employed individual? That is the question Canada Customs and Revenue Agency (CCRA) may ask if they ever question your expense deductions. CCRA will be satisfied if you can prove that you as the new entrepreneur have significant control over how you conduct your business. If, for example, you simply work in your home office under contract with your previous employer, but that employer has significant direction and control when you work, then in CCRA's eyes you are probably an employee.

Another procedure used by CCRA is to test whether your contribution to the company is so significant that there is a risk of profit or loss. Other questions that CCRA might want answered concern the number of clients you service out of your business, and whether you receive such things as dental plans and pension benefits from your previous employer. Because the number of people working from home has increased so dramatically, CCRA has hired a large number of additional auditors to look specifically at self-employed individuals.

If you are moving to self-employment under contract with your former employer, consult with a professional accountant so that your agreement conforms with the CCRA guidelines. In fact, it might be wise to get a ruling from CCRA about the tax status of your new relationship.

As a truly self-employed individual you can deduct a wide variety of expenses, including your automobile—gas, oil, insurance and its maintenance; business insurance; office equipment; a portion of property taxes; mortgage interest; hydro and telephone costs; and some entertainment costs, among others. However, there are also two main classes of employees who are not considered strictly self-employed: commissioned employees and salaried employees. If you fall into either of these two classes you will not be allowed to deduct all business expenses. For example, a commissioned salesperson can claim a portion of property taxes, insurance, maintenance and utilities but not mortgage interest or house depreciation. In contrast, if you fall into the salaried class you can only claim a portion of expenses such as heating and lighting, but not property tax, insurance and mortgage interest.

CCRA's small business page includes information on business publications including information concerning corporate income tax redesign as well as a *Guide for Canadian Small Business*, which includes information on how to set up a business, the GST/HST, excise taxes and duties, importing/exporting and much more.

Canada Customs and Revenue Agency

www.ccra-adrc.gc.ca/menu-e.html

Renovating the Home Office

If you want to be successful in working at home you need a well-organized work space that is separate from the rest of the house. The money you spend on your office may range from a few hundred dollars for the purchase of a desk and filing cabinets to tens of thousands of dollars for a renovated basement with all the bells and whistles of a modern office. If you need to see clients, extra care must be taken to ensure that your place looks professional with a waiting room, magazine racks, tables and comfortable chairs. The actual office must be neat and provide the client with the feeling that his or her business will be well taken care of, that an important contract will not be smothered under piles of paper, and so on. Many office furniture companies now sell office furniture for the home office with limited space.

When you plan for your home office you must take your work and needs into consideration. Also ensure that when you do renovate you do not violate local bylaws and zoning regulations.

Financing

We will discuss financing a small business later in the chapter and also in Chapter 9. Obtaining adequate financing is a major problem for individuals establishing a new business. However, if you set up your business and operate it from your home, most new business costs are either eliminated or kept to a minimum. Usually the money required comes from savings or from relatives. If that is not possible, a personal loan from a bank may be all that is required. For larger amounts, a mortgage on the home may be another way of getting the necessary funds. The credit card can be a means of financing supplies, office equipment and even small renovations. Some individuals may have received a buyout or severance from their previous employer and can use those funds to start their home business.

Office Equipment

Now that you are your own boss you no longer have to fight with the finance department when you want new equipment. You simply go and buy what you need—if you have the money, that is. It is important, however, to remember that equipment that does the job well is worth the money.

Office furniture is probably first on the list. Most important is the desk and chair where you will spend a considerable amount of time. If you spend eight hours a day in your chair, you will need one that is comfortable and encourages you to work for extended periods. It must be ergonomically designed to reduce the strain that your work places on parts of your body.

To ensure that you get what you need, prepare a list of the items required based on the functions you will be performing and the equipment you will be operating. Visit various office equipment places and try out the chairs and desks. Check that the desk is sturdy and that it has the drawers and shelves that you will need. Ensure that the height is appropriate for you and that it is sturdy when you work on it. Since most people now use computers, make sure that the desk has enough space for the computer, fax machine, printer, mouse and keyboard. Your chair should be adjustable for height and should allow you to swivel around. Be sure that it is ergonomically designed. A chair in which you will spend eight hours a day must be comfortable and you can expect to pay $450 to $550, although some ergonomically designed chairs can range from $700 to $1200.

Computer equipment is also an important item. If you need the latest technology because your business is into multimedia and graphics, where speed is all-important, then you should consider a Pentium II processor combined with as much RAM (random access memory) as you can afford. Machines with high-capacity hard drives, built-in fax modem and high-speed CD-ROMs and graphics cards are available at extremely good prices. Some computer stores include the operating system and a variety of software titles in so-called "office suites" that address most business requirements. But keep in mind that for most office functions such as word processing, spreadsheets, personal contact managers, database operation and accounting, older

Operating a Small Service Business in Alberta

www.cbsc.org/alberta/ op_servbus.html

computers that have first-generation Pentium central processing units (CPUs) such as P133's are sufficient when combined with at least 64 megabytes of RAM. If you require one or more of these machines, check out the used-equipment market. These older machines can be purchased with a SVGA colour monitor for $500 to $600. In addition, you will probably inherit all of the software that the previous owner had on the hard drive. The same holds for printers. Although laser printers have decreased dramatically in price, you may need a dot matrix printer because you print invoices in triplicate. For the accounting function you may want a wide-carriage dot matrix printer for reports. Some of these printers are available used for as low as $50. A good economical printer for business letters and reports would be an entry-level bubble jet if multi-part forms are not required.

The new multifunction machines available from a variety of manufacturers combine a free-standing fax machine, printer, scanner, copier and PC fax. Some of the newest machines contain the software for an entire communications centre that works with your computer. They range from $400 to $1700 and are a valuable addition to any home-based office. The fax machine can be connected to your regular telephone line but with distinctive-ring capability can accept faxes without any intervention on your part. Scanners allow you to scan in any type of logo or graphic and some models have OCR software so that you can convert memos, article and contracts into editable text. The copier allows you multiple copies with enlargement and reduction. You can also hook up this machine to your computer and use it as a printer or fax receiver. These machines come in versions that use laser, inkjet or thermal process for printing. Of the three types of technologies, the laser machine, although more expensive, gives you better copies at a much lower cost per page.

Communications

Can you think of a business that doesn't need a telephone? Not likely. The clients of many home-based businesses are aware of their status and don't object to limited communications facilities. However, as the business grows the communications capabilities must also grow or customers will become annoyed and take their business elsewhere. Today even a home business can have communications capabilities that rival those of a large corporation.

Basically the equipment you choose comes down to your needs. As a home business you can use your residential line and add distinctive-ring capability so that you can ascertain whether a call is for your business or for your residence. You can also use this capability for a fax machine for your business. A busy-line switch can be attached to extension phones in the rest of the house so that a business call cannot be interrupted.

As your business increases, you should consider a private business line. You can also add mailboxes so that customers can leave messages for various individuals. If you leave the office you can have call forwarding to your cell phone so that you are never out of touch with your customers. Equipment is also available so clients can get selected information through fax-back services. Depending on your business you may want to add an answering service, which provides the personal touch of a real operator but without the costs of hiring a person; perhaps this service is only necessary once your business grows to a certain size. Telephone companies have developed elaborate services and equipment to ensure that you and your clients can keep in touch through voice or fax at any time of the day or night if necessary.

One of the major expenses for home-based businesses is long-distance costs. Various telephone companies and telephone service providers have developed plans to suit most subscribers with discounts for various types of calls. An important consideration for some home-based businesses is the ability to let customers from other parts of the country call in without incurring long-distance charges. The 800 or 888 service is designed for businesses that are advertising out of their local calling area. For a small monthly charge as well as a per-minute charge, you can have this service.

One important communications factor is the Internet. The use of the Internet for business transactions is growing at a phenomenal rate. Some government estimates suggest Internet sales could reach US $3.2 trillion by 2003, a figure representing 17.5% of global sales. As of spring 1999, 37% of Canadians had Internet access, with 17% having made an on-line purchase in 1998. The opportunities to target untapped markets are endless. The Canadian government has announced the Canadian Electronic Commerce Strategy, which addresses four major goals:

1) Building trust in the digital economy

2) Clarifying marketplace rules

3) Strengthening the information infrastructure

4) Realizing the opportunities

**Electronic
Commerce in Canada**
http://e-com.ic.gc.ca
Industry Canada
http://strategis.ic.gc.ca

Insurance and Security

As your business moves to your home, it becomes even more important that you are protected from various unexpected disasters such as fire, floods or burglary. It is enough to lose valuable personal possessions without also losing your ability to earn a living.

Demand for home business insurance is rising steadily as more individuals are telecommuting or setting up their home business. Policies now offered provide for loss of equipment on a menu-type basis. In other words, you can choose your type of coverage. There are also policies for specific types of individual. For example, policies for consultants cover loss of equipment and records but not accidents or loss of income. Other policies cover you in the case of injury to clients who come to your home.

Long-term disability insurance may also be required in case you are unable to work. Some insurance companies provide this coverage but usually the owner must have several years of business earnings before he or she can be covered.

With a home-based business you should also protect yourself from burglary. Imagine that you have all of your accounting records, contracts, reports, database, and perhaps even confidential business information on your computer and a burglar takes it all. Where would you be? This underscores the importance of regular backups of your software and personal data. You may even want to use some type of encryption for confidential business information so that someone else cannot make use of it. With the growing number of people working at home, including financial analysts, software programmers and other specialists, more and more critical business information is stored on home-office computers. Some of this information could be of critical importance to competitors.

With so many computers connected to the outside by telephone, you must also consider theft of data from your computer. If outside individuals can access your computer hard drive via a modem, you must ensure that you separate what they can and cannot see. This is called setting up a firewall and it is becoming important as more and more personal computers are connected to the Internet. You don't want to expose your data to hackers or viruses.

Finally, if you keep valuable items in your home business, consider buying a safe or at least some lockable storage area that is difficult to access. Use it for your computer backups and all personal papers of value. Most safes also protect your valuable papers against fire and water damage. Fire-resistant record boxes cost $30 to $100 while small fire-resistant safes with combination locks are available from $200 and up—a small price to pay for the security of irreplaceable business information or personal valuables. Often insurance companies will not provide coverage for your business unless your premises are alarmed and monitored.

Motivation and Discipline

A home-based business may sound appealing for someone who has worked in a company facing a daily commute that can take an hour or more each day. And not having a supervisor looking over your shoulder may also be appealing. But working in your home office has its own problems.

Perhaps the major problem is the isolation that you will now have to cope with as you attempt to offer your services out of your home. Some individuals compensate by making more phone calls and attending more trade shows and other functions.

Some individuals adjust more easily to working at home. Those who enjoy their work and are in constant contact with others are not as likely to suffer from motivation problems. However, those who enjoyed their previous job because of the ability to socialize may miss the time spent chatting at the water cooler, copy machine or coffee and lunch breaks.

It is also more difficult to become motivated when working at home because household chores must be done and it is easy to put aside the business work for other tasks.

Companies that originally saw only increasing productivity from people who worked from the home because they were no longer exposed to commuting or worrying about their children, are now realizing that the social interaction at the place of business was an important part of work. Some companies now insist that their telecommuting employees come into the office to attend regular meetings. Those individuals who do not have an office to go to for socializing are establishing support networks. This may mean meeting for coffee or lunch several times during the week.

To stay motivated requires a clear purpose and strategy. In other words, know what you are doing and how you are going to go about it. However, this does not mean making a list of things to do because the easiest and most fun jobs on such a list usually get done first.

Another problem experienced by individuals who work out of the home is that they don't treat their work as a job. Sometimes friends drop in to chat when really they are trying to work. Children also should not interrupt what you are doing. That is why a separate office where you can shut the door is most important. A well-known author who had turned her garage into her office got into her car each morning, and drove around the block. Then she would park the car and sneak into her office and write. At lunch she would leave the office and get back into her car, drive around the block and park in the driveway. All of this was done so as not to let her three children know that she was in close proximity to them for fear of being constantly interrupted in her work.

Always being close to your work can be a real problem for the person working out of the home. Unless you set specific guidelines it may seem to you and your family as if your work overshadows your entire day. With some exceptions, of course, you should make it a habit to close your home office door as if you were leaving work. Lock the door and stay away until the next morning.

The Business Plan

The **business plan** helps you to organize your thoughts and provides a clear set of long-term objectives so you can focus on your activities. It requires you to analyze your product, market, management and finances. A business plan is important not only for those starting a business but also for the established entrepreneur who may be looking for more partners or more financing. The business plan is also important for a business that is either facing rapid change or is in serious trouble.

The business plan must always be kept current. It should be developed when a business is started and updated periodically as required. A business plan helps to ensure success, because all or most factors that may affect the business at the start-up stages or down the road have been thought about and provided for. Perhaps one of the most important reasons for developing a business plan is to get the financial resources required to start a business.

Although business plans come in many forms, for a new business you should provide answers to the following questions:

- What are your business objectives?

- What will be your market approach?

- Where will you be located?

- What are your physical facility requirements?

- What are your financial requirements?

- Will you need other employees?

- What is the legal basis upon which your firm will be established?

Business plan a detailed plan of a business's objectives, including a summary of its financial requirements.

The Business Plan

www.ca4it.com/magazine/
business.html

Establishing Your Business's Objectives

What are you trying to accomplish? Prepare clearly written and specific objectives that can be measured if and when they have been achieved. Indicate, for example, the expected size of your facilities, the amount of money to be spent on various aspects of the facilities and the number of employees required. Also determine production levels and performance levels in terms of sales, market share and profit.

Planning the Market Approach

Before starting a business, you must identify some key factors about your market. First, it is important to have a clear concept of your target market. You should develop a customer profile that includes factors such as age, income, occupation and social class. In addition, you may need to identify your customers' personality and lifestyle characteristics.

Second, you must understand the needs, wants and purchasing habits of your target customers before you can develop a marketing strategy. You might ask questions such as why, where and when the target customers purchase the product or service. What attributes about the product will influence them in their buying decision, and how much of the product will they purchase? The answers to some of these questions may be gathered from government reports or business publications. In some instances, you may have to get the information through questionnaires or by asking people directly.

Third, you should be aware of any uncontrollable factors that might affect the marketing of your product or service. Such factors could include pending provincial or federal legislation, the state of the economy or changes in competitive factors. Finally, you develop your marketing strategy, which deals with such aspects as method of distribution, promotion and pricing. We will discuss marketing further in Chapter 8.

Selecting the Location

Depending on the nature of your business, location can be critical to its success. A retailer must select a trading area with a sufficient customer base to support the business. For a small retailer, easy access to the premises by customers is of primary importance. For a manufacturer, natural resources, cost of land, utilities, appropriate sites, people with particular skills and the attitude of the people in the trading area to the new business may all be important. For many small businesses (particularly service businesses) operating out of the home has increasingly become a primary consideration and can drastically reduce the costs of starting a business.

Determining the Physical Facilities

A manufacturing firm typically requires greater financial resources for facilities, while a retailer requires a larger investment in inventory. In any case, detailed estimates of the financial resources required for building, equipment, furniture, fixtures and inventory (if required) must be prepared. In addition, plans should be made as to how purchasing will be implemented, how inventory will be controlled, how the production process will be carried out, how the interior of the facilities will be set up and how the finished product will be stored and distributed. Business functions are discussed in detail in Chapter 7.

Planning for the Financing

A crucial part of the business plan is the financial plan. In fact, a business plan is often drawn up only to acquire the necessary financing for a business. The feasibility of the business is evaluated with tools such as break-even analysis and a cash budget. Then a projected income statement is generated for one or more years into the future, as is a projected balance sheet and cash-flow statement. The end result is an estimate of the financial resources required to start and operate the business for a period of time, particularly during the early period when revenues are low. The amount that must be borrowed must be in balance with the amount that the owner(s) provide. If a new business is being established, then the accounting system to be used and the method of evaluating the financial results of the business must also be established. Chapter 9 will discuss financing in more detail.

Human-Resource Planning

Many small businesses are operated by the owner and immediate family members. If more people are required, then some thought must be given to the structure of the organizational hierarchy—who is responsible for particular aspects of the business and who reports to whom. Thought should be given to recruiting, hiring and training employees, as well as to establishing policies that affect the employees. We will discuss human-resource management in Chapter 10.

Legal Requirements

An important consideration when starting a business is determining the legal structure of the business. Will it be operated as a sole proprietorship, partnership or corporation? Each form will have implications for taxation and legal liability. We will discuss this matter in the remaining part of this chapter. The new owner must also determine what licences are required, and tend to other legal aspects such the filing for patent protection if necessary. Business owners must be constantly aware of legislation, both existing and pending, that will affect their particular business.

FIGURE 2.4

Components of a business plan

1. *Title page.* Name of company and location; telephone; date; person to contact.

2. *Summary.* A summary of the major points of the business plan.

3. *Table of contents.*

4. *Introduction.* A description of the product; why it is expected to be in demand, and why the loan is required.

5. *The company.* A summary of the company: its location; reason for establishment; number of employees, if already operating; principal owners or shareholders.

6. *Management.* A brief description of the principal members of the management group, along with their professional designations and expertise.

7. *The product.* A description of the product or service.

8. *The marketplace.* Areas where the product will be available; the major target markets; the major stores where the product will be available.

9. *Market size.* A discussion of the potential size of the market and its future growth.

10. *Competition.* A discussion of the major competitors; their product; their market share; advantages and disadvantages of their products compared to yours.

11. *Marketing strategy.* A description of the target market and how your product will cater to it; your pricing; distribution and advertising approach.

12. *Sales plan.* A discussion of your sales effort during the first year: what territory you will cover; whom you will approach first; the number of people to be employed in sales; the advertising campaign planned.

13. *Sales forecast.* An actual sales forecast indicating unit sales expected for a number of years in the future, along with the dollar amount. If sales territories are involved, they should be mentioned and a percentage breakdown given per territory.

14. *Sources of market information.* How the sales and market information was collected, along with sources of information.

15. *Product development.* Whether a prototype is available; what ongoing research and development is required; what testing is required before the product is salable.

16. *Production.* Where you will be located; the facilities and equipment required; engineering and design factors; how the product will be manufactured; parts to be purchased from other sources; the number of people required in the production process; special skills required, if any; manufacturing space required.

17. *Product costs.* A breakdown of manufacturing costs per unit; break-even analysis (see Chapter 9).

18. *Gross profit.* An analysis of the gross profit expected per unit. This takes into account the suggested retail price and discounts offered.

19. *Financial requirements.* An analysis of the financial requirements; money invested in the venture to date; the projected first-year total costs; revenue expected during first year.

20. *Pro forma financial statements.* Includes pro forma income statements for a number of years, balance sheet, as well as cash-flow projections and break-even analysis. (See Chapter 9 for a discussion of cash flow and an example of a cash-flow statement.)

21. *Support services.* Bookkeeping; accounting; computer systems.

22. *Appendices.* Attach any technical data on the product; market research data; customer/supplier lists; legal documents (incorporation documents, patents applied for, and other legal documents); personal dossiers on owners/major shareholders, management; names of consultants and advisers, and any reports prepared by them.

Setting Up the Business Plan

If the business plan is to be used primarily for your own purposes, then a less formal plan is appropriate. If you are preparing the business plan to get a loan, however, factors of concern to a banker or investor(s) must be addressed. Using experts (such as accountants or financial advisors from a management consulting firm) to help you project a positive image to potential lenders is also sound advice. You have to show that your business will be financially successful. The components of a business plan are listed in Figure 2.4.

The report must look professional. Several computer software programs are available that will help you to prepare a business plan. Simply fill in the appropriate information as presented on the screen and the program will format it and print it out. If you cannot use a computer, gather the necessary material and ask a professional to prepare the business report for you. The money spent on such help will be well spent if it helps you to get the loan.

For help in setting up a business plan, go to the Internet and look for the small business Web site of your provincial government. The British Columbia government has a Web site with excellent references about how to establish a business plan, and includes a sample plan.

**British Columbia
Business Service Centre**
www.sb.gov.bc.ca/smallbus/
sbhome.html

Financing a New Business

Getting adequate financing is a major challenge for most individuals who plan to open their own business. You require money to start a business and to finance it through the first year when expenses are high and sales are likely to be low. To ensure that your business survives the first few months or even the first year, you must carefully plan for the money you need and then reconcile it with the financial resources available before you even consider going into business.

Determine What You Need

Obviously, determining what you need is the first step in trying to get financing. You must consider two factors—start-up capital and operating capital.

Start-up capital is required to pay for land, buildings, renovations, fixtures, equipment licences, fees, permits, professional services such as lawyers and accountants, and so on. You may also require an initial inventory if you are opening a retail store. **Operating capital** includes such costs as payroll, utilities, rent and advertising.

A cash budget or cash-flow statement—a schedule of the money coming in and going out on a monthly basis—must be developed in order to calculate the money needed to cover operating expenses after the initial start-up. When expenses exceed revenue, money must be borrowed and repaid when revenues exceed expenses. We will discuss cash budgeting in detail in Chapter 9.

Types of Capital

Financing can be in two forms, equity or debt. **Equity financing** is money from the owner's own savings, borrowed from friends, relatives, business associates or partners, or from shareholders in the case of a corporation. We will examine the different forms of business ownership and what they mean in Chapter 3. Usually these funds are not secured, so the people who have lent this money have no claim on the business' assets. In other words, if the business goes broke and there are other loans outstanding from secured sources such as a bank, all assets available will be sold to pay off the other loans before any others can be repaid.

Start-up capital in the business sense refers to money required to start a new business and includes funds for renovations, purchase of fixtures, initial inventory purchases and various start-up fees.

Operating capital includes money for the ongoing costs of running a business including salaries, inventory purchases, utilities, rent, advertising and taxes.

Equity financing is money that comes from the owner's own savings, or is borrowed from friends, relatives, business partners or, in the case of a corporation, shareholders.

Debt financing means that the person borrowing money must repay it, along with interest, over a period of time. It is the time period that indicates whether it is short-term or long-term financing. A long-term loan is arranged to finance assets such as a building, a vehicle or furniture or equipment and the repayment is spread over a period longer than a year. The loan is also secured against these assets and they can be seized by the lender and sold if you default on your repayment. Short-term debt is usually for a period shorter than one year and is required to finance day-to-day costs of the business such as employee wages, advertising and inventory purchases.

The more equity money you have invested in the business, the easier it is to borrow money from other financial institutions or from investors—because you or your partners have a stake in the business and this shows that you are committed and prepared to share the risk with other lenders. Depending on your business and how carefully you have set up your plans, you may be able to borrow two to three times the amount of equity in the business.

Sources of Equity Financing

As discussed earlier, a large portion of equity financing is obtained from your personal savings, inheritances or a mortgage that you may have placed on your home. Friends, relatives and business associates may also contribute. If you need additional money you have two main sources: private investors and venture capitalists. You may be able to persuade an individual or other company to invest in your business.

Alternatively you may approach a **venture capitalist**—a private investor or firm that invests in promising new businesses. There are hundreds of venture capitalists in Canada, and they are always looking for investment possibilities. They generally expect rates of return of 30% to 40% on their new investments. While they sometimes provide financing only, in most instances they take ownership in the firm by buying shares. One problem with equity investors is that they may leave owners with little or no control over their firm. Thus, if you want 100% ownership, venture capitalists are not a source for consideration. However, today many equity investors only wish to invest in a new company from five to seven years to give them the 30% to 40% return they are looking for. The entrepreneur then must arrange to buy out the equity investor, usually through a public share offering.

There are now community-based venture capital groups that provide funding for new businesses. For example, the Metropolitan Ottawa Investment Venture is planning to make several smaller investments, $750 000 or less, and to co-invest with other groups including local investors. Other communities are also getting together to develop a second model of community-based funding. For example, a group of businesspeople is assembling an organization of sophisticated investors in the community to invest in high-technology companies in Kitchener-Waterloo, Cambridge and Guelph.

Sources of Debt Financing

Sources of debt financing include trust companies, credit unions, finance companies and chartered banks; the latter are by far the largest source of small business financing. The six chartered banks and a number of foreign banks account for 80% of all small business lending. Many of these banks have opened specialized business branches.

Although some banks have emphasized their commitment to lending to small businesses, it is still not easy to get a loan. Check out some of the bank Web sites for more information.

The federal government's main support program for small business changed on April 1, 1999. The *Small Business Loans Act* has been replaced by the *Canada Small*

Debt financing is borrowed money on which interest must be paid and the full amount of which must be repaid at some point. Common sources for debt financing are commercial banks.

Venture capitalists are private investors or businesses prepared to finance individuals who have a promising new product or service but lack the funds to start.

CIBC Small Business Services
www.cibc.com/english/business-services/small-business/index.html

Bank of Montreal
www.bmo.ca/business/business.html

Toronto Dominion Bank
www.tdbank.ca/business/Main$treet/index.html

Business Financing Act. Lending under this Act offers borrowers the same access to asset-based financing as the SBLA. The fundamental program parameters remain the same but an effort towards cost recovery will be maintained. The criteria of a CSBFA Loan include:

a) for amounts up to $250 000;

b) for the acquisition of fixed assets;

c) for a maximum term of 10 years;

d) for for-profit, non-farm businesses with annual gross revenue of less than $5 million;

e) CSBFA guarantees 85% of net losses incurred on defaulted loans.

Small business loans that are backed 85% by the federal government require banks to exercise what is called "due diligence on the company." This means that the bank will demand a business plan and personal financial history. The business owner may also have to put up a personal guarantee to cover the 10% of the loan not covered by the federal government. Some home-based businesses, most likely those that have operated for a few years and are considering expansion, may choose this route.

An excellent source that discusses the financing of your business can be found on the Internet at various Web sites of your provincial government.

Canada Small Business Financing
http://strategis.ic.gc.ca/sbla

Business Development Bank

Business Development Bank
www.bdc.ca

At the federal government level, the major small business lender is the Business Development Bank (BDB). The BDB is a federal-government institution that provides advice on the many federal and provincial loan and grant programs available to help finance small businesses. The bank also has consultants who prepare loan proposals for a reasonable fee. In addition, the bank offers long-term and operating loans to businesspeople who have been turned down by other financial institutions. That does not mean that the BDB makes loans to poor risks, but simply that it is a last resort for businesses that look promising but do not have the collateral or other securities that a chartered bank might want. On occasion, the BDB may take an equity position in the new firm.

When applying for a loan, it is important that you do not underestimate your requirements for fixed assets or for the operation. **Undercapitalization**—not having enough funds—is a common cause of failure in many small businesses. Remember that you will require money to live during the initial operating period when your business has little, if any, income. Unless you allow for your personal requirements, you will underestimate your financial requirements and, ultimately, hurt your business.

Undercapitalization means a business does not have sufficient funds to purchase the machines and equipment needed to operate the business and to see it through the initial start-up period.

Chapter Summary

1. The number of small businesses in Canada increased dramatically and small business comprises approximately 97% of all business. Firms with fewer than five employees make up 78.2% of all businesses while only 0.2% have over 500 employees. In the first eight years of the 1990s, self-employment expanded by an average of 4.2% per year. As of December 1998, 18% of the Canadian workforce was self-employed, representing almost 6.2 million workers.

2. Operating one's own business is a common aspiration. Unfortunately, three-quarters of all new businesses fail in the first five years of operation, primarily due to poor management skills and inadequate financing. Successful small business management depends on many factors, including acquiring a business education, planning, careful money management, keeping accurate records, effective marketing, organizing time and acquiring good employees. Although the overwhelming majority of small businesses do not grow appreciably in size, those that do employ particular strategies for growth.

3. A person may buy an existing business or start a new one. Buying an existing business has several advantages, such as an established clientele and premises, together with fixtures, equipment, machines, suppliers and inventory. To decide which way to go, you must evaluate the following factors: availability of existing businesses; amount of capital available; your willingness to take risks, the time required to get the business operating; the location of the existing business and its facilities; the reputation of the business; and the assistance required from the existing employees and owner.

4. Several steps are involved in buying an existing business. First, list the types of businesses in which you are interested and establish some criteria for evaluating businesses that are for sale. Then actively look for available businesses. After you have found a business, check that the facilities are in shape and that the staff and management are well trained. Talk to suppliers, customers and employees about the business and find out why the owner wants to sell. After this preliminary analysis, perform a complete financial analysis. Professional help from accountants and lawyers should be considered.

5. If an existing business cannot be found, then the only alternative is to establish a new business. There are advantages in starting your own business. You can tailor everything to your needs— location, facilities, fixtures, information system and so on. You can choose your own suppliers and hire and train your own employees. Although much more work is involved in starting your own business, you are not paying for the reputation of an existing business, nor do you have to make do with existing facilities or cope with existing problems.

6. Franchising is popular because the franchiser often assists the new owner in all aspects of starting and operating the business. Support in acquiring management skills can prevent business failure. The major disadvantages of franchises are the initial high cost of buying a successful franchise, strict adherence to policies and rules of the franchiser, and the royalty that must be paid on gross receipts.

7. The home business has become an important method for delivering services and products to other businesses or customers. Besides not having to fight traffic, an advantage is that normal business expenses can be deducted from income before paying taxes. Nevertheless, attention must be paid to setting up the home office properly. In most instances the costs of setting up a home office are minimal. With some forethought, used computer equipment can be purchased to reduce costs. An important factor is communications equipment so that you can stay in touch with your client. This includes telephones, fax machines, cellular phones and portable equipment for on-the-road use. You must ensure that your home office is properly insured and that you have made provisions for securing important items. An important factor for home office workers is motivation and discipline. Some individuals may find it hard to get their work

done because they have to cope with distractions from family members. Others may find it difficult to leave their work since it is so close at hand.

8. Developing a business plan is crucial because it forces you to set clear objectives. It also helps you to establish your market approach; select your location; and determine your physical facility requirements, your financial and human-resource needs and your legal form of business ownership. A business plan must be kept current because it is required to get financing and/or to attract new investors or partners.

9. Obtaining adequate financing is a critical task for anyone wanting to start his or her own business. It is important to first determine how much money is required. Often initial capital comes from the entrepreneur's own savings or from family and friends. Beyond that the potential business owner must determine if debt or equity financing will best serve the needs of the business. Debt financing means borrowing money from a financial institution. Equity financing means selling a portion of the business to other investors. The Business Development Bank can provide both types of financing and is usually a last resort. Venture capitalists will invest in a business for a portion of ownership. A proper business plan and financial plan is crucial to getting the money required.

KEY TERMS

Small business 39	Home business 55	Equity financing 64
Franchise 50	Business plan 61	Debt financing 65
Franchiser 50	Start-up capital 64	Venture capitalists 65
Franchisee 50	Operating capital 64	Undercapitalization 66

REVIEW QUESTIONS

1 Why are small businesses so important to Canada's economy?

2 What are the major problems faced by individuals operating a small business?

3 What are the seven areas of concern to which the owner-manager of a small business must pay particular attention?

4 What are the advantages of buying an existing business compared to starting a new business? What are some of the things one should check before actually making a final offer?

5 What is a franchise? What are the major advantages/disadvantages of purchasing a franchise?

6 What are some of the advantages of buying a franchise as opposed to starting one's own business?

7 What are some of the major advantages of running a business from your home?

8 What is a test for Canada Customs and Revenue Agency as to when a person operating out of the home is actually a business and not a contract employee?

9 What are some of the sources of capital for starting a new business or a franchise?

10 What is the difference between debt and equity capital?

11 What is the difference between getting start-up funds from venture capital as compared to a bank loan? Why do many business owners have problems in arranging financing? How can a business plan help an owner get a loan?

DISCUSSION QUESTIONS

1 Should the federal and provincial governments make a conscientious effort to help entrepreneurs start their small businesses? If so, in what areas might the government provide help?

2 When it comes to investing in a franchise, should the adage "Buyer beware" apply, or should the government bring in strict rules as to what franchisers must disclose to franchisees? Discuss.

3 What types of businesses would be ideally suited for operating out of the home? What do you think the future holds for the home business?

4 What might be some drawbacks to companies that encourage their employees to work out of their own home for one or more days of the week? What are some of the advantages for both employees and their companies?

5 Contact your local banker and determine the requirements for getting a small business loan. According to your banker, what are the major reasons why small business owners cannot get adequate financing?

Buying a Video Franchise

Two years ago, Tayreez Mushani decided to open a video rental store. Although she knew they were a dime a dozen, there were none in her neighbourhood (the nearest one was several kilometres away). She knew there were franchises available, but after investigating a few of them she decided to go it alone. The franchise fees were generally $25 000 to $35 000; there were also monthly fees based on sales revenue, amounting to 4% to 5%.

Tayreez was in the midst of developing a business plan—which she needed in order to get a loan from the local bank—when she received a call from a video rental franchise company, one that was relatively new. The company wanted only $10 000 as an initial fee, plus an additional $5000 in the second year of operation. Furthermore, there was a clause in the agreement that stated that the first 100 franchise owners would have to pay only a 2% monthly royalty on revenue for the first five years. The agreement further stated that if the franchise owner was not satisfied with the parent franchise company, he or she could terminate the relationship after five years for a fixed fee of $25 000 or 25% of the business' annual revenue in the fourth year of operation, whichever was lower. The franchise company offered this buyout as a reassurance that what they had to offer would be beneficial enough that the owner(s) would want to remain as part of the company.

Tayreez met with the franchise company president. So far the company had sold 14 franchises, but only two stores were in operation. These stores had once been independent, but had agreed to become part of the franchise chain. Tayreez was not told whether these stores had actually bought into the franchise chain or whether they had been wooed by the franchise company to enter it at no cost. Their business was good, according to the financial statements, but it was difficult for Tayreez to see how the franchise had helped these particular individuals.

The franchise company presented a prospectus that outlined the benefits she could expect. They were similar to those of other franchise operations she had looked at, but this company could not really prove their advantage in terms of either reduced costs for movie purchases or greater advertising clout, since there were only two stores at the time. However, the franchise president was aggressive and seemed to know his business.

Tayreez reviewed the franchise company's offer over the next several days and eventually decided to join. Now, two years down the road, she believes that she made the right choice. "I'm really happy with the franchise," she explains, admitting that she took a gamble when she signed a franchise agreement with a fledgling video company. She admits that there were frustrations, but the benefits far outweigh them.

But there were some other problems at the beginning. Because Neighbourhood Video was still in its infancy, it didn't have a central buying team or an advertising policy. This is typical of a small company, says Tayreez. Sometimes it was difficult to get management at the Canadian head office in Toronto to follow through on purchasing and financing because of a lack of staff. But several years of working with the people at head office have smoothed out the problems, and the franchise company has grown substantially.

A major benefit for the Canadian franchisers was the fact that the U.S. video franchise company helped Canadian operations tremendously in terms of buying power and advertising clout. For example, the U.S. offices of Neighbourhood Video are placing an ad this spring in *People* magazine, and the Toronto stores in the >>

Neighbourhood Video chain cooperatively bought two months of television advertising at a cost of about $48 000. "You don't do these kinds of things if you're on your own," she says. Other local efforts have included cross-promotional advertising with a Toronto retailer of VCRs, offering consumers who bought a VCR one free movie rental for every movie rented at Neighbourhood Video. Tayreez says that the campaign brought at least 200 new customers into her store.

When the Canadian franchise operation joined the U.S. company, the original franchise owners had to agree to some new costs. The initial fee required an investment of $15 000, and Tayreez now had to pay royalties for both the Canadian offices of Neighbourhood Video (as initially agreed), plus 2% of all revenues to the U.S. headquarters in Texas. There's also a 4% fee that goes toward paying for advertising in Tayreez's local area.

Even with the royalty payments, Tayreez has been able to make the firm grow and show a profit. In the first year of operation, video rentals brought in about $165 000. Sales and rentals of VCRs brought in approximately $65 000. Tayreez used virtually all profits to purchase more movies. She also redecorated the store, to show the corporate design of Neighbourhood Video, for about $6000.

Tayreez expects to do about 30% better in the second year and has invested another $40 000 in movies. She has also hired two full-time and four part-time employees to help ease the long hours. She is convinced that getting in on the ground floor with Neighbourhood Video was a smart move.

Questions

1 What were the advantages to Tayreez Mushani of buying a video rental franchise as opposed to opening her own video rental business? What might have been some of the disadvantages of buying this franchise?

2 If Tayreez had decided to open up her own video rental business instead of buying a franchise, what additional factors would she have had to consider?

3 Before buying this franchise, what factors should Tayreez have investigated?

4 Indicate how each of the seven factors of success applies to this business.

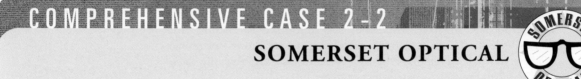

COMPREHENSIVE CASE 2-2
SOMERSET OPTICAL

In the 1990s, Mike Fowler and Peter Dewar were employed by Byway Optical Inc. Mike was an optician and Dewar was the manager of a Byway Optical retail store located on Somerset Street in Ottawa.

Byway Optical Inc. operated a number of retail optical dispensaries that sold fashion prescription eyewear, fashion sunglasses and contact lenses. All of the company's retail outlets were leased; the leases, while long term, were operating leases. Of the three outlets that Byway operated, the Somerset Street location ranked lowest in terms of volume sales.

The optical industry is a relatively close-knit group in which the main participants are well known among themselves. Most of the opticians in Ottawa know each other; most of the dispensing optical outlet managers and employees know each other; and most of the optical retail stores use the same suppliers. In this extremely aggressive competitive environment, the cost of inventory is usually differentiated only by volume discounts on inventory orders. Personal customer service is extremely important, because the selling price of eyewear is generally the same from one retail outlet to another. Success in this industry also depends on customer repeat business and a wide selection of inventory. Another factor of significance is the relatively low cost of purchasing inventory. Depending on volume, contact lenses may cost the retailer $7 to $14, while eyeglass frames can range from $15 to over $60.

The president of Byway Optical Inc. was an aggressive "marketeer" who opted for increasing volume sales; in exchange, he settled for a lower profit margin on sales. The idea was to generate volume sales and use the cash profits as reinvestment funds to acquire more retail outlets. Advertising was aggressive and was undertaken centrally for all of Byway's retail outlets. The longer-term plan was to develop scale economies such that Byway, because of volume alone, could offer to the public the most inexpensive frames at the highest possible quality. This strategy would perpetuate itself only if each Byway retail outlet experienced a certain threshold sales amount as determined by the management at Byway Optical Inc. For the Somerset Street location, this level of sales was established at $20 000 per month. Sales below this amount were not compatible with Byway Optical's overall plan.

In the first four months of operation, the Somerset Street location averaged $13 500 per month in sales, with its best month at $19 500. Because these results were well below the established sales threshold, the president of Byway decided to close Somerset and try a different location.

Peter Dewar felt strongly that if the Somerset Street location were to cater more to customer service and offer the services of a stellar optician, it could be made to meet the $20 000 per month threshold. The management at Byway Optical Inc. disagreed; pointing out that despite its downtown location, Somerset did not attract a large enough client base.

Dewar responded that perhaps the $20 000 threshold was only a theoretical amount; just because Somerset's performance was below this threshold did not necessarily mean that it was unprofitable. Byway management agreed that Somerset could be mathematically profitable, but its performance was not consistent with Byway's business plan.

Dewar continued to feel strongly about the potential success of the Somerset Street location. Eventually, Byway agreed to sell the Somerset location to Dewar for $12 000. Dewar would pay $2000 cash and Byway would finance the remaining $10 000 over the next 10 months, charging no interest. The price would include all inventory on hand at the time, and Dewar's new business would assume responsibility for all outstanding Somerset liabilities. The agreement was finalized, and on April 1, 1997, Somerset Optical was born.

SOURCE: By David H. Jones-Delcourt. Reprinted by permission of the author.

>>

Questions

1 In your assessment of this case study, discuss any areas where, in your opinion, business matters could have been handled more effectively.

2 Could Byway Optical Inc. be moving toward a franchise position? Advise Byway management on the most effective way to establish franchises, and discuss the advantages and disadvantages of the franchise. Would this industry be well suited to franchising?

3 Prepare a skeleton business plan for Byway Optical Inc. Use the information provided and add other information necessary to outline the key points in a business plan.

3

Forms of Business Ownership

Learning Objectives

After reading this chapter, you will be able to

1 Explain why it is necessary to have a legal form of business ownership.

2 Identify the basic characteristics of a sole proprietorship, partnership and corporation.

3 Explain why the corporate form of business ownership has become dominant today.

4 Explain why most large businesses are corporations.

5 Explain how a corporation is governed.

6 List the general steps required for incorporating in Canada, both federally and provincially.

7 Describe how businesses grow through vertical, horizontal and conglomerate mergers.

8 Explain why cooperatives have become increasingly important and how they differ from other forms of private business ownership.

The form of business ownership you choose is a legal prescription that indicates to the people with whom you are dealing who will be responsible for the operation of the business, and who will reimburse them in the event of loss. For example, the government wants to know whether your business profits should be taxed as part of your personal income or as part of the firm's income. If you are dealing with suppliers, they want to know who will be responsible for merchandise payment—if you were hit by a car or went bankrupt, how could they recover their money? Could they obtain it only from your business, or could they go to your private assets? Investors in large corporations want to know how their investment will be protected. How can they go about selling their ownership in the business to someone else? Finally, customers may also want to know who owns the business, in case they need recourse for defective goods or unsatisfactory performance of a service. The form of business ownership chosen is therefore very important, both to you the owner and to the people who will be dealing with your business.

Forms of Private Business Ownership

There are three major forms of private business ownership—the sole proprietorship, the partnership and the corporation. Each form has its advantages and disadvantages, depending on the business and the nature of the product or service. See Table 3.1.

Sole Proprietorship

A **sole proprietorship** is a business owned by one person. Usually this person operates and manages the firm, although he or she could hire someone else to perform that task. It is still the most common legal form of business ownership in Canada, perhaps because it is easy to set up and operate. The sole proprietorship is ideally suited for small-scale retail and service businesses (e.g., beauty salons, repair shops or service stations, especially those just starting out) that require flexibility in both operation and management.

Sole proprietorship—a business owned by one person who is responsible for the firm's operation and takes all risks of loss.

Comparison of forms of private business ownership

TABLE 3.1

Form of Ownership	Advantages	Disadvantages
Sole Proprietorship	1. Retention of all profits 2. Ease of formation and dissolution 3. Freedom and flexibility of management 4. Secrecy of operation	1. Unlimited financial liability 2. Limited financial resources 3. Management deficiencies
Partnership	1. Ease of formation 2. Complementary management 3. Greater financial resources 4. Employee incentive	1. Unlimited financial liability 2. Disagreements among partners 3. Lack of continuity 4. Complexity of dissolution
Corporation	1. Limited financial liability 2. Specialized management skills 3. Great financial capability 4. Unlimited life span 5. Ownership easily transferred 6. Capacity for growth	1. Difficult and costly to establish 2. Lack of personal interest by management 3. Legal restrictions and government regulations 4. Lack of secrecy in operation

The sole proprietorship is the most common form of business ownership in Canada >

The sole proprietorship is responsible for the firm's operation and assumes all risks of loss. The law does not distinguish between the owner as a private individual and his or her business. Legally, he or she is the business. Anyone dealing with the firm in effect deals with the owner. Should any legal problems arise between the owner and the people dealing with the business, they can usually be resolved by the courts through the laws of contracts and sales.

Advantages of Sole Proprietorships

The major advantages of sole proprietorship are:

- ease of formation or dissolution;
- management freedom;
- secrecy of operation; and
- retention of all profits by the owner.

A sole proprietorship is relatively easy and inexpensive to set up, primarily because it faces few legal requirements. Often a business licence from the local municipality is all that is required, the cost of which will depend on the type of business, its size and the municipality in which it is located. If the owner wants to use a name other than his or her own, or to use the words "and Company," the name must be registered with the provincial Registrar of Companies. If the name is already in use, another must be chosen. In the event that the owner wants to dissolve the business, a sole proprietorship is as easily dissolved as it is formed.

Freedom of management is a major advantage of the sole proprietorship. The owner is free to implement new operating procedures and policies, change the product or service or move the business to another location without consulting others. Future business plans can be kept secret, and, with the possible exception of employees, the owner is the only one who knows the amounts of the firm's assets and debts, profits and operating expenses, or any problems the business is having. Such privacy and secrecy of operation is particularly important for a business operating in a highly competitive environment.

Because no distinction is made between the business and the owner, all income for this person is considered personal income, whether it comes from one or more businesses or from other sources such as savings, stock investments or rental income. The individual pays taxes only on total personal income. If a business owned by this person incurs a loss, then this loss can be written off against the owner's total personal income to reduce income taxes paid.

Disadvantages of Sole Proprietorships

The major disadvantages of sole proprietorships are:

- unlimited financial liability;
- limited financial resources;
- possible limited management and technical skills;
- lack of permanence of the firm; and
- possible tax disadvantage.

Since the business and the owner are legally the same, the sole proprietor is liable for all financial losses or debts that the business may incur. In the event of **insolvency**—when a firm cannot pay its debts because it lacks the necessary funds— creditors can look to the owner's private assets to cover the losses. During the **commercial bankruptcy** proceedings, the insolvent business owner might be forced to sell his or her home, automobile or other belongings. **Unlimited liability** can mean financial ruin for the owner should the business fail, and is probably the major disadvantage of this form of business ownership.

A sole proprietor usually has little trouble borrowing moderate amounts of money, particularly if he or she has a good credit rating and if the business is reasonably successful. However, the large sums required to finance major growth or expansion are more difficult to obtain. Since most financial institutions demand some security, loans are limited by the amount of collateral available from the owner's personal assets. Given that insufficient financial resources represent one of the major reasons for small business failure, those assets are not likely to be enough. Thus, additional financing usually depends on the owner's personal savings or business profits, together with whatever loans can be obtained from friends and relatives.

The more successful the business becomes, the easier it will be to obtain additional financing. If growth is the objective, however, it may be best to consider incorporating, so that additional funds can be raised through the sale of shares to investors. Furthermore, while financial assistance is available to small businesses through various programs offered by both the federal and provincial governments, it is often available only to firms that have been incorporated.

In addition to financial difficulties, a sole proprietorship may also encounter management problems. The owner and manager—often the same person—may not have the business education or management experience necessary to perform the wide variety of management tasks required. The owner may simply dislike certain tasks or neglect some essential business function such as finance or marketing. Any shortcomings in the owner's management ability when the firm is small will lead to even more serious consequences as the business grows.

Another serious problem faced by the sole proprietorship is the lack of continuity of the business. When the owner dies, the business also legally terminates. The firm's assets become part of the deceased's estate and may have to be sold to pay estate taxes. However, selling the business quickly may be difficult, especially if its success

Insolvency means that a firm cannot pay its debts because it lacks the necessary funds.

Commercial bankruptcy is a mechanism for the orderly and equitable distribution of assets of an insolvent company and for its eventual reintegration into the economy.

Unlimited liability means that a person is liable for all financial losses or debts that a business may incur.

has depended on the special skills of the owner. If the business is very large, on the other hand, it may be difficult to find a buyer with sufficient funds to take it over.

Finally, a successful sole proprietor may be paying more taxes than if the business were incorporated, because all profits made in the business must be included in the owner's personal income for tax purposes. Incorporation may present a tax advantage for a business owner because of certain corporate tax provisions. This topic will be discussed further when we look at corporations.

Partnership

Partnership exists when two or more people combine their talents and resources in a business for the purpose of earning a profit.

A second major form of private business ownership, though less common than the other two, is the **partnership**. This is an unincorporated business owned by two or more people who have combined their talents and resources for the purpose of earning a profit. A partnership is almost as easy to establish as a sole proprietorship, and it suffers from many of the same disadvantages. Partnerships are most common in the professions—law, medicine, dentistry and accounting—but are also found in manufacturing, wholesaling and retailing, as well as in the trades (e.g., carpentry, painting and plumbing).

Formation of a Partnership

Partnership by express agreement means that the factors important to the partners are specified in writing.

A partnership is usually formed by two or more individuals who draw up an agreement as to how the partnership will operate. In a **partnership by express agreement**, the factors important to the partners are specified in writing and include the following:

- the name and location of the business;
- the names of the partners;
- how profits (or losses) are to be divided;
- the amount of the investment;
- the salary each partner is to receive prior to distribution of profit;
- the duties and authority of each partner;
- the life of the partnership; and
- how the partnership may be dissolved.

Partnership by implication may exist when two or more people act in a manner that a court of law deems to be a partnership, even if there is no written agreement.

General partners are business partners who may or may not be actively involved in running the business, but who are financially and legally responsible for its actions.

Limited partners are only liable for the amount they have invested in the business and may not take an active part in its operation.

A **partnership by implication** may also exist when two or more people act in a manner that a court of law deems to be a partnership, even though there is no written agreement. Often friends or co-workers may start a business but neglect to draw up a formal agreement. This can cause serious problems later should personal disagreements arise concerning the management or objectives of the firm. See the article "How Important Is a Partnership Agreement?" in this chapter.

Kinds of Partnerships

A partnership may consist of **general partners** who own the business, work in it and share the profits or losses. However, it may also include one or more **limited partners** who are liable only for the amount they have invested in the business. Limited partners may inquire into the operation of the partnership and make suggestions about its management, but they may not take an active part in its operation. While a firm may have many limited partners, it must include at least one general partner with unlimited liability.

General partners may be actively involved in the daily operation of the business, or they may be **silent partners** who have invested in the business but who neither involve themselves in its operation nor allow their names to appear in the firm's name. However, if the silent partner's name is important to the firm, the firm might be permitted to use it for a fee. A silent partner still has unlimited liability for any debts incurred by the firm in the event of bankruptcy.

Silent partners have the same responsibility as general partners, but do not become actively involved in the firm's daily operation. They may let their names be used for a fee.

Advantages of Partnerships

The major advantages of partnerships are:

- ease of establishment;
- complementary management skills of partners;
- greater capacity to raise funds; and
- incentive for employees.

A partnership is as easily formed as a sole proprietorship, and faces few, if any, legal or government rules and regulations. However, a written agreement specifying the terms of the partnership should be established. While this may be done by the partners themselves, they would be wise to seek legal advice. The time and money initially expended on this document may be far less than the expenses incurred later should a serious disagreement arise as to the partners' original intentions.

Since a partnership may include a wider range of management skills than a sole proprietorship, the chances of business failure may be lessened. Two or more partners can divide the management and operating duties among themselves. Doctors, for example, may form a partnership in which each is a specialist in a different field of medicine. Or two people may establish a retail business in which one partner is skilled in buying merchandise and in the administration of the business, while the other partner is highly proficient in sales.

A partnership can raise funds more easily than a sole proprietorship because collectively the partners can provide a larger amount of money to start their business. If additional funds are required, financial institutions such as banks are more likely to make larger loans to a partnership because the risk of business failure is lower. Even if the partnership were to fail, each partner remains financially liable for the total debts of the business.

Another major advantage of a partnership is its ability to retain valuable employees by making them partners in the business. Many accounting and law firms hire trainees with the promise of a partnership at some later date. The possibility of ownership and a share of the profits provides incentive for the trainees to work hard and contribute to the firm.

Disadvantages of Partnerships

The major disadvantages of partnerships are:

- unlimited financial liability;
- possibility of management disagreements among partners;
- limited ability to raise financial resources;
- lack of continuity in the firm; and
- complexity of dissolution.

How Important Is a Partnership Agreement?

An agreement, whether it concerns a partnership or one or more people that have incorporated, is an absolute must. It specifies before the business is started how disputes will be resolved, or how a person in the partnership or corporation can sell his or her share in the business. The agreement also specifies what happens if one partner dies or becomes disabled or retires.

A common occurrence is that a partner wants to leave a business or cannot get along with the others. In this case some method for evaluating the business share must be established. One method is to let the seller determine the price and all parties are then bound by that price. Another method is to set the price at an annual meeting after the yearly balance sheet has been drawn up and the price for the shares can be more easily determined. A third alternative is to get an independent business evaluator to set the price for the shares and all shareholders will be bound by that price. Each of these methods has its drawbacks, but it is better to have an orderly agreement drawn up initially than to have chaos when it finally happens.[1]

As in the sole proprietorship, a major disadvantage of a partnership is the unlimited liability of each general partner in the event of bankruptcy. In addition, all partners are liable, jointly and severally, for the total debts of the business. This means that while all partners are liable for the partnership's total debts, each member is also liable for the full amount if the other partners are unable or unwilling to pay. Furthermore, any single partner can bind all the others to agreements and contracts, even without their consent.

Perhaps one of the greatest problems in partnerships is the possibility of personal disagreements regarding the firm's management or objectives. For example, while one partner might be prepared to take greater financial risks in order for the firm to grow and expand rapidly, the other might prefer that the firm remain at its present size or grow more slowly to minimize risk. If one partner lacks interest or management skills, the entire workload may fall to the remaining partner(s). Sometimes another person can be found to come into the business; if not, the partnership may have to be dissolved.

Depending on the size and type of business, getting adequate financing may still be a problem for a partnership. Even though more individuals are available to contribute to the business, either through their own savings or through loans, the amount raised may still be far short of that required. A multiple partnership, for example, may have trouble raising the large amounts of capital required to establish even a small manufacturing company.

Like a sole proprietorship, a partnership is legally terminated when one member dies or is otherwise unable or unwilling to continue as a partner. Legally, this is not a major problem, because most partnerships specify in their written agreements how a new partner may be brought into the firm to replace another; thus, operations are not seriously affected. Nevertheless, it may be difficult to find someone who is acceptable to the remaining partners and possesses the skills or funds necessary to take the place of the individual who has left.

Finally, members of a successful partnership may also face higher taxes, since individual tax rates may be higher than those for corporations. Again, a point will be reached when incorporation may be advantageous in terms of taxation.

Corporation—an artificial person in the eyes of the law, with an unlimited life span, empowered by the federal or provincial government to carry on a specific line of business. It is owned by shareholders who are liable only to the extent of their investment in the company.

The Corporation

A corporation eliminates some of the disadvantages of both the sole proprietorship and the partnership. In the eyes of the law, a **corporation**:

- is a separate legal entity (with an unlimited life span) that is able to buy, sell, employ, borrow, loan and own property;

- must act through individuals;

- is owned by shareholders who may also be employees;

- distributes its profits through dividends that are taxed in the hands of the shareholders;

- is a taxable entity and must file returns and pay taxes.

Consequently, a corporation has the same legal rights as an individual. It can sign contracts, and sue or be sued. It can purchase, own or dispose of property and is generally subject to many of the same regulations that apply to individuals.

The first corporations were actually established in medieval Britain through the granting of charters to trading companies. The charter stated that no member was to be held liable for collective debts; in other words, those who owned the corporations were sheltered from being held personally liable for any debts incurred by the trading company. One of the trading companies to obtain this royal protection was the Hudson's Bay Company. In a 19th-century British court case, *Salomon v. Salomon,* the sheltering aspect of the corporation was strengthened through the court ruling that a creditor had no right to the assets of a corporation's shareholders, even if there was only a single shareholder.

Private and Public Corporations

Corporations may be either private or public. A **private corporation** may not have more than 50 shareholders. It may not offer its shares to the general public, and there are restrictions on the transfer of shares. These limitations do not apply to a

Private corporation—a corporation that may not have more than 50 shareholders. It may not offer its shares to the general public, and there are restrictions on the transfer of shares.

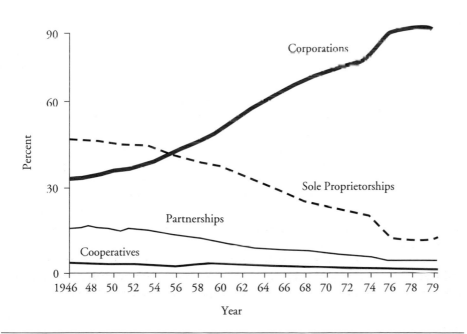

FIGURE 3.1

Change in percentage distribution of forms of business establishments, 1946–79

SOURCE: Adapted from *Manufacturing Industries by Type of Organization and Size of Establishment* (Ottawa: Statistics Canada, 1979), cat. no. 31-210. Although no data are available after 1979, there is a clear trend in the increase in the number of corporations.

Public corporation—a corporation that may sell or transfer its shares freely on Canada's stock exchanges, but which is subject to various government regulations designed to protect its shareholders.

public corporation, which may sell or transfer its shares freely on Canada's stock exchanges. However, the **public corporation** is subject to certain government regulations designed to protect the shareholder. These regulations include disclosing pertinent financial and operating information to its shareholders, having at least three directors and holding annual meetings for the election of board members and the appointment of an auditor.

Advantages of Corporations

The major advantages of corporations are:

- limited financial liability;
- greater ability to raise funds;
- easy transferability of ownership;
- unlimited life span;
- greater capacity for growth and expansion;
- greater ability to attract specialized management skills; and
- possible tax advantages.

The fact that a corporation is an artificial person means that there is a distinction between the business and its owners. An owner is called a shareholder, and this individual's liability is limited to the amount of money the shareholder has invested. The personal property of shareholders is not affected by a corporate business failure. Individuals dealing with a corporation are alerted to this limitation by the presence of one of the following words in the firm's name: "Limited," "Incorporated" or "Corporation" ("Ltd.," "Inc." or "Corp."). This word must be clearly displayed in the name and must appear on all invoices and stationery. **Limited liability** may well be the greatest advantage of incorporation.

Limited liability means that shareholders in a corporation are limited in loss by the amount of their investment. The personal property of shareholders is not affected by a corporate business failure.

It is important to remember, however, that incorporation cannot be used to evade creditors. For example, if a person were about to face bankruptcy and incorporated so as to safeguard his or her personal property, the Fraudulent Conveyances Act would disallow such a transfer. The Bankruptcy Act has a similar provision. The courts could also ignore the usual protection offered by a corporation if they suspected fraudulent or improper actions on the part of owners of the business. This doctrine is known as piercing the "corporate veil."

A corporation with a proven track record is better able than other forms of ownership to acquire greater financial resources. Since ownership in a corporation can be divided into many small parts, or shares, many small investors can purchase a part of the business. While an individual may hold as little as one share in a company, the total number of shares that may be owned is limited only by the total number of shares that the company has issued. Of course, the amount of financial capital that can be raised depends on investors' confidence in the firm's profitability. New corporations may actually have trouble raising capital because of the limited liability of the shareholders. Lenders in such corporations want the personal guarantee of the principal shareholders that their loan will be repaid in case of bankruptcy.

Another advantage of a corporation is the easy transferability of ownership. Millions of shares, representing ownership in hundreds of companies, are traded on Canada's stock exchanges every day. Since shares may change hands in hours or even minutes, investors need not worry that their investments will be tied up indefinitely should they decide to sell.

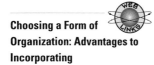

Choosing a Form of Organization: Advantages to Incorporating

www.ca4it.com

Strategis: Corporations Directorate Home Page

strategis.ic.gc.ca/sc_mrksv/corpdir/engdoc/homepage.html

Since the death of any one shareholder does not end the life of the corporation, it can concentrate on growth. Large corporations generally have a good credit rating and thus can borrow from financial institutions at lower rates of interest than smaller companies. Large corporations are also able to devote more money to research and development of new products, and can accumulate greater stores of the capital goods necessary for production. An indefinite life span also means that large corporations can promise long-term employment and thus attract experts in many areas, including management.

Because corporations are separate legal entities, they must pay both federal and provincial taxes on net profit before dividends to shareholders are paid. Shareholders must then include any dividends paid in their personal income and are taxed a second time. To prevent shareholders from being taxed twice, the federal government allows private individuals who receive dividend income to deduct a dividend tax credit from their tax payable.

Perhaps the prime reason for incorporating is the potential tax advantage. For example, instead of taking a large salary that would be taxed at high personal income tax rates, owners of corporations can pay themselves a token salary on a monthly basis. What they don't take out as salary they withdraw as dividends, which are taxed at a lower rate. Income splitting is also possible. For example, family members can become shareholders of the corporation and receive dividends that would be taxed at a lower rate.

Being incorporated may also give a business a better image and more credibility. The effort involved in incorporation may lead potential clients to believe that a business is more serious, and thereby result in increased business.

Another advantage of incorporation is the potential savings through the special tax treatment of small businesses. Instead of paying a federal tax rate of 38%, a small Canadian-controlled corporation is eligible for the small business deduction (SBD). This means that the federal tax rate is 12% on the first $200 000 of active business income annually. Even though the various provinces impose income taxes that vary from nil to 17%, the combined rate for small corporations ranges from 12.84% to 22.84%, significantly less than the 38% otherwise required.

On the other hand, a person who operates an unincorporated business and must include business profit in personal income could pay as much as 50% in Ontario and 59% in Quebec. Thus, incorporation offers a considerable tax advantage. However, even with these tax advantages there is general agreement among tax accountants and advisers that a person should not incorporate unless sales or billings exceed $60 000 to $70 000 per year. Some even suggest that $100 000 to $200 000 is a more realistic figure.[2]

Disadvantages of Corporations

The major disadvantages of corporations are:

- costs of incorporation;
- legal restrictions and government regulations;
- some lack of secrecy of operation; and
- lack of personal interest by management.

The major disadvantages of incorporation are the legal and accounting work required. Since a corporation is a separate legal entity, the requirements to establish it are more complicated and time-consuming. Both the federal and the provincial

Should You Incorporate Yourself?

As indicated above, incorporation can be relatively simple. You can buy incorporation guides or obtain the information from libraries or provincial information sources. However, unless the business is owned and operated by one person with little capital, you should seek the assistance of a lawyer. While this may raise the cost of incorporating from $300 to $1000 or more, a mistake or oversight made in self-incorporating may cost a lot more in legal fees to fix later. But by all means, shop around. Often an initial consultation is either free or carries a nominal $10 charge.

If a large firm is to be incorporated as a public company with many classes and types of shares, legal assistance is essential to ensure that all aspects of the organization and operation of the company are provided for.

governments require a fee for filing the necessary documents. Except for simple one-person corporations, a lawyer is required, who will probably charge about $2000 in legal fees and several hundred dollars per year to keep the books of the corporation. Owners of corporations must also complete annual reports, hold annual meetings and file federal and provincial tax reports. Even so, accounting fees for a small corporation will not necessarily be greater than those for a comparable unincorporated business.

In addition, both public and private corporations are subject to more legal restrictions and government regulations than sole proprietorships and partnerships. All corporations face a constant bombardment of government forms that must be filed both federally and provincially. To comply with these regulations and perform the required paperwork, a company may have to spend considerable time, money and effort.

Another drawback is the lack of secrecy. Because a corporation is owned by shareholders who must receive financial statements and other information about the company, it is difficult to keep all operations secret, which may give competitors knowledge about the corporation's activities. This is generally not a problem for small private corporations (with a few shareholders) where financial information need not be disclosed publicly.

Finally, larger corporations are usually operated by professional managers who are not shareholders. Without an ownership interest in the company, there may be less personal incentive for management and thus less personal involvement and responsibility than in other forms of ownership.

How to Incorporate

Companies may be incorporated by special acts of either the federal or provincial governments. This method of incorporation is primarily used for establishing firms such as banks and trust companies, where specific regulations are required to protect the public. The great majority of corporations are established under either the Canada Business Corporations Act or the various provincial Business Corporations Acts. If a business will operate in only one province, it should incorporate there. However, if it intends to operate in a number of provinces from the beginning, federal incorporation may be more advantageous.

Most provinces and the two territories use the **registration system** for the incorporation of companies. Individuals are required to register a document called a Memorandum of Association with the Registrar of Companies. The memorandum must be accompanied by the corporation bylaws, a Notice of Office and the required fee. In New Brunswick and the Yukon, a corporation is formed by issuing a document called the **letters patent**. The provincial secretary, acting under the authority of the lieutenant-governor, issues this document after obtaining the pertinent information

Registration system—a method of incorporation used by some provinces where individuals are required to register a document called a Memorandum of Association with the Registrar of Companies. The memorandum must be accompanied by the corporation bylaws, a Notice of Office and the required fee.

Letters patent—a method of incorporation used by some provinces. The provincial secretary, acting under the authority of the lieutenant-governor, issues a document called the letters patent after obtaining the pertinent information about the corporation from the application form.

about the corporation from the application form. In Quebec, a corporation may be formed by either drawing up the articles of incorporation or issuing a letters patent.

Incorporation in Ontario, for example, is quite simple. The Companies Branch of the Ontario Ministry of Consumer and Commercial Relations conducts the corporation registration. To register your corporation you must provide three things to the Companies Branch:

1. **Corporate Name Search Report**: an original Nuans report obtained from a private search house;

2. **Executed Articles of Incorporation**: duplicate copies of the Articles of Incorporation, and any needed consent forms;

3. **Government Fee**: $330 payable to Ontario Minister of Finance for corporation registration fee.

If you have all of the required information, your registration may take only a few minutes.

Incorporation for private companies may vary among provinces. To set up a corporation in British Columbia, for example, where the registration system is used, you begin by choosing three names that you would like to call the corporation. You submit these three names to the Registrar of Companies, where each name is checked against existing corporation names. If one or more of the names are not in use, they are reserved for you for a specific period of time to allow you to get the other documents together. This includes the Memorandum of Association and the Notice of Office (see Figures 3.2 and 3.3), and a set of bylaws. These forms are readily available in book stores as part of a package that explains all of the incorporation procedures. The bylaws specify how the firm is to be operated and seldom require changes. When all the forms are completed and signed, you then submit all three documents along with the required fee (approximately $300), which is based on the number of shares the company is authorized to sell. In a few weeks you should receive the charter, which signifies the legal establishment of the corporation. If you later have to make changes to any of the documents, you can do so by informing the Registrar of Companies.

Organization of the Corporation

Most large corporations are operated by professional managers. The owners—**shareholders** or **stockholders**—are primarily concerned with receiving an appropriate return on their investment and, especially in large corporations, are not directly involved in the operation of the company. The board of directors is the link between the owners and the managers. It is elected by the shareholders on the basis of one vote per share held and is responsible to them for the proper operation of the company. In practice, however, the board delegates the responsibility for actual operation to the firm's top managers, whom it hires, appoints or elects. The governing structure of the corporation is illustrated in Figure 3.4.

The Shareholders   Shareholders are the owners of a corporation. Since many private corporations are established as family businesses, the major shareholders are usually family members and sometimes long-time employees. The ownership of many of Canada's larger public corporations is usually spread among many shareholders.

A corporation may issue two major types of shares: common and preferred. **Preferred shareholders** usually receive a specified annual dividend per share that must

Shareholders or **stockholders** are the owners of a corporation who own either common and/or preferred shares.

Preferred shareholders usually receive a specified annual dividend per share and have first claim to any assets remaining after all other creditors have been paid. They generally have no voting rights.

FIGURE 3.2

Memorandum of association

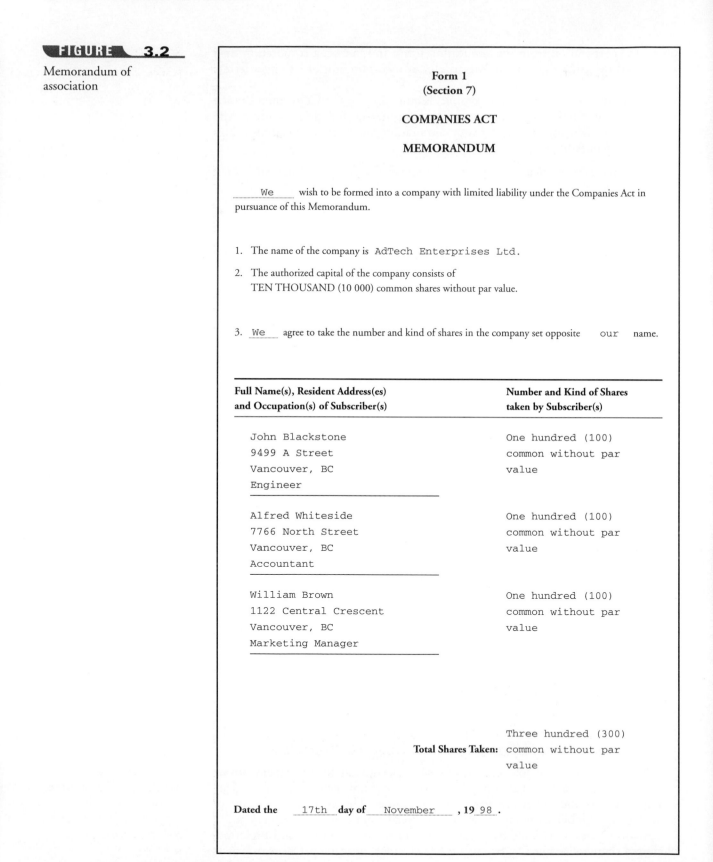

Form 1
(Section 7)

COMPANIES ACT

MEMORANDUM

____We____ wish to be formed into a company with limited liability under the Companies Act in pursuance of this Memorandum.

1. The name of the company is AdTech Enterprises Ltd.

2. The authorized capital of the company consists of TEN THOUSAND (10 000) common shares without par value.

3. __We__ agree to take the number and kind of shares in the company set opposite ___our___ name.

Full Name(s), Resident Address(es) and Occupation(s) of Subscriber(s)	Number and Kind of Shares taken by Subscriber(s)
John Blackstone 9499 A Street Vancouver, BC Engineer	One hundred (100) common without par value
Alfred Whiteside 7766 North Street Vancouver, BC Accountant	One hundred (100) common without par value
William Brown 1122 Central Crescent Vancouver, BC Marketing Manager	One hundred (100) common without par value
Total Shares Taken:	Three hundred (300) common without par value

Dated the ___17th___ **day of** ___November___ , **19** _98_ .

Form 3
(Section 10)

PROVINCE OF BRITISH COLUMBIA

Certificate of
Incorporation No. ....

COMPANIES ACT

NOTICES OF OFFICES

The offices of the Undermentioned company are located as follows:

Name of Company   AdTech Enterprises Ltd.
....

Registered Office:

Address   7766 North Street

          Vancouver

British Columbia

Records Office:

Address   7766 North Street

          Vancouver

British Columbia

Dated the   17th   **day of**   November   , 19 98 .

(Signature)   *Alfred Whiteside*

(Relationship to Company)   Director

FIGURE   3.3

Notice of office

General Information Required for Incorporation

Name Every corporation is required to have a name that must not be similar to that of an existing corporation and must not misrepresent the business the firm intends to practice. The name must be followed by "Limited," "Incorporated" or "Corporation," or the appropriate abbreviation, and it must be prominently displayed on all orders, invoices, contracts or other binding agreements to ensure that individuals dealing with the firm are aware of its limited liability.

Head Office The location of the head office must be stated and readily accessible to any shareholder, director or government agency. If the firm is incorporated federally, the head office may be anywhere in the country, but incorporation in a particular province requires that the head office be located there.

Directors A company must have a certain minimum number of directors to represent the shareholders. The names and addresses of the directors, and the number of shares each owns, must be specified.

Objects of the Company Corporations are granted the right to carry on a specific line of business—the sale of real estate, for example, or the manufacture of specific products. However, some provinces are fairly lenient regarding the restrictions of the charter, allowing a company to engage in a wide variety of activities without requiring that the charter be amended.

Authorized Capital A company is granted the right to issue a number of common and preferred shares, up to a stated maximum. Certain rights may be attached to both types of shares. The number and class of shares that the company decides to issue must be clearly stated in its Articles of Incorporation.

Other Matters The individuals incorporating the company are free to specify in the Articles of Incorporation any other matters pertaining to its organization or operation.

FIGURE 3.4

Governing structure of the corporation

SHAREHOLDERS

Shareholders elect a board of directors, who may or may not be shareholders.

BOARD OF DIRECTORS

The board of directors elects a chairman and other corporate officers such as vice-chairperson, secretary and treasurer.

TOP MANAGEMENT

The board also elects or appoints top management, who may or may not be directors of the company.

MIDDLE MANAGEMENT

Top management hires upper levels of middle management, who in turn hire lower levels of middle management.

SUPERVISORY MANAGEMENT

Middle management hires supervisory management.

be paid before common shareholders can receive any payment. In the event of the firm's bankruptcy, preferred shareholders have first claim to any assets remaining after all other creditors have been paid. **Common shareholders** have no particular right to any share of profits, nor any claims on assets, should the company go bankrupt. However, they do retain ownership of what remains after all creditors and preferred shareholders have been paid. Common shareholders have the right to attend at least one shareholders' meeting per year. They are also entitled to question the board of directors or senior management on any aspect of the company's operation. An example of a share certificate is shown in Figure 3.5.

If a shareholder is unable to attend the meeting in person, he or she may vote by proxy. A **proxy** (see Figure 3.6) authorizes another individual, usually a director, to vote on a shareholder's behalf. Often proxies are solicited by company officers, such as the board of directors, who are thus able to reelect themselves to office. It would be difficult and expensive for dissident shareholders to solicit proxies from others, particularly if the corporation is a large one with many shareholders. As a consequence, most corporate officers are able to perpetuate themselves in office, while shareholders are virtually powerless to challenge them regarding their method of operation or their performance. Often the only option for dissatisfied shareholders is to sell their shares; if the company's performance has been poor, however, its shares will not bring as high a price as the shareholders originally paid.

A company that intends to offer additional shares to the general public must prepare a prospectus for each new share offering. The **prospectus** provides information about the company, including comparative financial data for a number of past years, the movement of share prices over a period of time, the directors and their shareholdings, details of the company's operation, the reasons for the new share offering and the auditors' reports.

The Board of Directors   The **board of directors** represents the shareholders and is elected by them on the basis of one vote per share. Shareholders who own a large number of shares have considerable influence in electing board members, and may even stand for election themselves. The number of directors on the board of a public corporation may vary, from a minimum of three to 15 or 20 in large corporations. A private corporation requires only one director, who is usually the owner. Most boards of public corporations meet on a quarterly or semiannual basis. Once elected by the shareholders, the board elects its own chairperson, vice-chairperson and secretary.

Since board members are chosen for their business expertise, many are presidents or senior officers of other large companies. Individuals are not restricted in the number of directorships they may hold, as long as there is no conflict of interest. Their main function is to provide an outsider's point of view on major company decisions. In theory, the board of directors also has the power to manage the company, establish corporate policies and institute bylaws governing specific actions of the corporation.

The board of directors seldom initiates major courses of action for the company, but is often involved in making specific decisions concerning the extent of plant expansion, the timing and nature of company expansion into other regions or countries and the addition or deletion of particular product lines. The directors also decide on new share issues, the payment of dividends and the establishment and conduct of shareholders' meetings, including the issuance of proxies for voting.

The actual involvement of board members in the day-to-day management varies depending on the board. Particularly in smaller companies, board members often meet

Common shareholders have voting rights and retain ownership of all assets after other creditors and preferred shareholders have been paid.

Proxy authorizes another individual (usually a director) to vote on a shareholder's behalf.

Prospectus—issued by the company that intends to offer additional shares to the general public. It provides financial and other information about the company that is important for new shareholders.

Board of directors—elected by the shareholders to represent their interests. It has the power to manage the company, establish corporate policies and institute bylaws governing specific actions of the corporation.

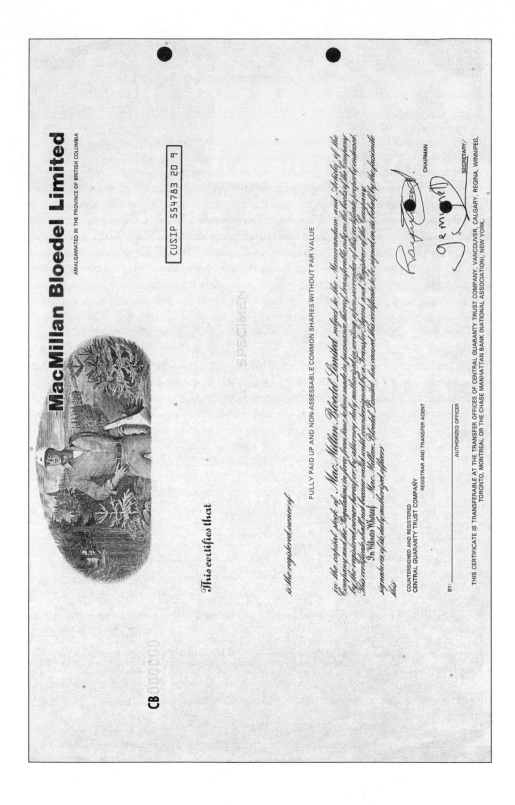

MacMillan Bloedel Limited

**Proxy Solicited by the Board of Directors for the Annual General Meeting of Common Shareholders
to be held at the Hotel Vancouver, Vancouver, B.C., on Thursday, March 28, 1991 at 10:00 a.m.**

The undersigned hereby appoints R.V. SMITH, or failing him, A.H. ZIMMERMAN, or failing him, R.B. FINDLAY, or

to be his proxy holder to attend the Annual General Meeting on Thursday, March 28, 1991 and any adjournment thereof, and to vote and act with respect to all common shares of the Company registered in the name of the undersigned as if the undersigned were personally present, and specifically on the items of business referred to in the Information Circular for this Annual General Meeting as follows:

1. To vote for all of the following nominees for election as directors ☐ except as withheld below:

D.C. Davenport, F.J. de Wit, J.T. Eaton, R.B. Findlay, R.E Harrison, G.H.D. Hobbs, R.T. Kenney, D.W. Kerr, C.C. Knudsen, J.A Pattison, A. Powis, J. St. C. Ross, R.V. Smith, D.W. Strangway, J.S. Wallton and A.H. Zimmerman or to withhold authority to vote for all nominees listed above ☐.

To withhold authority to vote for any individual nominee, write the nominee's name in the space following

2. To vote for ☐ or against ☐ or to abstain from voting on ☐ the appointment of Price Waterhouse as auditors with authority to the directors to fix their renumeration.

(Continued and to be signed on the other side)

(Continued from other side)

IF NO DIRECTION IS GIVEN WITH RESPECT TO THE ITEMS OF BUSINESS THE SHARES WILL BE VOTED ON A POLL FOR THE NAMED NOMINEES AND AUDITORS. HOWEVER, IF A DIRECTION IS GIVEN THE SHARES WILL BE VOTED ON A POLL IN ACCORDANCE THEREWITH. A SHAREHOLDER MAY APPOINT AS HIS PROXY ANY OTHER R PERSON, WHO NEED NOT BE A MEMBER, AND IF HE WISHES TO DO SO HE MUST STRIKE OUT THE PRINTED NAMES AND SUBSTITUTE THE NAME OF HIS APPOINTEE IN THE SPACE PROVIDED IN THIS PACKAGE.

The undersigned hereby acknowledges receipt of the notice of this Annual General Meeting and the accompanying Information Circular and ratifies all that his proxy may lawfully do by virtue hereof and revokes all former Proxies.

PLEASE PRINT NAME

SIGNATURE   1991

DATE

Please sign, date and mail promptly in the enclosed envelope.

Proxies must be received by the Company, Central Guarantee Trust Company or Shareholder Communications Corporation, at least 48 hours prior to the meeting.

SHS–21 (1–91)

FIGURE 3.6

Example of a proxy

frequently and have considerable say and control over the management of the firm. In most large companies, however, day-to-day management is primarily left to hired management. The board may select the president, who then runs the company subject to the approval of major courses of action by the board.

In an effort to safeguard shareholders, the federal and provincial governments have placed restrictions on the powers of the board of directors. In addition, board members are charged to act honestly and in good faith in carrying out their duties for the company. A public corporation is required to hold annual meetings, provide financial statements about its operation and submit the company's operation to an audit, where the accuracy of the information included in the financial statements is verified by an independent accounting firm.

Until recently, directors have not been liable for the actions of either the board or company officers/agents unless the action is illegal. However, for a number of years there has been growing public pressure for greater responsibility and liability for directors regarding company management. Some shareholders are insisting that board members address issues such as environmental pollution and the hiring and promotion of minorities and women. Company governance is a major issue today. To see how it has been affected, read the article "How Corporate Governance Is Changing" reproduced here.

Top Management   The board of directors hires, appoints or elects the **chief executive officer (CEO)**, who may be the chairperson of the board of directors or the corporation president, or both. The members of the board usually hire or elect the secretary and treasurer and, together with the president or CEO, hire other senior officers, usually titled vice-presidents or general managers.

Chief executive officer (CEO)— someone who is hired, elected or appointed by the board of directors. He or she may be the chairperson of the board of directors or the corporation president, or both.

How Corporate Governance Is Changing

For many years, boards of directors acted like rubber stamps. They met a few times a year, accepted the decisions of top management as they were presented and then were off for lunch. But that kind of board behaviour is no longer acceptable.

First, shareholders have become much more activist and have questioned top management and board decisions at annual meetings. Second, provincial laws have changed radically, making directors potentially liable for everything from environmental damage to employee vacation pay. Third, institutional investors have insisted that their shareholdings (which are often substantial) should give them a real say in how the companies are run. Fourth, regulators such as the Ontario Securities Commission have insisted that board members on a company's audit committee have a greater responsibility to shareholders than other board members because of their ability to examine a corporation's financial affairs.

As a result, a whole range of corporate governance issues are being examined, including

- the relationship between the board and management;
- how directors are chosen;

- how management uses the board and what the board should demand of management;
- the role of directors beyond their prescribed legal duties; and
- whether the same person should act as both chairperson of the board and CEO of the corporation.

Many directors unwilling to take responsibilities and the associated risks of being on a corporate board have resigned to protect themselves against any liability. For example, Ontario now permits class-action suits, which means that a small group of investors can sue on behalf of all investors and seek damages to the full amount raised. For example, directors of Standard Trust and Royal Trust and others have been sued for being derelict in their duties while they were on the board. Primarily because of this new liability and because of the work involved, it is becoming much more difficult for companies to find suitable directors. Those directors that are willing to serve have become much more active in understanding what their duties are and in carrying them out. Directors today are asking for power and are pushing management to be strategic thinkers.[3]

The various vice-presidents may be in charge of the major functional areas of the company such as finance, marketing, production or personnel. The **secretary** is in possession of the corporate seal and signs all corporate documents, either alone or with another officer. The secretary also attends all board and shareholders' meetings to take minutes. The **treasurer** is in charge of the corporation's finances, and in some companies is known as the **controller**.

The **president** and **vice-presidents** are responsible for the operation of the company. Their major responsibilities include short- and long-range planning, policy-making and the control of operations, particularly financial control. Another major task is the development of an organizational structure that will allow lower levels of management to look after the daily operations of the company. We will discuss the major management functions in later chapters.

Growth of Corporations

Although the overwhelming majority of businesses in Canada are small, a few are successful and grow into large corporations. Table 3.2 shows Canada's 50 largest corporations. Various Canadian business magazines regularly compile lists of the largest corporations, along with their ranking in terms of sales, net income, total assets, number of employees and the percentage of foreign ownership.

With business growth come many advantages for the firm. As the scale of operation increases and more units are produced, production costs usually decrease, since fixed costs pertaining to plants and equipment, management salaries, insurance, utilities and so on are spread over a greater number of units. When costs per unit are reduced, the company can reduce the product's selling price, in turn leading to increased sales and a greater market share for the company. A successful firm has little difficulty in obtaining funds for future expansion, while the prestige that accompanies success is often an incentive for both owners and top management.

Business growth is not achieved exclusively from within. It can also occur through the outright purchase of other companies or the acquisition of a majority of another company's shares. During the 1980s, mergers and takeovers were common. Some of these takeovers resulted in financial ruin for large, well-established companies.

Mergers, Acquisitions and Hostile Takeovers   A merger or acquisition can help a firm grow either vertically or horizontally. In a **merger**, two firms come together to create a new one. Usually both firms bargain for the best deal, and the existing shareholders receive shares of the new firm. In an **acquisition**, one firm attempts to acquire all, or a significant portion, of the shares of another company. The firm interested in the acquisition will usually offer the other shareholders a higher price for their shares than they were selling for in the stock market prior to the takeover announcement; alternatively, the acquiring firm might offer a share exchange with a cash bonus.

Not all takeovers are friendly. A **hostile takeover** is an unsolicited attempt by one company to acquire another company by purchasing its shares on the open market. In the 1980s, a number of individuals known as **corporate raiders** arrived on the business scene. These individuals have the ability to amass large amounts of financing, allowing them to make a **tender offer** to shareholders of a firm in the hope of acquiring a significant portion of the company's outstanding shares. Often their primary aim is to acquire control of a company, strip away its cash (if it has any), and then break up the company and sell off its parts to make a profit.

While some hostile takeovers can wreak havoc on a well-run company, others can turn a sprawling, poorly managed company into a smaller but more productive and

---

Secretary—the person who is in possession of the corporate seal and who signs all corporate documents, either alone or with another officer. The secretary also attends all board and shareholders' meetings to take minutes.

Treasurer or **controller**—the person in charge of the corporation's finances.

Presidents and **vice-presidents** are responsible for the operation of the company. Their major responsibilities include short- and long-range planning, policy-making and the control of operations, particularly financial control.

Merger   occurs when two firms combine their operations.

Acquisition—a firm's attempt to acquire all, or a significant portion, of the shares of another company.

Hostile takeover—an unsolicited attempt by one company |to acquire another company by purchasing its shares on the open market.

Corporate raiders—individuals with the financial capability to purchase a controlling portion of a company's outstanding shares.

Tender offer—a proposal to purchase all or part of a firm's stock at a price above the current market value.

Rank		Revenue ($MIL)	Profit ($MIL)
1	BCVE Inc.	19 656 000	5 459 000
2	Toronto Dominion Bank	15 683 000	2 981 000
3	Royal Bank of Canada	19 683 000	1 757 000
4	Bank of Nova Scotia	16 654 000	1 551 000
5	Bank of Montreal	16 685 000	1 382 000
6	Bell Canada	12 714 000	1 309 000
7	Cdn. Imperial Bank of Commerce	20 133 000	1 029 000
8	Seagram Co.	12 572 000	686 000
9	Manulife Financial	14 063 000	866 000
10	Rogers Communications	4 352 407	840 488
11	Power Financial	14 705 000	834 000
12	Thomson Corp.	5 823 000	532 000
13	Alcan Aluminum	7 503 000	460 000
14	Shell Canada	5 379 000	641 000
15	Magna International	9 403 000	430 000
16	Anglo-Canadian Telephone	619 500	685 800
17	Canadian National Railway	5 339 000	602 000
18	Canadian Pacific	11 437 300	593 900
19	Great West Life Assurance	13 326 000	588 000
20	Imperial Oil	9 160 000	582 000

TABLE 3.2 Canada's 20 largest corporations in terms of profit (1999)

SOURCE: Adapted from *National Post* Web site, www.nationalpost.com.

competitive entity. Often a company becomes a target for a hostile takeover because it is poorly managed, which depresses the price of its stock. After acquiring a controlling interest in the company, some raiders replace top management with a new group that will reduce operating costs. Sometimes this means that parts of the company or some of its assets must be sold. The main objective is to make the company more profitable so that its shares command a higher price in the future.

Obviously, a hostile takeover can often threaten the position of the existing top management, who may try to take evasive action. One method is to change the corporation's bylaws to increase the number of votes needed to enact a merger or acquisition. Management can also simply try to persuade its shareholders not to sell their shares because the price offered to existing shareholders is, in management's opinion, too low.

If these measures do not stop the takeover bid, top management can use other methods. The **poison pill** approach is designed to make the targeted firm less desirable as a takeover candidate. For example, management can threaten to issue more stock, which will make a takeover more expensive for the acquiring firm. Another approach is to seek a **white knight**—a third company that is interested in taking over the firm or parts of it. The white knight would probably give some assurance that the present management would retain its position and allow it to continue to operate the company as an autonomous entity.

When top management uses some of these evasive tactics to thwart a takeover, the shareholder is often the loser. For example, taking the poison pill approach to make the targeted firm less attractive to the raider can easily depress the value of the shares, which might not recover for some time.

Vertical and Horizontal Integration **Vertical integration** occurs if, for example, a manufacturing company producing kitchen appliances purchases a retail

Poison pill—an attempt by a firm targeted in a takeover struggle to make itself a less desirable candidate.

White knight—a firm that takes over a company already the target of a hostile takeover and allows the existing management and board to continue to operate the company as an autonomous entity.

Vertical integration occurs when a company purchases another company in a different phase of operation (e.g., a manufacturer purchasing a retail company).

company primarily engaged in selling such appliances to consumers. The manufacturing company is interested in diversifying into the retail field. On the other hand, a company that purchases another company in the same industry is practising **horizontal integration**. The manufacturer of kitchen appliances might buy out another kitchen appliance manufacturer, while a retailer might buy other retail companies. The Hudson's Bay Company, for example, engaged in extensive horizontal integration by purchasing a controlling interest in both Zellers and Simpsons, two large retail chains. Figure 3.7 shows the difference between vertical and horizontal integration.

Conglomerates   Sometimes one company will take over another in an entirely different industry. For example, a food processing company might purchase a retail chain or a trust company. The company seeking the merger may be interested in diversification for the sake of security in earnings, or simply to acquire profitable firms. The result is a **conglomerate**, which exercises control over the various companies through some centralized top management. Examples of Canadian conglomerates include Power Corporation of Canada, Bell Canada Enterprises and Canadian Pacific Ltd. The diversified nature of the latter conglomerate is shown in Figure 3.8.

Conglomerates have not performed well over the past 30 years and shareholders have been complaining. As a result, of the 12 conglomerates listed on the Toronto Stock Exchange, only five remain in 2000. Conglomerates have sold off some unprofitable companies in an attempt to refocus on their major business. Initially conglomerates were formed on the basis of the belief that when a number of diverse businesses are held it is unlikely that all of them will be affected equally in an economic downturn. Unfortunately, experience has shown that management is often not focused on any of the businesses, which results in poor performance. Shareholders have complained because the return on shares of conglomerates has reflected this non-focused approach in the company's performance. Furthermore, with the strong emergence of mutual funds, investors can let professional fund managers develop a much more diversified portfolio of companies, which will probably be less affected by an economic downturn than the traditional conglomerate.[4]

Horizontal integration occurs when a company purchases another company in the same industry.

Conglomerate—a firm consisting of many companies that produces different products. The main objective is to diversify operations.

Power Corporation of Canada
www.powercorp.com
Bell Canada Enterprises
www.bce.ca
Canadian Pacific Inc.
www.cp.ca

Factors to Consider When Choosing a Form of Business Ownership

Now that we have examined the three major forms of private business ownership, let us review some of the prime factors to be considered when choosing among them.

Vertical Integration—Two companies in different phases of the same business combine.

Horizontal Integration—Two competing companies combine.

 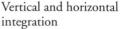

Vertical and horizontal integration

FIGURE 3.8

Canadian Pacific as a
diversified conglomerate

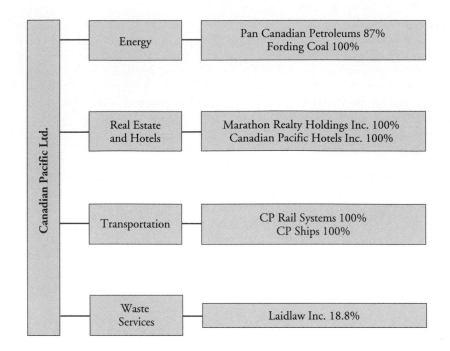

The Need for Limited Liability

The first consideration must be the need for limited liability. If you are considering a risky business that requires a large investment from creditors as well as yourself, it is imperative that you have limited financial liability; otherwise your private assets would be in jeopardy should the business fail. You would therefore be wise to incorporate. On the other hand, if your business provides a service with relatively little investment for equipment or inventory, and you therefore face little risk, a sole proprietorship or partnership might be adequate.

Availability of Financial Resources

In a sole proprietorship, your capacity to borrow funds is limited by the amount of personal assets you can offer as collateral. More funds would be available for a partnership since there are more owners who can invest. The greatest financial resources would be available to a corporation, however, since it could raise capital by issuing shares. Present shareholders would then lose some control over the company (unless they purchased some of the new issue to keep their percentage of ownership the same), and they would be obliged to share profits with new shareholders. Nevertheless, the new infusion of money from the share issue could be used to enlarge the operation and thereby increase total profits, meaning more for everyone.

The Need for a Variety of Management Skills

Individuals who lack management skills or experience in certain business functions would be well advised to seek out one or more individuals who have the complementary business skills and who may want to become partners. As an alternative, specialized personnel can be hired; however, this may be expensive for a new firm with limited financial resources.

Other Considerations

Though not as important as the preceding three factors, there are others to be considered before deciding on a form of ownership. First, there is the ease and cost of starting a business. While a sole proprietorship or partnership is relatively easy to establish, a corporation is more difficult and costly, and might face numerous government rules and regulations, both federal and provincial. On the other hand, the cost of incorporating may be small in comparison to the total money invested in the new business venture. Furthermore, the federal and provincial governments have special tax rules favouring small incorporated companies as opposed to sole proprietorships and partnerships. Both levels of government also provide special grants for new corporations to hire employees and for research and development.

Finally, a sole proprietorship or a partnership is always faced with the problem of continuity, since the death of the owner or one of the partners legally terminates the business. A corporation, on the other hand, continues regardless of what happens to its shareholders. In any case, a business established as a sole proprietorship or partnership can always be incorporated at a later date, once it has proven to be successful.

Member Ownership: The Cooperative

Cooperatives are business organizations owned by the members who use their services. Control rests equally with all members ("one member, one vote") and surplus earnings are shared by members in proportion to the degree they use the services. Cooperatives are structured in a democratic way that allows members to have a say in their actions. The members elect the board of directors and decide what should be done with any surplus that is generated in the cooperative. A cooperative's purpose is usually to supply its member-owners with products and services at a lower cost than would otherwise be possible, though sometimes a cooperative is established simply to provide a service that would otherwise not be available. Cooperatives can be either for-profit or not-for-profit enterprises. Since most cooperatives today are incorporated, they have both limited liability and an unlimited life span. In Canada, most cooperatives in the healthcare, childcare and housing sectors are not-for-profit cooperatives. While some cooperatives (such as family housing cooperatives) receive some government funding, co-operatives are not government organizations. Cooperatives are community-initiated organizations and businesses. Cooperatives in Canada are doing well and their numbers are increasing. Perhaps the fastest-growing area of cooperatives are the credit unions and their Quebec counterparts, the caisses populaires. Canada's credit union movement consists of 820 credit unions and 1351 caisses populaires, with more than 3700 locations and almost 3200 automated banking machines (ABMs). In 1998, the movement had about $110 billion in assets, or about 12% of the domestic assets of Canada's deposit-taking financial institutions.[5]

Credit unions actively compete with the chartered banks, and have led the way in providing members with chequing and savings accounts. In addition, they offer residential and commercial mortgages, personal loans and other services similar to those available at chartered banks. In terms of domestic assets held, credit unions they are comparable to the Toronto Dominion Bank, and combined they have more branch offices nationally than the Canadian Imperial Bank of Commerce. See Table 3.3 for a list of Canada's largest cooperatives.

Besides credit unions or financial cooperatives, there are also consumer co-

Cooperative—an incorporated non-profit business organized on a voluntary basis to meet the economic, social and cultural needs of its members.

Credit unions are financial cooperatives that actively compete with the chartered banks.

TABLE 3.3

Canada's largest financial and non-financial cooperatives in terms of assets (as of Dec 1999)

Financial Cooperatives	Profit	Revenue	Assets
Mouvement Caisses Desjardins	218 000	7 675 000	70 004 000
Caisse Centrale Desjardins	26 400	509 475	9 715 937
Vancouver City Savings Credit Union	23 742	462 071	6 410 978
FCPD de Mtl.	61 626	408 350	4 841 664
Co-operators Group	28 454	1 825 465	4 575 692
Credit Union Central of B.C.	11 928	173 897	2 986 076
Credit Union Central of Saskatchewan	4 186	189 509	2 603 158
Richmond Savings	7 726	135 452	1 857 986
Co-operator's Life Insurance	2 142	466 341	1 426 288
Pacific Coast Savings Credit Union	5 336	116 078	1 305 528
Non-financial Cooperatives			
Agricore Cooperative	2 928	3 087 360	1 277 094
Agropur Co-operative Agro-Al.	2 991	1 470 357	505 524
United Farmers of Alberta, Co-op.	13 469	609 800	254 089
Calgary Co-operative Assoc.	315	616 638	210 940
Co-op Atlantic	4 203	442 635	148 201
Lilydale Co-operative	4 320	458 071	131 143
Western Co-op. Fertilizers	31 477	335 783	128 809
Scotsburn Co-op. Services	n/a	183 083	56 062
Purdel Co-operative Agro-Alim.	1 339	99 122	44 070
Agrinove Co-op. Agro-Aliment.	(828)	158 274	33 170

SOURCE: Adapted from *The Globe and Mail* Web page, http://www.ronmagazine.com/top1000/other/coops.htm.

operatives that provide members with retail goods and marketing cooperatives that market products such as milk, poultry and wheat. Insurance cooperatives provide their members with life, fire and other types of insurance, while the various service cooperatives offer housing and legal services.

The Canadian Co-operative Association (CCA) is the national umbrella organization of anglophone co-operatives. Formed in 1987 through the merger of the Co-operative College of Canada and the Co-operative Union of Canada, the CCA supports and promotes cooperative enterprise in Canada and around the world. CCA's national office is located in Ottawa and its regional affiliate offices are situated in Vancouver, Edmonton, Saskatoon, Winnipeg, Toronto, and Moncton. The CCA also has offices located in eight other countries.

CCA supports its member organizations through the provision of the following services: government affairs and policy; business facilitation; planning and coordination; information; education and training; the provision of a "common table" to bring various cooperative sectors together; cooperative development; and communications. The CCA also holds a national Congress every three years that features workshops and forums, and presentations by leading cooperative and credit union experts and researchers. CCA's international development program is another key cornerstone of the association. Technical and financial assistance to cooperatives and credit unions in over 20 countries is provided through CCA and its network of volunteers and partners abroad.

Nevertheless, the cooperative movement has encountered some problems. Many cooperatives originally started as small local organizations in which members had complete control, and were the recipients of any profits that were generated by the

Canadian
Co-operative Association

www.coopcca.com

cooperative. Today, cooperatives have become big business and face many of the same problems as corporations—raising the capital required for expansion and operation, for example, and acquiring competent managers. At the same time, members appear to have less control over operations.

Chapter Summary

1. The sole proprietorship—a business owned by one person—is relatively easy and inexpensive to start. The owner has complete control and can keep operations secret. Among the disadvantages are the owner's unlimited liability, the limit on the amount of capital one individual can normally raise, the need for expertise in many business activities and the fact that the life of the business is limited to the owner's lifetime.

2. A partnership can help to solve some of the problems faced by the sole proprietor. Two or more partners can share responsibility for the business and provide a wider range of expertise. They can probably also raise a greater amount of financial capital. However, disagreements concerning management may arise, and any single individual has only partial control over the business. All partners still have unlimited liability. The partnership ceases to exist when one or more partners leave or die, and partners may have difficulty selling or transferring their ownership interest. A formal agreement, although not required, is recommended to resolve some of the above problems.

3. The corporation has become a favoured form of ownership for a number of reasons. Legally, a corporation is an artificial person with all the rights, powers and obligations of a private individual. A business may be incorporated provincially or federally, depending on where it intends to operate. If there are fewer than 50 shareholders, the corporation is private. The cost of incorporating is relatively low, and there are generally few rules and regulations to be followed. A public corporation, on the other hand, has more than 50 shareholders, requires at least three directors and must follow specific rules and regulations in order to keep shareholders informed of the company's financial operation.

4. The owners of the corporation are the shareholders, who receive either common or preferred shares in return for their investment. A public corporation can also borrow money through the sale of bonds or by issuing notes to lenders. Individuals who own common shares are entitled to elect a board of directors to represent them. The board of directors in turn is responsible for the proper operation of the company and for the hiring of top management, including the president and various vice-presidents.

5. A major advantage of incorporation is the limited liability provided to shareholders. Once a business is established as a profitable corporation, shares can be sold to raise additional financial capital. Ownership is easy to transfer, and the life of the corporation does not depend on individual shareholders. Among the disadvantages are the limited control that shareholders have over the company, as well as the tendency of professional managers who run large corporations to take less personal interest than the owners in the well-being of the company. In addition, large corporations are subject to more government rules and regulations than sole proprietorships and partnerships, and lack some secrecy in operation.

6. Another form of ownership is the member-owned cooperative, which is established to provide services such as product marketing, life insurance or financial services. Although many are incorporated, a basic difference between the cooperative and the corporation lies in the voting and distribution of earnings. In the cooperative, each member receives only one vote, while earnings are distributed according to the amount of business each has done with the cooperative over a period of time.

KEY TERMS

Sole proprietorship 75	Limited liability 82	Merger 93
Insolvency 77	Registration system 84	Acquisition 93
Commercial bankruptcy 77	Letters patent 84	Hostile takeover 93
Unlimited liability 77	Shareholders/stockholders 85	Corporate raiders 93
Partnership 78	Preferred shareholders 85	Tender offer 93
Partnership by express agreement...78	Common shareholders 89	Poison pill 94
Partnership by implication 78	Proxy 89	White knight 94
General partners 78	Prospectus 89	Vertical integration 94
Limited partners 78	Board of directors 89	Horizontal integration 95
Silent partners 79	Chief executive officer (CEO) 92	Conglomerate 95
Corporation 80	Secretary 93	Cooperative 97
Private corporation 81	Treasurer/controller 93	Credit unions 97
Public corporation 82	Presidents/vice-presidents 93	

REVIEW QUESTIONS

1 Why is it necessary to choose a form of business ownership?

2 What is the advantage of establishing a business as a sole proprietorship and incorporating, if necessary, at some later time?

3 What are the advantages/disadvantages of establishing a partnership as opposed to a sole proprietorship?

4 Distinguish between general partners, limited partners and silent partners.

5 Explain joint and several liability for business debts in a partnership.

6 Distinguish between (a) a public and a private corporation and (b) preferred and common shareholders.

7 How can a company increase in size? Distinguish between a merger and an acquisition.

8 Distinguish between (a) horizontal integration, (b) vertical integration and (c) a conglomerate.

9 What are a cooperative's chief characteristics?

DISCUSSION QUESTIONS

1 "Large corporations are good for Canadians!" Discuss both sides of this issue.

2 What major problems might occur if one of the members in a successful partnership wanted to sell his or her portion of the business, assuming that no written agreement exists?

3 In most elections, every person eligible is allowed to cast one vote. Shareholders in a corporation, however, are entitled to cast as many votes as shares owned. Why should this be so?

4 What powers should shareholders have over the board or directors and chief executive officer? What powers do they actually have?

5 Should board members be personally liable for the actions of a company? Why or why not? Discuss.

Deciding on a Form of Business Ownership

Victor Kovacs was promoted to service manager for a major auto dealer. By trade he was a mechanic, and fixing and modifying cars and engines was his favourite pastime. After working as service manager for a little more than a year, he realized that he was not enjoying his work. All day long he had to deal with customers who, it seemed, were never satisfied. He longed to be back at his bench so he could fix his cars and leave the customer problems to someone else. His dissatisfaction grew worse each day, and after more than a year at his new job he seriously considered quitting. One day on his drive home, he saw an empty warehouse located in an area that he felt was ideally suited for an auto repair shop. The next day he inquired about the terms for leasing the empty warehouse, and they sounded reasonable. But he had to decide quickly because others were also considering the site.

Victor visited his banker to get some idea of how difficult it would be to obtain financing. He laid out the financial requirements as far as he knew them. He needed approximately $300 000 to have the warehouse renovated and to purchase the necessary equipment for a two-bay workshop. He also needed approximately $30 000 for some initial inventory, although virtually all necessary parts were purchased as required. His monthly lease costs would be $2500. Monthly wages for another mechanic, a helper or apprentice and a person in the office to handle phones, make up invoices and so on would amount to approximately $7500. Victor's wife would handle the accounting. There would be monthly costs of approximately $4000 for water, supplies, taxes, and so on.

Victor could raise $70 000 as initial cash and would require a bank loan of $230 000 plus $30 000 for meeting the cash requirements during the first few months of operation when sales would be slow. He was counting on many of his customers from his other place of business to come to him for their repairs: they had always been happy with his work, both as a mechanic and as a service manager. He could not forecast, however, when his monthly revenues would equal his monthly expenditures.

Victor's banker looked up from the three typewritten pages that Victor had given him to read at the start of their meeting. "On the basis of this analysis," he said, "I have a few questions that I think you will have to answer both for yourself and for the bank.

"I know that you are a good mechanic, and I would be one of the first people to bring my car to you for repairs. But do you have any idea how much work you have to perform to cover the monthly operating costs? Can you make that amount with only two mechanics? If you are one of the mechanics, who would look after the other aspects of the business such as advertising, customer relations, work scheduling and so on?

"If we gave you a loan—and, believe me, we want to have you as our customer— we need some safeguards. We would need collateral for the loan. I don't see where you brought the loan costs into your analysis. Also, what form of business organization did you plan to have?"

Victor looked at the bank manager questioningly. "What do you mean?" he asked.

"I think we should sit down and review your proposal so we can get some better figures. Perhaps we can trim the loan requirement or some of the monthly costs, or both. We will try to put together a rudimentary business plan that you will have to flesh out."

Questions

1 What are some of the problems that Victor faces in starting his own business?

2 How could a business plan help Victor to establish his business? What information would he gain from a business plan?

3 Evaluate the advantages and disadvantages of each of the three forms of business ownership in relation to the business that Victor wants to enter. (It would be helpful to review the section in this chapter entitled "Factors to Consider When Choosing a Form of Business Ownership" before answering this question.)

4 What form of business ownership should Victor choose? Why?

COMPREHENSIVE CASE 3-2

SOMERSET OPTICAL

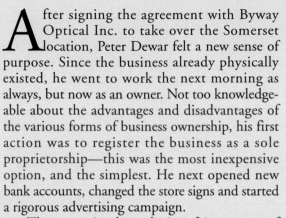

After signing the agreement with Byway Optical Inc. to take over the Somerset location, Peter Dewar felt a new sense of purpose. Since the business already physically existed, he went to work the next morning as always, but now as an owner. Not too knowledgeable about the advantages and disadvantages of the various forms of business ownership, his first action was to register the business as a sole proprietorship—this was the most inexpensive option, and the simplest. He next opened new bank accounts, changed the store signs and started a rigorous advertising campaign.

The campaign brought in a fair amount of business. Dewar soon realized that he could reduce his costs considerably and make a greater profit or charge lower prices by cutting his own lenses. Laboratory services, while offering timely and high-quality work, were relatively expensive. Mindful of the regulations governing optical dispensing, Peter Dewar undertook an intensive campaign to hire an optician.

Mike Fowler had become increasingly unhappy working for Byway Optical Inc. For some time he had thought about opening his own optical business, but felt uneasy about the risks involved. A certified laboratory technician and a seasoned professional optician with a wide client base, Fowler was well regarded as one of Ottawa's finest contact lens fitters. When he head about Dewar's search for an optician he arranged a meeting and the two men hit it off. They agreed on a salary— $40 000 per year—and a 50% ownership in Somerset Optical. An effective retail manager, with skills in merchandising and advertising, and a certified optician appeared to be a winning combination. For Fowler it was the chance to be in business yet not accept all of the risk by himself.

Instead of changing the provincial business registry, Fowler and Dewar prepared a contract that, among other things, described Mike as a partner and formalized the partners' respective salaries at $40 000 and $18 000. The firm was now set to embark on what was to be a memorable learning experience.

SOURCE: David H. Jones-Delcourt. Reprinted by permission of the author.

Questions

1 Comment on the appropriateness of the sole proprietorship that Dewar established. What are the advantages and disadvantages of this form of ownership for this particular type of business? Would a corporation be more beneficial? Explain.

2 Does the signed contract between Dewar and Fowler change the form of business ownership of Somerset Optical from a sole proprietorship into a partnership? What factors should be stated in such an agreement?

VIDEO CASE—PART 1

BEER MITTS

How difficult can it be to come up with a new product or service? At one time or another most of us have probably searched for an item that would perform a particular job, or we desperately needed a service that no one was offering.

There are people who spend a lifetime coming up with the "perfect product"—the brilliant idea that should have no problem selling itself. Others just stumble upon it. But there is a huge gulf between having an idea of a product that one could offer and actually getting that product ready for sale to the public. The video *Beer Mitts* effectively outlines the efforts required to bringing a new product to market. It also takes a glimpse at the problems that its three featured partners run into while attempting to launch their product.

SOURCE: Based on "Beer Mitts," *Venture* 718 (September 14, 1999).

Questions

1 What problems did the three partners encounter in getting their Beer Mitts to market? How were these problems resolved?

2 Of the seven factors for business success discussed in Chapter 2, which appear to be the most troublesome for the three partners in their new venture?

3 The partners mention that their business plan was rejected a number of times. Chapter 2 lists the critical items that must be addressed in a business plan. Which of these items' information might have been difficult to obtain for the Beer Mitts product?

2

Business and Management

Business organizations are at the core of our economic system. They are human creations bringing together the factors of production to make useful products or services. Managers play a key role in business organizations. They are responsible for developing the goals of the organization and for planning its future course. To achieve goals and objectives, they establish an organizational structure, coordinate the efforts of all involved, and ensure that raw materials, machines and equipment are available as required. Finally, managers ensure that the organization is on the proper course by comparing plans with actual achievements.

In Chapter 4, we examine the nature of management and the specific tasks of managers. We then focus on two of the four major functions of management: planning and controlling. Finally, we look at the role of computers in business and how managers can benefit from the organized information computers provide.

In Chapter 5, we look at another essential management function: organizing, or establishing the organizational structure best suited to achieve planned objectives. This structure is established by dividing the total work to be accomplished into manageable units, and then assigning a manager to each unit. Depending on the size of the organization, several levels of management may be necessary to coordinate the various tasks.

In Chapter 6, we look at the leading function of management. Since any enterprise needs people who will perform their jobs willingly and in the best interests of the organization, managers must provide employees with motivation and leadership.

4

Management, Planning and Controlling

Learning Objectives

After reading this chapter, you will be able to

1 Explain why management is the most important ingredient for success in a business.

2 Identify the three types of managerial skills—technical, human and conceptual—and indicate their relative importance to each of the three levels of management.

3 Identify and explain the four functions of management: planning, organizing, leading and controlling.

4 Identify the elements of planning.

5 List the four steps in the planning process, and indicate the difference between long- and short-range plans.

6 Explain the purpose and process of control, and why control is closely related to planning.

7 Explain why an effective management information system is important for proper control of operations.

8 List and explain the various budgetary and non-budgetary methods of control.

9 Recognize why computers are important to business, and describe how managers can use computers in their operation.

10 Explain how you should go about choosing the appropriate computer hardware, software and vendors.

Contact!
The Canadian Management Network

strategis.ic.gc.ca/sc_mangb/
contact/engdoc/homepage.html

What Is Management?

Movies and television dramas often focus on giant corporations and the conflicts of top executives. We become familiar with the spacious offices and oak-panelled boardrooms of multi-storied corporate buildings, but see little of management in action, nor do we learn about what a manager's job entails. In fact, we may get the impression that managers are involved only in intrigue and political manoeuvres. What about the owner of the local television repair shop, or the local service station, both of whom are in business for themselves? Are they managers? What is their function? This chapter explains the functions of management and points out its importance to the successful operation of a business.

Managers are members of an organization—a university, a business, a sports team, a religious group, or government agency. These organizations must achieve particular goals or purposes. To do so requires people and materials. Managers must ensure that organizational goals are accomplished by getting other people to perform the necessary tasks.

One of the tasks managers perform is planning—thinking about the goals and objectives they want their organization to achieve and how to go about doing so. Another task is to bring together people, material and financial resources so that the activities that will lead the organization toward desired objectives can be performed. Managers must also provide leadership and influence their people so they perform their tasks efficiently and effectively. To this end, it is important to establish a proper working environment and atmosphere so that subordinates want to do their best. Finally, managers must ensure that the organization is, in fact, moving toward its goals. If some parts of it are not doing so, it is up to managers to find out why and correct the problem.

We can provide a more comprehensive definition of **management** by saying that it is a process of planning, organizing, leading and controlling the efforts of organization members in using organizational resources so as to achieve organizational goals in the most efficient and effective manner. A process is a systematic way of doing things (see Figure 4.1).

Management is a process of planning, organizing, leading and controlling the efforts of organization members in using organizational resources so as to achieve organizational goals in the most efficient and effective manner.

The Importance of Management

In our constantly changing world, even the best-laid plans can go amiss. Since organizations are subject to many outside forces, including competitors, business cycles, government policies and changing consumer demands, managers must constantly reassess established goals and objectives in relation to the social and economic environment. They must be aware of trends and changes so that they can direct employees toward realizable goals within the constraints of the financial, human and material resources available. Furthermore, as problems arise, the manager must make decisions to resolve them.

Unfortunately, business decisions are not always easy to make. If a manager consistently makes the wrong decisions or fails to understand all that his or her job entails, if he or she neglects planning for the future, has a loose control system and provides poor leadership, the organization is likely to show poor results. In the long run, the organization may face loss of profits or even bankruptcy. Even in organizations where bankruptcy is precluded—government organizations or hospitals, for example— poor management may be reflected in inadequate and inefficient services.

Poor management is a particular problem for small firms where the owner-manager is often required to perform all management tasks. As discussed in a previous

FIGURE 4.1

The management process within an organization

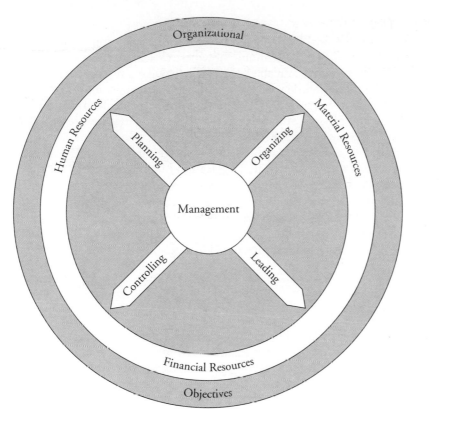

chapter, the great majority of business failures can be attributed to poor management. Even if a small firm is successful, management may be unable to maintain effective control as the firm grows. In fact, growth may reveal management deficiencies that were not evident when the organization was small.

One of the greatest deficiencies of management in growing organizations is poor or inadequate planning. Giant corporations can go bankrupt if top management has been unable to forecast future economic conditions accurately. One example is the Chrysler Corporation, whose financial problems were largely the result of poor economic forecasting and consequent failure to meet consumer demands for smaller, better-built, more fuel-efficient cars. New management revised plans and objectives, produced an automobile that met consumer demands, and made the company profitable again.

The Functions of Management

Managers perform somewhat similar tasks, whether they are managing a business, government department, hospital, political party or non-profit organization such as the Red Cross or the Salvation Army. We can classify a manager's tasks into four basic **functions of management**: planning, organizing, leading and controlling. While these functions are listed as separate and distinct activities, and even though at any given time a manager may be preoccupied with one or another, he or she is likely to engage in all of them during the course of a day.

Functions of management—all the tasks that managers perform can be classified into four main activities or functions: planning, organizing, leading and controlling.

Planning

Planning involves establishing objectives that the organization should accomplish by a future date, and then determining how best to achieve those objectives with the organizational resources available.

Planning involves establishing objectives that the organization should accomplish by a future date, and then determining how best to achieve those objectives with the organizational resources available. A manufacturing organization wishing to expand its operation from Ontario to western Canada, for example, must first determine the potential increase in revenue and profit that it can expect from such a venture, and then assess the physical, financial, personnel and managerial resources required. Does the company have the necessary capacity in its present manufacturing facilities to produce the additional product? Does it have the necessary financial resources to open a sales office, advertise its product and hire the people for sales and support activities? Can it spread its managerial resources thinner so that the move to western Canada will not jeopardize its existing operation?

After evaluating these and many other factors, the company might decide to establish a regional sales office in one of the Prairie provinces or British Columbia to test the market, and subsequently expand from there should the test prove profitable. Closely related to planning, therefore, is decision making, or choosing a course of action from a number of available alternatives to achieve a desired result.

Organizing

Once managers have established objectives and developed plans to achieve those objectives, an organization must be developed to carry out those plans. Depending on the objectives, different kinds of organizations will be required. A company manufacturing auto parts will be different from a hospital organization or a university. Auto parts, for example, usually require assembly lines for efficient production, which is hardly the case for hospitals or educational institutions. So managers must be able to determine what kind of organization is required, hire the appropriate people and lead those people to accomplish the objectives. We will examine the **organizing** function in more detail in Chapter 5.

Organizing involves creating a formal structure of tasks and authority.

Staffing is the recruitment and placement of qualified people to perform an organization's work.

One of the most important organizing activities is **staffing**. Managers must recruit and place qualified people in the various job positions under their authority. However, acquiring adequate human resources is no simple task, and personnel matters are complex and time-consuming. Employees quit or retire, business conditions may dictate a reduced work force, or the company may decide to consolidate in one area and expand in others. Therefore, virtually all large organizations (and many medium-sized ones as well) include a personnel department where specialists supervise the recruiting, selection, hiring, training, compensation and termination of employees. Nevertheless, the final choice as to who should fill a particular job is the responsibility of the manager directly in charge of that position.

Because staffing has become such an important function, one that requires specialized skills and knowledge, the matter of personnel is treated as a special business function. We discuss staffing as part of the personnel function in Chapter 10.

Leading

Leading, or **directing**, involves guiding the actions and performance of people to achieve the organization's goals.

An organization cannot achieve its goals without people. **Leading**, or **directing**, involves guiding the actions and performance of people to achieve the organization's goals. It means helping to bring out the best in workers, ensuring that they are happy and satisfied with their work, and thus motivating them to work willingly toward achieving the organization's goals. It includes assigning work to employees, explaining procedures and helping to correct errors. Managers must be able to communicate ideas and directions to others to achieve desired results. In fact, the greatest proportion of a manager's time is spent in directing employees.[1] The leading function, or "people-managing," is discussed more fully in Chapter 6.

Controlling

The fourth function of management is controlling—a term not always readily accepted because it suggests imposing restrictions on individuals. Although we use the term "controlling" in this book, "evaluating" is also often used.

Controlling means ensuring that actual performance is according to plan and that organizational objectives are being met. For example, given that a specific level of profit is a major objective for most businesses, the factors that can affect profit (e.g., actual sales and expenses) must be constantly checked against the plan so that corrective action can be taken if any discrepancies appear. If sales are slow, for example, management may need to promote advertising or hire more salespeople. Thus planning and controlling are closely related.

> **Controlling** means ensuring that actual performance is according to plan and that organizational objectives are being met.

Levels of Management

Even though all managers—from the president of a large corporation to the owner of a local service station—perform the same functions, their jobs differ according to the size of their organization. Large organizations have many different tasks to be performed and thus require more people than small organizations. As the number of tasks to be coordinated increases, more managers are required. Organizations therefore develop a **managerial hierarchy**, and managers are classified according to the level of the hierarchy on which they operate. These levels can be divided into three categories: top management, middle management and operating or supervisory management.

> **Managerial hierarchy** consists of three main levels of managers—top management, middle management and operating or supervisory management—whose tasks are defined by their particular level.

There are usually many supervisory managers on the bottom level of a large organization, but as one moves up in the hierarchy each level includes fewer managers. At the top of the hierarchy is the president, who has total responsibility for the operation of the organization. Figure 4.2 shows an organizational or management hierarchy.

> < The number of managers required increases as the number of tasks to be co-ordinated grows

FIGURE   4.2

The management hierarchy

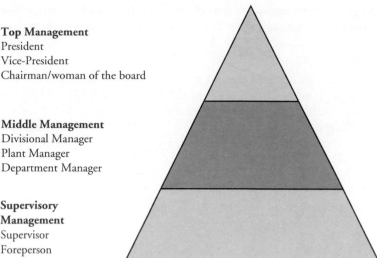

Top Management
President
Vice-President
Chairman/woman of the board

Middle Management
Divisional Manager
Plant Manager
Department Manager

**Supervisory
Management**
Supervisor
Foreperson

Top management is responsible for the overall management of the organization.

Middle management is responsible for translating top management's overall plans into action plans for their own departments. These action plans are carried out by operating or supervisory management.

Operating or **supervisory management** directs operating employees only. They are responsible for putting into action the detailed plans developed by middle management.

Technical skills are associated with the actual mechanics of a job and may include the use of tools or specialized knowledge.

Human skills are essential to the success of managers' interaction with employees. Managers must understand employee needs and motivate them to work toward the goals of the organization.

Depending on the size of the organization, **top management** may include the president, the chairperson of the board, the vice-president and, in the case of very large companies, the general managers in charge of various divisions. These managers devote most of their time to long-range planning on such matters as plant expansion, international operations, major financing problems and the addition or deletion of major products or product lines. Top management is also the level directly involved with external affairs, including relations with government and the community.

Middle management, which includes division and department managers, is concerned with more specific operations. It must develop the specific plans and procedures required to implement the broader plans of top management. A middle manager might be concerned with purchasing new equipment or raw materials, establishing inventory maintenance systems and personnel policy, and determining personnel requirements.

Operating or **supervisory management** is directly involved with workers on a departmental level. Included in this group are production supervisors and hospital ward nurses. Managers on this level assign workers to specific jobs, provide training and evaluate performance. They are responsible for putting into action the detailed plans developed by middle management. As they are involved directly with the workers, they must be able to deal quickly with a constant stream of problems, both major and minor. Much of a supervisor's time, therefore, is spent communicating directly with employees.

Managerial Skills

All managers should possess three basic skills: technical, human and conceptual.[2]

Technical skills are associated with the actual mechanics of a job and may include the use of tools or specialized knowledge. For example, a supervisor in a machine shop may need to know how to operate a lathe, an accountant must know how to keep the firm's books, while a data-processing manager must have some knowledge of computer programming.

Human skills are essential to the success of managers' interaction with employees. Managers must understand employee needs and motivate them to work toward the goals of the organization. Human skills are particularly important to managers because they accomplish their job through the work of others. To perform their own jobs well, they must be able to communicate effectively in both written and oral form.

Conceptual skills refer to an individual's ability to perceive the organization as a whole and see how the various parts work together to achieve long-range goals. Managers must be able to envision how their actions will affect the entire organization.

Technical skills are most important to operating and supervisory managers concerned with the daily operation of the business. Supervisory managers in the plant and managers in charge of specific business areas such as accounting and advertising, for example, need technical skills to deal with specific problems as they arise. Human skills are most important to supervisory and middle managers who interact directly with employees. Conceptual skills, on the other hand, are most important to top managers who are involved in long-range planning and decision making, as well as in maintaining relations with outside organizations. The relative importance of specific skills thus depends on the manager's level in the organizational hierarchy. Figure 4.3 indicates the relationship between the three management levels and the managerial skills generally required for each.

Since all managers at any given level perform similar functions, they can move from one position to another at the same level, or from one organization to another. Top levels of management probably find it easiest to move from one organization to another because at this level conceptual skills are of prime importance, while technical knowledge is virtually unnecessary. A top-level manager, for example, could move from a manufacturing organization to become a senior government official, the head of a bank, or the president of a university. All of these positions involve long-range planning, communication with other organizations and responsibility for decisions on the general direction of the organization.

Technical skills are not as readily transferable between organizations. For example, a retail department store supervisor could not assume the job of a nursing supervisor because he or she would not have the necessary technical skills. However, the store manager of a large retail chain might be quite capable of assuming the position of hospital administrator, since at this level the managerial skills required are similar.

Conceptual skills refer to an individual's ability to perceive the organization as a whole and see how the various parts work together to achieve long-range goals.

FIGURE 4.3

Skills required at various management levels

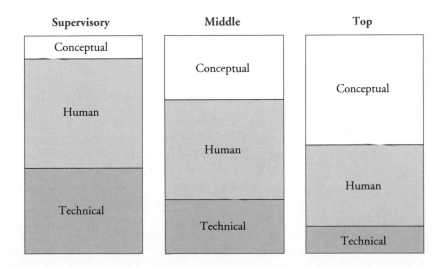

What Is a Manager's Job? An Alternative View

A different method of categorizing managerial tasks was developed by Henry Mintzberg, a Harvard University researcher. In a 1975 study, he surveyed the existing research on how managers spend their time and perform their work, and integrated his own research on the activities of five chief executive officers. The total survey included all kinds and levels of managers, from factory supervisors and sales managers to administrators and presidents. Mintzberg concluded that the jobs of managers at all levels are similar. According to his study, the formal authority and status of managers in the organization enables them to perform roles in three major areas: interpersonal, informational and decisional (see Figure 4.4).[3]

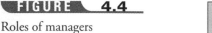

FIGURE 4.4

Roles of managers according to Mintzberg

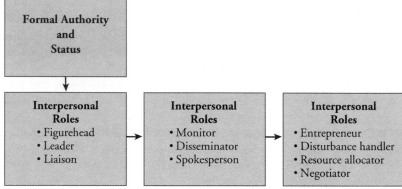

INTERPERSONAL ROLES	INFORMATIONAL ROLES	DECISIONAL ROLES
These roles are routine and keep the organization running smoothly.	These roles provide a manager with information for decision making.	The most important role of a manager is decision making.
Examples: – ceremonial duties – motivating workers – dealing with people outside of the organization, such as clients and suppliers	*Examples:* – looking for useful information – distributing information to subordinates – transmitting information to individuals outside the organization	*Examples:* – responding to situations beyond the manager's own control – deciding distribution of resources – working out agreements between two parties – making the unit grow and expand

SOURCE: Reprinted by permission of *Harvard Business Review*. An excerpt from "The manager's job: folklore or fact" by Henry Mintzberg (July–August 1975). © 1975 by the President and Fellows of Harvard College; all rights reserved.

Managers and Decision Making

One of the major tasks of managers is **decision making**, the process of choosing the best course of action from two or more alternatives. In fact, management and decision making are so closely linked that the two are often equated.

Managers are required to make decisions, major and minor, on a daily basis. Minor decisions can be made quickly, while decisions of major consequence for the firm require deliberate thought and analysis. A manager may be able to decide quickly where to hold an emergency meeting, for example, but it is more difficult to decide on a response to a competitor's newly introduced product that threatens to take a significant share of the firm's market. Deciding which alternative action to take is difficult because a manager cannot be certain of the future consequences of his or her decisions. He or she will likely choose the best alternative on the basis of the risk factor associated with each decision.

Decision making is the process of choosing the best course of action from two or more alternatives.

Programmed and Non-programmed Decisions

We can distinguish between two types of decisions—programmed and non-programmed. **Non-programmed decisions** deal with unusual or unique problems, and therefore few, if any, guidelines exist to help a manager make these decisions. Examples of non-programmed decisions include planning a course of action for the future that may involve a large part of a firm's resources, or meeting a competitor's product challenge. The ability to make non-programmed decisions is more important for high-level managers because they must handle these decisions more frequently.

Non-programmed decisions deal with unusual or unique problems, and therefore few, if any, guidelines exist to help a manager make these decisions.

To ensure that managers make the best possible non-programmed decisions, a specific process is usually followed that includes five major steps:

1. recognizing and defining the problem;

2. collecting and gathering data;

3. analyzing data and developing alternative courses of action;

4. evaluating alternative courses of action; and

5. selecting and implementing one course of action.

Occasionally the process includes a sixth step—the follow-up—to determine whether the decision was effective or whether it requires a change. However, the follow-up is also a step in the management function of planning and control, and therefore we will not include it in the process of decision making itself.

Decisions of lesser importance that managers may be required to make routinely as part of their daily operational tasks are known as **programmed** or **administrative decisions**. Because managers often encounter these types of decisions, organizations establish guidelines known as policies. As we will see later, policies are designed to limit the number of alternatives that a manager would otherwise be obliged to consider before making a decision. Although policies may appear to limit managers' freedom to act, they are established to facilitate decision making. Customer complaints, for example, can be resolved much more quickly if policies have been established specifying what a manager should do.

Programmed or **administrative decisions** are decisions that managers may be required to make as part of their daily operational tasks.

Planning and Management

Planning is an important function of management. Managers who do not plan where they want their organizations to go illustrate a familiar adage: "If you don't know

A New Manifesto for Management

In a recent article in the *Sloan Management Review*, the authors suggest that management is moving away from the old model of the 3 Ss: crafting strategy, designing the structure to fit, and building supporting systems. Although this model served management well for many years, the "real world" no longer corresponds to these theories. In the 1980s companies were driven by fierce competition and the focus was on continuously improving their operating efficiency. Shareholder return and management salaries have increased but at what cost? The bond of trust between corporations and employees, and corporations and their suppliers has been broken in what the authors call the dismemberment of the organization. The uncertainty concerning today's corporations is exemplified by the fact that both Bill Clinton and Tony Blair have set up reviews of companies' roles. Big business is often portrayed as the villain rather than the hero, with public furor raging over such topics as executive salaries. Managers are consistently ranked lower than either politicians or journalists on ethical standing when polls are conducted.

The "real world" has changed and at a pace that can render an organization's structure obsolete overnight. The quality of management is of critical importance as firms move toward a new moral contract, not only with employees but also with society, on a course of shared destiny. The authors propose a new model, the 3 Ps: purpose, process and people. Rather than creating strategy, managers can establish a sense of purpose. Rather than designing a formal structure in the organization, managers can focus on the processes. And managers can become developers of people rather than builders of systems. The new focus of management can be centred on creating rather than cutting as corporations pursue a higher purpose.[4]

where you want to go, then any road will take you there." Without specific objectives and plans, firms may lose potential profits or produce goods and services that no longer meet consumers' needs. According to studies, organizations that have poor planning processes, or worse, no planning at all, are far more likely to go bankrupt than organizations that plan ahead.

The Need for Planning

Planning is essential in helping to minimize the uncertainty and risk associated with changing economic and political conditions. By looking to the future, management can identify both potential threats to the organization and new business opportunities to be exploited.

Planning also enables everyone in the organization to focus on goals and objectives, and the means of achieving them. A clear idea of the organization's objectives helps both managers and employees to coordinate the organization's resources and use them more effectively and efficiently. Without the sense of direction provided by clear objectives, the aimlessness of the organization is likely to be carried over to all levels of management and to the employees, which will affect their motivation to perform well. If they don't know what they are to achieve, they have nothing on which to base their performance and no one to give them direction. The result is a waste of effort and resources.

Finally, planning and plans are the basis upon which control systems are established so that management can determine the organization's performance. The plans and the dollar budgets derived from those plans form the base or standard against which future performance can be measured to ensure that the organization is achieving its goals.

Flexibility in Planning

Although planning is essential, the plans made cannot be carved in stone. Plans must be flexible so that they can be changed as conditions change, both inside and outside the organization. During the planning process, efforts must be made to forecast factors that can affect a firm's operation. Not only must plans take these factors into account; alternative plans, which can be implemented immediately should the new conditions arise, may have to be established.

For example, a firm planning to do business in a country with a quickly changing political picture, such as Russia or China, must have alternative plans developed for different political situations. Or, if a business's success depends entirely on the personal characteristics of one individual, the possibility that he or she may die, retire or leave the organization must be taken into account. If risks are recognized when plans are made, alternative courses of action may be established to minimize detrimental effects.

Since the environment in which the organization operates is changing constantly, planning must also be done on a continuous basis. Managers must always be aware of changing conditions and be ready to adjust organizational goals and the methods for achieving them.

Types of Plans

There are two basic types of planning processes—strategic planning and tactical planning. Both terms are taken from the military, where a strategic plan is developed to achieve a set of larger objectives and is based on actions that the enemy may or may not invoke, and a tactical plan is developed to achieve a particular military objective that is a part of the overall strategy.

When it comes to business, **strategic planning** is particularly important when an organization with limited resources faces strong competitors and a rapidly changing environment. In strategic planning, key objectives and plans on how to achieve them are developed with a view to the possible actions of competitors and the resources available to the organization. **Tactical plans** then translate these overall business unit strategies into detailed plans that can be implemented over a shorter period of time. Tactical plans, also known as **action plans** or **short-range planning,** include budgets, individual departmental action plans, proposed changes in organization structure (discussed in Chapter 5), control systems and so on.

Long- and Short-Range Planning

Any organization with long-term survival as an objective must attempt to forecast what factors may affect its operation in the future. **Long-range planning** may attempt to look five to fifty years into the future depending on the organization. For example, to meet its power requirements a utility company must have long-range plans because new hydroelectric plants can take a decade or more to build. However, since the future is difficult to predict, especially when forecasts are made far into the future, a long-range plan must remain flexible so that all or part of it can be adjusted if forecasted conditions change.

Strategic planning may be long- or short-range planning depending on the nature of the business environment. For example, in the areas of computer hardware and software development, a strategic plan may be outdated in a matter of months because technology advances so rapidly, with new competitors going in and out of business and new products constantly entering the market. On the other hand, a government-regulated utility company with no competitors and a product that is unlikely to change for a long period may develop a strategic plan that will remain viable for decades.

Strategic planning is a formalized planning process whereby an organization selects specific goals and objectives and develops methods for achieving them, taking into account the available resources.

Tactical, action or **short-range planning** covers specific objectives of the strategic plan to be accomplished over a shorter period of time, usually one year.

Long-range planning, extending five to fifty years into the future depending on the organization, is done to identify factors that might affect the organization's operation in the future.

Short-range planning, also known as tactical and action planning, usually covers specific objectives to be accomplished for a period of one year or less. Short-range plans include advertising campaigns, employee hiring and training programs, sales incentive programs and expenditures for specific activities such as building a warehouse or new sales offices in other regions of the country. Short-range plans outline the specific actions that an organization must take in the near future to achieve strategic plans or plans with longer-range objectives. These plans are developed through a monthly, quarterly or semiannual planning process that involves all levels of management. Once short-range plans are formed, a budget is drawn up. The budget specifies the financial resources needed to implement the plans, and provides a guide for income and expenditures.

Elements of Planning

During the planning process, management focuses on the specific goals of the organization, including its purpose, mission and objectives. To achieve these goals, an organization requires a strategy that involves both single-use plans (programs, projects and budgets) and standing plans (policies, procedures and rules). Figure 4.5 indicates the relationship between these planning elements.

Establishing Goals and Objectives

The terms "goals" and "objectives" are often used interchangeably and can be confused. We will therefore use the term **goals** as a broad category including purpose, mission and objectives.

The **purpose of an organization** is the fundamental reason for its existence. It is a broad aim that applies to all organizations engaged in a similar kind of activity. In a free enterprise economy such as Canada's, for example, the purpose of business organizations is to produce goods and services in order to earn a profit. The purpose of a university, on the other hand, is to pursue knowledge through research and to communicate it through formal teaching programs, while the purpose of a hospital is to provide health care.

Goals as a broad category include purpose, mission and objectives.

Purpose of an organization— the fundamental reason for an organization's existence. It is a broad aim that applies to all organizations engaged in a similar kind of activity.

FIGURE   4.5

The elements of planning

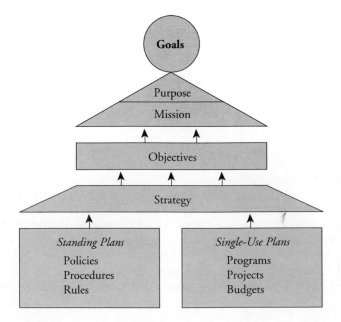

The **mission of an organization** is the particular aim that sets it apart from other organizations with the same purpose. For example, although universities in Canada may have the same purpose, the mission of one might be to specialize in engineering and technical areas, while the mission of another might be to focus on medical research and training. In the same way, business organizations have many different missions. Some manufacturing firms produce cars and trucks; others make furniture or kitchen appliances.

An organization must define its mission carefully. Too narrow a definition might prevent management from taking advantage of new opportunities. Faced with changing environmental conditions, an organization may be unable to survive if it does not redefine its mission.

In the last few decades, many railways have experienced serious operating problems that have been attributed to a failure on the part of management to adapt

> **Mission of an organization—** the particular aim that sets one organization apart from other organizations with the same purpose.

Canadian Pacific Railway: A Company That Redefined Its Mission[5]

A number of U.S. railways have failed to adapt to changes in transportation, but the Canadian Pacific Railway does not appear to have fallen into this trap. Founded more than 100 years ago, it was given the task of tying eastern and western Canada together. By the 1950s, however, the company realized that the highly regulated transportation business in Canada could not be relied upon for increased profitability. Thus, while it has continued to pour hundreds of millions of dollars into railway equipment and track maintenance, at the same time expanding its shipping, airline, trucking and telecommunications subsidiaries, CPR has also embarked on a program of diversification into areas not regulated by government.

It was in the late 1950s that the CPR first turned to the oil and gas industry, and in 1962 it incorporated Canadian Pacific Investments, later known as Canadian Pacific Enterprises Ltd., as a holding company for its non-transportation investments. By 1979 the company owned or had invested in coal mining, oil and gas exploration, iron and steel, logging, pulp and paper, various manufacturing companies, hotels and a real estate development company, among others. CPI's assets in that year totalled $5.7 billion and accounted for more than 60% of the revenues of the parent company, Canadian Pacific Ltd. (CP).

In 1985 CP president and chief executive officer Bill Stinson and his management team switched emphasis from the acquisition of companies to the prime concern of profitability— to put it more precisely, an acceptable and sustainable return on shareholder investment.

The change in strategy was to dispose of corporate holdings that did not fit in with the new CP, either because they tended to make profits volatile or simply because there was no place for them in the new hierarchy. CP sold its 52% interest in Cominco in 1986. It also sold CP Air to Pacific Western Airlines in the same year. In 1987, the company sold Maple Leaf Mills, but turned around and bought CN Hotels, as well as the outstanding 40% of Fording Coal. In 1993 it sold its holdings in Canadian Pacific Forest Products Limited and in 1994 sold its trucking operation (CP Trucks) to its employees. In 1995 it sold off its common shares in Dominion Industries Limited and wrote off its investment in Unitel Communication Holdings Inc. as a loss. To strengthen its core business in shipping it bought the container business from the Cast Group as well as an outstanding interest in Canada Maritime Limited.

CP now has three core business areas: transportation, energy, and real estate and hotels. It also has a minor business in waste services.

Transportation	**Energy**
CP Rail	PanCanadian Petroleum Ltd.
CP Ships	Fording Coal Ltd.

Canadian Pacific Hotels and Real Estate
Pacific Hotels and Resorts Inc.
Marathon Realty

Waste Services
Laidlaw Inc.

The new holdings will tend to lessen the cyclical effect of economic activity, which occurs every five or six years, and had severely affected the company's profits. CP also reduced its debt load by almost $2.2 billion. The most critical change according to the president, however, has been a process of renewal and regeneration. Right across the company, the subsidiaries have been shedding old product lines for new ones, finding new markets and increasing productivity. This has had a profound effect on profitability. CP's earnings from its remaining operations climbed 324% to $636 million, even though its revenues from those operations had changed very little. The conclusion is that most of the things CP did were significantly more profitable.

How Wisconsin Central Is Practising Its Mission Statement

In a recent article in *Railway Age*, the author relates how Wisconsin Central (WC) took its mission statement to heart and grew in size and profitability by doing so. The mission statement consists of only 21 words but each element relates to the success of the company. The statement is as follows: "To offer superior transportation consisting of more frequent, dependable train service, at competitive prices, with proper equipment, accomplished by customer-minded employees." The WC story exemplifies the importance of building value to your customer, which will in turn lead to value to the shareholder. Each element of the mission statement relates to customer value. For example, frequent service in the railway shipping industry is critical for competitive advantage; dependability also connotes an advantage for customers as they attempt to move their products on to the end-consumer. Proper equipment is a clearly visible commitment to the shippers as WC continues to purchase new boxcars and hoppers. Moody's Investor Services notes the focus on a high level of customer service by WC and recognizes WC's service-oriented workforce.

With their success in North America as an impetus, WC exported its expertise to the freight operation of British Rail. By recognizing the different environment in which they were operating, WC was able to adopt the mission statement in their UK operations with an expected tripling of business in the next few years.

By adhering to a well-thought-out practical mission statement, WC succeeded in their domestic market and transported the concept to a less favourable environment, succeeding there as well.[6]

---

the missions of these organizations to changing conditions. Management continued to see the organizational mission specifically as providing rail service rather than more broadly as providing general transportation services. The latter definition might have allowed the organizations to diversify into other areas.

Objectives are the specific ends that the organization must achieve to carry out its mission. It might be a company's objective, for example, to increase total sales by 10% over the next year, or to increase its share of the market by 3%. The various company divisions each formulate objectives that are in line with these overall objectives. In turn, departmental objectives are established in accordance with divisional objectives. As shown in Figure 4.6, objectives become more specific as we move down the organizational hierarchy from top management to the lower levels.

It is important that objectives be as specific as possible so that their achievement can be measured; otherwise they may not be particularly meaningful. For example, a company objective specifying that "to provide better service to customers, the sales staff in XYZ department will be increased by five people over the next six months," is much more meaningful than an objective that states simply: "We would like to provide better service to our customers by increasing our sales in the future." It would be difficult to gauge when, if ever, the latter objective had been accomplished.

How to Achieve Goals

Once objectives that reflect the organization's overall goals have been established, management must choose a strategy to achieve them. A **strategy** creates a unified picture of the organization's future course by ensuring that its objectives complement one another, and by specifying how resources are to be used. However, while a strategy provides the framework for the overall action of the organization, nothing could be achieved without outlining both standing and single-use plans. **Standing plans** include policies, procedures and rules; **single-use** plans include programs, projects and budgets.

Standing Plans

Many activities in the everyday operation of an organization are repetitive. A bank, for example, loans money to people for many reasons, and although each case differs

---

Objectives are the specific ends that the organization must achieve to carry out its mission.

Strategy creates a unified picture of the organization's future course by ensuring that its objectives complement one another, and by specifying how resources are to be used.

Standing plans include policies, procedures and rules. They enable employees to carry on everyday business efficiently without subjecting each individual case to a lengthy process of decision making.

Single-use plans include programs, projects and budgets. Once the objectives of a single-use plan have been achieved, the plan is terminated.

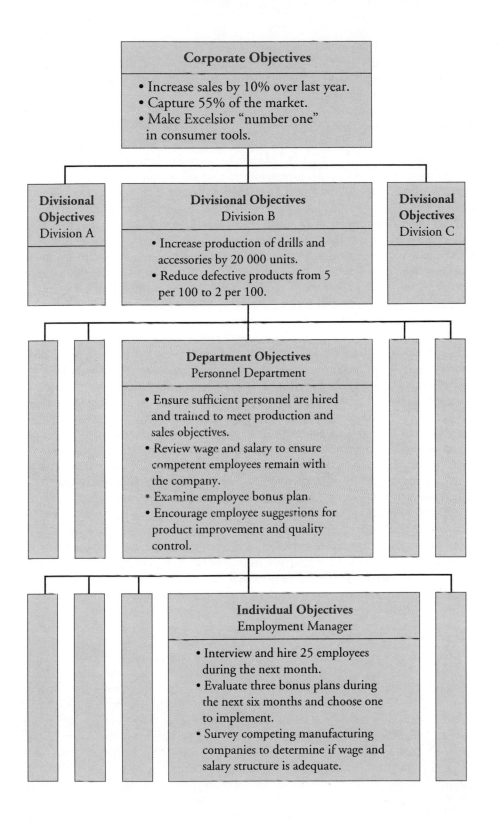

FIGURE 4.6

Hierarchy of objectives

Corporate Objectives

- Increase sales by 10% over last year.
- Capture 55% of the market.
- Make Excelsior "number one" in consumer tools.

Divisional Objectives
Division A

Divisional Objectives
Division B

- Increase production of drills and accessories by 20 000 units.
- Reduce defective products from 5 per 100 to 2 per 100.

Divisional Objectives
Division C

Department Objectives
Personnel Department

- Ensure sufficient personnel are hired and trained to meet production and sales objectives.
- Review wage and salary to ensure competent employees remain with the company.
- Examine employee bonus plan.
- Encourage employee suggestions for product improvement and quality control.

Individual Objectives
Employment Manager

- Interview and hire 25 employees during the next month.
- Evaluate three bonus plans during the next six months and choose one to implement.
- Survey competing manufacturing companies to determine if wage and salary structure is adequate.

Policy—a general guide that helps managers in decision making by placing limits on possible courses of action.

in some aspects, the process used to determine the applicant's creditworthiness is identical in all instances. If an individual or a company meets certain criteria, the loan is granted. The entire credit-granting function is based on standing plans established by middle and top management. Standing plans enable employees to carry on everyday business efficiently without subjecting each individual case to a lengthy process of decision making. These plans include policies, procedures and rules.

A **policy** is a general guide that helps managers in decision making by placing limits on possible courses of action. Managers can make their decisions more rapidly when they need consider only those solutions that fall within set limits. For example, a major retailer may follow a policy of building regional shopping centres only in cities or areas with a population of at least 200 000. Such a policy eliminates the large number of possible locations that management would otherwise be obliged to consider, and allows it to concentrate on evaluating a smaller number in greater depth.

Policies may be broad or narrow. For example, a policy stating simply that the customer must always be satisfied is very broad compared with a policy that customer satisfaction will be guaranteed by replacing the defective product or refunding the purchase price. In the first instance, the manager has wide discretion in satisfying the customer; in the second case, his or her discretion is limited.

Policies are established for all levels of management. By setting policies, top management may delegate decision making to lower levels without losing control entirely. At the same time, the delegation of responsibility fosters individual initiative and allows managers discretion in solving problems as they arise. However, policies must also be revised continually as company objectives and environmental conditions change. If they are not, managers may continue to make decisions based on outdated policies, and the results could be detrimental to the organization.

Procedure—provides a detailed set of instructions for performing repetitive actions. It is a sequence of steps intended to streamline operations and control the actions of employees by describing the most efficient way to perform specific tasks.

A **procedure** provides a detailed set of instructions for performing repetitive actions. It is a sequence of steps intended to streamline operations and control the actions of employees by describing the most efficient way to perform specific tasks. A procedure may outline how to handle customer complaints or hire employees, for example.

Rules state exactly what may or may not be done in a particular case. They do not serve as guides to decision making, since they allow no discretion. While some rules are necessary to prevent mistakes, too many of them may limit creativity and imagination, and prevent employees from finding new and better ways of doing things. Rules should be carefully examined before implementation and reviewed periodically to determine whether they are still required.

Rules state exactly what may or may not be done in a particular case.

Program—a single-use plan that embodies a complex set of goals, policies, procedures and rules, together with the people, activities, raw materials and other elements necessary to implement a desired course of action.

Single-Use Plans

A **program** is a single-use plan that embodies a complex set of goals, policies, procedures and rules, together with the people, activities, raw materials and other elements necessary to implement a desired course of action. A program is usually supported by a budget to cover operating and capital expenditures. Programs vary in scope, in cost and in the time required for completion. For example, the federal government may establish an employment program, either for the entire country or for selected regions, to last a specified length of time. An oil company may set up an exploration and drilling program for the coming year, while other businesses may initiate long-term research and development programs. As a single-use plan, a program is terminated once the objectives have been reached.

Project—a miniature program or part of a larger program. It might include the same steps as the program, but not encompass as many activities.

A **project** can be regarded as a miniature program or as part of a larger program. It might include the same steps as the program, but not encompass as many activities. For example, a company program of expansion across Canada might comprise a

"After spending 1.6 billion dollars and ten years on this project. I've lost interest in it."

SOURCE: Cotham—Copyright, Singer Media Corporation, San Clemente, CA 92672.

number of projects, including the building of sales offices and plants or the expansion of warehouse facilities. If the company were to establish a branch office in Halifax, that particular project could be independent or it could represent a part of the general program of expansion.

A **budget** is a single-use plan specifying the financial resources that have been set aside for one particular operation and how the resources are to be allocated. Business organizations often call their budgets "profit plans," since they indicate how much of the expected revenue may be used for expenses while still providing a profit. Once budgets have been established, they can be used for control purposes, to determine how actual performance compares to the plan. In this sense, budgets are used as a standard for organizational performance.

Budget—a single-use plan specifying the financial resources that have been set aside for one particular operation and how the resources are to be allocated.

The Planning Process

All planning must be approached in a systematic manner. The **strategic planning process** differs in several ways from the process used to develop tactical or action plans.

First, the activities involved in strategic planning generally require a longer period of time in terms of both implementation and feedback on their results. Second, the eventual impact of these activities is of greater significance. Third, to carry out an effective strategy, an organization might focus on a fairly narrow set of actions, which in all likelihood will reduce the resources available for other activities. Fourth, strategic planning usually requires decisions that complement one another over a period of time. Finally, a strategy usually covers a wide range of activities, from resource allocation to day-to-day operations; because these activities must be applied consistently over a period of time, all levels of the organization must act so as to reinforce the strategy.

Strategic planning process— consists of four basic steps: establishing the mission and major goals; analyzing the external environment; evaluating the organization's internal strengths and weaknesses; and developing a strategy for achieving the established goals.

Strategic Planning and Small Business

Small business cannot ignore strategic planning. For a number of reasons, the strategic planning process is simpler for small organizations than it is for large organizations. First, a small business usually offers only a limited number of products and services with a fairly defined market. Second, there are fewer people—the owner(s) and key employees only—who must be involved in the actual planning process. Finally, a small business has fewer resources and thus a limited number of options to consider.

The strategic planning process itself can be a simple response to the following questions:

- Where are we?
- Where do we want to go?
- Can we get there?
- What do we have to do to get there?
- How can we control our performance?

Small businesses may also face problems in the planning process, however. The owner-manager may be reluctant to share with key employees his or her ideas about the future of the company. In addition, a small business may lack the resources needed to analyze both the strengths and weaknesses of the company, and the forces in the environment. Key employees may also shy away from systematic procedures and instead rely on their experience and intuition.

Both small and large firms require strategic plans. The article "Strategic Planning and Small Business" explains how small firms can implement strategic planning on a regular basis. "Hickson Moves into a Recovery Strategy," on page 127, on the other hand, shows how a large firm introduced a new strategy to help it recover from bankruptcy.

The strategic planning process can be reduced to the four steps shown in Figure 4.7.

Step I: Establishing the Mission and Major Goals

A strategy is based on the organization's mission and major goals. Major goals specify what the organization hopes to achieve in the medium to long term. Usually, the return to stockholders is the primary goal. Supporting the top goal are secondary goals. For example, a private business may consider market share, new products or services, or expansion into other markets to support its profit objective. Non-profit organizations will have different goals. For example, a hospital might aim to specialize in the treatment of certain illnesses or to perform specialized operations in addition to offering regular health care.

FIGURE 4.7

The planning process

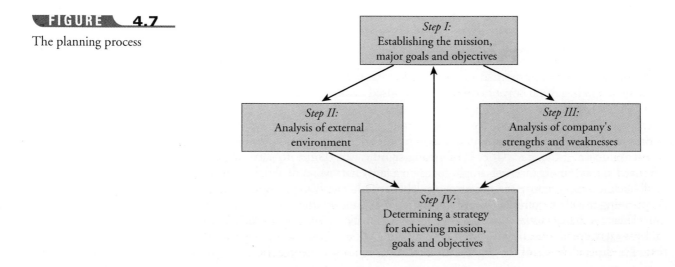

The organization's mission and major goals are always determined by top levels of management. Even if no changes are planned, the existing strategic plans and goals should be re-examined to ensure that they are still in line with the mission and with what has been achieved during the past year. Then the short-term objectives to be achieved during the next year must be established for the organization as a whole.

Step II: External Analysis

The purpose of analyzing an organization's external environment is to identify any strategic opportunities and threats. Management must understand the organization's major competitors and anticipate their potential actions. Other factors that must be considered are possible changes in economic conditions, technology, population, lifestyles, social values and customs, or the political and legal environments, along with changes in world conditions as a whole. While some of these factors may have little impact on a company's short-range plans, their effect could be considerable in the long run.

Although management is unlikely to be able to influence environmental factors, it can protect the organization by preparing alternative plans. For example, Canadian firms have little influence on the price of oil charged by the OPEC countries, but they can look at alternative sources of energy or sources of crude oil. Firms can also plan for changes in social habit. Faced with decreased demand for cigarettes because smoking has become less socially accepted, for example, many tobacco companies are diversifying into other areas.

Step III: Internal Analysis

An internal analysis of the organization identifies strengths and weaknesses in terms of the quantity and quality of resources available. Such an analysis must determine whether the organization's goals and objectives can realistically be achieved with its available financial, human and managerial resources. Many businesses have over-extended themselves because they failed to anticipate the strain that trying to achieve unrealistic objectives would place on the organization. If resources appear adequate, then the preliminary objectives can be firmly established. Otherwise they must be revised and brought into line with what can reasonably be achieved.

Step IV: Determining a Strategy for Achieving Objectives

The fourth step in the strategic planning process involves developing a series of alternative strategies that takes into consideration the organization's internal strengths and weaknesses and its external threats and opportunities. In evaluating the alternative strategies, the costs and benefits associated with each must be balanced. The final choice may not be the optimum strategy, since management cannot have adequate information and knowledge of all the factors involved. Rather, decisions will be based on available information, general experience and the judgement of top management. In any event, the strategy chosen should be flexible enough that it can be changed should future conditions make it unusable.

Once a strategy has been chosen, a program for implementing the strategy must be developed. An organization must ensure that the organization structure is appropriate for the plan. If not, then changes to the structure must be made. We will discuss organization structure in Chapter 5. The article "Strategic Management" lists the steps in both strategy formulation and strategy implementation.

Strategic Management

Strategic Formulation

1. Agree on a clear definition of the business.

2. Size up the key internal factors (purpose, strategy, functional operations, results, organization resources) and assess their strengths, weaknesses and congruency.

3. Size up the business environment, that is, identify, analyze and assess important external trends, and analyze competitors, including forecasts of their expected strategies.

4. Identify and analyze key success factors and make a self-assessment relative to competitors.

5. Identify and analyze competitive strengths, weaknesses, opportunities and threats ("SWOT" analysis).

6. Develop, analyze and evaluate strategic alternatives.

7. Prepare the strategic plan, including goals, objectives, business strategies, programs and financial forecasts.

8. Prepare the detailed operating plan, outlining the necessary actions and expected results related to implementation of the first year of the strategic plan.

Strategic Implementation

1. Develop a program for management of change, that is, define what should be done. Outline integrated plans for major changes needed in strategy, operations, organization and resources to improve results as required to achieve purpose. Outline tactics, timing, sequence and priorities in terms of urgency and importance.

2. Specify the action necessary to implement the strategic and tactical plans. Make the action plan clear, sharp and focused in terms of the "Who? What? Why? How? When? and Where?"

3. Monitor whether the management of change is successful. Assess performance and results against plans and budgets. Determine whether procedures for control, feedback and corrective action are satisfactory. Make reviews and follow up to ensure successful execution of plans.

4. Ensure that there is continuous improvement. Develop increased and upgraded participation, commitment and understanding among all members of the management team.

5. Start again on a new planning-action cycle. Update the entire process.

SOURCE: Donald H. Thain, "Strategic management: the state of the art," *Business Quarterly* (Autumn 1990): 98.

Action Planning and Budgeting

Profit plan—a forecast of the total sales and total expenses, along with the profit the firm must earn.

Action plans are developed by individual divisions and departments. Each division sets objectives in line with organizational objectives and the general profit plan, and each department, in turn, establishes objectives geared to achieving divisional objectives.

Once the strategy has been chosen, tactical planning can get under way. Usually top management will develop a general profit plan for the year. The **profit plan** is a forecast of the total sales and total expenses, along with the profit that the firm must earn to satisfy its shareholders. The organization is then ready to establish detailed action plans specifying how the objectives of the general profit plan will be achieved. **Action plans** are developed by individual divisions and departments. Each division sets objectives that reflect organizational objectives and the general profit plan, and each department, in turn, establishes objectives that are geared to achieving divisional objectives.

After objectives have been broken down for divisions and departments, detailed budgeting can begin. Supervisory or operating managers become involved at this stage. Because of their intimate knowledge of specific work processes and daily operations, they can determine such matters as individual workloads and costs for labour and raw materials. They also establish detailed monthly budgets for employee wages and salaries, including provisions for holidays and estimated sick days (see Chapter 9).

Departmental managers review these budgets with their supervisors before submitting them to their divisional managers for inclusion in the division's budget.

When the division budget is complete, it is submitted to top management. If there are any discrepancies between divisional budgets and the original profit plan, they must be resolved. Depending on the nature of the discrepancy, the entire planning process may have to be repeated.

In 1995, Hickson International was on the brink of bankruptcy. What happened to reverse the spiralling debt and rescue the company? With a debt of $164 million and a debt-to-equity ratio of over 100%, the company recorded a multimillion-dollar loss. The creditor banks intervened and Chairman James Hann began to build a rescue strategy, which involved pure survival at the outset with a debt-reduction program being implemented, involving the sale of some of the company's businesses. By early 1998, seven businesses had been divested, reversing the acquisition binge of the late 1980s and early 1990s. The sale of these businesses reduced indebtedness to 25–30%, reduced sites from 38 to 16 and decreased headcount to half of former levels. The selection of the four businesses retained by Hickson was based on the company's global positions, market shares and growth prospects. By 1998, Hickson had begun a five-year growth plan. Some of the new strategies included forming market alliances, introducing new products where a demand had been identified, outsourcing some production units and refocusing into higher-margin areas. By reducing their debt and pursuing growth strategies consistent with careful environmental scanning, Hickson has managed to pull back from disaster and, according to new CEO David Wilbraham, the company may see double-digit returns during their new five-year plan.

Hickson Moves into a Recovery Strategy

SOURCE: Adapted from Natasha Alperowicz, "Hickson moves into recovery mode," *Chemical Week* (Apr 21, 1999): 49–52.

Planning and Controlling

There is a close relationship between planning and the other management functions of organizing, directing and, in particular, controlling. Since planning involves the uncertainties of the future, actual results are unlikely to follow precisely according to plan. Conditions can change so quickly that discrepancies could easily arise.

On the other hand, the plan might have been wrong for any number of reasons. For example, management may have planned for an unrealistically high increase in sales without considering sales incentive programs for their employees or the action of competitors. A new government could also affect a company's profits by introducing changes (in tax rules or business incentives) that the company did not anticipate. Many factors can cause actual results to differ widely from those planned.

A system of controls is therefore required to indicate when actual results deviate from plans. Although the control system may be established by anyone in the organization, in each particular case the responsibility for controlling results falls to the manager who established the plans. Managers at every level of the managerial hierarchy are responsible for controlling their own part of the operation.

The Process of Control

To **control**, in a business context, means to compare one thing to another. Golfers compare their scores to what is par for the course; this tells them where they stand in relation to a good golfer playing that particular course. Similarly, in business, actual operations are compared to a plan that has been translated into a numerical dollar budget. The budget becomes the standard against which actual performance is measured. If actual performance differs from the standard, corrective action must be taken.

Many standards are used in business. Virtually all industries have established standards against which other businesses in that industry can measure themselves. Among these standards are inventory turnover, profitability and return on investment. When standards are derived from a large number of companies, they can be considered absolute standards and usually vary little over time.

National Quality Institute

www.nqi.ca/english/index.htm

Control—a process that consists of four basic steps: establishing standards, measuring actual performance, comparing actual performance against standards and taking action to correct deviations from standards.

Total Quality Management —Does it Work?

Recent independent research conducted by major consulting firms suggests that only about one-fifth to one-third of TQM programs in North America and Europe have achieved significant or even tangible results. While quality is essential for organizational success, TQM is only one way to achieve it. Why doesn't TQM work? The following 10 reasons have been suggested by author and researcher Oren Harari:

1. TQM focuses attention on internal processes rather than on external results. The day-to-day operation of a TQM system requires employees to focus on the internal processes despite the turmoil that is occurring outside the organization. Hence the firm may become more efficient but less responsive, innovative and flexible, a veritable death sentence in today's fast-paced environment.

2. TQM focuses on minimum standards. The goals of zero defects and no rework efficiency are only minimum objectives to compete in the global market of the twenty-first century.

3. TQM develops its own bureaucracy. To maintain the order and predictability of a TQM system, staff must be in place to monitor the program. This leaves no opportunity for the gut-wrenching re-engineering often necessary for a quality turnaround.

4. TQM delegates quality to experts rather than to real people. The importance of empowered employees and involved customers cannot be underestimated for shaping quality interventions.

5. TQM does not demand organizational change. If you are serious about quality improvements, a flattening of the structure is necessary to free up line management and front-line people so that they may be less constrained by functional boundaries.

6. TQM does not demand changes in management compensation. As long as quality is not tied directly to compensation, it will not receive the attention necessary.

7. TQM does not demand entirely new relationships with outside partners. With the advent of subcontracting and outsourcing, concepts such as trust, honesty and openness become essential in a working relationship among partners.

8. TQM appeals to those looking for a quick fix. In some instances, TQM has been marketed as a clean, orderly, logical, easy way to attain quick results.

9. TQM drains entrepreneurship and innovation from the corporate culture. The standardization and routine of a TQM program is acceptable in a standard and routine world; however, this is not the definition of the global marketplace of the twenty-first century.

10. TQM has no passion. TQM attempts to ensure quality via a logical, organized, methodical path. True quality is derived from love of the company and the product, enthusiasm for the task, excitement for the process of creating and a sense of accomplishment and joy. TQM has no soul.

SOURCE: Adapted from: Oren Harari, "Ten reasons TQM doesn't work," *Management Review* (January 1997):38-44.

ISO Online

www.iso.ch

Although budget is not an absolute standard but rather an expected outcome, it is a useful measure of performance because at the time it was established it was believed to be achievable. Deviations of actual performance from the budget may be the result of either poor budgeting or poor performance, or both. A manager must recognize these problems and take them into account when evaluating results.

In fact, as Figure 4.8 shows, the control process is a continuous cycle consisting of four basic steps:

1. establishing standards;

2. measuring actual performance;

3. comparing actual performance with standards; and

4. taking action to correct deviations from standards.

The control process is not complete unless corrective action is taken. Plans may have to be revised when economic conditions or other factors change and result in year-end figures that differ substantially from the plan. On the other hand, the main plan may be correct and the supporting ones wrong. If sales are down, for example,

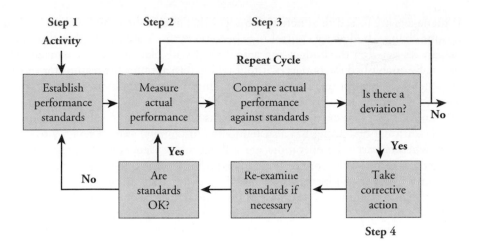

FIGURE 4.8

The control cycle

management may need to revamp the advertising campaign, increase sales commissions or hire more salespeople. In extreme cases, the entire plan may have to be revised, even in the midst of actual operations. Replanning gives the organization the opportunity to re-examine its objectives in light of new conditions.

Control Techniques

There are two general types of control techniques: budgetary and non-budgetary. Budgets are plans that have been converted into dollar figures and that cover specific activities over a given period of time. A budget usually includes total revenues, total expenditures and expected profit. For non-profit organizations, budgets simply indicate expected expenditures for all divisions and departments. Non-budgetary methods of control include personal observation, reports, external and internal auditing, ratio and break-even analysis, Gantt charts, Program Evaluation and Review Technique (PERT) and Critical Path Method (CPM).

Budgetary Control Techniques

All organizations, profit or non-profit, require money to operate. A budget serves to translate all organizational activities into monetary terms, with dollars as the common denominator for a wide variety of factors. Individual budgets can be used in all departments of an organization. At every level, budgets allow an organization to compare goals and objectives with the plans designed to achieve them.

A budget is also a useful coordination tool. In any organization, responsibility for various expenditures rests at specific points in the managerial hierarchy, and all individuals are accountable to their superiors for the proper use of budgeted financial resources. The budget provides a check on both spending and plans, since any over-expenditure must be fully justified.

Since budgets are expressed in numerical terms, they encourage precision in planning. If a manager wants two extra people in the sales department to help promote sales, the increase in labour costs must be weighed against the expected increase in sales. Later, a comparison can be made with the previous year to determine whether actual sales were worth the extra labour expenses incurred. Thus, a budget can be a useful tool for both planning and control.

If budgets are too rigidly followed, however, they can be detrimental to the organization. Budgets are subject to errors because they deal with the future.

If managers are forced to adhere to a budget that allows them no flexibility if conditions change, budgetary control may become dysfunctional. At other times, discrepancies between the budget and actual results are blamed on the manager who originally established the budget, without taking into account the reasons for the discrepancies. To protect themselves against blame and inflexibility of superiors, managers may develop unrealistic budgets. For example, they might project lower sales or plan for higher expenses to avoid problems when the final results come out.

Traditional budgeting has also tended to discourage annual reviews to determine whether particular operations are still necessary. Generally, the previous year's budget is assumed to be correct, with any additions to the budget defended as being necessary to cover cost increases. To guard against perpetuating unnecessary activities, a technique known as zero-base budgeting may be used. Under this budgeting process, a manager must justify all activities planned for the coming year. Previous budgets, or the activities they covered, are of no consequence in the new plan.

Non-budgetary Methods of Control

Experienced managers can often detect problems simply by inspecting a particular operation. **Personal inspection** remains a primary tool of control because some problems (e.g., unnecessary activities) cannot be detected by looking at the budget. Sometimes major problem areas are known, but specific causes are not. Careful study may be required, and findings and solutions can then be presented in a special report. Occasionally, personal observation of a minor problem may lead to the discovery of more serious problems. Thus, a special study can result in significant savings.

Auditing, another non-budgetary method of control, involves a detailed and systematic examination of a company's procedures. There are two types of audit: internal and external. **External auditing** is a verification of an organization's financial records performed by an outside accounting firm, usually on behalf of stockholders or for a bank considering a loan. **Internal auditing** is conducted by an organization's own personnel. Both types of audit are designed to encourage employee honesty and safeguard the company's financial or physical resources. However, an internal audit can also bring to light outdated or inefficient procedures, and usually provides recommendations for improvements.

A third non-budgetary method of control is **ratio analysis**, which is used to compare current financial (and sometimes non-financial) results with those of previous years or with those of other organizations. For example, ratio analysis may show that an expenditure that appears exceptionally high when compared with previous years is actually normal when compared to that made by similar organizations for the same year. The ratios most commonly used by an organization are liquidity (ability to pay current debts), financial leverage ratios (ability to meet long-term debt), profitability (a measure of return on investment) and activity ratios (designed to evaluate and control various aspects of the organization's activities, such as inventory and accounts receivable). We discuss these ratios in detail in Chapter 9.

Break-even analysis shows graphically or algebraically the point at which the costs of producing a service or a particular amount of a product are covered by sales revenue. Managers can thus study the relationship between costs, sales volume and profits. Break-even analysis is discussed in detail in Chapter 9.

The **Gantt chart** is a graphic representation of the major tasks to be accomplished in the course of a particular project. It indicates the tasks that overlap and can be worked on simultaneously, and those that must be completed before work can begin on the next. It graphically emphasizes the time required for individual operations and

---

Personal inspection—careful study, leading to corrective action, of why a particular problem occurs.

Auditing involves a detailed and systematic examination of a company's procedures.

External auditing is a verification of an organization's financial records performed by an outside accounting firm. It is designed to encourage employee honesty and safeguard the company's financial and/or physical resources.

Internal auditing is conducted by an organization's own personnel. It is designed to encourage employee honesty and bring to light outdated or inefficient procedures.

Ratio analysis is used to compare current financial (and sometimes non-financial) results with those of previous years or with those of other organizations.

Break-even analysis shows graphically or algebraically the point at which the costs of producing a service or a particular amount of a product are covered by sales revenue. Managers can thus study the relationship between costs, sales volume and profits.

Gantt chart—a graphic representation of the major tasks to be accomplished in the course of a particular project.

for the completion of the project as a whole. Gantt charts are most often used in a production department. They are examined in more detail in Chapter 7.

Finally, two other control techniques also discussed in Chapter 7 are PERT and CPM. The **Program Evaluation and Review Technique (PERT)** was first used by the U.S. Navy in the development of the Polaris weapons system, while the **Critical Path Method (CPM)** was developed by DuPont to control large, complex industrial projects. Both techniques are used to monitor the accomplishment of a series of stages, when each event requires a specific time for completion. These techniques are most useful when time is a crucial consideration, and for projects that are large and unlikely to be repeated.

Program Evaluation and Review Technique (PERT) and **Critical Path Method (CPM)** are techniques used to monitor the series of stages in large, complex industrial projects.

Management Information System (MIS)

To have effective control, managers require specific and accurate information. A vast data-processing department equipped with the most modern computers churning out realms of printouts may be meaningless unless managers receive the necessary information and know how to use it to correct problems. In other words, a **management information system (MIS)** is needed. To be useful, computer information must be:

Management information system (MIS) provides managers with specific and accurate information about the operation of the business, thus enabling them to correct problems as required.

1. *Timely.* A manager does not benefit from discovering in July that sales were down in May, if it is too late to correct the problem.

2. *Reliable.* Although computers can compile data into meaningful information accurately and rapidly, their output can be only as correct as the data that are fed into them. Inaccurate data are of little value.

3. *Objective.* If managers are to draw effective conclusions from information, it must be objective. Figures can be presented in any number of ways, depending on their intended effect. Sheer numbers must not be allowed to hide a drop in quality, as exemplified in the story of the plant manager who consistently exceeded his production quota of sewer covers because he made them thinner.

4. *Channelled.* Information should be sent to the manager who is responsible for the operation and has the authority to make the necessary changes.

5. *Organized.* The amount of information gathered must not be so great as to make it difficult for managers to decide what is relevant. Information should be gathered only from those points in the organization where deviations from standards would cause the greatest harm. A few strategically placed controls can provide all the information required for determining harmful conditions, without necessarily using a sophisticated data-processing system.

6. *Efficiently gathered and distributed.* Gathering and distributing information that is of little consequence is a waste of money. Even though computers can tabulate information quickly, someone must convert the raw data and feed them into the computer; the computer's printouts must be distributed to management before managers can even begin to interpret the data. If the control system costs the organization more to operate than it saves, it must be redesigned.

Computers in Business

There was a time in the mid-1980s when one person could have a fairly good understanding of computers and the available software. Word processing was a

Computerization allows managers to access a large amount of current data for use in planning, controlling, and decision making

primary function and many managers were just learning how to use spreadsheets in preparing their budgets. Driven by these two applications, personal computers developed rapidly into useful business tools. By 2000, Pentium computers and thousands of useful business programs proliferated. The once-mighty mainframe computer, costing millions of dollars and requiring special rooms and operators, slowly gave way to networked personal computers. In the following section we will briefly look at personal computers with emphasis on the software that is available for managers.

Data Gathering and Information Processing

Data—raw, unorganized facts collected from a variety of sources.

Businesses and scientific institutions must gather data. **Data** refers to raw, unorganized facts collected from a variety of sources. For example, a business may collect thousands of receipts from customer payments on accounts. However, the receipts tell managers nothing about overdue accounts, or whether the cash receipts are sufficient to cover the firm's expenses for the coming week or month. Not until the receipts have been organized in some manner will they become meaningful.

Information—data that have been processed and organized.

Information is data that has been processed and organized and can be used by management for decision making. For example, a daily summary report of cash receipts from customer payments will tell management if enough cash is coming in to meet normal operating expenses, or if a bank loan is required. It will also show over-due accounts so that management can take action to collect outstanding debts.

Accessing information is essential for managers. To prepare budgets, managers need information from the previous year on sales, labour costs, raw material costs and other expenses involved in the manufacture of their product. They also need factual information about competitors, customers and government policies to make accurate forecasts of sales and costs. Data can be gathered from many sources, including salespeople, trade journals and surveys, but organizing the facts into meaningful information is difficult without a computer.

Managers who make use of computers can manage their time more efficiently

Mainframes, Minicomputers and Microcomputers

In the past, the data processing needs of large companies were handled by a centralized data processing department using **mainframe computers**. These computers, still used today, can manipulate large volumes of data quickly. However, conflicts often arose between those operating the data-processing department and those wanting to use information in the computer. Often information was not readily available in the required form and had to be compiled. Even if the appropriate information was available as requested, the manager had no way of manipulating it or combining it with new data except to return it to the data-processing department. The shuffling of information often resulted in confusion, delay and extra cost.

Minicomputers in combination with **microcomputers** went a long way to eliminate this computing backlog. As microcomputers evolved from a relatively low-power Intel 8086, 8-bit processor, powering a machine with 64K RAM and no hard drive to today's Intel Pentium III or AMD's powerhouses, the need for minicomputers faded. True distributed computing came to fruition with these high-powered desktop machines. This in combination with powerful network operating systems (NOS) such as Novell and Microsoft's Workgroup product have led to a new computing device called the network server, which spawned the proliferation of local area networks (LAN). According to Novell Inc., local area networks are a collection of devices that can store and manipulate electronic data, interconnected in such a way that network users can store, retrieve and share information with each other. Commonly connected devices include microcomputers, minicomputers, mainframe computers, terminals, printers, various data storage devices and a host of other equipment.

LANs allow workers to create smart networks where they could collaborate on projects and receive instant feedback from co-workers and management. With the use of advanced communications devices such as routers, bridges and multiplexers, group members working on a joint project need not reside in the same physical area.

Mainframe computers can perform functions rapidly and have a large memory capacity to store data.

Minicomputers can perform many of the functions of mainframes, but are significantly smaller as a result of technological advances in integrated circuits.

Microcomputers are small, relatively inexpensive, stand-alone computers that are designed for a single user.

The Internet is a good example of this concept, but due to its size the Internet is classified as a WAN or Wide Area Network. Sales of networking gear reached $37.4 billion in 1999, reflecting the increased demand for connectivity and the increased reliance on the Internet as a communications and business tool.[8] The network would also provide access to the mainframe so managers could extract billing, general ledger and inventory management information and download this information to their own PCs. Once this information is stored on their PCs, managers can do the required analysis using PC-based software tools such as spreadsheets independent of the data-processing department. In the past, managers had problems accessing timely information from the data-processing departments, but now that they need not rely on others to obtain this information, managerial decision making can be speeded up.

How Managers Can Use Computers

It is rare today to see a desk in a business office that doesn't have a computer on it. Managers in particular have found computers invaluable in performing their job. Many write their own reports, prepare their budgets, make sales calls and prepare multimedia marketing presentations. The Internet, virtually unknown to most individuals in the early 1990s, is today a valuable tool for sending e-mail around the world or across the street. Web pages provide companies with a readily available marketing tool for their products and provide customer information on a 24-hour basis. And **intranets**—the networks that tie companies together on a countrywide or worldwide basis—have improved communications among offices separated by distance.

Today's portable computers fit into a briefcase and leave room for a small printer and the brown-bag lunch. They are powerful machines and in combination with a cellular phone, enable individuals to receive faxes, make calls to customers, and send and receive data from their car or hotel room. Together with the appropriate software, laptop and desktop computers can help managers make decisions and use their time more efficiently. Sophisticated programs for word processing, contact management, spreadsheets and database management are helping managers carry out their responsibilities quickly and efficiently.

Intranet—a company's computer network. The computers may be interconnected either within a building or across geographical areas to facilitate communication and information sharing among employees.

Managers rely on computers, along with the appropriate software, to help them make decisions and use their time more efficiently

In addition, more and more of these notebook computers have pen-based software, which allows the user to write on the display area with a specialized pen—the computer interprets the writing and stores it in a file. Alternatively, computers can display a form on the screen that can be filled in with a pen.

Handheld computers finally came into their own in 1996 with the introduction of the Palm Pilot and other similar devices using the CE operating system developed by Microsoft Corporation. Handheld computers are useful for contact management, scheduling and note taking. Back in the office, the handheld device is connected to the desktop and data are transferred between the two so both computers are always up-to-date.

Budgeting and Financial Analysis

Perhaps the biggest "killer" application program is the electronic spreadsheet. The Visicalc spreadsheet made the Apple Computer prominent; the Lotus spreadsheet program did the same for the IBM PC. These spreadsheets took over the tedious task of making calculations, allowing managers to focus instead on "what if" questions and forecasting.

Cash budgeting is made particularly easy, because a spreadsheet can be prepared once and then updated on a regular basis to match receipts with expenditures. Any discrepancies can be located quickly and projections can be recalculated on the basis of the new information. To determine whether the financial performance of the firm is up to par, the computer can be used in ratio analysis. Sophisticated graphs can be developed and printed out for overhead projection to a large group or to make figures more meaningful.

Time and Contact Management

Computers can help managers use their time to best advantage through group appointment scheduling and contact management software. Some software can calculate time spent with a client and can be used directly for billing purposes. The new generation of personal information managers (PIMs) provide calendars, to-do lists and telephone directories, and allow managers to import information from other files and reorganize it in a variety of ways for their own use.

Word Processing

The word processor makes it easier for many managers to write their own notes and letters because editing is easy. Copies can be saved and changed easily for other clients or purposes. As a result, less time is spent in transcribing and retyping by secretaries, which makes the whole process of developing written communication more efficient.

Data Management

The storage of data and the recall of it in useful form has always been a problem. But the easy-to-use database software allows managers to store virtually any type of information and recall it as needed, print it out, update it and/or analyze it. As storage media have increased in capacity and decreased in price, large volumes of information can be stored on desktop micros. The rapid expansion of CD-ROM as a medium makes huge amounts of data available on a single disk. With the development of removable storage and large hard drives, document management is finally becoming easier. Virtually any piece of paper can be scanned into a computer and stored on disk either as an image or as editable text.

Inventory Management

In the past, inventory management was a mainframe or minicomputer function. But the newest computers can be used for inventory management in small to medium-sized firms, keeping track of items in stock and the handling of reorders.

Inventory programs allow a manager to routinize order placements and delegate the responsibility to other employees. Furthermore, computers can project the costs of stocking too much or not enough of a particular item. An inventory model—incorporating the time it takes to receive an order from the supplier, the economic order quantity and the rate of consumption—allows the manager to determine the best time to place an order. He or she can thus minimize out-of-stock conditions, keep inventory items fresh and at the same time reduce inventory carrying costs.

In addition, inventory turnover—so crucial in a retail business—can be analyzed easily with a computerized system. On-line accounting software can keep track as merchandise is sold and received from suppliers. Managers can then access up-to-the-minute financial information on the performance of their business.

Presentations

Many managers make their presentations today using presentation software such as Powerpoint from Microsoft Corporation. Instead of preparing lifeless overhead transparencies, a Powerpoint presentation can animate images. New information is displayed by touching a key on the computer. Images of all kinds as well as video and sound can be integrated into a presentation to make it interesting for the listener and easier to convey for the presenter.

Statistical Analysis and Graphics

Computers are particularly useful for engineers and quality controllers who can feed in data and quickly develop criteria for rejecting or accepting materials. Connected to a measuring device, a computer can also automatically determine whether a product is within statistical controls and provide a complete record on disk that can be printed out in reports or stored for later analysis.

Sophisticated graphics packages allow a manager to graph operating figures for analysis (see Figure 4.9). Analytic graphics clearly illustrate relationships and help managers in decision making. Presentation graphics, on the other hand, are useful to get a point across to others about company operations.

Project Management

Another area where software is helping the engineer and manager is in planning and scheduling a variety of projects. You can begin with a starting date and determine when the project will be completed, or start with a deadline and, working backward, determine when the project needs to be started. A project management program forces a manager to anticipate every step in a project, eliminating surprises.

Once the activities necessary to carry out a project have been determined along with their completion dates, the computer generates a critical path diagram and

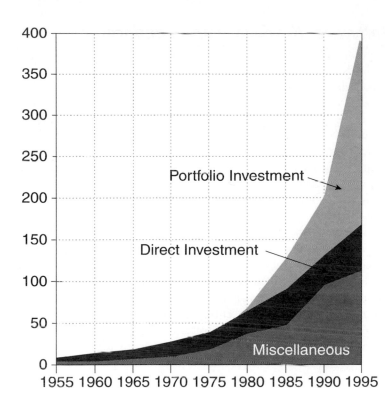

FIGURE 4.9

A graph prepared with an electronic spreadsheet program

Gantt charts. The cost of additional human resources is also calculated and updated as required. When completion dates change, the manager can input the criteria and new dates, and the computer quickly recalculates the schedules and resource costs. A particular project schedule can be saved and reused later as a template for planning similar projects. Without computers, the daily or weekly updating of project schedules would require a considerable amount of a manager's time. A project schedule is shown in Chapter 7.

Data Communications

One of the major advantages of computers is their ability to communicate with other computers. Most companies today have tied their computers together in a network on which data can be readily exchanged. Intranets (described earlier) allow rapid transfer of information between offices of a company no matter where they are located. In fact, intranets can access information not only from other microcomputers in the company but also from outside databases—of which there are a growing number that store information for doctors, lawyers and other professionals. Using these sources eliminates the time and expense of searching through volumes of library material.

The ability of branch managers to access data at head office from thousands of kilometres away cuts down on the necessity of bringing branch managers together in one location. Also, with either intranets or an **Internet** connection, e-mail is available: you simply address your communication to the proper person and it is transferred to that person's computer directly, or indirectly via a mainframe or minicomputer.

Doing Business on the Internet

www.loc.gov/global/internet/inet-business.html

Internet—a worldwide computer network which allows any individual with a computer and direct access or access through an Internet service provider to reach any other computer on the network for information sharing or e-mail, and increasingly for commercial transactions.

Choosing Software, Hardware and Vendors

An important and potentially costly task is to choose the appropriate software and hardware.

Software is a program or series of programs that perform(s) a particular task such as word processing, spreadsheet analysis, database management or accounting functions.

The **software** includes *application programs* and *operating systems,* which tell the computer what to do. An operating system is what allows you or your application software to interact with the computer. It allows you to manage files, see on-screen what you are typing at the keyboard and access your hard drive. Application software is a program or series of programs that perform(s) a particular task such as word processing, spreadsheet analysis, database management or accounting functions. Thousands of programs are available for different computers, and some perform highly specialized tasks. Many software packages are similar in their function, but have a variety of different features.

Hardware consists of the physical parts of the computer, including the keyboard, the monitor, the disk drives, the printer and the metal box that houses the central processing unit (CPU) and internal memory.

Hardware consists of the physical elements and related parts of the computer. These elements include the keyboard, the monitor, the disk drives, the printer and the metal box that houses the central processing unit (CPU) and internal memory.

The latest development in hardware is the NC or network computer. It is a bare-bones device that may or may not have a hard drive, so that most or all of its programs are accessed over a network from a central computer. The NC has evolved due to the constant change in hardware and software. The cost of acquiring and installing new hardware or software has become prohibitive, especially when a company's computers number in the thousands. With NCs, the systems manager can update the software on the main server only and users can access it from there.

While an NC is not necessarily the answer for all company employees, a significant number of them use only word processing, spreadsheet or accounting software; it is not necessary for them to have a stand-alone system. With an NC the systems manager can also control the types of programs that employees have and the time they spend on activities that are not really related to their job (such as unauthorized Internet use or computer games). The cost savings are expected to be significant.

Most consultants advise choosing hardware after your software requirements have been determined. For example, if the accounting function is your major reason for computerizing, you should first identify the software that best performs those particular functions for your firm and then choose the hardware that can best run that software.

To purchase the appropriate software package for your business or for private use, you should first clearly establish your needs. For example, there are many contact managing programs on the market; however, each one may have different features. One particular program may be more suited to your special needs. In some instances—for example, with accounting software—you may want to know whether the software can be configured for your needs, or if the company can customize it to your requirements.

You should also ensure that the program has a clearly written reference manual, instructions on how to install and use the program, and perhaps a tutorial. Since you often cannot know before trying it if the software suits your needs, can you return the program package to the developer or retailer if it doesn't suit you? You should also be aware of the company's update policy: How often are the updates being performed? Do they have an upgrade policy? Do they have a technical support service you can call if you have problems installing or using the software? How do they handle the problem of fixing errors (bugs) and getting the corrected software to the customers? Do you have to purchase the upgrade and fixes or are they available as a download over the Internet?

The **World Wide Web (WWW)** is a collection of digital information, graphics, sound and video assembled into electronically linked *pages* or *Web sites*. Each page/site has a unique address (e.g., www.income.com). It is on the WWW that communication and advertising opportunities exist on the Internet.

Of course, consumers have the ability to access only what is of interest to them, avoid ad messages and interact as they choose. Furthermore, it is accessible whenever they want—24 hours a day for the entire year. Perhaps the reason the WWW is so popular is that it puts control of the medium in the hands of consumers.

History of the Internet

The Internet had its beginnings in 1966, when, to minimize the risk of storing valuable information on a single mainframe, the U.S. Department of Defence decided to duplicate it on several computers around the country. The computers were then linked with telephone lines. In the event of attack and destruction of one or several installations, this data and communications network could continue to function. Soon other governments, educational institutions and scientific researchers around the world developed similar networks.

At this stage, use of the "Internet" was restricted to scientific researchers conversant with the arcane language required to navigate it. To remedy this situation, researchers at CERN (the European Laboratory of Particle Physics) developed the "World Wide Web," in 1989.

Because of the diversity of existing systems, researchers also needed a "common interface" that would allow access to all types of information, and so by the end of 1991 CERN had developed a text-mode "browser," soon to be followed by the graphical browsers being used today.

In 1992 CERN began publicizing the WWW project. As corporations, publishers and consumers saw what a great idea it was, they began creating their own web "servers"—computers that make their information available on the Web.

By the summer of 1994 the WWW had become one of the most popular ways to access Internet resources. Today, over five million computers are linked on the WWW, and the Web is growing by 25% per month. At this rate, it is expected that by the year 2000 over 100 million computers will be linked.

Advertising on the WWW grew to $12.4 million in the fourth quarter of 1995. It is estimated that the interactive industry generated $5.7 billion in 1994, a number expected to reach 14.2 billion by the end of the decade—almost triple. By 1997, normal credit card purchases were possible over the Internet. By the year 2000, it is estimated that on-line purchases will amount to one billion dollars.

Internet Access

Access to the Internet can be had in three ways:

1. *A direct connection* uses a dedicated computer gateway to connect to the Internet. It gives full access to all services, and is the method primarily used by government, educational institutions and scientific research organizations and Web servers housing significant sites.

2. *A direct service* provider allows you to access the Internet through their own gateway. This type of service provider generally uses a modem or dedicated telephone connections with high-speed lines.

3. *An indirect (on-line) service provider* is an online company such as America Online, CompuServe or Microsoft Network that allows you to subscribe to a range of Internet services. This access method is chosen by many consumers because of the other information services that are offered by the company.

At the present time, to access the Internet you need a computer, a modem and communications software. You also need a browser so you can navigate the net easily. Many different browsers are available—the most popular being Netscape and Microsoft's Internet Explorer. Both of these browsers are available free of charge from a variety of sources. High-speed Internet access is also now available either through cable or through your telephone company

Common Internet Services

The most used service today is **e-mail (electronic mail)**, which provides direct communication between registered users via computer. Although e-mail is provided with your hookup to an Internet service provider (ISP), you can also acquire email accounts free of charge at other places. Microsoft's Hotmail, for example, provides an e-mail account that can be accessed from anywhere in the world and it is free. Newsgroups are electronic bulletin boards on which information may be posted by companies, associations or private individuals. In addition, almost any type of information—text files, computer programs, graphics files—may be downloaded to your computer using FTP (file transfer protocol). Chat programs are offered through a variety of sources. They allow you to communicate with someone anywhere in the world in real time. This means that you can type on your computer and as you do, it appears on the other person's monitor, who in turn can answer immediately.

What Is the Internet?

World Wide Web (WWW)—a collection of digital information, graphics, sound and video assembled into pages or web sites that are electronically linked.

E-mail (electronic mail) gives the ability to send messages to another person through a computer link to a network. This network may be a company intranet or the Internet. It is already possible to transmit images and sound over these computer networks.

Vendor—a company or individual that supplies the computer hardware, software and related services, and often provides training and maintenance.

In choosing the **vendor**, a number of considerations should be kept in mind. Is the company likely to be in business in the foreseeable future? Can the vendor maintain the equipment and provide software support including possible customization of programs? Will the vendor provide assistance in converting the present operation? A final consideration should be the vendor's past performance with other clients.

Often, new uses for the computer will be discovered once it is operating. It is therefore important to choose a system that can be expanded and a vendor who can adapt the system to meet future requirements.

Chapter Summary

1. A manager achieves the goals and objectives of an organization by coordinating human, material and financial resources. Poor management has been responsible for many business failures; at the least, it can result in poor or inadequate service with conspicuous waste.

2. As an organization grows, a managerial hierarchy develops with three levels—top, middle, and operating or supervisory. Regardless of their level, all managers perform similar functions including planning, organizing, leading and controlling. In addition, managers require three kinds of skills—technical, human and conceptual. The relative importance of these three skills depends on a manager's level in the hierarchy.

3. A major task of managers is decision making—the process of choosing the best course of action from two or more alternatives. Non-programmed decisions deal with unusual problems and managers have no guidelines to help them make these decisions. Programmed or administrative decisions are those that must be made frequently, and therefore guidelines, called policies, are established to help managers make these decisions more quickly.

4. Managers plan the goals and objectives of an organization and the methods of achieving them. Without planning, resources cannot be properly utilized. The organization is also exposed to more risk if no attempt is made to forecast the future. Long-range plans apply to periods longer than one year, while short-range plans are made for periods of a year or less. Short-range plans include budgets, procedures, rules and specific policies. All plans must be flexible, so that they can be altered should conditions change.

5. In strategic planning, key objectives and plans on how to achieve these objectives are developed keeping in mind the possible actions of competitors and the resources available to the organization. It is important particularly for companies operating in a fast-changing environment. It requires carefully defining an organization's mission so management is better able to focus on its direction and activities. Strategic planning consists of two phases: strategy formulation and strategy implementation. A strategic plan covers a lengthy time period for implementing various activities and seeing the results; will have a significant impact; requires a concentration of effort and resources on a narrow range of activities; requires a series of consistent decisions over time; and requires a commitment by all levels of management in the organization to carry out activities that are supportive of the strategy.

6. Planning elements include goals and objectives, mission, strategy, standing plans and single-use plans. Standing plans change infrequently and guide the actions of managers and employees on a daily basis. They include policies, procedures and rules. Single-use plans are developed to support a particular strategy and are no longer used once they have been achieved or the strategy has changed. They include programs, projects and budgets.

7. The strategic planning process consists of four major steps: establishing the mission and major goals and objectives, analyzing the organization's external environment to determine any opportunities or threats, analyzing the organization's internal environment to determine if there are any strengths or weaknesses, and developing a series of alternative strategies and choosing the best one to achieve the goals and objectives. Once the strategy has been chosen, tactical or action plans are developed to achieve part of the strategy during the coming year.

8. Once plans have been established, organizational performance must be evaluated. The control function of managers involves establishing standards, measuring performance against standards and correcting performance if necessary. An important standard for control is the budget, which is an action plan converted into dollar terms. To control operational aspects that are not budget-based, non-budgetary control techniques are used, including personal observation, special reports, external and internal auditing, ratio and break-even analysis, Gantt charts, PERT and CPM.

9. Many businesses use computers to process data and provide management with information for decision making. The minicomputer has made computerization possible for many small and medium-sized firms and the microcomputer or personal computer has become an invaluable aid to managers in their daily management function. The new network computers are expected to reduce costs of maintaining hardware and software in a company.

10. Most managers and employees today use computers on their job. This includes spreadsheets, word processing, data management, contact and time management, inventory management, graphics and presentations. When computerizing, a company must evaluate hardware and software requirements, and choose a vendor who will service the system after it is installed.

KEY TERMS

Management 108
Functions of management 109
Planning 110
Organizing 110
Staffing 110
Leading/directing 110
Controlling 111
Managerial hierarchy 111
Top management 112
Middle management 112

Operating/supervisory
  management 112
Technical skills 112
Human skills .112
Conceptual skills 113
Decision making 115
Non-programmed decisions 115
Programmed/administrative
  decisions .115
Strategic planning 117

Tactical/action/short-range
  planning .117
Long-range planning 117
Goals 118
Purpose of an organization 118
Mission of an organization 119
Objectives 120
Strategy 120
Standing plans 120
Single-use plans 120

Policy	122	Auditing	130	Information	132
Procedure	122	External auditing	130	Mainframe computers	133
Rules	122	Internal auditing	130	Minicomputers	133
Program	122	Ratio analysis	130	Microcomputers	133
Project	122	Break-even analysis	130	Intranet	134
Budget	123	Gantt chart	130	Internet	137
Strategic planning process	123	Program Evaluation and Review Technique (PERT)/Critical Path Method (CPM)	131	Software	138
Profit plan	126			Hardware	138
Action plans	126	Management information system (MIS)	131	World Wide Web (WWW)	139
Control	127			E-mail (electronic mail)	139
Personal inspection	130	Data	132	Vendor	140

REVIEW QUESTIONS

1 Explain the importance of management in an organization.

2 How do the four functions of management help organizations achieve their goals?

3 What are the three types of managerial skills? How important is each to the various management levels?

4 Why can top levels of management move to different organizations more easily than middle and supervisory levels?

5 What is decision making? Distinguish between programmed and non-programmed decisions.

6 Explain the importance of planning in an organization.

7 Why should plans be flexible?

8 Why is strategic planning important? Distinguish between strategic planning and tactical or action planning.

9 What is the difference between an organization's purpose and its mission?

10 What is a strategy? How are standing and single-use plans related to strategy?

11 What are the four steps in the strategic planning process? What is management trying to determine during external analysis of its environment?

12 What is the difference between strategic formulation and strategic implementation?

13 Why is strategic planning important for both large and small firms?

14 Explain why planning and controlling are closely related.

15 Outline the steps that make up the control process.

16 Distinguish between budgetary and non-budgetary methods of control.

17 Explain how various businesses use computers.

18 What are the differences between mainframe, mini- and microcomputers? Describe three major uses of microcomputers for managers.

19 What are the three major factors a firm must consider before installing a computer system?

DISCUSSION QUESTIONS

1 "The future is so uncertain that any long-range planning is just a waste of time—plans have to be changed anyway. I might as well wait until things really happen, and then act accordingly." Discuss.

2 "To be a good manager, you have to be born for the job." Discuss.

3 "Planning is the most important function of a manager." Discuss.

4 How can business managers make sure that they have the information they need to control an organization's performance?

5 Keeping in mind the job managers have and who they represent, what would be the impact on business organizations if managers unionized or formed an association? How might this affect the daily operation of firms? How might a manager's union or association help him or her to do a better job of performing the management functions?

CASE

4-1

Planning—Who Needs It?

Quality Press was established 47 years ago and had been operated by two sisters who took over the business when their father died some 27 years ago. Quality Press had been able to hold onto some customers for decades because it turned out quality products, even though its equipment was, as one customer said, "from Gutenberg days."

Bill Cranshaw, a salesperson with the firm for 16 years, attributed much of the company's success to his outgoing personality, his knowledge about the printing business and the personal service he offered his customers. He put in an inordinate amount of unpaid time looking after his customers, motivated by the promise of the two sisters that he would eventually be able to buy them out. Although in their eighties, the two sisters came to the office faithfully each day, performed all of the office work and managed the overall enterprise. The printing supervisor had also been with the company for a long time and was well liked by the seven workers in the print shop.

Eventually, Bill's dream came true. He managed to strike a good deal for buying out the firm. Because of his love for selling and his desire to be on the front lines, he continued as salesperson, giving his customers the high level of service they were accustomed to. His printing supervisor, now in his early sixties, continued to supervise the print shop. He also handled any problems that came up in the office, since Bill was out on the road almost all of the time. Virtually all of the workers in the shop remained with the new owner, except for one who retired. The office work was handled by two employees whom Bill had hired after the sisters left.

Within two years, the revenues of Quality Press had increased substantially. Bill's unrelenting drive as the new owner resulted in the acquisition of a number of new customers, including three large banks, three insurance companies, two major retailers and a large number of small firms.

One day Bill and a friend discussed, over lunch, the prospects for an economic recession that some were predicting would begin as early as next year. Bill's friend asked him if he had plans for a possible business downturn, and what his plans were for the long run.

"No, I can't see anything happening to my business, even if a recession occurs," Bill replied. "As far as the long run is concerned, this company has been in business for over 50 years. I have expanded the customer base. It is profitable. Why waste my time planning for the 'long run,' as you call it?"

"That's great, Bill, but what if things should suddenly change? You're relying on these large firms for the bulk of your work. What if they decide to have their printing done at head office, or what if some other large printing company offers them a better deal? Have you considered possible competition from the many small print shops that use personal computers to prepare forms and small print jobs—jobs that at one time had to be done by shops like yours? Have you considered all of these factors?"

"I'm not really concerned, John. I've talked with all my customers and they're happy with my work and the prices I charge."

>>

Nine months later, the largest of the three banks doing business with Quality Press entered into a long-term contract with another large national printing company. Two of the three insurance companies installed a computerized print shop that would handle almost 80% of the printing they had previously given to Quality Press. The third insurance company closed its office as the company was restructured. Many of the other businesses told Bill that their printing requirements would in all likelihood be reduced amid growing concern about the recession. Within a few months, Quality Press revenues dropped substantially, and Bill Cranshaw began to worry about how he would pay for the recent expansion to his plant and for his two new printing presses.

Questions

1 What does the case indicate about Bill Cranshaw's management ability? What potential problem might arise in the future?

2 Could strategic planning have prevented the problems Bill now faces? Explain.

3 Assume that Bill had another salesperson working for him. How should he have conducted his strategic planning process?

4 Based on the information given in the case, are there any factors Bill could not have foreseen even if he had engaged in strategic planning?

CASE

4-2

Tyller Gorman & Sons Moving and Storage

Tyller Gorman was the president and founder of Tyller Gorman & Sons Moving and Storage. Located in Arnprior, Ontario, since 1958, the firm specialized in residential moving contracts between major cities throughout Ontario. While Gorman managed the overall company and the storage warehouse, his three sons—Adam, Bob and Tommy—drove the firm's three moving vans.

Since 1958, Tyller had been very successful with his moving and storage activities. He had managed to win a number of federal and provincial contracts to move transferred employees. Occasionally, a few large companies in the Ottawa area asked him to move large pieces of equipment from one location to another. These types of moving contracts were particularly appealing to Gorman because they did not require a lot of time, and because the work was typically heavy the firm enjoyed a very high profit margin.

In recent months, Gorman's revenues from residential moves had begun to fall off. He thought a good substitute might be to develop commercial moving services, and proposed that one truck of the three be specifically used for this purpose. As well, he also proposed reserving one-half of the warehouse storage space specifically for commercial applications.

Gorman also decided he would immediately launch an advertising campaign to inform larger companies about his new business activity. Adam Gorman also suggested that they purchase another moving van, hire another three drivers and offer their regular residential moving services across Canada instead of just within Ontario. Tommy Gorman suggested that instead of restricting their commercial moving activities to the Ottawa area, they should branch out to include Ontario, Quebec and the Maritimes. To do this, he suggested that they purchase at least two or three new moving vans and hire at least five new drivers.

Bob Gorman thought that with all its experience driving eighteen-wheelers, the company should also offer training courses and train not only their own drivers, but also other individuals who were interested in becoming professional truck drivers.

Although Tyller thought that these different plans were very sound, he had difficulty conceptualizing how all of them could be effectively implemented. Bob Gorman said he knew a management consultant with considerable planning experience. Monique Daigle, he was sure, could provide some consultative advice concerning these important anticipated operational and strategic plans.

SOURCE: By David H. Jones-Delcourt. Reprinted by permission of the author.

Questions

1. You are Monique Daigle. What is your opinion on the activities planned by the Gormans?

2. What information would you require in order to advise them on a particular strategic direction?

3. Assume that all the Gormans' suggestions are to be implemented. Develop a detailed plan, together with a "time line," and set out how and when the new activities could be implemented.

COMPREHENSIVE CASE 4-3

SOMERSET OPTICAL

In June, about two months after Somerset Optical commenced operations, it became obvious to Peter Dewar and Mike Fowler that considerably more attention would have to be paid to matters of management, planning and control. Sales were increasing steadily, but orders were being lost and the paperwork was in shambles.

While Fowler was a stellar optician and a talented contact-lens fitter, he was not an administrative manager. Dewar, on the other hand, was a first-class salesperson who generated considerable sales as a result of his professional and personal skills. Like Mike, however, he was neither particularly interested in, nor well suited for, management, planning or control.

Fowler and Dewar decided to contract out accounting and administrative duties to a professional consultant with a certain level of expertise in the optical industry. Ruth Suboski, president and founder of Suboski and Associates, and a personal friend of Fowler's, agreed to assume this important consultative role for a bargain-basement monthly fee.

Ruth quickly formalized what she referred to as levels of "internal managerial skills." For example, Fowler was unquestionably the "technically skilled" manager while Dewar had well-developed skills in sales as well as in conceptual thinking. Although Dewar was able to conceptualize and perceive the organization as a whole, he had difficulty applying what he conceptualized.

Ruth recommended that Fowler and Dewar decide on a mission statement that would set out in clear and concise terms the organization's strategic scope. After considerable discussion, the mission of Somerset Optical was formulated as follows: "To market superior-quality fashion and functional eyewear at the most competitive prices possible and with the highest level of customer service."

Ruth then recommended that the partners develop a strategy that would enable the company to deliver on their mission statement. The strategy was a simple one, and was finalized as follows:

Standing Plans (addressing policies and procedures)

1. It is the policy of Somerset Optical to ensure that its suppliers meet maximum trade quality standards and to dispense only those products that meet or exceed the maximum trade policy standards.

2. It is the policy of Somerset Optical to ensure complete customer satisfaction and to either replace products with which customers are dissatisfied or refund the purchase price.

3. All accounting operations shall be computerized and the records maintained off-site, with weekly financial statements and analyses provided to management.

4. All sales information and customer files will be computerized with a backup cardex system; all files remain on site.

5. All decisions relating to administration will be made upon mutual agreement or compromise by the partners.

Single-Use Plans

1. The consultant will develop a detailed operating budget and report actual progress against budget on a monthly basis. The partners will be responsible for their own banking for deposits and for the operation of a petty cash fund, but the consultant will hold and prepare all cheques.

2. The consultant will stop in once a week, pick up all incoming mail concerning the financial accounts, pick up copies of daily sales reports

>>

for the week, drop off any necessary cheques for signature (two signatures required) and post all new details to the financial system.

3. The partners will take a physical inventory once every six months to allow the consultant to prepare accurate financial statements.

4. The consultant and the partners will develop a comprehensive business plan to map out the intended progress of Somerset Optical.

It was also decided that the company would acquire a personal computer that could be linked to the consultant's computer by modem. Although the consultant could not access the customer files, she could access, on "view-only" mode, daily sales records. Similarly, the partners could access, on "view-only" mode, financial records, including ledger accounts and the financial statements that were updated weekly.

SOURCE: By David H. Jones-Delcourt. Reprinted by permission of the author.

Questions

1 How applicable is the planning process to very small companies such as Somerset Optical?

2 What types of problems can occur when applying the planning process to very small companies?

3 Evaluate the mission statement of Somerset Optical. Is it realistic?

4 Evaluate Somerset Optical's strategy. In your opinion, what key issues are not being addressed? Identify the pros and cons of the strategy. Rewrite the strategy for Somerset Optical, addressing those shortcomings that you have identified.

5 Describe how a personal computer can both help and hinder a small business. Evaluate how the personal computer will be used in the case of Somerset Optical, as described above.

Organizing for Management

Learning Objectives

After reading this chapter, you will be able to

1 Explain why an organizational structure is necessary.

2 Recognize the difference between formal and informal organizations.

3 Understand the purpose of an organization chart.

4 Understand the meaning of departmentation and the various methods used.

5 Explain why it is necessary to distribute authority and responsibility among the various levels of management.

6 Understand the major factors involved in the effective distribution of authority, and explain the meaning of span of control, delegation, accountability and chain of command.

7 Compare a centralized organization to a decentralized one, and explain why it is important to balance the two.

8 Understand the meaning of line and staff departments, and explain the relationship between them.

9 Understand the difference between groups and committees, and how they can be used in planning and decision making.

10 Explain the importance of e-commerce and its impact on organizational structure.

The Formal Organization

Schools, universities, government, hospitals, sports teams, churches and businesses are only a few of the organizations we come into contact with every day. By combining the efforts of many individuals to achieve specific objectives, organizations can accomplish goals that would be difficult or impossible for single individuals to achieve. Organizations offer several advantages. First, they acquire information and knowledge and preserve it for future use. Second, the knowledge gained and the resources available to organizations can be used to develop and improve products. Finally, they provide people with job opportunities, career development and income for basic needs and other consumer goods; in doing so, they raise the standard of living.

An **organization** is formed whenever people join together to achieve one or more objectives. For example, the Greenpeace Foundation was established in 1971 by a group of anti-nuclear demonstrators who sailed to the Alaskan Aleutian Islands to try to stop American atmospheric nuclear tests. The group, known as the "Don't Make a Wave Committee," had a strong commitment to accomplish a specific objective. A single individual protesting against these tests may not have been noticed, but as a group the Greenpeace demonstrators were effective in raising public awareness of nuclear tests and their possible consequences.

A group of homeowners who get together to protest increasing property taxes is another example of an organization. Their objective is to tell their government to hold the line on tax increases. They may show their solidarity by marching to city hall and presenting their demands to city council.

It is not unusual for individuals to get together to support a particular cause and then disband when the task has been accomplished. But if an organization has long-term objectives, then a formal structure must be established to sustain the initial interest and effort of all involved.

To create a **formal organization**, someone (usually the founder) must develop a written description of how the organization should work. Jobs are defined along with the experience and education required to carry them out. Management positions are established along with the authority relationships that indicate who reports to whom in the organization. This formal record of organizational relationships is known as the organization chart.

Organization—a structure that is formed whenever people join together to achieve one or more objectives.

Formal organization is a written description of the jobs and management positions in an organization.

Organization Charts

An **organization chart** is a graphic representation of various management positions in a formal organization. Figure 5.1 shows an organization chart. Each box represents a management position and shows a title that provides a general idea of the manager's tasks. The lines between the boxes indicate the flow of authority through the various levels from the top to the bottom of the managerial hierarchy.

The major purpose of the organization chart is to give a bird's-eye view of the formal organization structure, showing clearly what management positions exist and how they are related to one another. The organization chart can also be used to determine whether too many positions exist, or if there is an imbalance of responsibility anywhere in the organization.

An organization chart does have some shortcomings, however. It does not show the exact title and position of everyone who works in the organization, nor does it specify the responsibilities of each position. The title shown gives only a vague idea of what each manager should accomplish and does not indicate the limits to authority and actions. The major shortcoming of an organization chart is that it does not

Organization chart—a graphic representation of various management positions in a formal organization.

show the informal organization, which often determines who has the real power. In addition, since an organization structure does not remain static, the organization chart must be updated periodically, as responsibilities and duties in the organization shift.

The Informal Organization

The **informal organization** is the result of social interactions between employees and managers inside and outside the workplace. These interactions create informal channels of communication. For example, a manager and a worker might belong to the same church or political organization; employees may meet regularly for coffee breaks; some employees may join a company softball team; others may simply get together because of similar educational backgrounds or skills. During this interaction, employees may discuss company operations and exchange information. The "grapevine" is the best example of an informal channel of communication.

The informal organization can help to create a pleasant working environment by satisfying social needs on the job. Friendships that cut across departmental lines can also benefit the organization because they facilitate communication between people and help solve problems. Furthermore, social relationships can encourage teamwork and build morale. Peer pressure also encourages employees to work toward common goals. In fact, the informal organization is largely responsible for the firm's smooth functioning on a daily basis. On the other hand, unless management learns to minimize its disruptive aspects—the spreading of false information, for example, and the setting of inadequate production limits by the work groups—the informal organization can have a negative influence.

While the formal organization chart shows who should, in theory, hold the power, the informal organization determines who actually exercises it. An ineffective department manager may be ignored by employees, who instead approach the assistant manager for all major decisions; the informal group leader may have the power to speed up or slow down production, depending on how he or she views management decisions. Managers have failed because they have been unable to gain the support of their workers.

To succeed, managers must take the informal organization into consideration and ensure that its leaders are included in the decision-making process whenever possible. All employees should be encouraged to make suggestions for improving operations. The particular technique chosen to improve communication between employees and management is not important, as long as managers receive feedback on what people in the organization are thinking. A technique called "sensing" is used by some organizations. Sensing allows top management to get into contact with employees and hear their problems firsthand.

The Importance of Organizing

An organization's success depends on what it can accomplish with the limited funds available. Wasted or unnecessary effort cannot be tolerated. Every job must be accomplished as efficiently as possible. Each person's effort should complement the efforts of others so that everyone works together toward the same end. Every employee needs to know what his or her job entails and how it is related to all other jobs in the organization. By establishing formal relationships, organizing helps to clarify the work environment for employees.

Informal organization is the result of social interactions between employees and managers both inside and outside the workplace.

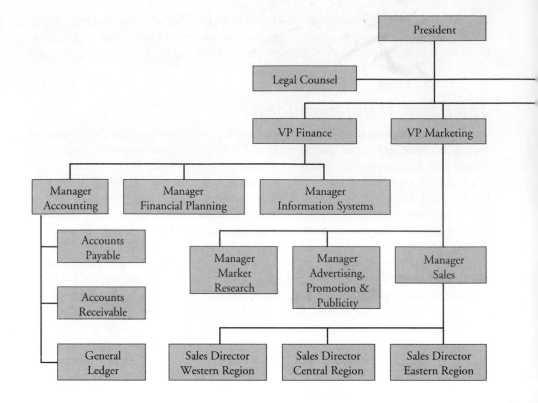

FIGURE **5.1**

Typical organization chart for a manufacturing company

A second result of organizing is the coordination of work groups. Related activities are grouped into departments headed by a manager who is responsible for ensuring that all the people in the department work together to achieve particular objectives. In large organizations, related departments are further grouped into divisions under a divisional manager. The divisional manager thus coordinates the activities of the various department managers. In very large organizations, divisions may be further grouped under a general manager. The president at the top of the organization has ultimate responsibility for the successful performance of the entire organization. As Figure 5.2 illustrates, organizations have a pyramid-shaped structure.

The third result of organizing is to establish permanence and stability of relationships. Every member of the organization knows who is responsible for performing various tasks. Even if an employee leaves the organization, the position

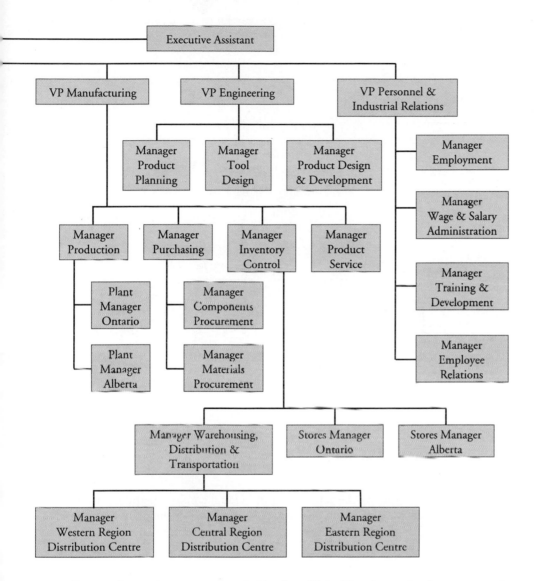

usually remains and a new person is hired to fill it. If a change in the structure is necessary because of a change in plans—as when a new department is created for producing and distributing a new product—this change is formally communicated to all employees so that everyone knows where to turn.

The Relationship Between Planning and Organizing

The purpose of strategic planning is to define the organization's mission and long-range objectives. Operating or short-range plans are then established to outline specific methods of achieving long-range objectives. Plans in themselves, however, accomplish nothing. It is the people in the organization who ensure that the organization meets its objectives. To ensure that everyone fulfills his or her role, an organizational structure is established. Managers are placed in charge of various

FIGURE   5.2

An organization has a
pyramid-shaped structure

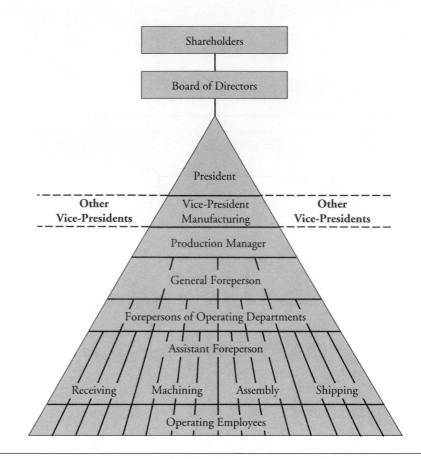

SOURCE: Henry L. Sisk, *Management and Organization,* 2nd ed. (Cincinnati: South-Western Publishing Co., 1973):
271. Reprinted by permission.

work groups to coordinate the activities of individual employees and to ensure that
everyone works toward the goals and objectives outlined in the plans. When plans
change the structure must be changed, or at least examined to ensure it is still
appropriate for the required task.

Building an Organizational Structure

Businesses generally start small, with an owner and a few employees. Because of the
small size, communication between the owner and employees is usually direct and
face-to-face. Everyone knows the firm's objectives and everyone has a specific job
to perform; some employees may also take on supervisory duties. If problems arise,
they can be resolved quickly through direct interaction between employees and
managers. As the organization grows, however, more employees are needed, including managers to coordinate the increased number of activities. While an owner
may be able to oversee most aspects of an organization while it is small, as it grows
he or she must bring in others to manage various aspects of the organization such as
the sales force and the production facilities, for example. Figure 5.3 depicts the
stages in an organization's growth.

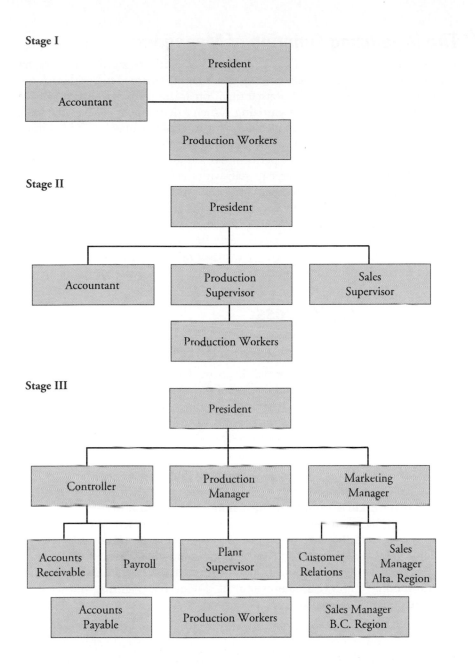

FIGURE **5.3**

How an organization's structure changes with growth

Organizational growth thus tends to separate employees from top management, making it increasingly difficult for employees to identify with company objectives. Management may also find it difficult to ensure that all activities performed by employees are contributing to the company's objectives. The **organizational structure** must therefore be changed to solve specific problems arising from growth, a shift in plans or a change in organizational strategy.

While assuring the company's overall performance, the structure must allow all concerned to focus clearly on their own contributions. Broad company objectives must be broken down into divisional, departmental and individual worker objectives. Figure 4.6 in the previous chapter shows the breakdown of objectives.

Organizational structure—how component parts and positions in an organization are arranged and how they are interrelated.

The Organizing Function of Managers

Managers of a fast-growing organization are frequently engaged in the organizing function as new jobs are added, existing departments enlarged or combined, or new management positions created. Rather than "organizing," therefore, it may be more appropriate to use the term **reorganizing**. When a department has become too large for one manager to coordinate effectively, for example, it may be divided into two separate departments. Often the natural development of an organization leaves some departments with fewer jobs to perform. As a result, management may decide to dissolve the department and merge its staff with that of another department needing support. A company might also choose to emphasize some previously neglected facet of its business by creating a new department, then assigning a manager and a group of employees. As the new department grows, more managers and staff may be added.

Reorganizing is an ongoing task of managers. It ensures that the structure of the organization is best able to meet the organization's current objectives.

Organizing is not a daily managerial exercise—the task arises periodically as conditions make it necessary. Nevertheless, a manager must keep the organization structure in mind whenever plans are changed, to ensure that it is adequate for the new situation.

The Organizing Process

Whether a new organization is established or an existing one reorganized, the organizing process should follow a series of logical steps:

1. *Identify the work that must be done to accomplish the organization's goals.* The first step relates to the purpose and mission of the organization and the plans that have been established in the strategic planning process. Plans and objectives must be clearly understood so that tasks required to achieve objectives can be identified. For example, equipment may have to be purchased, people hired, buildings rented or built and relationships established with outside organizations.

2. *Divide the total workload into individual jobs.* Since organizations are established to accomplish objectives that could not be accomplished by single individuals, the total workload must be divided among the organization's members. Special care must be taken to ensure that the workload is divided evenly and that jobs are given to individuals who have the necessary expertise to carry them out. Some jobs (e.g., building plants or purchasing and installing new equipment) may exist only while the organization is being established. Others, such as hiring and training employees, manufacturing, financial accounting and sales, are required on an ongoing basis.

3. *Classify and group activities.* In the third step of the organizing process, the basic organization structure is established by grouping related activities. Welding, machining and painting may be grouped under production, for example, while recruiting, training and compensating employees are grouped under personnel. Activities are classified according to two basic principles: division of work and specialization of labour. **Division of work** refers to the breakdown of work activities into individual tasks. A number of these tasks are then assigned to individual employees. Division of work results in **specialization of labour**, in which employees develop particular skills and become experts in carrying out specific tasks. Specialization of labour can increase productivity.

Division of work—the breakdown of work activities into individual tasks.

Specialization of labour occurs when employees develop particular skills and become experts in carrying out specific tasks.

Departmentation is the grouping of related tasks into appropriate units.

Departmentation is the grouping of logically related activities. For example, all employee matters are grouped under the personnel department. Departments in turn may be grouped into divisions, depending on the size of the organization. Departmentation gives rise to the basic organization structures based on

An organizational structure ensures that every person in an organization knows who to report to

functions—personnel, marketing, finance and production; on the products produced; or on the geographic location of the firm's operation. We return to these basic structures later in this chapter.

4. *Establish a coordinating mechanism to ensure that all organization members work together.* Once the basic divisional and departmental structure is established, managers can be assigned responsibilities and given the necessary authority to carry them out. In this step, the various management levels—supervisory, middle and top—and the relationships between the various departments and divisions are established. These levels indicate the chain of command—who reports to whom and who can adjudicate if problems arise between departments. They also define the "span of management," which refers to the number of subordinates that directly report to each manager. The formal organization structure is thus established and an organization chart can be drawn up.

5. *Monitor and adjust the organization structure for maximum effectiveness.* Since organizing is not a one-time activity but an ongoing process, each step must be monitored and evaluated with respect to its effectiveness in steering the organization toward its goals and objectives. As organizations grow and the environment changes, the existing organization structure must be re-evaluated and reorganized as necessary.

Horizontal Division of Labour: Departmentation

As stated earlier, grouping related tasks into appropriate units is known as departmentation. Departmentation has two major advantages. First, it can increase productivity, since employees are able to specialize in performing specific, related tasks. Second, it promotes communication, since members of the same department work in proximity and can exchange ideas or give each other support. There are three major types of departmentation: functional, product and geographic, and project and matrix.

Functional Departmentation

When a business is organized around the major business functions of production, marketing, finance and personnel, as shown in Figure 5.4, the grouping is known as **functional departmentation**. Each of the major functions or activities may have more specialized departments on a lower level. Marketing, for example, may include the lower-level departments of market research, advertising and sales. A university, on the other hand, is usually departmentalized by major subject area—English, business administration, physics and so on.

Functional departmentation promotes specialization in basic activities and allows an organization to build valuable expertise. However, exclusive specialization in one area should be avoided. If an employee's interest, understanding and loyalty are limited to his or her own department, the organization cannot benefit from the interaction between departments, and the situation will hinder the employee's opportunities for promotion to a general managerial position. Functional departmentation may also give rise to conflicts as various departments compete for financial resources.

Product and Geographic Departmentation

Businesses that produce two or more major products tend to group their activities and personnel around those products. General Motors, for example, practises product departmentation. Each of GM's five major divisions—Chevrolet, Pontiac, Oldsmobile, Buick and Cadillac—is responsible for the production and marketing of one particular make of car. As shown in Figure 5.5, each product division may then be further departmentalized on a functional basis.

Product departmentation allows a large organization to concentrate on and promote the growth and development of each of its major products. In effect, each product division becomes a separate business with its own profit and product objectives. Each division competes not only with other auto manufacturers, but also with other divisions in the same company. The variety of activities that must be performed in such a division provides excellent training for general managers.

On the other hand, top management relinquishes considerable control when it allows divisional management levels to make major decisions. Furthermore, product departmentation requires a large number of general managers in addition to those with specific management skills. For smaller companies, the cost in salaries may be prohibitive. Finally, product departmentation may mean considerable duplication of effort and expense as each division follows its semi-autonomous course. Functions such as market research, advertising, and product research and development may have to be duplicated in each division.

When an organization is spread over a large geographic area or has operations in different countries, **departmentation by geography** or territory may be appropriate. This type of departmentation is used when local decision making is important.

Functional departmentation occurs when a business organizes itself around the major business functions of production, marketing, finance and personnel.

Product departmentation occurs when a business produces two or more major products, and groups its activities and personnel around those products.

Geographic departmentation occurs when all activities of an organization are performed in the region where the unit operates. It allows local managers to make decisions quickly on such matters as labour supply, customers, language and governments.

FIGURE 5.4

Departmentation by function

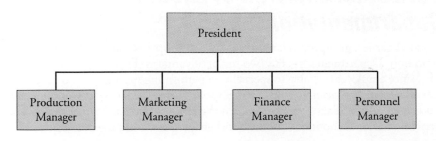

FIGURE   5.5

Departmentation by product

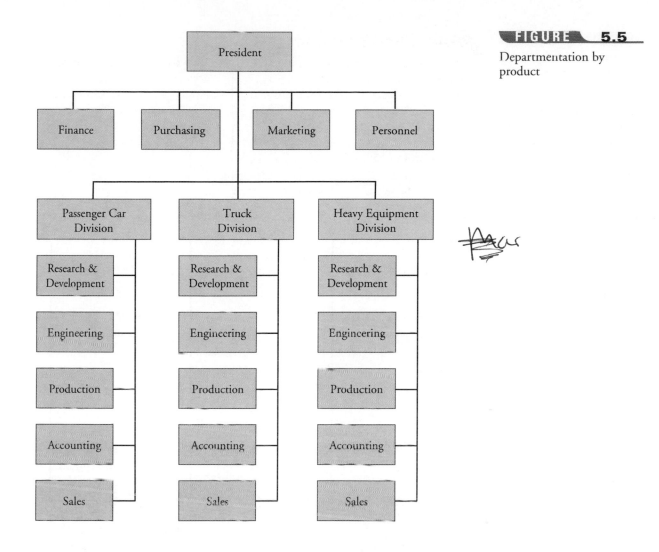

Regional managers can deal effectively with local concerns (e.g., labour supply, customers, language and governments), since they have the power to make most operating decisions immediately, without waiting for approval from head office. The disadvantages are similar to those associated with product departmentation: top management experiences some loss of control; there may be duplication of services; and more managers with general skills are required, meaning higher costs.

Geographic departmentation is similar to product departmentation, as a comparison of Figures 5.5 and 5.6 will show. Instead of product divisions, there are geographic divisions. Each geographic division may, however, be further departmentalized by function and by product or customer. Retail chain stores, national bakeries and dairy companies are among the businesses organized on a geographic basis.

Project and Matrix Structures

Organizations that regularly undertake special projects use a **project structure**—a smaller, self-contained unit with specific objectives set up by the parent organization (see Figure 5.7). The project structure is usually based on functional departmentation

Project structure uses self-contained units that have specific objectives to operate independently and draw on resources from either inside or outside the parent organization.

FIGURE 5.6

Departmentation by
geography or territory

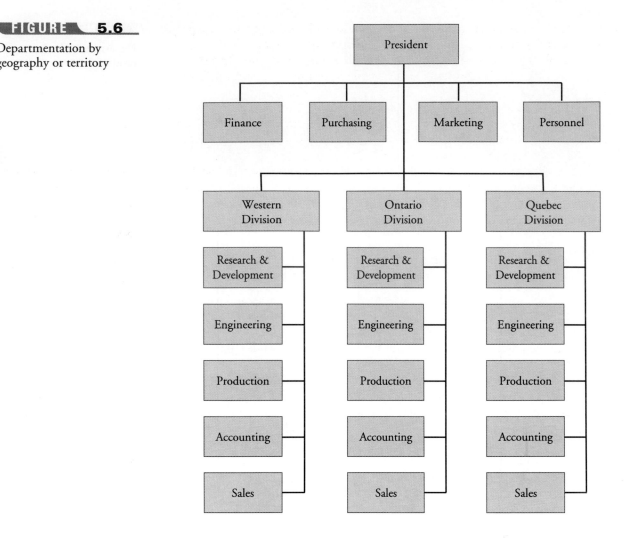

FIGURE 5.7

Project organization

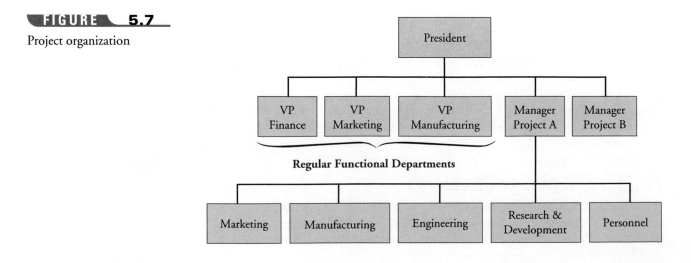

and headed by a project manager who is given considerable authority over the project and who is free to draw on resources from either inside or outside the parent organization. Sharing a clear purpose and objectives, employees in a project structure often become a close-knit team, one that benefits from informal communication and high morale.

Nevertheless, the project structure does have problems. Setting up a new structure can disturb the parent organization. For example, facilities are often duplicated and resources often used inefficiently. For employees, there is always the problem of job security when the project is completed.

A **matrix structure** is intended to resolve some of the problems of functional and project departmentation. A horizontal structure is superimposed on the functional hierarchical structure shown in Figure 5.8. The project manager acts as a coordinator, specifying what is to be done while allowing the functional department to decide how it is to be done.

The major benefit of the matrix structure is that it allows the firm to bring together a group of people with specialized skills to work on a particular project. The problems of coordination are minimized because the individuals working together have clearly defined objectives. The structure also helps to reduce costs and allows the firm to be flexible in using personnel, since only a limited number of employees are assigned to a project at any one time. A matrix structure thus allows an organization to use its own human resources effectively without hiring outsiders for jobs that may be of relatively short duration.

The major problem with the matrix structure is that it violates the principle of unity of command, according to which each employee should report to only one superior. If both the functional department head and the project manager request an employee at a meeting, for example, who takes priority? Conflicts can also develop between the project managers and functional department heads. Project managers may feel that they have little authority over functional departments, while functional department heads may feel that project managers are interfering in their territory. To minimize problems with the matrix structure, the roles, responsibilities and authority of all involved must be clearly defined.

> **Matrix structure**—a horizontal structure superimposed on the functional hierarchical structure. The project manager acts as a coordinator, specifying what is to be done and allowing the functional department to decide how it is to be done.

Other Types of Departmentation

Departmentation may also be accomplished by simple number, by time, by customer, or by process.

When the number of workers is the major consideration, *simple number departmentation* may be used. For example, an organization's fund drive may be launched by assigning a manager a certain number of volunteers to visit households in a given section of the city. In the same way, particular work gangs may be formed by giving a supervisor a certain number of people for a particular job.

When the workforce must be divided into shifts to cover the entire 24-hour day, then *departmentation by time* is used. An example is the police department, where most support services and activities are made available for each shift.

Departmentation by customer allows a firm to concentrate on the needs of its customers. For example, a firm that manufactures products for both industrial customers and private consumers may require two different sales forces to sell its products effectively. Retailers are another example. Products may be grouped into men's, ladies' and children's wear for the convenience of the various groups of customers.

Departmentation by process means grouping activities around specific equipment or procedures. In many organizations, for example, data processing is a separate

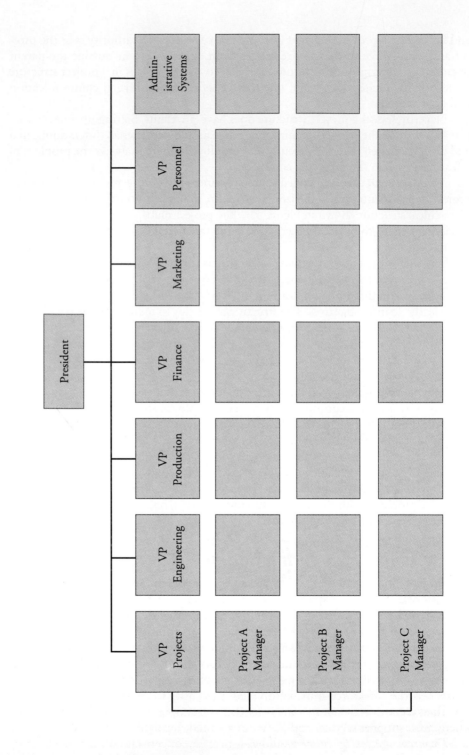

FIGURE 5.8

Matrix organization

department that handles the information processing of all departments. Automobile manufacturers may establish special departments to manufacture parts, assemble motors or perform service and inspection functions. The major advantage of grouping activities by process stems from specialization of labour; greater efficiency results when both workers and machines perform closely related tasks.

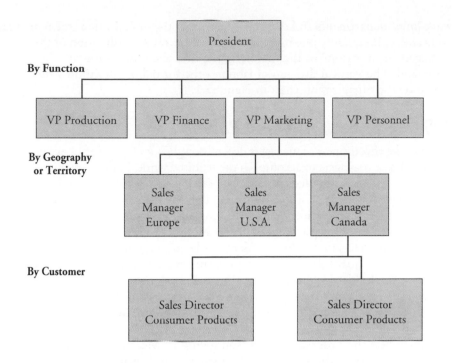

 **FIGURE** **5.9**

Example of a firm using
several forms of
departmentation

Combining Methods of Departmentation

Often an organization will use more than one method of departmentation. For
example, a major automobile manufacturer with branch plants in a number of
countries may use geographical departmentation; in turn, each branch plant may use
departmentation by product, while each product division may use departmentation
by function. Figure 5.9 shows how a hypothetical firm might use the various methods
of departmentation.

Vertical Division of Labour: Establishing Authority Relationships

Once the basic form of departmentation has been established, the next task is to
ensure that the various departments and groups work together to achieve the
organization's objectives. This requires coordination to ensure that individual work
groups accomplish the objectives of their departments, and that departments
accomplish the objectives of their divisions. **Coordination** is the process of integrating
the objectives and activities of these separate departments or functional areas to
ensure that the objectives and goals are accomplished efficiently.

Coordination is the responsibility of managers. For example, a division consists
of a number of departments, with each department having its own objectives. The
divisional manager acts as coordinator between the divisions, higher management and
the various department managers that report to him or her, and ensures that there
is communication flowing both ways—from the departments up to the division,
and from the top of the organization down—so that everyone knows what they
must accomplish and how well they are performing.

Setting up the coordination mechanism is step four of the organizing process.
Management positions are established and managers placed in charge of individual

Coordination is the process of
integrating the objectives and
activities of individual
departments or functional areas
to ensure that an organization's
objectives and goals are achieved
as efficiently as possible.

work units, departments and divisions. The larger the organization, the more managers and, consequently, the more management levels. Coordination of the various management positions in the hierarchy requires the establishment of a chain of command. The vertical division of labour—the formal organization structure—is shown on the organization chart in Figure 5.1.

Influence, Authority and Power

Influence is the ability of managers to encourage employees or subordinate managers to accomplish the required work.

Much of the effectiveness of managers depends on their ability to **influence** employees or subordinate managers to accomplish the required work. In most cases, a manager's influence stems from the formal authority arising out of his or her position in the management hierarchy. Formal authority allows managers to ask their employees to perform specific tasks while they are working for the organization. Formal authority is passed down from the president of the organization to lower management through the process of delegation. The president has been granted his or her authority by members of the board of directors, who in turn receive their authority from shareholders. Shareholders' rights are rooted in the laws of society, according to which private individuals may own property and do with it as they wish.

An alternative view of formal authority—the subordinate acceptance theory—holds that subordinates may or may not accept a superior's directives depending on how they view the order and the person giving it. Most employees will accept a manager's directives if they believe the requests are legitimate and based on the accepted job description. For example, employees would comply with a manager's request for periodic reports or for the performance of routine duties. However, if the request is illegal or against the employee's moral values, it is likely to be refused. Nevertheless, some subordinates may be so devoted to the corporation that they consider its needs above all else and engage in activities that run counter to their personal convictions.

Power is the ability to exert influence.

The relationship between authority, power and influence is shown in Figure 5.10. The amount of influence a manager has depends on the sources of power available to him or her. **Power** is the ability to exert influence. According to one study, there are five major types of power: legitimate, reward, coercive, expert and referent.[1]

Legitimate power is equivalent to formal authority and resides in the position occupied by the individual manager in the organizational hierarchy.

Legitimate power is equivalent to formal authority and resides in the position occupied by the individual manager in the organizational hierarchy. Legitimate power is the most important source of power because it provides the basis for operating the organization. It gives appointed managers the authority to ask their employees to perform specific tasks. It also gives managers **reward power**, since they are able to reward employees by raising their salaries, for example, or by giving them other privileges for good performance. Legitimate power also gives managers **coercive power**, or the authority to discipline employees by withholding rewards or by firing them. In addition, all managers enjoy some degree of **expert power** because they are assumed to have considerable knowledge in their functional areas.

Reward power allows a manager to influence behaviour by giving subordinates tangible rewards such as increases in salary or promotions.

Coercive power allows a manager to influence behaviour by disciplining subordinates or by firing them.

Expert power allows a manager to influence the behaviour of subordinates because they accept the manager's expertise or knowledge in a particular field, which may be important in carrying out their own job.

The only source of power that managers do not acquire as a result of their formal position in the organization is **referent power**, which depends primarily on a manager's individual personality and style. A manager with referent power or charisma can inspire a strong sense of loyalty and enthusiasm in employees.

Referent power allows a manager to influence subordinates because they admire the manager's personal characteristics or personality.

It may be difficult for Canadians to deal with the concept of power. We have an aversion to being used to accomplish goals that are not our own goals. This fear of being manipulated, however, can be detrimental to an organization if it prevents a manager from accomplishing legitimate organizational objectives. A manager must use the sources of power available to channel the efforts of employees in the

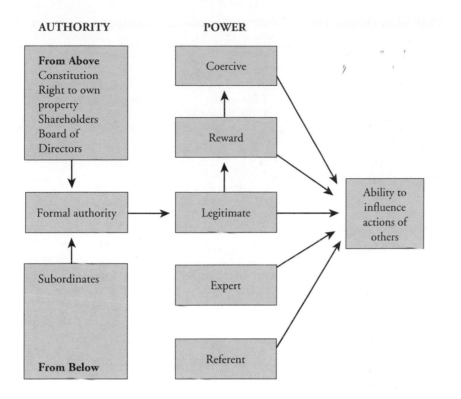

FIGURE 5.10

The relationship between authority, power and influence

appropriate directions. A manager can thus use power positively to encourage employees to develop the skills, competence and strengths needed to achieve organizational goals as well as their own personal goals.. Good managers exercise power to encourage teamwork, support their subordinates and reward their achievements, all of which raise morale.

Types of Authority

While all managers have formal authority, we often distinguish between line authority, staff authority and functional authority. The advantages and disadvantages of each type of authority are listed in Table 5.1.

Line Authority

The authority relationship that exists between those engaged in the primary activities of the organization is known as **line authority**. The shaded boxes in Figure 5.11 show the line management positions. Here the chain of command extends from the board of directors through the president and down to the workers and salespeople through the departments of finance, production and marketing. These three business functions are engaged in the primary activities of the firm—production and sales. In the case of a university, the line organization would consist of the board of governors, the president, the dean of instruction and the faculty. Since the primary activity is teaching, student services, the registrar and the business office are known as service or support departments.

　　Line authority organizations usually develop naturally as organizations grow. When a business is first started, the owner usually handles such secondary activities as public relations, personnel and legal problems, in addition to personally directing

Line authority is the authority exercised by those managers in the organization who are directly responsible for achieving organizational goals.

TABLE 5.1 Comparison of line, line and staff, and functional organization structures

Organizational Structure	Advantages	Disadvantages
Line	1. Simple organization structure. 2. Clear division of authority. 3. Decisions can be made quickly. 4. Subordinates are responsible to only one person.	1. Expert advice not readily available. 2. Line managers must be generalists. 3. Not suitable for a large organization.
Line and staff	1. Expert advice is readily available to line. 2. Line managers can concentrate on their main managerial task.	1. Staff managers have no direct authority over line managers and can only recommend a course of action. 2. Conflicts may develop between line and staff managers.
Modified functional	1. Expert advice is available to line managers. 2. Staff managers have authority to make decisions in specified areas. 3. Line managers can concentrate on their main managerial task. 4. Reduces conflicts between line and staff managers.	1. Employees may have more than one superior. 2. Conflicts and misunderstandings may arise unless authority relationships are clearly defined.

FIGURE 5.11

Line organization

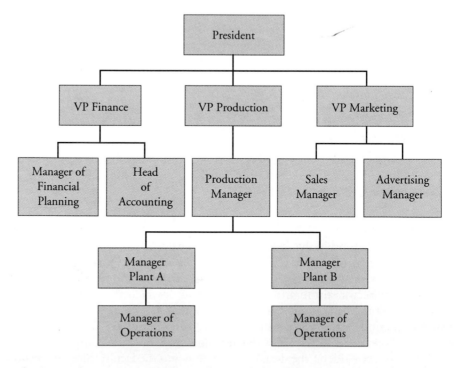

employees in the primary activities of production and sales. As the business grows, however, the need for specialized assistance becomes evident. In fact, the many supporting activities once performed by the owner may become so specialized and technical, and amount to such a great workload, that one person can no longer handle them effectively. At this stage many "assistant to" positions are created.

Individuals in these positions have no authority over others in the organization, but handle special assignments and projects as necessary.

The major advantage of a line authority organization is its simplicity. Everyone knows who is responsible for what and who reports to whom. Decisions can be made quickly because each subordinate has only one superior, and no additional advice or consent is required. The major disadvantage is that each manager must be skilled in many different areas. There are no specialists to offer advice on legal matters or personnel, for example. It may be difficult, therefore, for the various divisions and functional areas—such as sales, marketing and finance—to coordinate tasks that require specialized knowledge and expertise. In view of these disadvantages, the pure line organization is seldom found in large organizations.

Line and Staff Authority

As organizations grow larger and the need for additional services becomes evident, staff departments are created to provide services that support the line function. **Staff departments** may include personnel, production, planning and control, purchasing, engineering, research and development, quality control, accounting, budgeting and planning, plant maintenance, legal affairs and public relations. Managers in charge of staff departments have only **staff authority**, which means that they have no direct authority over line managers. The dark boxes in the organization chart in Figure 5.12 show the staff departments that have been added to the original line structure.

Line and staff organization allows authority and responsibility to be clearly defined throughout the chain of command, but gives line managers the opportunity to obtain expert advice from staff. For example, the production manager who constantly requires new workers can leave most of the work involved in recruitment, selection, training and other personnel matters to the personnel department, and conduct face-to-face interviews only with the most promising applicants. Similarly, the accounting department will assist the production manager by setting up control procedures and collecting data for his or her evaluation.

A line and staff organization often causes conflict, however. While staff experts may believe very strongly that their advice must be taken, they lack the authority to ensure that line managers accept it. Line managers, on the other hand, may resent having to seek staff advice that they often feel obliged to accept.

Functional Authority

One way to eliminate many of the problems between line and staff positions is to extend **functional authority** to certain staff managers. With functional authority, staff managers may exercise in their specialized areas direct authority over line managers. The arrows shown in Figure 5.13 indicate that some staff departments have authority over line departments. For example, the personnel manager may have the functional authority to order salary increases for any group of employees in the company, or to insist that all personnel matters be handled through the personnel department. The accounting department may be given the authority to require that all departments and divisions follow certain reporting procedures when preparing budgets or submitting daily operating figures. Keep in mind that, in practice, organization charts do not show these arrows. Instead, the functional authority of various staff departments is outlined in the company's policy manual.

The pure functional form of organization was developed in the late 19th century by Frederick Taylor, known as the father of scientific management, in an attempt to overcome the problems of the pure line organization. Instead of requiring one

Staff departments are established to provide services and advice to line managers.

Staff authority is the authority exercised by those individuals in an organization who provide line managers with advice and services.

Line and staff organization allows authority and responsibility to be clearly defined throughout the chain of command, while giving line managers the opportunity to obtain expert advice.

Functional authority allows staff managers to exercise direct authority in their specialized areas over line managers.

5.12

Line and staff organization

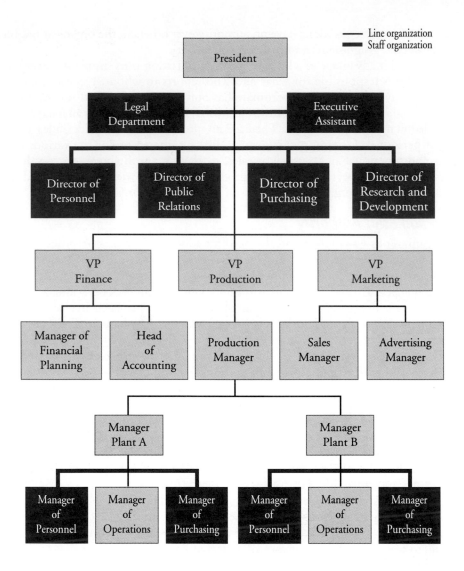

manager to become a generalist in many areas, which could reduce efficiency, Taylor believed that an organization should include many specialists to whom workers would report as their jobs required.

The major disadvantage of Taylor's pure functional organization is that each worker has many superiors. As a result, conflicts of authority, shirking of responsibilities and general confusion may arise. Functional organization in its pure form is rarely found, but the modified form discussed above and shown in Figure 5.13 is common in many organizations.

Delegation

Delegation of authority and responsibility is necessary because the amount of work that one person can do is limited. Managing even a small business becomes difficult if all of the coordinating tasks are the responsibility of the owner. As the business grows, some of the owner's duties and responsibilities must be given to others. More managers and management levels are needed as organizations become larger.

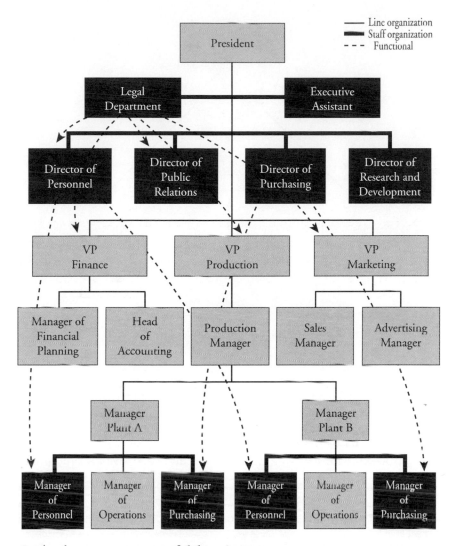

— Line organization
■ Staff organization
--- Functional

FIGURE **5.13**

Modified functional organization (staff positions have functional authority)

In the three-stage process of **delegation**, a manager:

1. assigns duties and responsibilities to a subordinate manager who is willing to accept them;

2. grants the subordinate manager the necessary authority to carry them out; and

3. holds the subordinate manager accountable for fulfilling his or her duties and responsibilities properly.

Responsibility and authority must be in balance when they are delegated to others (see Figure 5.14). Subordinates should not be held responsible for the performance of duties unless they have also been given the permission or authority to take the necessary actions. For example, a manager who has been made responsible for increasing production, without the corresponding authority to hire, fire, raise wages or reassign work, may be unable to fulfill his or her responsibilities.

If responsibility and authority are balanced, employees are accountable to their superiors for the performance of their duties. In other words, they must answer for the work that has been delegated to them and accept any criticism or credit for their performance.

Delegation is the assignment of authority, responsibility and accountability that enables subordinates to carry out specific activities.

FIGURE **5.14**

The delegation process (responsibility and authority must be balanced)

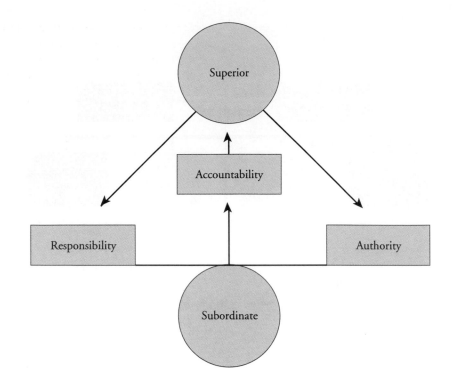

Accountability means that employees must answer to their superiors for the performance of the work that has been delegated to them, and accept any criticism or credit for their performance.

Accountability is the factor that differentiates between delegation and simple abdication of responsibility. A manager cannot simply grant authority to subordinates, making them responsible for performing the assigned duties and then blaming them if their performance causes problems for the organization. The superior manager remains responsible for the work he or she has delegated, even if subordinates in

Whistle-blowing and Organizational Structure

Whistleblowing is described as the reporting of a perceived wrongdoing within an organization's control by a current or former member of the organization to internal or external sources that may be able to correct the wrongdoing. External whistleblowing is viewed to be more detrimental to the company as the recipient of the report may be members of the media, government officials, members of public support groups, and so on. Since observers of wrongdoing may not report the behaviour due to communication barriers, the structure of the organization may be an important variable to consider. For example, in a bureaucratic structure, with formal lines of authority, whistleblowing may be seen as dissenting behaviour and therefore discouraged. Also, the climate may be threatening to one who does not play by the corporate rules. Therefore, the whistleblower is more likely to report externally to the media or other body. However, if the organization operates a decentralized management style within the centralized system, the opportunity may be presented to report internally.

Within a matrix structure each employee reports to two managers, therefore a choice may be offered to the whistleblower when a wrongdoing is observed. If the wrongdoer is manager A, then the complaint could go to manager B. However, if clear and proper channels are not perceived by the complainant, then the report is likely to be made externally.

In a divisional structure, due to the departmental autonomy, observers of wrongdoing may be more inclined to use internal disclosure channels.

If an organization wishes to minimize the risk of external whistleblowing, a clear and proper channel to handle perceived wrongdoings should be created and communicated to all employees. The creation of such a channel may also serve to enhance relations between organizational levels. If the structure itself prohibits such a channel, perhaps the organization should consider an ombudsperson, an internal review board, an organizational development consultant, EAPs, hotlines, etc. to encourage employees to report observed unethical behaviour internally, without fear of retribution.[2]

turn have delegated parts of their management tasks to others. A good example is the captain of a ship who is responsible for the actions of every crew member. Even though his personal performance may be impeccable, he must accept responsibility for accidents that may result directly from the neglect of one of his crew members. Therefore, although managers delegate **operating responsibility**, they cannot delegate **ultimate responsibility**.

Chain of Command

Delegation creates authority relationships between levels of management in the form of a hierarchy known as a **chain of command**. An organization chart shows the chain of command through the lines that connect the various management positions, indicating who can delegate to whom and who is responsible to whom. The chain of command connects the president at the very top of the hierarchy with every worker in the organization. In effect, each worker carries out the orders of the president through the orders of managers at each of the various levels.

When problems arise between individuals or departments, the chain of command aids in the adjudication process by passing the matter up through the hierarchy until it reaches a level of management where one person with authority over both factions can make a decision to solve the problem. The decision is then passed down to the worker or department in question through the same channel. If any managers are bypassed, their authority may be undermined. If they are bypassed frequently, the balance between their responsibility and authority is upset, and it may be difficult to hold them accountable for the operation of their departments.

In practice, of course, links in the chain of command are often bypassed. Operations would quickly bog down if the complete chain of command had to be followed for every minor problem. Individual workers or managers in different departments resolve daily operating problems themselves without consulting their superiors. In an emergency situation requiring immediate action, the superior manager who has been bypassed is notified as soon as possible. Under normal circumstances, however, any problems out of the ordinary should be passed through the chain of command.

Span of Control

How many subordinates can a manager supervise? The answer depends on the organization and the type of people in it. Managers with many subordinates reporting to them have a wide span of control; managers with few subordinates have a narrow span of control (see Figure 5.15). The **span of control**, also known as the **span of management**, determines the height of the management hierarchy and the number of management levels within it. If managers in a particular organization generally have a narrow span of control, a greater number of management levels is required than in a similar organization where each manager has a wider span of control. Many levels of management mean a tall organization structure, which increases costs not only in managers' salaries but also in support staff, office space and other facilities. Furthermore, with too many levels of management, effective communication may become impaired. The communication barriers responsible for distorting messages are discussed in Chapter 6.

A wide span of control, on the other hand, means fewer levels of management, resulting in a flat organization structure. However, an inadequate number of levels may not be efficient either, and could also be costly. If a manager is responsible for

Operating responsibility is the responsibility to properly carry out duties that have been delegated.

Ultimate responsibility means that the manager who has delegated operating responsibility to others is still responsible for how they carry out their work.

Chain of command—the authority relationships between levels of management.

Span of control or **span of management**—refers to the number of subordinates reporting to a manager.

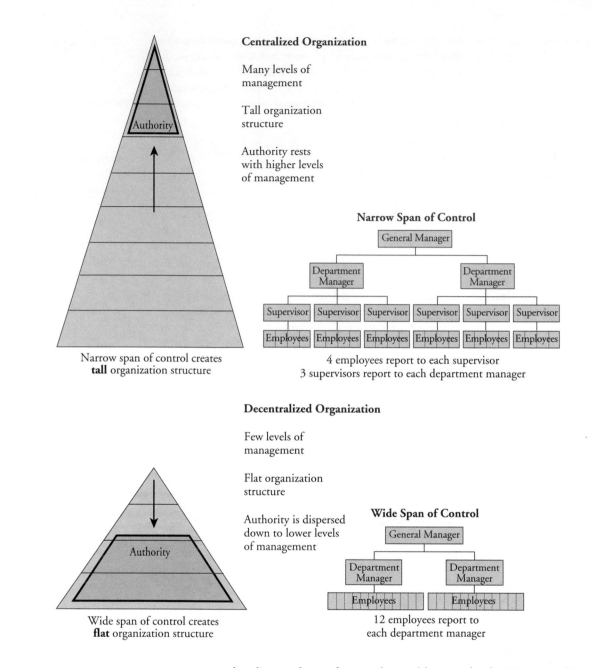

Centralized Organization

Many levels of management

Tall organization structure

Authority rests with higher levels of management

Narrow span of control creates **tall** organization structure

Narrow Span of Control

4 employees report to each supervisor
3 supervisors report to each department manager

Decentralized Organization

Few levels of management

Flat organization structure

Authority is dispersed down to lower levels of management

Wide span of control creates **flat** organization structure

Wide Span of Control

12 employees report to each department manager

FIGURE 5.15

Span of control determines height of organizational structure

too many subordinates, he or she may be unable to make decisions quickly, consult with subordinates thoroughly or otherwise give them sufficient support. The entire organization may suffer as opportunities slip by and necessary actions are delayed.

In practice, a common span of control covers five to nine subordinates. The span varies, however, with the particular level on which the manager operates. The number of subordinates that top management can effectively supervise is generally fewer than the numbers supervised by middle and lower levels of management. The optimum span of control depends on the manager's personal skills, in addition to how well subordinates understand the organization's plans and objectives, and how clearly their jobs are outlined. A wider span of control is possible when the organization is operating in a stable environment, since there is less need for close communication between superior and subordinate. A manager's span of control can also be wider if employees are highly motivated and tend to work well on their own, thus requiring less supervision.

Decentralization and Centralization

The terms "decentralization" and "delegation" are often confused. While there is a definite relationship between them, the two concepts are not identical. As discussed earlier, organizational growth requires that some responsibility and authority be delegated to other individuals.

Decentralization refers to the amount of authority that has been delegated to lower levels of management, and is reflected in the kinds of decisions lower-level managers are allowed to make. If top management is confident of the abilities of lower-level managers to make important decisions, it may delegate considerable authority to them. If top management prefers to retain responsibility for all major decision making, keeping close control over the actions of subordinates, operations are said to be **centralized**.

The degree of decentralization may also depend on other factors—the environment in which the organization operates, for example, or its size and rate of growth. In an environment where markets and competitive relationships are relatively stable, decision making can be more centralized because top management has more time to direct operations itself; the same is true of a medium-sized organization with a fairly stable rate of growth. On the other hand, in an industry where technology is changing rapidly, as in the case of computer manufacturers, decentralization is essential if the firm is to react quickly to the actions of its competitors.

It is important that firms strike a balance between centralization and decentralization. A decentralized organization helps to train and develop managers by allowing them to make decisions and learn from their mistakes; greater freedom for creativity also increases their value to the firm. Moreover, most daily operating decisions can be made more quickly—hence efficiently—when left to lower levels of management.

Decisions that may affect long-term prospects of the organization, however, should be retained by top management. These decisions include the setting of long-range objectives and goals, policy development, acquisition of financial resources, capital expenditures, new products, international expansion and organizational change. Although major decisions can sometimes be made at lower levels of management, they could prove costly unless an effective control system has been established to keep top management informed.

Committees

A **committee** is a group of people brought together to perform a particular task. An increasing number of organizations now use committees to solve specific problems, to perform ongoing organizational activities or simply to share information. Committees may also be used to make recommendations to upper management and to establish policy for the organization.

Committees offer a number of advantages. First, they often make better decisions than individuals because members are able to share their knowledge. Second, committee decisions are more likely to be accepted because most of the organization's members have had some input in the decision-making process. Finally, committees tend to make their members more aware of how the organization functions; exposure to others and their operations often leads to better coordination between departments.

Decentralization refers to the amount of authority that has been delegated to lower levels of management, and is reflected in the kinds of decisions lower-level managers are allowed to make.

Centralization refers to the decisions and the authority that has been retained by higher levels of management.

**Mintzberg:
Organizational Coordinating Mechanisms**

http://sol.brunel.ac.uk/~jarvis/
bola/mintzberg/mintstru.html

Committee—a group of people brought together to perform a particular task or share information.

One of the major advantages of committee decision making is its acceptance by a broad group of people in an organization

Committees also have disadvantages, however. Decision making is often slow and time-consuming. Moreover, many decisions tend to be compromises, due to the conflicting interests of various members. Perhaps most important, committees lack accountability. Should a decision prove to be wrong after it has been implemented, it is difficult to hold any one member responsible.

Nevertheless, because of the trend to more participation in decision making, committees will likely be used even more in the future, in all types of organizations. Managers must therefore understand how committees can function efficiently. The first major step is to establish clearly the committee's goals and objectives so that members can focus on the task at hand. The authority of the committee must also be clarified so that members know whether their decisions will be implemented or simply used for advisory purposes. Finally, formal procedures covering frequency, place, dates and times should be established for meetings.

If the committee is to be permanent, a secretary must be assigned to handle all communications and correspondence. The agenda and correspondence should be distributed well before the meeting so that all members have time to study the material. Finally, all meetings should start and end on time. It is best to set a predetermined time limit for the meeting and reconvene later, if necessary, to ensure that all members can give their undivided attention to matters. If meetings are long and appear to be unproductive, members may become distracted with other business or with personal matters.

The second major consideration is the committee's composition—it must not be so large as to be unmanageable. The leader, responsible for ensuring that formal procedures are followed, must be carefully chosen. Leaders must have the people skills needed to elicit ideas and discussion from the group; they must encourage timid members to contribute, while tactfully keeping monopolizers under control. The committee members must listen carefully and evaluate all suggestions fairly; they should try to avoid illogical compromises. Most important, members should approach their task in a cooperative spirit, rather than one of competition, if they hope to arrive at solutions.

Those who extol the virtues of small business often say that big businesses hold meetings to plan how they're going to hold meetings. Pretty funny stuff, huh?

I thought so, too, until I attended eight half-day training sessions on group process dynamics and interaction management several years ago.

There's some logic in doing this. In most big companies, employees attend a gaggle o' meetings every week, so making meetings more productive pays off. When managers learn the basics—have an agenda, review old action items at the beginning and new ones at the end, seek out the ideas of those folks who routinely don't contribute to conversations—meetings will become more productive.

Knowing how to run a meeting is as much a part of the manager's basic toolkit as a saw is for a carpenter.

You can make your meetings even more productive if you follow the guidelines in this column. Warning: What follows requires sophisticated mathematics and isn't for the faint of heart.

Step No. 1: Cut the average number of meetings in half. Here's how you got into this mess. At some critical point it became difficult to call meetings because everyone's schedule had become clogged with other meetings. What's the logical response? Establish a standing meeting, so everyone will reserve time in advance on their calendars. The consequence: having too many meetings leads to more meetings.

Here's what else happens: Everyone spends so much time in meetings that they have too little time to get work done at their desks. The result: Meetings become working sessions, not review sessions, leading to a need for ... yet more meetings.

Then a pernicious effect sets in: employees, and especially managers, lose the habit of time management. Instead, their appointment calendar manages them, and they go from meeting to meeting until the week has ended. Free time actually becomes a psychological threat.

Break this logjam. Encourage everyone to say no. It isn't all that hard. Once you have 20 hours of meetings on your calendar, make appointments with yourself for the rest. Say, "Sorry, I'm tied up the rest of this week. How else we can handle this?" Or, "You don't need me. I trust you to do the right thing."

Now you can convert meeting work to individual work. Brainstorming sessions are a prime candidate; psychologists have proven they rarely work anyway. Substitute a process in which individuals develop ideas independently and e-mail them to a central "idea facilitator" who organizes them, eliminates duplicates, and publishes a consolidated list for independent review and evaluation, prior to a meeting to decide on final solutions.

Step No. 2: Cut the average meeting size in half. This is simple. The bigger the group, the slower the progress. Two people in a group is best; you can bounce ideas off each other without having to wait your turn too much. As many as seven participants is acceptable. Ten people is the maximum for anything other than a presenter/audience format.

So why do we have big meetings? Lack of trust. People tend to refuse to accept any result unless they had a hand in its creation. All constituencies must be represented in the process or they won't accept the conclusions.

What's the cure? Design each team to have the smallest number of participants possible, while still containing the expertise needed to get the job done. Everyone else? Put them on a steering committee that meets monthly, or even quarterly, to review and comment.

These two simple steps—reducing both the number of meetings and their attendance—are simple to state, but achieving them will take commitment, vigilance and strong leadership.

The benefit is awesome. In some companies, managers spend more than 30 hours each week in meetings. The program described in this column would cut that to fewer than 10 hours—that's 20 additional hours per week per manager of real work.

You could spend 10 of them procrastinating and still be way ahead.

Two Radical Steps Can Save Hours of Time Spent in Meetings

The Next Evolutionary Step

In the 21st century people are often no longer required to be physically in the same location in order to complete their tasks. The old hierarchical structures created in response to industrialization are inappropriate for many types of businesses. As the world changes, so must the structure of many organizations. The key to success in the 21st century is flexibility and responsiveness. With the advent of e-commerce, a competitive advantage may last only a few days rather than months or years. In order to reconfigure our organizations to be more responsive, the structural model may become more of a network than a pyramid. This model is referred to as a network organization, virtual organization or boundaryless organization. With the availability of many communication options, virtual teams comprising a virtual organization can be effective, efficient and flexible. While some degree of hierarchical structure will obviously be necessary in complex network organizations, many organizations will move away from the bureaucratic constraints more readily than others. The choice of a structure depends, of course, on the particular kind of work being done. The key is to add the horizontal links necessary to facilitate communication and response to change within the required hierarchy.

The formation of virtual teams has been made possible by utilizing the technological advances in communication that allow the members to work toward a common purpose irrespective of time zones, distance or organizational boundaries. The virtual team model consists of three components: purpose, people and links. By expanding this model, the "people" node can become a group of people or an entire organization. The purpose of the virtual team must be of a nature sufficiently compelling to hold the team together without bureaucratic rules, regulations, policies and procedures. The purpose is crucial to the effective functioning of the team. The people are the core of the team and must be able to work effectively alone as well as interdependently. The leadership of the team tends to rotate among the members depending on the particular skill set dominating the work at that time. Linking the team to the rest of the organization has been facilitated by technology but is not limited to it. Face-to-face conversations and the formation of trusting relationships add to the richness of the virtual team's experience and functioning. Positive social outcomes may or may not result from the team's efforts.

The virtual organization or network organization may also be characterized by outsourcing or the contracting-out of non-core functions. This process involves renting or buying these functions from specialists. This approach has received mixed reviews as some critics believe that outsourcing alienates the work force as workers watch entire departments disappear from their organization. Others feel that it is the way of the future to ensure the desired flexibility. With the outsourcing approach, the organization consists of a hub of core functions joined by contract to the non-core functions. Theoretically this enhances flexibility by allowing the hub to retain or not retain the outsourced functions as the hub deems necessary for success of the business endeavour.

While this configuration offers some benefits in the form of cost savings and economies of scale, a mutually satisfying relationship with the contract partners may be difficult to maintain as the goal of the hub is often to reduce costs at the partner's expense. Another problem could result from the fact that the partner employees, performing the work of the network hub, feel no allegiance or loyalty to it as the relationship is indirect. Thus control over the productivity, efficiency and effectiveness of these employees has been removed from the core or hub and placed in the hands of the contract partner who may or may not address the issue. Therefore, while the network organization permits some degree of flexibility, it has difficulties inherent in the formation of the contractual relationship that must be addressed. See Figure 5.16 for an example of a network organization.[3]

The Virtual Organization. . . . To be or not to be?

Is the virtual organization the way of the future? Let's examine some advantages and disadvantages as well as some factors contributing to the success of virtual organizations.

Virtual organizations offer the following advantages:

1. Reduced investment can result as companies utilize the assets of their contract partners.

2. The focus is on the core competencies of each partner; therefore each is a specialist in his or her own functional area.

3. The virtual organization offers flexibility and responsiveness, which is highly valued by customers.

Virtual organizations offer the following disadvantages:

1. Participating partners have access to each other's trade secrets, technology and data.

2. Old managerial styles are ineffective in virtual organizations.

3. Conflicting corporate cultures of partner organizations can create difficulties in achieving shared goals.

4. Operations are often bound by contractual obligations, which can constrain the functioning of the organization.

The success of virtual organizations depends on the following key factors:

1. A focus on customer needs.

2. The choice of the right partners with the right core competencies.

3. Pursuit of a win-win outcome for all participating organizations.

4. Trust.

5. Communication of information.

6. Protection of company's proprietary information.

7. A new kind of organization structure that is lean and flexible to respond to customer needs.

8. A new breed of leader capable of facilitating and supporting rather than dictating orders.

9. A new breed of worker who is able to work effectively in a team with minimal supervision and direction.

With the appropriate blend of all factors, a successful virtual organization may emerge with partners who share skills, technology, costs and access to one another's markets to the benefit of the organization and the customer.[4]

Chapter Summary

1. An organization is a group of people with an objective. It becomes a formal organization when management is added to direct the activities of people toward achieving the organization's objectives. An organization structure ensures that employees know to whom they are responsible, and that established authority relationships are relatively stable and permanent. The formal organization structure is shown by an organization chart that indicates the different management positions, titles and authority flow.

2. People performing the various tasks in an organization can be grouped together into units—a process known as departmentation. The most common groupings are by function, product, geography or territory, project or matrix, customer and process. The type of structure chosen will be the one best suited to achieving the organization's objectives.

3. To ensure that all organization members work toward the objectives and goals of the organization, managers must be able to influence their actions. Managers base their authority on five types of power: legitimate, reward, coercive, expert and referent. Legitimate power is equivalent to formal authority and gives managers the right to act. Reward power is a manager's authority to give employees tangible rewards; coercive power is a manager's authority to discipline employees. Expert power comes from a person's knowledge and experience in a particular field, while referent power stems from an individual's personality.

4. We can distinguish between line, staff and functional authority of managers. The managers who are directly in charge of the organization's major activity are line managers. As organizations grow, managers require more expertise in specific areas and thus staff positions are created. When staff managers obtain authority over specific aspects of their job, they have functional authority.

5. Since the head of the organization cannot perform all the work, some duties and responsibilities must be delegated to other managers, along with the authority to carry them out. Subordinate managers in turn are accountable to their superiors for the performance of their duties.

6. Through delegation, a managerial hierarchy known as the chain of command is established. The hierarchy can be either tall or flat depending on the number of managers in the organization and the span of control of each. A narrow span of control means that one manager is responsible for only a few subordinate managers; a wide span of control means that one manager is responsible for many subordinates. The optimum span of control refers to the number of subordinates one manager can most effectively supervise. Effectiveness depends on the abilities of both the superior and subordinate managers, the type of activities being performed and the closeness of communication required. Generally, the wider the span of control allowed to managers, the greater the degree of decentralization in decision making within the organization.

7. A committee is used when representation or input from a variety of areas is required. Although the decisions made by committees are generally of superior quality, committees are costly to use. Many decisions are compromises, and they can take a long time to make. Committees also tend to lack accountability. Nevertheless, committees are now being used in the management of organizations, and managers should understand how to make them function effectively.

8. A network organization, virtual organization or boundaryless organization is a more flexible organizational structure with fewer hierarchical levels. With the advent of the Internet and E-commerce, organizations need to be more responsive to environmental factors to maintain their competitive advantage. Outsourcing, which involves renting or buying non-core functions from specialists outside the company, may also be characteristic of virtual organizations.

KEY TERMS

Organization 150	Project structure 159	Staff authority 167
Formal organization 150	Matrix structure 161	Line and staff organization 167
Organization chart 150	Coordination 163	Functional authority 167
Informal organization 151	Influence 164	Delegation 169
Organizational structure 155	Power 164	Accountability 170
Reorganizing 156	Legitimate power 164	Operating responsibility 171
Division of work 156	Reward power 164	Ultimate responsibility 171
Specialization of labour 156	Coercive power 164	Chain of command 171
Departmentation 156	Expert power 164	Span of control/span of management 171
Functional departmentation 158	Referent power 164	Decentralization 173
Product departmentation 158	Line authority 165	Centralization 173
Geographic departmentation 158	Staff departments ....,.,..167	Committee 173

REVIEW QUESTIONS

1 Why are formal organizations necessary?

2 Explain the difference between formal and informal organizations.

3 What is departmentation? When would a firm use product departmentation? Geographic departmentation?

4 Explain the terms authority, responsibility and accountability. How are they related?

5 Explain one of the errors commonly made in the process of delegation.

6 Distinguish between influence, power and authority.

7 What are some of the dangers in bypassing the chain of command?

8 Why would the dean of instruction at a college or university have a wide span of control? Why would the president of a very large corporation have a narrow span of control?

9 Distinguish between centralization and decentralization. When is decentralization appropriate?

10 What is the difference between line and staff positions? Why might conflicts develop between individuals in each of these positions?

11 What is a matrix organization structure? Name some kinds of organizations that might employ a matrix structure. Describe some of the problems involved in using this structure.

12 What are the advantages and disadvantages of committees? Will the use of committees to make management decisions increase in the future? Give reasons for your answer.

DISCUSSION QUESTIONS

1   If organizational structures are established to allow people to perform their jobs more effectively, why is it that they can also cause so much conflict and friction?

2   How can technology affect a company's organization structure? Provide some examples.

3   "The principle underlying delegation is simple, yet delegation is often a major factor of management failure." Discuss.

4   "There should be a balance between centralization and decentralization in a company." Why might this balance be difficult to obtain in a rapidly growing company?

5   "More of management's work should be done through committees, since a group of people can make better decisions than one person alone." Evaluate this statement on the basis of the information provided in the last two chapters.

The Greenpeace Foundation at 20

In 1971, a small group of activists sailed from Vancouver to Alaska to protest the Amchitka nuclear tests being conducted by the Americans in the Aleutian Island chain. By 1998 the Greenpeace Foundation had evolved into a worldwide organization represented in 40 countries with 2.4 million financial supporters. In one of the newest offices, China, the number of donors increased substantially, with more than 3000 additional regular supporters.

Until 1979, the Greenpeace head office was located in Vancouver. But a significant amount of infighting among various groups loosely connected to Greenpeace almost destroyed the organization. The battle between the U.S. and Canadian organizations over the use of the name Greenpeace cost over $400 000. The final showdown in court was averted when David McTaggart, a Canadian yachtsman and Greenpeace activist, offered to pay off all debts and bring the various factions together if the Vancouver group would relinquish its head-office status and accept an international coalition with him at the helm. This ultimately led to the formation, in 1979, of Greenpeace International, with its headquarters in Amsterdam. The Council is the major decision-making body for Greenpeace International. Each Greenpeace officer appoints a representative to the Council, which meets once a year to approve the budget of Greenpeace International for the following year and to make decisions on the overall direction and policy, especially for the longer term.

Greenpeace's success against nuclear testing, and the virtual elimination of commercial whaling and sealing, raised the organization's world membership to almost four million. International support rose dramatically after the 1985 bombing of the group's flagship, the *Rainbow Warrior*, which resulted in the death of a Greenpeace photographer. The ship had been on a mission to sabotage French nuclear testing in the South Pacific.

Over the years Greenpeace became a closely knit network of national and regional offices, coordinated from its headquarters in Amsterdam. Greenpeace International is funded by the national offices. These, in turn, are financed almost entirely by small contributions from supporters in 158 countries, and by sales of merchandise. By the end of 1998, Greenpeace worldwide was in a solid financial situation. Net income was stable at US$101 million. A surplus was recorded worldwide of US$7 million, which will be used towards modernizing the Greenpeace fleet and investing in the development of new Greenpeace offices in non-OECD countries.

Some observers charge that Greenpeace is spending too much of its resources on its own growth, and too little on the activism that garnered its reputation. Patrick Moore, a founder, left after 15 years to take up fish farming. Paul Watson and Robert Hunter, both founding members, have also left the organization, claiming that Greenpeace has become a multinational corporation. According to Watson, the organization cranks out millions of pieces of junk mail as part of their fund-raising, yet engages less and less in the confrontation that earned them a global reputation.

The current executive director, an MBA from Montreal's McGill University, insists that frontline combat is still the central activity of Greenpeace. In fact, in 1990 he personally manoeuvred an inflatable zodiac to tag the British aircraft carrier *Ark Royal* in Halifax as a carrier of radioactive material. He and Canadian Greenpeace employees argue that a large international organization is needed because environmental abuses are a global problem. Nor is it possible today to run an international organization in the ad-hoc manner favoured by the early Greenpeace effort.

SOURCE: Adapted from John Fox, "The business of Greenpeace," *The Financial Post* (January 7, 1991): 5, and the Greenpeace Web page at http://www.greenpeace.org

>>

Questions

1 What type of organization structure would be best suited for Greenpeace? Keep in mind that the organization is largely voluntary and relies for its financial support on individuals' concerns about the environment.

2 Draw an organization chart for the Greenpeace Foundation that includes its head-office departments and international branches. How many types of departmentation might Greenpeace use? Keep in mind that some functions must be coordinated from head office.

3 Most of the people who work for Greenpeace are volunteers. What problems relating to authority might this cause for the chief officers of the Greenpeace organization? Explain how much they could rely on each of the sources of power to influence the behaviour of Greenpeace members.

4 What kinds of activities should be centralized/decentralized in this organization?

Surprise, Surprise!

Many managers are afraid to delegate. They feel more comfortable doing the "important" tasks themselves and leaving the routine ones to others. In the case that follows, Jo-Anne is thought to be a "good" manager because "the report" always gets out on time. This perception, however, is inaccurate. This fear of delegation could have long-term consequences for both Jo-Anne and George.

For the 100th time, Jo-Anne thought:

"If I tell George to do that he'll screw it up! Then Mr. Sims might be on my back. Better write the damn report myself."

So she delayed her vacation once more, hoping the snow wouldn't be gone from the mountains when she finally made it.

For the 100th time, George sighed as he bent over his computer terminal:

"More routine and more routine! I think I'm going mad! . . . data entry and gophering. Wish I could get out of this dump, but there's a recession on. I wonder how Jo-Anne stands it ... seems to put in endless hours. Wish I understood what she was doing— I'd sure like a crack at doing the report."

For the 100th time, Mr. Sims felt a sense of satisfaction:

"The report is due tomorrow, but Jo-Anne's group always comes through. Precisely at two o'clock, George will deliver it, all neatly and correctly presented. There's a new position coming up that would be a considerable promotion for Jo-Anne. Yes sir! It was real nice to have such competent people on payroll. George should be able to take over Jo-Anne's job."

Ten days later, Mr. Sims was on the phone:

"George, I've just had some terrible news! Jo-Anne's broken her leg skiing . . . multiple fractures. She'll be in traction for at least three months. You'll have to take over the group while she's gone. The report is due out next week, but I know I can count on you! Are you there, George? . . . hello? . . ."

At that precise moment, George had the distinct feeling he was going to throw up.

SOURCE: By Dr. P. C. Wright, Faculty of Administration, University of New Brunswick, Fredericton, N.B. Reprinted by permission of the author.

Questions

1 Might Mr. Sims have a different opinion of Jo-Anne's competence by the time she returns?

2 How might Jo-Anne's career be affected?

3 What might happen to George? Whatever happens, would it be George's fault?

4 Using this case incident as an example, discuss the general principles of delegation as Jo-Anne should have applied them. Discuss Mr. Sims' involvement in this situation. Should he have acted differently?

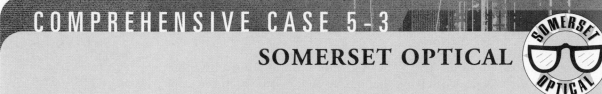

COMPREHENSIVE CASE 5-3

SOMERSET OPTICAL

As Somerset Optical began to enjoy steadily increasing sales and to establish itself as a serious contender in the Ottawa optical market, the president of Byway Optical had second thoughts about his decision to sell the outlet to Dewar.

In July 1998, John Claymore paid a surprise visit to Somerset Optical. He was impressed with the store's look: a good mixture of high-quality frames and premium contact lenses, among other things. A steady stream of customers came through the door while he was there. In fact, he thought he recognized a few of his own customers!

Claymore was indeed surprised to learn that Fowler and Dewar were averaging $23 000 per month in gross sales since they started the business on April 1. In view of the deep discounts Somerset was offering its customers, had the goods been sold at the full retail price, gross sales would have been double the amount reported. But Claymore knew very well that no one ever paid full retail price for eyewear. Even so, using the discount scheme offered by Byway Optical Inc. (which was not quite as deep as the one offered by Somerset), the level of sales under the Byway scheme could be expected to gross at least $29 500 in sales.

Claymore suggested that Dewar and Fowler could benefit considerably by participating in the volume discounts available to Byway Optical Inc. He offered to take back 51% ownership of Somerset Optical, cancelling the remaining $6000 owed to Byway for the purchase agreement and refunding the $6000 paid to Byway to date. In return, 51% of all profits from Somerset would go to Byway Optical Inc. and the remaining 49% would be split between Fowler and Dewar. Furthermore, Claymore would pay Fowler a salary of $50 000 per year if he agreed to provide services to Byway's four existing locations. Somerset Optical would change its name to Byway Optical, but the partners could run the Somerset operation without interference from Claymore.

Ever the pragmatic conceptual manager, Dewar asked Claymore to describe how his company was now organized. Dewar described the organization of Byway Optical Inc. as follows.

"Reporting to the president [Claymore] are the managers from each of the four Byway retail outlets, the manager of the Byway Optical Laboratory, the administrative manager, the financial manager, the internal accountant, the external accountant (as adviser and auditor) and the marketing assistant. Reporting to each retail outlet manager is the optician. We also employ two physicians whose practices are limited to treatments of the eye. While operating as separate business entities, these practices report to the president of Byway. The doctors' receptionists report directly to the respective physicians. There is also an eye-examination centre operated by an optometrist who reports directly to the president of Byway. Two of the four retail outlets are being restructured so that the manager will own 49% of the retail outlet. All stock orders, bills and leasing matters are dealt with and administered by Byway Optical's downtown location.

"The optical laboratory is located in the retail outlet in the east end of the city. Byway employs at least two opticians per location and at least five full-time and four part-time sales clerks. There is also a delivery person who delivers stock orders to the respective locations. This delivery person reports to the president. All capital equipment is centrally leased and dispersed to each location. In addition, the opticians can work in any of the locations with the approval of the president. The marketing manager handles all leasehold details and all advertisements on behalf of all locations. All accounting functions are centralized at the downtown location. The profit structure is different

>>

for each store depending on each manager's personal investment in his or her retail outlet, and none of the proposed 51-49% ownership splits have been legally established. This structure provides for maximum flexibility and maximum growth potential."

After Claymore left, Dewar and Fowler called their consultant and relayed the above information and "offer," seeking her advice on whether or not the offer was a good one.

SOURCE: By David H. Jones-Delcourt. Reprinted by permission of the author.

Questions

1 Design an organization chart for Byway Optical as described by Claymore. What are your general impressions of the firm's organization?

2 How would you modify Claymore's organizational structure to make it more efficient and effective?

6

Managing People

Learning Objectives

After reading this chapter, you will be able to

1 Explain the meaning of motivation and identify the key ideas of the major theories that have been advanced to explain how people are motivated.

2 Explain the relationship between motivation and leadership.

3 Explain the difference between Theory X and Theory Y managers.

4 Briefly explain the leadership continuum, the managerial grid, Fiedler's contingency theory of leadership, the path-goal theory and the life-cycle theory.

5 Identify the criteria that organizations should use to select leaders.

6 Compare Japanese management techniques to North American techniques.

7 Recognize the importance of good communication and identify ways of overcoming communication barriers.

8 Explain the relationship between motivation, morale, job satisfaction and productivity.

9 Explain how organizations can redesign work to make it more interesting for employees and improve morale.

10 Identify the steps in the management by objectives process and discuss the problems involved in implementing this process in organizations.

Motivation

Imagine standing on a bridge in New Zealand, some 60 metres above the water. Your legs are tied together by a bungee cord that will expand and slightly cushion your fall as you dive toward the water below. As you freefall, you experience a feeling of terror: what you are doing goes against all your instincts for survival.

Individuals who perform such death-defying acts often do not receive any tangible rewards. So why do they do it? What motivates them?

To gain a better understanding of what makes people do things, we must examine the meaning of motivation. Motivation can refer to an individual's condition, as when we say, Louise is highly motivated and therefore does well in her job. Managers are concerned with motivation as a process. What factors brought Louise to her motivated condition?

We can thus define **motivation** in general terms as that which causes, channels and sustains a person's behaviour. The cause may be a person's drives, desires, needs and wishes. A simple example is hunger, which drives us to satisfy the need for food by finding something to eat. In our example, Louise may have felt the need or desire for a reward: material, social or psychological, and believed that doing her job well would satisfy the need. Motivation thus also involves goal-oriented behaviour, or the drive to satisfy a need. Figure 6.1 is a simplified representation of the motivation process.

Motivation is that which causes, channels and sustains a person's behaviour.

How to Motivate People

All individuals have needs that require satisfaction. The need perceived to be strongest at any given time will dictate current behaviour. A manager can motivate employees by showing them that their needs can be satisfied best by working toward the organization's goals. He or she must convince them that by doing their jobs well they can benefit through money, status, good social relationships or some other psychological reward. But how can a manager motivate all employees to work toward the same organizational objectives when no two individuals have the same needs at the same time? A look at some of the motivation theories that have been advanced may give us some ideas.

Classical Theory of Motivation

Proponents of the **classical theory of motivation** considered people as purely economic creatures with money as their prime motivator. They believed that people worked to satisfy their need for basic necessities—food, clothing, shelter—and to raise their standard of living by acquiring other material goods. To motivate people to work toward organizational goals, then, a manager would need only offer more money.

One of the chief proponents of the classical theory of motivation was Frederick W. Taylor, known as the father of **scientific management**. In 1898, Taylor began a series of studies on the specific tasks performed by workers in a steel company metal

Classical theory of motivation holds that money is the primary motivator of people in the workplace.

Scientific management is a management approach that attempts to establish in a scientific manner the best methods for performing a task, and for selecting, training and motivating workers.

Simple motivation process

cutting, handling iron and shovelling. The results of his studies were published in a series of scientific papers. In 1911, Taylor published *The Principles of Scientific Management* in which he proposed (1) that jobs should be scientifically studied to determine what they entail; (2) that workers should be scientifically selected and trained; (3) that there should be cooperation between workers and management to ensure that all work is done according to scientific principles; and (4) that the total work should be divided between management and workers according to what each is best able to do.

Taylor believed that if all work were divided into small activities, any person could learn the tasks easily and eventually perform them rapidly. By studying the physical movements required to perform a specific task, Taylor was able to calculate the standard production rate for the average worker. Workers who achieved the standard level of output received the standard rate of pay, but any higher level of output was rewarded with a higher rate calculated according to each additional unit produced. This was Taylor's **differential piece rate system**. He believed that since workers could double their earnings, they would be strongly motivated to increase productivity.[1]

The classical theory of motivation was most effective during the latter years of the Industrial Revolution when workers were relatively poor and jobs were hard to find. By working faster, employees could increase their earnings and lead a more comfortable life. However, as the workers' standard of living improved, management noticed that their productivity no longer increased as rapidly, regardless of the monetary incentives that were offered. At first, managers were puzzled by this change, but eventually they learned that the process of motivating human beings is far more complex than was previously believed.

Human Relations and Elton Mayo

From 1927 to 1933, Elton Mayo, a Harvard professor of industrial research, and his associates conducted motivation experiments at the Hawthorne plants of the Western Electric Company near Chicago. In one study, the researchers set out to determine the relationship between physical working conditions and productivity. They divided the female workers into two groups: an experimental group and a control group. The experimental group was subjected to changes in working conditions and incentives. As rest periods were added and lighting conditions improved, for example, productivity increased. When incentives were later withdrawn, productivity still continued to increase. Surprisingly, similar productivity increases, although not as great, were obtained with the control group that did not receive better rewards and did not experience changes in working conditions.

After rechecking their experiments and results, the researchers attributed the consistent level of productivity to two factors: a feeling of importance among the female workers in both groups and a trust in the researchers and management. The females were proud to have been chosen for such an important project, and also came to believe in what management said about the state of the company. A feeling of involvement in the actual operation of the firm motivated them to work harder. Mayo concluded that, regardless of working conditions, productivity tends to increase when management gives special attention to workers. This tendency became known as the **Hawthorne effect**.

In another experiment at the same company, a different phenomenon was discovered. Researchers found that workers restricted their output to a level that could reasonably be met by all members of the group. The workers as a group

Differential piece rate system is Frederick W. Taylor's system of compensating more efficient workers by paying them higher wages in accordance with their increased production.

Hawthorne effect is the tendency of productivity in a workplace to increase, regardless of working conditions, when management gives special attention to workers.

established their own standards, and group pressure kept individuals from performing above or below the norm. Individuals who exceeded the group norm were called "ratebusters" while those who produced less were termed "chiselers." Since most workers adhered to the group norm, Mayo concluded that individuals have a strong need to be liked and accepted by their fellow workers, and would choose to earn less money rather than be excluded from the work group.

The results of experiments by Mayo and others have shown management that workers have needs other than money and job security. The importance of social needs must be recognized and the work environment made conducive to good social relationships. Management must recognize the importance of the informal work group and seek employee input when considering changes that will affect the work environment.

Maslow's Need Hierarchy

Further explorations into motivation and human needs were conducted by psychologist Abraham Maslow. In the 1940s, Maslow developed a need hierarchy based on the need-satisfaction theory discussed at the beginning of this chapter. Maslow believed that while a strong need is a motivator, once that need is satisfied the individual will no longer be motivated by it, and will then attempt to satisfy another need. Thus, he arranged the major categories of needs in order of their importance to the individual. As an individual satisfied one level of need in part, attention would be turned to satisfying the next level. Maslow's hierarchy of needs—physiological, safety, social, esteem and self-actualization—is shown in Figure 6.2.

Physiological Needs

Physiological needs are those basic to sustaining life—food, clothing and shelter—and must be satisfied, at least to some degree, before an individual can consider

Money and Motivation

www.mapnp.org/library/guiding/ motivate/basics.htm

Physiological needs are those basic to sustaining life-food, clothing, shelter-and must be satisfied, at least to some degree, before an individual can consider higher-level needs.

FIGURE 6.2

Maslow's hierarchy of needs

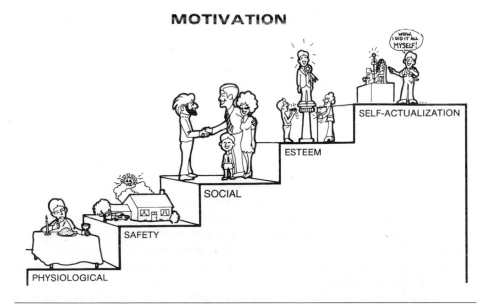

SOURCE: Reproduced by permission of the Instructional Communications Centre, McGill University, Montreal, Canada.

higher-level needs. Since money can buy the necessities of life, it is a prime motivation at this stage. However, it loses some of its importance as the individual becomes aware of higher needs that money cannot satisfy.

Safety Needs

Once satisfaction of physiological needs is achieved, the next most important concern is to maintain the basic level of life. Workers will seek to satisfy **safety needs** by protecting themselves from dangers on the job, by ensuring continued earnings and job security, and by maintaining a basic income required to support their lifestyle. Today, safety needs are satisfied by programs such as workers' compensation, employment insurance, pension plans and various government subsidies.

Social Needs

Human beings need to be liked by others, to be needed and to have friends. **Social needs** are thus strong motivators and, as shown by the Hawthorne experiments, they are not readily satisfied by money. Once physiological and safety needs have been reasonably satisfied, an individual's desire to be accepted by fellow workers tends to be stronger than the desire for higher income.

Esteem or Ego Needs

Esteem or **ego needs** follow social needs in Maslow's hierarchy. Individuals must feel that they and their work are important, and that they are respected and have the support of others. All of these factors are essential for an individual's self-confidence. Sometimes esteem needs are satisfied by status, which refers to an individual's standing within a particular group or within society generally. Status can be acquired through wealth, education, accomplishment or occupation. Some people, for example, seek status by acquiring material possessions. Others may work long hours in a corporation to win an impressive promotion that promises an increase in prestige as well as money and power.

Self-Actualization Needs

At the top of Maslow's hierarchy are **self-actualization needs**—the needs to grow and achieve one's full potential, and to use one's talents, abilities and interests to the fullest. Self-actualization is the desire to become everything one is capable of becoming. Self-actualization needs differ from esteem needs in that a person seeking satisfaction at this level is not interested primarily in status or power, but rather in fulfilling an intensely personal goal. Of course, in the process of satisfying self-actualization needs, an individual may also satisfy ego needs.

The Individual and the Need Hierarchy

Maslow's need hierarchy is not a rigid structure applying equally to every individual. Some people require more of one kind of satisfaction than another. Some never go beyond satisfying their social needs, while others may consider safety needs all-important. Others still may strive to fulfill all five needs at the same time.

North American workers generally receive good wages, pension plans, employment insurance and other benefits to satisfy their physiological and safety needs. Many also have social needs satisfied, either on or off the job, through membership in informal work groups, unions or other organizations outside the workplace. However, needs for esteem and self-actualization are not as easily fulfilled in the

---

Safety needs include the need for safety, order and freedom from fear or threat.

Social needs include the need for love, human contact and feelings of belonging.

Esteem or **ego needs** include the need for self respect, self-esteem and the respect and support of others.

Self-actualization needs include the need to grow, to use talents, abilities and interests to the fullest and to achieve one's full potential.

Goals and Needs

Goals Related to Physiological Needs

- ON THE JOB: Money for purchase of basic goods; acceptable physical surroundings at work; vacations and personal time off from job; subsidized cafeterias.
- OFF THE JOB: Availability of adequate stores of the basic necessities; adequate living space; availability of physicians; time to relax and sleep; recreational facilities.

Goals Related to Safety Needs

- ON THE JOB: Health and medical care packages; social security; safe workplace; job security; automatic cost-of-living salary increases.
- OFF THE JOB: Protection against crime and fire; a savings account; an orderly family life; a freezer stocked with food.

Goals Related to Social Needs

- ON THE JOB: Association with peers; involvement with committees; group travel; staff meetings; team incentives; contacts with other departments.
- OFF THE JOB: An adequate social and family life; involvement in community and social clubs; intellectual stimulation; recreation facilities.

Goals Related to Ego Needs

- ON THE JOB: Promotions based on performance; special assignments; responsibility and independence to schedule one's day; respect from one's co-workers and superiors; pay; contacts with other departments; development of unique expertise; doing better than last year.
- OFF THE JOB: Gaining the respect of people one admires; being elected to the board of education; repairing the kitchen faucet; helping with homework; learning how to paint; having people appreciate one's sense of humour.

Goals Related to the Need for Self-Actualization

- ON THE JOB: Setting one's own goals and standards; attending training programs; doing satisfying work; devising feedback systems to determine one's effectiveness on the job; feeling free to be open with one's peers and superiors.
- OFF THE JOB: Achieving self-set standards of performance in leisure-time activities; being accepted by the family for what you are; taking night courses "just for fun"; doing volunteer work; starting one's own business; trying something new; managing time well; upgrading existing skills.

SOURCE: Andrew H. Souerwine, "Motivation and career strategy: giving direction to commitment." *Management Review* (November 1977): 57. Reprinted by permission of the publisher. © 1977 by AMACOM, a division of American Management Association. All rights reserved.

workplace, largely because many workers perform jobs that are boring and repetitious, particularly in the service and manufacturing industries. It is also doubtful that workers will be able to fulfill all of their needs at work in the foreseeable future. Nevertheless, a manager should attempt to determine the needs of individual employees and allow them opportunities to satisfy their upper-level needs whenever possible.

Some Additional Ideas on Maslow

The author of a recent article in the *Journal of Humanistic Psychology* suggests that those studying Maslow's hierarchy of needs theory be wary of the differentiation between the need for esteem from others and the need for self-esteem. The need for esteem from others encompasses performing roles well as we look to others for our standards and how well we rate with them. A person pursuing this type of esteem wants regular structure and relevant others with higher status; that is, they want to be respected by those whom they respect. Satisfaction of this need leads to enhanced self-image and sometimes can be accompanied by the wearing of a mask to enhance this image of the false or public relations self. In order to move to the level of self-esteem, personal examination of our role playing to attain the esteem of others is necessary.[2] Another article describes Maslow's theory in terms of deficiency motivation (needs) and abundance motivation (seeking new and fresh stimulation). Maslow wrote and spoke more of deficiency motivation in the satisfaction of needs and in coping in general. He referred to abundance motivation as "being-values" and felt that it is more apt to be found at the self-actualization level of development. Maslow believed that all lower-level needs are contained within the higher ones, and that our lower-level needs never really disappear but rather become background rather than foreground issues.[3] Although Maslow's hierarchy of needs may seem relatively simplistic at first glance, further investigation reveals an in-depth study of human motivation culminating in self-actualization as the highest goal for healthy, striving humans.[4]

Herzberg's Motivation-Hygiene Theory

In the late 1950s, psychologist Frederick Herzberg conducted a study to understand better what motivates people in their jobs. In a questionnaire, he asked several engineers and accountants to indicate the factors that made them either satisfied or dissatisfied with their jobs. Herzberg found that dissatisfaction could be generally attributed to factors in the work environment. On the other hand, satisfaction could be attributed mainly to the nature of the work. On the basis of these results, Herzberg proposed his motivation-hygiene or two-factor theory.

Herzberg's study indicated a distinct difference between the work environment and the nature of the work-hence the term "two-factor." He found that individuals may be highly motivated by their work, but very dissatisfied with their organization.

The elements that caused people to feel dissatisfied with their jobs Herzberg labelled **hygiene factors**. They include quality of management, company policy, working conditions, wages and salary, status and job security. For example, hazardous

Hygiene factors are those factors that contribute to job dissatisfaction. They include quality of management, company policy, working conditions, wages and salary, status and job security.

FIGURE **6.2**

Employee job satisfaction and dissatisfaction: two views

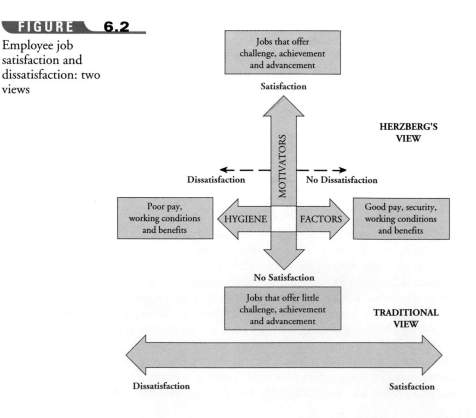

working conditions and low wages caused dissatisfaction. When these conditions were improved, workers were no longer dissatisfied, but they also did not have job satisfaction because Herzberg's hygiene factors do not act as strong motivators.

The positive satisfactions associated with the nature of the work Herzberg called **motivators**. These include responsibility, advancement, growth in the job, challenging work, recognition and achievement. Although motivators tend to make people satisfied with their work, their absence does not necessarily cause dissatisfaction with the organization.

Herzberg found that, in the case of **job satisfaction** at least, the opposite of satisfaction was not dissatisfaction, as was traditionally believed. Simply eliminating some of the dissatisfying characteristics of a person's job environment did not necessarily make that job more satisfying. Herzberg concluded that a dual continuum was involved—one for motivators and one for hygiene factors. The dotted line in Figure 6.3 indicates that motivators can be present whether hygiene factors are satisfactory or not.

What role does money play in job satisfaction? According to Herzberg, money is a hygiene factor. Employees who are not adequately paid may become extremely dissatisfied with the organization. They may, however, derive a high level of motivation from the job itself if it offers a feeling of importance and responsibility. On the other hand, employees who are highly motivated because of their jobs will not be motivated further by a higher salary or more fringe benefits.[5]

Figure 6.4 shows a comparison of Herzberg's two-factor theory and Maslow's hierarchy of needs. It is interesting to note that Herzberg's hygiene factors correspond to Maslow's physiological, safety and social needs, while his motivational factors correspond to Maslow's esteem and self-actualization needs.

Motivators are those factors that contribute to job satisfaction. They include responsibility, advancement, growth in the job, challenging work, recognition and achievement.

Job satisfaction stems from the total job situation. In addition to the work itself, factors involved in the total situation include pay and benefits, supervision, opportunities for promotion and relations with co-workers.

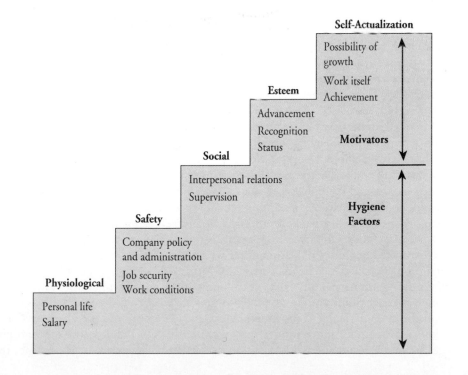

 **6.4**

Herzberg and Maslow: A comparison

Eight Ways to Improve Your Managerial Skills

www.smartbiz.com/sbs/arts/bly54.htm

McGregor's Theory X and Theory Y

In 1960, Douglas McGregor published a book entitled The Human Side of Enterprise[6] in which he proposed that the treatment of workers by managers is based on one of two sets of assumptions, which he labelled Theory X and Theory Y.

Theory X

1. The average person dislikes work and will avoid it whenever possible.

2. The average person has little ambition, shuns responsibility and prefers to be directed.

3. Therefore it is necessary to control employees through coercion and threats of punishment.

Theory Y

1. Work is as natural as play or rest; under proper conditions, people will not only accept responsibility, but actively seek it.

2. People committed to organizational objectives will exercise self-direction and self-control, and will find satisfaction in achieving the goals.

3. Commitment to organizational objectives is a function of the rewards associated with goal attainment.

4. Many people have the capacity to use creativity, imagination and ingenuity to solve organizational problems; unfortunately, the intellectual potential of the average human being is only partially utilized.

Individual leadership style and methods of motivating employees will obviously depend on the degree to which a manager subscribes to either set of assumptions. **Theory X managers** tend to be authoritarian leaders who establish tight controls to ensure that employees produce. Their motivational technique is a "carrot-and-stick" approach. Those employees who perform well are rewarded with more money, greater job security and other tangible rewards. Those who do not perform are threatened with the loss of these rewards, or perhaps the loss of their jobs. Theory X managers clearly believe that physiological and safety needs are the most important to their employees.

Theory Y managers focus on workers' needs. While they do not underestimate the importance of hygiene factors, they know that emphasis on lower-level needs will not motivate employees to do their best. Motivation can be accomplished only by encouraging employees to work towards satisfying their higher-level needs. Theory Y managers, then, give employees responsibility, allow them to use their creativity and ingenuity, and offer them the opportunity for advancement. Rather than establish tight controls over their performance and subject them to constant supervision, Theory Y managers allow their employees to exercise as much self-control as possible.

If we asked ourselves which manager we would prefer to work for, most of us would probably choose a Theory Y manager. But it is important to keep in mind the realities of organizational life. First, not all individuals are able to control and direct themselves easily. Some employees prefer to do only what they are told, with as little responsibility as possible. Many individuals want job security above all else. While workers might prefer more interesting jobs, many would choose to receive high wages for more mundane work, satisfying their higher-level needs off the job, in

Theory X managers contend that people dislike work, engage in it only to sustain themselves and avoid it whenever possible.

Theory Y managers contend that the expenditure of physical and mental effort is as natural as work and play, and that people will work to achieve job objectives if they are properly rewarded.

Theory X and Theory Y

www.accel-team.com/human_relations/hrels_03_mcgregor.html

< According to McGregor, Theory X managers establish tight controls over employees, while Theory Y managers focus on workers' needs

outside organizations or the pursuit of hobbies. Moreover, many jobs are by nature tedious, and there may be little management can do to make them more interesting for employees.

Thus, while managers may prefer to apply Theory Y assumptions when dealing with their employees, they should not ignore the above factors. Unfortunately, evidence suggests that many managers underrate their employees, tending toward the

ISSUE

Money, Recognition and Other Rewards

Is money the only motivator? Or even the most effective motivator? Some researchers have found that money does not seem to significantly motivate individuals to improve performance until it exceeds 20% of base pay. Obviously this would be a tremendously expensive approach for most organizations. The pay cheque, as a motivating factor, can be ranked as low as eleventh by employees, following such items as recognition, open communications, ability to challenge status quo and opportunity for personal growth. Recognition can be extremely important to employees and can include a combination of recognition by both peers and superiors, recognition in the form of some physical symbol (plaques, certificates) and recognition in the form of a **significant** monetary reward.[7] Another popular incentive is increased vacation time. This incentive has been reported to reduce absenteeism and increase performance prior to the time off. Given the incredible costs involved to effectively motivate with cash, perhaps increased vacation time is a viable option provided that the employee does not need to be replaced by a casual worker during his or her absence. Other possible motivators include increased pension contribution, increased health care options and provision of child care.[8] Having motivated and productive employees can lead to increased sales, reduced absenteeism, lower costs and creative thinking, to name just a few of the benefits.

Theory X approach. They use minutely detailed job descriptions and work assignments, and have carried work specialization to the point where jobs are nothing more than boring, unchallenging routines. Some organizations allow employees little control over their work environment, which makes them passive and gives them little incentive to assume responsibility for achieving organizational goals.[9]

Leadership

Theory X and Theory Y indicate two opposing views of employees. The view managers hold will influence their methods of motivation and their leadership style.

Leadership is the process of directing and influencing people to channel their efforts toward specific goals. Although this definition is straightforward, effective leadership is often difficult to achieve. Should managers be authoritarian, telling their people exactly what to do? Or should they ask employees for their opinions and suggestions? Should they maintain a forceful image and keep their distance from employees? Or should they make an effort to be part of the group? If they do, will employees lose respect for them? To understand leadership, we must examine some of the major theories that have been proposed.

Theories of Leadership

It was long believed that successful leaders possessed certain personal characteristics—intelligence, courage, leadership—that distinguished them from followers. Yet out of the many studies on leadership, no single set of specific **leadership traits** has emerged. Researchers have therefore concluded that specific personal traits represent only one factor in the leadership phenomenon; the situation in which the individual functions presents other factors. Situational factors include the nature of the work; the expectations, needs and attitudes of the followers; and the general environment in which all are operating.

Managerial Grid: A Behavioural Theory

Unable to isolate any specific traits that contributed to effective leadership, researchers began to wonder whether certain types of behaviour might be responsible for making some managers more effective leaders than others. Perhaps there was an optimum method of motivating employees, delegating tasks and communicating with subordinate managers—one method that would best achieve the goals of the organization. If so, this kind of behaviour, unlike traits, could be learned.

After conducting a number of studies, researchers discovered two general leadership styles, which were labelled as "task-oriented" and "people-oriented." A **task-oriented leader** is primarily concerned with getting the job done in the most efficient manner, and will therefore arrange working conditions so as to minimize interference by the human element. The **people-oriented leader**, on the other hand, pays careful attention to the human need for satisfying relationships, in the hope that a comfortable, friendly organization will achieve the best results.

These two leadership styles were used by Robert Blake and Jane Mouton to develop what they called the managerial grid shown in Figure 6.5.[10] The horizontal axis indicates the task-oriented style of management; the vertical axis indicates the people-oriented style. Each dimension is then divided into nine parts, from low concern to high, providing a total of 81 different leadership styles. While it would be impractical to describe each of them in detail, five main styles can be readily identified.

Leadership is the process of directing and influencing people to channel their efforts toward specific goals.

Leadership traits—the theory that successful leaders possess certain personal characteristics-intelligence, courage, leadership-that distinguish them from followers.

Task-oriented leader—a leader who is primarily concerned with getting the job done in the most efficient manner, and who will therefore arrange working conditions so as to minimize interference by the human element.

People-oriented leader—a leader who pays careful attention to the human need for satisfying relationships, in the hope that a comfortable, friendly organization will achieve the best results.

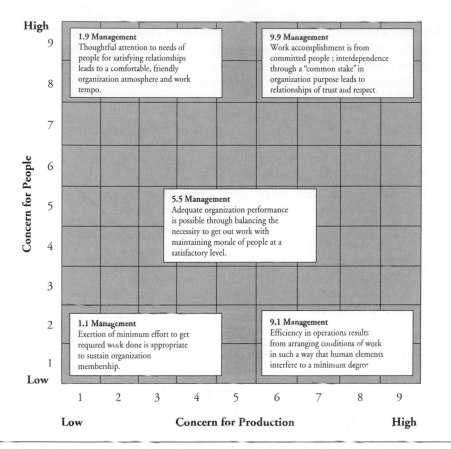

SOURCE: Reprinted by permission of *Harvard Business Review*. An exhibit from "Break-through in organization development" by Robert R. Blake, Jane S. Mouton, Louis B. Barnes and Larry E. Greiner (November-December 1964). 1964 by the President and Fellows of Harvard College; all rights reserved.

FIGURE 6.5

The managerial grid

1. *Style 1.1.* Impoverished management— little concern for either production or people is shown. Little is accomplished, since there is no direction and all employees can do as they please.

2. *Style 9.1.* Task-oriented leadership—the accomplishment of the job is the only concern, regardless of the consequences for employees.

3. *Style 5.5.* Middle-of-the-road management—people and production are equally important.

4. *Style 1.9.* Country-club management—leaders are primarily interested in being liked by their followers; accomplishing the job is of secondary concern.

5. *Style 9.9.* Followers trust the leader and are committed to getting the job done because they feel they have a stake in the organization.

The **managerial grid** indicates how a more balanced approach between the two extremes of task- and people-oriented management can make leadership more effective. Blake and Mouton insist that a 9.9 style of management will result in improved employee performance, lower absenteeism and turnover, and high employee satisfaction, regardless of the situation. However, other researchers believe that situational factors are as important as any given style of management in determining a leader's effectiveness.

Managerial grid identifies various ways in which managers provide leadership based on different combinations of two leadership styles-task-oriented and people-oriented.

The Leadership Continuum: A Situational Approach to Leadership

Leadership continuum identifies various leadership approaches, the selection of which depends on how a manager is influenced by his or her background, knowledge and experience; the characteristics of subordinates; and the general situation in the workplace.

Researchers Robert Tannenbaum and Warren Schmidt used a **leadership continuum**, shown in Figure 6.6, to classify leadership according to the proportions of authority and freedom involved.[11] In effect, the classification is similar to the task- or people-oriented distinction.

Managers can choose various styles of leadership that lie between the extremes of authority and freedom. Their choice will ultimately depend on three sets of forces:

1. *Forces within the manager*—personal values, knowledge, or experience.

2. *Forces within the subordinates*—their knowledge and experience vis-a-vis the job they are doing; their interest in taking responsibility and making decisions; their desire for independence and freedom of action.

3. *Forces in the situation*—the nature of the work, the pressure of time and the clarity of goals and objectives. An important factor is the general climate within the organization, which is a reflection of how upper management believes the firm should be run.

According to Tannenbaum and Schmidt, the most important factor in choosing a leadership style is that it be appropriate to the situation. There is no single optimum style; an effective leader is flexible, capable of adapting to any situation.

FIGURE 6.6

Leadership behaviour continuum

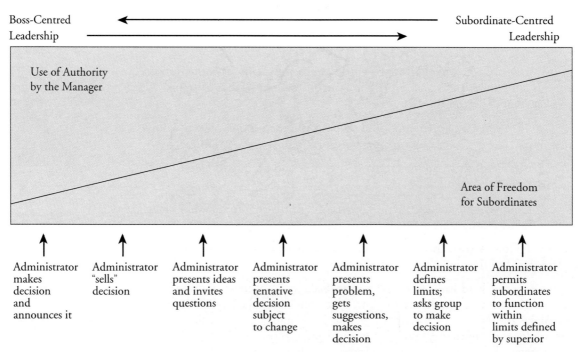

SOURCE: Reprinted by permission of *Harvard Business Review*. An exhibit from "How to choose a leadership pattern" by Robert Tannenbaum and Warren H. Schmidt (May-June 1973). 1973 by the President and Fellows of Harvard College; all rights reserved.

Fiedler's Contingency Theory

Research seems to suggest that managers should adopt a leadership style appropriate to the situation. Managers should be trained, then, to become both task- and people-oriented. However, one leadership researcher, Fred Fiedler, believes that it is difficult, if not impossible, for a manager to change his or her personality and leadership style to suit a situation.[12] Even if some change could be brought about, it would be a slow process and its effectiveness could not be guaranteed. Rather, Fiedler recommends either changing the leadership situation itself or choosing a manager with the appropriate leadership style for a particular situation. In essence, he believes that any managerial leadership style can be effective in the right situation.

To prove his situational or **contingency theory of leadership**, Fiedler examined many work situations. He identified three key variables that would define a particular leadership situation:

1. *Leader-member relation*-indicates how well leaders are accepted, trusted and respected by followers.

2. *Task structure*-identifies how specifically the followers' tasks are laid out.

3. *Position power*-indicates the formal power that the leader has in the organization and how it can be used to gain employees' compliance.

These three variables can be combined into the eight possible situations shown in Figure 6.7. Leader-member relations can be either good or bad, tasks can be either structured or unstructured, and the leader's position power can be either strong or weak.

Having identified the possible situations, Fiedler then surveyed the leaders of more than 800 work groups to determine whether they were task-oriented or people-oriented. He then classified their leadership situation according to the eight possibilities and attempted to identify which type of leader was most effective in each situation.

> **Contingency theory of leadership** states that any leadership style can be effective if used in the appropriate situation.

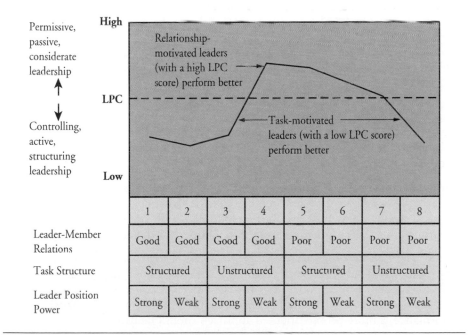

SOURCE: Adapted from Fred E. Fiedler and Martin M. Chemers, Leadership and Effective Management (Glenview, Ill.: Scott, Foresman, 1974): 80. Reprinted by permission of Fred E. Fiedler.

FIGURE 6.7

How the style of effective leadership varies with the situation

As Figure 6.7 indicates, Fiedler found that task-oriented leaders were most effective in situations 1, 2, 3 and 8, where they had either great or minimal power and influence. People-oriented leaders were most effective in situations 4, 5, 6 and 7, where they had moderate or little influence and power.

The Path-Goal Theory

Path-goal theory of leadership requires that the leader clarify for subordinates how they can achieve high performance and reap the rewards associated with that performance.

According to the **path-goal theory of leadership**,[13] the leader must decide on the leadership style that will most effectively motivate employees to achieve organizational goals. Since leaders have defined the organization's goals, they can communicate to subordinates what must be done and then reward good performance. The path-goal theory attempts to predict how different types of rewards and leadership styles affect the motivation, performance and satisfaction of employees and subordinate managers.

A people-oriented manager, for example, offers not only pay and promotion as rewards, but also support, encouragement, security and respect. He or she is also sensitive to the fact that different individuals have different needs and desires, and therefore tailors rewards to particular individuals. In comparison, a task-oriented manager emphasizes rewards and performance by clarifying the level of performance that must be attained to gain salary increases, bonuses and promotions. He or she offers a more limited, less individualized set of rewards.

An organization's environmental factors can also influence motivation. These factors include the type of task the subordinate must perform, the organization's formal authority system and the subordinate's work group. Thus, a manager's leadership style should either complement or compensate for the deficiencies in the work environment. For example, if a task is repetitive and the employee knows exactly what to do, then a manager who places too much emphasis on directing the employee is using an inappropriate style.

The Situational Theory of Leadership

Situational theory of leadership describes how managers should adjust their leadership style as their employees show a greater desire for achievement and responsibility, and gain greater experience in performing their jobs.

According to the **situational theory of leadership** developed by Paul Hersey and Kenneth H. Blanchard,[14] a manager must evaluate the development of his or her subordinate before deciding on the appropriate leadership style. Development in this instance does not mean age and emotional stability, but rather refers to an individual's desire for achievement, willingness to accept responsibility and past work experience.

Figure 6.8 shows that the relationship between a manager and subordinate changes as the subordinate develops. The level of development is indicated by the horizontal line along the bottom of the diagram. The leadership style a manager should use is determined by drawing a line straight up from a point on the development line to intersect the curve.

PHASE I: High task-low relationship   When employees first join an organization, they usually need direction and require specific instructions as to what they are supposed to do. They must also become familiar with the organization's policies and procedures. A task-oriented leadership approach is therefore most appropriate.

PHASE II: High task-high relationship   The task-oriented leadership style remains important even as subordinates are learning their jobs, as long as they are not willing or able to accept full responsibility for their performance. Nevertheless, as the manager becomes more familiar with subordinates and puts more trust in their performance, a more people-oriented approach should be used.

PHASE III: Low task-high relationship   As the subordinates' abilities and performance become more evident, and as experience increases and subordinates

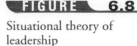

FIGURE **6.8**

Situational theory of
leadership

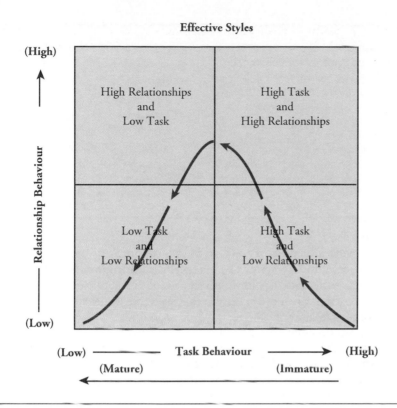

Effective Styles

SOURCE: James A. F. Stoner, *Management*, 2nd ed (Englewood Cliffs, N.J.: Prentice-Hall, 1982): 487. Adapted
from Paul Hersey and Kenneth Blanchard, *Management of Organizational Behavior: Utilizing Human Resources*,
3rd ed. (Englewood Cliffs, N.J.: Prentice-Hall 1979): 165. Reprinted by permission of Prentice-Hall.

actively seek greater responsibility, the manager can relax the close direction—task-
oriented style—of the previous two stages. However, the manager should continue
to be supportive and encourage subordinates to take on greater responsibility.

PHASE IV: Low task-low relationship   Once subordinates have reached the point
at which they are self-directing, confident and experienced in their jobs, the manager
can reduce the amount of support and encouragement previously provided.
Subordinates are now on their own and no longer need or want a directive relationship
with their manager.

Matching the Leadership Style with the Situation

What do Fiedler's leadership theory, the path-goal theory and the situational theory
tell us about the effectiveness of a particular leadership style? All three are contingency
theories that attempt to identify the appropriate leadership style based on the existing
situation. They indicate that any leadership style can be effective if used in the
appropriate situation. But there are differences. According to Fiedler's contingency
theory, leadership styles are relatively fixed and individuals have difficulty adapting
to a new leadership style, if and when required. Therefore, leaders should be chosen
by matching their leadership style with that required by a particular situation.

On the other hand, the situational theory suggests that individuals can indeed
change their leadership style, and should do so as their subordinates become more

Visionary Leadership

In the case of visionary leadership, leaders create positive future visions and transmit these effectively to the employees. Some indications of visioning ability in a leader include future time perspective and a positive outlook, which suggests that some leaders may be naturally more inclined than others to be visionary. However, vision training programs can also help.[15] The top leadership competency identified by a panel of leaders when asked to look five to ten years into the future was the ability to create a shared vision. This competency embodies many aspects of visionary leadership including:

- *communicating* the vision to the organization
- *empowering* employees to achieve the vision
- *inspiring* employees to commit to the vision
- *developing* strategy to achieve the vision
- *encouraging* participation in decision making to achieve vision[16]

Visionary leadership could have a profound impact on management practice in the 21st century as managers lead their organizations and members with vision and strategic insight.

familiar with their job and take on greater responsibility. The path-goal theory links motivation and leadership style. The manager's most important task is to analyze the factors that either enhance or diminish the subordinate's level of motivation in a particular situation. Then the manager can choose the leadership style that provides the highest possible level of motivation.

Criteria for Choosing Leaders

Given the complexity of the leadership phenomenon, organizations must become more sophisticated in their selection of managers. When a management position becomes available, the leadership style required for that situation should be identified. Only those individuals with either the appropriate leadership style or the ability to be flexible in adopting a particular leadership style should be considered. Such individuals can be identified beforehand through tests and questionnaires, or through observation of their reactions to various simulated leadership situations.

According to Fiedler, the organization can thus match a manager's leadership style to the situation rather than attempt to change an individual's style through leadership training. The success of the latter approach is doubtful, he says, due to the time required to change a person's attitude. While training may expose managers to alternative leadership styles and thereby make them more aware of their own leadership behaviour, research has failed to show that training leads to any significant, long-term change in leadership behaviour and effectiveness. Furthermore, training often lasts only a few days, after which managers return to their previous environment. Since there has been no change in the environment or situation, the manager is likely to revert to his or her original leadership style.

Promotions within an organization can also cause leadership problems. Promotions are often based on an individual's performance in a particular operating position. Thus, good workers are promoted to supervisors, good salespeople to sales managers, good accountants to controllers and good teachers to principals. But good operating personnel do not necessarily make good leaders. A good "doer" is not necessarily a good manager, since the tasks are different. Similarly, managers who are promoted may find that their leadership styles are not appropriate to new situations. An organization may thus lose an effective worker or manager in one job, only to gain an ineffective worker in another.

Obviously, some managers will have less difficulty than others adjusting to situations that require different leadership styles. Flexibility is important for the path-goal and life-cycle theories of leadership. When necessary, managers must attempt to change their leadership style if they experience a situation in which their subordinates clearly do not perform and are uncooperative. In these instances, leadership training can be helpful in that it makes individuals aware of the meaning of leadership and gives them the ability to diagnose problems in a leadership situation. They can then alter their leadership style as necessary.

Japanese Management Techniques

Japanese companies have been particularly successful in marketing their products internationally. Their automobiles, cameras, stereo and video equipment have gained an excellent reputation for quality and value. The phenomenal growth of Japanese industry and Japanese technological advances has been studied extensively. A major factor contributing to the success of Japanese companies appears to be the relationship between companies and their employees.

Theory Z

What is the relationship between Japanese employees and their companies? In *Theory Z: How American Business Can Meet the Japanese Challenge,* William G. Ouchi explains the meaning of **Theory Z**. In contrast to McGregor's Theory X and Theory Y, type-Z organizations are characterized by lifetime employment, extensive training and development programs, frequent and clear performance reviews, less formal control systems and slower promotion. Instead of relying solely on modern management information systems, formal planning, management by objectives and quantitative techniques, more emphasis is placed on judgments based on experience, with decision making taking into consideration the entire organization and the long-term view.

Theory Z is a management style that emphasizes individual responsibility, open communication, and decision making as a participatory activity for more employees.

Individual responsibility is emphasized as management constantly seeks to build greater trust between individual and company. Open communication is encouraged, and employees participate frequently in decision making. The company's influence does not stop when the workday is finished but extends to the family and social life of individual employees.[17]

Entering the 21st century, the pillars of Japanese management systems remain the same: lifetime employment, promotion by seniority and consensus decision making. The system received much attention in the past due to the fact that Japan's major exporters, automotive manufacturers and consumer-electronics manufacturers adhered to the system. These companies included up to 30% of the working population but due to their high profile it was often assumed that all Japanese companies adopted the Japanese management system. Today, with a different economic environment to deal with, Japanese management may see a new evolution. The current environment includes an unstable yen, increased internal competition within Japan, increased competition from Asian neighbours and the high cost of doing business in Japan. Given this new and ever-changing environment, Japan industry leaders are faced with major management challenges such as:

1. An expensive seniority system

2. Rising unemployment

3. Lack of individual initiative

4. Hierarchical, inflexible structures

5. Lack of creativity

Considering what we have learned thus far concerning the new global marketplace, it is evident that the key factors of flexibility, adaptability, creativity and innovation must be addressed in order for Japan to remain competitive in the future. An interesting fact that may contribute to Japan's problems in the 21st century is that there is very little entrepreneurship in Japan. Top students still believe that the best career path is to join a large established organization. Given the lack of flexible, speedy decision making, individual initiative, and creativity in the Japanese system, changes are necessary. One such change is the implementation of a philosophy known as management by objectives (MBO).

MBO is discussed in detail later in the chapter but basically involves participative goal setting, a previously unknown concept in Japanese management. Another approach involves attempting to provide an environment conducive to creativity. Also, increased emphasis on the best deal rather than the best relationship is evolving between buyers and sellers. A combination of the best elements of western and Japanese management along with the dedication of Japanese employees may lead to Japan once again becoming a major global competitor with increased white-collar productivity.[18]

Communication

Clearly, no organization could function without communication. Goals, objectives and plans developed at the top must be communicated to lower levels of management for implementation, and eventually to employees. The control process also depends on communication. Information must be gathered from actual operations and passed on to managers for evaluation. Thus, managers can perform their duties as coordinators only through communication with others in the organization.

Problems with Communication

The communication process consists of three basic elements: a sender, a message and a receiver. A failure in any one of these elements can cause poor communication.

A model of the **communication process** is shown in Figure 6.9. The sender who initiates the communication must have the skill to translate his or her wishes, needs and desires into a verbal or written message that the receiver can understand and use to reconstruct the sender's ideas. If communication is face-to-face, the sender may use words, actions, gestures and other body actions to transmit the message. Even so, the receiver may misinterpret the sender's actions, words or expressions, resulting in failed communication. If the receiver concentrates on the sender's facial expressions rather than on the spoken word, for example, the message that he or she receives may be entirely different from the one intended.

The chances of misunderstanding or misinterpretation are even greater in written communication. When the sender is not present, the receiver cannot rely on gestures or facial expressions to clarify the message; nor can the receiver check his or her interpretation by asking questions. With no opportunity for feedback, a message can easily be misunderstood.

Poor communication is not the fault of the sender alone; the receiver is often equally to blame. For example, one of the major reasons for poor communication is failure to listen. This is partly due to simple physical limitations in human beings. While an average person may speak at the rate of only about 150 words per minute, his or her listening capacity may be 900 words per minute. As a result, the listener may become bored and "tune out" the speaker, especially if the listener is preoccupied with other issues.

Communication process refers to the process by which the sender who initiates the communication must translate his or her wishes, needs and desires into a verbal or written message that the receiver can understand and use to reconstruct the sender's ideas.

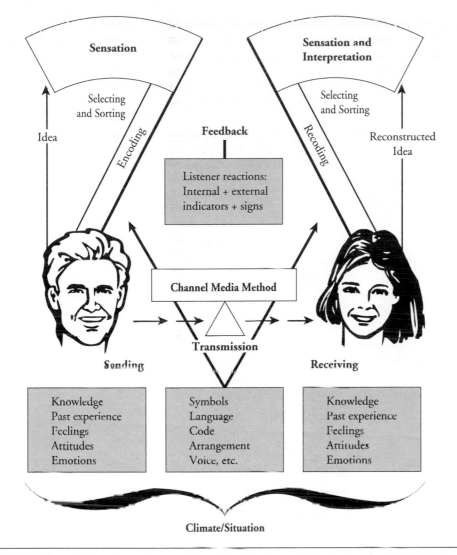

SOURCE: Raymond S. Ross, *Speech Communications,* 5th ed. (Englewood Cliffs, N.J.: Prentice-Hall, 1980): 14. Reprinted by permission of Prentice-Hall.

Overcoming Barriers to Effective Communication

Difficult as communication is, however, some of the barriers can be overcome. Three techniques are particularly effective: feedback, repetition of the message and the use of simple language.

As shown in Figure 6.9, feedback is the reaction of the listener to the sender's message. Visible reactions, such as a raised eyebrow, a puzzled look, anger and so on, tell the sender whether the message was understood as he or she intended. If these reactions are contrary to what the sender feels they should be, he or she can restate the message and clarify any misunderstandings. *Feedback* can be used in both written and oral communication. Teachers, for example, receive feedback from their students through written examinations that indicate whether they have understood the material.

Another way to ensure better communication is to *repeat the message as often as possible* using different methods and media. Advertisers use television, radio and newspapers; teachers use lectures, films, videotapes and guest lecturers. A manager may announce a change in policy by communicating it orally to his or her employees, and then back it up with a written memo to be read at leisure.

Finally, *language must be simple* and easily understood. The message should be as brief as possible, and it must be written or spoken clearly. Multi-syllabic words do not impress readers, who may have trouble understanding them. A two-page memo that could be reduced to a few sentences may be more confusing than helpful. Moreover, readers tend to shun lengthy communications. Busy people may only skim a long memo, missing the important points it was intended to convey, or they may simply put it aside for another time. In either case, the communication will have been ineffective.

Improving Listening Skills

Poor communication can also be due to poor listening habits on the part of the receiver. People hear on average 600 words per minute but even the fastest talker can only manage 100 to 150 words per minute. So, what are we doing during the gap between hearing and speaking? We are probably letting our minds wander to other topics, perhaps related, perhaps not. To become better listeners, we must first understand the barriers to effective communication which have already been discussed. Through this understanding we can move on to improving our listening skills.[19]

Techniques for improving listening skills include:

1. *Attending.* Prepare yourself physically and mentally.
2. *Offering appropriate silences.* Wait until you are sure the speaker is finished before you comment.
3. *Making supportive statements.* Acknowledge the speaker both verbally ("Yes, I see,") or non-verbally (nodding).
4. *Asking questions.* Ask *relevant* questions.
5. *Rephrasing.* Repeat what the speaker has said in your own words.
6. *Expressing empathy.* Try to understand where the speaker is coming from.
7. *Sharing experiences.* Briefly relate similar experiences to show empathy.
8. *Labelling conflicts.* Clear the air by ensuring what the speaker says is what they mean in accordance with the tone of the message.[20]

E-mail and Communicating in the 21st Century

Effective communication has always been critical to an organization's success. However, with the huge amounts of information bombarding us today it is even more difficult for organizations to ensure that employees receive the information they need to do their jobs. Due to this "information overload," critical information may be lost or not given the proper attention due to skimming and ineffectual information sorting techniques. In a recent study of 900 organizations, e-mail was cited as the most frequently used medium for employee communication (90%). Yet, even though e-mail was the most popular choice, it was not the most effective; the study showed that ongoing publications are the most effective method (70%)

followed by group meetings (60%).[21] Key components of an effective communication system include the following:

1. Feedback
2. Use of repetition
3. Active listening

E-mail often does not include a feedback component. Use of repetition in e-mail is likely to be ineffective since the recipient may ignore subsequent messages, believing that they have been re-sent in error. As a result, the sender of the message cannot assume that the message was understood by the recipient as the sender intended. Active listening that includes listening for content and feeling and recognizing both verbal and non-verbal information, often requires face-to-face communication.

E-mail is sometimes misused in organizations. For example, the following list provides guidelines for using e-mail appropriately:

1. Do not attempt to solve employee problems through e-mail.
2. Do not confront an employee using e-mail.
3. Do not use e-mail to "pass the buck."
4. Use e-mail to take responsibility—not to cover your tracks.
5. When appropriate, use hard copy as a follow-up to an e-mail message.

E-mail provides management with a powerful tool that sets the stage for a virtual environment that excels in the straightforward and wide distribution of vast amounts of information, leading to greater flexibility in information management. However, corporate guidelines outlining the appropriate use of e-mail may be necessary to assist the transition to this environment.[22]

Morale

Morale is the mental attitude of employees toward their jobs and their organization. Employees will be cheerful and enthusiastic if they believe in what the organization is doing, if they think the work they are doing is contributing to those objectives and if their jobs also contribute to their personal goals. When employees view the organization as providing them with satisfaction, results are likely to include low employee turnover and absenteeism, few grievances, improved productivity and greater individual interest in reducing waste.

But what can managers do to ensure that their employees' morale is high? If management waits until grumbling starts, it may already be too late and valuable employees may have one foot out the door. Some ways to boost morale include the following:

1. Commit budget funds to morale boosters.
2. Develop an ongoing plan.
3. Get to know your people.
4. Find out what employees value as a morale booster.
5. Don't overlook less expensive options such as spot bonuses, lunch on the house or an afternoon off.

Morale is the mental attitude of employees toward their jobs and their organization.

Morale and the Bottom Line

www.toolkit.cch.com/text/ P05_7105.asp

Getting the Message: How to Make Sure You're Understood

To do their job, managers must constantly communicate ideas, information and instructions—and be understood. For many of them, that's a daily exercise in frustration. Language and its precise use are the hurdles that trip them up.

Examine 400 common words in a dictionary and you'll discover more than 14 000 meanings—about 35 per word. Yet as a manager, you must select from this jungle of confusion words to which the receiver ascribes the exact meaning or interpretations you intended.

The odds of this happening are astronomical.

Experts define communications as: "The transmission and reception of messages." They define management communications as: "The transmission and reception of messages having the objective of achieving desired results through people." They define effective management communications as: "The transmission and reception of messages that succeed in persuading people to act as the communicator wants them to act-and like it."

Clear? Yes. Easy? No. But here are a few suggestions that'll help.

- *Think it out before you speak.*
  Decide what you want to achieve before you put your tongue in gear. Clarify the objective. It takes time, but the offspring of a pregnant silence is often comprehension.

- *Get their attention.*
  You don't need a sledgehammer. A creative approach, a stated benefit, an expression of appreciation, use of a name, a pithy question, a little excitement, a smile-they're all attention grabbers.

- *Remember Murphy's Law of Communications.*
  Whenever you communicate, you automatically deal with partial information, inaccurate interpretations and inaccurate assumptions. Therefore, make it simple and specific. Use the listener's language, not your own. You don't wear your tuxedo to a barn dance; don't wear your graduation gown to the office.

- *Don't assume you are understood.*
  Get feedback. Listen to the response. Watch the reaction. Ask questions. You won't insult the receiver's intelligence and you'll guarantee comprehension.

- *Check the communication environment.*
  If the communication is private, make it so. Is it

the right time? Are you in tune with custom and tradition? Is it the right place—should you be yelling to compete with the noise?

- *Think in terms of "you" and "your."*
  Speak or write in terms of the benefits to be enjoyed by the listener or reader. Find out his or her wants and show how they can be obtained by what you are saying or writing. Next to one's own name, the word "reward" is the dictionary's best.

- *If you want understanding, have empathy.*
  Put yourself in your listener's place. How will your message sound to him or her? Would you understand it? Accept it? Reject it? All of these are simple suggestions, but they make good common sense.

Still, if you don't have the following six skills, you're in trouble in any management function:

- *Telling:* There's a 3-C formula—clear, concise, cogent. Simple words, few of them, expressed with impact. Remember, however, this is one-way communication; it lacks feedback.

- *Asking:* This is management's responsibility. It clarifies, complements, produces ideas, advice and action, and shows recognition of the receiver's importance.

- *Listening:* Study listening skills. You'll be astonished. It's 45% of the communication equation, but you'll search a long time to find a college or university that teaches it. Attend a listening-skills seminar.

- *Observing:* Observe reaction, behaviour, commitment. You'll get the feedback you need to check understanding levels. Use all five senses and don't hesitate or apologize. Your career could depend on it.

- *Understanding:* Perceiving is one thing; understanding what you perceive is another. It occurs only when you correctly interpret the meaning of what you perceive. That may occur after perception, after your mind has processed the information perceived. Whether instantaneous or delayed, it simply must be present before the communication becomes effective.

- *Convincing:* Sincerity underpins conviction. It means believing in the truth of what you are saying or writing. It's aided by enthusiasm and by the action you take to prove your own conviction.

SOURCE: Gordon A. Shave, "Getting the message: how to make sure you're understood," *The Financial Post* (July 21, 1979). Reprinted by permission of the author.

Factors in morale as ranked by managers and employees

TABLE 6.1

Morale Factor	Management Ranking	Employee Ranking
Good wages	1	5
Job security	2	4
Promotion and growth with company	3	7
Good working conditions	4	9
Interesting work	5	6
Management loyalty to workers	6	8
Tactful disciplining	7	10
Full appreciation for work done	8	1
Sympathetic understanding of personal problems	9	3
Feeling "in on" things	10	2

SOURCE: Adapted from Paul Hersey and Kenneth H. Blanchard, "What's missing in MBO?" *Management Review* (October 1974).

6. Designate an employee advocate.

7. Communicate, don't just act.

8. Follow through on all promises.[23]

One study found that management and workers had to rate the various factors that can contribute to high morale (see Table 6.1). The comparison showed that managers generally view the satisfaction of employees' lower-level needs as contributing to high morale, while employees tend to cite higher-level needs.

Morale, Job Satisfaction and Productivity

Clearly, it is in the best interest of any organization to ensure that employees' morale is high, to reduce behaviour (turnover, absenteeism, tardiness, waste) that is detrimental to the achievement of organizational goals and objectives. High morale develops when employees receive satisfaction from their total job situation. In addition to the work itself, factors involved in the total situation include pay and benefits, supervision, opportunities for promotion, and relations with co-workers. Employee satisfaction may result from any of these factors, alone or in combination.

Thus, there is a definite positive correlation between job satisfaction and morale. Does the same kind of relationship exist between job satisfaction and productivity or performance? Traditionally, managers believed that rewards such as pay and benefits or good working conditions would give employees satisfaction, which in turn would improve performance and productivity. Many managers today still subscribe to this view, and indeed it seems plausible that a happy employee should also be a productive one. In the late 1960s, however, a different view was proposed—namely, that high performance leads to rewards that in turn result in a certain level of employee satisfaction. These rewards can be either intrinsic or extrinsic. **Intrinsic rewards** include a sense of accomplishment from a job and increased self-esteem. In effect, they are like a pat on the back for a job well done. **Extrinsic rewards**, on the other hand, are based on the individual's performance as evaluated by superiors or group members, and may include bonuses, salary increases or promotions.

Intrinsic rewards include the sense of accomplishment and increased self-esteem that individuals desire from their jobs.

Extrinsic rewards are based on the individual's performance as evaluated by superiors or group members, and may include bonuses, salary increases or promotions.

Building Morale in Tough Times

When times are tough, building morale is even more crucial. Since morale depends on many factors other than pay, it can be nurtured even during downsizing and mergers. During mergers, it is common for employees to be left out of the communication loop, which leads to a significant drop in morale. Employees feel uncertain about their jobs and their future with the company. Yet, companies such as Boeing, Exxon, and Seagram's have all managed to conduct major downsizing while still maintaining worker morale. How did they do it? Through a combination of communication benefits and company activities. Other companies experiencing layoffs have also managed to successfully maintain high levels of morale. Some of their strategies are listed below.

1. Creation of a new employee orientation program.

2. Formation of "morale committees" that are responsible for developing programs such as awards and work citations, education programs and "fun" activities.

3. Communication of a vision of corporate goals and empowerment of remaining employees to achieve the vision.

4. Creation of a learning environment to help offset the stress of increased workloads.

5. Establishment of trust between management and workers. Since perceived breach of trust is one of the main causes of decreased morale, it is critical to re-establish the bond.[24]

To re-establish morale, management must be prepared to keep promises, communicate openly and honestly, and involve employees in solving problems. Failure to reach these goals can result in the loss of the remaining employees.

Some research studies, however, have indicated that rewards may lead to both performance and job satisfaction; furthermore, future performance may depend on how current performance is rewarded. In other words, an employee will repeat the kind of performance that is rewarded, regardless of whether it is high or low. The implications for management are great. If managers continue to reward individuals with the aim of making them satisfied employees, then they will be likely to reward low performers and high performers more or less equally. Thus, if a low performer is rewarded, he or she will continue to perform poorly. As high performers will tend

FIGURE 6.10

Job performance, rewards and job satisfaction

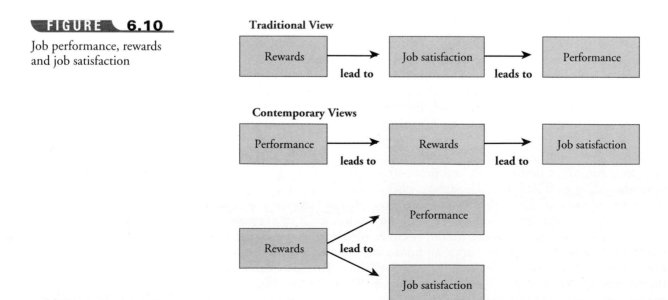

to see this practice as inequitable, they will eventually either reduce their own performance or seek more satisfying employment elsewhere. The various views of the relationship between job performance, rewards and job satisfaction are shown in Figure 6.10.

Redesigning Work

Artists and craftspeople take great satisfaction in their work because they enjoy what they are doing and because they have total control over their actions. Their entire effort is concentrated on producing a finished product. However, many jobs in industry allow workers neither freedom of action nor the satisfaction of creating a finished product. Most jobs, both white-collar and industrial, are boring and repetitious. They offer only those rewards that satisfy lower-level needs: higher wages, fringe benefits and job security. Any satisfaction of higher-level needs can stem only from outside the organization.

Many organizations have recognized the problem of job boredom and its associated costs, both to the employees and the organization. As a result, some companies are trying to do something about it by **redesigning work**.

Redesigning work is undertaken to reduce the boredom associated with routine and repetitive work and thereby eliminate alienation, absenteeism and high turnover.

Management by Objectives

Job dissatisfaction affects managers as well as clerical and blue-collar workers. Although managers may have a better perspective than other employees on the organization's direction and objectives, they often experience conflicts between their personal goals and those of the organization. They may become frustrated when their own ideas are not implemented or when their needs are left unsatisfied.

In an attempt to reduce management dissatisfaction and raise low morale, the concept of **management by objectives (MBO)** became popular in the late 1950s. MBO allows managers and other employees to set their specific job goals in line with the overall goals and objectives of the organization.

Management by objectives (MBO) allows managers and other employees to jointly set their specific job goals in line with the overall goals and objectives of the organization

---

With its Wisconsin door plant floundering, Weyerhauser decided to try intranet technology as a last-ditch effort to save the plant. Skyrocketing costs, slumping sales and low morale had all combined to create what Weyerhauser V.P. Jerry Manigel referred to as a "dead dog of a plant." The situation deteriorated to the point where the plant was operating at half capacity. A new management team decided to install a state-of-the-art in-house communication network to compare prices and track orders and deliveries. Since its implementation in late 1995, the system, known as Door Builder, has helped to double production and improve delivery service to customers. The intranets link workers to databases of information such as factory-floor operations, supplier inventory, price lists and order taking. For example, the task of order taking had historically been a complex job as each door is custom-built according to

two million different configurations. Yet, the company was buried in information and this area had become a bottleneck. Door Builder can now sort through the information in seconds and customers tied in to the Weyerhauser system can submit their own orders. The system results in fewer errors, less haggling, the elimination of guesswork and favoritism and the refusal of orders that had been costing the company money. Many of Weyerhauser's distributors have a direct link to Door Builder with a dedicated phone line and trained in-house order-placers. The return on their investment includes on-time deliveries, which are a critical component on the success formula for the distributors. The Weyerhauser example suggests that even the most unlikely candidates can benefit from new communication technology and suggests that those who do not get on board will probably be left in the dust.[25]

Weyerhauser's Intranet System Opens the Door to Profits

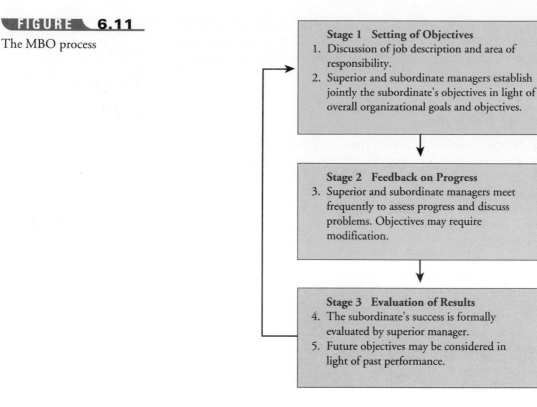

FIGURE 6.11

The MBO process

Stage 1 Setting of Objectives
1. Discussion of job description and area of responsibility.
2. Superior and subordinate managers establish jointly the subordinate's objectives in light of overall organizational goals and objectives.

Stage 2 Feedback on Progress
3. Superior and subordinate managers meet frequently to assess progress and discuss problems. Objectives may require modification.

Stage 3 Evaluation of Results
4. The subordinate's success is formally evaluated by superior manager.
5. Future objectives may be considered in light of past performance.

The MBO Process

The MBO process consists of a number of stages and steps, as shown in Figure 6.11. In the first stage, superior and subordinate managers discuss job descriptions to ensure that they both agree on the area of responsibility, the level of performance that will be acceptable and the method of evaluation. Then the subordinate establishes short-term objectives in consultation with his or her superior; all objectives should be specific (in numerical terms whenever possible). By mutually setting these objectives, both managers may become aware of factors inside and outside the organization that could interfere with their achievement.

During stage two, which is the ensuing operating period, both managers should meet frequently to discuss the subordinate's progress. Actual performance should be evaluated at predetermined checkpoints to determine whether the objectives can be achieved as planned or will require modification.

The third stage comes at the end of the operating period, when superior and subordinate jointly evaluate the results of the latter's total effort. Future objectives for a new cycle may be considered at this stage, in the light of past performance.

One of the most important activities in a successful MBO program is planning. Dale McConkey, an executive involved with MBO seminars, is quoted on planning in the article "The Role of Planning in MBO."

Benefits of MBO

Perhaps the greatest benefit of MBO is that it allows subordinates to participate in setting goals and objectives for their own area of responsibility. In addition, it provides

MBO is a philosophy that suggests a business has many objectives with one objective common to all, customer satisfaction. MBO emphasizes outputs, the productivity, rather than inputs, the work efforts, thus making managers and employees alike accountable for their results. The control feature of MBO is self-control as employees strive to attain goals set by themselves in consultation with their supervisors. MBO embraces the behavioural-science findings that all workers want freedom to participate and share in the work experience. With proper application MBO can also result in increased employee esteem, development of goals by teams of employees, and motivation accruing from open access to information. All of these results are desirable in the organization of the twenty-first century. With increased emphasis on flexibility, creativity and empowerment, organizations must move in this direction. The MBO philosophy of employee participation, goal specificity, feedback and evaluation is consistent with organizational movement toward a flexible, creative organization with empowered employees motivated by feelings of participation and control. "A quick-fix management toy of Christmases past"? Probably not.[26]

MBO: Is it Yesterday's News?

them with a better understanding of how their own efforts relate to the goals and objectives of the whole organization. Once their objectives and the methods of achieving them have been clearly identified, the subordinate managers know what is expected of them and how their performance will be evaluated. As a result of the close contact between superior and subordinate managers in the MBO process, communication throughout the organization is also enhanced. Finally, the constant review of job descriptions, responsibility and authority improves the whole process of delegation in that the accountability of subordinate managers is emphasized when their responsibility for achieving objectives is clearly specified.

Problems with MBO

The greatest drawback of the MBO process is the time, money and paperwork it requires. Thus, an MBO program is likely to fail unless top management encourages participation and commits the resources required to support it. In addition, authority relationships may have to be restructured to give managers sufficient authority to achieve their objectives. Control systems to measure accurately how objectives are being achieved must also be established. Finally, individual rewards may cause problems unless they are based on the achievement of predetermined objectives; many organizations reward not performance, but other factors such as good work habits, individual appearance and the ability to get along with others. If an MBO program is to succeed, both top management and the participants must be convinced of its benefits.

The MBO system is not a solution to all of an organization's ills. Nevertheless, it does allow some integration of individual and organizational goals, and provides a better basis for evaluating and rewarding managers; many organizations today use some form of MBO.

Chapter Summary

1. Without people, organizations could not function. However, people may not perform to their full potential unless they are motivated, and therefore their needs must be satisfied. At one time, managers believed that money was the prime motivator, but the Hawthorne experiments proved that social pressure and social needs are often more important than higher wages.

2. Maslow proposed that there are five levels of needs that people attempt to satisfy-physiological, safety, social, esteem and self-actualization needs. Only the two lower levels of needs can be entirely satisfied with money, and only those needs that have not been satisfied will motivate people to work harder.

3. Herzberg discovered similar needs in workers. His "hygiene factors" correspond to Maslow's physiological and safety needs, as well as to some social needs, including money, job security, quality of management, company policy and adequate working conditions. His "motivators" correspond to higher-level needs and include the actual work that employees do, responsibility, advancement, recognition and achievement.

4. McGregor's Theory X and Theory Y have implications for both motivation and leadership. A Theory X manager attempts to motivate employees through satisfaction of lower-level needs. A Theory Y manager prefers to allow them the opportunity to satisfy higher-level needs. Similarly, a Theory X manager will tend to be authoritarian, exercising close control and supervision, whereas a Theory Y manager allows employees considerable self-control and participation in decision making whenever possible.

5. Leadership refers to the process of directing and influencing people to channel their efforts toward specific goals. Research has shown that leaders tend to be either task-oriented or people-oriented. Both the managerial grid and the leadership continuum show a range of leadership styles that lie between the two extremes, and indicate that a balanced approach may be the most desirable. On the other hand, Fred Fiedler believes that all leadership styles can be effective provided they are used in the appropriate situations.

6. The path-goal theory links motivation with leadership style. A people-oriented leader tries to match rewards with the needs of individuals. The task-oriented leader tries to create a strong link between rewards and performance, focusing little attention on individual needs. The situational theory bases a manager's leadership style on the development level of the subordinate. As a new employee comes to know the job and takes on more responsibility, the task-oriented leadership style should slowly give way to the people-oriented style. Ultimately, the employee will require little of either style as he or she becomes intimately acquainted with the job.

7. Poor communication is a common problem on the part of sender and receiver alike. Communication barriers can be overcome by using clear language that is easy to understand, by repeating the message through various channels and by using feedback.

8. Employees with high morale feel that the organization provides them with job satisfaction. The results may include low employee turnover, low absenteeism, few grievances and less waste of resources. No clear-cut relationship has been found as yet between job satisfaction and productivity, but evidence suggests that employees who are properly rewarded for their performance and have well-defined goals receive greater job satisfaction.

9. Unfortunately, many jobs are tedious, boring and monotonous. To make jobs more interesting and thereby raise morale, managers have introduced job rotation, job enrichment, flexible working hours and several other techniques. Similar

steps have been taken to help managers identify more closely with the organization and see the results of their work. One major technique is management by objectives, in which managers establish goals jointly with their superiors and then participate in evaluating their progress in meeting these goals.

KEY TERMS

Motivation 187
Classical theory of motivation 187
Scientific management 187
Differential piece rate system 188
Hawthorne effect 188
Physiological needs 189
Safety needs .190
Social needs .190
Esteem/ego needs 190
Self-actualization needs 190
Hygiene factors 192

Motivators 193
Job satisfaction 193
Theory X managers 194
Theory Y managers 194
Leadership 196
Leadership traits 196
Task-oriented leader 196
People-oriented leader 196
Managerial grid 197
Leadership continuum 198
Contingency theory of leadership . . .199

Path-goal theory of leadership 200
Situational theory of leadership 200
Theory Z 203
Communication process 204
Morale 207
Intrinsic rewards 209
Extrinsic rewards 209
Redesigning work 211
Management by objectives (MBO) 211

REVIEW QUESTIONS

1 What is motivation?

2 What is the classical theory of motivation? Why was this theory successful for so long?

3 How did the Hawthorne studies revolutionize theories of motivation?

4 Explain Maslow's theory of human needs.

5 Explain what Herzberg means by hygiene factors and motivators.

6 Contrast a Theory X manager with a Theory Y manager. What are some of the problems each manager might face in a modern organization?

7 Explain the trait theory of leadership.

8 Compare the effectiveness of the leadership continuum and the managerial grid in helping an individual choose a leadership style.

9 What is Fiedler's contingency theory of leadership? How does he view an individual's ability to adopt a different leadership style? How does he view leadership training?

10 Briefly explain the path-goal theory and the situational theory of leadership. What is the major difference between these two theories and Fiedler's theory?

11 What is a Theory Z organization?

12 Identify some of the major communication problems. How can they be overcome?

13 What is morale?

14 What is the relationship between morale and productivity?

15 Why are organizations today interested in redesigning work?

16 What is management by objectives? Describe what happens in each of the five steps that makes up the MBO process.

17 Describe the benefits of MBO to an organization. Why is MBO often not successful?

DISCUSSION QUESTIONS

1 "Good managers tend to be good leaders, but good leaders are not always good managers." Discuss.

2 Why does the selection of managers become more important, but also more difficult, at the upper levels of the organizational hierarchy?

3 Consider your own motivations and needs. How do they correspond to Maslow's hierarchy?

4 Identify a variety of management positions in different types of organizations, then describe the leadership style that would be most effective for each position. How should managers for these positions be selected?

5 What Japanese management techniques do you think could be adapted for Canadian companies? Explain.

The Devil Would Know!

"I just can't seem to get them to pay attention to detail!" lamented Jerry as he stood in the subway train, next to his friend Archie. "I pay them decent wages. Not the highest, to be sure—I just can't afford more. But no one's starving."

"Maybe a little yelling and screaming might help—let them know you're serious," replied Archie.

Jerry didn't answer right away; the subway car banked into a steep turn, and he hung on to a post to keep his balance. Finally, relaxing his grip, he said, "How will that help, Arch? Look, I tell a worker how to fold the wires and put a little clip around them, nice and neat. Then I show him or her how to put them in the casing in just the right place—but every now and then when I take a machine apart, the inside looks like a hair-curler basket!"

"Fire one of them!" Archie said. "That'll teach the lot a lesson. Nothing like a little fear to keep someone's mind on the task at hand."

"Sure, great! And how am I to choose which one? They're all equally guilty. I really can't put my finger on any one person. Besides, jobs are hard to find right now. I have two single parents, one employee with a disability and another with four kids who helps support a sick mother. How would *you* choose?"

Archie shrugged. "I don't know how you stay in business, Jerry. You're too nice a guy."

"Why do I have to be heartless to be in business?" Jerry exclaimed. "Why can't I just tell somebody once and have them do what I want, every day? It's a simple job— a monkey could do it!"

The subway stopped. Realizing that it was his stop, Archie bounded for the door, his briefcase narrowly missing the head of a frantically dodging child. "I'd still get tough if I were you ... " And he was gone, sprinting for the stairs to avoid the crowd.

"Great!" thought Jerry. "I go in this morning, choose someone at random, chew either his or her ear off and my problems are supposed to be solved."

"But if those wires keep getting loose, one of them could short out or cause a machine to overheat. Then we could have a fire and ... what about those government inspection people? Someone could complain; we might lose our certification." Jerry's eyes glazed slightly as he thought of the possible effects of a fire, and the subsequent investigation, on his liability insurance rates. He knew he would have to do something soon. Three more stops ... How the devil did you get people to do what you wanted them to do?

SOURCE: By Dr. P. C. Wright, Faculty of Administration, University of New Brunswick, Fredericton, N.B. Reprinted by permission of the author.

Questions

1 Discuss the possible effects of Archie's motivational style.

2 Using some of the theories discussed in this chapter, answer Jerry's question: "How did you get people to do what you wanted them to do?"

3 What might happen if Jerry gives his employees a raise? Will they fold the wires more neatly?

The Painted Meaning of Life

"I never really know what I'm supposed to do. Take yesterday, for example. Heather said that I was to paint the seminar room. So I went and got myself all set up in Seminar Room E (that's the one that looks the grubbiest) and got about halfway through when she came along. Well, you'd think I had painted over the *Mona Lisa* with a broad brush. She had wanted Seminar Room D painted! She had a group coming in for a training seminar this evening. I had screwed up her entire schedule and when she told the manager I'd be dog meat!"

"He's done it to me again! He knows that we repaint those seminar rooms in strict rotation. A, B and C were done last month, does it take a brain surgeon to figure out that D comes after C? The guy needs a cerebral implant; he acts as if brains were loose change and he had a hole in his pocket!"

"I wish we could get some good help around here. I think I'll recommend to the manager that he be let go; this is the umpteenth time I've had a mess to clean up! Take last week, for example; we were expecting 500 folks for that dog-grooming convention. What did he do? He sets up and starts to paint that spot in the lobby over the front desk. And when I got all excited and tried to clear him out of there, he got mad! The man just doesn't understand what guest service is all about, and temper tantrums I don't need. I was being perfectly sensible!"

"I'll bet she tells the manager about that little problem last week at the front desk. I ask you, is it my fault? I'm sitting there half-asleep (it was my break time); my kid had gone into the hospital at 4:00 a.m. to get his appendix out. She sticks her head in the door and says something about the spot where the broken pipe had damaged the wall in the lobby; she was still talking when she walked down the hall. Anyway, I thought she wanted me to get at it right away; I try to be helpful. Boy, was I wrong! And she wouldn't let me finish! Wouldn't listen when I told her I'd be done in five minutes. I got mad! Do you blame me?"

SOURCE: By Dr. P. C. Wright, Faculty of Administration, University of New Brunswick, Fredericton, N.B. Reprinted by permission of the author.

Questions

1 What parts of the communication process have broken down?

2 Discuss the sender's faults. How could she have acted differently?

3 Discuss the receiver's responsibilities. How could he have acted differently?

COMPREHENSIVE CASE 6-3

SOMERSET OPTICAL

By September 1998, Somerset Optical had grown considerably. The company now employed a full-time staff of four sales clerks and two opticians (excluding Mike Fowler and Peter Dewar). In addition to the administrative/financial consultant, the firm also retained a marketing manager under contract.

Sales were averaging $28 000 per month, and Somerset had an average monthly growth rate of 12%. The administrative consultant, together with Fowler and Dewar, made a conscious effort to create a very positive working environment in order to retain staff for the longest possible time. They instituted, for example, a system of base salary plus commission for all salespersons and opticians. As well, it became company policy (1) that no employee would work more than 7.5 hours per day; (2) that each would receive a paid lunch period of 1.5 hours per day; and (3) that no employee would work more than five consecutive days. Any employee who worked Saturday would have Monday off; all employees were required to take turns working Saturdays.

The company provided for all employees a full benefits package that included a dental and drug plan. Each employee enjoyed three weeks' paid vacation and was allowed paid sick leave when the illness was certified by a physician. In addition to these benefits, the company reimbursed employees for any continuing education course or program that was relevant to the business, as well as for any personal-interest training up to a maximum of $200 per employee per year.

The company also offered an in-house training program in partnership with the government and an optician training college. This program, which was partially subsidized by a government agency and made available to the top performing sales clerk every year, allowed the candidate to take a three-year leave of absence to attend optician's college. While the company would not pay salary during this time, it offered the candidate a job on successful completion and paid all tuition costs associated with the course. The candidate was required to guarantee the company one year of service for every year the company paid fees.

Somerset Optical also held staff "pub crawl" nights and sponsored a slow-pitch baseball team, not only for Somerset staff members but also for staff members of other retail optical outlets in the city.

In addition to the extensive benefits offered, all employees received regular in-house training that encompassed the latest selling techniques, product improvements and new product developments. In addition, Dewar and Fowler were giving serious consideration to either expanding into a second retail outlet outside the city or going into the eyewear import business, supplying their own outlets and perhaps other eye wear retail outlets such as Byway Optical. Most Somerset employees were convinced that all personnel required for any new undertaking would be selected from within, so that advancement was a very good possibility.

Not surprisingly, Somerset Optical was heralded as *the* place to work in Ottawa's optical sector.

SOURCE: By David H. Jones-Delcourt. Reprinted by permission of the author.

>>

Questions

1 How does management at Somerset Optical attempt to motivate people? Contrast the situation as described above with both Hertzberg's and Maslow's theories of motivation, noting similarities and differences.

2 Discuss the style of leadership displayed by Dewar and Fowler as it relates to the managerial grid theory of leadership. What style of leadership are they using?

3 How does Somerset Optical's work environment relate to the path-goal theory of leadership?

4 Use the life-cycle theory of leadership to analyze the leadership style of Somerset Optical's management.

5 What level of morale would you expect to find at Somerset Optical? Give reasons for your answer.

PART 3

The Business Functions

All organizations in some way perform the four major business functions—production, marketing, finance and personnel. The production function is necessary to physically produce the goods or services; the marketing function to determine what to produce and then sell or otherwise convey to consumers; the finance function to provide funds required for all aspects of the operation; and the personnel function to ensure that people with all the required skills are available.

In Chapter 7, we look at the production function and its two major tasks—establishing the necessary physical facilities and managing daily production operations.

In Chapter 8, we examine the marketing function and its role as intermediary between the business organization and the consumer. We see how a business determines what products and services to produce, and we learn what the producer does to convey the product to the consumer.

In Chapter 9, we look at the finance function and the major tasks of the finance department. The finance department controls all financial operations, ensuring that enough money is available for day-to-day business operations and acquiring the necessary funds for long-term growth.

In Chapter 10, we survey the personnel function. In addition to recruiting, hiring and training employees, the personnel department is responsible for compensating employees for their services, and for evaluating their performance in view of continued employment, promotion or, if necessary, termination.

7

Production and Operations Management

Learning Objectives

After reading this chapter, you will be able to

1 Explain the meaning of economy of scale, mechanization, standardization and automation, and how they contribute to mass production.

2 Identify the five major types of production processes.

3 Explain why capacity planning is one of the major long-term decisions.

4 List and explain the factors that must be considered when deciding on plant location.

5 Know when a product layout should be used as opposed to a process layout.

6 Explain the purpose of work design.

7 Recognize why demand forecasting is crucial to efficient production.

8 Explain why inventory management is important.

9 Explain how distribution planning can minimize transportation and production costs.

10 Explain the purpose of aggregate planning.

11 Explain how MRP and just-in-time inventory contribute to efficient production.

12 Explain how scheduling is different in high-volume production systems as compared to job shops, and explain the difference between loading and scheduling.

13 Know the importance of the purchasing department in an efficient manufacturing operation.

14 Identify the major factors to be considered in establishing optimum systems for quality control and maintenance.

15 Describe how the automated factory works and how it can increase productivity and result in a higher-quality product.

The Production Function

Imagine for a moment that you could get virtually any product delivered to you almost instantly, personalized to your own taste, yet as inexpensive as if it were mass-produced. That is what the factory of the future will be able to do.

A customer's requirements will be fed into a computer that alters an existing design and sends the information to the machines on the shop floor, which will instantly readjust themselves and begin manufacturing the product ordered. The manufacturing process will be performed by clusters or cells of multi-purpose machines run by computers and served by nimble-fingered robots. Required parts will be supplied by remote-controlled vehicles.

These types of factories were built by companies such as General Motors, General Electric and IBM. In the 1980s, all three companies developed highly automated plants that allowed huge increases in output, productivity and higher quality. While the results were astonishing, the cost of building these factories was uneconomical. Nevertheless, the lessons learned were invaluable for future factory automation.

The core of activity in any business organization is the production of goods and services. As Figure 7.1 shows, **production** is the process of converting resources—raw materials, human resources, capital, technology and information—into products and services. The conversion process, also known as the technical core, varies depending on the nature of the firm. An automobile manufacturer requires huge plants, assembly lines and specialized machines and equipment. A restaurant requires considerably less equipment to prepare its various menu items. The feedback and control function in the production process provides information about the quality of the outputs and about the efficiency of the production operation.

When we speak of production the first thing that comes to mind are automobiles or steel or stereos. But it may come as a surprise that roughly seven out of ten Canadians work in the service industry, such as medical, educational, retail, transportation and food services. Keep in mind that lawyers, hairdressers and consultants also operate in the service sector of the economy.

Production is the process of converting resources—raw materials, human resources, capital, technology and information—into products and services.

FIGURE 7.1

The production system

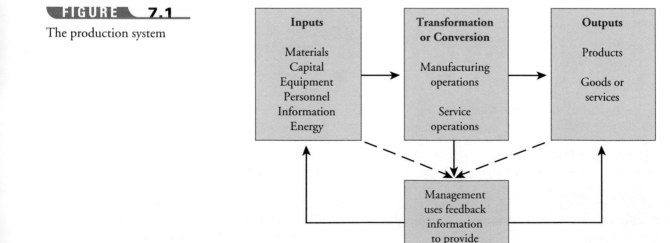

Management gathers information through feedback, evaluates it and decides if changes are required.

Service businesses differ from manufacturing businesses in two major ways. First, in a service business the customer is involved in the production process. A bus transports a person from one place to another, while a hospital treats a patient. Second, service outputs cannot be stored in inventory as can manufactured products. A lawyer cannot prepare a case for a non-existent client, nor can a doctor diagnose a non-existent patient.

Like a good product, a good service doesn't just happen. It must be planned and managed from the original design of the service to its ongoing delivery. The performance of the service must be monitored to ensure that its quality remains high. While in manufacturing, machines and technology play a key role, in the service industry the individual employee plays a much greater role since it is that person's skill or personality that influences directly or indirectly the customer's perception of the quality of the service.

Nevertheless, manufacturers and service organizations face the same problems—for example, scheduling, whether of patients or of production workers and raw materials; the acquisition of materials and supplies; and quality and productivity the output must satisfy the customer, and it must be produced at the lowest possible cost.

Mass Production and Technology

Mass production is the manufacture of goods in large quantities. An assembly line is expensive to build, but once it is operating it can churn out vast quantities of cars, refrigerators, radios or televisions at prices many people can afford. Mass production allows us to achieve economies of scale by matching plant capacity with required output. To understand the concept of **economies of scale**, we must remember that a manufacturing plant is built to produce a specific number of units of a product based on present and anticipated sales for perhaps five or ten years into the future. Up to maximum production capacity, the costs of maintaining and operating the plant (fixed costs) remain fairly stable. The variable costs, such as wages of production workers and costs of raw materials and parts used, vary directly with the number of units produced.

As an example, consider a flowerpot manufacturer. Suppose the plant can produce 200 000 flowerpots at maximum production capacity. The plant costs $100 000 per year to operate; this figure represents fixed costs. Let us assume that variable costs are $1 per flowerpot, including the cost of raw materials and labour. Therefore, 100 000 flowerpots would cost $200 000 to produce, and the cost per flowerpot would be $2. However, if we produced 200 000 flowerpots, which is the maximum capacity for the plant, our total production costs would be $300 000 and the cost per flowerpot would drop to $1.50. Thus, by producing more units, we would actually decrease the cost of producing one flowerpot. The same principle holds for virtually all products that can be produced and sold in large quantities.

Mass production is best illustrated in the production of automobiles using an **assembly line**, a device that automatically moves the automobile along a fixed route past various workers. Each worker performs a small part in the total manufacture of the car. By introducing assembly-line techniques, along with standardized interchangeable parts in 1913, Henry Ford was able to reduce the building time per car from more than 12 hours to just over one hour. He thus also reduced the price per car to the consumer by almost 10 times. As a result, many more people were able to buy cars, and the increased sales revenues helped to increase profit. To stem the large employee turnover caused by the monotony of assembly-line work, Ford doubled the standard daily wage rate of the industry from about $2.50 to $5.

Service businesses, in comparison to manufacturing businesses, involve the customer in the production process; as well, service outputs cannot be stored in inventory.

Mass production is the manufacture of goods in large quantities.

Economies of scale are achieved when production approaches maximum plant capacity because fixed costs are spread over more units.

Assembly line—a device that automatically moves a product along a fixed route past various work stations where additional production steps are performed.

Introduction to Operations Research

mscmga.ms.ic.ac.uk/jeb/or/intro.html

The assembly-line process was soon adopted by other manufacturers with suitable products. Today, the assembly line is used in countless manufacturing processes, from the bottling of soft drinks to the assembly of complex electronic products.

However, while the assembly line increases efficiency in manufacturing, it does little to enhance workers' motivation. Many assembly-line jobs are repetitious and boring. To relieve frustration in a tedious, unchallenging job, workers may resort to absenteeism or even sabotage.

Automobile manufacturing companies have recognized the problem of boredom, however, and have instituted various schemes to make jobs more interesting. For example, workers now often perform a larger part of the assembly process and form work groups to take over supervision. Many job enrichment and job enlargement programs were pioneered by Volvo in Sweden and have since been implemented in North America by manufacturers of various products.

Mechanization

Mechanization refers to the use of machines to perform work previously done by human beings or animals.

Mass production depends on **mechanization**, or the use of machines to perform work previously done by humans or animals. Without mechanization most industries in our modern industrial economy could not operate. Cranes, for example, are essential to move heavy objects and build skyscrapers, while modern earth-moving equipment makes it possible to build many kilometres of freeways in a few months—an achievement that was unthinkable in the days of pick-and-shovel gangs. Mechanization also means that fewer people are needed to grow, harvest and process food than in the past, particularly in industrialized countries. By freeing the vast majority of people from the production of their own food requirements, mechanization allows many to work in the manufacturing or service industries, which increases the gross national product and the standard of living.

Standardization

Standardization means that, through precise production control, component parts can be mass-produced and later assembled interchangeably.

Standardization is an important factor in reducing the cost of producing complex products. Precise control over production processes allows mass production of virtually identical parts and components. These parts and components can later be assembled into finished products or can be used to repair products that are currently in service. Think how expensive car repairs would be, for example, if each replacement part had to be built or modified by hand before it could be installed in your car.

Automation

Automation refers to the process whereby one machine, usually a computer, regulates and monitors another, so that no human operator is required to be present.

Automation refers to the process whereby one machine (usually a computer) regulates and monitors another so that no human operator need be present. The monitoring computer can quickly analyze machine operations or production processes and command the machine either to stop a certain activity or to correct a particular process. For example, oil refineries are almost entirely automated. At each step in the refining process, information is fed into a computer that analyzes it and responds with the appropriate command to keep the production process on course. Automobile manufacturers also use computers and robots to automate particular assembly operations such as welding. Computers that control machines and robots are already being used in factories to automate various processes, including the machining of parts.

Custom Production

Mass production does not mean that only identical products can be produced at any one time. Although assembly lines are ideally suited for this function, the

< Computer-controlled robot welding line

production process can be adjusted so that items can be customized or built to order. As long as the products are not too dissimilar, **custom production** can be achieved through careful production planning and scheduling, as we will discuss later. For example, General Motors produces thousands of cars per year, but few are identical in every respect. Individual cars may vary by model, in the equipment ordered by the customer, or in outside appearance such as trim and paint. The custom order is scheduled into the production process so that the appropriate equipment arrives at the work station at the same time as the chassis, thereby allowing a high degree of customization on an otherwise inflexible assembly line.

Custom production refers to the making of products according to customer specifications.

The Job Shop

By far the greatest number of manufacturing establishments are **job shops** that produce small quantities of a product. A customer may request one particular item from a machine shop or a small batch of identical items. To process these small quantities, job shops position machines in work centres so that specific operations can be performed at one time. When that operation is completed, the entire batch of semi-finished product moves to another work station. Unlike mass-production operations, which operate continuously, these small operations often must wait until a customer order arrives. This presents particular problems in scheduling of jobs, inventory management, purchasing and controlling other production costs.

Job shops produce one particular item or a small batch of identical items according to a customer's order.

Organization of the Production Department

Production department activities must be organized to function effectively. Small manufacturing firms usually have a line organization structure. A small firm does not have the resources to hire a variety of specialists; nor are specialists particularly necessary, as often only one product is manufactured. The owner, who usually has considerable experience in the manufacture of the product, provides as much of the necessary expertise as possible.

As the business grows and the owner must pay more attention to other areas, he or she may hire a production manager. The production manager in turn may hire an assistant production manager, who may also be known as production superintendent or general foreperson. The lower-level foreperson would then report to the assistant, allowing the production manager to spend more time on the general aspects of production—planning, product design, quality control, maintenance and production cost control.

As a manufacturing firm grows and enlarges its product offering, the organization structure must be changed. Large manufacturing firms require specialists, since a line operation does not allow the time or expertise required for both planning and controlling production. A large firm must spend considerable time planning for new products, new production processes and for changes in plant and equipment. These three planning functions are known as product engineering, process engineering and plant engineering respectively.

Controlling the various aspects of production is also more complex in a large manufacturing firm. Production control is necessary to maintain production at the specific volume required for maximum utilization of resources. Quality control is essential to ensure that the quality of the products is satisfactory. Finally, the firm must exercise control over all production costs, a function known as cost control.

Thus, a large firm will have augmented its original line structure with various staff positions, as shown in Figure 7.2. One drawback of the structure illustrated is the wide span of control given the production vice-president. Seven subordinates report to this individual, who, in addition to his or her responsibilities for coordinating major activities of the firm with other managers, may have difficulty managing the production function effectively.

FIGURE 7.2

Line and staff organization for production

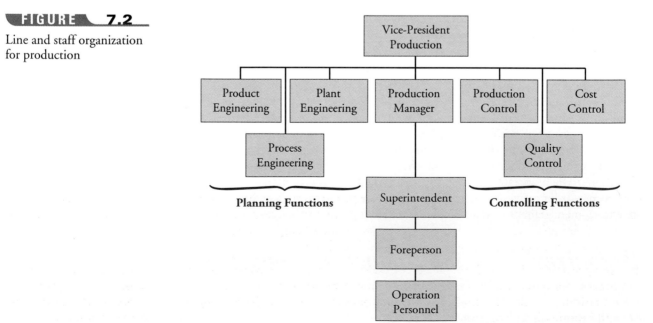

The line and staff organization may also encounter many of the authority problems discussed in Chapter 5. For example, if the products coming off the assembly line are found to be defective, should the quality control manager (usually a staff position) have the authority to stop the line? If the line is stopped, the number and cost of defective products would be reduced immediately, but staff and machines would be idle. Given that the assembly-line manager, who must answer for any cost overruns, has the actual authority to stop the line, perhaps he or she should be notified first. But the delay may waste precious time, during which a stream of defective parts continues to roll off the line. Thus, in a line and staff structure, it is essential that responsibility and authority be clearly specified to minimize conflicts.

Designing Production/Operations Systems

New products or services often require new facilities that may be either added to the existing plant or built at another location. Management must make decisions about plant capacity and location, plant layout, the machines and equipment required, product and service design and work systems design. These are all major decisions, which are costly and can have long-term effects on a firm, since they commit it to a course of action that cannot easily be changed. Because they are so significant, such decisions are generally made by top management, although production staff and management are usually heavily involved in fact-finding, analysis of information, and recommendations for building specifications, the type of machines and equipment to purchase and so on.

We will now discuss the above decisions as they relate to the establishment of production facilities. Then we will look at the operating production decisions—decisions that must be made on an ongoing basis.

Product/Service Planning and Design

Products and services have life cycles. Depending on customer demand, products have to be changed and redesigned, or new products developed. Similarly, new services are provided as the need arises. New or changed products require detailed specifications, which are developed by the production division through its research, engineering and development department to determine costs and physical production requirements. During this product development stage, marketing (which will be discussed in Chapter 8) and production work closely together to ensure that the product or service will meet the requirements of the customer and that it will be of an acceptable quality, at a price customers are prepared to pay.

Production Processes

A firm's choice of products determines the **production process** required, which in turn has a major influence on long-term production decisions. For example, a kitchen appliance manufacturer requires different facilities than a firm in the oil refining industry. The five basic production processes are listed below:

1. *Analytic process.* The **analytic process** divides a particular raw material into its component parts, resulting in one or more different products. For example, in oil refining, crude oil is broken down into gasoline, kerosene, lubricating oil and heating oil for homes.

Production process refers to the method of transforming inputs into outputs.

Analytic process—divides a particular raw material into its component parts, resulting in one or more different products.

Extraction process—raw materials are taken from either the earth or water.

Synthetic process—combines various raw materials chemically to form a new product.

Fabrication process—changes the form of a given raw material.

Assembly process—combines a number of fabricated components to form a new product.

2. *Extraction process.* In the **extraction process**, raw materials are taken from either the earth or water. Examples include coal mining and the recovery of salt or other minerals from sea water.

3. *Synthetic process.* In the **synthetic process**, various raw materials are combined chemically to form a new product. For example, iron ore, coke and other materials are combined at high temperatures in the production of steel. In the production of plastics, various hydrocarbons are combined.

4. *Fabrication process.* The **fabrication process** changes the form of a given raw material. Typical examples include making bottles from raw glass, weaving cloth, making steel beams and manufacturing paper from wood pulp. Most manufacturing involves fabrication.

5. *Assembly process.* The **assembly process** combines a number of fabricated components to form a new product. The resulting goods are usually complex (e.g., automobiles, appliances and machinery). Some components may themselves require assembly; these are called subassemblies. For example, the automobile engine is usually assembled in a separate plant and then shipped to the main assembly line for installation into the chassis.

Some firms may use more than one production process, either on the same premises or in a different plant. For example, Sherritt-Gordon, a nickel mining and fabricating company, extracts its nickel ore in Manitoba and refines it in Alberta using the analytic process. The company also fabricates commemorative coins, as well as nickel and silver blanks for shipment to other countries where the coins are minted.

Service organizations use different processes according to the service provided and the number of people using the service. For example, fast-food restaurants, cafeterias and university registration areas are similar to assembly-line operations, because a large number of people move through a similar activity. These are known as service-based operations. On the other hand, a fixed-position service is provided when a customer remains at one station through the entire service or when the service must be performed at a particular location. Beauty treatments, landscaping and dental services are examples.

A process-based service combines the two types. A large number of people are moved through particular operations in batches. Higher education is an example in which students take a variety of paths to get their degree or diploma. Classes are grouped by discipline and students move from class to class depending on the subject being taught.

Capacity Planning

Capacity planning involves determining the maximum desired production capacity of a plant based on expected production volumes.

Determining the maximum production capacity of a plant is the most fundamental decision production managers must make. In **capacity planning**, management must take into account present and future demand for its products. It must decide what the maximum capacity should be and how long the present plant should last. Management must also keep in mind the swings in production volume due to seasonal variations. This means that the plant should be designed with flexibility in mind so that production volume can be increased or decreased readily, depending on customer demand.

Deciding on maximum capacity is a crucial decision. It costs millions of dollars to build a brewery, a hospital or an assembly plant for cars or household appliances.

The initial plant size not only determines the initial construction cost but also affects the operating or overhead costs. The larger a plant, the greater its fixed operating cost. We discussed this cost factor earlier under mass production and economies of scale. A plant that is built to accommodate production requirements 10 years into the future may be too large for today's production volume. Therefore, the operating cost per unit is higher, which means that either the price to the customer must be greater or the firm earns less profit. It is probably less costly to expand an existing facility at a later date than to operate a plant at half capacity for years into the future. Ideally, demand and capacity should be matched as closely as possible to minimize operating costs. We will discuss how this is done later in the chapter.

Plant Location

Another major long-term decision is plant location. An existing firm might find it easier and less costly to relocate and build a new plant than to modernize its existing facilities. A plant's decision to relocate might also stem from continuing labour problems at its present site, shifts in market demand for its product, increased transportation costs for shipping raw materials or finished goods or simply a desire to expand into other geographical areas. Whatever the reason, location decisions must be considered carefully —once made, they are difficult and expensive to change.

Many factors can enter into a location decision, but often one or a few factors overshadow the others. Once the most important factors have been determined, a firm will attempt to locate a suitable geographic region. Then a small number of communities where appropriate sites are available will be considered. We will first examine regional factors and then community factors.

Choosing a site for a service business differs in many ways from choosing an industrial location. For product manufacturing, minimizing costs is the primary consideration, because manufacturing costs can vary substantially between various locations. For private-sector service businesses, revenue maximizing is the primary focus, because costs generally vary little within a particular region.

Regional Factors

The major regional factors that must be considered in location decisions are raw materials, markets and labour considerations. The source of raw materials and the market for its product are two of the major factors that a firm must consider when seeking a location for its plant. In both cases, the cost of transportation is critical.

Raw Materials—Sometimes a firm finds it necessary to locate near its source of raw materials because a product is highly perishable or because of high transportation costs. Mines, farms, fish canning plants, cement plants and food processors are obvious examples of operations that must locate near their raw material sources.

Another critical factor is the cost and supply of energy. A ready supply of natural gas at reasonable cost is the reason Sherritt-Gordon located near Fort Saskatchewan, Alberta, even though its nickel mine is situated in northern Manitoba. In addition, the ammonia produced as a byproduct of the natural gas is required in large amounts for nickel processing. Thus, a source of energy that included a necessary production ingredient outweighed higher transportation costs as a consideration in plant location.

Location of Markets—Locating near a firm's market is important if the products are perishable or bulky to ship. Firms that distribute fresh produce want to be as close to their markets as possible to minimize spoilage of their product on long shipping routes. Sand and gravel firms and cement processors must locate in their market areas due to the bulkiness of their products.

In the case of products such as televisions or calculators, where transportation costs are small in relation to the total cost of the product, and where the product is a manageable size and is not perishable, transportation cost is a less important factor.

Labour Factors—A firm must decide whether it needs skilled or unskilled workers in its production process. If only unskilled workers are required, it may locate near a large population centre, where labour costs are low. Sometimes the existence or strength of labour unions is also a consideration. On the other hand, if access to a large pool of skilled labour is a major requirement, then a company's choices are more limited. Particular industries are often found clustered together in one region where skilled labour is readily available. For example, automobile manufacturers and firms that make parts for cars locate in proximity. Another well-known example is Silicon Valley, the heart of the computer industry located outside San Francisco. Many new computer hardware manufacturers have set up offices there.

Community Factors

Many communities are anxious to attract new firms to their area because of the taxes they would pay and the jobs they would offer. However, communities as a rule do not want businesses that cause pollution or otherwise endanger the local residents or lessen the quality of life in the community. There is considerable debate, for example, over the location of nuclear power plants, chemical plants and pulp and paper mills. On the other hand, the federal, provincial or municipal governments may offer tax concessions to companies that locate in particular communities and thus lessen unemployment or expand industrial activity. A firm might also consider a given community in terms of the facilities it offers (e.g., schools, shopping, recreation, housing, entertainment, police and fire protection and availability of medical services).

Site-Related Factors

The major considerations with respect to the site of the location are the land, transportation and local zoning restrictions. Soil conditions and drainage ability may be critical, depending on the type of building to be erected. Other factors, such as room for future expansion, available utilities and sewer capacity, and transportation access for trucks and rail, are often critical. For particular types of operations, such as light manufacturing or assembly work, and warehousing and customer service facilities, industrial parks are ideal locations.

Industrial Parks

The automobile, which facilitated the exodus of families from cities to the suburbs, also assisted the fledgling industrial parks that were beginning to develop in Canada in the 1950s. **Industrial parks** are established by private companies and by municipal governments. Access roads and railway spurs are provided to facilitate the transport of raw materials to plants and finished goods to markets. Water and sewers are provided, in addition to police and fire protection. Most industrial parks today strive for an agreeable working area and a visually pleasing environment.

Canada's first industrial park, Ajax Industrial Estates, located 40 kilometres outside Toronto, opened in 1953. The park had an area of 50 hectares—about a third was used for services and roads, and the remainder for development. After five years, the park had leased a quarter of its sites. The 120-hectare industrial park, Malton, located on the western fringes of Toronto, took only 10 years to fill. Another one of the early indus-

Industrial parks are established to provide facilities for manufacturing plants or other types of businesses along with an agreeable working area and a visually pleasing environment.

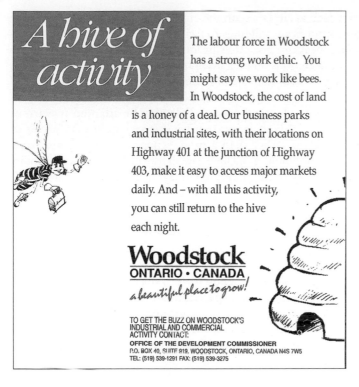

> Industrial parks are established by private companies and by municipal governments

trial parks was the 480-hectare Annacis Industrial Estates, which opened on Annacis Island in British Columbia's Fraser River area in 1955. A newer development is Lake Erie Industrial Park in southern Ontario. The major reasons for the growth of industrial parks are the significantly lower cost of land, expansion possibilities, amenities and lower taxes as compared with sites away from industrial parks.

For municipalities and small communities, industrial parks provide a major source of tax revenue, even though many communities initially offer tax concessions to businesses as an incentive to locate there. Eventually, however, firms provide additional tax revenue and a more balanced tax base (commercial and residential) for the community. An industrial park may also attract new residents to a small community, together with retail stores and other supporting businesses.

Plant Layout

The production process to a large extent determines the layout of the plant. Continuous processing is used to produce highly standardized products, such as televisions and videocassette recorders, in large volume. Operations are often highly repetitive, requiring low-skilled labour. Although they are expensive, specialized equipment and machines can be used because the high volume of production makes the cost per unit relatively low. Intermittent processing, on the other hand, involves low-volume jobs and frequent setting up of machines for new products. General-purpose equipment is used to satisfy a variety of processing requirements. Semi-skilled or skilled workers are required to operate the equipment.

Plant layout involves the positioning of facilities, material storage space, machines and other equipment so that raw materials and semi-finished work flow through the plant as rapidly as possible for maximum production efficiency. Production processes that use gravity feeding systems require multi-storied buildings. Heavy

Plant layout involves the positioning of facilities, material storage space, machines and other equipment so that raw materials and semi-finished work flow through the plant as rapidly as possible for maximum production efficiency.

machines or large objects such as airplanes, on the other hand, are normally fabricated and assembled in large ground-floor buildings to facilitate the movement of materials and parts to the assembly location. For other products such as automobiles, which are best moved past the work stations on long assembly lines, the plant may be a long, narrow building or large hall, with the assembly line snaking back and forth.

Since one of the main objectives in plant construction and layout is to reduce cost, it is important to choose a production process that may be adapted to various building shapes. For example, if land is inexpensive, management may prefer to build a large single-storey plant rather than a more expensive multi-storied one. Other advantages of single-floor buildings include ease in moving materials, availability of natural lighting and flexibility in modifying plant layout to future requirements. On the other hand, multi-storied buildings can reduce handling costs through the use of gravity feeding systems to move raw materials.

Types of Plant Layout

The two basic types of plant layout shown in Figure 7.3 are known as process and product layout. A **process layout** is usually chosen when manufacturing depends on custom orders, and the same machines and space are used to produce a number of different products. Machines of similar type are grouped together and the raw materials and finished goods are shifted from one department to the next as required for each mechanical process. A process layout allows flexibility in plant layout since material and product movement do not have to follow a fixed route. It is also less expensive to set up because there is no need for costly assembly-line equipment. However, since the semi-finished goods often must be physically moved from one work station to another, a process layout can increase the cost of material handling.

A **product layout** is used for mass production involving continuous runs of similar products. With a product layout, which is basically an assembly line, the product moves along fixed routes, past various work stations, according to the sequence of operations to be performed. A product layout reduces material handling costs and saves space, but it is not particularly flexible and the cost of altering a product line at a future date may be high. Furthermore, the failure of one machine may hold up an entire production process, and may be expensive if workers and machines in the rest of the product line are idled.

For some manufacturing operations, it may be advantageous to combine the two types of layouts. Thus, a process layout may be used to manufacture parts of the product, which are then brought together at the beginning of a product line for further assembly.

Machinery and Equipment

Often the type of plant layout determines the machinery required. There are basically two types of machines: general-purpose and special-purpose. **General-purpose machines** can perform a variety of operations, and are thus useful in process layouts, since the equipment can be adjusted as required. Metal lathes, for example, are used for a variety of machining operations. Since they are so versatile and can be sold to different manufacturing firms, general-purpose machines can be produced in large quantities and costs can be kept down. However, general-purpose machines are generally slower in their operation than special-purpose machines. They may also require skilled labour, since they must be set up and adjusted for each new process.

In contrast, **special-purpose machines** are specially designed to perform one operation. Thus, they lend themselves to integration into a product layout—the

---

Facility Layout

mscmga.ms.ic.ac.uk/jeb/or/ faclay.html

Process layout groups similar machines together and shifts the raw materials and finished goods from one department to the next as required for each mechanical process.

Product layout is used for mass production involving continuous runs of similar products.

General-purpose machines can perform a variety of operations, and are thus useful in process layouts, since the equipment can be adjusted as required.

Special-purpose machines are specially designed to perform one operation and are primarily used in assembly lines.

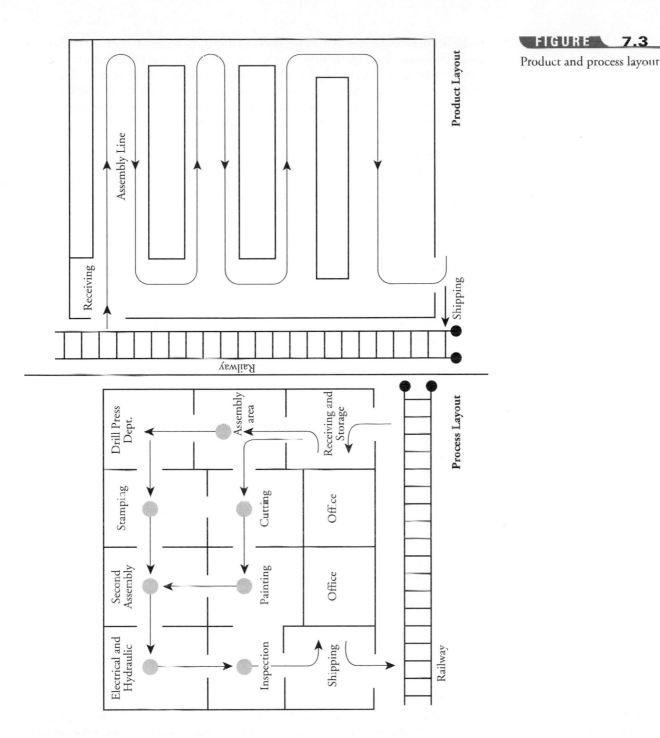

FIGURE 7.3

Product and process layout

speed of operation can be adjusted to coincide with the movement of the product along the assembly line. Soft-drink manufacturers, for example, incorporate bottling machines that perform only one function—the filling of bottles—but they accomplish this task at high speed. Special-purpose machines generally do not require skilled operators, as they seldom need resetting or complicated adjustments.

The type of machinery purchased and its cost depend largely on the product. For example, it may be possible to design a particular product so that it requires less complicated machinery but more skilled labour. If skilled labour is available at reasonable cost, a company may decide to forego costly specialized machinery. On the other hand, a firm may find it less expensive in the long run to design machinery that will mechanize a production process, thus permitting the use of unskilled labour or eliminating the need for labour entirely. By eliminating labour, productivity can often be increased, and the cost of the product may be reduced.

Layouts for Retail Firms

Retailers have found through experience that some areas in a retail store draw more customer traffic than others. Obviously then, the most profitable products should be placed in high-traffic areas if possible. Certain types of products (e.g., convenience goods such as toothpaste) are found closer to heavier customer-traffic flows. Shopping goods and specialty goods—furniture, cameras—for which people are willing to spend more time investigating before buying are placed in the rear or in more inaccessible parts of the store. How merchandise is displayed on shelves is also important. Goods placed at eye level and at the end of aisles generally sell better.

Two general types of layouts are used by smaller retail stores—the grid layout and the free-flow layout. Supermarkets and hardware stores generally use a grid layout because it provides maximum convenience for customers and highest productivity for the retailer. For goods that are purchased at more leisure (e.g., clothing and furniture), a free-flow layout is used. Larger retailers, especially department stores, will use combinations of these types of layouts.

Layouts for Service Firms

The great variety of service firms means that there is no standard layout for these types of firms. Where service is the primary function, as in restaurants, a retail-type layout is generally used. For repair businesses, where the required repair space is large compared to the customer area, a modified production layout may be used.

Work System Design

Work system design attempts to determine how to perform a given job in the most cost-efficient manner, while at the same time ensuring that the job is not so simplified that it causes boredom and worker dissatisfaction.

An organization depends on human effort to achieve its goals. The purpose of **work system design** is to determine how to perform a given job in the most cost-efficient manner, while also ensuring that the job is not so simplified that it causes boredom and worker dissatisfaction. The end result of work system design is to establish for each job time standards on which worker compensation is based. Work system design is a complicated process, but consists primarily of job design and work measurement. A brief look at each factor will provide some insight.

Job Design

Job design is concerned with specifying the tasks to be performed by a worker and how those tasks are to be done.

Job design is concerned with specifying the work activities of an individual or group in the organization. The emphasis is on performing a job in the most efficient manner possible in order to reduce costs. Ideally, each product should be designed so that it can be produced on an assembly line with workers performing simple, repetitive tasks. However, workers who must perform highly routine operations become bored very quickly. This leads to lapses in concentration, which results in poor assembly of parts and higher costs due to scrapping products, rework or after-sales service. Since the 1950s, emphasis has been placed on making jobs more interesting and giving workers more control over their jobs.

Job design is based on a **methods analysis** of a particular operation. The operation to be performed is studied along with the machines, equipment and materials used. The operator may be asked to provide input as to how he or she is performing the job. Sometimes **motion studies** may be used to systematically study the human motions used to perform an operation. These studies may be implemented either through personal observation or through the use of motion pictures or video that can later be reviewed in slow motion. Each movement and action is detailed on a process chart that can be studied to determine if better methods can be used to perform an existing job. If workers are found to perform unnecessary motions, they can be retrained in a new procedure. Sometimes unnecessary actions can be eliminated by repositioning machines and tools to reduce delays between the time that one unit leaves and another unit arrives at the worker's station.

Work Measurement

While job design, methods analysis and motion studies focus on how a job is done, **work measurement** focuses on the length of time required to complete the job. The firm requires knowledge about job times for performance evaluation and for determining how workers should be compensated. Information on how long it takes to perform a job is also required for personnel planning, estimating labour costs, scheduling, budgeting and designing incentive systems. For the worker, time standards provide an idea of expected output.

A common method of work measurement is **time study**, developed by Frederick W. Taylor in 1881 and still widely used today. The various component activities of a particular job are timed, filmed, videotaped or otherwise measured with some type of recording device. This procedure is repeated several times and the results are averaged. The averaged times for each component are then added together to get an average total time for the completion of the entire job. Allowance is usually made for worker fatigue and personal needs. A typical job performance is also taken into consideration; a worker who is unusually fast or slow in performing the job can skew the results such that the study loses its applicability to other workers performing the same job.

Operating Production Decisions

The daily operation of the plant is primarily the responsibility of the middle and supervisory management of the production division, and includes activities such as demand forecasting, inventory management, distribution planning, production planning, scheduling of customer orders, purchasing of raw materials and parts, maintenance of machines and equipment and control of product quality. In addition, one of the prime responsibilities of production management is the control of both fixed and variable production costs to ensure efficiency. We will now look at each of these functions in greater detail.

Demand Forecasting

Let us imagine, for a moment, a shoe manufacturer with factories in Montreal and Winnipeg. This manufacturer also has six regional warehouses, one at each of the factories and four others located in Vancouver, Edmonton, Toronto and Halifax. These regional warehouses supply shoe stores in their region. To simplify the discussion, assume that the firm manufactures only one style of shoe. Retail shoe

Methods analysis is the study of how a particular operation is performed along with the machines, equipment and materials used.

Motion studies are used in manufacturing companies to study how production workers perform their jobs. The objective is to eliminate any unnecessary motions and make workers' efforts more productive.

Work measurement focuses on the length of time required to complete a particular job.

Time study is used to determine how long it takes to perform a particular job.

stores order the quantities that they believe they will be able to sell and send their orders to the regional warehouses. The retailers assume that their orders will be filled promptly according to the shoe company's policy.

To meet the demand, the shoe manufacturer faces several problems. First, sufficient raw materials and semi-finished components must be ordered to meet the required demand. Second, the shoes must be manufactured, which takes time. If production capacity must be increased, additional time may be required to buy more machinery and train more production workers. Third, the shoes must be delivered to the regional warehouses from which retail orders will be shipped. If the manufacturer has not correctly anticipated the quantities ordered by the shoe stores, production will be less than demand, which means that sales (and, consequently, profit) will be lost.

To guard against this potential loss, the shoe manufacturer can (1) carry a large inventory so that even an unusually high demand of shoes can be met, if necessary; or (2) either increase or decrease production depending on whether demand is increasing or decreasing. Either alternative poses problems. In the first case, it costs money to carry a large amount of inventory, and if sales never materialize the manufacturer will be stuck with out-of-style shoes that may have to be scrapped. The second alternative is not very practical either. It takes time to recruit, interview, hire and train new workers. It may also take weeks or months before sufficient raw materials and parts can be acquired. New machines may also have to be specially ordered or reconditioned.

Fortunately, most manufacturers, including our shoe manufacturer, can get a reasonably accurate picture of future demand by engaging in **demand forecasting**. Forecasts of expected sales are usually made for a 12-month period. These forecasts are usually prepared using previous years' sales as a basis for determining sales in the coming year. For example, if sales have been rising steadily over the years, then the company will probably assume that sales will continue to rise in a similar manner. Each warehouse prepares a forecast using historical data, which is called a **time series analysis** (see Figure 7.4A). Then these forecasts can be examined and adjusted based on other criteria. For example, salespeople in the field will have a good idea what demand will be because they are constantly in touch with the people who are doing the ordering. Future economic conditions can also be taken into account and forecasts adjusted accordingly.

Since there is always the possibility that a demand forecast may be inaccurate, and that the actual demand may be greater than the forecasted demand, a **safety stock** is incorporated into the forecast. The size of the safety stock is a policy decision of management based on its desire not to lose sales or have dissatisfied customers.

When individual warehouse forecasts are complete, they are merged into a total forecast for each of the factories so that material requirements and production capacity can be determined (see Figure 7.4B). By forecasting a year in advance, the firm can gear up its production schedule and order the necessary raw materials. As actual sales are realized, these new figures are used to update the forecast. With a good idea of what future sales might be, the shoe company can adjust its production capacity and inventory sufficiently far in advance to avoid a production crisis.

Inventory Management

For production operations, **inventory management** is a complex activity. The inventory manager must ensure that enough of the raw materials and parts that are primary inputs into the production process are available as needed. At various stages,

Demand forecasting for manufacturers is necessary to ensure that sufficient raw materials and semi-finished components will be available and that the product will be ready for shipment when needed.

Time series analysis—a forecast that uses historical data.

Safety stock is an additional amount of inventory carried to minimize the costs of running out of stock due to inaccurate demand forecasts.

Inventory management is the planning and control of physical stocks of raw materials, semi-finished goods and finished products.

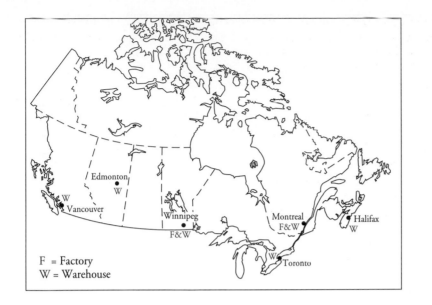

FIGURE 7.4A

Demand forecast for the
Edmonton warehouse

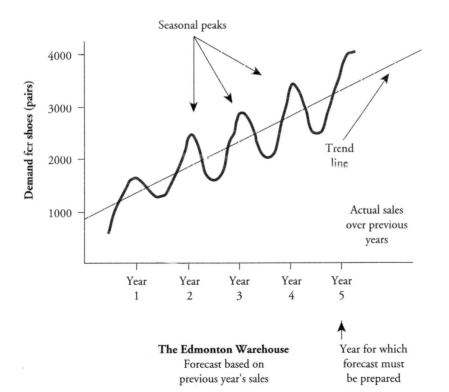

For each warehouse, the sales figures from previous years are used to
make a forecast of expected sales for the new year, year 5 in the above
example. As you can see by the trend line, which slopes upward, sales
appear to be increasing over the years. The trend line and sales forecast
for each month can be calculated using regression analysis.

FIGURE 7.4B

Company sales forecast

Warehouses	Jan.	Feb.	Mar.	Apr.	May	June	July	Aug.	Sept.	Oct.	Nov.	Dec.	Total
Vancouver	2 780	2 800	2 810	3 000	3 800	3 800	4 150	4 680	4 460	4 100	4 100	3 900	44 380
Edmonton	2 560	2 690	2 820	2 950	3 240	3 610	3 840	4 010	3 730	3 630	3 510	3 440	40 030
Winnipeg	2 100	2 160	1 800	1 940	2 360	2 890	3 250	3 460	3 400	3 020	2 900	2 700	31 980
Winnipeg Factory	7 440	7 650	7 430	7 890	9 400	10 300	11 240	12 150	11 590	10 750	10 510	10 040	116 390
Montreal	8 540	8 750	8 530	8 990	10 500	11 400	12 340	13 250	12 690	11 850	11 610	11 140	129 590
Toronto	13 500	13 850	13 480	14 250	16 760	18 260	19 830	21 350	20 420	10 010	18 620	17 830	198 160
Halifax	4 960	5 100	4 950	5 260	6 260	6 860	7 490	8 100	7 730	7 160	7 000	6 690	77 560
Montreal Factory	27 000	27 700	26 960	28 500	33 520	36 520	39 660	42 700	40 840	29 020	37 230	35 660	405 310
Total Production	34 440	35 350	34 390	36 390	42 920	46 820	50 900	54 850	52 430	39 770	47 740	45 700	521 700

the production process yields semi-finished products that may have to be stored for use as inputs into the production process at a later stage. Finally, the amount of finished goods in inventory must be great enough to ensure that normal customer orders can be filled.

What Quantity Should the Firm Buy?

The quantity of material purchased is normally dictated by the rate at which the material is used. If raw materials or parts are used at a constant rate, a firm may buy often and in small quantities. This strategy is known as **hand-to-mouth buying**. Buying in large quantities that will last a long time is termed **forward buying**.

Both strategies have their advantages and disadvantages. When prices are in a decline, buying in small quantities will contribute to lower material costs over time, and, with less money tied up in inventory, storage costs may also be reduced. Buying in smaller quantities allows greater flexibility if a firm must change a raw material. However, the purchaser also runs the risk that suppliers may be unable to ship the materials when necessary. Moreover, since smaller quantities are purchased, the supplier may not offer volume-price concessions.

Buying in large quantities, or forward buying, is often done during inflationary periods when prices are certain to increase over time. Forward buying also offers some protection against problems such as supplier strikes or material shortages. It may allow a firm to continue production for as long as it takes to resolve the problem. Thus, utilities and steel companies stockpile enough coal to allow production for as long as three months, in case supply is suddenly cut off.

Carrying Inventory Costs Money

A firm could guard against running out of raw materials or finished goods by always having large quantities on hand. However, carrying inventory costs money. If the firm must borrow the money to buy the inventory, it must pay interest on the borrowed funds. If the firm uses its own money, there is an opportunity cost in that the money tied up in inventory cannot be used for other purposes that may generate income. It also costs money to store inventory and insure it against hazards such as fire and theft, and with some items there is always the possibility that it will spoil or become obsolete.

On the other hand, too little inventory can also cost the firm money. A shortage of raw materials may cause expensive delays in the production process. In the case of a retail business, potential customers will be lost, perhaps permanently, if they find that common merchandise or parts are out of stock.

Establishing an Inventory Control System

In manufacturing, some raw materials or components may be used up faster than others, while retailers may find that certain dress styles and sizes, for example, are sold more frequently than others. Since it is critical to carry the right amount of inventory at all times, knowing how much to order, and when, is crucial. A system is required to monitor how quickly inventory is moving and when a new order must be placed.

With a computerized inventory management system, sales are recorded when purchased by the customer and the item is then deducted from inventory records. When the items in inventory drop below a certain minimum level, a new order, automatically developed by the computer, is then mailed to the supplier. This minimum level, as well as the amount to reorder, must be determined for every item so as to minimize the cost of carrying inventory as well as the cost of reordering.

Hand-to-mouth buying occurs when a firm buys materials often and in small quantities.

Forward buying occurs when a firm buys materials in large quantities that will last a long time.

Sales Forecasting

www.inventorymanagement.com/fcstg1.htm

www.inventorymanagement.com/fcstg2.htm

Inventory being taken at Upjohn Company of Canada >

The Economic Order Quantity and the Reordering Process

For a better understanding of the inventory and reordering process, refer to Figure 7.5. The amount of product used in manufacturing can be determined from the production order or, in the case of a retailer, from past experience or sales forecasts. In our example, it takes six weeks to use 60 units of an item and reach the reorder point when a new order is placed. The **reorder point** is chosen so that there is enough product on hand to meet sales demand or manufacturing requirements until the new order arrives in stock. The **lead time**—four weeks in our example—represents the time needed to mail the order to the supplier and have it filled, shipped and placed into stock. The purchasing department must know the lead times for all items because they may vary for different products and suppliers. If inventory management and purchasing are separate departments, close cooperation between the two is required.

The **economic order quantity (EOQ)** is the lowest order size that will minimize the total annual cost of carrying inventory in stock and the reorder cost. The annual **inventory carrying cost** includes costs of insurance, storage, spoilage, obsolescence and interest charges on the money tied up in inventory. Some of these costs are known or can be calculated, while others are estimates.

The annual **ordering cost** includes the cost of issuing an order to a supplier, as well as the cost of receiving it in the warehouse. For example, the larger the order size, the greater the average inventory carried during the year and hence the greater the cost of carrying that inventory. On the other hand, the larger order size means a decrease in the number of orders that must be issued during the year and received in stock. Therefore, reorder costs decrease. Figure 7.6 shows how the EOQ is basically a trade-off between inventory carrying cost and reorder cost.

The EOQ for the firm may or may not agree with the quantity sold by suppliers. For example, even though the economic order quantity for a particular item is five dozen, it may be available only in gross lots such as 144 dozen. In other instances, a supplier may offer discounts to encourage the purchase of large quantities.

Reorder point is chosen so that there is enough product on hand to meet sales demand or manufacturing requirements until the new order arrives in stock.

Lead time represents the time needed to mail the order to the supplier and have it filled, shipped and placed into stock.

Economic order quantity (EOQ) is the lowest order size that will minimize the total annual cost of carrying inventory in stock and the reorder cost.

Inventory carrying cost includes costs of insurance, storage, spoilage, obsolescence and interest charges on the money tied up in inventory.

Ordering cost includes the cost of issuing an order to a supplier, as well as the cost of receiving it in the warehouse.

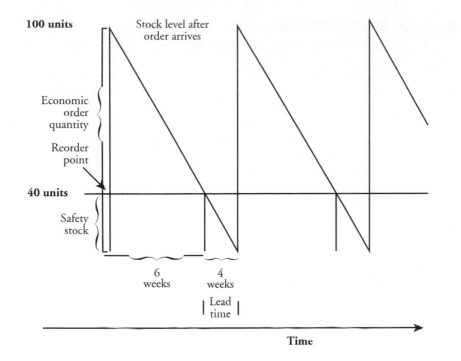

FIGURE 7.5

Stock movement and reordering

The inventory manager must then make a decision on the quantity to order. There would be little advantage in ordering 100 units of a product simply because the supplier offers a small discount, if only 50 units are sold per year. The cost of carrying the inventory, together with the potential cost of spoilage or obsolescence, could easily outweigh the discount.

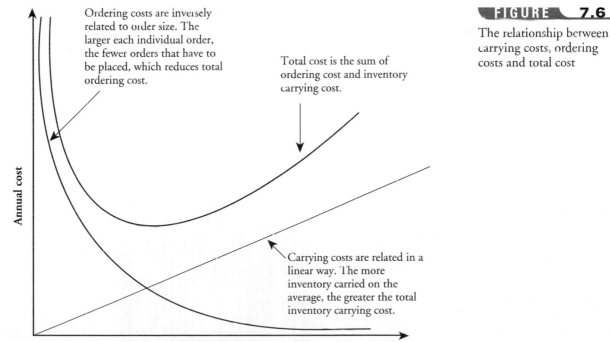

Inventory Control Methods

Periodic inventory control system—involves counting the inventories at specified time intervals to determine how much is left.

Perpetual inventory control system—shows the inventory in stock at any given time, since additions to and withdrawals from inventory are noted on special cards or are controlled by a computer.

Two general methods can be used to track inventories. The **periodic inventory control system** involves counting the inventories at specified time intervals to determine how much is left. By adding purchases to beginning inventories and subtracting ending inventories, a firm can determine the actual amount sold. Although costly, this process is required at least once each year for tax purposes.

In a **perpetual inventory control** system, inventory is tracked on a continual basis. When goods are sold, the item and dollar value is immediately deducted from inventory. Similarly, when a purchase is received it is immediately added to inventories. Today, additions to and withdrawals from inventory are controlled through a computer, which can be programmed to reorder when the quantity drops below a minimum point. Small firms may record additions and withdrawals on special cards.

Perpetual inventory control is practised by modern department stores with computerized inventory systems. All cash registers are linked to the central computer, where the inventory files are contained. As merchandise is sold, the cashier enters both the inventory number and the price of the item into the register. The computer deducts this item from inventory. When the stock level drops to a predetermined reorder point, the computer automatically produces the order, which is then mailed to the supplier. Thus, the reordering process can be largely automated if the computer is given specific criteria as to what inventory levels are to be maintained. However, the computer cannot make judgments as to how consumer demand may be affected by future economic conditions or consumer habits. These must remain decisions of management.

Universal product code (UPC) is a series of light and dark bars printed on the package of a product and designed for use in a computerized perpetual inventory system.

The **universal product code (UPC)**—the series of light and dark bars printed on many items—is designed for a computerized perpetual inventory system. An item is passed over a light in a counter or a cash register clerk draws a light wand across the bars, signalling the computer. The computer then registers the type of product, price and so on, and automatically reduces the inventory level. Two major advantages of computerized perpetual inventory management are the speed at which the information becomes available for management and the reduction in tedious work for clerical employees.

Physical Inventory Count

Regardless of how sophisticated an inventory system is, a physical count is still required at least once a year to determine the actual level of inventory on hand. Even a perpetual inventory system cannot know how much is lost due to theft or lost in other ways. The physical count is then compared to the perpetual inventory figures. Any difference must be accounted for by the inventory manager. Large deviations are usually the result of errors in paperwork, but they could also be caused by theft or by the loss of materials in transit.

Bar Codes

www.adams1.com/pub/ russadam/upccode.html

A universal product code is > designed for a computerized perpetual inventory system

0   5781287711   5

Distribution Planning

A firm with only one factory has few distribution problems as long as there are adequate transportation facilities to ship its product to market. However, if a firm has a number of factories and warehouses in various locations across the country, then **distribution planning** becomes an important production decision. The objective is to minimize the total distribution costs (e.g., the costs of moving product to the various warehouses from the various factories).

For example, let us return to the shoe manufacturer with two factories and six regional warehouses. Figure 7.7A shows the location of these facilities. To simplify, assume that each factory produces only two types of shoes, the eastern sandal and the western boot. Assume further that each factory can manufacture both styles and can ship to any of the six warehouses if necessary.

It is the task of production management to determine the lowest-cost method of distributing its product, based on transportation cost and demand for the two types of shoes. It may be that both factories should produce both types of shoes and supply their own regions—the Winnipeg factory supplying both styles of shoes to the West and the Montreal factory supplying them to eastern Canada. This pattern is shown by the solid lines in Figure 7.7A. Or, it might be advantageous to specialize production of the western boot in the Winnipeg factory and that of the eastern sandal in the Montreal factory. Then each factory would ship its product to any of the six warehouses. The dotted lines in Figure 7.7A indicate this situation. Either of

Distribution planning is required when a firm has more than one factory and/or warehouse. The objective is to minimize the total distribution costs (i.e., the costs of moving product to the various warehouses from the various factories).

FIGURE 7.7A

Shoe company factories, warehouses and transportation routes

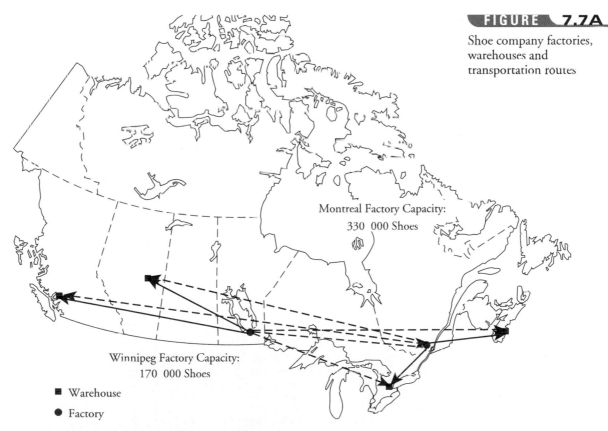

Montreal Factory Capacity: 330 000 Shoes

Winnipeg Factory Capacity: 170 000 Shoes

■ Warehouse

● Factory

Dotted lines indicate that any factory can supply any warehouse if necessary.
Actual supply and manufacturing depend on transportation costs.

these two approaches would depend on transportation and manufacturing costs. If each factory can reduce its costs of production by manufacturing only one type of shoe, and if this reduction in manufacturing costs is greater than the increased cost of shipping one type of shoe to all warehouses from one factory, then it would be a viable alternative.

Distribution planning may also become important under another circumstance. Assume that Winnipeg's production facilities produce only the western boot because demand in the West for the eastern sandal is very small. In the past, this demand has been met by the Montreal factory, which has shipped the eastern sandal to the various western warehouses, even though shipping costs per pair are quite high.

Let's now assume that demand for the eastern sandal in western Canada increases dramatically. While Montreal can gear up its production to meet the increased demand, shipping costs from Montreal to the West are much higher compared to shipping costs from Winnipeg to the western warehouses (see Figure 7.7B). Because of the lower shipping costs, it may be advantageous for Winnipeg to begin to produce the eastern sandal, even if this initially requires overtime. Figure 7.7B shows that the total cost to manufacture a pair of eastern sandals using overtime at the Winnipeg plant, and to ship them to the three western warehouses, is less in all instances than to have the Montreal factory supply the West with these sandals.

Production Planning and Control

Planning and controlling are two important functions of managers in manufacturing firms. The production department generally incurs the greatest costs because it usually employs the largest number of people, including managers. It is responsible for virtually all purchasing requirements, and it generally has a large investment in raw materials and semi-finished or finished goods. Inefficient methods in the production process may add greatly to variable costs, and consequently increase the price to the

FIGURE 7.7B

Cost matrix for Canadian Shoe Company, Inc.

From (factory) **To** (warehouse)	**Winnipeg** OT TC	**Montreal** OT TC	**Warehouse capacity** (pairs of shoes)
Vancouver	$1.10 $0.80	$1.80 $2.30	50 000
Edmonton	$1.10 $0.50	$1.80 $1.90	50 000
Winnipeg	$1.10 $0.10	$1.80 $1.40	80 000
Toronto	$1.10 $0.70	$1.80 $0.30	110 000
Montreal	$1.10 $1.10	$1.80 $0.10	150 000
Halifax	$1.10 $1.40	$1.80 $0.70	30 000
Factory capacity (pairs of shoes)	170 000	330 000	

OT = Overtime cost to produce one pair of shoes
TC = Shipping and handling cost per pair of shoes

consumer, which could affect product sales. Shaving a few pennies off production costs, perhaps through product redesign, may result in substantial dollar savings for a product that is produced in large quantities. A better-designed machine to make the production process more efficient might be worth the expense in the long run.

Production planning starts with demand forecasts (usually for a period of one year) to ensure that general capacity is available for the expected demand. This aggregate plan is broken down into a master schedule that contains detailed production planning for specific models and covers a specific time period, whether hours, days, weeks or months. The master schedule is used to determine the materials and parts required for production. The master schedule is also used to develop the basic production schedule, specifying which work centres will be used to produce specific orders and the time required in those work centres. We will now examine this process in more detail.

Aggregate Production Planning

Aggregate planning, also known as medium-range planning, is the first step in the actual production planning process. (Figure 7.8) Its purpose is to translate demand forecasts into planned production levels. The focus, however, is on families of products rather than individual products. Our shoe manufacturer would plan in terms of total numbers of eastern sandals and western boots, but would not be concerned at this stage with colours and sizes. Similarly, an appliance manufacturer will plan for output requirements of refrigerators, stoves and dishwashers. Later on, in the short-range planning process, when the master schedule is prepared, these broad categories are broken down into specific models such as frost-free, side-by-side or energy-efficient refrigerators.

Aggregate planning is designed to translate demand forecasts into planned production levels.

FIGURE 7.8

Aggregate planning and the planning cycle

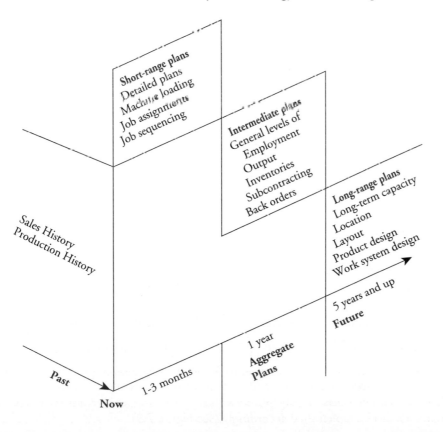

Thus, aggregate planning is concerned with having enough production capacity to meet demand for the upcoming 12- to 18-month period. The manufacturer has a number of options available.

1. *Vary the workforce size.* If demand rises and falls, production can be increased or decreased by hiring and firing workers as required. This increases hiring and layoff costs, costs associated with finding qualified employees, interviewing and training, and eventually the costs associated with laying them off again when production levels return to normal. On the other hand, the firm reduces the cost of building up and carrying inventory to meet the increased demand.

2. *Hold the workforce constant but vary its utilization.* Production can be increased with overtime work or a shortened work week. While this strategy reduces hiring and layoff costs, it means greater payroll costs because of overtime and associated costs. Furthermore, when employees work longer hours, there is usually a drop in productivity and a greater possibility of accidents because employees are more fatigued than usual. Another factor is equipment failure, or downtime of equipment, since it is used more intensively.

3. *Subcontract.* An outside manufacturer can be used to produce component parts.

4. *Hold the workforce constant and use inventories to absorb demand fluctuations.* Inventories will be built up during periods when production exceeds demand. During periods when demand increases, product will be drawn from inventory to meet the higher demand. By using this strategy, the firm incurs greater inventory carrying costs. There will be higher storage costs, and money will be tied up in inventory, which is not available for other purposes.

**Materials
Requirements Planning**

mscmga.ms.ic.ac.uk/jeb/or/
mrp.html

Master schedule—a detailed, short-term production plan that states the quantity and types of items to be produced during a specific time period, which may be hours, days or weeks.

Material requirements planning (MRP) is a computerized process that requires information from the master schedule, bills of materials and inventory records to determine when orders must be placed with suppliers, so that inventories of parts and materials can be replenished accordingly.

Material Requirements Planning

Developed from the aggregate plan, the master schedule is a detailed, short-term production plan that states the quantity and types of items to be produced during a specific period. For example, it would specify to our appliance manufacturer detailed production rates, on a daily or weekly basis, for specific models of refrigerators, stoves and so on.

The aggregate plan and **master schedule** will provide rough estimates of the labour, facilities and equipment that will be needed to produce the various quantities of product. However, the various raw materials and parts are not actually accounted for in these plans and schedules. One approach is to ensure that enough of what a company uses is always in inventory. As already discussed, however, carrying large inventories is costly, and even large inventories do not ensure that a company will not run out of a crucial item used in the production process.

To ensure that the master schedule can be executed without huge inventory levels, a company must plan to have the necessary materials, parts and assemblies available in time for use in the production process. This requires answers to two basic questions:

1. What parts and raw materials are needed to make the end item?

2. How much of those parts and raw materials do we have on hand?

Material requirements planning (MRP) is a computerized process that requires information from the master schedule, bills of materials and inventory records to determine when orders must be placed with suppliers, so that inventories of parts and materials can be replenished accordingly (see Figure 7.9).

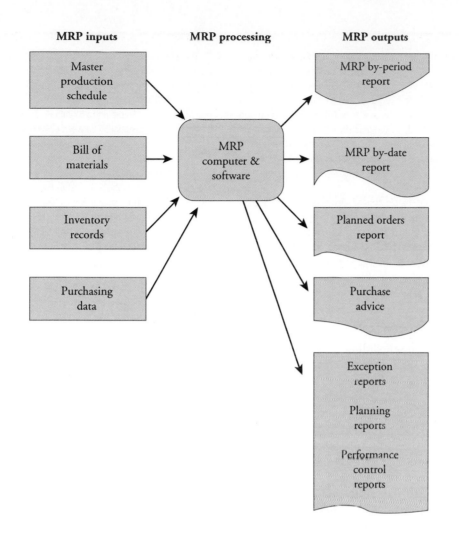

FIGURE 7.9

The material requirements planning (MRP) process: inputs and outputs

Each finished product has its own **bill of materials** that lists all the assemblies, sub-assemblies, parts and raw materials that are needed to produce one unit. The inventory records file is used to store information on the status of each item by time period. Typical information stored in an inventory records file includes part number, on-hand quantity, on-order quantity cost data and procurement lead time, economic order quantity and lot size. Furthermore, information about the supplier is also usually included. The **inventory records file** is linked to production and purchasing so that updates can be made to orders, receipts and issues from stock.

If MRP is to be successfully implemented, the firm must have a computerized information system, since a large amount of data must be stored and processed. Information fed into the system must be accurate. If wrong figures are entered regarding quantities on hand and future needs, then the system will break down. Once processed, various reports and schedules are produced, including planned order schedules, order releases and changes, performance control reports, planning reports and exception reports. These outputs are also shown in Figure 7.9.

Scheduling

Scheduling, the final step in the production planning process, involves assigning priorities to manufacturing orders and allocating workloads to specific work centres.

Bill of materials—lists all the assemblies, sub-assemblies, parts and raw materials that are needed to produce one unit of a product.

Inventory records file—stores information on the status of each item by time period, including part number, on-hand quantity, on-order quantity, cost data and procurement lead time, economic order quantity and lot size.

Scheduling—the final step in the production planning process—involves assigning priorities to manufacturing orders and allocating workloads to specific work centres.

Just-in-Time Inventory

Just-in-time inventory (JIT), or Kanban, stems from Japan. The idea is to have suppliers deliver raw materials and/or parts at the exact time they are needed, so as to keep inventories of the manufacturing facility at zero (or as close to it as possible). This system also keeps goods-in-process inventories to a minimum because goods are produced only as needed for the next production stage. Finished-goods inventories are also minimized by matching production closely with sales demand.

Under the old system, also called the batch-push system, each work station in the production process produced at a constant rate regardless of what the next stage required. The excess was put into inventory. In contrast, with JIT, also known as the demand-pull system, each work station produces its product only when the next work station requires more input.

The advantage of JIT is that the financial capital not tied up in inventories can be directed toward other company uses. For example, General Motors has used JIT since 1980 and has reduced its annual inventory-related costs from $8 billion to $2 billion. Successful JIT requires total coordination between all work stations of the production process as well as precise scheduling to ensure that product arrives when needed (otherwise the next station cannot produce). It also requires motivated employees who are good at teamwork and able to perform different jobs and to help out in any area that has fallen behind. Under JIT, workers experience increased job satisfaction because they have responsibility for making the system work and can influence changes and improvements in it.

Through scheduling the production manager attempts to balance conflicting goals, which include efficient use of staff, equipment and facilities, while minimizing customer waiting time, inventories and process time. Scheduling challenges the operations manager to adjust his or her production output to changes in customer orders, equipment breakdowns, late deliveries from suppliers of parts and raw materials, and various other disruptions.

Scheduling is a problem for both manufacturing and service organizations. Consider one of the more difficult scheduling problems—scheduling passengers on an airline. Each plane has only so many seats available, depending on the type of aircraft used. The airline must ensure that it doesn't overbook seats. Some customers book months in advance, while others book only a few hours before flight departure. The reservation system, essentially a scheduling system, must therefore keep track of the many flights months in advance, allowing quick updating of reservations or cancellations from anywhere in the country, sometimes even across international boundaries.

In manufacturing, scheduling depends on the nature of the production process. Different scheduling problems are experienced by high-volume production processes and job shops. We will discuss project management later in the chapter.

High-Volume System—High-volume operations such as assembly lines pose the fewest scheduling problems. The product follows a fixed path, produces a limited number of products and needs little work-in-process inventory. Highly specialized tools and equipment are designed to enhance the flow of work through the system. However, since jobs are highly specialized, worker boredom and fatigue, absenteeism, turnover and so on may disrupt the smooth flow of work through the system.

Another scheduling problem with high-volume systems is due to the fact that not all products are identical in model and style. An automobile manufacturer, for example, may schedule a variety of models into the assembly line and produce two- and four-door models with varieties of decor and optional equipment. This may mean that some work stations take longer than others to perform their task, which could hold up other work stations farther down the line. The work station is thus said to be "out of balance" with the regular line. Scheduling can ensure that the various models go through the line so that the workload per work station is relatively balanced. Scheduling must also take into account the different parts and materials required by each model. If the production line is to operate smoothly, the flow of these various parts and materials to the particular work station must be coordinated.

Scheduling must also take care of disruptions such as equipment failure, material shortages, accidents and absences. It is not usually possible to compensate for lost production time by speeding up the assembly line, which is designed to perform at a fixed rate. Thus, a firm will have to schedule overtime or subcontract. Similarly, if production has exceeded demand the line cannot be slowed down; the alternative will be to operate the line for fewer hours.

Job Shops—In a job shop, products are made to order and orders usually differ considerably from those found in high-volume operations in terms of processing requirements, materials needed, processing time and processing sequence or set-up. Therefore, scheduling in job shops is usually complex. Furthermore, little can be done prior to receiving the actual job order. Thus, the major concern for job shops is to distribute the workload among work centres (loading) and determine in what sequence orders should be processed (sequencing).

Loading

Loading refers to the assignment of jobs to work centres. Problems arise for the operations manager when two or more jobs are to be processed and a number of work centres are capable of performing the required work.

A **Gantt chart** is often used for loading and scheduling. The name derives from Henry Gantt, who pioneered the use of these charts for industrial scheduling in the early 1900s. A Gantt chart can be used to organize and clarify actual or intended use of resources over a given period of time. The time scale is shown horizontally and resources to be scheduled are listed vertically. How the resources are used is indicated in the body of the chart.

A **load chart** shows when a particular machine or work centre is either available or in use at any given time. Some work centres may be idle for long periods between jobs. With a load chart, a manager can reassign jobs to make better use of the work centres. For example, a new job may be inserted or the work for one particular centre can be rearranged in preparation for a large order. The load chart in Figure 7.10A shows which work centres are fully loaded and which ones are available.

In contrast to a load chart, a **schedule chart** is often used to monitor the progress of jobs. The horizontal axis shows time while the vertical axis shows work in progress. The chart indicates which jobs are on schedule and which are behind or ahead. Figure 7.10B shows a schedule chart for a particular job. A major task for operations people is to update these charts continually to keep them current and thus meaningful.

Sequencing

Sequencing specifies the order in which the jobs waiting at a given work centre are to be processed. If work centres are lightly loaded and all jobs require the same amount of processing, then sequencing represents no particular difficulty. However, if work centres are heavily loaded, and there is a mix of short and long jobs that must be processed at these work centres, then sequencing becomes critical. For example, a number of small jobs requiring different processing set-ups may be ahead of a large job that should be out by a certain date if a contract is to be met. Thus, some

Loading refers to the assignment of jobs to work centres.

Gantt chart—can be used to organize and clarify actual or intended use of resources over a period of time.

Load chart—shows when a particular machine or work centre is either available or in use at any given time.

Schedule chart—often used to monitor the progress of jobs.

Sequencing specifies the order in which the jobs waiting at a given work centre are to be processed.

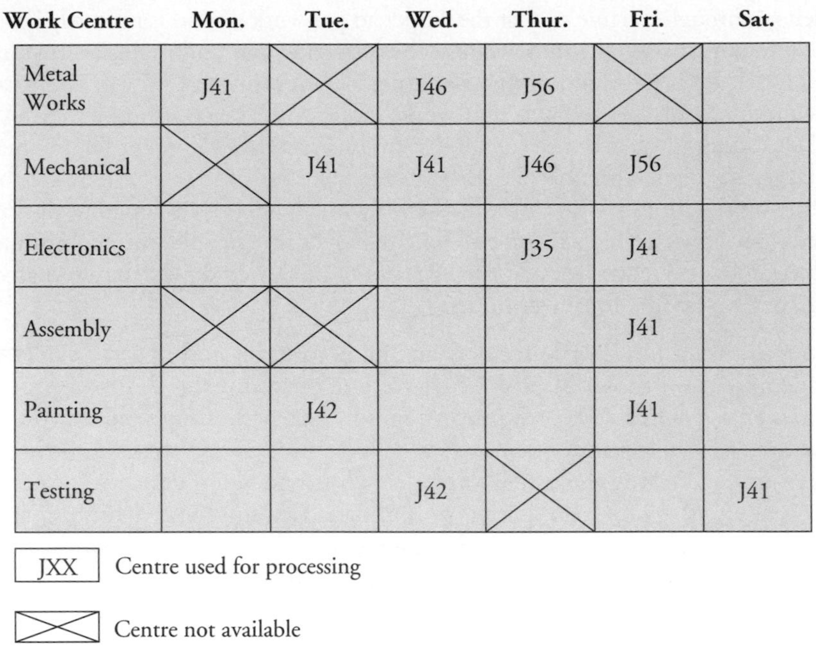

FIGURE 7.10A

FIGURE 7.10A

A Gantt load chart

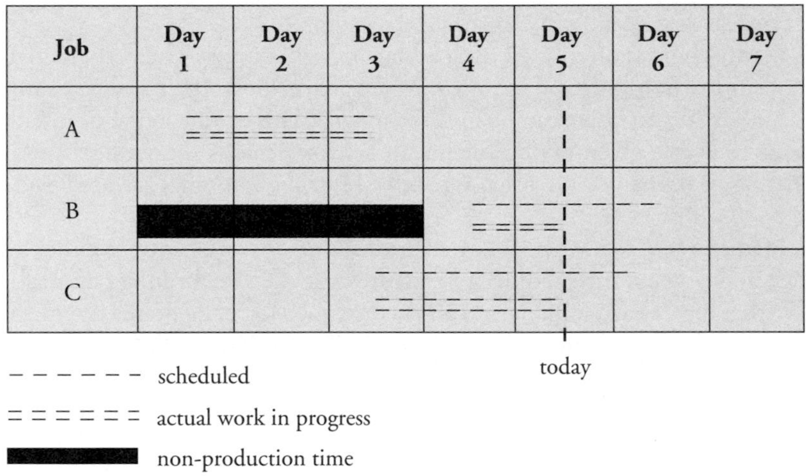

Work Centre	Mon.	Tue.	Wed.	Thur.	Fri.	Sat.
Metal Works	J41	✕	J46	J56	✕	
Mechanical	✕	J41	J41	J46	J56	
Electronics				J35	J41	
Assembly	✕	✕			J41	
Painting		J42			J41	
Testing			J42	✕		J41

JXX	Centre used for processing

✕	Centre not available

FIGURE 7.10B

A Gantt scheduling chart for jobs

Job	Day 1	Day 2	Day 3	Day 4	Day 5	Day 6	Day 7
A							
B							
C							

– – – – – – scheduled

= = = = = = actual work in progress

■■■■ non-production time

today

work centres could be sitting idle while others are overworked.

Operations managers have developed four rules that are used to determine sequencing order.

1. *FCFS (first come, first served).* Jobs may be processed on a first-come, first-served basis.

2. *SPT (shortest processing time).* Jobs may be processed according to processing time at a machine or work centre, with the shortest job being first.

3. *DD (due date).* Jobs may be processed in order of due date, with the earliest due date being processed first.

4. *RUSH.* An emergency order or a preferred customer may receive priority processing.

Purchasing

Improper attention to **purchasing** can mean losses for a firm. An inexperienced purchasing agent concerned only with material costs, for example, might buy low-quality raw materials or components that break down in the production process, causing delays and driving up production costs. If quantities purchased are too large, the firm may face stockpiles of obsolescent materials. If purchases are made from new suppliers without a proper check on their ability to meet shipping dates and quantities, the production process may again be delayed.

On the other hand, astute purchasing managers can reduce costs. Through bargaining and volume purchasing, they can often negotiate a good price for raw materials or parts, and if they watch economic conditions closely they may be able to purchase large quantities of a product before a major price increase. Moreover, through careful analysis of the materials and parts used, the purchasing manager may be able to substitute less costly materials and still achieve the same quality in the final product. The latter task is known as value analysis.

In **value analysis**, engineering and purchasing personnel work together to examine materials used in the manufacture of a given product. Engineers examine the product design and proposed materials to determine whether less expensive materials could be substituted without affecting the quality of the finished product. For example, the sheet metal used in automobile bodies today is thinner than that used 20 years ago and reduces the cost of production for the manufacturer. Yet the metal is equally effective, and because it helps to reduce the total weight of the car it also contributes to fuel economy. Similarly, value analysis may show that a plastic gear performs as well as a more costly brass one. Any small saving in cost per individual item can amount to a large total saving on mass-produced items and result in lower prices for the consumer.

Purchasing involves obtaining and managing incoming materials and parts for use in the production process.

Value analysis involves examining the product design and proposed materials to see if less expensive materials could be substituted without affecting the quality of the finished product.

Suppliers

A major function of the purchasing department is finding suppliers for the materials required by the production firm. A supplier may be chosen on the basis of price, quality of product, ability to provide supplies as needed, speed of delivery and other services. Sometimes a firm uses only one supplier to gain the advantages of volume purchase. Such a strategy may be risky, however, if the supplier becomes engaged in a strike or is otherwise unable to supply the product; it may then be difficult for the firm to change to other suppliers, who may have prior commitments to steady customers.

Firms using sophisticated inventory management techniques such as MRP and JIT are placing new emphasis on long-term stable relationships with their suppliers. Since the supplier's production is so closely linked to the buyer's consumption, cost of parts and materials is no longer the sole criterion for choosing a supplier. The supplier must be able to provide consistent delivery of materials. As delivery times are so crucial, local suppliers are increasingly relied upon to supply all of a firm's requirements for a particular raw material or part. Needless to say, quality of product is also a major consideration.

Make-or-Buy Decisions

Manufacturing firms that use components from outside suppliers are often faced with a **make-or-buy decision**. If facilities are large enough and a firm has the financial and human resources to make the product itself, then it might save money in the long run. Some firms have no choice, if buying parts elsewhere means giving away a secret production process, or if no other firm has the expertise or resources required to produce the parts. Other reasons for a firm's decision to manufacture its own

Make-or-buy decision—a production decision about whether to make components or to purchase them from outside suppliers.

Quality control inspector monitors the measuring of pharmaceutical products >

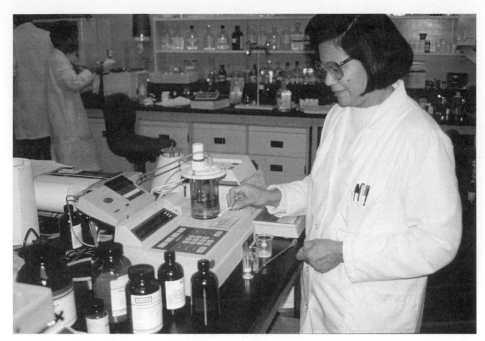

components include control over quality, elimination of supply problems or control over supply costs. A make-or-buy decision can be of major importance to a firm, and is usually not made without upper-management approval.

Quality Control

Quality Control

mscmga.ms.ic.ac.uk/jeb/or/
qcontrol.html

Quality control is an attempt to find defective products, either during or after the production process, before they reach the customer.

Most products today must meet stringent manufacturing standards. Otherwise they may perform improperly, wear out too quickly or break down. Producing a poor-quality product can be costly if a firm must repair the product even before it is sold to customers, or if extensive warranty repairs are necessary. Sometimes the entire production run may have to be scrapped if the product cannot be repaired. Besides incurring these direct costs, a firm may lose customers, and thus revenue and profit, if it consistently produces inferior products.

To ensure that product quality is high, manufacturers usually inspect the products at various stages of assembly. **Quality control** can be accomplished through visual inspection to check for defects or poor workmanship. Often quality control also involves measuring various aspects of the product and comparing it with predetermined standards, which could be based on technical requirements and engineering standards, industry standards or customer expectations concerning operating life. For products such as appliances, quality control is performed by actually operating the product for a specified period of time. Television sets, for example, are "burned in"—that is, turned on for a specific period during which any defects usually become apparent. Some products, however, can be checked only by dismantling or physically destroying them. Quality control then involves taking a random sample of the manufactured product.

Regardless of how a product's quality is measured, a quality control function requires people, space and costly measuring equipment—all additional expenses for a firm. Without quality control, however, a firm could incur even greater costs, since a poor-quality product could result in the loss of customers and reputation, as well as in a substantial direct loss if the defective product has to be repaired or scrapped. Thus, a firm must balance the cost of exercising quality control against these other costs.

Figure 7.11 shows the relationship between the cost of establishing a quality control function and the possible cost of producing defective products. The vertical axis represents costs in dollars while the horizontal axis represents additional units of quality control, such as quality control inspectors. The downward sloping curve represents the cost of producing defective products. These costs include scrap loss, repairs and loss of potential revenue from dissatisfied customers. Without a quality control function, these costs could be extremely high.

The establishment of a quality control department with inspectors to check product quality and standards on the assembly line also incurs a cost; the upward-sloping diagonal line in Figure 7.11 indicates that as the number of inspectors increases, so does the cost of the quality control function in terms of salary, office space and testing equipment. However, quality control costs will be offset because (1) poor-quality production runs are detected more readily, which reduces scrap loss; (2) both customer alienation and after-sale repair costs will be reduced if fewer defective products reach the market.

There is a limit to the number of inspectors a firm can have in quality control. The cost of salaries and other expenses could rise to the point where they offset any additional savings from increased inspection. The firm incurs the lowest possible cost, taking both inspection and poor quality into account, at the lowest point of the U-shaped total cost curve. The curve first declines as the quality control operation reduces the costs of producing defective parts, but starts to rise again as the costs of inspection begin to outweigh the savings.

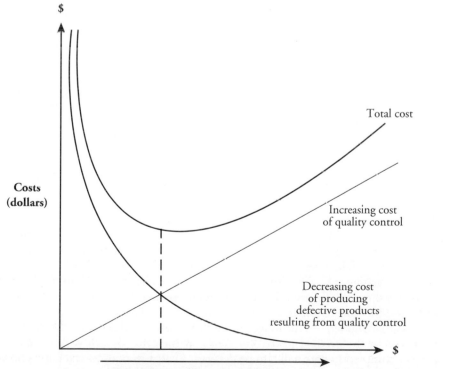

FIGURE 7.11

Effects of a quality control function on costs associated with defective products

Maintenance

Most manufacturing processes are heavily dependent on machines. If a machine breaks down, especially one performing a crucial task, an entire production line could be shut down, costing the firm many thousands of dollars as workers stand idle while the machine is repaired. The risk of such breakdowns is minimized through **preventive maintenance**. Machines are periodically inspected and adjusted even if they are not defective. Any parts that appear defective or worn are replaced, although the machine may still be operable. Preventive maintenance thus helps a firm to avoid the additional expense of unexpected disruptions in a production schedule.

In preventive maintenance, as in quality control, management must strike a balance between the cost of the maintenance function and the potential cost of unexpected machine failure and its effect on the production process. A chart similar to Figure 7.11 could be used to determine the optimum amount of preventive maintenance. The optimum amount would again be at the lowest point on the total cost curve, where the decreasing costs of machine failure are offset by the increasing costs of the maintenance function.

Project Management

Building large, complex projects—power dams, high-rise office complexes, a new airplane, ship or space vehicle—presents a particular problem for the production manager. Few of these projects are ever alike, and unforeseen problems could arise at any time, delaying completion of the project and costing the firm considerable sums of money when contract deadlines are not met. Other firms involved in the project could also be affected.

Any major project can be broken down into specific tasks that must be completed over a period of time with the resources available. Some tasks can be started only after others are completed. Other tasks can be worked on simultaneously. **Project management** involves establishing a **project schedule**, or **network**, that specifies the tasks that must be completed, the time required for each task and the sequence in which the tasks have to be completed. In addition, the resources available for completing each task—people, equipment, space and so on—are also specified.

One common technique for planning major production projects and for controlling their completion time is **PERT (Program Evaluation and Review Technique)**. First used in the production of guided missiles for the Polaris submarine, PERT was quickly adapted for use in industry. A second technique, **CPM or Critical Path Method**, was developed by DuPont for the planning and control of complex industrial projects.

The two techniques, PERT and CPM, are essentially similar, except for their method of establishing the time required for the completion of the various segments of the project. PERT is used when the completion times for various project tasks are unknown or difficult to estimate. Statistical methods are then used to determine the longest, most likely and shortest probable time for completing a particular task. CPM, on the other hand, is used in projects where the completion times for various tasks are reasonably well known.

To illustrate, a CPM network for the construction of a custom-designed automobile is shown in Figure 7.12. The completion of each task is shown by a separate path, and the time required to complete each task, in days, is indicated. The sequence of tasks that will require the longest time to complete, indicated by the thick arrows, is known as the **critical path**. Any delay in the critical path will mean that the project completion date will also be delayed. Delays in non-critical paths, however, may not cause delays in the total time required to finish the project.

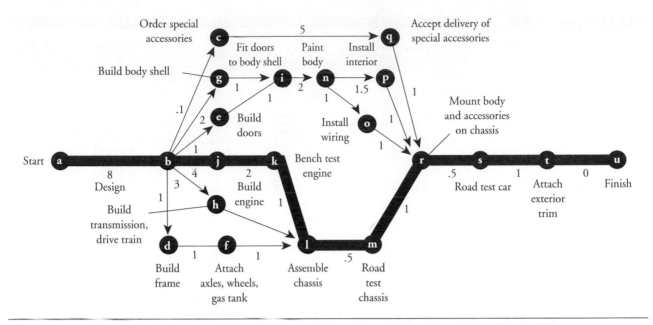

Order special accessories — c

Fit doors to body shell — i

Paint body — n

Install interior — p

Accept delivery of special accessories — q

Build body shell — g

Build doors — e

Install wiring — o

Mount body and accessories on chassis — r

Start — a — Design 8 — b

j — Bench test engine — k

s — Road test car — t — Attach exterior trim — u — Finish

Build transmission, drive train — 3

Build engine — 2

Build frame — d — Attach axles, wheels, gas tank — f — Assemble chassis — l — Road test chassis — m

SOURCE: James A. F. Stoner, *Management* (Englewood Cliffs, N.J.: Prentice-Hall, 1978): 640. Reprinted by permission of Prentice-Hall.

CPM and PERT networks are complex and difficult to establish. Before computers, they had to be drawn by hand and updated manually, which was extremely time-consuming and subject to errors in calculations. Since updating was such a difficult chore, it was done only infrequently. Eventually, mainframe computers were used for the planning and control of major projects where the expensive computer time could be justified. However, managers of smaller projects had difficulty accessing the costly mainframe computers.

With today's powerful computers, project management programs can help production managers schedule and coordinate projects of virtually any size. The project manager can readily develop complicated project networks. He or she enters into the computer the required information: tasks, time for completion, sequence, resources to be used and their cost. The project manager can then view the information in a variety of ways, as shown in Figure 7.13A.

The computer program known as SuperProject shows the various tasks, the people involved, and the estimated time required to complete the tasks (both graphically, through the bars in the Gantt chart, and by date). Figure 7.13B shows some of the same information as part of a PERT or network chart calculated by the program to show the critical path. As the project gets under way, the project manager can monitor on the screen or through a variety of printed reports including Gantt, PERT, status, task, resource and cost reports.

Once it is established, the manager can quickly update the network schedule hourly, daily or weekly, as completion times and resource requirements change. Updated reports can also be prepared quickly for analysis and/or distribution to other managers.

FIGURE 7.12

CPM Chart

Computers in Production

The first computer dedicated to business data-processing applications was UNIVAC I, and its first major use was in the U.S. Census Bureau. Even though business data

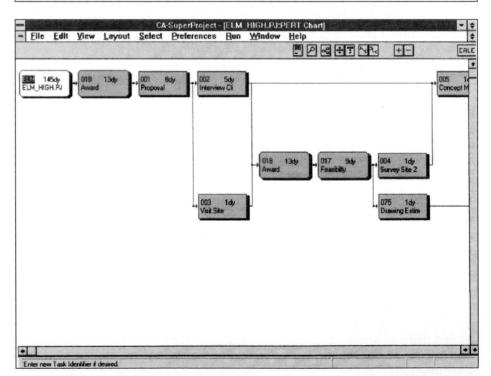

FIGURE 7.13

Establishing a project management schedule using SuperProject

processing was possible, the first-generation computers were still oriented primarily toward scientific applications. Their tremendous mathematical capabilities made them suitable for number crunching, but they were not very efficient at business data processing, which requires the input of large volumes of data on which simple calculations are performed.

The importance of computers to business was nevertheless soon realized. The first major uses were in production planning and scheduling, and in inventory management. Today, computers are a major part of a firm's management information system: accounting, planning and budgeting are largely computerized. In production departments, computers are an integral part of the entire system. They are used for production and distribution planning, MRP and inventory management, production scheduling and the keeping of central databases.

On the shop floor, many machines are already controlled by computers. There are computer-controlled stacker cranes, automatic materials-handling equipment, direct computer-controlled machine tools, and automatic inspection and test equipment including computerized quality control. However, due to high costs, only a few large corporations have integrated all of these machines and computers into a highly automated manufacturing facility. Nevertheless, giant technological strides are being taken to make the automated factory more prolific.

Computers and Automation

Computers are the critical element in automating the production process. Because of computers' ability to manipulate vast amounts of data, manufacturing processes can be regulated constantly to ensure that the quality is consistent and thus reduce scrap costs. It also allows processes to be operated at an optimum speed, which reduces manufacturing costs because of the efficient use of machines and other capital equipment. For example, it was found that in traditional manufacturing operations, the average product spends only 5% of its time in the machine; 95% of the time it is moving between work stations and waiting for further processing. This raises the costs of processing inventory, which can be as high as 22% of annual sales. If the product spent less time in the actual manufacturing process, inventory carrying costs would be reduced and the final product would reach the customer sooner.

Let us look briefly at the automated factory of the future and how products are likely to be produced in a completely automated environment.

CAD/CAM, Robots and the Automated Factory

What will the automated factory of the future look like and how will it work? The basic machine will be the CNC (computerized numerical control) machine tool. Hooked to a computer, this machine allows a manufacturer to make as many different types of components as there are computer programs that can tell the machine what to do. The CNC can be simple and perform only a few related activities, or it can be highly complex and perform a variety of tasks such as drilling, boring, milling, tapping and threading without changing its grip on the piece being machined.

The factory becomes further automated when smart robots and AGVs (automated guided vehicles) join the CNCs on the shop floor. AGVs are used primarily to ferry parts and components between work centres or fetch them from inventory. Robots would provide the arms and movement often required in manufacturing products. The movements can be precisely controlled by a computer so that processing time is reduced as much as possible.

Automating the manufacturing process is one thing—developing the product design in the first place is another. Although some designers continue to use drawing boards and develop the design on paper, more than a decade ago there emerged **CAD/CAM** (a term used to indicate the relationship between computers and manufacturing). CAD stands for computer-assisted design; CAM for computer-assisted manufacturing, sometimes also called CIM (computer-integrated manufacturing).

CAD/CAM are terms used to indicate the relationship between computers and manufacturing. CAD stands for computer-assisted design; CAM refers to computer-assisted manufacturing.

The factory of the future >

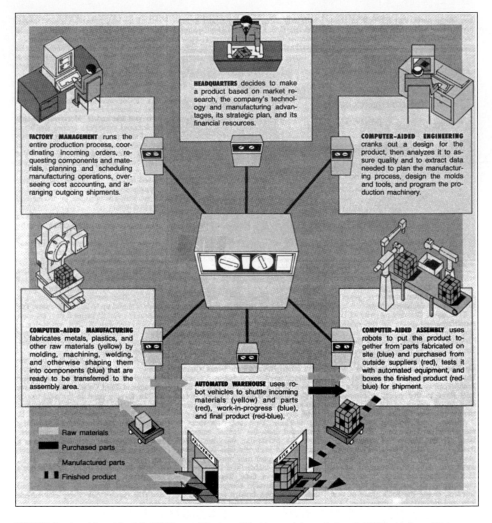

SOURCE: Reprinted from March 3, 1986 issue of *Business Week* by special permission. © 1986 by McGraw-Hill Inc.

CAD provides a technological advance that increases the productivity of designers and engineers dramatically. The designer makes sketches on a computer screen using either a light pen or a mouse. Crooked lines are straightened automatically by the computer. The software program contains hundreds of standard shapes that can be called up by the designer. If necessary, any of these shapes can be easily changed. A new rectangle can be drawn by simply specifying three corners, and a new circle can be drawn by specifying the centre and radius. Figure 7.14 shows a machine part designed with CAD. Given that one designer using a computer screen can do the work of 3.8 designers using drawing boards, CAD is likely to replace traditional manual drafting skills soon.

For example, an architect using CAD can design a house in three dimensions, view it from the front as a simple line drawing with all lines exposed, then remove view lines that would not be seen if the house were solid; he or she can shade the roof with crosshatching, mark off the chimney and make it smaller if required, colour the garage door blue, rotate the house to view it from a corner (in perspective), add new windows, and even pull a drainpipe from a library of symbols and install it under the eaves.

FIGURE 7.14

Machine part designed using an AutoCAD program and reproduced on a plotter

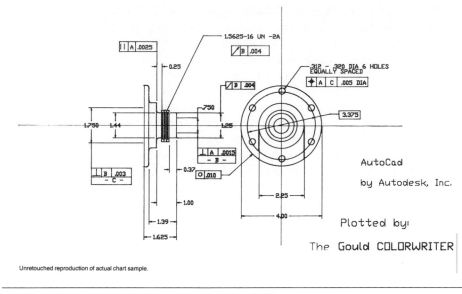

Unretouched reproduction of actual chart sample.

SOURCE: Reproduced courtesy of Gould Electronics, Recording Systems Division.

CAD can be used to design many items, from auto parts and blue jeans to wide-bodied aircraft and paper mills. For its 777 program, Boeing set up a computer network capable of accessing a sophisticated three-dimensional computer-aided design program from France, known as Catia. By linking 500 IBM work stations and two mainframe computers, Boeing will produce the first commercial jet fully designed on a computer. Whereas stress analysis of an airplane strut once required that engineers spend hours reading through pages of computer-printed numbers in search of stress concentrations, with the 3-D Elfini stress analysis system areas of high stress are identified by different colours on the computer screen.

< Using CAD/CAM in machine design

Canadian General Electric's Cobourg plant was the first in North America to use CAD/CAM to make moulds for producers of plastic parts. The first step in the CAD/CAM mould-making process is to draw a design (e.g., for a circuit-breaker mould) on the computer screen. This design is then fed into the computer operating the milling machines (computer numerical control), which in turn produce the mould, based on the computer's commands, at high speed. The operator simply loads the machine, monitors its operation and unloads it when the job is done. A similar process is used to control robots for welding or spray painting.

The communications network that ties together the design process, the computer, the robots, AGVs and CNCs so that they can all communicate with one another is called a **manufacturing automation protocol (MAP)**. MAP is a set of rules that governs how, in an ideal world, machines of any make would communicate with one another. MAP was pioneered by General Motors and has since been embraced by firms producing industrial computers and communications, as well as by major users of machine tools in other industries. More than 1000 manufacturers worldwide now adhere to the MAP standard.

Manufacturing automation protocol (MAP) is a communication network that ties together the design process, the computer, the robots, AGVs and CNCs so that they can all communicate with one another.

Robots provide the arms and movement required in manufacturing products. The movements can be precisely controlled by a computer to reduce.

The Problems of Automation

While computers and **robots** make production processes more efficient, they also alter many people's jobs and contribute to the unemployment problem. In addition, automation has made the marketplace more competitive: many firms must either automate or face bankruptcy.

The forest industry in British Columbia faced severe financial difficulties because its outmoded plants and equipment raised production costs and made its products uncompetitive. In response, more and more mills have introduced computers to measure logs electronically and direct saws to cut them so as to produce the greatest amount of lumber. The computer is more accurate than a human sawyer and reduces waste by 10%. In addition, the mill can be reprogrammed quickly to produce various types of lumber, depending on customers and their needs. One mill was able to produce as much with 350 employees as an non-automated mill employing 500. While some may argue that automation caused the loss of 150 jobs in the forest industry, others argue that it resulted in saving 350 jobs because without increased productivity the entire mill would have been shut down.

In both Canada and the United States, robots have been strong in automotive manufacturing since 1961. Robots can significantly increase productivity for automotive manufacturers. For example, Japanese automakers using many robots can produce a car in about 57 hours; in North America, the same process (without robots) takes, on average, 100 hours. Although the robots used by the automotive industry work well and are exceptionally efficient, such has not been the experience of many manufacturers outside that industry. In the past, robots were designed first and then fitted to various applications. Often they were put into positions assembling parts that were previously assembled by hand. To make them work, manufacturers had to redesign and modernize entire assembly lines at great cost. The end result was less-than-spectacular performance by the robot, which was often replaced by human assemblers.

With greater computing power and new software, robots can now be integrated more readily into many production lines. For example, robots can now be integrated into conveyor belt lines because the new programming allows interaction between the speed of the conveyor belt and the robot. Other manufacturers, such as food and beverage, pharmaceuticals and electronics, are starting to apply robots to their manufacturing lines. For example, Asea Brown Boveri Inc.'s flexible automation division, for one, has made a firm commitment to moving its robots into the packaging industry. The Burlington, Ontario-based company has made a commitment to be a leader in the area of picking, packing and palletizing.

Robots are evolving in other ways as well. Since gripping-device technology has improved, robots now have soft-sided grippers with much better sensors so they can actually perform much more complex or delicate functions—such as lifting cheese without damaging it. With the increased sensing ability of robots, they are being used increasingly in the automation of printed circuit-board (PCB) assembly and injection moulding applications.

Much of the drive towards more robots is because the manufacturing community is beginning to realize that they must be more productive and more efficient in their factories. In the last five years, robot sales have risen 172% in units and 136% in dollars during that time. The primary reason is that the price of robots has come down substantially and their performance continues to improve with increased reliability, user friendly controls and advancements in vision technology.

The use of robots is partly a function of labour shortages and economics. A country with low-cost labour readily available is less likely to employ robots than one that has a shortage in skilled labour and relatively inflexible work forces such as Japan. Another factor that enters into this is the cost of buying robots and integrating them into the production line. In many industries, low production levels preclude the use of robots because of their cost. And if production levels are very high, manufacturing is more likely to move offshore. However, more and more low-cost robots are used in light assembly and manipulation tasks such as packaging and food processing.

There are no easy solutions to the automation dilemma. Workers displaced by automation will require retraining or early retirement. As more aspects of manufacturing are automated, fewer managers will be required. However, it is not likely that the computer will ever fully replace managers. Computers are incapable of making the intuitive judgments that managers often must make; instead, they are valuable tools managers can use to evaluate data and make better decisions. Because computers reduce the drudgery of many tasks, they may help managers become more creative as well as more productive. If this is to happen, however, managers will have to become computer-literate and able to use the sophisticated business software as it becomes available.

Chapter Summary

1. The material well-being of many Canadians is largely a result of high productivity through mass production. Mass production of goods is made possible through mechanization, the assembly line, standardization and automation.

2. Production management is faced with two major types of decisions: production system design decisions and operating production decisions. Production system design decisions include product planning and design, capacity planning, plant location and layout, and work system design. These long-term decisions always involve top management; they are major decisions and, once made, are difficult and costly to change. Marketing and production (particularly the research and development department) work closely together to determine, on the basis of customer demand, what to produce. The product determines to a large extent

what type of manufacturing process will be used. Determining plant capacity is a critical decision because it affects operating costs and, ultimately, the price of the final product. Plant location requires careful analysis of the firm's markets, the availability of labour, energy and transportation, proximity to raw materials, and community and site factors. The type of production operation will also determine plant layout and machines, and work system design.

3. The major operating production decisions are medium- and short-range production planning, distribution planning, inventory management, aggregate planning, material requirements planning and production scheduling. Demand forecasting provides production management with the information it needs to plan production requirements for the coming year. On the basis of this demand forecast, inventory requirements and distribution plans for finished goods are made. This in turn provides information for aggregate production plans, which ensure that sufficient raw materials and adequate plant capacity, labour and machinery will be available for production. The aggregate plan is the basis for developing the master schedule, which contains material requirements planning as well as daily production scheduling.

4. Since the production department is the major purchaser of raw materials and may have large inventories of semi-finished and finished products, the purchasing and inventory functions are particularly important. The purchasing department must buy the right material and components, at the right price, for fabrication or assembly. Occasionally, it must decide whether to make a component part or buy it. Inventory management must ensure that sufficient raw materials and finished goods are available at all times, while minimizing the cost of carrying the inventory and ordering. An inventory control system is needed to keep track of inventory and orders placed. The more sophisticated production facilities have a highly computerized inventory management system to ensure that raw materials, parts and components are available for production as required. To reduce inventory carrying costs, just-in-time inventory systems are increasingly being used.

5. Production scheduling is the attempt to coordinate labour, materials and machinery for maximum production efficiency. Production scheduling is critical because it makes the optimal use of machines and equipment and ensures that customers receive orders on time. A Gantt chart can be used to organize and clarify actual or intended use of resources over a period of time, as well as for loading and scheduling. A load chart shows the loading and idle times of a group of machines. It can show that a particular machine or work centre is either available or in use at a particular time. A schedule chart is often used to monitor progress of jobs. The charts indicate which jobs are on schedule and which one are early or late.

6. Quality control is another major concern for production management. Waste and loss of reputation associated with the production of defective products and extensive after-sales repair costs can be reduced through quality control. Another critical function is preventive maintenance—that is, the periodic inspection and replacement of parts in crucial machines to prevent machine breakdown and avoid costly delays in normal production.

7. Computers have automated many functions in the manufacturing firm. CAD (computer-assisted design) makes the design process more efficient, while CAM

(computer-assisted manufacturing) uses computers to control machines previously controlled by people. Robots are also increasingly being used on production lines. In addition to automating the production process, computers are used to check quality control, maintain inventory and reorder automatically when necessary. Managers use microcomputers to aid in budgeting, data management and break-even analysis. Computers also figure prominently in project management—the planning and controlling of large projects. Project management software for microcomputers can handle large projects, allow easy updating if there is a change in task completion time or in resources used, and enable the manager to prepare a large variety of reports for analysis.

KEY TERMS

Production 224
Service businesses 225
Mass production 225
Economies of scale 225
Assembly line 225
Mechanization 226
Standardization 226
Automation 226
Custom production 227
Job shops 227
Production process 229
Analytic process 229
Extraction process 230
Synthetic process 230
Fabrication process 230
Assembly process 230
Capacity planning 230
Industrial parks 232
Plant layout .233
Process layout 234
Product layout 234
General-purpose machines 234
Special-purpose machines 234
Work system design 236

Job design 236
Methods analysis 237
Motion studies 237
Work measurement 237
Time study 237
Demand forecasting 238
Time series analysis 238
Safety stock .238
Inventory management 238
Hand-to-mouth buying 241
Forward buying 241
Reorder point 242
Lead time 242
Economic order quantity (EOQ) 242
Inventory carrying cost 242
Ordering cost 242
Periodic inventory control
    system 244
Perpetual inventory control
    system 244
Universal product code (UPC) 244
Distribution planning 245
Aggregate planning 247
Master schedule 248

Material requirements
    planning (MRP) 248
Bill of materials 249
Inventory records file 249
Scheduling 249
Loading 251
Gantt chart 251
Load chart 251
Schedule chart 251
Sequencing .251
Purchasing 253
Value analysis 253
Make-or-buy decision 253
Quality control 254
Preventive maintenance 256
Project management 256
Project schedule or network 256
PERT (Program Evaluation and
    Review Technique) 256
CPM (Critical Path Method) 256
Critical path .256
CAD/CAM 259
Manufacturing automation
    protocol (MAP) 262
Robots 262

REVIEW QUESTIONS

1 How do service businesses differ from manufacturing businesses?

2 How can mass production contribute to an increase in the standard of living?

3 Briefly define mass production, mechanization, standardization and automation.

4 Why is capacity planning a critical decision in the design of production systems?

5 What are some of the reasons for relocating a plant? What major factors should be considered in plant location?

6 Distinguish between product and process layout.

7 What is work system design? How might motion study be used in job design?

8 Why is demand forecasting important for a manufacturer? How might a manufacturer react to uncertain demand?

9 Distinguish between hand-to-mouth buying and forward buying. What are the advantages and disadvantages of each?

10 Distinguish between a periodic and a perpetual inventory control system. What role can computers play in inventory control?

11 What are the consequences of carrying too much or too little inventory? Explain why the economic order quantity is the order size that will minimize the sum of the annual costs of holding inventory and the annual costs of ordering inventory.

12 When is distribution planning an important consideration for manufacturing companies?

13 What is aggregate planning? What four major strategies can the production manager use to meet the requirements of the aggregate plan?

14 What is material requirements planning? What information is required by MRP?

15 Explain why scheduling can be viewed as both a planning function and a control function. Why is scheduling for high-volume systems relatively easy compared to scheduling for the job shop?

16 Discuss the difference between loading and sequencing.

17 What is the significance of the purchasing function in a manufacturing firm?

18 Explain how a make-or-buy decision can resemble a plant location decision.

19 Why is quality control necessary? What are the factors to be balanced in practising quality control?

20 Explain how the process of finding an optimum level of preventive maintenance resembles determining optimum quality control.

21 What is project management? How is a project schedule created? How can a computer help managers both to create a project schedule and to update it as the project advances?

22 How does CAD relate to CAM? How are computers used in automating the manufacturing process? What are the implications of automation for unemployment and productivity?

DISCUSSION QUESTIONS

1 How will continued automation affect production management?

2 Name a few factories located near your community. Identify and explain the factors likely to have led to the location of each.

3 "A firm should ensure that its products are of the highest quality possible." Discuss.

4 If technological change, for example, CAD/CAM, can make production more efficient and thereby raise our standard of living, why are labour unions generally opposed to such change, particularly automation?

5 What might be the impact of the automated factory on our standard of living?

Martin's Quick Oil Change Limited

Robert Martin founded Martin's Quick Oil Change Limited in the spring of 1992. He operated the oil-change service business for two years before he heard about automated equipment that would allow him to reduce labour costs significantly. He evaluated two machines that would allow him to reduce labour costs over his present manual system and allow him to offer service 16 hours per day in two eight-hour shifts, six days per week.

Martin reviewed the manufacturer's specifications on two different automated oil-change units. The comparative specifications were as follows:

	The Greasy Greaser	**The Change Agent**
Purchase cost	$285 000	$350 000
Useful life	15 years	20 years
Oil-change technicians	2 persons per shift	1 person per shift
Utilities (monthly expense)	$980	$1 150
Depreciation/year	$19 000	$17 500
Time for oil change per vehicle	9 minutes	7 minutes

Market research had shown that Martin could expect a weekly demand for his services of 195 vehicles per day. In his experience, two or three Saturdays per month are busy days with frequent lineups. To accommodate the expected increase in demand he would use an extra two service bays that would not use the automated equipment. He would require two additional oil-change technicians and an additional customer service agent. All three would be brought in for an eight-hour shift from 9 a.m. until 5 p.m. on Saturday. This additional bay could accommodate an average oil change in 20 minutes. Rest periods would be covered by the other employers so that there would be no interruption of service.

Each oil change averaged $19.99 in revenues for Martin. By buying his oil and grease in bulk, he reduced costs of materials to $7 per oil change on average. Martin paid his oil-change technician employees $9 per hour. In addition to the direct labour shown above, he would also require two customer service agents at $6 per hour for either machine.

SOURCE: By David H. Jones-Delcourt. Reprinted by permission of the author.

>>

Questions

1 Which version of automated oil changer should Martin purchase? Evaluate all aspects of using either of the two machines (excluding tax considerations) in arriving at your recommendation.

2 In Martin's experience, only two or three Saturdays are busy enough to require the three additional people and the extra service bays. Because it was not possible to forecast in advance when the lower demand would occur, Martin decided to always bring in the three extra people on Saturday. How many additional cars must Martin service each Saturday to break even on his extra labour costs?

3 What are the benefits of having the extra crew on Saturday even when there are days where demand is normal and could be handled by the existing crew using the automated oil-change machines?

CASE

7-2

Pacific Boat Works

Pacific Boat Works was started in 1958 on the Fraser River south of New Westminster, British Columbia. In the beginning, the company manufactured small aluminum boats for large fishing vessels. By 1991, its major business was building seiners and gillnetters, boats up to 30 metres in length.

The plant and offices are housed in a steel shed, and company personnel numbers approximately 40 people, depending on the amount of work to be done. Orders for the large boats are handled by Sheldon Abramsky, the owner and president, together with a marine engineer who is a major shareholder. After the price and plans for a new boat have been finalized with the customer, the supervisor orders materials and schedules production.

The supervisor has been with the company since the beginning and owns about 10% of the shares in the company. At age 56, he prides himself on being from the old management school. He carries a heavy workload and is one of the most knowledgeable people in the boat-building business. When the work has to get out, he drives his workers, who on more than one occasion have charged him with unfair treatment. While Mr. Abramsky had to reprimand him a number of times for driving his workers, no one has been found to replace him, and there is no assistant supervisor.

In 1985, the company's fortunes improved when it received a number of orders for large fishing vessels. With additional employees and the crowded plant, Mr. Abramsky noticed that costs were starting to soar. He knew that few records were kept. The workers' time slips were used only to calculate wages. Since the workers belong to unions, their wages are negotiated on an industry-wide basis. However, though the supervisor claims he knows who the top performers are, there is no way of comparing workers' productivity. No attempt has been made to specialize the workers, most of whom perform whatever jobs are required.

>>

As long as the firm was producing only small aluminum boats, the lack of a production system was not a problem. Material requirements were generally consistent and ordering was handled by the foreperson, who knew what was required. When the firm began to produce large boats, however, large volumes of parts and raw materials were required. The lack of an inventory system often meant that all those workers assigned to a large boat had to be shifted to various other jobs because raw materials and parts had not arrived or had not been ordered.

The major problem remained production control. For example, the firm knew how many hours it took to build a large fishing vessel, but no one knew if any of the hundreds of jobs could be done more efficiently. Since there was no specialization, the same tasks were regularly done by different workers. Thus, no one person acquired expertise in a particular operation. In addition, a number of profitable projects had to be turned away because they could not be handled under the present production control system.

Although management had received advice on establishing a production control system, it was reluctant to install the system. Mr. Abramsky and the board of directors did not want to hire the additional staff and add to overhead costs. The supervisor was adamant that such a system was simply not necessary: he worked as hard as was humanly possible and did not have the time to fool around with more details. Management also felt that since the company was so small, the existing informal system might actually be the most efficient way to operate, even if it meant turning away a few orders. Although Mr. Abramsky had contemplated expansion, he had some doubts as to whether the present organizations could be expanded without a complete reorganization. He also wondered whether a change in management methods should be made before or after expansion.

Questions

1 What is wrong with management's and the supervisor's arguments against implementing a production control system? What would the advantages of such a system be?

2 The company has three choices on how to devise and install a production control system: (a) assign the task to the supervisor; (b) employ a qualified worker from another company; or (c) use a firm of consulting engineers. What are the merits of each alternative?

3 If you were asked to outline a production control system for Pacific Boat Works, what major factors would you take into consideration? (Keep in mind the future expansion of the firm.)

4 How would you answer Mr. Abramsky's question of whether the production control system should be changed now or after expansion?

5 How might a computerized production control and inventory system help the company? How would you go about implementing the system?

COMPREHENSIVE CASE 7-3

SOMERSET OPTICAL

In October 1998, Somerset Optical was approached by a competitor who operated three dispensing optical outlets in Ottawa. Interested in getting out of the business, the competitor offered both stores to Somerset Optical for extremely good terms. The management of Somerset Optical, with the blessing of their administrative consultant, closed the deal in late October and from that point on operated three outlets.

As Somerset's sales volume increased, Mike Fowler and Peter Dewar decided it would be much more beneficial to the company if they were to grind their own lenses on-site. This would provide an important service to customers in that they would spend much less time waiting for their glasses. Three lens-grinding machines could be leased and installed in the basement of Somerset's largest location.

To purchase the necessary equipment, Somerset would pay an initial amount of $5000 and lease payments of $1200 per month for five years. After five years, Somerset could purchase the machines from the lessor for $1. The combined volume of sold frames was now 1300 per month, which represented gross monthly sales of $188 500. The cost of the frames was $64 935. This figure excluded the costs of the lenses and laboratory costs of approximately $55 250. Straight laboratory costs for grinding the lenses and applying chemical treatments such as anti-reflective and scratch-resistant coatings amounted to $32 500 of the $55 250. If Somerset were to undertake its own laboratory services, it could save a large portion of the monthly laboratory costs. As well, with on-site laboratory services, it was expected that the overall volume of sales could increase to 1500 frames per month from all locations.

The total costs of setting up the Somerset laboratory were as follows:

1.	Acquisition of three machines	$5 000
	Monthly lease payments	1 200
2.	Set-up costs	8 000
3.	Laboratory technician's salary (per year)	32 000
4.	Laboratory assistant's salary (per year)	25 000
5.	Monthly cost of chemicals	9 000
6.	Depreciation cost on equipment (per month)	642

Somerset Optical opted for a process layout because the manufacturing would depend on custom orders. Each set of lenses would be different: the thickness would vary, as would customers in their requests (or lack of requests) for anti-glare/anti-static coating; tinting; anti-scratch coating; and other special features.

Somerset Optical would serve the demand for raw lenses by installing a just-in-time inventory system. Bryce Glass and Plastics of neighbouring Hull, Quebec, would supply each day's order of raw lenses the next morning in response to a fax order sheet sent out the night before by Dewar. Bryce Glass would also provide, at a substantially higher cost, emergency delivery service at any time during the workday.

SOURCE: By David H. Jones-Delcourt. Reprinted by permission of the author.

Questions

1 Analyze the costs that Somerset would incur (a) by using a laboratory and (b) by producing its own lenses. Which option is more cost-effective?

2 Prepare a process layout for Somerset Optical.

3 Discuss Somerset's in-house production arrangement as it relates to each of the following: inventory control system; quality issues; aggregate planning; and the reliability of the raw plastic/glass supplier.

8

Marketing Management

Learning Objectives

After reading this chapter, you will be able to

1 Describe the functions of marketing.

2 Explain the marketing concept and how marketing research is used to select a target market.

3 Identify the four basic components that make up the marketing mix.

4 Describe the differences between consumer and industrial markets, and list the types of goods appropriate for each market.

5 Explain the concept of product life cycles and their effect on a firm.

6 Explain how a firm actually sets the price for a new product, and describe the two major pricing strategies that may be used to introduce a new product.

7 Identify and describe the four major types of promotion.

8 Recognize when to use mass advertising as a major promotional tool, and when to use personal selling.

9 Describe how goods get from the product to the consumer or industrial customer.

10 Explain the function performed for manufacturers and retailers by wholesalers.

11 List the major types of retail outlets.

12 Identify the major problems involved in the physical distribution of goods.

The Importance of Marketing

We have all seen television commercials—some insult our intelligence, others are witty and appropriate. The objective of a commercial is to have us take notice of a product. An advertisement may stimulate a desire for the product, or it may simply remind us of the product as we pass the supermarket shelf. Either way, if we are influenced to buy the product, the commercial—whether or not we like it—has been successful.

Advertising is the aspect of marketing that makes consumers aware of existing products. But marketing encompasses many more activities. It involves contacting consumers and businesses to identify products that are needed and in demand. Marketing is also responsible for pricing, advertising and sales promotion, and for getting the product to the customer through one or more channels of distribution, including wholesalers and retailers.

Marketing products and services is costly and often accounts for more than half the cost of a product. Therefore, we might ask, why not reduce marketing activities and thereby reduce the product's price for the consumer? Surely lower prices would give a producer an edge over the competition. In fact, some firms do reduce the marketing function to a bare minimum. An example is the mail-order house, which allows the customer to shop conveniently at home by ordering through a catalogue.

However, many of us want to look at products, feel them, try them on and compare prices when we shop. Before we buy a best-selling novel, for example, we read the back cover. Before we invest in a new car, we test-drive it and compare various makes. Thus, some marketing functions are essential and could not be eliminated, regardless of how much a producer may wish to cut product costs. Marketing is as basic a business function as production, finance and personnel.

The Functions of Marketing

Marketing is "the performance of business activities that direct the flow of goods and services from the producer to the consumer or user."[1] To ensure that these activities are carried out, specific functions must be performed, each of which adds value to the product for the consumer. This value, or **utility**, represents the ability of goods and services to satisfy a human want or need. The marketing function adds three types of utility: time, place and ownership utility. To add **time utility**, marketers determine what products the customers want available at particular times. Having the product available at a convenient location for purchase adds **place utility**. **Ownership utility** is created by facilitating the transfer of title for the product from seller to buyer. A fourth type of utility, known as **form utility**, is created by the production function, which converts raw materials into useful products for consumers or businesses. Refer to Figure 8.1.

Marketing is the performance of business activities that direct the flow of goods and services from the producer to the consumer or user.

Utility represents the ability of goods and services to satisfy a human want or need.

Time utility is created by having the product available when the consumer wants it.

Place utility is created by having the product available at a convenient location for purchase.

Ownership utility is created by facilitating the transfer of title for the product from seller to buyer.

Form utility is created when a firm converts raw materials into useful products for consumers or businesses.

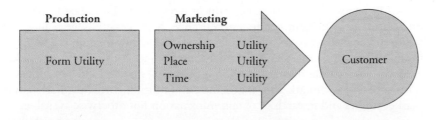

FIGURE 8.1

Marketing adds utility to products

There are eight marketing functions:

1. *Buying.* Before a business can produce or resell products, it must buy raw materials, parts or finished goods. It must seek out suppliers and purchase the right product in the right quantity. Retail buyers, for example, take a number of factors into consideration, including style, size, colour, quantity, quality and brand. Buying entails risk, and mistakes can be costly if products remain on the seller's shelf because they do not appeal to customers.

2. *Selling.* Before a business can make a profit, it must sell the products it has bought or produced. Thus, potential buyers must be made aware of the product's existence, usefulness and price. Sellers may therefore offer various services to make the product more attractive. A producer, for example, may provide the retailer or wholesaler with advertising allowances, demonstrate use of the product to customers and maintain inventory. Both the producer and retailer may provide consumers with warranties, credit, delivery and servicing facilities.

3. *Transporting.* A product must be transported from the place where it is produced to a location that is convenient for the customer. The gasoline in an Alberta refinery, for example, is of no use to the motorist in Toronto unless it is made readily available through service stations.

4. *Storing.* Retailers and wholesalers, as well as specific marketing institutions such as warehouses and transportation agencies, store goods to ensure they are available when customers are ready to buy. Thus, goods as diverse as fresh fruit, books and furniture are readily available almost anywhere in Canada.

5. *Risk-taking.* Buying, selling, transporting and storing all entail some risk. Some stocked items may not sell, goods in transport may be damaged and goods in storage may spoil. The producer, wholesaler or retailer must then bear the loss. Businesses can protect themselves against specific risks by purchasing insurance.

6. *Financing.* Many consumers and businesses either cannot or do not wish to pay immediately for the products they purchase. The seller therefore provides the buyer with credit for a specified period of time following receipt of the goods. A retailer buying a product from a manufacturer, for example, may be able to resell it and make a profit before he or she is required to pay for it.

7. *Standardizing and grading.* Many products are priced according to standards of quality, size and colour. When the manufacturer or producer standardizes and grades goods, the seller need not inspect every unit he or she receives. Turkeys, eggs and fruits are graded according to size, quality or condition, and many other goods are manufactured according to standards established either by the industry or by government. For example, all products with the stamp "CSA Approved" are manufactured to meet certain minimum standards established by the Canadian Standards Association.

8. *Information gathering.* Information on products and consumer needs is essential, since a firm may prosper or go bankrupt depending on its ability to adjust to market demands. The marketing department is responsible for gathering information on consumer needs and product acceptance. Sales generally give an accurate indication of product acceptance, while other product information can be gathered from retailers and wholesalers who are in close contact with customers. Marketing executives also gather information about products, markets and consumers from trade journals and marketing magazines. In addition, firms regularly conduct market studies and research to obtain information not otherwise available.

The Marketing Concept

In the past, business firms were not as concerned with consumer needs as they are today. The early phase of marketing, now known as **production marketing**, lasted until the late 1930s. During this phase, the marketing function was of minor importance, as indicated by Henry Ford's famous statement, "They can have their Model T in any colour, as long as it's black." Consumers had few alternative products to choose from, but the demand for goods was enormous. More goods gradually came on the market, however, and prices began to drop as a result of mass production. Advertising media were developed to inform the public of available goods. Hence, the sales function of marketing became increasingly important as competition for the consumer's dollar increased. Producers concentrated on selling products using sophisticated sales techniques, thus ushering in the **sales-oriented marketing** era, which lasted through World War II.

After World War II, something akin to a marketing revolution occurred. Once consumer goods could be produced on a mass scale, new products became available at relatively low prices. Competitors could take an existing product, improve on it and offer it to the consumer, often at a lower price than the original product. With many products to choose from and a better-educated consumer market, old-style sales techniques were no longer successful. Companies that ignored consumer needs and wants found themselves out of business, while firms that listened to consumers prospered. Thus, the **marketing era** began. Salespeople and marketing executives studied customers to determine their needs and wants; once these were known, a firm could channel all of its resources into producing the most suitable product or service.

Marketing Research

If a firm intends to gear its entire activity toward producing goods and services for its customers, it must find out specifically what forms, colours, packaging, prices and retailers the consumers want, as well as what types of advertising, public relations and selling practices appeal to them. **Marketing research** is the systematic gathering, recording and analyzing of data related to the marketing of goods and services.

Production marketing refers to the time when consumers had few alternative products to choose from, but the demand for goods was enormous.

Sales-oriented marketing refers to the time when competition for the consumer's dollar increased and producers began selling products using sophisticated sales techniques.

Marketing era —a firm attempts to determine the needs and wants of the consumer and channels all of its resources into producing the most suitable product or service.

Marketing research is the systematic gathering, recording and analyzing of data related to the marketing of goods and services.

< Market shelves display a variety of products competing for the consumer dollar

FIGURE 8.2

Steps in marketing research

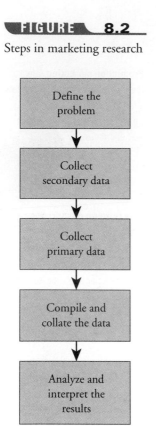

Define the problem

↓

Collect secondary data

↓

Collect primary data

↓

Compile and collate the data

↓

Analyze and interpret the results

Comprehensive market research consists of five basic steps:

1. *Defining the problem.* This first step is the most important, and often the most difficult, job of the marketing researcher. It is easy to mistake symptoms for the problem. Defining the problem may take time, but if the wrong problem is examined, money and effort are wasted. Consequences may be serious if a solution to a wrong or non-existent problem is implemented. For example, a drop in sales could result from a variety of problems, including inadequate advertising, poor-quality product or a lack of salespeople. Sometimes market research is also used to determine whether a problem exists. For example, a sales analysis may indicate increased sales over previous years, but after further market analysis the firm may find that it is actually losing market share.

2. *Gathering secondary data.* The next step is to gather secondary data from company records, trade magazines, government and private information sources, library sources or similar market studies. If a problem can be resolved at this stage, it will cost far less than gathering primary data.

3. *Gathering primary data.* If secondary data do not provide the answer, or if more data are required, then primary data must be gathered. Primary data are gathered through observing people; through experiments such as test marketing a product in a particular area to see how consumers react; or through surveys in which individuals are questioned by telephone, mail or in personal interviews.

4. *Compiling data.* The fourth step consists of compiling the data that have been gathered. At this stage, the marketing department clarifies relationships between various factors. For example, researchers may try to establish a relationship between income and the type of product purchased. Extensive correlations are facilitated by the use of computers.

5. *Interpreting the information.* The final step is the interpretation of the data. A mistaken interpretation may prompt management to take the wrong action. For example, it may reject a potentially successful product or decide to produce a product that consumers will not buy.

Marketing Strategy

As noted earlier, a business cannot simply produce what it thinks is a good product and hope that a large number of people will buy it. A successful company, large or small, builds a product or offers a service that satisfies the needs and wants of its customers. The marketing manager thus establishes a plan or **marketing strategy**, which consists of two parts:

Marketing strategy consists of identifying the target market and developing a marketing mix for that target market.

1. *Identifying the target market.* Since not all consumers will be interested in a particular product or service, the group(s) most likely to buy a product because it fits their needs or wants must be identified.

2. *Developing a marketing mix.* The marketing mix is the assortment of variables that the marketing manager can adjust to suit the specific target market. It involves making a product with specific features that customers want; choosing a price or range of prices they are prepared to pay; selecting an effective method of promotion to reach the customers; and distributing the product in the most appropriate way. The marketing mix is often referred to as the four P's of marketing: product, price, promotion and place.

Identifying the Target Market

All individuals have needs and wants for particular goods and services. Marketers classify groups of consumers with similar demands so they can develop variations of a given product to satisfy the particular demands of each group. For example, a television manufacturer may produce a variety of models, including both expensive, high-quality sets with many features and simpler, lower-priced models. Each model is designed to appeal to particular groups of people or **target markets**. Some consumers prefer a low-priced small-screen television, while others are in the market for an expensive, feature-laden home-theatre system.

Dividing the total market into a number of target markets based on specific criteria is known as **market segmentation**. Before a market can be segmented, a company must know some of the characteristics of the consumer market.

1. *Demographic characteristics* include age, income, education, occupation and residence location.

2. *Lifestyle characteristics* include the activities, interests, opinions and personalities of consumers.

3. *Purchase characteristics* include what, when, where and how much of a product the market purchases.

4. *Purchase motivations* indicate what factors influence a person to buy a particular product and could include family, social group, cultural background and so on.

Once some of the above information about the market has been obtained, it is easier and more effective to develop a marketing strategy that is geared to a particular consumer group.

The consumers who comprise the target market for one product may be entirely different from those in a target market for another product. For example, people in the target market group for a feature-laden colour television may or may not belong to the target market for an instant breakfast designed to appeal to the single working person.

In Canada, marketers for certain products may be concerned with the various ethnic markets, particularly the French- and English-Canadian markets. One or the other of these two major target markets may prefer some products over others. For example, Quebec leads all provinces in expenditures for clothing and cosmetics, and has the highest per-capita sales of sweets in Canada. When these markets are segmented, particular attention is paid to cultural and language criteria because there are significant differences in consumer attitudes and behaviour.

Developing the Marketing Mix

Once the characteristics of the target market are known, the next step in the development of a marketing strategy is the creation of the **marketing mix**. The firm can vary its marketing mix—product characteristics, pricing strategy, promotion and distribution channels—to suit each target market or market segment. Of course, the marketing mix must also take into account management's objectives for the firm, competition, social values and customs, and legal constraints.

The marketing mix, as illustrated in Figure 8.3, shows that the **four P's** focus on the target market. It is important to note that the initial combination of the four P's is not necessarily the best and may need adjustment over time. For example, a dress manufacturing firm may find that its line is so well received by customers that the original advertising strategy can be altered and advertising costs reduced. It may also find that it can reduce the number of styles and colours offered, if only a few styles sell well.

Target market —a group of consumers with similar demands that the firm attempts to satisfy with specific variations of a product.

Market segmentation attempts to divide the total market into a number of target markets, based on specific criteria.

Marketing mix —represents the best possible combination of product, price, promotion and place in order to satisfy a particular target market.

Four P's of marketing refer to the marketing mix of product, price, promotion and place.

FIGURE 8.3

The Four P's of marketing

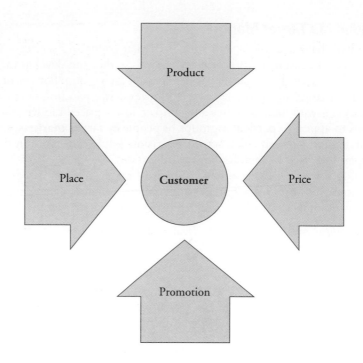

The Four P's of Marketing

Product
In addition to the basic characteristics appropriate for the target market, the product also includes the proper packaging, branding and labelling, colour, size, delivery and any warranty or service that may be required.

Price
The product must be priced so as to appeal to the target market while providing a reasonable profit for the firm.

Promotion
The promotion campaign must be geared to the specific target market, which may mean either mass advertising or personal selling, or some combination of the two. A firm might also use other sales promotion techniques, and attempt to stir up publicity for its product through newspaper or television reporting.

Place
A channel of distribution must be determined to make the product available to the consumer or business customer. The producer may sell directly to the retailer or else hire the services of a wholesaler to distribute the product to retail stores. Often both methods are used.

Consumer and Industrial Markets

The total market for goods can be divided into two categories: consumer and business or industrial markets.

Although many products are used by both sectors, business products are put to more strenuous use and must be more durable; hence they are usually more expensive than consumer products. A photocopier, for example, is heavily used in business offices, while a student may use it only occasionally.

Since many businesses make products for both consumer and business use, it is important that the marketing department understand the difference between the two markets. When sales in both categories are substantial, the marketing activities of a firm may be divided into separate consumer and industrial departments. The firm can thus gear its marketing effort specifically to each group of buyers.

When a new home entertainment product such as a video disc player or giant-screen television is made available for purchase, who will actually buy it? That is a big question for manufacturers. One common method marketers use to segment the population to determine the various target markets is to consider income and family life-cycle stage. Because of its development and marketing costs, a new product is usually high-priced when it first comes on the market. However, as demand for the product increases over a few months or years, the price slowly drops. This makes income a key criterion—someone in a high-income bracket is better able to afford an expensive new entertainment product.

The family life-cycle stages consist of the following:

1. bachelor stage (young single people);
2. young married couples with no children;
3. young married couples with children;
4. older married couples with dependent children living with them;
5. older married couples with no children; and
6. older single people either still working or retired.

Missing from this classification is one group quite common today: the young single mother with children. Depending on the product, marketers may or may not include this group in their market analysis. High-priced electronic entertainment systems will probably not be purchased by this group to any great extent.

Figure 8.4 shows the market grid for the video disc player. Across the top are various family life-cycle stages, while down the left side are the various income groups. Each family life-cycle stage can now be surveyed to determine their desire for the product and also their willingness to pay the price to own it. If the marketer already believes that only certain segments will be interested in the product, then only those segments will be surveyed.

High-income families or individuals, for example, are quite likely to be interested in a video disc player. This target market may want a feature-laden product and have little concern about price. On the other hand, this product may also appeal to lower-income groups, for example, young married couples with children, wishing to avoid the expense of babysitters and the other costs associated with going out to a movie. This target market may be very concerned with the price and thus prefer a basic unit with few frills but good performance. In fact, these two groups might represent the two primary target markets.

There may also be smaller target markets that the company can satisfy by changing the product mix slightly. For example, manufacturers of colour televisions produce a large variety of types and styles to suit every conceivable target market.

Once the actual product and the price have been determined, the marketer will develop an appropriate promotional plan that is geared to each target market. This plan may specify advertising on television, in selected magazines, newspapers, radio and other media, depending on which target market the company wants to reach.

Making the product readily available for purchase is the marketer's final concern. In the case of an entertainment product, department stores and specialty retail stores are the most likely places where this product would be sold initially. As the product becomes more accepted and sought out, discount stores may also carry it. Manufacturers of entertainment equipment are usually large companies, with their own distribution centres and sales force that sell the product directly to the various retail outlets. They seldom use wholesalers or other intermediaries. This puts them closer to the customer and provides a much better idea of how the product is selling.

Segmenting the Market for a Video Disc Player

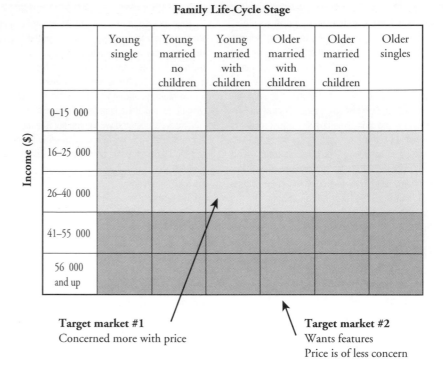

FIGURE 8.4

Segmenting the market for a video disc player

Consumer Goods

The market for consumer goods is generally large and geographically widespread. **Consumer goods** directly satisfy the needs and wants of the purchaser. Consumers often buy goods on the basis of emotional or psychological factors such as fear or the desire for prestige. Many consumer purchases are made on the spur of the moment, a practice known as impulse buying. Consumer goods can be classified into three categories: convenience, shopping and specialty goods.

Consumer goods directly satisfy the needs and wants of the purchaser.

- *Convenience goods.* **Convenience goods** are products that are needed often and are bought without much deliberation (e.g., bread, cigarettes and razor blades). No one wants to hunt for these products, and they are expected to be widely available.

Convenience goods are products that are needed often and are bought without much deliberation.

Shopping goods are usually expensive products for which the consumer is prepared to spend considerable time comparing quality, price, colour and after-sale warranties.

- *Shopping goods.* Since **shopping goods** are usually expensive, the consumer is prepared to spend considerable time comparing quality, price and, when necessary, after-sale warranties. Shopping goods include automobiles, furniture and television sets.

Specialty goods are products that the consumer is prepared to make a special effort to buy.

- *Specialty goods.* **Specialty goods** are products that the consumer is prepared to make a special effort to buy. Brand names are often important, and the consumer may be unwilling to accept a substitute. High-priced and imported cars usually fall into this category; a person wishing to buy a Mercedes, for example, may go to great lengths to locate a dealer. For people who favour a particular brand (e.g., clothing by Pierre Cardin, or a Nikon camera), there may be no substitute.

Two factors must be kept in mind when classifying consumer goods. First, what is a specialty good to one person may be a shopping or convenience good to another. For example, the affluent household may regularly buy T-bone steak at the local market regardless of price, while the university student may be able to afford this luxury only occasionally and only after carefully comparing prices at a number of stores. Second, what was considered a shopping or specialty good in the past may be considered a convenience good today. Many non-food items such as children's toys or low-priced cameras and film are now found on supermarket shelves because consumers expect them to be readily available.

Industrial Goods

Industrial goods are purchased by many types of profit and non-profit organizations, including manufacturers, building contractors, wholesalers, retailers, hospitals and schools as well as government departments. Some industrial products are used to facilitate production and last a considerable length of time before they need to be replaced. These are called **capital goods**. Most goods in this category are costly and extremely complex and technical in nature. Therefore these types of industrial products are often bought by purchasing agents; engineers and other personnel who are well informed about the technical aspects of available products may also be involved. Another category of industrial goods are consumables (e.g., printer paper, pencils, cleaning supplies), also known as **expense goods**.

Professional purchasing decisions are based largely on economic considerations rather than on emotional or convenience factors. Since industrial products are complex and since there are fewer industrial customers than consumers, the marketing approach for industrial goods is different from that for consumer goods.

Besides being classified into capital and expense goods, industrial goods can also be divided into six major categories: installations, raw materials, parts, accessory equipment, supplies and services.

- *Installations.* Installations include large and costly capital goods such as heavy machinery, airliners, freighters, blast furnaces and turbine generators. Since these items are purchased infrequently and are expensive, their suitability is carefully examined prior to purchase, and they are often built to specifications.

- *Raw materials.* Raw materials may include grains, minerals, timber or cotton. Because they are used constantly and in large quantities, these materials must be readily available; even small variations in price can be significant. Other considerations important to the buyer include grading, storage and transportation.

- *Parts.* Firms that assemble products such as automobiles often buy sub-assemblies, or parts, from other businesses. Some parts may be manufactured according to the buyer's specifications, while others are of standard design. For example, in the automobile industry, manufacturers buy parts from thousands of different suppliers. Each major manufacturer, however, may buy the same part from one supplier and the part may be standard or designed for a specific automobile.

- *Accessory equipment.* Accessory equipment includes the tools and equipment needed in manufacturing, along with items such as fax machines, computers and copiers. Accessory equipment is often bought by individual department heads through the purchasing department. Expensive equipment may require careful analysis in terms of price and capability for the job.

- *Supplies.* Supplies are items not used in the actual manufacturing process, and include maintenance and office supplies such as paper, printer cartridges, and labels.

- *Services.* In order to function, a firm requires many additional services provided by people who are not employees. Included are legal services, maintenance or repair services, consultants and advertising agencies.

Industrial goods are those goods purchased by businesses for their own production purposes.

Capital goods are industrial products used to facilitate production. These goods last a considerable length of time before they need to be replaced.

Expense goods are a category of industrial goods that are consumed either directly in the production process or in support services.

Differences Getting Too Much Attention

Yes, it's true, there are many differences between the Quebec and the Canadian consumer.

For more than 30 years now, the Quebec marketing and advertising industry has been striving to prove that Quebec is a different and unique consumer.

It is, and that's a very good thing, indeed. If it weren't, many of us wouldn't have jobs. Everything could be managed, decided and translated directly from Toronto—or maybe even New York.

The differences are many and affect all areas of consumer behaviour. Who among us hasn't heard that Quebecers eat more pasta, but less canned spaghetti sauce (we prefer the homemade variety). Or that we like cookies with a chocolate coating better than plain cookies. Or—and here's an interesting find—that we have the largest number of estheticians per capita in North America. It's not really that we need them especially, we're simply more preoccupied with how we look like.

Yes, the Quebec consumer consumes differently.

We have certain personality traits that reflect our Latin genes. The eternal "joie de vivre," for instance, a characteristic that has become a cliché with time, is nonetheless always present, says Alain GiguFre of the research firm CROP. Quebecers, as a general rule, are more hot-tempered and demonstrative. Our emotions sometimes outweigh our logic. According to researchers, our life in Quebec is full of falling in love, being impulsive and passionate.

On the other hand, this same Latin influence means that our men are more macho than yours. I guess we can't have everything.

But maybe for once—just once—it would be helpful to consider the things we have in common, not only with each other, but with our neighbours to the south.

In North America, we share a continent and a certain standard of living, but we also share an important demographic phenomenon that completely upset the entire social order—the baby boom. This phenomenon, by its size alone, has been bringing about extraordinary changes for some 40 years. And these changes, at the North American consumer level, will continue to be felt well into the next decade.

Several new North American trends have emerged over the last little while, but according to sociologists and trend-followers, there is one that, in its own special way, stands above the rest.

This trend will mark consumers well into the nineties, whether they are Americans, Canadians or Quebecers. And that trend is the return to true, solid values.

More than ever, the consumer of tomorrow will want to rediscover the serenity, morality and gentleness of traditional values.

Faith Popcorn, of the Brain Reserve, N.Y., named this decade the Decency Decade, and this is perhaps the best designation so far. It's a decade in which people will take themselves in hand, regain control of their personal and professional lives and basically clean up the havoc created in the eighties.

Here we are, at the threshold of the nineties, tired and disillusioned, especially we baby boomers, many of whom are approaching age 40, the age where we want to start relaxing a little. Because of this, everywhere in North America, we're sensing the emergence of the need for calm, order, control, equilibrium and simplicity.

The consumer of tomorrow will feel less inclined to want to impress his neighbour. He'll want to feel good, as opposed to wanting to look good. Restraint will be appreciated in most consumer areas and people, less preoccupied by appearance and "what will they say?" attitudes, will feel more at ease in showing their individual tastes and personalities.

The consumer of the nineties will also demand fair play. After witnessing the aftermath of stock-market finagling, after seeing top business gurus toppled from their empires, after seeing one too many elected politician caught with his hand in the till, and one too many members of a religious order with his hands where they shouldn't be, people have just about had enough.

In the 1990s, we're finally going to find a balance between body and spirit, and between careers and home life. And, since the body was revered and taken care of to a large extent in the eighties, with jogging, aerobics, squash, it will be spirit and intelligence that will be cherished in the coming years.

Workaholics will be shelved. People will be looking for quality of life and a lifestyle that is simpler, more relaxed and less pompous. Simplicity, truth, honesty, tenderness, serenity, balance—these will be the "in" words of the nineties.

Above all, we in advertising must remember that this is a business—a business where we solve marketing problems with brilliant ideas. We North Americans share basic values and marketing tenets. The differentiating factors are our methods of communication and the stimuli that trigger responses.

Good business sense dictates that the best way to convince someone is to adapt to their personality. The fact that Quebecers are more hot-tempered, more passionate and more emotional are tools that we, as advertisers who know the market, can use to sell our products.

The content of the product remains the same. The product's container, or how we sell it, varies from region to region. Advertising from Montreal will be a bit more emotional, a bit more passionate, because it reflects our own distinct emotional, passionate personality.

Yes, the Quebec consumer is different. Yes, there are logical, legitimate reasons for having those differences exploited and enhanced by people who work and live here. But don't forget. Some powerful trends and tendencies transcend provincial and national borders.

We must emphasize the differences, while underlining the similarities. We must look at our basic shared values and communicate them in our own inimitable style.

And then, maybe 30 years from now, different issues can be discussed.

SOURCE: Anne Darche, "Differences getting too much attention," *Marketing* (March 25, 1991): 21.

Creating the Product

When we hear the word "product," the first thing that comes to mind is probably some physical object—a bicycle, a book, a computer. But if we buy such a product, we buy it for the satisfaction that we expect from its use. For example, a student who buys a personal computer for developing term papers may look forward to easier editing, a nicer-looking term paper and, therefore, better grades. A person buying a bicycle may be thinking of benefits such as recreation, physical exercise or transportation. The marketing manager can therefore make a product more attractive by emphasizing benefits such as quality, packaging, detailed instructions on use, credit, delivery, brand name, product warranties and after-sales servicing. Anything that heightens the benefit to the buyer becomes part of the product. New automobile manufacturers, for example, from Europe or Asia need to establish a comprehensive service network in North America before they can expect to have substantial sales.

Although service is important as part of the purchase of a physical product, a large portion of our purchases consist of services only. The product of a medical doctor is a service, as is the product of a lawyer or an accountant. In all instances, the buyer of the service may receive nothing more tangible than advice.

Product Mix and Product Line

Some firms produce and sell only one consumer or industrial product, but many firms manufacture or sell a product line. A **product line** may consist of products that are similar in design or use, or that are intended for a similar market. A kitchen appliance manufacturer, for example, may produce toasters, steam irons and electric kettles as part of its product line. A product line can be expanded with additional related products or services.

In deciding whether to offer more products or product lines, a firm's resources obviously play a major role. For example, a firm may specialize in one product either to make production more efficient or because financial resources are limited. On the other hand, increasing the **product mix**—providing a greater number of products that are not related—might be prudent for a company whose sales depend on consumer tastes and economic conditions. For example, a firm that handles only one product could be severely hurt by a sales slump. On the other hand, if this firm handled a broader product mix, a sales slump in one product or product line might not seriously affect its financial position if other products continued to sell well.

Product line —consists of products that are similar in design or use, or that are intended for a similar market.

Product mix —the assortment of products that a firm provides.

Product Planning and Development

A firm must constantly ensure that all of its products contribute to the goal of profitability. Therefore management engages in **product planning** to determine whether

Product planning is required to find new products or determine ways of improving existing ones.

new products can be produced or existing ones improved. The ideas for new products can come from customers, retailers and wholesalers, or from market research.

Once the product planning function is established, **product development** becomes an ongoing activity involving six stages: generating new product ideas, screening, concept testing, business analysis, test marketing and commercialization.

New product ideas can be generated in a variety of ways, from soliciting information from retailers and wholesalers to primary market research. All new product ideas are subjected to *screening*, which assesses a product's general usefulness to the consumer and decides whether it should be considered for further study. *Concept testing* is then conducted. Ideas on how the product may be used and an estimated price are presented to a small group of potential consumers who are asked to comment. Even a negative response from the sample group is likely to be followed up with further study.

After concept testing, a thorough *business analysis* is undertaken to determine whether the product could be commercially successful. The analysis focuses on product features, estimated sales and profitability, competitive strength and potential for growth. The firm's current resources for producing and distributing the product are also examined.

Following the business analysis, the product is produced in limited quantity and tested for quality and performance. Often the product is tested by having consumers use it or compare it with an existing product. Test marketing may or may not be conducted depending on the results of the product tests. In *test marketing,* the company introduces the product for sale to consumers in selected geographical areas and studies responses. During this stage, any design, production or distribution problems can be corrected.

Once test marketing has been completed, *commercialization*—launching the product in the general market—must follow quickly; otherwise competitors could gain the upper hand in sales and profit, since they have been spared the cost of testing a similar product. Management may therefore bypass test marketing if it is confident that the product will be profitable. However, the gamble could be expensive; studies have shown that only two of every 100 product ideas result in successful commercial products. By omitting the test-marketing stage, a company may spend millions of dollars introducing a product, only to see it fail on the market.

Product Life Cycles

Since products have a limited life span, product planning and development are ongoing activities. A new product spawned by a fad may last only a few months on the market, whereas demand for a product such as the automobile may continue indefinitely. Nevertheless, a product may change radically over time, reflecting changes in technology, competition, economic conditions and consumer tastes. Hence, even products in constant demand require ongoing product planning and development. A firm that ignores this function could lose customers. The Chrysler Corporation, for example, did not adapt its product to economic conditions and customer needs until bankruptcy was imminent; it continued to produce large cars when consumers were demanding smaller, more fuel-efficient vehicles.

The **product life cycle** shown in Figure 8.5 consists of four stages: product introduction, market growth, market maturity and sales decline. During the *product introduction stage,* the firm's primary objective is to make potential customers aware of the product's existence. Managers therefore develop an appropriate promotional campaign, which may include mass advertising, personal selling and various methods of sales promotion. At first, promotion costs are high in relation to product sales and profits. Video camcorders and high-definition televisions, for example, are products now in the introduction stage.

Product development is an activity that usually includes six stages: generating new product ideas, screening, concept testing, business analysis, test marketing and commercialization.

Product life cycle —consists of the four stages (product introduction, market growth, market maturity and sales decline) that all products go through.

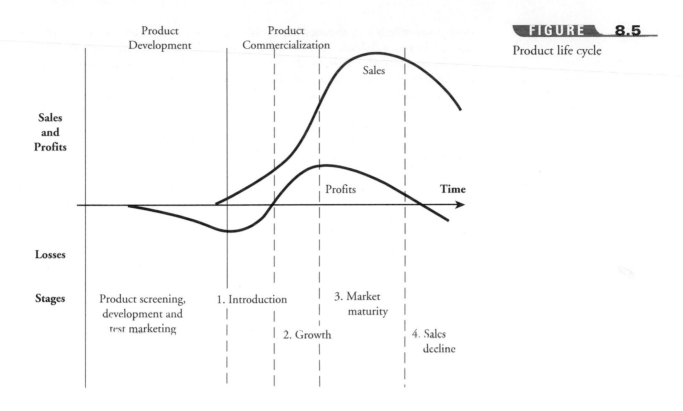

FIGURE 8.5

Product life cycle

If the product survives the introductory stage and customers accept it as useful, sales will increase. The product is then in the *market growth stage*, when the firm that introduced the product must recover its development costs and make a profit. As product prices tend to remain high, competitors are drawn into the market, each claiming a better product design. By the end of this stage, a wide variety of products are available and total product sales are still increasing. However, the profit for the original company is now reaching its peak, which marks the beginning of the end for the product.

In the *market maturity stage*, competition among manufacturers becomes more intense, as many similar products compete for the consumer's dollar. As each firm tries to obtain a greater market share through increased advertising, price cutting and product differentiation, profits begin to decline. Some manufacturers may drop out of the market altogether, as their sales and profits decrease. Most firms will concentrate on developing new products to replace the old. At the end of the market maturity stage, the market is saturated and total product sales begin to decline slowly (colour television reached this stage in the late 1970s).

In the final stage of *sales decline*, new products introduced to the market cut into sales of established products. Nevertheless, through vigorous price competition, a few firms may continue selling an established product that may remain profitable for many years before it is withdrawn from the market. Consumer loyalty and specific need often account for continued sales. Even today, for example, slide rules are still available, often at higher prices than sophisticated calculators.

Effect of Product Life Cycles on a Firm

The concept of product life cycles means that a company cannot rely on a successful product for long periods. Technological advances, for example, rapidly make many products obsolete and shorten product life cycles. Competitors may also make a successful product obsolete by introducing a simple modification such as a change in flavouring or a new package design. Competitors who seize the opportunity to improve a product can hasten the decline of profits and sales for the pioneering firm.

Thus, companies must continually develop new products and adjust the marketing mix to take advantage of high profits in the early stages of a product's life cycle. A firm must introduce its product quickly and see it to the market growth stage before competitors introduce their version. Otherwise a firm may not recover its investment in product planning and development.

Finally, the firm must be acutely aware of consumer needs and translate these needs into products. It must also plan for the decline of a product in the latter part of its life cycle; rather than simply withdraw the product from the market and replace it with a new one, the firm might be able to improve or repackage it. Thus, product life cycles are an essential consideration in a firm's marketing strategy.

Branding, Packaging and Labelling

Included in the total product concept are three factors that are important throughout the product life cycle: branding, packaging and labelling.

Branding

Brand —identifies a firm's products by a name, sign, symbol or any combination, and serves to differentiate a firm's products from those of its competitors.

A **brand** serves to identify a firm's products; it can be a name, sign, symbol or any combination that differentiates one firm's products from those of its competitors. Virtually everyone recognizes the McDonald's golden arches, for example, or the brand names "Ford" and "Coca-Cola." When symbols and names are registered with the federal government, the original firm retains sole and exclusive use. Without such protection, competitors could exploit an established brand name with no regard for the product, and the original firm would lose the recognition value associated with the product.

"The name's Fred Wilson, not Pierre Cardin or Yves Saint Laurent—now show me a shirt with a fancy FW on it and you've got yourself a sale."

SOURCE: Trevor Hutchings, *Marketing Magazine*, reproduced courtesy of the artist.

A successful brand name can also contribute to a firm's future marketing success and profitability; however, the predictability of customer loyalty is becoming less of a sure thing. One study suggests that only 58% of men and 55% of women regularly use well-known brand names. The pursuit of value is becoming more important than the status symbol.[2] Companies must be careful not to confuse brand loyalty with simple repeat behaviour. Loyalty leads to repeat behaviour, but repeat behaviour is not necessarily an indication of loyalty.[3] Discounts, premiums and other factors can lead to repeat behaviour, but not necessarily customer commitment. What has caused this change in consumer behaviour? Several factors can be cited to explain it:

1. More products on the market has resulted in greater choice for consumers.

2. Better-quality products are now available, which means that it is more difficult for consumers to differentiate on quality alone.

3. Greater cultural emphasis on change over conformity, and an expectation of instant gratification.

4. Increased influence of information technology.[4]

Packaging

Some products have led consumers full circle from scooping sugar and flour out of a sack to multiple-size packages and back round again to scooping sugar and flour out of bulk bins.

Packaging can be a significant product characteristic if it offers consumers additional benefits. A package designed to be resealed can protect products from becoming stale or spoiling, and one that can be used as a container makes storage easy. Packaging may also be a boon to the retailer. A well-packaged product is easy to handle, can be displayed in a small space and attracts customers' attention.

If a change in packaging improves the total product, it can be as effective as a new product in increasing sales. A new package may appeal to a new target market without losing the previous market; for instance, food packaged in smaller quantities may attract the growing single-person market while continuing to appeal to the original family market.

"Green" packaging is closely related to the issue of pollution prevention and is being recognized as a viable marketing focus. Costs savings to the producer may also be achieved by introducing more recycled materials into the packaging. UPS, a shipping company, recently reported the following results from an eight-month program that introduced a range of "green" express packages:

1. Amount of post-consumer recycled material used in the UPS box has almost doubled.

2. UPS is using 80% recycled material in its Express Letter.

3. Bleached paper is no longer used.

4. Air pollution associated with the manufacture of UPS express packaging will be reduced by 50%.[5]

5. Waste-water discharge has been reduced by 15%.

6. Energy consumption has been reduced by 12%.

In addition to these environmental advantages, from a business perspective UPS estimates total savings to be in the range of $1 million.[6]

Dismantling the Brandocracy: Restoring Relevance to the Marketing Department

www.strategy-business.com/strategy/95403/

Packaging —the physical container of a product—can be a significant product characteristic if it induces consumers to buy.

Labelling

A **label** provides information about the product or its manufacturer. Information may include instructions for use (especially important in the case of drugs) or a list of the product's ingredients.

The label may also attempt to provide information concerning the grade of the product. However, new labelling terms such as "ultra," "light," "high fibre" and "reduced fat" have led to more consumer confusion than enlightenment. Consumer advocates are continually pressuring regulators for more stringent laws with respect to labelling, particularly when there are major health concerns for consumers. For example, some critics charge that consumers should be advised of which types of foods are not being irradiated, so that they may make educated purchasing decisions.

Pricing the Product

In Chapter 2, we stated that a product's price is determined by the interaction of supply and demand in the marketplace. Theoretically, that statement is true. But firms require more concrete methods of setting prices for their products; they cannot simply place the product in stores and set the price according to the number of people who buy the product. The producer or manufacturer must know the price of a product in order to plan for production and profit. Wholesalers and retailers must also know product prices in order to plan their resale prices and to determine their profits.

Product pricing directly affects a company's profit and therefore requires careful analysis. The marketing manager must know the costs of manufacturing, sales and overhead as well as the profit objectives of the firm. He or she must also have a pricing strategy for each product. We now examine pricing strategies and how specific prices can be set.

Pricing Strategies

A pricing strategy depends on the specific objectives of a firm but may follow two general trends: skimming the market and penetration pricing.

A **skimming the market** pricing strategy is used when a new technological product, such as video recorders or home computers, is introduced into the consumer market. Due to initially high research, development and production costs and a low anticipated sales volume, the price of this product will be relatively high when it is first introduced. The skimming strategy is based on the assumption that some people, usually those with relatively high incomes, want the latest that technology has to offer and are willing to pay the high price for ownership of a new product. By "skimming" these customers off the top of the market, a company can maximize profits on new products. As demand for the product increases and greater quantities are produced, manufacturing costs drop along with prices. Prices may also be affected as competitors introduce similar products at a lower price in the hopes of gaining a share of the market.

A skimming strategy may also be dictated by the existing level of technology to mass-produce the product. Sometimes new products require considerable labour in their manufacture, which raises costs. Nevertheless, a company may want to be first on the market with a new product regardless of the initial price. Subsequently, it can improve production techniques, thereby reducing production costs and lowering consumer prices.

A second strategy is **penetration pricing**, in which a company introduces a product at a low price to gain a large portion of the market quickly. If customers accept the product, then the company can benefit from economies of scale in production and lower its costs. If the firm can establish the new product on the market in this manner, profits could be high. At a later date, the firm could introduce one or more similar products at higher prices and gain greater profits. At the same time, the low price of the initial product and the strong market position may discourage competitors from entering the market since they would likely be faced with low profit per unit.

Penetration pricing is used when a company introduces a product at a low price to gain a large portion of the market quickly.

Pricing Approaches

It is a difficult task to price products so that they will both attract consumers and provide a profit. There are two basic approaches to setting prices. The price to the consumer can be set on the basis of costs of production (the cost approach). Alternatively, the demand or market approach can be used; under this approach, prices are based on what consumers are willing to pay for the product and/or how market factors (e.g., the competition) affect prices.

Cost Pricing

Under the cost approach, the costs of doing business are the primary determinants of price: for a manufacturer, the cost of producing the product; for a retailer, the cost of buying and selling merchandise; and, for a service company, the cost of providing the service. In addition, the firm's general administrative expenses and an amount for profit must be included. In some instances, the initial pricing structure must also take into account the costs of research and development as well as the cost of introducing the product to the market, including extensive advertising and promotional schemes. There are two basic methods of **cost pricing**: mark-up and break-even analysis.

Cost pricing takes all fixed and variable costs into consideration and then adds an amount for profit in order to calculate an appropriate return for the company.

Mark-Up Pricing In **mark-up pricing**, which is generally used by retailers, a certain amount is added to the cost of the product to arrive at the selling price. Mark-up is usually expressed as a percentage and can be based on the cost or retail price of the product.

$$\text{Mark-up at cost} = \frac{(\text{Selling price} - \text{Cost})}{\text{Cost}}$$

Mark-up pricing means that an amount, usually a percentage, is added to the cost of the product to arrive at the selling price.

For example, if an item costs $1 and is sold for $2, then the mark-up at cost represents 100%.

$$\frac{\$1 \times 100}{\$1} = 100\%$$

Using the same example, but calculating the mark-up at retail, we get a mark-up of 50%.

$$\text{Mark-up at retail} = \frac{(\text{Selling price} - \text{Cost})}{\text{Selling price}}$$

$$\frac{\$1 \times 100}{\$2} = 50\%$$

Mark-up at retail or mark-on is also known as the retail method of pricing.

A cost plus method of pricing is also often used when selling to government. The seller determines his or her costs of production and adds a certain amount for a profit.

Break-Even Analysis Pricing   **Break-even analysis pricing** shows the minimum sales volume required at a particular price in order to cover all costs. Total costs are made up of both fixed and variable costs. *Fixed costs*, up to a point, remain unchanged regardless of production volume. They include costs such as insurance, utilities, managerial salaries and a variety of overhead costs. Total *variable costs*, on the other hand, increase directly with the volume produced. Included are items such as direct labour and raw materials required to produce each unit. Total revenue is determined by multiplying price by the number of units sold.

Figure 8.6 shows a break-even calculation and the *break-even point.* The break-even point, where total costs and total revenue are equal, is 110 000 units. At that volume, the total revenue received from selling that number of units at $10 each is equal to the total cost (fixed and variable) of producing that number of units. If the volume of product sold is above the break-even point, the firm will make a profit. As shown in the diagram, if 150 000 units were sold, then the total profit produced would equal the amount shown in the shaded portion between total revenue and total cost. Once a schedule has been established, the marketer can compare various profit results with various prices for the product, then choose the price most compatible with the target market and develop a pricing strategy. Break-even analysis is discussed in greater detail in Chapter 9.

The cost approach to pricing is relatively simple, but the resultant price may turn out to be too high for consumers. Competitors selling a similar product also have to be taken into account and the price adjusted accordingly. On the other hand, if this method produces a price lower than what customers are prepared to pay, the firm may lose potential revenue.

Break-even analysis pricing
shows the minimum sales volume required at a particular price in order to cover all costs.

FIGURE   8.6

Break-even method for pricing products

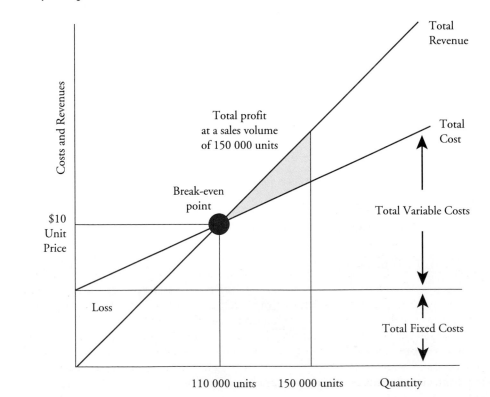

Demand or Market Approach

The ability to cover all costs and achieve a profit is an ideal way of pricing a product. Unfortunately, a competitive marketplace does not often allow that. The most important consideration must be **prevailing market prices**. Many manufacturers of standardized products such as convenience goods adhere to established market prices. **Customary pricing** is another method used for items that are of low cost and purchased frequently (e.g., chocolate bars and soft drinks). For years, the nickel-and-dime chocolate bars remained at that price even though costs of production rose gradually. Manufacturers absorbed these costs until a price increase was absolutely necessary.

Another method is the **flexible pricing** approach, where a careful analysis is made of potential sales based on different prices. If the price is lowered, for example, the increase in total revenue from higher sales could more than offset the drop in the price per unit. On the other hand, raising the price of the product may have little or no effect on sales revenue. Even though flexible pricing will set the ultimate price in the marketplace, a cost-pricing method may be used to determine the initial price that the firm needs to cover its production, distribution, research and development costs, as well as make a profit. Once this price is established as a floor price or reference point, the actual price will be determined by customers in the marketplace.

Since most firms sell a variety of products, one product may be used as a loss leader. The objective of a loss leader is to attract consumers to the product in the hope that they will eventually buy a higher-priced model. Thus, sales of other products increase and profits rise.

Suggested and going-rate pricing are relatively simple, but both are subject to problems. With **suggested pricing**, also known as **list pricing**, the seller uses the manufacturer's recommended price. Often the list price is then used as a base for discounts, a method often used to sell stereo and video equipment. Consumers seldom pay list price for these items.

Going-rate pricing places emphasis on the competition and the prices that people appear willing to pay. For example, when there is a bumper crop of apples, prices are low to entice people to buy more apples. At a public market, prices vary constantly based on demand. The alternative is to transport the product home again and risk spoilage.

Under either suggested or going-rate pricing, the risks are high for the producer if there is strong competition or if there are forces beyond the seller's control that determine demand for the product. For example, most manufacturers attempt to keep their list prices reasonable; nevertheless, an important consideration for the individual store owner is that his or her expenses are in line with those of the industry. If they are not, then list prices may yield a low profit.

Other Pricing Considerations

Consumers tend to believe that price and quality are related—the higher the price of a product, the better the quality. Marketers must keep this price-quality relationship in mind when pricing a product. If an item is priced too low, a large segment of the target market may assume that quality is also low and may not purchase the product.

Another factor often considered is **psychological pricing**. In pricing products at 79 cents, $9.95 or $29.95, instead of 80 cents, $10 or $30, marketers hope that the customer will unconsciously view $9.95 as significantly less than $10.

Psychological factors have not been proven conclusively, but odd pricing also functions as a control factor. For example, if an item cost an even $10, a sales clerk could pocket the money without ringing it into the till. Firms therefore set odd prices since the clerk is usually obliged to make change.

Prevailing market prices are used by manufacturers of standardized products such as convenience goods to adhere to established market prices.

Customary pricing is used for items that are of low cost and purchased frequently (e.g., candy bars and soft drinks).

Flexible pricing attempts to determine what effect different prices will have on sales.

Suggested/list pricing —the seller uses the manufacturer's recommended price and adjusts it as necessary to the prices of the competition.

Going-rate pricing is based on the competition and the prices that people appear willing to pay.

Psychological pricing is based on the customer unconsciously viewing a price such as $9.95 as significantly less than $10.

Promoting the Product

Promotions are the communications used to increase the sales of a product or service.

We are bombarded from all directions by various kinds of **promotions**—the communications used to increase sales of a product or service either directly or indirectly. Products are promoted on billboards, on television, in newspapers and magazines, and through displays and demonstrations. Promotion is not restricted to products, however, it also extends to ideas. Institutions use various methods of promotion to tell us what they do, political parties use promotion to persuade us to vote for a particular candidate and government uses promotion to publicize its services.

One major criticism of promotion comes from consumers who believe that producers spend an excessive amount of money to sell their products. The advertising techniques used to influence consumers in their buying behaviour are also frequently questioned.

Promotional Mix

Promotional mix —the combination of mass advertising, personal selling, sales promotion and publicity used to appeal to the target market.

The **promotional mix** is the combination of mass advertising, personal selling, sales promotion and publicity used to appeal to the target market.

1. *Mass advertising.* Marketers may use various media such as radio, television and newspapers to reach a large group of consumers.

2. *Personal selling.* Salespeople use a one-on-one approach to deal directly with customers in an attempt to sell a product or service.

3. *Sales promotion.* Techniques other than advertising are used to increase sales or the awareness of a product or service. Marketers may attend trade shows, arrange attractive displays in retail stores or offer contests or rebates to either the customer or the retailer.

4. *Publicity.* The media can generate interest in a product or service through newspaper, radio or television reports. Since publicity is an unpaid activity, marketing managers may have little influence over what is said about the product; sometimes publicity is adverse.

The promotional methods chosen by the marketing manager will depend primarily on the target market and the product offered. Industrial customers almost always require personal selling because of the technical aspects of the product and because the target market is relatively small. For consumer products, on the other hand, advertising is often the most effective means because the objective is to reach a large number of people and to inform them about a product that is usually simple to use and relatively inexpensive.

Often, of course, the two techniques are combined. Automobile manufacturers use all four methods, for example. They rely on mass advertising to tell consumers about the new cars available, and use personal selling once the customer enters a dealer's showroom. At that point, various sales promotion techniques may come into play, including rebates, extended warranties, attractive displays, contests and giveaways.

Automobile manufacturers also receive frequent publicity for their advances in technology and new model changes and gadgets, even though the publicity is sometimes adverse. The financial difficulties of Chrysler, for example, may have discouraged some customers from buying Chrysler cars for fear that the company might be forced to close down its operation. Similarly, people may have hesitated to purchase a Ford Pinto after hearing reports that the gas tank had exploded in a number of car accidents.

< Effective promotion can
increase sales of a product

Advertising

Advertising is a paid, non-personal promotional activity requested and paid for by a sponsor. The most important feature of advertising is its ability to reach large numbers of people through the use of mass media such as television, newspapers, radio and magazines. Advertising can also reach particular segments of the population by selective use of media. Thus, Mercedes-Benz might use *National Geographic* magazine and financial newspapers to advertise its cars, while Ford will use television and newspapers to advertise its lower-priced models that appeal to a larger segment of the population.

Mass advertising is not as expensive as it may appear. A colour newspaper supplement may cost a retailer hundreds of thousands of dollars, but considering that it reaches the majority of households in Canada, the cost per household is very small. Similarly, the high cost of sponsoring a major television production or movie may turn out to be small on a per-capita basis. Furthermore, by advertising during a particular television program, a company may gain exposure to a large portion of its specific target market. Table 8.1 shows the top magazine categories for advertising spending in January and February 1999.

Advertising is a paid, non-personal promotional activity requested by a sponsor.

Top magazine ad categories, January/February 1999

TABLE 8.1

Leading National Advertiser Industry Class	Spending ($M)	%Change from '98
Direct response	119.3	+10.8
Automotive/accessories & equipment	117.3	- 9.8
Computers & software	80.3	+27.3
Medicines & remedies	65.4	+27.5
Media & advertising	59.9	+19.2

SOURCE: J. Masterton, "Autos running second in ad-spending race," *Mediaweek 9,* (II) (March 15, 1999), p. 39.

Advertising agencies specialize in planning, producing and placing advertisements in various advertising media for their clients.

Account executive —the key intermediary between a client and an advertising agency who plans the advertising campaign and coordinates the work of the other advertising professionals involved.

Advertising media include newspapers, television, radio and magazines used to carry a particular message about a firm's product or service to potential customers.

Geographic selectivity indicates an advertising medium's ability to reach people in a particular geographic region.

Qualitative selectivity indicates an advertising medium's ability to reach specific types of people such as doctors, lawyers or homemakers.

Most commercial advertising is prepared by **advertising agencies** that specialize in planning, producing and placing advertisements in various advertising media for their clients. An agency typically consists of copywriters, artists, TV directors and media buyers. The **account executive** is the key intermediary between the agency and the client plans the ad campaign and coordinates the group of professionals involved. Agencies are normally paid a 15% commission based on the cost of the advertising placed in the media.

Advertising Media

Advertising can be analyzed in terms of the **advertising media** used to reach particular target markets. Each medium has advantages and disadvantages, depending on the product and its market. The popularity of the various media is best illustrated by the percentage of total advertising dollars spent on each. Figure 8.7 shows how the total advertising revenue in 1990, which amounted to $10.86 billion, was distributed among the various media. It also shows how total advertising revenue for each particular medium has changed on the basis of expenditures in 1980, 1985, 1990 and 1994.

Among the factors to be considered in choosing an advertising medium are cost, flexibility, length of life, quality of reproduction, and the amount and type of creative services and assistance provided. Levels of geographic and qualitative selectivity may also be important factors. An advertising medium that reaches most of the people in a particular geographic region is said to be high in **geographic selectivity**. **Qualitative selectivity** means that the medium is successful in reaching specific types of people such as doctors, lawyers or homemakers. Table 8.2 lists the major types of advertising media, together with the various characteristics that the advertising manager must consider in choosing among them.

Marketing on the Net

The Disney Web site is a booming place. It is estimated that 50% of users make a purchase on the site, with orders averaging double those of retail locations and triple those of catalogue sales. The site focuses on personalization, product customization and automated order processing.[7] Other companies have not experienced similar success. Why? Some authors suggest that failing to recognize the importance of the customer is still a fatal error, either with or without Internet technology. Some companies mistakenly assume that the consumer's thought processes somehow change

TABLE 8.2 Characteristics of various advertising media

Media Characteristics	Newspapers	Television	Radio	Direct Mail	Magazines	Outdoor
Geographic selectivity	High	Good	Good	High	High	High
Qualitative selectivity	Low	Moderate	Moderate	High	Moderate	Relatively low
Cost	Relatively low	High	Relatively low	High	High	Relatively low
Flexibility	Good	Poor	Good	Good	Poor	Poor
Length of life	Short	Short	Short	Generally short	Relatively long	Long
Quality of reproduction	Poor	High	No visual stimuli	Advertiser has choice	High	High
Creative services and assistance	Generally provided	Not generally provided	Some services provided	Left to advertiser	Left to advertiser	Usually provided

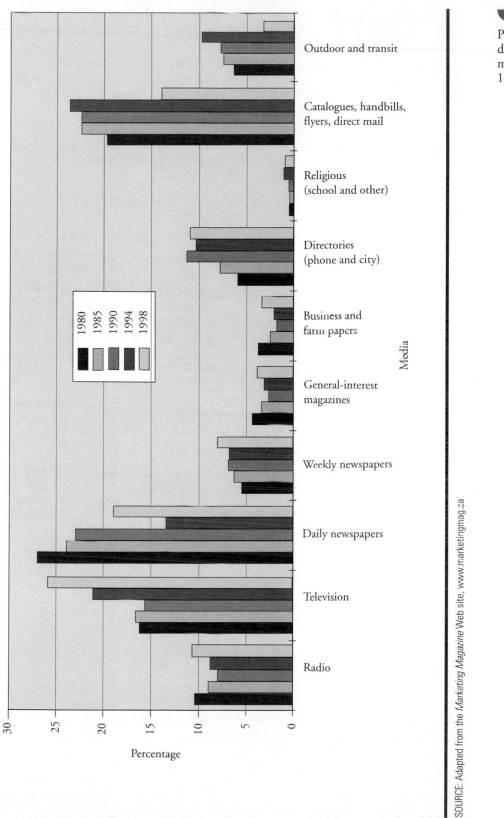

SOURCE: Adapted from the *Marketing Magazine* Web site, www.marketingmag.ca

FIGURE 8.7

Percentage of advertising dollars spent on various media, 1980, 1985, 1990, 1994, 1998

when they browse a Web site. Instead, marketers need to better understand the unique attributes of this audience in order to gain the attention they desire. The most successful Web sites are interactive. Customers are exposed to the advertising of the product on the banner ad space but can also request more information, request telephone call backs, purchase the product and post comments about the product without ever leaving the original Web site.[8]

Just how popular is Internet advertising? In a recent Quicken.com survey, 66% of companies report spending more in traditional advertising media, 19% have an even mix and 6% are spending more on online marketing than traditional media. The top three reasons cited by companies for increasing online advertising are

1. To acquire new customers (78%)

2. To drive revenue (22%)

3. To retain customers (19%).[9]

One author estimates that the Internet is growing at a rate of over 100% per year and that by 2006, there will be 900 million computers and other devices on the Net. Companies appear to progress through three stages of Internet use: first, businesses offer information about themselves and their product; second, business transactions are exchanged with suppliers and customers; and finally, the company undergoes fundamental operational changes as a result of the Internet.[10] Disney appears to be in the second stage of this development, and will soon proceed into the final stage. With these predictions of growth, writer Alan Rosespan proposes that there will be only two types of companies in the future: the quick and the dead. The power is in the hands of consumers. Now, before making a major purchase, many people search the Net so that they are armed with information not only on the company in question but also possibly five or more of its competitors. To survive in the future, Rosespan suggests four strategies for companies:

1. Become a seeker of knowledge—What are your competitors doing? What is happening in the industry? What is new in technology?

2. Innovate, don't imitate. By the time you have copied another company's model, the model will have changed.

3. Get to the future fast. Speed is essential.

4. Be more creative than ever before. This strategy includes not only advertising and marketing, but also every component of your business.[11]

Personal Selling

Personal selling uses a one-on-one approach between salesperson and customer to sell a particular product or service.

The main advantage of **personal selling** is face-to-face contact with the potential buyer, in contrast to the impersonal nature of mass advertising. In personal selling, the sales approach can be tailored to fit different situations: the salesperson can answer questions about the product, handle customer objections and, above all, gain a great deal of information about the customer's requirements. A salesperson can establish a relationship of trust with the customer, persuading the customer that his or her personal satisfaction and welfare are uppermost in the seller's mind. The major disadvantage of personal selling is its high cost; each salesperson commands a fairly high salary, but can call on only a limited number of customers. Personal selling is therefore generally restricted to industrial, wholesale and large retail customers, whose potential purchases amount to a substantial dollar value.

The Sales Process

Personal selling may bring to mind the travelling salesperson who uses his or her practised pitch to persuade customers to buy. While the sales approach still follows a basic process, the salesperson must identify the particular sales situation and make necessary adjustments to the basic presentation. The sales approach follows seven basic steps:

1. *Prospecting and qualifying.* Potential sales depend on the number of new prospective customers a salesperson can identify. The customers must have a potential interest in the product and be financially qualified to purchase.

2. *Approach.* Information about the prospects must be gathered and analyzed, so that the salesperson can prepare for the first meeting with the potential customer.

3. *Presentation.* When making the presentation, the salesperson must stimulate the customer's interest in the product. He or she provides information concerning the main features of the product, its advantages to the customer and evidence of other consumers' satisfaction.

4. *Demonstration.* A demonstration allows the customer to see the product or service in actual operation. The benefits of the item may also be explained with the aid of graphs, charts or pamphlets.

5. *Handling objections.* Experienced salespeople welcome customer objections, since they provide an opportunity to set the customer's mind at ease through detailed explanation of the product's use.

6. *Closing.* Unless a sale is closed, even the most knowledgeable salesperson and the best sales approach may come to nothing. Once the five previous steps have been completed, the salesperson must adopt the positive attitude that the customer will indeed purchase the merchandise. Walking to the cash register or starting to write up the order can help to remind a hesitant customer of his or her decision to buy.

7. *Follow-up.* Follow-up is the link between the first sale and future sales. The salesperson must ensure that the order is processed quickly and that all terms of the sale—delivery dates, installation and service—are carried out.

Sales Management

Large or small, a sales force must be coordinated by a manager. The sales manager performs all management functions, including planning for future sales personnel needs and recruiting and hiring salespeople. The training and development of salespeople and the evaluation of their work are particularly important. Leadership and motivation also play a major role; since salespeople generally enjoy their freedom and do not like close supervision, a good sales manager must be able to exert control without stifling initiative.

Sales Promotion

In addition to personal selling and advertising, various types of **sales promotion** can help stimulate consumer buying through specific one-time sales efforts. The most common technique is **point-of-purchase advertising**, which includes displays and demonstrations of a product, usually close to where it can be purchased. Another common promotional technique is **specialty advertising**, which involves giving

Sales promotion—an activity that is directed at increasing sales or the awareness of a product or service.

Point-of-purchase advertising includes displays and demonstrations of products usually close to where the products can be purchased.

Specialty advertising involves giving away inexpensive articles—pens, calendars and the like—that bear an imprint of the firm's name.

Trade shows are geared to retailers and wholesalers, but are usually open to the public

Trade shows are designed to provide the general public and buyers with information about the firm's products and services.

away inexpensive articles—pens, calendars and the like—that bear an imprint of the firm's name. Some companies may also use training seminars and **trade shows**. While these are usually geared to retailers and wholesalers, the general public may be invited to view the firm's products and services. The fashion industry often uses this kind of promotion. Contests for cash or merchandise prizes are also often offered. Other techniques designed to build customer loyalty for a product or service include merchandise samples, coupons, premium merchandise and trading stamps.

Publicity

Publicity is media communication about newsworthy products or services. It may or may not influence product sales.

New products, particularly those stemming from breakthroughs in technology, are newsworthy and frequently receive coverage in major newspapers or television. This **publicity** is, in effect, free advertising. While publicity can increase product sales when the news is favourable, adverse reports can result in decreased sales. Many trade magazines also provide publicity by printing articles about specific products, which may attract consumer interest. Manufacturing firms often go out of their way to make products available for testing in the hope that articles written about them will be beneficial.

Distributing the Product

Channel of distribution refers to the method used to get the product to the customer.

Would you order a can of peaches or a tube of toothpaste through a catalogue? We usually need these items quickly, and are not prepared to wait a week or more for delivery. Thus, many small retail stores exist alongside larger retailers; all are interested in attracting the customer with a variety of merchandise readily available for sale.

To get the merchandise to the consumer, producers can choose between the various **channels of distribution** shown in Figure 8.8. They can sell their product to the consumer through door-to-door sales, through catalogues, or through intermediaries such as agents, wholesalers and retailers.

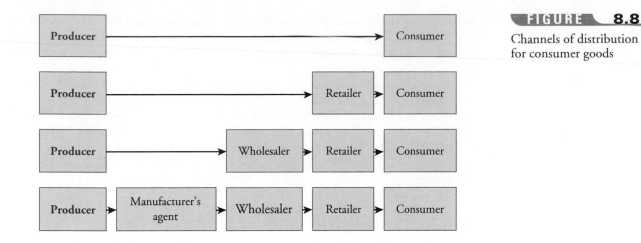

FIGURE 8.8

Channels of distribution
for consumer goods

Channels of Distribution for Consumer Goods

Producer-Consumer

The most direct route is to sell to the consumer without the use of intermediaries. Some producers establish retail outlets or catalogue stores and supply them directly. Others, such as Avon and Fuller Brush, use door-to-door salespeople. Artists, craftspeople and artisans often sell their wares through their own stores, as do fruit and large produce growers. While direct distribution can mean lower prices for the consumer, it is usually more expensive for the producer, who must perform many of the marketing functions normally handled by intermediaries. Moreover, the producer may not have the expertise or capital required to establish the retail outlets or sales forces necessary for adequate distribution. Most producers, therefore, choose to leave the distribution function to intermediaries.

Producer-Retailer-Consumer

Rather than sell directly to consumers, many manufacturers prefer to deal only with retailers. The producer may have a sales force to sell directly to retail stores (particularly large chain stores) and thereby exert more control over the selling situation. For example, if a retailer wants special concessions in return for a large order, the salesperson can communicate directly with head office to get approval for the sale under the specified conditions. Most large chain stores—particularly furniture and appliance stores—also have their own buyers who visit the manufacturer's premises to negotiate purchases.

Producer-Wholesaler-Retailer-Consumer

Most consumer products are distributed through this chain, particularly low-priced items such as toiletries and cigarettes. The producer may employ a sales force to sell to wholesalers, who generally buy in bulk. The wholesaler in turn employs a sales force to sell to the thousands of smaller retailers in a given geographical area. Because the wholesaler distributes a wide variety of products, the cost per item of the additional sales force is relatively low.

Producer-Agent-Wholesaler-Retailer-Consumer

Small manufacturers who cannot afford their own sales forces, yet sell their products over a large geographical area, often use a manufacturer's agent as an intermediary between themselves and the wholesaler. The agents employ sales forces to sell to wholesalers and large retailers. A manufacturer's agent may represent a number of producers with non-competing products, and receive a commission from each producer.

Producers may use any or all of the above channels to distribute their product. The choice will depend on the target market they want to reach. The Firestone and Goodyear tire companies, for example, have established retail outlets to sell directly to the consumer, and use wholesalers to sell to service stations and independent tire outlets. They also have sales forces to sell to automobile manufacturers and institutional markets, including government, the armed forces and taxi or car-rental companies.

Channels of Distribution for Industrial Goods

Producers of industrial products may sell their products to industrial customers directly, through manufacturer's agents or through wholesalers. They may also use a manufacturer's agent to sell to wholesalers who then distribute the product to various industrial customers. Figure 8.9 illustrates these channels.

The direct channel accounts for the greatest dollar volume in sales of industrial goods. Large installations such as nuclear power plants, turbine generating stations and locomotives are always sold directly to the user. On the other hand, office equipment/supplies and building materials are usually sold through industrial distributors. A producer without a marketing department may use agents to sell directly to industrial users or industrial distributors.

Wholesalers

Wholesalers reduce manufacturers' distribution costs by providing a sales force to sell a large variety of products to several retailers. In addition, many wholesalers store and deliver the merchandise, relieving the producer of responsibilities for warehousing and transportation. Retailers can thus also keep lower inventory levels and reduce their inventory costs. In addition, the wholesaler provides retailers with trade credit and other merchandising assistance. Wholesalers can be classified into two general categories: merchant wholesalers and manufacturer's agents.

> **Wholesalers** reduce manufacturers' distribution costs by providing a sales force to sell a large variety of products to several retailers.

FIGURE 8.9

Channels of distribution: industrial goods

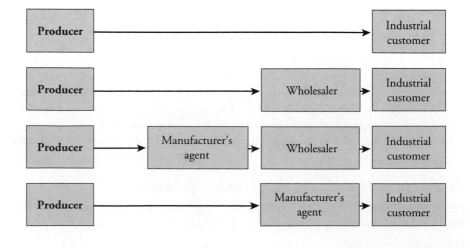

Merchant wholesalers take title to the products they buy from producers or manufacturers. They therefore own the merchandise outright. As temporary owners, they offer a full service to both producers and retailers, paying the producer for the product, storing it until it is sold to retailers, shipping it to retailers and providing them with trade credit and, when necessary, grading and sorting. Because of the risks they take and the services they perform, merchant wholesalers may charge a fee amounting to 25% of the retail price.

Manufacturer's agents do not take title to the goods they distribute, and seldom take possession of the goods. Their major function is to provide the producer with a marketing service by employing a sales force to cover a particular territory. Manufacturer's agents often handle the products of various non-competing producers. Because the service they provide is limited, agents charge a lower fee or commission, perhaps 5% of sales.

The producer must determine the need for either or both of these channels of distribution. Producers who lack a sales force are likely to use both kinds of distributors.

> **Merchant wholesalers** buy the products from producers or manufacturers and offer a full service to retailers, including storing, shipping, trade credit and, when necessary, grading and sorting.

> **Manufacturer's agents** do not buy the goods they distribute, but provide the producer with a marketing service by employing a sales force to cover a particular territory.

Retailers

The retailer is the intermediary who meets the consumer face-to-face; as such, he or she is the most important link between producer and consumer. **Retailers** buy their merchandise from the producer or wholesaler, and then resell the goods to the consumer. Since they are so close to the consumer, they can provide the producer with information about both the product and consumers' changing needs and wants.

Retailing is a competitive business. Small retail stores can be established with little capital, and educational and legal requirements are few. Moreover, retailing requires virtually no previous experience. While these factors attract many people into retailing, the rate of failure is high. Retailers must have a keen ability to forecast consumers' demands. In addition, successful retailers must be imaginative; they must be astute buyers, efficient in their operation and able to provide good service to customers.

> **Retailers** buy their merchandise from the producer or wholesale, and then resell the goods to the consumer.

Retail Chain Stores

Many retail stores have grown into large **chain stores** with branches in the shopping centres of virtually all major cities. In 1956, independent stores handled 81.8% of total retail sales in terms of dollars; the remaining 18.2% was handled by chain stores. By 1985, chain stores had increased their share of total retail sales to 42%.[12] Table 8.3 presents a comparison of retail sales in millions of dollars for various retail categories, in January and February 1999.[13]

One major advantage that chain stores have over the independent small retailer is their buying power. Almost all chain stores use some form of **centralized buying**. With a central buying office receiving orders from all of the chain's branches, specialized buyers can comb domestic and world markets and buy merchandise in large quantities. Volume purchases in turn allow these retailers to receive quantity discounts, and the savings can be passed on to the consumer.

Another advantage of chain stores is their capacity for large-scale—often nationwide—advertising. Large-scale advertising reduces costs of television commercials, newspaper advertisements, catalogues and special promotions. Although costly, these advertisements amount to little per dollar of sales when spread over many stores and a large total sales volume.

> **Chain store** —a retail store with two or more branch stores.

> **Centralized buying** is used by retail chains where purchases are handled through a central office and specialized buyers buy merchandise in large quantities in order to receive quantity discounts.

FIGURE 8.10

Retail trade in
Canada, 1999

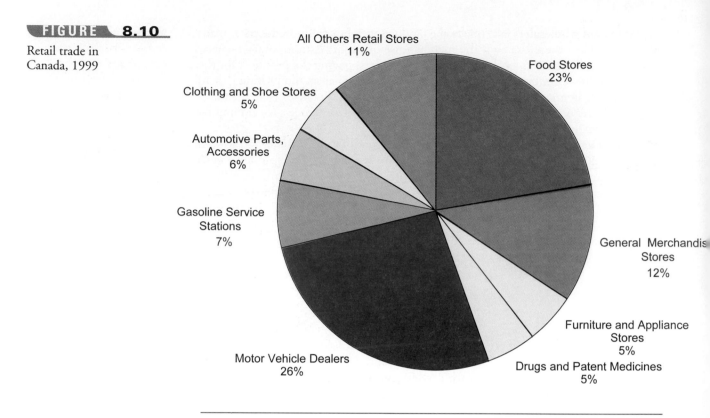

SOURCE: Adapted from Statistics Canada, *Canadian Economics Observer* (July 2000), Cat. no.
11-101XPB.

TABLE 8.3

Retail sales in Canada (Jan/Feb 1999) [14]

Category	Jan 99($M)	Feb 99($M)	%Change
Food	4 851	4 837	-0.3
Medicine Stores	1 102	1 109	0.6
Clothing	1 168	1 175	0.6
Furniture	1 096	1 095	-0.1
Automotive	8 060	8 073	0.2
General Merch.	2 491	2 427	-2.6
Total Retail Sales	21 099	21 008	-0.4

Retail chains are also able to hire professional managers to specialize in the merchandising of specific products, from carpets and rugs to housewares and men's clothing. Department managers know their merchandise well; they can watch for subtle changes in consumer preferences and quickly relay them to the central buying office.

While chain stores have a number of advantages due to their size, independent retailers are able to concentrate on those areas in which chain stores are deficient: close customer relationships, personal service and specialized merchandise. For example, small clothing retailers attune themselves to their customers' needs and wants, call them when specific clothing items appear in the store and ensure a proper fit. Chain

< Hudson's Bay Company is a chain store with branches in almost every major Canadian city

stores are not particularly adept at providing personal service, nor do they generally handle merchandise that does not appeal to a mass consumer market.

The Retail Franchise

In an attempt to combine the advantages of large chain store retailers with those of the small independent retailer, **retail franchising** has become popular. A retail franchise allows centralized buying of merchandise, supplies and equipment, while retaining the virtues of independent ownership. For an initial investment, which may range up to $200 000 or more, the franchisee or independent owner can take part in the success of a well-known firm with a well-known product. In addition, he or she can benefit from centralized buying, training and management services, as well as assistance in locating advertising and inventory control. If a building is required, plans and building expertise are available; any equipment required is furnished by suppliers who are aware of the specifications. Retail franchises are discussed in more detail in Chapter 2.

Retail franchising allows centralized buying of merchandise, supplies and equipment, while retaining the virtues of independent ownership

Types of Retail Operations

There are several types of retail operations, each with advantages and disadvantages.

- *General stores.* The earliest retailers, general stores offer a wide variety of merchandise and are still common today.

- *Department stores.* Department stores are, in effect, large general stores with merchandise grouped in departments, each headed by a manager responsible for buying and selling the department's merchandise. Department stores may be either large independent stores or parts of a chain.

- *Supermarkets.* Supermarkets are large retailers that offer a variety of food and other merchandise, self-selection and lower prices than most independent markets.

- *Discount stores.* Discount outlets usually offer a variety of merchandise at substantially lower prices than regular stores. There are generally few services such as credit or delivery, and little by way of elaborate displays or wrappings.

- *Convenience stores.* Convenience retailers offer a limited selection of food and non-food items, and are established in convenient locations to save people time and travel. Convenience stores remain open for long hours and may charge relatively high prices for their merchandise.

- *Specialty stores.* Specialty stores carry only one particular kind of merchandise such as sporting goods, suits or cameras. By narrowing their total merchandise offering, they can provide a more thorough selection, together with technical expertise and service. Prices are generally higher because of the wider selection and superior service.

- *Vending machines.* Merchandise such as soft drinks, sandwiches and candy bars can be sold in vending machines at a low operating cost. Entertainment can also be provided in the form of pinball machines, various electronic games and videocassette rentals.

- *"Big box" stores.* These are big warehouse outlets that either sell a broad group of merchandise or provide an extensive selection in a certain category such as office supplies, sporting goods or arts and crafts. They provide virtually no customer services. Some, such as Price-Costco, do not advertise but charge a membership fee.

- *Mail order.* A wide variety of merchandise is available through catalogues and is shipped to the consumer by mail. Mail orders offer convenient shopping from virtually anywhere, and delivery is usually rapid.

- *Electronic or home shopping.* This allows individuals to order goods displayed on a television screen by telephone or by using a computer interactively with an electronic order board.

Changing Retail Concepts

Wheel of retailing refers to the cycle that retailers go through as they mature. By adding products and services to satisfy their customers, they become vulnerable to undercutting by newer outlets offering lower prices and fewer services.

Scrambled merchandising occurs when retailers add different types of merchandise to their original product mix in order to attract more customers.

The classification of retail operations is becoming difficult to apply, since modern retailers are in a continual state of transition. Many outlets start by offering relatively low prices and a minimum of service. As they mature, they tend to add services to satisfy their customers, which tends to increase prices. These retailers then become vulnerable to undercutting by newer outlets offering lower prices and fewer services. These outlets eventually reach the same maturity stage and are then faced with new competition. This retail cycle is called the **wheel of retailing**.

A second factor that confuses retail classifications is the concept of **scrambled merchandising**, a type of merchandising that occurs when retailers add different types of merchandise to their original product mix in order to attract more customers. Thus, drug stores come to resemble small department stores as they add cameras, stereo equipment, toys, kitchenware, small appliances, books and CDs to their basic stock. Supermarkets too have begun to expand into non-food items such as T-shirts, running shoes and stationery. Service stations are also beginning to offer a variety of merchandise and services in addition to gasoline sales and car repairs.

Physical Distribution

So far in our discussion we have considered only the channels of distribution and their members, without focusing on the physical task of transporting products. **Physical distribution** encompasses all the activities involved in transporting finished goods from the producer to the final consumer, as well as moving raw materials from their source to the producer. In addition to the transportation of goods, physical distribution involves warehousing, physical handling, packaging for shipment, inventory control, order processing and customer services.

Physical distribution must be considered from a total cost point of view, keeping in mind the level of customer service desired. Transportation is often the most costly aspect of the total physical distribution cycle, but the least expensive method is not necessarily the best. The product and the customer must also be considered. Thus, while railways may be the most efficient means of handling large, bulky items such as household appliances, they are not ideal for shipping the latest fashion goods, which must get to the market quickly. Air freight may be more cost-effective. A comparison of the major types of transport is shown in Table 8.4.

Storage is another major concern, particularly for producers who supply a large area. The lower costs of shipping by rail must be compared to greater storage cost incurred because of the need for regional warehouses. In contrast, the higher transportation costs of trucking may mean lower storage and inventory costs.

Physical distribution is the aspect of marketing that encompasses all the activities necessary to move products efficiently.

The four major forms of transportation ranked by characteristic

TABLE 8.4

	Best	Second	Third	Worst
Speed	Plane	Truck	Train	Ship
Availability	Truck	Train	Plane	Ship
Delivery flexibility	Truck	Train	Plane	Ship
Bulk transportation capability	Ship	Train	Truck	Plane
Cost	Ship	Train	Truck	Plane
Frequency	Truck	Plane	Train	Ship
Dependability	Truck	Train	Ship	Plane

Chapter Summary

1. Marketing concerns the movement of goods and services from the producer to the consumer. It consists of eight specific functions: buying, selling, storing, transporting, standardizing and grading, financing, risk-taking and information gathering. Most firms today that cater to the consumer are marketing-oriented (e.g., geared toward producing the goods and services wanted by consumers).

2. Since a firm's success depends on satisfying the customer's needs, marketing managers must develop a marketing strategy. First, they must determine, through market research, the characteristics of the market. They then select a target market and determine the particular combination of product features, price, promotion and distribution channel best suited to satisfy the targeted market. This combination is known as the marketing mix. A different marketing strategy is usually required for consumer products as opposed to industrial products.

3. Products have a life cycle consisting of four stages after product development: product introduction, growth, market maturity and sales decline. Some product life cycles are short, while others may last for decades. In most instances, a firm must constantly plan for the development and introduction of new products. It must also determine the particular product mix that it wishes to sell. The product mix may consist of a single product line or a number of product lines, each made up of products with similar physical characteristics or uses. Other important marketing considerations include branding, packaging and labelling, all of which are significant product characteristics.

4. Another key marketing decision involves pricing. A firm may choose from two general strategies: skimming the market and penetration pricing. To determine specific product prices, a firm may use the cost method or the demand method. There are two basic cost methods of pricing-mark-up pricing and break-even analysis pricing. With mark-up pricing, the firm adds an amount to the basic cost of development and product introduction to cover sales expenses and profit. With break-even analysis pricing, a firm can determine the profit earned at various sales volumes based on its fixed and variable costs. An appropriate price can then be selected based on the sales volume expected. Demand and market conditions must also be taken into account when pricing products. This includes prevailing market prices, customary pricing and going-rate pricing. Other considerations in pricing include price-quality relationships and the effects of psychological pricing.

5. The third element of the marketing mix is promotion, which includes advertising, personal selling, sales promotion and publicity. Advertising takes the largest chunk of the promotion budget, but because it reaches the largest number of customers it can mean a relatively low cost per person or household reached. The largest amount of advertising money goes to newspapers, with television next, followed by other media. Personal selling includes retail sales, door-to-door selling and sales to industrial customers. Sales promotion is intended to increase sales by supplementing a firm's basic sales effort through displays, demonstrations, specialty advertising, trade shows, samples, coupons, premiums or promotional contests. Publicity is unpaid advertising for a company or its products that is provided by trade publications and consumer media; although reports are often favourable, adverse news can be detrimental.

6. Placing the product means getting it from the manufacturer to the consumer or industrial customer. The manufacturer can choose one or all of the channels available—manufacturer's agents, wholesalers and retailers. Wholesalers are the intermediaries who store products, take credit risks and provide market information. The wholesaler makes it more convenient for retailers and industrial customers to get products as required. Retailers buy goods from manufacturers or wholesalers for resale to consumers.

7. Most retail stores are small, but a few chain stores in Canada account for a substantial proportion of total retail sales. There are many types of retail operations, including department stores, discount stores, supermarkets, convenience stores, mail order, automatic vendors and the so-called "big box" stores.

8. The most common means of transporting products are trucks, railway, planes and ships. The cost of transportation is important, but other factors such as warehousing, selling and financing must also be taken into consideration.

KEY TERMS

Marketing 273	Product line 283	Advertising agencies 294
Utility 273	Product mix 283	Account executive 294
Time utility 273	Product planning 283	Advertising media 294
Place utility 273	Product development 284	Geographic selectivity 294
Ownership utility 273	Product life cycle product lifecycle ...284	Qualitative selectivity 294
Form utility 273	Brand 286	Personal selling 296
Production marketing 275	Packaging 287	Sales promotion 297
Sales-oriented marketing 275	Label 288	Point-of-purchase advertising 297
Marketing era 275	Skimming the market 288	Specialty advertising 297
Marketing research 275	Penetration pricing 289	Trade shows 298
Marketing strategy 275	Cost pricing 289	Publicity 298
Target market 277	Mark-up pricing 289	Channel of distribution 298
Market segmentation 277	Break-even analysis pricing 290	Wholesalers 300
Marketing mix 277	Prevailing market prices 291	Merchant wholesalers 301
Four P's 277	Customary pricing 291	Manufacturer's agents 301
Consumer goods 280	Flexible pricing 291	Retailers 301
Convenience goods 280	Suggested/list pricing 291	Chain stores 301
Shopping goods 280	Going-rate pricing 291	Centralized buying 301
Specialty goods 280	Psychological pricing 291	Retail franchising 303
Industrial goods 281	Promotions 292	Wheel of retailing 304
Capital goods 281	Promotional mix 292	Scrambled merchandising 304
Expense goods 281	Advertising 293	Physical distribution 305

REVIEW QUESTIONS

1 What functions does the marketing department perform?

2 Distinguish between production marketing and sales-oriented marketing. How did the marketing era develop?

3 How can market research be used to select target markets?

4 What is involved in establishing a marketing strategy?

5 Why may each target market require a different marketing mix?

6 Distinguish between consumer and industrial markets.

7 Define each of the three categories of consumer goods.

8 Distinguish between product mix and product line.

9 How important is the concept of product life cycles to a firm? Describe each of the four stages in the product life cycle. Suggest some products currently associated with each stage.

10 Distinguish between the two pricing strategies—skimming the market and penetration pricing. Suggest some relatively new products that might have been successfully introduced by each of these strategies.

11 Distinguish between the cost pricing and market pricing approaches.

12 What is the difference between calculating mark-up at cost and calculating it at retail?

13 How can break-even analysis be used in pricing a product?

14 Why is the cost approach to pricing not always used?

15 What is meant by promotional mix? Identify some product examples and indicate the best promotional mix for each.

16 Describe two forms of sales promotion.

17 Under what circumstances is advertising the most appropriate promotional tool? Personal selling?

18 Why should a salesperson follow the basic sales approach? Explain the importance of each step in the basic sales process.

19 What is a channel of distribution? Define the three channel members.

20 Why does an industrial product distribution channel differ from the distribution channel for a consumer convenience product?

21 What advantages do retail chains have over small independent retailers? How can franchising provide small retailers with the advantages enjoyed by chain stores?

DISCUSSION QUESTIONS

1 "Marketing costs too much." Discuss.

2 What are the pros and cons for the consumer of allowing large Canadian retailers to become even larger through mergers with smaller retail chains?

3 In what aspects of marketing do you favour more government regulation?

4 Discuss the impact of eliminating intermediaries for consumer products.

5 Is marketing a more important function than production? Debate this issue.

Digital Video Disc: Success Finally

If you rent videotapes regularly, recently you may have noticed ever more racks offering DVDs for rent. The same size as a music CD, a DVD offers a minimum of seven times the data storage of a music CD. A double-layered disc can hold up to four hours of continuous play. The largest-capacity DVD disc can hold up to nine hours of prerecorded programming.

Besides capacity, compared to VHS tape, the picture resolution is twice as good as current VHS-taped movies and better than the almost defunct laserdisc and satellite video. Many DVDs contain a standard size 4:3 aspect ratio, which is the standard television screen size in North America, and on the reverse side, a wide-screen image that shows the movie on your screen as you are likely to see in a movie theatre. Most DVD movies also contain the theatrical trailer, an explanation of how special effects were achieved in the movie, and other features. In addition, movies can be multilingual, since a DVD has the capacity of presenting soundtracks in eight languages with up to 32 distinct subtitles. Movie producers can even include multiple story lines on one DVD so the viewer can determine the outcome of the movie plot in a truly interactive way. Some discs may also offer multiple camera angles, making it ideal for teaching sports such as tennis and golf by showing a variety of angles. Instead of a censoring chip to lock out certain material, various versions of a movie may be produced on the same disc, allowing parents to lock out a more adult version for a more sanitized PG version. All DVDs will have surround sound, with sound quality superior to that of today's CDs.

There was a time when the success of the DVD was in doubt. Content providers were afraid of illegal copying because the quality of the DVD is so high. But eventually agreement was reached on a copy protection method, which spelled the eventual end of videotape. As more movies began to appear on DVDs, the prices of DVD players also declined rapidly. At the beginning of 1999, a mid-priced DVD player still cost approximately $700, but by mid-2000 the price had dropped to half that amount. Matsushita, Philips, Sony, Pioneer and Sharp, to name only a few manufacturers, now have DVD players in various price ranges depending on features. DVDs are now starting to flood into retail stores and are expanding rapidly into video rental stores as well.

Questions

1 If you were the marketing manager at Matsushita, Philips, Sony, Pioneer and Sharp, what criteria would you use to determine the various target markets for the new DVD players? What types of consumers would initially be in these target markets?

2 Taking into consideration the rapid changes in technology, identify the major concerns of any manufacturer of a new home entertainment product such as a DVD player.

3 What general pricing strategy are the manufacturers using when marketing new home entertainment products? Why are they using this strategy?

4 Which of the pricing method would be adopted initially by a manufacturer of DVD players? How might this pricing strategy change as more manufacturers put DVD players on the market?

5 Explain how a manufacturer might use the four promotional techniques to promote the DVD players.

The Bottomfeeder

Roscoe Girrard was an engineer who operated Front Street Telecommunications Inc. While all the competition was investing madly in new product research and development, cellular technology, satellite communications and fibre optics, Roscoe was making a very good living selling "old technology."

"The issue," said Roscoe, "is that someone, somewhere, must service the needs of those customers who are still using old technology. Take, for example, a small company that is using an old telephone switchboard system. Just because it's outdated doesn't mean it doesn't work. These companies don't have the money to invest in all this newfangled technology, and really, why should they? For their needs, the old stuff works fine and it will continue to work fine. The problem occurs when they need repairs. The innovators' ideas are easy but not cheap—replace everything with new technology! But to actually fix this old junk? You've got to be joking ... and so the story goes. I am proud to be one of the only telecommunications firms in the country that can service old technology."

In addition to Roscoe's parochial and domestic success, he was also experiencing substantial growth in his company division, which purchased old telecommunications technologies and sold them to developing countries. Because companies and competitors were only too anxious to offload this old technology on anyone dumb enough to be interested in purchasing it, Roscoe was able to obtain an almost endless supply of equipment at such low cost that he could resell it to developing countries for an enormous profit, but at prices still cheap enough for the developing country to consider it a bargain price.

SOURCE: By David H. Jones-Delcourt. Reprinted by permission of the author.

Questions

1 Discuss Roscoe's experience with respect to the product life cycle.

2 Discuss Roscoe's experience with respect to market segmentation, target marketing and the marketing mix.

3 Do you think that the market for old technology will continue for any definite period of time?

COMPREHENSIVE CASE 8-3

SOMERSET OPTICAL

In early April 1999, Somerset Optical began to notice a drop in sales. This was of particular concern in view of the company's recent expansion activities. By then Somerset Optical consisted of three dispensing optical retail outlets and a full-service optical laboratory.

At a management meeting, it was suggested that the company should pay particularly close attention to marketing. Somerset Optical clearly had the right people, the right suppliers, the right equipment and the right intention. It was felt, however, that the original marketing plan put in place before Somerset expanded was now largely inappropriate. The marketing plan would have to be modified to more accurately reflect Somerset's current operating realities.

The administrative consultant defined a marketing strategy, in simple terms, as a plan that identifies a target market and develops the appropriate mix. The development of the target market usually follows a philosophy of market segmentation as opposed to market aggregation. The former involves breaking down a large market into its different segments, whereas the latter groups segments together as one market. The administrative consultant explained that market aggregation would occur in instances where a company was attempting to mass-market a relatively generic product to the widest range of consumers. Market segmentation, on the other hand, would break down the larger market into smaller markets. The strategic options discussed were mass-marketing a product to customers in a particular market segment, or niche-marketing to a particular segment. Finally, target marketing would pinpoint those in the market segment who would be likely consumers of the product.

After considerable discussion, Fowler and Dewar defined as their target market the middle-to mature-aged customer who is simultaneously health- and fashion-conscious, who has the resources available to purchase higher-end eyewear, and who would not be opposed to paying a higher price on the margin for a higher level of personal service. The target market was also proposed as being the general area surrounding each of the three stores within a 15-kilometre radius.

Following considerable discussion of the marketing mix, Fowler and Dewar made the following decisions:

1. *Product.* Somerset would carry no deep-discount frames as they did not seek to compete with volume eyewear discounters. Their products would be brand-name, of excellent quality, backed by the best available warranties and available in a wide selection of styles and colours.

2. *Price.* Somerset would set an aggressive market price to attract undecided buyers. The aim was to sell eyewear at a price that would provide the firm with a minimum $50 profit on each pair of glasses sold, and a minimum $40 profit on each pair of regular, daily-wear contact lenses sold.

3. *Place.* Somerset would dispense glasses and contact lenses from each of its three locations.

4. *Promotion.* Somerset would promote its products through a combination of personal selling and mass advertising. In addition to advertising in elevators and local newspapers, the company would send literature to the offices of ophthalmologists and optometrists.

SOURCE: By David H. Jones-Delcourt. Reprinted by permission of the author.

>>

Questions

1 Evaluate Somerset's marketing strategy.

2 Where would you expect to find eyewear in the product life cycle?

3 Discuss two pricing approaches available to Somerset in pricing their product.

4 Recommend what you consider to be an optimum promotional mix for Somerset Optical.

5 What would be the most effective type of advertising for Somerset Optical?

9

Accounting and Financial Management

Learning Objectives

After reading this chapter, you will be able to

1. Identify the three major functions of the finance manager.

2. Explain the meaning of cash flow, and prepare a cash budget for a new business. _Definition Cash Flow_

3. Identify the major sources of short-term financing.

4. Explain the purpose of an accounting system, and why financial statements are essential to any organization.

5. Explain the function of each of the three major accounting statements: balance sheet, income statement and statement of changes in financial position. _3 key terms Definitions_

6. Identify the most common financial ratios, and explain how they are used for control purposes.

7. Compare debt financing to equity financing.

8. List the advantages and disadvantages to a company of issuing stocks or bonds for raising money.

9. Identify the difference between common and preferred shares.

10. List and explain the major factors that a financial manager must consider before deciding between stocks and bonds as a means of raising long-term funds.

11. Describe the basic operation of the stock and bond market.

The Function of the Finance Department

Money management is one of the most crucial aspects of operating a business, be it large or small. While small firms often suffer from not having enough money to meet their daily requirements or modernize their operation, large firms may run into money problems because they have miscalculated the financial implications of a major new venture or a takeover of an existing firm.

Financing is the business function involved in acquiring and managing funds effectively. In a small business, the owner usually handles finances and arranges for loans as necessary. In a large corporation, finance is a separate department, usually headed by a vice-president with one or more middle managers who perform specialized functions.

The three major functions of the finance department are:

> **Financing** is the business function involved in acquiring and managing funds effectively.

1. *Acquiring operating funds.* A business must have cash available at all times to handle expenditures incurred in normal operations. Employees expect to be paid for the work they do, and suppliers expect to be paid for the raw materials or finished products they provide. In addition to these payments, the firm has various other financial obligations such as rent, utilities and services provided by other firms, not to mention provincial, federal and municipal taxes. If the firm is unable to meet these payments, it could face bankruptcy.

2. *Analyzing operations.* The finance department performs a regular analysis of the firm's operation to ensure that it is functioning efficiently. This analysis requires an accounting system and the collection of financial data, which are summarized at regular intervals in the form of accounting statements. The three major accounting statements used in financial analysis are the income statement, the balance sheet and a statement of changes in financial position, which shows how funds were acquired and used over a period of time. Management uses the information in these statements to determine how the firm is doing and to compare performance with previous years, or with other businesses in a similar industry. Except in small businesses, the accounting function is usually a separate department. The manager in charge of the accounting department usually reports to the firm's top financial executive, often the vice-president of finance.

3. *Acquiring long-term funds.* Even gradual growth may require large amounts of money that the firm can repay only over a long period of time. To expand its operation to another province, for example, a business may require a few million dollars more than the regular operation can supply. The finance manager must raise the required funds either by borrowing or by selling shares of ownership in the company to investors.

Ensuring Financial Solvency

Profits are obviously a key indicator of a successful firm. But even profitable firms can be mismanaged and become bankrupt. Profits shown on financial statements do not mean that a firm has managed its funds efficiently. A firm may be unable to pay its suppliers if sales are too low and too much money is tied up in accounts receivable and inventory, or if money was invested in additional plant capacity, equipment and machinery. If a firm has no cash to pay its operating debts, creditors could petition the courts to have the firm declared bankrupt. Thus, the most important function of the finance department is to ensure that the business remains **financially solvent**, so that it can pay its bills as they come due.

> **Financial solvency** refers to the ability of a business to meet its financial obligations as they come due.

Working Capital and the Cash Budget

Cash is basic to the operation of any business. As Figure 9.1 indicates, cash is used to purchase **fixed capital**—buildings, machines, equipment and furniture—necessary for the firm to operate. But cash is also required in current operations, to generate sales revenue through either the manufacture of goods or the provision of a service. Cash used for these purposes is known as **working capital**. In a retail business, for example, cash is used to buy inventory and to pay for wages, salaries and the many other expenses incurred in its regular operation. When merchandise is sold, the firm once again receives cash, either at the point of sale or when a customer pays his or her bills. As **cash flows** in this circular pattern, for a profitable firm each dollar generates a small amount of profit.

Management has little control over sales since it cannot force people to buy. But a firm can gear its operation to anticipated sales by controlling the amount of inventory purchased, the number of people on the payroll, the collection of accounts

Fixed capital is the buildings, equipment and machinery required in a business.

Working capital is the cash used in the daily operation of the business and includes inventory and accounts receivable.

Cash flow describes the cycle through which cash is converted to inventory and then to accounts receivable, thus generating the firm's profit.

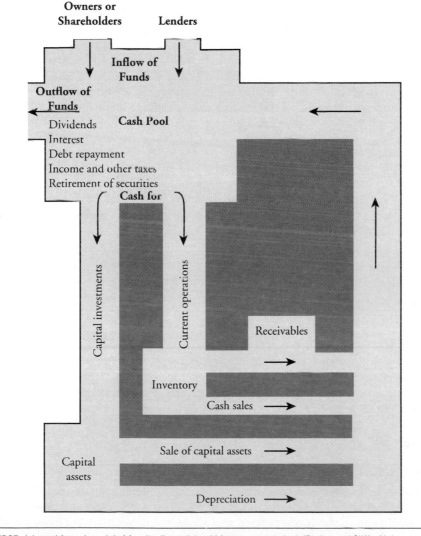

SOURCE: Adapted from Joseph L. Massie, *Essentials of Management*, 3rd ed. (Englewood Cliffs, N.J.: Prentice-Hall): 203.

FIGURE 9.1

How cash flows through a business

receivable and other expenses. Planning and sales forecasting are therefore important. If planned sales revenue does not provide sufficient funds to meet expected expenses and/or debt repayments, the firm can plan to borrow money to continue operating during slow periods.

Cash budget shows expected inflows and outflows of funds over a period of time.

Expected inflows and outflows of funds over six months to a year are summarized in a **cash budget**, as shown in Figure 9.2. The estimated receipts for each month are added up and the estimated expenditures deducted to establish the monthly cash inflow from operations. This net balance is added to the beginning cash balance. The result is compared to the minimum cash balance desired at all times. Plans can then be made to either borrow money or repay a short-term loan depending on the amount of money available.

A cash budget usually covers 12 months or more and indicates to the finance manager when there may be a shortage of cash, and how much the shortage might be. This will allow him or her to make arrangements with a bank or other financial institution to borrow money when necessary and repay loans during the months when there is a surplus.

The cash budget in Figure 9.2 was developed on a computer using an electronic spreadsheet. By setting up a model and entering the appropriate formulas, the finance manager can develop various scenarios of revenue inflows and expenditure outflows and quickly see the results as the cash balance increases or decreases and as loan requirements change. Once a cash budget is finalized, the finance manager can enter the actual cash inflows and outflows for the previous month to get an up-to-date picture of the present and forecasted financial situation.

Short-Term Borrowing

As the cash budget for Wombat Ski Equipment Company Inc. shows, receipts and expenditures are not always in line. In fact, while expenses are fairly constant throughout the year, sales revenue fluctuates widely. Since Wombat sells only ski equipment, sales are very low from May through October. Nevertheless, the firm must continue to pay rent, utilities, salaries and a host of other expenses. Once the ski season is in full swing, sales revenue will quickly exceed expenditures. To cover expenses in the off-season, Wombat borrows money, which it repays during periods when sales revenue is high.

Short-term financing is required when a firm needs money to meet its current operating expenses or for special purposes.

Many businesses, large and small, regularly borrow money to tide themselves over during periods when expenses may be greater than the cash inflow from sales. Alternatively, a company may need **short-term financing** to purchase inventory for anticipated sales increases due either to growth or to a sudden economic upswing. A firm may also need short-term financing to meet expenses during a strike, or to take advantage of a new business opportunity. The major sources of short-term funds are trade creditors, commercial banks, factor companies, sales finance companies, other businesses and investors, and the federal government. We now examine how each of these sources can serve a business.

Sources of Short-Term Funds

Trade Credit

Trade credit arises out of the practice of allowing purchasers of inventory or supplies a certain amount of time before payment has to be made to the supplier.

An established business that has built a reputation for sound operation and has a good credit rating can buy inventory, raw materials or other supplies on **trade credit**. The supplier ships the goods ordered and allows the buyer a certain length of time to pay for them. This period of time may vary from one week, as is customary for meat and produce, to three months or more for some raw materials. For most items, a 30-

FIGURE 9.2

Wombat Ski Equipment Co. Inc.—Cash budget for the year 2001

	Jan	Feb	Mar	Apr	May	Jun	Jul	Aug	Sep	Oct	Nov	Dec	Total
Sales:													
Ski equipment cat 150	67 000	57 000	51 000	36 000	22 000	14 000	14 000	22 000	64 000	92 000	126 000	136 000	701 000
Equipment rentals cat 250	13 000	9 000	7 000	3 000	3 000	3 000	3 000	5 000	10 000	14 000	25 000	31 000	123 000
Travel packages cat 300	8 000	8 000	4 000	4 000	4 000	4 000	6 000	6 000	12 000	18 000	22 000	25 000	118 000
Other income	2 000	2 000	2 000	3 000	3 000	3 000	3 000	3 000	3 000	3 000	3 000	3 000	33 000
Total sales	**90 000**	**76 000**	**64 000**	**46 000**	**32 000**	**24 000**	**20 000**	**36 000**	**89 000**	**127 000**	**176 000**	**195 000**	**975 000**
Collections:													
During month	54 000	45 600	38 400	27 600	19 200	14 400	12 000	21 600	53 400	76 200	105 600	117 000	585 000
One-month lag	33 000	27 000	22 800	19 200	13 800	9 600	7 200	6 000	10 800	26 700	38 100	52 800	267 000
Two-month lag	9 600	11 000	9 000	7 600	6 400	4 600	3 200	2 400	2 000	3 600	8 900	12 700	81 000
Total collections	**96 600**	**83 600**	**70 200**	**54 400**	**39 400**	**28 600**	**22 400**	**30 000**	**66 200**	**106 500**	**152 600**	**182 500**	**933 000**
Expenditures:													
General & administrative:													
Rent	2 000	2 000	2 000	2 000	2 000	2 000	2 000	2 000	2 000	2 000	2 000	2 000	24 000
Management salaries	3 000	3 000	3 000	3 000	3 000	3 000	3 000	3 000	3 000	3 000	3 000	3 000	36 000
Clerical salaries	1 500	1 500	1 500	1 500	1 500	1 500	1 500	1 500	1 500	1 500	1 500	1 500	18 000
Utilities	520	520	520	520	520	520	520	520	520	520	520	520	6 240
Office supplies	300	300	300	300	300	300	300	300	300	300	300	300	3 600
Legal & accounting	350	350	350	350	350	350	350	350	350	350	350	350	4 200
Miscellaneous	500	500	500	500	500	500	500	500	500	500	500	500	6 000
Total gen. & admin. expenses	**8 170**	**8 170**	**8 170**	**8 170**	**8 170**	**8 170**	**8 170**	**8 170**	**8 170**	**8 170**	**8 170**	**8 170**	**98 040**
Selling:													
Wages	5 200	4 500	3 000	3 000	3 000	3 000	3 000	3 000	5 000	8 000	12 000	12 000	64 700
Advertising	4 500	2 000	500	500	500	500	500	800	2 000	2 500	3 500	4 000	21 800
Supplies	1 000	1 000	700	700	400	400	400	400	700	900	1 300	1 400	9 300
Delivery	1 000	800	700	500	300	200	200	600	900	1 200	1 700	1 900	10 000
Miscellaneous	800	800	500	500	500	200	200	200	200	300	600	1 200	6 000
Total selling expenses	**12 500**	**9 100**	**5 400**	**5 200**	**4 700**	**4 300**	**4 300**	**5 000**	**8 800**	**12 900**	**19 100**	**20 500**	**111 800**
Total expenses	**20 670**	**17 270**	**13 570**	**13 370**	**12 870**	**12 470**	**12 470**	**13 170**	**16 970**	**21 070**	**27 270**	**28 670**	**209 840**
Cash flow from operation	96 600	83 600	70 200	54 400	39 400	28 600	22 400	30 000	66 200	106 500	152 600	182 500	933 000
Less:													
Total expenses	20 670	17 270	13 570	13 370	12 870	12 470	12 470	13 170	16 970	21 070	27 270	28 670	209 840
Purchases (net)	44 000	37 000	36 000	21 000	15 000	15 000	24 000	104 000	136 000	146 000	135 000	96 000	809 000
Net cash flow	**31 930**	**29 330**	**20 630**	**20 030**	**11 530**	**1 130**	**(14 070)**	**(87 170)**	**(86 770)**	**(60 570)**	**(9 670)**	**57 830**	**(85 840)**
Balance beginning month	23 140	55 070	84 400	105 030	125 060	136 590	137 720	123 650	36 480	5 000	5 000	5 000	
Cumulative cash end of month	55 070	84 400	105 030	125 060	136 590	137 720	123 650	36 480	(50 290)	(5 280)	610	62 220	
Minimum cash balance required	5 000	5 000	5 000	5 000	5 000	5 000	5 000	5 000	5 000	5 000	5 000	5 000	5 000
Surplus or (deficit)	**50 070**	**79 400**	**100 030**	**120 060**	**131 590**	**132 720**	**118 650**	**31 480**	**(55 290)**	**(10 280)**	**(4 390)**	**57 220**	
Bank loan required									55 290	10 280	4 390		69 960
Bank loan repayment												57 220	57 220

day period is standard. Providing credit, however, represents a cost to the supplier. To induce the buyer to pay sooner, the seller often grants a discount shown as "2/10 net 30" on the invoice—the buyer can deduct two percent from the total amount of the invoice if he or she pays within 10 days of the billing date. Otherwise the full invoice amount must be paid within 30 days.

Advantage of Cash Discounts

Cash discounts—reductions of a certain percentage of the invoice amount offered by suppliers to encourage purchasers to make early payments.

If you can take advantage of **cash discounts**, you in effect obtain a reduction from the supplier on the price of the product. If you were offered 2/10 net 30 on a $1000 invoice, for example, you would save $20 by paying within 10 days. While you would lose the use of the $1000 for 20 days, the discount means more than a 36% return per annum since there are slightly more than 18 20-day periods in a year. Thus, it is to your advantage to borrow $1000 from the bank at 10% in order to earn 36% from supplier discounts.

Types of Trade Credit

Open book credit allows a purchaser to obtain goods from the supplier and pay for them after a specific period of time.

Open Book Credit Most trade credit is given on the so-called "open book account." **Open book credit** allows a purchaser to obtain goods from the supplier and pay for them after a specific period of time. The buyer phones or mails in an order, which the seller fills and ships together with an invoice for the goods. The seller then enters the amount of the purchase in a sales ledger and waits for the buyer to send the payment according to the terms and conditions established at the outset of their business dealings. However, this form of trade credit is usually extended only to firms with a good credit rating.

Consignment means that the buyer does not have to pay for the goods until they are sold. The seller retains ownership.

The procedures for setting up an open book account may be stringent or easy, depending on the supplier. For example, a supplier might find that liberal credit policies mean sales increases proportionately greater than the potential losses from firms that do not pay their debts. Thus, it may be in the seller's interest to be relatively lenient in granting credit.

Promissory note—a written agreement that states the terms of the sale. It is made out by the seller and signed by the customer, who pledges to pay the seller a certain sum of money on a specified date.

Consignment   When goods are purchased on **consignment**, the seller retains ownership since the buyer does not pay for the goods until they are sold to customers. The seller also absorbs the cost of credit and any losses that may be incurred, unless otherwise specified.

Promissory Notes   A **promissory note** is a business "I.O.U." Some sellers prefer to have a written agreement made out and signed by the customer. The customer pledges to pay the seller a certain sum of money on a specified date. A promissory note also states the rate of interest payable until the principal is paid. It is generally used for sales of valuable goods or when the customer has been slow in paying for merchandise on the open book account.

Trade draft—combines the advantages of allowing customers to order merchandise on the open book account with the relative security provided by a promissory note.

Trade Drafts and Trade Acceptance   A **trade draft** combines the advantages of allowing customers to order merchandise on the open book account with the relative security provided by a promissory note. Upon receiving the order, the seller, or drawer, originates a draft and sends it along with the merchandise to the customer, or drawee. If the drawee accepts the draft, he or she writes his or her name across the face of it. In the case of a **time draft**, the customer has a specified period of time in which to pay for the merchandise. When the document is signed, it becomes a **trade acceptance**. On the other hand, a sight draft, as shown in Figure 9.3, requires the customer to pay on presentation.

Time draft—a trade draft that specifies that the customer has a specified period of time in which to pay for the merchandise.

Trade acceptance—a trade draft signed by the customer that signifies acceptance of the terms of the sale.

Trade or commercial drafts are commonly used when goods are sold to customers, often foreign, whose credit rating is either poor or unknown. The seller then sends

SOURCE: Reproduced courtesy of the Royal Bank of Canada.

to the customer a **sight draft** together with an order bill of lading—a receipt from the shipping company. When the customer presents the order bill of lading to the shipping company, he or she can take possession of the goods provided the sight draft has been paid.

Sight draft—requires the customer to pay for the merchandise on presentation.

Loans from Chartered Banks and Other Financial Institutions

Although trade credit is the most common source of short-term credit, businesses often need money to make an outright purchase, to pay debts or to buy additional materials for manufacturing or merchandise for sale. If the money is needed for a period of less than one year, a business is likely to turn to a chartered bank for a short-term loan. Repayment terms are usually flexible and are often geared to cash flow.

In Canada, there are six Canadian-owned banks chartered by Parliament, and approximately 60 foreign-owned banks. Banks are closely regulated by the federal government. The "Big Six"—the Royal Bank of Canada, Canadian Imperial Bank of Commerce, Bank of Montreal, Bank of Nova Scotia, Toronto Dominion Bank and National Bank of Canada—have over 7000 branches across the country. In addition to the banks there are provincial government financial institutions, including the Province of Ontario Savings Office (established in 1922) and the Province of Alberta Treasury Branches (established in 1938). There are also trust and mortgage companies and credit unions.

Secured Bank Loans

As discussed in Chapter 3, a basic requirement for a loan is a business plan. It provides the bank manager with information about the business and the owners. But even if a loan is granted based on the business plan, the bank will usually want some security, known as collateral. **Collateral** refers to items of specific value that may be signed over to the bank for as long as the loan is outstanding, and that can be seized and sold if the borrower is unable to repay the loan. This is referred to as a **secured loan**. If the business can provide little collateral, which may be the case for a newly incorporated business, the borrower may be asked to provide a personal guarantee to repay the loan. Alternatively, the borrower may be asked to pledge personal assets as security, apart from the assets of the business.

Collateral refers to items of specific value that may be signed over to the lender for as long as the loan is outstanding, and that can be seized and sold if the borrower is unable to repay the loan.

Secured loan—means that the borrower has pledged some form of security, known as collateral, for the loan.

Types of Collateral

Accounts Receivable Accounts receivable are monies owed to the business—monies it expects to collect from customers in the near future. A firm's representative signs a statement promising the lender the receivables until the loan is repaid. Customers continue to send their payments to the business, and the business in turn forwards them to the bank.

Inventories A company with a large inventory of products that are not required for sale immediately may use the inventory as collateral for a short-term loan. The inventory is stored in an independent warehouse that gives the company a trust receipt. The receipt is then signed over to the lender by the borrowing company. Before the borrowing firm can recover its inventory for sale, it must pay off the loan to the bank, which will then return the trust receipt to the borrower. Should the borrower default, the bank may sell the inventory to cover the loan.

Other Property Any valuable property can be used as collateral: buildings, automobiles, trucks or farm machinery. However, for this kind of collateral the bank may require that the business sign a chattel mortgage agreement in addition to the normal loan agreement. With the chattel mortgage, the borrower has the use of the equipment and is responsible for it, but the lender has the legal right to seize it if the borrower does not repay the loan as specified in the agreement.

Demand loan—granted by a bank after the borrower signs a demand note. The bank may demand payment at any time.

Line of credit—allows the business to borrow up to a prearranged maximum over a fixed period of time.

Stand-by fee—covers the bank's cost for having the financial resources available at any time the business requires further loans under a line of credit.

Types of Loans

The most common business bank loan is the **demand loan**, for which the borrower signs a demand note. See Figure 9.4 for an example. Under this arrangement, the bank may demand payment at any time—for example, if it loses confidence in the firm's financial situation.

Often a demand loan is combined with a **line of credit** that allows the business to borrow up to a prearranged maximum over a fixed period of time. The advantage of the line of credit is that the business need borrow only what is required; what remains in the line of credit is available at any time during the life of the agreement. This will reduce the total amount of interest the firm would otherwise have to pay. However, the bank charges a **stand-by fee** to cover its costs for having the financial resources available at any time the business requires further loans under the agreement.

FIGURE 9.4

Example of a demand note

SAMPLE ONLY

FORM 1442 (9-55)

January 2 19 98 $ 175,000.00

ON DEMAND AFTER DATE FOR VALUE RECEIVED we PROMISE TO

PAY TO THE ROYAL BANK OF CANADA OR ORDER

AT THE ROYAL BANK OF CANADA **10-3** Main Branch, Royal Centre, 1025 W. Georgia St., VANCOUVER, B.C. THE SUM OF

-- ONE HUNDRED & SEVENTY-FIVE THOUSAND -- DOLLARS

WITH INTEREST ON $ 175,000.00 PAYABLE MONTHLY AT THE RATE OF 8 PER CENTUM PER ANNUM AS WELL AFTER AS BEFORE MATURITY.

NAME Razzle Dazzle Spindle Co.		
CR. ACCT. # 007	CASUAL DISCOUNT ✔ ☐	MGR. INIT.
REN.$		

Ronnie Fantastic

SOURCE: Reproduced courtesy of the Royal Bank of Canada.

In some instances, the bank may require that the business maintain a **compensating balance**—a fixed percentage of the line of credit—in an interest-free account. A compensating balance, in effect, raises the cost of borrowing for the firm, since the funds tied up are not available for use in the business. Meanwhile, the bank is free to use the funds without having to pay interest on them.

Compensating balance means that the business must maintain a fixed percentage of the line of credit in an account for which the business receives no interest.

Unsecured Bank Loans

If the bank manager is willing to give the business an **unsecured loan**, no collateral is required. The bank manager is satisfied that the borrower will repay the loan according to the agreement, usually because the firm has a good credit rating. However, the bank will also consider factors such as the firm's future profitability and the amount of the owner's equity in the business. If the equity is substantial, the bank's risk is reduced.

Unsecured loan—the lender receives no security or collateral for the loan.

Acquiring Funds through Factoring

A factor company may take over a firm's accounts receivable, thereby assuming the credit risk. The service offered includes record-keeping, credit assessment of existing and new customers and collection of accounts receivable. For this service, the factor company charges the firm one to two percent of sales depending on sales volume, average invoice size, terms of sale and customer mix.

A business that uses a factor for its credit sales eliminates the risk of customers not paying for goods shipped; it is also given immediate access to the funds in its accounts receivable immediately. **Factoring** is particularly popular during recessions, when bankruptcies increase. Small businesses with sales between $1 million and $5 million comprise most of the factor company's clients. Instead of individual businesses having to check constantly on the credit risk of their clients, they can leave that task to the factoring company, which has a thorough knowledge of the industry and the creditworthiness of individual customers.

Factoring is used by a business to raise money by selling its accounts receivable directly to a factor company at a discount. The factor company then collects the money from the firm's customers.

The principle of factoring also underlies bank-sponsored credit cards such as MasterCard and Visa, which allow customers to purchase merchandise from a wide variety of retailers. When these retailers deposit their credit-card receipts with their bank, their account is credited with the amount of the customer's purchase less a handling charge of up to six percent. Although the charge may appear high, these credit cards provide merchants with a large number of customers and insure them against the risk of customers not paying their accounts.

Loans From Finance Companies

Finance companies serve both private individuals who purchase material goods and businesses that require short-term funds. The interest rates charged by finance companies tend to be higher than those charged by banks, because finance companies will lend money in higher-risk situations (e.g., to companies that do not have good collateral). Several of the finance companies operating in Canada today are owned in part by chartered banks.

Finance companies finance the purchase of business assets or provide short-term loans for businesses, usually at interest rates higher than those charged by banks.

Loans by finance companies are most often made against collateral such as accounts receivable, inventories or the equipment to be purchased with the borrowed funds. Finance companies also provide outright financing for machinery and equipment through conditional sales contracts. If a business can make only partial payment for an item, the finance company will draw up an agreement specifying the number of installments required to repay the loan, the interest rate charged and where ownership of the machinery or equipment will lie for the term. Similar conditional sales contracts are used when a consumer purchases a car, for example.

Finance companies can also provide money to businesses by discounting trade drafts and promissory notes. Both of these financial instruments represent money owed to the firm by customers or other debtors, to be paid at a future date. A business that needs the funds immediately may sell the financial papers to a finance company in return for the face value of the note less a discount. When the note comes due, the finance company collects the full amount owed from the original issuer.

Loans from Investors and Other Businesses

Commercial or corporate papers are promissory notes issued by large companies requiring short-term funds.

Large companies requiring short-term funds may borrow in the short-term money market by issuing promissory notes, also known as **commercial** or **corporate papers**. Investment dealers play a large part in these transactions because they bring borrowers and lenders together. For example, a large company with a cash surplus may be prepared to lend to other firms for 30, 60 or 90 days or more. Both the lender and the borrower benefit: the lending company earns interest on its surplus funds, while the borrower can usually obtain the funds at an interest rate lower than that offered by financial institutions, and often free from many of their restrictions.

Sources of Funds from the Federal Government

The federal government has established a number of agencies and organizations to provide direct loans or loan guarantees to businesses. Loans may be for business improvements; to help specific industries threatened by international competition; to help manufacturing and processing industries located in regions with particularly high unemployment; and to support businesses dealing with foreign purchasers of Canadian goods and services. The Federal Business Development Bank (FBDB), for example, provides loans to businesses that may be unable to obtain financing from conventional sources.

As noted earlier, borrowing money for business operations is an important, often essential requirement for almost all businesses, regardless of size. Nevertheless, many small businesses find it difficult to raise money, primarily because they are ill-prepared for presentations when they approach financial institutions.

Controlling Financial Operations

Ensuring that sufficient cash is available to meet debts as they arise is the most important control requirement of any business. However, a business also must know how well it is operating—how profitable it is, and whether its assets are increasing or decreasing. To this end, the firm must establish an accounting system. Accounting is the process of recording, gathering, organizing, reporting and interpreting data and information. As such, it describes the operation of the firm and helps in the decision-making process.

Financial accounting keeps track of the firm's resources in dollar terms and prepares financial reports for anyone interested in the firm's operation.

Accounting can be broken down into two major functions: financial and management accounting. **Financial accounting** keeps track of the firm's resources in dollar terms and prepares financial reports, which can be shown to owners, potential investors, the tax department, lenders, managers and others interested in the performance of a firm.

Management accounting provides information that is used primarily by internal managers in decision making. For example, it involves overall budgeting, forecasting and break-even analysis, and the evaluation of investments to determine those that are profitable. Management accounting can help management isolate and resolve problems in production, sales, finance and inventory.

Accounting and Bookkeeping

Accounting is often mistaken for bookkeeping. **Bookkeeping** is the clerical task of recording, on a daily basis, the firm's financial transactions. **Accounting** is the task of summarizing the recorded data into meaningful information and reporting on the firm's operation. **Accountants** may specialize in particular aspects of accounting such as cost accounting, auditing or taxation. They acquire expertise relative to their business or industry and help in financial decision making.

Financial Accounting

The **accounting system** provides financial information essential for managers in decision making. Financial statements show where the firm stands in terms of profit and loss at a particular time, and can indicate future directions. Owners and shareholders can see how much profit the firm has made during a particular month or year. Financial statements are also required by government for tax purposes, by lenders to ensure their loan is secure and by suppliers before they grant trade credit. Last, but certainly not least, financial information is needed to substantiate the firm's tax liability to Canada Customs and Revenue Agency.

The Accounting Process

In the first part of this chapter, we emphasized the inflow and outflow of cash resulting from business transactions. A day's sales in a department store, for example, may consist of thousands of transactions between the firm and its customers. A method must be developed to record the individual sales made in various departments. Records must also be kept on payments made to employees and suppliers, and on the hundreds of merchandise shipments received by the firm.

Specific accounts are set up to record individual transactions. The transactions are usually summarized monthly, and reports are made to management. Management, for example, must know the total sales and expenses of each department. It must also know whether inventories and customer credit accounts have increased or decreased during the month, so that appropriate action can be taken. For example, if sales decreased from the previous month while inventories increased, then too much money may be tied up in merchandise; management must then ensure that the firm does not face a cash shortage. Financial statements for outside parties such as shareholders and investors are usually prepared quarterly, semi-annually or annually.

Accounting Statements

Although every business prepares a variety of financial statements, three statements are standard: (1) the **balance sheet**, which shows the firm's financial standing at a particular point in time; (2) the **income statement**, which summarizes business transactions over a period of time, showing sales, expenses and the profit or loss

Management accounting provides information that is used by managers in decision making.

Bookkeeping is the clerical task of recording, on a daily basis, the firm's financial transactions.

Accounting is the task of summarizing the recorded data into meaningful information and reporting on the firm's operation.

Accountants acquire expertise relative to their business or industry and help in financial decision making.

Accounting system—a system that provides financial information essential for managers in decision making.

Balance sheet—shows the financial condition of a firm at the beginning and end of a particular period of time.

Income statement—shows the net profit or loss resulting from the operation of the firm over a period of time, usually a month or year.

Statement of changes in financial position—shows management how cash was obtained during a given period of time and how it was used in the operation of the business.

that has been realized during that period; and (3) the **statement of changes in financial position**, which shows how the firm obtained and spent the cash received during a particular period of time. Figure 9.5 illustrates the relationship between the income statement and two balance sheets, one for the beginning and one for the end of the year.

The Balance Sheet

The balance sheets in Figure 9.6 show the financial condition of Wombat Ski Equipment Company Inc. at the beginning and end of the year. Each balance sheet shows the firm's total assets in dollars and indicates how much of the total belongs to owners of the business and how much to creditors. Total assets include all property that belongs to the business: cash, accounts receivable, inventory, buildings, furniture and fixtures. Since our example is a retail business, assets such as plant, equipment and machinery (which would be included in the balance sheet of a manufacturing firm) do not appear.

The liabilities or debts owed by the business include money the firm owes to suppliers and employees, rent to the landlord and taxes to the tax department. Shareholders' equity represents the book value or equity that the owners or stockholders have in the business. The book value of a business is based on cost data and may differ substantially from the market value of its assets.

The total dollar value of the assets must always be equal to the total dollar value of liabilities, plus the equity of the shareholders, as shown in the following equation:

$$\text{Assets} = \text{Liabilities} + \text{Shareholders' equity}$$

The two sides must always balance, as all the firm's assets must belong to someone, whether to owners or to creditors such as suppliers, banks or mortgage companies.

Current assets consist of cash, accounts receivable, inventory and other prepaid expenses that make up the working capital used in the firm's regular business operations.

Current and Fixed Assets   The assets section of the balance sheet contains two major categories: current and fixed assets. **Current assets** consist primarily of cash, accounts receivable, inventory and other prepaid expenses that make up the working capital used in the firm's regular business operations.

Accounts receivable represent money owed to the firm by customers who have made their purchases on credit. Usually accounts are paid monthly. If an account is not paid within the time allotted, then the firm must take immediate action to recover its money. A lax policy of collecting outstanding accounts could lead the firm into bankruptcy since it may not have enough cash to meet its debts.

Inventories represent merchandise, raw materials or parts that have not as yet been sold. As discussed in Chapter 7, proper inventory management is important because excess inventory ties up a firm's cash; money may not be available, then, should the firm wish to take advantage of other business opportunities or to pay debts. Prepaid expenses represent cash outlays, usually for services that have not as yet been used (e.g., insurance, rent or utilities).

Fixed assets include items such as plant, equipment, machinery and trucks, which are used in daily business operations.

Depreciation represents management's estimate of how much an asset deteriorates during its operating period.

Fixed assets include items such as plant, equipment and machinery, trucks and office equipment, which are used in daily business operations to produce goods or services for sale. Fixed assets are always valued at their initial cost to the firm. As they are used and wear out, they depreciate in value.

Depreciation is a regular operating expense and appears on the firm's income statement (see Figure 9.7). The total depreciation of each fixed asset as of a particular date is shown on the balance sheet.

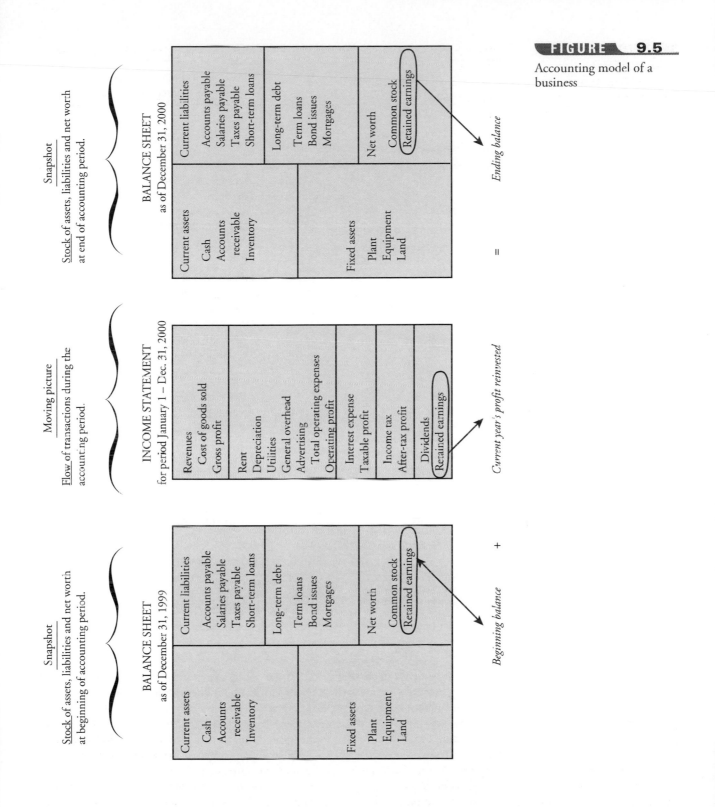

FIGURE   9.5

Accounting model of a business

FIGURE 9.6

Comparative balance sheets at two different time periods

WOMBAT SKI EQUIPMENT CO. INC.

Balance Sheet As at December 31, 2000		Balance Sheet As at December 31, 2001	
ASSETS			
CURRENT ASSETS		CURRENT ASSETS	
Cash	8 894	Cash	23 140
Marketable securities	40 000	Marketable securities	45 000
Accounts receivable	93 240	Accounts receivable	137 340
Inventory	187 450	Inventory	127 030
Prepaid expenses	8 900	Prepaid expenses	13 500
Total current assets	338 484	**Total current assets**	346 010
FIXED ASSETS		FIXED ASSETS	
Land	0	Land	0
Buildings	0	Buildings	187 000
Less: Accum dep	0	Less: Accum dep	18 700
Equipment & fixtures	76 600	Equipment & fixtures	86 450
Less: Accum dep	15 320	Less: Accum dep	29 546
Total fixed assets	61 280	**Total fixed assets**	225 204
TOTAL ASSETS	399 764	**TOTAL ASSETS**	571 214
LIABILITIES			
CURRENT LIABILITIES		CURRENT LIABILITIES	
Accounts payable	115 948	Accounts payable	122 530
Loans payable	23 000	Loans payable	35 000
Accrued liabilities	19 934	Accrued liabilities	23 450
Total current liabilities	158 882	**Total current liabilities**	180 980
LONG-TERM LIABILITIES		LONG-TERM LIABILITIES	
Long-term loan on equip	85 300	Long-term loan on equip	72 000
		Mortgage on buildings	98 653
TOTAL LIABILITIES	244 182	**TOTAL LIABILITIES**	351 633
SHAREHOLDERS' EQUITY		SHAREHOLDERS' EQUITY	
Common stock	100 000	Common stock	100 000
Retained earnings	55 582	Retained earnings	119 581
Total shareholders' equity	155 582	Total shareholders' equity	219 581
TOTAL LIABILITIES & EQUITY	399 764	**TOTAL LIABILITIES & EQUITY**	571 214

Capital cost allowance (CCA) represents Revenue Canada's maximum allowance for yearly depreciation for particular classes of assets.

The federal tax department states how much a firm may depreciate a fixed asset for tax purposes, which is known as the **capital cost allowance (CCA)**. Methods of depreciation allowed by the tax department may or may not be identical to methods the firm uses for its own purposes. For example, the tax department may allow a firm to take CCA on an automobile at 30% per year on a decreasing balance basis. The firm could claim the 30% CCA as an expense against its income to calculate income subject to taxes. However, for its own statements, the firm may believe that a straight-line depreciation will better indicate to shareholders the worth of the firm and the income for the year. In straight-line depreciation, the total cost of an asset minus expected salvage value is divided by its expected life in years; the resulting amount is then charged off as depreciation. A $10 000 truck expected to last for five years, for example, would be depreciated at the rate of $2000 per year. Under these circumstances, the firm would maintain two sets of records—one for the tax department and one for its own shareholders.

Once the truck is fully depreciated on the firm's books, it will no longer represent any dollar value as an asset, even though it may still be useful. When the truck is eventually sold, the proceeds, if any, must be shown as income—an extraordinary gain from the sale of fixed assets. Fixed assets are not ordinarily turned into cash except when equipment or a building is no longer required for regular business operations, or when a firm experiences a severe cash shortage with little chance for borrowing the money.

Current and Long-Term Liabilities   The liabilities section of the balance sheet is also broken into two main categories: current and long-term liabilities. **Current liabilities** represent the debts that the business has incurred in the regular course of operations. They include accounts payable (amounts owed to suppliers for raw materials and merchandise purchased), wages to be paid to employees and taxes payable to the government based on current operation. They may also include rent or billings for advertising, and any other debts to be paid during the coming year. Liabilities are current if they are expected to be paid off within the year.

Long-term liabilities are debts such as bank loans, mortgages on buildings, or payment for trucks or other equipment. The payments will be made over a number of years. Only the current year's payments are included as current liabilities.

Shareholders' Equity   The category known as **shareholders' equity** shows the amount of money that the owners or shareholders have invested in the business. The amount listed opposite common stock in Figure 9.6 is the total money raised from the initial sale of shares to the owners. **Retained earnings** represent profits not taken out of the company.

Shareholders' equity can also be regarded as the amount of money that would remain for the owners if they were to sell their assets at book value and pay off all liabilities. For a firm that is not incorporated—a sole proprietorship or partnership—the term "owners' equity" or "partnership equity" is used.

The Income Statement

The income statement shows the net profit or loss resulting from the operation of the firm over a period of time. Figure 9.7 shows a typical income statement for a one-year period.

Gross sales represent the dollar value of all sales made to customers during a particular period. Net sales represent actual sales after all returns and customer allowances have been deducted from gross sales.

The cost of goods sold—the cost of the actual merchandise sold to customers—is deducted from net sales, leaving an amount called the **gross profit**. The cost-of-goods-sold figure may be calculated by adding net purchases for the period to the value of the initial inventory and then subtracting the value of the final inventory. Both inventory figures are usually arrived at by physically counting the value of the stock.

Expenses incurred in the course of regular business operations are then deducted from the gross profit, to give the net profit before taxes. Expenses may be broken down into operating expenses and general/administrative expenses. The distinction is generally not important in a small business, but in a large firm with many departments, general and administrative expenses are those that pertain to the firm as a whole (e.g., salaries and office expenses for support personnel, head office personnel—including the president—and research and development). These expenses are distributed among departments based on some method, such as the percentage each department has sold of total sales.

Current liabilities are debts that are expected to be paid off within the year.

Long-term liabilities are debts for which repayment will be made over a number of years.

Shareholders' equity shows the amount of money that the owners or shareholders have invested in the business.

Retained earnings represent profits not taken out of the company by its shareholders.

Gross profit is what remains after the cost of the actual merchandise sold to customers is deducted from net sales.

FIGURE 9.7

Income statement

WOMBAT SKI EQUIPMENT CO. INC.

Income Statement
Year Ended December 31, 2001

		$	%
Net Sales		889 560	100.0
Cost of Goods Sold		516 145	58.0
Gross Profit		373 415	42.0
Operating Expenses:			
Selling expenses	96 345		10.8
Advertising	11 190		1.3
Supplies	7 810		.9
Insurance	6 940		.8
Rent	36 000		4.0
Utilities	5 470		.6
Administrative expenses	35 330		4.0
Depreciation	32 926		3.7
Bad debts	2 700		.3
Miscellaneous	6 230		.7
Total Operating Expenses		240 941	27.1
Operating Income		132 474	14.9
− Expenses		30 725	3.5
Taxable Income		101 749	11.4
− Income Tax		37 750	4.2
Net Income		63 999	7.2
− Dividends		0	.0
Increase in Retained Earnings		63 999	7.2

Net profit is the amount that remains after deducting all business expenses and corporate income taxes from gross profit.

If the business is a corporation, it is a separate legal entity and will be taxed as such. The **net profit** is the amount that remains after corporate income taxes have been deducted. This profit belongs to the owners or stockholders of the business. Dividends, for example, are paid from the net profit. In a sole proprietorship or a partnership, on the other hand, the business profit is not taxed. The net profit becomes the personal income of the owner(s) and is taxed on the basis of individual income tax rates.

The net income is arrived at through the following calculations:

> Sales
> − Cost of goods sold
> = Gross profit
> − Operating expenses
> = Net profit before taxes
> − Income taxes
> = Net profit
> − Dividends
> = Retained earnings

The net profit shown on the income statement is not necessarily cash. As stated earlier, a profitable company can become bankrupt if it is unable to meet its expenses because too much cash has been tied up in fixed assets. The cash dividend paid to shareholders, for example, would depend on the amount of cash available—the cash not required for operations—rather than on the net profit shown on the income statement. In Figure 9.7, no dividends were paid; the net profit, then, is an addition to retained earnings, as shown in the retained earnings section of the balance sheet.

Statement of Changes in Financial Position

The statement of changes in financial position shows management how cash was obtained during a given period of time and how it was used in the operation of the business. The information is obtained by comparing the dollar amounts of various categories of assets and liabilities in two consecutive balance sheets, and from the income statement and statement of retained earnings for the same period. The statement of changes in financial position explains the change in cash (or cash equivalent) from one balance sheet statement to the next. "Cash" is considered to be actual cash, plus short-term investments, minus short-term loans.

Net income and depreciation both represent a *source* of funds from the income statement, while dividends paid represents a *use* of funds. When reviewing a balance sheet, remember the following rules:

1. An increase in an asset account means that a use of funds has occurred.

2. A decrease in an asset account means that a source of funds has occurred.

3. An increase in liability and net worth accounts means that a source of funds has occurred.

4. A decrease in liability and net worth accounts means that a use of funds has occurred.

A reconciliation of the change in cash, and a statement of changes in financial position for Wombat Ski Equipment Company Inc., is shown in Figure 9.8. We see that the net change in cash to be reconciled in the statement of change in financial position arose from an increase in cash and marketable securities (short-term investments) and a decrease in loans payable (short-term loans).

Cash provided by operations results from an adjustment of net income for non-cash items such as depreciation, as well as from an adjustment of all accruals arising in the current asset and liability accounts. Increases in asset accounts represent a use of cash; an increase in liabilities represents a source of cash because that firm has, in effect, borrowed on a short-term basis.

We can see from the statement of changes in financial position in Figure 9.8 that operations and financing provided cash in the amounts of $118 743 and $85 353 respectively, whereas cash was used in investing activities—purchasing more fixtures, equipment and buildings.

The financial data in a statement of changes in financial position thus summarize data present in other statements. The summary gives managers a clear idea of how funds were used in the past and allows them to plan for future requirements. A statement of changes in financial position can also be used to establish a cash budget, as discussed earlier in this chapter.

Statement of change in
financial position

WOMBAT SKI EQUIPMENT CO. INC.

Changes in Cash

	2000	2001
Cash	8 894	23 140
Marketable Securities	40 000	45 000
Loans Payable	(23 000)	(35 000)
	25 894	33 140
Increase in Cash in 1998	7 246	
	33 140	

WOMBAT SKI EQUIPMENT CO. INC.

Statement of Changes in Financial Position
For the Year Ended December 31, 2001

Net Income from Operations		$ 63 999
Add:		
Depreciation	32 926	
Increase in Accounts Payable	6 582	
Decrease in Inventory	60 420	
Increase in Accrued Liabilities	3 516	103 444
Deduct:		
Increase in Accounts Receivable	(44 100)	
Increase in Prepaid Expenses	(4 600)	(48 700)
Cash Provided by Operation		118 743
Investing Activities		
Purchase of Buildings	(187 000)	
Purchase of Fixtures & Equipment	(9 850)	
Cash Used in Investing Activities		(196 850)
Financing Activities		
Payment on Equipment Loan	(13 300)	
Mortgage on Building	98 653	
Cash Provided by Financing Activity		85 353
Increase in Cash		$ 7 246

Financial Analysis

Once the financial statements have been prepared, what do they actually tell us about the business? The income statement will tell us whether we have made a profit and how much, but is this profit adequate for the investment in the business? Another question is the operating efficiency of management. Is it using the funds to the best advantage? Analysis of financial statements can provide valuable information on a firm's profitability and financial strength.

There are two main ways to analyze a company's financial statements. We can calculate a variety of ratios and compare them to standard ratios for the industry and to the company's previous financial data. A second method is to analyze a company's operation by turning its key figures into percentages, which allows easy comparison of income statement and balance sheet figures to previous years and to industry standards. To illustrate financial analysis, we will use the balance sheets and the income statement for Wombat Ski Equipment Company Inc.

Ratio Analysis

In **ratio analysis**, a ratio is used to compare two quantities against a predetermined standard. If the ratio is above or below the standard, it provides a general idea of the current status of the business. Although there exist over 400 different ratios, a few key ratios are sufficient to give an owner or financial manager a reasonable indication of the firm's financial health. Most ratios mean little in isolation, but are used to follow the trend within a business, and to compare an individual firm's performance with other firms in the same industry. To help us in our ratio analysis, we will use the following figures, which show information for all industries, as well as for the retail and wholesale industries in Canada.

Ratio analysis is used to compare two quantities against a predetermined standard to provide an insight into various aspects of a business's operation.

Industry	Current Ratio	Total Debt to Equity	Collection Period	Sales to Inventory (days)	Gross Margin %	Profits on Sales %	Profits on Equity %
All firms	1.1	3.0	52	5.9	31.6	5.6	11.9
Retail trade	1.3	2.2	11	6.4	26.7	3.3	28.8
Wholesale trade	**1.2**	**2.4**	**37**	**6.4**	**16.8**	**1.6**	**12.5**

The ratios can be classified into four groups. The ratios in each group provide information about a particular aspect of the firm's financial operation. Some key ratios in each group are as follows:

- *Liquidity ratios*
  1. Current ratio
  2. Quick or acid-test ratio

- *Activity ratios*
  1. Inventory turnover ratio
  2. Average collection period

- *Financial leverage ratios*
  1. Debt ratio
  2. Debt-equity ratio

- *Profitability ratios*
  1. Gross profit margin ratio
  2. Net profit margin ratio
  3. Return on investment
  4. Return on stockholders' equity

Liquidity Ratios

A firm's ability to meet its short-term financial obligations is often a critical concern to management and lenders. The cash budget we already discussed provides the best picture of a firm's ability to pay; however, liquidity ratios are a quick measure of a firm's ability to provide sufficient cash to carry on business in the immediate future.

Current Ratio The **current ratio** indicates the firm's ability to pay its short-term debts.

Current ratio—indicates the firm's ability to pay its short-term debts.

$$\text{Current ratio} = \frac{\text{Current assets}}{\text{Current liabilities}} = \frac{\$338\ 484}{\$158\ 882} = 2.13$$

A rule of thumb often cited is that this ratio should be 2, implying that the firm could meet its short-term obligations through its current assets. This ratio is important to creditors, who would not wish to see a firm in a short-term financial crisis, forced to sell its fixed assets to meet its current liabilities.

Wombat's current ratio of 2.13 in 2000 is well above the industry average of 1.1. For every dollar of current liabilities, there are slightly more than two dollars of current assets, which, if necessary, could be used to pay off the firm's liabilities. At the end of 2001, this ratio dropped to 1.91—not a serious drop, but one certainly meriting investigation. A current ratio much below two could signify that the company will have difficulty meeting its short-term debts through its current assets. However, it is important to examine the current assets that make up the ratio. If a large portion of the assets represent inventory, which may be difficult to turn into cash quickly, even a large current ratio may not be meaningful. In such cases, the acid-test ratio is often used.

Quick or acid-test ratio— excludes prepaid expenses and inventory from current assets to provide a stringent test of a firm's ability to meet its current liabilities.

Quick or Acid-Test Ratio   The **quick** or **acid-test ratio** provides a more stringent test of a firm's ability to meet its current liabilities, since it excludes prepaid expenses and inventory from current assets, which may be difficult or impossible to convert into cash quickly when necessary. The remaining resources—cash, accounts receivable and marketable securities—are known as quick assets.

$$\text{Quick (acid-test) ratio} = \frac{\text{Current assets (Inventories} - \text{Prepaid expenses)}}{\text{Current liabilities}} = \frac{\$142\ 134}{\$158\ 882} = 0.89$$

A common standard is one dollar of quick assets to cover each dollar of current liability. Wombat was just slightly below that standard in 2000, with quick assets of 89¢ to cover every dollar of current liabilities. By the end of 2001, this ratio went up to 1.14, which means that the firm could quite easily pay off most of its current liabilities with its liquid assets (see Figure 9.6).

Activity Ratios

Activity ratios indicate how efficiently a firm is using its assets to generate sales. By comparing activity ratios for the various asset accounts of a firm with established industry standards, a person can determine how efficiently the firm is allocating its resources. The two ratios we will examine are inventory turnover and average collection period. In both instances, cash is tied up either as inventory or receivables.

Inventory turnover ratio— measures the number of times the average dollar value of inventory carried during the year is sold or replaced in that period.

Inventory Turnover Ratio   The **inventory turnover ratio** measures the number of times the average dollar value of inventory carried during the year is sold or replaced in that period. An adequate inventory ratio is particularly important since inventory is generally a sizable investment; poor management may result in high costs of carrying—storing and handling—the inventory. Moreover, merchandise that does not sell may become shopworn or obsolete.

$$\text{Inventory turnover} = \frac{\text{Cost of goods sold}}{\text{Average inventory}} = \frac{\$516\ 145}{\$157\ 240} = 3.28$$

The average inventory carried during the year, or during each month of the year, must be calculated from the figures in the beginning and ending balance sheets for the period. Generally, the higher the inventory turnover, the more profit the firm makes, since inventory is converted to cash rapidly. However, it could also mean that the firm is frequently running out of stock and losing sales to competitors.

The inventory turnover ratio varies for different types of businesses. For example, a grocery store with a small profit margin on each item may turn over its inventory 20 times per year; in a furniture store, where the profit margin on each item is significantly greater, inventory may turn over only three times per year.

Due to the seasonal nature of the ski business, the inventory turnover ratio for Wombat may not be meaningful—the average inventory was calculated over a 12-month period, even though for five of these months the inventory carried was low. Hence, the average monthly inventory is higher, resulting in a relatively low inventory turnover ratio. The turnover ratio would be more meaningful if it were calculated only for the seven-month ski season. In Wombat's case, then, the inventory turnover ratio is significant only if it is compared with ratios of previous years as well as with ratios of other firms in the industry.

Average Collection Period   A business that provides credit to its customers must carefully control the length of time that the accounts are outstanding; otherwise it may find a high rate of non-payment on the outstanding accounts. If the customary credit period is 30 days, any accounts not paid within that period require notification. If no response is received, collection procedures must be implemented quickly.

The average collection period is the average number of days an account receivable remains outstanding. We can calculate it by dividing the year-end receivables balance by the average daily credit sales, which are based on a 360-day year.

Receivables can be controlled by determining the number of days' sales that total accounts outstanding represent (a usual and realistic period is 30 days). If this period of time increases, the firm may face losses because money is tied up in unpaid accounts. Individual accounts can also be analyzed as to the length of time each has been outstanding.

To determine the number of days' sales represented by accounts receivable, the net sales figure from the income statement is divided by the value of the outstanding accounts receivable, to give a turnover rate for the receivables per year or month. The following example uses Wombat's net sales for 1996 and the amount of receivables outstanding at the end of 2001.

$$\text{Average collection period} = \frac{\text{Accounts receivable}}{\text{Annual credit sales}/360} = \frac{\$137\ 340}{\$889\ 560/360} = 55.8 \text{ days}$$

On the average, therefore, Wombat's accounts receivable represent 56 days of sales. Again, the seasonal nature of the ski business means that the ratio should be based on only seven months rather than 12, since the firm does virtually no business during the five summer months. The receivables outstanding would thus be reduced to 32 days' sales, which is below the industry average for wholesalers. Wombat considers its accounts receivable to be well managed; only its wholesale customers—other ski shops—are granted credit, and no account has required more than 35 days to pay for purchases.

Financial Leverage Ratios

Whenever a firm borrows money to finance its fixed assets through stocks, bonds or leases, it is using financial leverage. In other words, management is using someone else's money to carry on business in an attempt to increase the firm's profit. Financial leverage ratios measure the degree to which the firm is using financial leverage. These ratios are important to creditors and owners or shareholders. We will discuss financial leverage in more detail later in this chapter.

Debt ratio—measures the proportion of a firm's assets that is financed with borrowed funds.

Debt Ratio

The **debt ratio** measures the proportion of a firm's assets that is financed with borrowed funds. In these instances, debt includes all short-term and long-term borrowing.

$$\text{Debt} = \frac{\text{Total debt}}{\text{Total assets}} = \frac{\$351\ 633}{\$571\ 214} = 0.615$$

A debt ratio is stated as a percent. In Wombat's case, the debt ratio at the end of 2001 is 61.5%. This means that Wombat's creditors are financing 61.5% of Wombat's total assets, while the owners or shareholders have an equity only of 38.5%. As the equity base declines, investors are more hesitant to put money into the firm because they are simply acquiring more debt. The only way such a company might be able to continue borrowing money is if it can show that it is capable of high growth and will have relatively stable future earnings.

Debt/equity ratio—indicates the relationship between the amount of a firm's debt financing to the amount of owner financing.

Debt/Equity Ratio

The **debt/equity ratio** indicates the relationship between the amount of a firm's debt financing to the amount of owner financing.

$$\text{Debt/equity ratio} = \frac{\text{Total debt}}{\text{Total equity}} = \frac{\$351\ 633}{\$219\ 581} = 1.60$$

The debt/equity ratio is similar to the debt ratio and is also stated as a percentage. Wombat's debt to equity at the end of 2001 is 160%. This means that Wombat has raised nearly $1.60 from creditors for each dollar invested by owners. When compared to industry ratios, Wombat is considerably lower than all firms, where this ratio is 3, and for retailers and wholesalers, where it is 2.2 and 2.4 respectively.

Profitability Ratios

Profitability ratios measure how effectively a firm's management is generating profits on sales, total assets and stockholders' investment. This is important to investors who are expecting long-run adequate returns in the form of dividends and share appreciation.

Gross profit margin ratio—measures the relative profitability of a firm's sales after the cost of goods sold has been deducted.

Gross Profit Margin Ratios

The **gross profit margin ratio** measures the relative profitability of a firm's sales after the cost of goods sold has been deducted. The gross profit must be enough to cover expenses and provide a reasonable profit for the firm after payment of taxes. The ratio is calculated by dividing gross profit by net sales and multiplying the result by 100. This ratio reveals management's effectiveness in making decisions regarding pricing and the control of production costs. The ratio may be calculated monthly, quarterly or yearly.

To calculate the gross profit margin ratio, we use income statement figures. The ratio is defined as follows:

$$\text{Gross profit margin} = \frac{\text{Sales} - \text{Cost of goods sold}}{\text{Sales}} = \frac{\$373\ 415}{\$889\ 560} \times 100 = 41.9\%$$

An increase in the gross profit margin ratio over time indicates that the spread between net sales and the cost of buying the goods is increasing. It means that the business is buying at lower prices, or selling at higher prices or both. In contrast, a decreasing gross profit ratio indicates a decreasing spread—the business is either selling at prices that are too low or paying too much for the merchandise, or both.

To see how the gross profit margin is moving it is best to compare income statements in percentage terms. Figure 9.9 does this for Wombat Ski Equipment Co.

WOMBAT SKI EQUIPMENT CO. INC.					
Comparative Income Statements	1999	2000	2001	Industry Average	Deviation Ind-2000
Sales	100.0%	100.0%	100.0%	100.0%	0%
Cost of goods sold	63.3%	56.9%	58.0%	55.0%	3.0%
Gross profit	39.9%	43.1%	41.9%	45.0%	–3.0%
Operating expenses	25.7%	28.3%	27.1%	31.0%	–2.8%
Net income before taxes	14.2%	14.8%	11.4%	14.0%	–.2%
Net income after taxes	7.4%	7.7%	7.2%	6.3%	.9%

FIGURE 9.9

Comparing Wombat's current income statement with previous two years and with industry standard

Ltd.—key income statement figures for three years, as well as a comparison to the industry, are shown as percentages.

Net Profit Margin Ratio   The **net profit margin ratio** uses figures from the income statement to measure the amount of profit in each sales dollar. It measures how profitable a firm's sales are after all expenses, including taxes and interest, have been deducted.

$$\text{Net profit margin} = \frac{\text{Net profit}}{\text{Sales}} = \frac{\$63\ 999}{\$889\ 560} \times 100 = 7.19\%$$

Net profit margin ratio— measures the amount of profit in each sales dollar.

The ratio is directly influenced by the firm's gross profit and operating expenses, which should be analyzed if the net profit ratio declines. The net profit ratio is most useful when compared with previous years or with other firms in the same industry. This ratio should be compared to the industry standard. Wombat has a net profit margin of 7.19%, which is good compared to industry standards.

Return on Investment   The **return on investment ratio** measures the firm's net income after taxes compared to total assets invested.

$$\text{Return on investment} = \frac{\text{Earnings (after taxes)}}{\text{Total assets}} = \frac{\$63\ 999}{\$571\ 214} \times 100 = 11.2\%$$

Return on investment ratio— measures the firm's net income after taxes compared to total assets invested.

While this ratio measures the return on total assets, return on investment can also be measured in terms of stockholders' investment. For Wombat in 2001, this would be $63 999/219 581 = 29.1%.

Investors can then compare the resulting percentage with returns on other types of investments available to them, such as the interest rate paid on bank savings accounts. If a bank would pay 10%, while their investment in the business returns only 7%, it might be advantageous for them to withdraw their money from the business and put it into a savings account or else buy Canada Savings Bonds. Another consideration for investors is the return compared to the risk involved. Money earning 10% at the bank is relatively safe, but a 10% return from a business is not as secure. Because of this risk factor, investors may require a return of 18 to 20% on their investment.

In Wombat's case, it should be remembered that the firm is a new enterprise in a recreation area that in geographical terms is relatively new. It is unlikely that the 29% rate of return on stockholder's equity will persist once competitors have become established. Even if Wombat remains the only ski equipment business in the area, the return on investment ratio could decline over the coming years as expenses and investments rise.

Comparative Analysis of Accounting Statements

All dollar figures on balance sheets and income statements can be turned into percentages for comparison with previous years. Many companies provide this information so that investors can see how the firm has progressed over a period of time. A percentage comparison can be revealing if sales are designated as 100% and all other items—cost of goods sold, all expenses, taxes and net profit—are shown as percentages of sales.

In Figure 9.9, for example, the comparative income statements for Wombat show that gross profit in 2001 was down from the previous year, but still higher than in 1999. However, Wombat's gross profit has never approached that of the industry, which is 45%. Expenses have followed a similar path as gross profit and have risen and declined along with gross profit. In terms of expense as a percentage of sales, Wombat looks good compared to the industry as a whole. Another important point is that net income after taxes has remained fairly steady for Wombat and is significantly higher than it is for the industry.

Forecasting and Budgeting

> **Forecasting** is an active attempt to reduce future uncertainty by forecasting possible developments.

A business cannot wait for the future to happen; it must make an active attempt to reduce future uncertainty by **forecasting** possible developments during the planning process (described in Chapter 4). Once plans have been made, the cost of carrying them out can be determined and set out in a budget. A **budget** states in financial terms the course of action planned for the coming year. Budgets show all expected cash inflows from sales, borrowings and owner investments, as well as all outflows, such as expenses, withdrawals (dividends) and loan repayments. Even though budgets are made for the entire year, they are often broken down into three- or six-month segments. Budgets are considered firm commitments and are not meant to be altered except for unforeseen changes in the level of operations or in the economic environment.

> **Budget**—states in financial terms the course of action planned for the coming year.

> **Budget forecast**—provides financial data for a projected income statement and a projected balance sheet for the year.

The **budget forecast** provides financial data for a projected income statement and a projected balance sheet for the year. These projected financial statements, together with detailed budgets, are used during the operating period as standards in the control process. Thus, actual results can be compared against planned results and any discrepancies between the two can be corrected.

The Budgeting Process

Budgeting usually starts three months before the end of the fiscal year—the business's operating period—to ensure that the budgeting process can be completed before the new operating period begins. As Figure 9.10 shows, the budgeting process begins when the sales department makes its forecast for the year. All other budgets are developed from the sales forecast and culminate in pro-forma financial statements. The budgeting process varies somewhat from business to business, depending on whether the firm is manufacturing, retail or service. We now look at the budgeting process in more detail.

Sales Forecasting

Since the entire operating plan of an organization depends on planned sales, accurate forecasting of future sales is critical. The finance department, usually in charge of the budgeting process, provides both planned and actual sales figures for the previous and current year. In large companies, the marketing department also spends considerable time in economic forecasting, taking into account governmental policies, the general

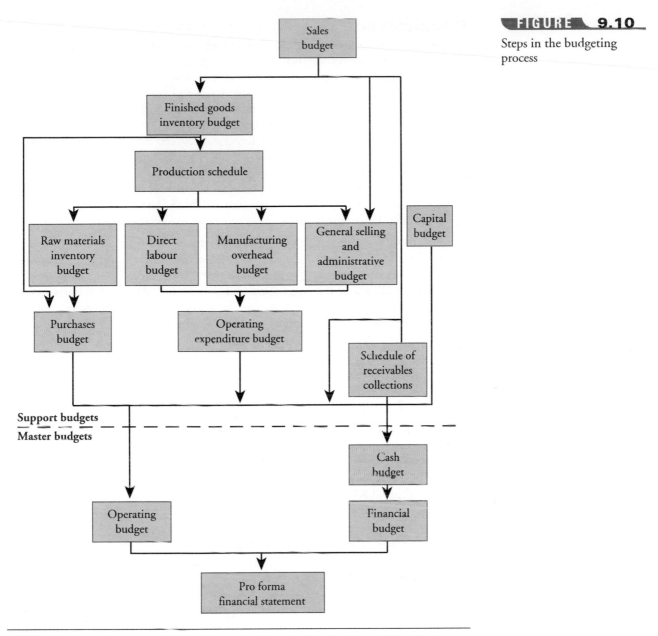

SOURCE: A. Thompson Montgomery, *Managerial Accounting Information* (Reading, Mass.: Addison-Wesley, 1979): 60. Reprinted by permission. © 1979.

FIGURE 9.10

Steps in the budgeting process

economic outlook, the industry and the competition. The result is a market-based forecast not only for the current year but also for future years, since market factors may influence plans for expansion and thus affect the capital budget. The firm also develops a sales-based forecast for the coming year. The sales forecast is based on each salesperson's expected total monthly sales for each product. Many small firms may use only a sales-based forecast for budgeting.

Once the sales budget has been established, other budgets are developed, including the selling and administrative expense budget, the capital budget and the production or manufacturing budgets.

Manufacturing Budgets

Marketing and sales must work closely together, particularly if the product is subject to spoilage or rapid obsolescence. Production must then be geared directly to sales to keep inventory low. On the other hand, if the product can be stored, the volume of production can be more uniform, which tends to lower production costs because plant facilities are not overworked during some periods and idle during others. Costs of hiring and laying off employees are also reduced. Finally, productivity often increases because hiring and training costs are reduced and workers have higher morale because of greater job security.

The manufacturing budget is based on the inventory required according to the sales forecast, taking into account spoilage, and storage and productive capacity. Once the number of units to be produced has been determined, the budgets for raw materials, direct labour and factory overhead can be drawn up.

Raw Materials Budget With the level of production established, the quantities of raw materials or parts required can be determined. A purchases budget is thus developed by the purchasing department, which is in close touch with suppliers and has a good idea of the costs of materials and parts. Again, if materials can be stored, the purchasing department does not have to strictly follow the production cycle and may take advantage of seasonal or volume discounts.

Direct Labour Budget The direct labour budget projects labour requirements based on the sales and production plan. As the various production times to produce one unit are generally known, labour costs can be determined by multiplying the person-hours required per unit by the total number of units to be produced and then multiplying the result by the rate of pay for labour.

Factory Overhead Direct labour and direct materials do not cover all expenses associated with manufacturing. Expenses such as rent, insurance, repair and maintenance, supervisory salaries and utilities would be incurred regardless of the level of production. These expenses are known as factory overhead. Sometimes freight and the costs of purchasing, receiving, handling and storing materials are also included in factory overhead since it may be difficult to break these costs down per unit.

The Operating Expenditures Budget

The operating expenditures budget includes all sales revenues and all expenses, including direct labour costs, manufacturing overhead, selling expenses, and general and administrative expenses. Selling expenses include the costs of promoting, selling and distributing the products. They are usually broken down by product lines, sales regions, customers, salespersons or some other method. General and administrative expenses are the costs of maintaining a head office, and the associated salaries and expenses. These costs are charged against various departments or products depending on the type of business. Nevertheless, individual budgets are prepared for comparison with previous years and for control purposes.

The Capital Budget

Capital budget—indicates management's estimate of when plant and equipment will need to be replaced and how the necessary funds will be raised.

An operating budget does not take into account that the assets used in the firm's operation plant, equipment and machinery wear out and must eventually be replaced. A **capital budget** is thus established, indicating management's estimate of when plant and equipment will need to be replaced and how the necessary funds will be raised. For example, if the firm knows that it must replace five trucks in three years' time, it can set aside a certain amount from profits each year to cover the purchase.

The capital budget is somewhat outside the main budgeting process. It includes detailed plans for the acquisition or disposal of major capital assets either through purchase, lease or construction. Although the capital budget pertains only to the current year, capital investment and planning will extend beyond one year depending on the long-term plans of the firm. For example, a firm that intends to expand its plant 10 years hence can detail its plans to raise the money in a capital budget. Thus, the year prior to expansion, the capital budget will indicate the amount of money the company plans to take from earnings for the expansion and the amount to be obtained through loans or through the direct sale of bonds or shares to investors.

The Cash Budget

With the completion of the capital budget, all the necessary schedules are available to develop the cash budget. A cash budget is a forecast of all expected cash receipts and expenditures for the year. If sales are made on credit, a separate schedule of receivables may be prepared based on the firm's history of collections. This schedule compares dates on which cash from sales is received with dates on which the product was originally sold. Thus, management can control overdue accounts and cash flow, thereby ensuring that adequate cash is always available to pay bills as they come due.

The Master Operating Budget and the Financing Budget

The **master operating budget** combines the various operating components of the total company—manufacturing, purchasing, sales, administration personnel—and shows the anticipated revenues and expenditures for the coming year. If the master operating budget calls for capital expenditures (sales may be expected to increase dramatically over the next few years), then a financing budget will be established to indicate how money will be raised for the additional financial outlays required. The **financing budget** lists the capital expenditures from the capital budget, as well as the total expected cash inflows and outflows from the cash budget. These cash out flows take into account expected payments of dividends to shareholders. The financing budget then indicates how any cash shortfalls will be met, most likely through borrowing, but also possibly through an additional share offering. The financing budget can take the form of a projected statement of changes in financial position, which is similar to the statement of sources and uses of funds discussed earlier in the chapter.

Master operating budget—combines all sales revenues and all expenses, including direct labour costs, manufacturing overhead, selling expenses and general and administrative expenses.

Financing budget—indicates how money will be raised for the additional financial outlays required.

Pro-Forma Financial Statements

Large companies develop the master operating budget into **pro-forma financial statements**: a forecasted income statement and a balance sheet that represent the final step in the budgeting process. The projected income statement consists of the sales forecast, with some adjustments for sales returns, and the forecasted costs-of-goods-sold statement. The difference between net sales and cost of goods sold is the gross margin, which will have to cover all expenses and provide the before-tax income for the firm. Then the various operating expenses sales and administrative are deducted to arrive at the operating income figure. Net income is, of course, the income after taxes. The projected balance sheet indicates the firm's financial position at the end of the coming year. The projected income statement, projected balance sheet, cash budget and financial budget are collectively known as the firm's master budget. Small and medium-sized companies often do not have a master budget and develop only the pro-forma financial statements.

Pro-forma financial statement—a forecasted income statement and a balance sheet that represent the final step in the budgeting process.

How Budgeting Benefits the Organization

The operating budget, in that it forces all levels of management to forecast possible future developments and their effect on the firm's sales and revenue, is a valuable planning tool. Once established, it serves to coordinate the activities of the various departments and divisions, since the planned dollar figures provide the limits within which each must operate. At the same time, the budgeting process itself gives the various managers involved a better idea of the firm's purpose and direction.

Finally, the operating budget serves as a standard in the control process. Although it is generally drawn up to cover a six-month or one-year period, a time, the operating budget is usually broken down into monthly budgets. Thus, actual sales and expenses for each month can be compared with planned sales and expenses. In the event of discrepancies between the two sets of figures, management can decide whether corrective action is necessary. In some cases, unforeseen events may make it necessary to rework the total company operating budget. However, if only certain areas are affected, the required overexpenditure in one department or division can be offset by reducing expenses in other areas.

Break-Even Analysis

Break-even analysis determines the feasibility of starting a new venture by calculating the amount of sales needed to make a profit.

An important tool in sales forecasting and budgeting is **break-even analysis**, which indicates the amount of sales needed to make a profit and gives management some idea of the relationship between sales, costs and profits. The relationship between these three factors can be demonstrated graphically or algebraically. Computers have made break-even analysis especially easy. By using an electronic spreadsheet a manager can enter a variety of different costs and revenues, and instantly see the results of these actions on screen or on a printout.

Break-even analysis is based on the fact that all operating costs can be divided into fixed and variable costs. **Fixed costs**, also called **overhead**, are those that are relatively constant regardless of the volume of goods produced or sold. For example, a manufacturing firm will have to pay for utilities, interest charges on plant and equipment, rent, insurance and clerical and management salaries regardless of how much the firm produces. Even if the plant closed down for a period of time, some of these costs would continue to be incurred. A magazine publisher must pay for the production of the monthly magazine, including the cost of the articles, without knowing how many issues it will actually sell for any particular month. A retail store must pay rent, utilities and sales staff salaries even if sales for a particular month are very low.

Fixed costs, or **overhead**, are those costs that are relatively constant regardless of the volume of goods produced or sold.

Variable cost—any cost that can be apportioned on a per-unit basis.

A **variable cost**, on the other hand, is any cost that can be apportioned on a per-unit basis. Included are wages of workers involved in producing goods or services and the cost of raw materials or shipping. For example, if it takes a worker 15 minutes to machine-produce an item, then it is a variable cost because the cost of labour per unit can be clearly identified. To calculate the total variable cost, we simply multiply the cost per unit times the number of units to be produced. Thus, total variable cost increases as more units are produced.

To illustrate how break-even analysis can be used to assess a new venture, consider the following example. The owner of Wombat Ski Equipment Company Inc. intends to establish a new business renting skis from the Snow Valley Ski Lodge. Given that her main concern is the profitability of the operation, she would have to determine how many ski packages, including skis, bindings, boots and poles, she would have to rent per day or week to make a profit.

Since she cannot earn a profit until all fixed costs are covered, she would start by designating all costs as either fixed or variable, as follows:

Fixed Costs

Annual depreciation expense on skis	$ 3 780
Rent in ski lodge	3 400
Advertising	1 500
Liability insurance	1 750
Manager's salary	9 350
Other fixed labour	730
Miscellaneous	1 750
Total fixed costs	**$22 260**

Variable Costs

For every 10 sets of skis rented:

Repairs per day	$ 30
Additional labour costs per day	20
Total variable costs	**$ 50**

Wombat's owner anticipated that she could rent skis for seven months of the year, from October to May, although business in the first and last months would probably be light. He would thus have 210 days in which to rent skis. Daily fixed costs would be $106, while total variable costs would be $50 per day for every 10 sets of skis rented. The rental charge to the customer for each set of skis would be $9.

How many units would have to be rented per day to break even on this operation? The break-even point can be computed by using the following formula:

$$\text{Break-even point (BEP)} = \frac{\text{Fixed costs}}{\text{Selling price} - \text{Variable cost per unit}}$$

$$\text{BEP} = \frac{\$106}{\$9 - \$5}$$

$$\frac{\$106}{\$4} = 26.5 \text{ or } 27 \text{ sets/per day}$$

The above calculation shows that each set of skis rented contributes $4 toward recovering fixed costs. Once sales have exceeded the BEP, this money goes toward increasing total profit.

If, on average, the owner can rent more than 27 sets of skis per day during the seven months, she would make a profit. Knowing this break-even figure, she can now look at the market more closely. If she finds that the demand for rentals is much greater than that required to break even, then she should proceed as quickly as possible to start the venture. If, on the other hand, initial demand is not be sufficient, she could try to reduce some of her fixed costs or else consider increasing the charge for each rental. Alternatively, she could simply accept the low revenues until demand improves.

Break-even analysis can also be done graphically. Figure 9.11A shows revenue and costs along the vertical axis, and the number of units of skis rented, in sets of 10, along the horizontal axis. Variable costs are then plotted on top of fixed costs at the rate of $50 per 10 sets of skis rented. The diagonal line originating at "0" indicates revenue and varies directly with the number of sets of skis rented.

At the break-even point, total fixed plus total variable costs are equal to the total revenue and Wombat makes no profit. If the number of rentals per day is below the break-even point, the firm suffers a loss. Rentals above the break-even point bring a profit that increases with the number of sets of skis rented.

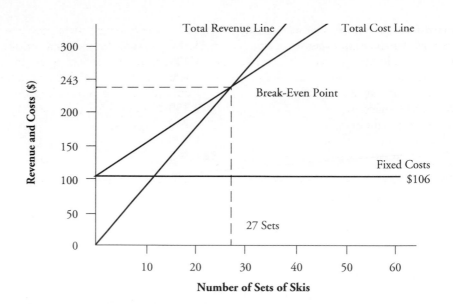

Break-even chart for
Wombat Ski Equipment
Company Inc.

Calculating the break-even
point using the Microsoft
Excel spreadsheet program

Another way to calculate the break-even point is to use an electronic spreadsheet program as shown in Figure 9.11B. You provide the input for the various costs and parameters for calculation. The program then provides the results showing the cost, revenue, profit/loss and unit cost along with the break-even point.

Acquiring Long-Term Funds

Individuals who purchase a major asset such as a car or home usually borrow the money and repay the loan over a period of years. Similarly, for long-term growth most firms must borrow money to finance new plants or purchase major new assets such as expensive equipment and machinery. They repay these loans over a period of years from the profit made in the operation. A large, financially strong company can raise long-term funds by selling its own corporate securities. Smaller companies can borrow long-term funds from a variety of financial institutions, including the chartered banks. However, if they are incorporated, they may issue their own shares to interested investors.

Types of Corporate Securities

The two major types of corporate securities are bonds and stocks. Bonds represent debt for the company, and therefore are known as **debt capital**. Common or preferred stocks represent ownership in the company and are known as **equity capital**. A comparison of stocks and bonds is shown in Table 9.1.

Bonds

A **bond** is a certificate issued by a company and traded to another company or to private individuals in return for an amount of money known as the **principal**. A bond certificate, as shown in Figure 9.12, states the **maturity date** when the company must repay the face value of the bond. A bond may reach maturity in five to 50 years, although the usual time period is 10 to 30 years. The certificate also states the amount of **interest** the company must pay to the bondholder each year. Most corporate bonds are sold in $1000 denominations, but a portion of each issue may be in denominations of $5000, $10 000, $50 000 and $100 000. The latter amounts are usually purchased by other large corporations, or by insurance companies and pension funds.

Bonds may be in either registered or bearer form. When a company issues a **registered bond**, it knows the owner's name and mails interest cheques directly to the bondholder when they are due. A **bearer bond**, on the other hand, has attached to it dated coupons that the bondholder uses on the specified dates to collect the interest owing. The interest is not usually paid directly by the issuer, but by the institution (often a trust company) that acted as a distributor for the bonds.

What Backs a Bond?

When you borrow money to purchase a car, the bank or finance company will usually require the car as collateral. The lending institution can then seize the car to make your payments. Similarly, a company that borrows money by issuing bonds must usually provide the lender with some security. Bonds backed in this manner are called secured bonds, meaning that the company has pledged specific property or fixed

---

Debt capital is borrowed money that has to be repaid after a period of time, along with a specific amount of interest.

Equity capital is raised by selling ownership in the firm and therefore is not repaid.

Bond—a certificate issued by a company and traded to another company or to private individuals in return for an amount of money—known as the principal—repayable in a stated number of years, with interest paid yearly at a stated rate.

Principal—the amount of money a firm borrows.

Maturity date—the date on which the company that has issued a bond must repay the full amount.

Interest—the amount of money a company pays for the use of borrowed money, stated in percentage terms.

Registered bond—the owner's name is known and interest cheques are mailed directly to the bondholder when they are due.

Bearer bond—has dated coupons attached to it, which the bondholder uses on the specified dates to collect the interest owing.

Comparison of stocks and bonds

TABLE 9.1

Stocks	Bonds
1. Represent ownership	1. Represent debt
2. No principal is repaid	2. Principal repaid upon maturity
3. May pay dividends	3. Must pay interest
4. Any dividends are paid after taxes	4. Interest is paid before taxes
5. Stockholders usually have some say in management	5. Bondholders have no say in management

FIGURE 9.12

Bond certificate (specimen)

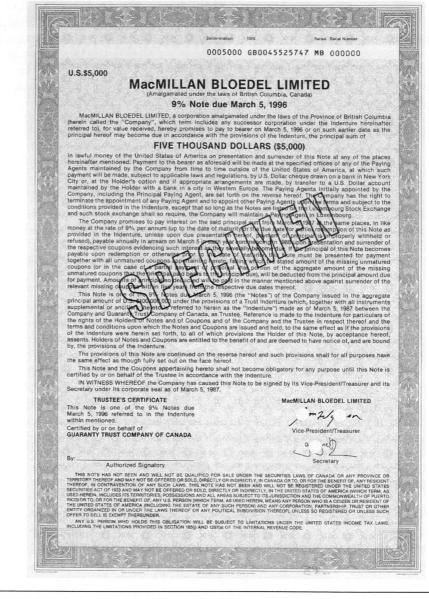

SOURCE: Reproduced courtesy of MacMillan Bloedel Limited.

assets that could be seized by the bondholder if the company is unable to repay the principal on the date specified in the bond issue. The security may be a piece of real estate, or specific equipment or machinery.

On the other hand, a company may issue unsecured bonds, backed not by specific collateral, but rather by the name and financial strength of the firm. Should the company fail, the bondholders will be repaid prior to any stockholders. However, lenders with claims on specific assets will be repaid before unsecured bondholders.

Unsecured bonds are also called debentures. **Debentures** are usually issued by financially strong companies, whose credit rating is judged to be exceptionally good by a firm such as Dun and Bradstreet—which specializes in analyzing and rating the financial condition of various companies.

Debentures are bonds not secured by specific collateral.

How Are Interest Rates Set on Bonds?

The interest rate that the issuer must pay on a bond issue is determined by the firm's financial strength and by whether the bond is secured or unsecured. It also depends on the general level of interest rates in the country at a particular period; when interest rates are rising, the company will have to pay a higher rate of interest to make the issue attractive to investors. However, the final decision on what rate to pay is made by the board of directors.

Calling and Converting

Calling and converting are two features occasionally included in a bond issue. By making a bond callable (redeemable), a company has the option to recall it before the maturity date, which may be done in the event that interest rates drop. For example, let us suppose that a callable bond was issued to pay 10% over a 20-year period, but after three years interest rates dropped to 7%. The company could then recall the bond as specified on the bond certificate, pay off the bondholders and issue new bonds at a lower interest rate.

The company then gains a substantial saving in interest payments. Suppose that the interest rate dropped from 10% to 7% within a five-year period, and the company had issued $100 million worth of bonds at 10%. If the firm called the bonds after five years and issued new ones for the remaining 15 years, thus saving three percentage points per year, the annual saving would amount to $3 million, or $45 million for the remaining 15 years. The call value of a bond is usually above face value because the issuer pays a premium to bondholders for the privilege of recalling the bonds before maturity date.

Convertibility is another feature that may benefit both the investor and the corporation. It allows the holder to convert the bonds to common stock. If all investors took advantage of convertibility, the company would not be required to repay the funds originally borrowed. Furthermore, the investor is assured of a continuing income from the bond and at some time has the option to participate in the company's financial success by sharing in any profits and capital appreciation of shares. Convertible bonds are thus considered a good investment, and companies can usually issue them at interest rates lower than those for regular bonds.

How Are Bonds Converted?

Let us suppose that a company issues a $1000 bond convertible to 50 shares of common stock when its shares are worth $15 each. At the time of issue, it would not be worthwhile for the investor to convert the bond to stocks, because their value would be only $750. If, however, over a period of five years, the stock rises to $25 per share—perhaps because the company promises to be very profitable—the investor could convert the bond to common stock. The $1000 bond would then be worth $1250—a $250 appreciation for the investor in addition to the interest received on the bond for the previous five years. If the company's financial outlook continues to be good, the shares could continue to appreciate in value.

Common Stock

Stocks are shares of ownership in a company. When a business incorporates, it can specify the number of **authorized shares** that it intends to offer. But the number of shares the firm is authorized to sell is often different from the number of **issued shares**, or shares sold to shareholders. Any shares not sold initially are available to future investors. For example, a small company that has recently incorporated with three

Authorized shares are the amount of shares that the company originally was authorized to sell.

Issued shares are the actual number of shares the company sold.

Common stock are shares of ownership in a company. It may or may not pay dividends.

equal shareholders might issue 100 shares of common stock to each individual. Since the minimum number of authorized shares is usually 10 000, 9700 shares of stock would be left for sale to other investors.

An investor who purchases **common stock** gives money to the company in return for a stock certificate, which represents shares of ownership in the company and indicates the number of shares bought, the name of the shareholder and the special characteristics of the stock. A sample share certificate is shown in Chapter 3. Common shareholders almost always hold voting rights and may vote for directors at the annual meeting. However, common shareholders have no special rights or privileges vis-à-vis dividends, and they are the last to be considered in the event that the company goes bankrupt. Furthermore, common shareholders have only last claim to undistributed profits, should any remain.

Given these disadvantages, why do people buy common stock? The major reason for purchasing common stock is its potential for appreciation. When a company is profitable and its earnings outlook is good, common stock can appreciate rapidly; prices have been known to double and triple in a matter of weeks.

Many companies also pay good dividends, which is another reason for investing in common stocks. If a company has had an exceptionally profitable year, common shareholders may also receive an additional special dividend from the surplus of funds. However, it is important to note that a company is not obligated to pay dividends to its shareholders.

The common shareholder may also benefit from a stock split, a procedure that companies often use to reduce the price of stock that has risen over a period of time. Splitting makes the stock more accessible to the small investor. For example, a stock that has risen from $30 to $100 may be attractive to more investors if it is split into four shares, each worth $25. Thus, all previous common shareholders also receive four times the number of their original shares. A stock split often causes another rapid rise in the new share price, since many more investors are now able to buy the stock.

Finally, an investor may benefit from appreciation of his or her stock when another firm attempts to gain control of the company, either through the purchase of shares on the open market or through a direct offer to existing shareholders. Usually the company attempting the takeover will offer a high premium over the current selling price of the stock, giving shareholders the opportunity to sell their stock for substantial capital gains.

Common shareholders also enjoy what is known as residual right to a company's earnings. When all interest has been paid to holders of bonds and other long-term debt certificates, and all payments have been made to preferred stockholders, the remaining earnings are available to common shareholders.

However, while common shareholders can sometimes gain substantial rewards from their stock, they are also prone to sudden and equally large losses. When a company becomes bankrupt, the common shareholder is not protected. If the firm has outstanding mortgages, or if it has many bondholders or preferred shareholders—all of whom have first claim to assets—there may be no funds left for common shareholders, who may lose their entire investment. Stock prices may also fall drastically during periods of economic recession or when there are poor economic forecasts that may affect a company's profit outlook. Since low profits may also mean a restriction on the payment of dividends, stock prices could drop further still.

Thus, common stock may be a sound investment when the company and the economy are doing well, but during difficult economic times shareholders may receive little income, and the value of their shares may drop substantially. In extreme instances, they may lose their entire investment.

When a shareholder receives a dividend from a Canadian corporation, the amount reported as taxable income is greater than the actual dividend. This grossed-up amount represents a portion of the income taxes paid by the corporation, since dividends are a distribution of profit after tax. In turn, the investor can then claim a dividend tax credit against federal tax payable, which also reduces provincial income tax payable. The effective rate of tax thus paid is less than the rate paid on other income. Under the new tax system, the dividend tax credit has been reduced from 22% to 16 2/3% of the actual dividend. That means that the top personal income tax rate on dividends will be about 30%

compared with the top rate on other income of about 45%. These rates vary from province to province because of the different provincial income tax rates.

The reason for the dividend tax credit is mainly to do away with double taxation—once when the corporation is taxed on its net income and then again when the investor has to report his or her income from all sources, including dividends. However, it is also an incentive to invest in Canadian corporations that pay dividends because income earned through dividends is taxed at a lower rate than income earned through employment or interest earned in savings accounts, term deposits or bonds.

What Is a Dividend Tax Credit?

Preferred Stock

To provide greater security and a steadier income for investors, yet still allow them some appreciation of their investment if the company is did well, preferred shares were developed. **Preferred shares** pay a dividend to shareholders, the amount being specified on the stock certificate. The dividend is either a fixed dollar amount or a percentage based on the issued price of the stock. For example, a preferred share may be issued at $25 with a $2.50 dividend, which represents a 10 percent return. Each share receives the specified dividend each year, usually paid quarterly, regardless of whether the value of the stock has gone up or down. Preferred shares may be issued in any denomination.

Preferred shares, along with common stock, tend to rise and fall depending on the financial fortunes of the company or the industry. However, the fluctuations are considerably less on preferred shares, primarily because of the fixed dividend that is paid. To some extent, the fixed dividend resembles a rate of interest. Preferred shares tend to fluctuate in their value as interest rates fluctuate. For example, if bank interest rates go up, then the price of preferred shares must go down in order to keep their relative return vis-à-vis interest paid at the bank. Similarly, the price of preferred shares goes up if bank interest rates go down. Preferred shares and common shares, however, are eligible for the federal dividend tax credit, which reduces the tax on dividends from Canadian corporations and thus effectively raises the return on dividends compared to interest received from bonds or bank savings accounts. Above all, preferred shares pay a fixed dividend that is often considerably higher than dividends paid to common stockholders.

To make preferred shares even more attractive, particular features may be added. For example, cumulative preferred shares guarantee that even if a dividend is omitted for one or more years, the company must first pay the dividends in arrears owed to preferred shareholders before paying common shareholders. Participating preferred shares entitle the holder to receive a further share of the company's earnings once common shareholders have received dividends equal to preferred dividends. The amount of this additional dividend is either specified on the share certificate or left to the discretion of the board of directors.

A company may also issue convertible preferred shares, which allow the holder to convert preferred stock into common stock prior to a specified date. If the price of the common stock rises to a specified price before the expiry date, then conversion will usually take place although by that time the preferred stock will have risen

Preferred shares pay to shareholders a dividend that is usually expressed in percentage terms based on the amount specified on the stock certificate.

to an equivalent price. Convertibility may make a preferred stock issue more attractive to investors because to the receipt of a good dividend is added great potential for capital appreciation.

Preferred shareholders have claim to dividends and assets before common shareholders, particularly in the event of company bankruptcy. Whatever remains after bondholders and other creditors have been paid goes to preferred shareholders. Any remaining funds may then be paid to common shareholders. Preferred shareholders usually do not have the voting rights that common shareholders do, although some issues may include voting rights on matters that concern preferred shareholders, such as the sale of a major part of the corporation, mergers or takeovers. However, this type of voting right must be specifically stated in the prospectus for the preferred share issue or in the articles or bylaws of the corporation.

Choosing the Type of Security to Issue

When financial managers need to raise long-term funds, they must consider the three major types of securities—bonds, preferred stocks and common stocks—and choose between additional debt or equity. Choosing additional debt through a bond issue creates another fixed annual cost for the business, since interest must be paid to the bondholders each year. Moreover, the face value of the bonds must be repaid on the maturity date. On the other hand, if a new stock issue is chosen, the firm is not obligated to pay any dividends or to repay the principal. However, the existing shareholders must share the company's profits with the new shareholders. All these factors must be considered in long-term financial decisions; the wrong decision could have severe consequences for both the firm and the common shareholders, whose interests are the financial manager's main concern.

Another factor in financial decision making is the concept of **financial leverage**, also known as **trading on the equity**. Common shareholders can gain through financial leverage if the firm is able to borrow at a rate of interest lower than the rate of return on investment generated by the firm's operation. For example, if a company can issue bonds at an interest rate of 10% and earn 16% by using these borrowed funds in its operation, then the difference of six percent goes into the company earnings from which common shareholders benefit.

Table 9.2 shows in more detail how financial leverage works. Both Company A and Company B plan to expand their operation by acquiring an additional $100 000,

Financial leverage, or **trading on the equity**, refers to the ability of a firm to earn money by using borrowed funds at a rate of interest lower than the rate of return from the firm's operation.

TABLE 9.2 Comparative rates of return using debt and equity financing

	Company A	Company B
Initial investment	$100 000	$100 000
Additional investment:		
Common stock	$100 000	$0
Bonds (10%)	0	100 000
Total investment	**$200 000**	**$200 000**
Earnings (20%)	40 000	40 000
Less: Bond interest	0	10 000
Net profit before tax	**40 000**	**30 000**
Return on shareholders'	$\frac{40\,000}{200\,000} = \textbf{20\%}$	$\frac{30\,000}{100\,000} = \textbf{30\%}$
equity (before tax)		

which would bring their total assets to $200 000. Company A will raise the funds through the issue of additional common stock, while Company B will issue bonds at an interest rate of 10%. If we assume that the earnings of both companies after the expansion will remain at 20% of investment, then Company B, which issued bonds, will earn a greater return on the total investment before tax.

Company B makes the greater return because money was borrowed at 10% and used by the company to earn 20%. Thus, the shareholders of Company B have increased their potential share of profits by 10% without any additional investment on their part. However, financial leverage can also work against common share-holders when company earnings drop. For example, if the earnings of both companies dropped to 10%, both companies would still show a 10% return on shareholders' investment. But the drop in return would have been twice as high for Company B, which financed its expansion by issuing bonds. If earnings dropped to zero, Company A would break even, but Company B would suffer a $10 000 loss because it had to pay that amount in bond interest.

Thus, financial leverage must be used with caution, particularly by companies that face considerable fluctuations in earnings. The increased return on investment from financial leverage could become a financial nightmare for a company with a fixed high-interest payment if its earnings were suddenly to drop. With the concept of financial leverage in mind, we can now briefly examine five of the factors that the financial manager must consider before deciding on a method of raising long-term funds. These factors are:

1. Cost of financing;
2. Taxation;
3. Voting control;
4. Risk;
5. Ease of raising capital.

Cost of Financing

As we have just seen, one of the foremost considerations for the financial manager is the rate of interest to be paid on a bond issue. If annual interest rates are high, a bond issue could become a liability if earnings take a sudden drop and the company still has to meet high interest payments each year. Thus, a company, particularly one with irregular earnings, may decide against issuing bonds and look to raising long-term funds through stock issues instead.

Taxation

Bonds offer an advantage to a corporation because bond interest is considered a business expense and can be deducted from corporate income before the calculation of income taxes. Dividends paid to shareholders, however, cannot be deducted since they are considered not an expense but rather a distribution of profits after taxes. The tax advantage of bonds compared to stocks is illustrated in Table 9.3. Although both companies had the same before-tax earnings, in the end Company B has retained earnings that are 50% greater than those of Company A. Company B raised funds through a bond issue, for which the interest payable is considered a before-tax expense. In contrast, Company A raised funds through a stock issue and, instead of interest, had to pay dividends, which come out of after-tax earnings. The treatment of bond interest as an expense is a major reason for the popularity of bond issues as a means of long-term financing.

TABLE 9.3 **Effect of corporate income taxes on equity and debt capital**

	Company A	Company B
Earnings	$ 40 000	$ 40 000
Less: Bond interest	0	10 000
Profit before tax	40 000	30 000
Less: Tax at 50%	20 000	15 000
Net profit	20 000	15 000
Less: Dividends	10 000	0
Retained earnings	**$10 000**	**$15 000**

Voting Control

Raising funds through a bond issue does not mean that existing shareholders lose control of the company, since bondholders have no voting rights. However, the original shareholders do lose some control of the company when additional shares are sold and the number of shareholders increases, unless they maintain their original proportion of outstanding shares by purchasing more of the new issue.

Risk

Businesses assured of steady earnings year after year, such as government-regulated public utilities, prefer bond issues since they have no difficulty meeting fixed interest payments or repaying the principal of the bonds at maturity. However, steel, construction and manufacturing companies, whose earnings may fluctuate considerably with business cycles, must be careful when issuing bonds. They may have difficulty meeting their fixed interest charges in years when earnings are low. Financial managers in these companies must pay particular attention to financial leverage and the debt/equity ratio.

Ease of Raising Capital

Decisions on long-term financing through debt or equity issues may be influenced by the existing market conditions for the sale of stocks and bonds. During buoyant economic periods, when stock prices are rising and investors feel positive about the stock market and the economy, a corporation may have no problem selling new stock issues. When the economic outlook is poor and stock prices are falling, however, new stock issues may be more difficult to sell, as investors trying to protect their investment will look for a more secure income. A corporation may then prefer to sell bonds, even though it may mean paying a higher rate of interest.

Marketing Corporate Securities

Once the best type of corporate security to raise the required financial capital has been chosen, the stock or bond issue is sold to potential investors. The finance manager then enlists the aid of a **securities underwriter**, who is responsible for marketing the new securities to the general public, to insurance companies or to other financial institutions such as those dealing in pensions and mutual funds.

    For example, suppose a company has decided to raise $10 million through a new share issue. The underwriter's first step is to investigate the firm's operation

Securities underwriter— markets a new securities issue to the general public, insurance companies, pension funds, mutual funds, brokers and investment dealers.

(particularly its financial condition) with the assistance of accountants, financial analysts and various individuals with expertise in the business. If the analysis shows that all is in order, the underwriter then negotiates details of the share issue with the firm. Once negotiations are complete, the underwriter usually purchases the share issue, either alone or in partnership with other investment companies.

Private Placement

Although a relatively unknown way of raising capital in Canada until the 1980s, **private placement** is becoming prominent in the 21st century. Increasingly, the big money pools—financial institutions, pension funds, insurance companies and investment firms—are bypassing private dealers to get a better deal. Since these securities are not sold to the general public, lengthy prospectuses are not needed and the cost of issuing securities is significantly reduced. A major drawback of private placement occurs when an investment is made in a company that becomes shaky. Because it is not an investment in a firm's shares, the lender cannot simply sell out, but must instead become involved in solving the problems of the borrowing firm.

Private placement means that large investors lend to qualified borrowers directly without involving the services of a private investment firm.

One critical task of the underwriter is to peg the stock at the right price for sale. Accurate forecasting is essential, as the stock could easily rise or fall between the time the price is determined and the time the shares are actually put onto the market. The underwriter also assists in obtaining approval for the share issue from the various government agencies concerned and from the securities commission. In addition, the underwriter aids in the preparation of the prospectus, which is a detailed description of the company and the new share issue. The prospectus, which must be issued to each potential buyer of the new shares, provides the investor with all the necessary information about the company. The underwriter's fee, also known as the spread, is the difference between the price for which he or she sells the issue in the market and the price at which he or she bought it from the firm. The spread will, of course, depend on how difficult it is to sell the stock.

The Securities Markets

Stocks and bonds are popular investments because they can be converted into cash quickly. However, an investor who has purchased shares or bonds issued by a company cannot get his or her money back from the firm, since in the meantime it will have purchased fixed assets or otherwise used the funds in its operation. Therefore, the holder sells his or her shares, through a securities or stock market, to others who are willing to purchase them. A **stock market** provides a means for buyers and sellers to meet and exchange securities at mutually agreeable prices.

Stock market—provides a means for buyers and sellers to exchange securities at mutually agreeable prices.

The world's oldest stock exchange, in Amsterdam, began operations in 1611 when the Dutch East India Company first sold its shares to the general public. In London, stockbrokers met in various coffee houses to sell stocks until 1773, when they moved to Sweeting Alley, which became known as the Stock Exchange Coffee House. Since the "Big Bang" in October 1987, this exchange has been known as the International Stock Exchange of the United Kingdom. Other cities with well-known stock exchanges are Paris, Tokyo, Zurich, Frankfurt, Melbourne, Copenhagen, Hong Kong, New York, Chicago, Montreal and Toronto. The network of securities markets as a whole consists of stock exchanges, over-the-counter markets and a variety of financial institutions, including chartered banks, brokerage firms, investment companies and security dealers.

Stock Exchanges

A **stock exchange** is essentially a marketplace for corporate securities. Members of the exchange purchase or sell securities, either for themselves or for clients.

Canada has four stock exchanges, in Toronto, Montreal, Winnipeg and Calgary. The Toronto Stock Exchange (TSE), started in 1852, is the largest and most active capital market in Canada. It accounted for 89% of all equities traded in 1998 for a total of 26 billion shares with a value of $460 billion.

At one time traders on the floor of the TSE shouted out buy and sell orders to each other; however, that was changed on April 23, 1997. On that day, the TSE changed over to a fully electronic trading environment where traders could access trading on the TSE from anywhere, through their computers. This move has made trading on the TSE more accessible and efficient.

Not only has trading moved on-line but the TSE, as an organization, is also on-line. TSE.com was launched in the fall of 1997 and has become one of the most popular financial sites. It receives over one million page views per day from people looking for information about the TSE and the capital markets, listed companies and participating organizations and how the market is performing.

How Securities Are Bought and Sold

Suppose you received a gift of $2000 and decided to try your hand at investing in the stock market. How would you go about it? Obviously, you would have to determine which stock to buy, either by reading about various companies in financial newspapers, or by asking individuals who are informed. You might also evaluate firms by researching their products, financial condition and future profit outlook.

Another source of information is a **stockbroker**. Listings can be readily found in the yellow pages of the telephone book. In addition to buying stocks or bonds for you, the broker can serve as an advisor and counsellor, suggesting stocks that may be appropriate and providing other current information about securities and the operations of various companies. Stockbrokers, mostly known as account executives, can also make stock purchases for their clients once accounts have been opened with them. As in opening an account with a department store, some personal information will be required.

Let us assume that after establishing an account with a local brokerage firm, you have decided to purchase 100 shares of stock in Canadian Pacific. The shares are trading at a price of $38.56 per share. Your broker will send the order via the Internet to their traders at the TSE. These traders will then enter the order into their computers. If another trader has these shares for sale at that price, then the order is filled automatically. A confirmation of the transaction is sent automatically to your broker and the purchase is recorded in your account.

On the settlement day, (usually three to five days later), you must make payment to your broker. Since the total cost of the stock you have purchased is $3856 plus the broker's commission, but you have only $2000, you will need to margin, or borrow, the remainder from your broker at a monthly interest charge. The commission, typically 3% of the value of the total stock transaction, is the payment for the work the brokerage house and the account executive have done for you in purchasing the stock. Investors who purchase large blocks of shares are usually able to negotiate the commission and receive a lower rate.

The Over-the-Counter Market

Only approximately 10% of Canadian companies have their stocks listed on any

How to read the stock tables

FIGURE 9.13

Typical stock quotations

Equities on Canadian exchanges are shown in decimals. NYSE, Amex, Nasdaq, and Unlisted stocks closing at less than $5 are shown in decimals, those closing at more than $5 are shown in fractions.

Stocks in bold type closed at least 5% higher or lower than the previous board lot closing price. Stocks must close at a minimum $1 and trade at least 500 shares to qualify.

Underlined stocks have traded 500% or more above their 60-day average daily volume.

1. Up/down arrows indicate a new 52-week high or low in the day's trading

2. 52-week high/low: Highest and lowest inter-day price reached in the previous 52 weeks

3. Stock names have been abbreviated

4. Ticker: Basic trading symbol for primary issues (usually common)

5. Dividend: Indicated annual rate. See footnotes

6. Yield %: Annual dividend rate or amount paid in past 12 months as a percentage of closing price in past 12 months

7. P/E: Price earnings ratio, closing price divided by earnings per share in past 12 months. Figures reported in US$ converted to C$

8. Volume: Number of shares traded in 00s;

	1		2	3	4	5	6	7	8	9	10	11	12
	52W high	52W low		Stock	Ticker	Div	Yield %	P/E	Vol 00s	High	Low	Close	Net chg
↑	x29.25	21.15		MaxStocknaMAX		f0.50	1.96	7.4	210501	27.25	27.05	27.20	+0.10
n	39.25	31.15		**MaxStockna**	MAX	f1.00	2.83	10.3	210501	37.25	37.05	37.20	+0.10
↓s	49.25	41.15		MaxStockna	MAX	f1.50	3.30	13.2	210501	47.25	47.05	47.20	+0.10

z – odd lot; **e** – exact no. of shares

9. High: Highest inter-day trading price
10. Low: Lowest inter-day trading price
11. Close: Closing price
12. Net change: Change between board lot closing price and previous board lot closing price

If a Canadian listed stock doesn't trade, its last bid and ask price can be found in the bid/ask table

Footnotes
* – traded in $US **x** – stock is trading ex-dividend **n** – stock is newly listed on exchange in past year **s** – stock has split in past year **c** – stock has consolidated in past year **a** – spinoff

company distributed as shares **↓** – shares carry unusual voting rights

Dividend footnotes
r – dividend in arrears **u** – US$ **p** – paid in the past 12 months including extras **y** – dividend paid in stock, cash equivalent **f** – floating rate, annualized **v** – variable rate, annualized based on last payment

Data supplied by Star Data Systems (905) 479-STAR and FP DataGroup (416) 350-6500

Historical Nasdaq supplied by DataStream

―――――― **How to read the options, index options, futures prices and futures options tables** ――――――

P/C – Option put or call. Futures prices open interest reflects previous trading day. **CBOT** – Chicago Board of Trade, **CDNX** – Canadian Venture Exchange, **CME** – Chicago Mercantile Exchange, **COMEX** – New York Commodity Exchange, **FINEX** – Financial Instruments Exchange, **IMM** – International Money Market, **CSCE** – Coffee, Sugar, Cocoa Exchange, **KBOT** – Kansas City Board of Trade, **MPLS** – Minneapolis Grain Exchange, **ME** – Montreal Exchange, **NYCE** – New York Cotton Exchange, **NYME** – New York Mercantile Exchange, **NYFE** – New York Futures Exchange, **r** – option not traded, **s** – no option offered, **TSE** – Toronto Stock Exchange, **TFE** – Toronto Futures Exchange, **WPG** – Winnipeg Commodity Exchange.

SOURCE: *National Post*, 2000

of the country's four exchanges. A listed stock must be approved by the provincial securities commission, and the exchange itself must approve it for trading. To obtain approval, the corporation must meet the exchange's minimum financial standards and show a reasonable management performance. Prices for stocks listed on the stock exchanges are available at all times; most major newspapers list the high, low and closing prices of every stock as it is traded during the day. Also, many cable television companies broadcast stock trades as they happen and provide a summary listing similar to that in newspapers.

For the other 90% of Canadian corporations whose stock is not listed on the stock exchanges, there is another method of trading known as the **over-the-counter market**. The over-the-counter market is a network of securities dealers and brokers who buy and sell unlisted securities for clients. Prices are established by supply and demand for each security. In the past, information on a small number of these stocks was available only to investors from day-old newspapers or from brokers who had to telephone other traders for the latest prices. However, in 1985 the over-the-counter market became automated. Brokers can now publicly display quotes on all over-the-counter stocks and report and store information. Figure 9.14 shows some over-the-counter stocks as displayed in newspapers.

Over-the-counter market—a network of securities dealers who buy and sell securities of companies not listed on a regular stock exchange.

Why Buy Stocks and Bonds?

Although the stock market is sometimes used by speculators who hope to make large gains quickly, it is primarily intended to raise money for business investment. Companies offer shares of ownership to the public, and potential investors hope to receive dividends from their investment, as well as appreciation of their shares if the firm is profitable. The businesses, in turn, use the money raised from the sale of stock to improve and expand their operation and thereby increase production and profits. Prospective investors have a wide choice of securities available to them,

Trading Stocks on the Internet

Following the lead of several U.S. stock-trading companies, Toronto-Dominion Bank's Green Line Investment Services Inc. was the first to offer Internet stock trading in Canada in 1997. The primary benefit to investors is the significantly lower brokerage fee. That does not mean, however, that investors must sacrifice information for lower fees. A company's home page on the Internet can provide useful information that investors can read or download at no cost to the brokerage company. Other information such as a prospectus for a new stock offering can be made available to investors for reading on-line or for downloading to his or her computer.

An Internet stock transaction is relatively simple. The investor completes a form on-line with details of the buy or sell order. The company's computer then confirms the order and a broker quickly reviews it and then passes it on to the appropriate stock exchange. Once the order is executed, the client receives an e-mail message to that effect. For more information, see, for example, the Toronto Dominion Bank brokerage Web site at www.tdwaterhouse.ca.

including common shares, preferred shares and bonds, each offering a variety of features.

Investing in the stock and bond market is risky. Since stock prices are determined by supply and demand in the market, sudden fluctuations can occur because of company misfortunes or because of economic or political events that might affect the company's profits. Nevertheless, certain companies promise to return to investors more than the interest received from the bank on a similar deposit in a bank savings account. Proper investment provides a greater return, but the risk is also higher. Preferred shares and bonds can reduce this risk considerably. Some stock investments have rewarded their investors handsomely over the years, while others have been a disaster. Common and preferred stocks do offer the investor some protection against inflation. Companies can increase the prices for their products to ensure that their profits increase relative to inflation.

An important consideration for many investors is the liquidity of their investment—the ease with which it can be turned into cash. Because of the network of stock

A trader's work station showing the computerized trading system at the Toronto Stock Exchange >

CDN UNLISTED 08.18.00

Figures supplied by Star Data Systems Inc.

Stock	Ticker	Vol 00s	High	Low	Cls	Net chg
AVL Info	AVLL	680	0.34	0.31	0.31	-0.02
ActFitcom*	ACTF	450	0.34	0.32	0.32	+0.02
Advntxcl*	AXCL	6	0.28	0.28	0.28	
AkroAsh	AAGM	10	0.19	0.19	0.19	
Alive Int	ALIV	26	2.75	2.25	2.25	-0.50
AlphaGrp	ALFG	500	1.15	1.15	1.15	
Ansil	ANSL	2400	0.15	0.15	0.15	
Armace	ARMC	107	1.75	1.50	1.75	
ArmstcRs	ACIG	93	0.02	0.02	0.02	
Asian TV	ATNL	255	0.40	0.35	0.35	-0.15
Asquith	ASQH	11	0.20	0.20	0.20	
AsstMgmtS	AMSS	363	0.70	0.55	0.62	+0.02
AtlanSys	ASGT	195	1.45	1.40	1.40	-0.05
Belzberg	BELZ	60	7½	7½	7½	-½
Betacom	EYEE	120	1.65	1.60	1.60	-0.10
BfkPearl	BLKP	250	0.20	0.20	0.20	+0.05
BluGld	BGII	45	0.05	0.05	0.05	
Brazln	BZIN	390	0.80	0.70	0.80	+0.10
Brckrdg	BREK	20	0.005	0.005	0.005	-0.03
CME Tel	CMET	18	8¾	8¼	8¼	-½
CdnArrw	CAML	6	0.15	0.15	0.15	
Cancall	CCCA	1850	0.15	0.10	0.15	+0.05
Canfibre	CFGL	355	0.43	0.25	0.35	+0.05

Stock	Ticker	Vol 00s	High	Low	Cls	Net chg
CapturNet	CAPN	100	0.50	0.50	0.50	
CarmaFin	CARM	70	0.70	0.69	0.70	
CheniRes	CHBI	40	1.00	1.00	1.00	+0.20
ColmMtl	COML	635	0.75	0.65	0.70	-0.05
CRMnet	CRMT	989	0.75	0.65	0.75	
Cymat	FOAM	70	1.55	1.45	1.55	+0.05
DavTisd	DDTS	70	0.30	0.30	0.30	
Dotcom2000	DCKK	5	0.60	0.60	0.60	
E21 Grp	EPRO	460	0.20	0.15	0.15	-0.05
EWMC	EWMI	263	0.55	0.45	0.55	+0.05
EleTel*	LETL	150	0.30	0.30	0.30	
eNblast	ENBL	250	0.17	0.17	0.17	-0.01
EnrVisn	ENVN	100	0.15	0.10	0.10	-0.05
eStation	ESTN	299	0.68	0.65	0.65	-0.10
EuroNet	ERNL	625	0.04	0.03	0.035	
Fareport	FARE	100	0.30	0.30	0.30	+0.05
Findor	FGRL	103	0.45	0.20	0.45	+0.09
1stmart	FSSC	90	0.25	0.25	0.25	
Funtime	FUNZ	110	0.50	0.50	0.50	+0.03
GalxyOnLn	GOLI	531	1.50	1.40	1.47	-0.01
Gastar Ex	GAST	128	21¼	19	21¼	+1¾
Gemstar	GSTR	30	0.15	0.15	0.15	+0.05
GemStone	GMSX	8	4.45	4.25	4.45	+0.20

Stock	Ticker	Vol 00s	High	Low	Cls	Net chg
GibSpring	GSPR	250	0.30	0.30	0.30	+0.15
GldHope	GNHM	40	0.65	0.65	0.65	
Grntree	GGOL	100	1.10	1.10	1.10	
HallTrn	HTRN	300	0.06	0.06	0.06	
HiAmGld	HIAM	10	0.09	0.09	0.09	+0.04
Homeprjct	HPCI	81	1.35	1.20	1.30	+0.10
Hucamp	HUCM	1325	1.40	1.35	1.40	
Hydrmet	HMEA	420	0.06	0.05	0.05	-0.01
HYWY	HYWY	40	0.75	0.60	0.75	-0.05
ICON*	ILEC	10	1.75	1.75	1.75	
IMI Intl	IMIN	24	4.30	4.15	4.30	
Inouye	ITII	97	0.17	0.17	0.17	+0.02
Interoil	INOL	76	3.35	3.00	3.00	-0.50
Interrent	HOUS	166	2.15	1.75	1.85	-0.30
Isee3D	EYEC	3014	0.30	0.25	0.28	+0.01
iWave.com	IWAV	1240	0.28	0.24	0.26	+0.01
JavaJoes	JVAJ	50	0.10	0.10	0.10	-0.05
Jetcom	JTCM	450	0.15	0.15	0.15	
KWG Res	KWGR	262	0.10	0.08	0.08	-0.02
KingPrd	KINK	230	0.50	0.48	0.48	-0.02
Krystal	KBON	550	0.25	0.25	0.25	
Lakota	LAKO	40	1.15	1.10	1.15	
Landmark	LMKG	8	1.00	1.00	1.00	
LifeTECH	LFTK	490	0.55	0.50	0.55	+0.04
Lignex	LGNX	1141	0.23	0.21	0.23	
MagAlloy*	MGAC	500	0.07	0.07	0.07	
Manitex	MNTX	45	1.35	1.25	1.35	+0.10
MplMnrl	MAPM	10	0.08	0.08	0.08	-0.02

FIGURE 9.14

Listing of industrial and other stocks trading over-the-counter

SOURCE: *National Post*, 2000

exchanges, most stocks and bonds can be sold within hours if the investor requires cash quickly. For investments in real estate or other assets, on the other hand, buyers are not as readily available.

Chapter Summary

1. In general, the most important function of the financial manager is to ensure that the firm survives. Even a well-managed company occasionally has to borrow to meet its financial obligations. The financial manager must examine the future cash flow of the business and establish a cash budget to indicate when the business will need to borrow money to survive, such as during periods when cash outflow exceeds inflow. The principal sources of short-term funds are banks, various financial institutions and other businesses. These sources may provide funds on a secured or unsecured basis; security can be provided by accounts receivable, inventories or other property. Another important source of short-term funds is trade credit, which is often extended on an open-book basis, though sometimes promissory notes or trade drafts are required.

2. The financial manager must also keep track of the performance of the business. An accounting system is thus established, one that provides information that is used to compare current performance with that of previous years and other businesses. Methods of financial analysis include ratio analysis and comparisons of income statements and balance sheets. Management also uses information from these analyses, and from break-even analysis, in decision making.

3. The two most basic financial statements are the balance sheet and the income statement. The balance sheet gives an indication of the firm's financial position at a particular point in time. The income statement shows the results of business transactions between two particular periods of time, and shows the income earned through the firm's operation. However, neither the income statement

nor the balance sheet specifies where cash came from, or where it went. This information is provided by a statement of changes in financial position, which is used by management to plan for future cash requirements. The financial manager is also responsible for establishing operating and capital budgets, and for comparing actual performance with budgetary plans.

4. To raise long-term funds to purchase fixed assets, a firm can resort to either debt or equity capital. A bond signifies that the company issuing it has borrowed money from investors, which must be repaid at a specific time in the future, and that interest must be paid on a yearly basis. Stocks or shares represent equity capital and indicate ownership in the company. Shares can be either preferred or common. Preferred shareholders receive specified dividends and have rights to assets before common shareholders should the firm go bankrupt. They also receive dividend payments before common shareholders. Common shareholders have no particular rights to dividends but have residual rights and voting rights to elect board members.

5. In deciding how to raise long-term capital, the financial manager must consider current interest rates, the respective advantages of bonds and stocks in terms of taxation, future earnings of the company, the voting control exercised by common shareholders, as well as general economic conditions, which may favour either stocks or bonds at any particular time.

6. Investors purchase stocks and bonds to obtain a return that is potentially higher than bank interest rates because of the potential capital appreciation of the shares, and because of the speed with which stocks and bonds can be turned into cash if necessary.

KEY TERMS

Financing 314	Compensating balance 321	Shareholders' equity 327
Financial solvency 314	Unsecured loan 321	Retained earnings 327
Fixed capital .315	Factoring 321	Gross profit 327
Working capital 315	Finance companies 321	Net profit 328
Cash flow 315	Commercial or corporate papers . . .322	Ratio analysis 331
Cash budget .316	Financial accounting 322	Current ratio .331
Short-term financing 316	Management accountin 323	Quick or acid-test ratio 332
Trade credit 316	Bookkeeping .323	Inventory turnover ratio 332
Cash discounts 318	Accounting 323	Debt ratio 334
Open book credit 318	Accountants .323	Debt/equity ratio 334
Consignment .318	Accounting system 323	Gross profit margin ratio 334
Promissory note 318	Balance sheet 323	Net profit margin ratio 335
Trade draft 318	Income statement 323	Return on investment ratio 335
Time draft 318	Statement of changes in financial position 324	Forecasting 336
Trade acceptance 318	Current assets 324	Budget 336
Sight draft 319	Fixed assets .324	Budget forecast 336
Collateral 319	Depreciation .324	Capital budget 338
Secured loan .319	Capital cost allowance (CCA) 326	Master operating budget 339
Demand loan .320	Current liabilities 327	Financing budget 339
Line of credit .320	Long-term liabilities 327	Pro-forma financial statement 339
Stand-by fee .321		Fixed costs/overhead 340

KEY TERMS

Variable cost 340
Debt capital 343
Equity capital 343
Bond 343
Principal 343
Maturity date 343
Interest 343

Registered bond 343
Bearer bond 343
Debentures .344
Authorized shares 345
Issued shares 345
Common stock 346
Preferred shares 347

Financial leverage 348
Securities underwriter 350
Private placement 351
Stock market 351
Stock exchange 352
Stockbroker .352
Over-the-counter market 353

REVIEW QUESTIONS

1 Describe the three major functions of the finance department.

2 What is meant by fixed capital? Working capital?

3 What is meant by financial solvency? Why must a business sometimes borrow money?

4 Explain the meaning of cash flow. How is cash flow responsible for generating profit?

5 Why is a cash budget necessary for a business? How is it established? How can a computer help in cash budgeting?

6 Why is short-term borrowing often required?

7 Why is trade credit included as a source of short-term funds? What are the various types of trade credit?

8 Why might a firm take advantage of trade discounts?

9 Explain the difference between a secured and an unsecured bank loan.

10 Explain the difference between a demand loan and a line of credit.

11 What is a factor company? Why would a business use the services of such a company?

12 What is accounting? What is the difference between financial and management accounting? Why does a business, regardless of size, need an accounting system?

13 Explain the importance of a balance sheet and an income statement. What is the purpose of a statement of changes in financial position?

14 What is the purpose of ratio analysis? Identify five common ratios. How are they useful in analyzing a firm's operation?

15 Why is forecasting and budgeting important? What are the key components of the total budgeting process?

16 Why is break-even analysis a useful tool for business forecasting and analysis? Distinguish between fixed and variable costs.

17 Why does a business distinguish between short- and long-term financing?

18 Distinguish between equity capital and debt capital. Under what circumstances would a company prefer equity to debt capital?

19 What is a bond?

20 Distinguish between common and preferred stock.

21 Explain the concept of financial leverage. Why is financial leverage an important consideration for the financial manager who must choose between debt and equity financing?

22 How do cost of financing, taxation, voting control, risk and ease of raising capital influence the decision about debt or equity financing?

23 How are corporate securities marketed? What is the function of the securities underwriter?

24 What is the purpose of a stock exchange? Of a brokerage firm?

DISCUSSION QUESTIONS

1 Which financial statement—the balance sheet or the income statement—do you think would be more useful to banks and other institutions considering whether to grant a loan to a business.

2 "It is more important to have firm control over cash flow than to have an accurate picture of profits." Do you agree or disagree with this statement? Give reasons for your answer.

3 One way of getting around the problem of choosing between debt and equity financing for a new plant, office building or warehouse is to let someone else build it and then lease the facilities from them for a fixed number of years at a regular monthly charge. Explain how leasing might be advantageous for a company.

4 After studying both the management and the finance function of a business, can you explain why these two areas represent the major reasons for business failure?

CASE
9-1

Raising Money for Publishing

Sylvie Bouchard and David Wong had known each other since university. For the past eight years Sylvie had been working as a market research analyst; she was particularly involved in lifestyle research. David had been teaching a college business communication course; for the past four years, he had also been editor of a publication called *Business Communication Today.* Sylvie and David decided to produce together a new monthly magazine called *Today's Environment.* Since the topic was of considerable current interest, they thought the project could make money; they were both also keenly interested in the venture and looked forward to considerable job satisfaction.

Magazine publishing is not an easy venture. Newsstand sales and subscriptions alone will not make it profitable, and Sylvie and David would have to get a fair amount of revenue from advertising to cover all costs and eventually make a profit for the business.

Today's Environment would include each month one feature article on some aspect of the environment. Sylvie and David would pay $3000 for the article, which they would solicit from freelance writers. They also wanted up to six shorter supplementary articles for which they would pay $600 each. Additional costs for pictures and copyrights were estimated at approximately $2000 per issue. Sylvie and David expected to do the monthly layout themselves, which would cost approximately $450 for the cover and $1600 for the magazine. After receiving estimates for printing costs from a number of printers, they settled on one who charged $870 per 1000 copies for the first 10 000 copies and $690 per 1000 copies for the next 20 000 copies. They were assured that these costs would not change for at least one year. Thus, they were reasonably certain about their printing and production costs.

During the first month, they expected to sell 4000 copies on the newsstand. These sales were expected to increase by 600 copies per month for the first year. Thereafter, they expected sales to level off. In addition to newsstand sales Sylvie and David expected the following subscription sales:

Month	Subscriptions	Month	Subscriptions
1	0	7	400
2	400	8	300
3	600	9	200
4	800	10	100
5	800	11	100
6	700	12	100

The costs of distributing the magazine to newsstands and through the mail averaged 40¢ per copy. From an advertising agency, Sylvie and David learned that they could expect net advertising revenues of approximately $6000 per month after the first year. During the first year, they expected advertising revenues to increase by $500 per month.

Sylvie and David studied the magazines that were similar to their own and felt that initially a price of $2 per issue would be satisfactory. Based on this price, they decided to sell a yearly subscription (12 issues) for $20. They rented an office for $300 per month, and hired a part-time secretary for $600 per month. Telephone, power and miscellaneous costs were estimated at about $150 per month. They also hit upon a novel advertising idea. The print run during each of the first three months would be 15 000 copies. Any copies not sold on the newsstand or through subscriptions would be distributed free of charge to selected households in and around the city during the following month. They hoped this tactic would encourage subscriptions.

All in all, Sylvie and David felt they had a good idea of what was involved in the venture. They had talked to a number of acquaintances with some knowledge of the business, and they had done considerable research on publishing. They each had $8000 to contribute to the venture and were confident that any chartered bank would be happy to give them a loan if and when necessary. They were also confident that they could raise money by selling shares to investors.

Both were confident of their future success. Sylvie left her job to devote herself full-time to the publishing venture. She would take $600 per month to cover her expenses. David felt he could continue to teach and edit the magazine at the same time. He did not expect to take any money out of the business for at least the first year.

After two-and-a-half weeks of operation, Sylvie and David realized they would have financial problems. The sale of advertising space in the magazine was extremely slow; they had difficulty both in deciding on the kinds of material to put into the magazine, and in attracting suitable articles from freelance writers. Recognizing that more money was needed, Sylvie and David wasted no time drawing up a cash budget and putting together a proposal to establish a line of credit at the bank.

Questions

1. What did Sylvie and David overlook before initiating this venture?

2. If Sylvie and David approach a lending institution to borrow money, what kind of information would they be required to provide before they could receive a loan? Before they could expect an investor to buy shares in the company, what would they have to do?

>>

3. Prepare a break-even analysis for this operation. To simplify matters, treat all subscriptions as if they were newsstand copies. Also, for the purpose of break-even analysis, ignore the fact that Sylvie and David get a price break for printing over 10 000 copies. Indicate, however, how these two factors will influence your break-even point. How will you treat advertising revenue in your calculation? Explain how break-even analysis can be used in financial planning for the company.

4. Prepare a cash budget for the first year of this publishing venture. Indicate if and when Sylvie and David need to borrow money and when the loans might be repaid. Assume for this exercise that they always want to have a minimum balance of $2000 in their account. Assume that all subscriptions begin the month following receipt of the order, and that all print runs have to be in thousands of copies. Distribution costs are 40¢ per copy regardless of the means of distribution.

Prairie Industrial Corporation

The following pertains to the Prairie Industrial Corporation, a manufacturing company.

	December 31, 2000	December 31, 2001
Accounts payable	$ 60 030	
Plant and buildings	320 000	
Equipment	95 300	
Inventory (finished goods)	115 430	
Accounts receivable	35 470	
Prepaid expenses	7 600	
Notes payable	110 000	
Accumulated depreciation on plant	128 000	
Accumulated depreciation on equipment	23 600	
Accrued liabilities	32 260	
Current portion of long–term notes payable	20 000	
Common stock (issued at $10 initially)	80 000	
Retained earnings	187 450	
Cash	43 540	
Marketable securities	24 000	
Revenue from manufacturing		764 350
Other income from operations		47 250
Interest income		2 900

The following additional information is provided to help establish financial statements for Prairie Industrial Corporation for the 2001 fiscal year.

1. Accounts payable increased by $14 400 during the year.

2. There were additions to the plant of $65 000, which can be depreciated by 5% in 2001.

3. There were additions to equipment of $33 000, which can be depreciated by 7.5% in 2001.

4. The current portion of long-term notes payable was paid at the beginning of the year.

5. At the end of 2001, the rest of the notes payable were repaid.

6. During 2001, 10 000 additional shares of stock were issued at $16 per share.

7. The existing plant annual depreciation rate is 10% per annum (straight line).

8. The existing equipment annual depreciation rate is 15% per annum (straight line).

9. Inventory of finished goods increased by $8000 in 2001.

10. Accounts receivable decreased by $9500.

11. Prepaid expenses increased by $2300.

12. Accrued liabilities pertaining to 2001 amounted to $53 600.

13. Cost of manufactured goods amounts to 61% of revenue from manufacturing.

14. Taxes payable amount to 20% of net income under special federal tax rules.

15. Provincial taxes amount to 11% of net income.

16. Operating expenses amounted to $146 430 (excluding depreciation).

17. General and administrative expenses amount to $32 720.

18. Securities decreased by $14 000.

Questions

1. Develop a comparative balance sheet for Dec. 31, 2000 and for Dec. 31, 2001.

2. Develop an income statement for the fiscal year 2001.

3. Develop a statement of changes in financial position for the fiscal year 2001.

4. Compute the following ratios:
   a. current ratio for beginning and end of period;
   b. acid-test ratio for beginning and end of period;
   c. inventory turnover ratio;
   d. average collection period;
   e. debt ratio;
   f. debt/equity ratio;
   g. gross profit margin ratio;
   h. net profit margin ratio;
   i. return on investment.

COMPREHENSIVE CASE 9-3

SOMERSET OPTICAL

The discussion about redefining Somerset Optical's marketing strategy in the face of declining sales lead to an examination of the firm's finances. Somerset Optical's unaudited financial statements appear below.

Based on cash-flow analysis, Somerset Optical determined that it needed an immediate cash infusion of $125 000, to be held for a period of one year. Four options were available to the company:

1. Obtain a bank loan for $125 000. Cost of borrowing to Somerset would be 12.5% per year.

2. Sell its accounts receivable to an agent for 75% of their reported balance sheet amount, making up the difference through a bank loan at 12.5% per year.

3. Obtain a loan from an independent investor for 13.8%.

4. Issue share capital to a private investor.

The above financial statements were sent to Somerset's bank manager in advance, in case the company elected to exercise the bank loan option. The bank manager compared the operating results presented by these statements to industry averages in a few key ratios in deciding whether Somerset Optical was healthy enough to service the loan. The industry averages in the key ratios were as follows:

- Current ratio — 1.8
- Total debt to equity — 2.9
- Net profit margin — 4.0%
- Return on investment — 19.5%

SOURCE: By David H. Jones-Delcourt. Reprinted by permission of the author.

SOMERSET OPTICAL INC.
CONSOLIDATED STATEMENT OF INCOME
FOR THE PERIOD ENDED MARCH 31, 1999

Net sales		$435 000
Cost of goods sold		165 300
Gross profit		$269 700
Operating Expenses		
Advertising	$19 000	
Supplies	5 400	
Insurance	6 000	
Building leases	14 700	
Utilities	3 200	
Depreciation	72 000	
Bad debts	8 000	
Salaries and wages	80 000	
Telephone	1 200	
Vehicle leases	4 300	
Accounting services	4 500	218 300
Pre-tax operating income		$ 51 400
Income tax (38%)		19 532
Net income		$ 31 868
Less: Dividends		0
Increase in retained earnings		$ 31 868

>>

SOMERSET OPTICAL INC.
BALANCE SHEET
AS AT MARCH 31, 1999

Assets

Current Assets

Cash	$ 32 500	
Marketable securities	28 000	
Accounts receivable	43 000	
Inventory	99 500	
Prepaid expenses	5 400	
	$208 400	

Plant & Equipment

Vehicles under capital lease	$ 24 000	
Less: Accumulated depreciation	9 000	15 000
Buildings under capital lease	235 000	
Less: Accumulated depreciation	56 500	178 500
Equipment	59 000	
Less: Accumulated depreciation	6 500	52 500

TOTAL ASSETS		$454 400

Liabilitites and Shareholders' Equity

Current Liabilities

Accounts payable	$ 35 000	
Loans payable	115 000	$150 000

Non-current Liabilities

Obligations under capital leases:

Vehicles	$ 15 000		
Buildings	178 500		
Equipment	52 500	246 000	$390 000

Shareholders' Equity

Common stock	$ 26 532	
Retained earnings	31 868	58 400
Total Liabilities and Shareholders' Equity		$454 400

Questions

1. Are there any other options available to Somerset Optical to raise the necessary cash?

2. Based on the information provided, is Somerset Optical in financial trouble?

3. What are the costs associated with each option available to Somerset Optical?

4. You are the bank manager. Would you approve the loan on the basis of the information provided above?

5. What are the advantages and disadvantages should Somerset Optical issue stock as a means of raising the necessary funds?

10

Human Resource Management

Learning Objectives

After reading this chapter, you will be able to

1 Identify the major activities of the personnel department.

2 Explain how personnel managers plan for future employee requirements.

3 List the various methods of recruiting employees.

4 Contrast the two major selection processes and identify the specific methods used to select future employees from the available candidates.

5 Explain the purpose of human-rights legislation and the major issues involved in employment discrimination.

6 Explain the purpose of orientation programs.

7 Recognize the importance of employee training and the various methods used to train employees and develop managers.

8 Identify the key factors in a good compensation plan, and the various methods of compensation.

9 Recognize the importance of employee benefits and health and safety programs for both the employee and the organization.

10 Recognize the necessity for staff evaluation and the problems associated with it.

11 Explain the meaning of career development.

12 Explain the meaning of promotion, transfer, dismissal and retirement.

Human Resource Management

Although money and materials constitute the resources of an organization, their effective utilization depends on the people in the organization. It is people—human resources—who are responsible for productivity increases and profitability. It is people who establish businesses; design, produce and market the goods and services; allocate financial resources; and set objectives and develop strategies for achieving them. This is true for a hockey or football team as well as for a university or hospital. Because of the tremendous importance of human resources to an organization's effectiveness, managing those human resources is a major activity of every organization.

As mentioned in previous chapters, staffing—or placing people in the various positions that must be filled to achieve organizational objectives—is an essential task for any manager. Many managers, however, lack expertise in personnel functions, which have become increasingly specialized. In many small firms, for example, managers have the technical expertise to produce goods or services, but lack the specific skills required for personnel or human resource management. Their only recourse, then, is to rely on outside agencies that will recruit and hire staff.

Human resource management, or personnel management, involves the recruitment, selection, development and motivation of human resources. Because of its increasing complexity and the importance of people to an organization's success, human resource management has become a specialized function, particularly in large organizations. Large firms must continually plan for future personnel needs, meet the requirements of government legislation and deal with the increasing demands of unions. Large firms therefore usually employ various personnel specialists or human resource professionals such as employment managers, training managers, wage and salary administration managers and labour relations specialists. Figure 10.1 provides an overview of human resource activities.

Human Resources: A Staff Department

While production, marketing and finance are considered line departments, the personnel department is a staff department. It performs a support function in relation to the line departments. As a staff department, it has four main functions:

1. *Policy initiation.* The personnel manager establishes new policies to solve recurring problems or to prevent anticipated problems. These policies are designed to aid other managers in making decisions about employee matters such as working hours or performance standards.

2. *Advice.* Personnel specialists counsel line managers on matters such as handling grievances or disciplining employees.

3. *Service.* Service responsibilities include recruitment, hiring, training, and wage and salary administration. For example, the personnel department plans and sets up training programs and maintains all employee records.

4. *Control.* The personnel department carries out control functions such as monitoring other departments to ensure that they are following established personnel policies, procedures and practices.

Although the human resource department provides support for line managers, it does not take over the staffing responsibility. Staffing is a management function. Managers make the final decision on who will work for them, and they are responsible for ensuring that employees are productive and are working toward established goals.

Human Resources Development Canada Library

www.hrdc.gc.ca/cgi-bin/AT-Nationalsearch.cgi

Human resource management, or personnel management, is the recruitment, selection, development and motivation of human resources.

FIGURE 10.1

The human resource function

Human Resource Planning	Determining future personnel needs
	Forecasting
	Examining present personnel resources
	Developing a personnel strategy

Job analysis
Establishing job specification
Establishing job description

Acquiring Human Resources	Recruitment
	Selection
	Hiring and orientation

From within the organization
Newspapers and professional journals
Employment agencies—public and private
Union offices

Application form
Screening interview
Testing
Reference checks
Medical examination

Final interview
Employee is formally entered on company records
Individual is made aware of company operation

Development of Human Resources	Worker training
	Management development
	Performance appraisal

On-the-job
Apprenticeship
Vestibule
Job rotation
Classroom
Seminars
Superior-subordinate discussion
Appraisal by results

Employee Compensation	Establishing a pay structure
	Establishing an incentive system
	Establishing benefits and service programs

Wages
Salaries
Commissions
Bonuses
Profit sharing
Production sharing
Employee stock ownership
Insurance
Pensions
Holiday and vacations
Others

Continued

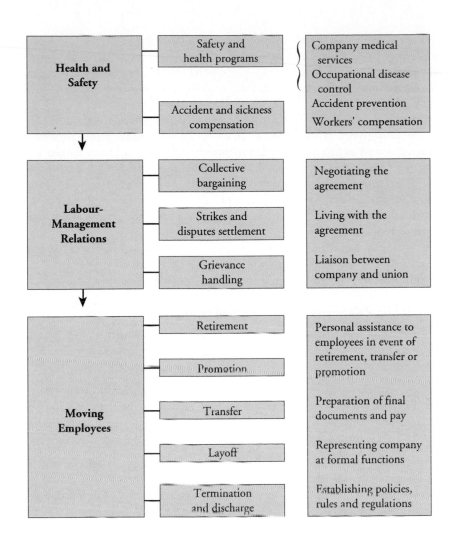

FIGURE 10.1

Continued

Human Resource Planning

When a firm develops long-range corporate objectives, it must take into account its human resources. Employees must possess the skills and education necessary to achieve the firm's objectives. In light of the firm's plans, the human resource manager must analyze future personnel requirements, taking into account current and past employee performance, as well as the future supply of qualified candidates. This analysis is particularly important for new firms starting up or for firms in industries that require special skills. Specialists may be in short supply even when overall unemployment is high. Some skills, such as those of qualified machinists, have a history of being in short supply. When booming economic times create a general shortage of workers, it may also be difficult to find qualified, motivated workers. This may drive up the costs of recruiting employees dramatically as supply and demand forces salaries for many occupations to rise sharply.

A recent article in the *New York Times* suggests that the scramble for highly qualified people in the technological sector has reached new proportions. For example, due to a severe shortage of engineers who design hardware and software and create Web pages, recruiters are resorting to various tricks to lure technical staff from their current employers. Some aggressive recruiters have even gone so far as to call each employee listed on the company's Web site, offering positions with salaries exceeding the engineer's current level as well as other attractive perquisites. Other recruiters search Internet job-placement services for newly posted resumes while others withdraw business cards from restaurant free-lunch draws in order to find possible job candidates.[1]

A business facing recruitment problems must plan well in advance to obtain necessary employees. It may have to develop special training and apprenticeship programs, as well as provide various incentives to attract and keep employees.

Human resource or **personnel planning** helps to ensure that the organization has neither a shortage nor a surplus of employees. Having too many employees can be a serious financial drain on a company, and union agreements or government regulations may make it difficult to trim employees from the payroll when economic conditions require it.

As with all planning processes, human resource planning is not a one-time exercise. As long-range corporate objectives change or are adjusted on the basis of short-range results, long-range personnel plans must also be revised.

Sidenote: **Human resource** or **personnel planning** helps to ensure that the organization has neither a shortage nor a surplus of employees.

The Human Resource Planning Process

1. *Determining future personnel needs.* Future needs will be based on the organization's objectives, taking into account plans to expand or reduce operations. The nature and number of new positions required should become evident during this first step.

2. *Evaluating current personnel resources.* The personnel manager evaluates the skills and productivity of current employees to determine the organization's human resources. The turnover rate, the ages of employees and the potential impact on the company of any impending retirements are also considered.

3. *Forecasting.* Having determined both future company objectives and current human resources, the personnel manager can estimate how much current employees can contribute to future plans, and the number of new employees and skills that will be required.

4. *Establishing a personnel strategy.* The information acquired in the forecast can be used to establish specific programs for recruiting and training new employees and for retraining present employees to meet future objectives.

Job Analysis, Job Specification and Job Description

Before an individual is hired for a new position, a **job analysis** is made. Generally, a job analysis is conducted by an analyst with a questionnaire who interviews employees and supervisors about the nature of the job and the work to be performed.

Sidenote: **Job analysis**—performed to determine the nature of the job and the work to be performed.

The information gained from a job analysis serves many purposes:

1. It is used to tailor training programs to the qualifications required to perform the job.

2. It allows interviewers to better assess the fit between a potential candidate and the job.

3. It helps interviewers choose the appropriate tests with which to gather objective information from applicants.

4. It helps to ensure that performance evaluation measures are based on job-related criteria.

5. It is often a first step in determining the worth of a job for pay purposes.

6. It can help a company comply with, and defend against, actions brought under human-rights legislation.

7. It provides clear and detailed information for career planning.

8. It provides information that can be used to establish safe job procedures.

9. Job analysis information is used in job design to develop and modify the basic requirements, duties and tasks of a specific job.

From the job analysis the personnel manager develops a job description and a job specification. The job description and specification may be combined in one document, but both are invaluable for hiring. Figure 10.2 shows the relationship between job analysis, job description and job specification, and outlines what each contains.

The data collected through a job analysis are used to develop a **job description**. The job description, exemplified in Figure 10.3A, outlines the job and lists the employee's duties and responsibilities as well as the machines and tools used. A duty-related job description simply describes the position and lists the typical duties that must be performed. However, these kinds of job descriptions are generally vague, provide few clues as to working conditions and do not set standards for minimally acceptable employee performance. They thus provide managers with little useful information for recruitment, orientation, MBO goal-setting or performance evaluations. Employees also find these job descriptions of little help for orientation or performance improvement. Duties are only briefly described, and employees must wait until they are actually on the job to learn about working conditions and standards. The failure to provide a clear performance expectation from the beginning may cause unrest between organizations and their employees.

A more effective approach is known as **results-oriented job descriptions (ROD)**, which expresses job duties in relation to the results desired. An ROD should contain the following:

> **Job description**—outlines the job and lists the employee's duties and responsibilities as well as the machines and tools used.

> **Results-oriented job description**—expresses job duties in relation to the results desired.

FIGURE 10.2

Job analysis leads to job description and job specification

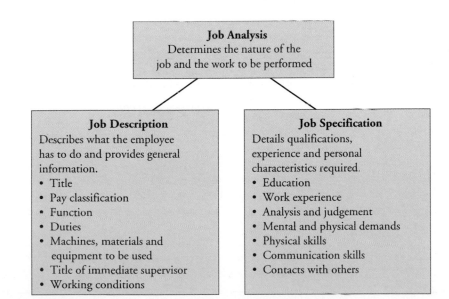

1. *Tasks.* What behaviour, duties or functions are important to the job?

2. *Conditions.* How often is a particular task done? What conditions make the task easy or hard to complete? What written or supervisory instructions are available to aid the employee in performing a task?

3. *Standards.* What objectives and performance expectations are attached to each task? Standards of quantity, quality and timeliness should be clearly related to organizational objectives.

4. *SKAs.* What skills, knowledge and abilities are required to perform each task at the minimally acceptable level?

5. *Qualifications.* What education and/or experience (length, level and type) are needed to ensure that employees will have the SKAs required for optimum performance?

Job specification—details the special qualifications (education, experience and personality) required to perform the job satisfactorily.

The personnel manager will also develop a **job specification** outlining the special qualifications, education, previous work experience and training needed to perform the job satisfactorily (see Figure 10.3B). The job description and job specification may be combined in one document, but both are invaluable for hiring. The job description in particular offers guidelines for recruitment and selection by identifying requirements and specifying the qualifying level for each.

Acquiring and Training Human Resources

Consider this scenario. You have just finished reading your secretary's letter of resignation. Surprised and dismayed, you urge this indispensable employee to reconsider, even offer an increase in salary, but to no avail. Eventually, you resign yourself to the fact that you will simply have to find and train someone else. After all, there must be many qualified secretaries looking for a job.

How Do RODs Affect Organizations?

Advantages of RODs
Results-oriented job descriptions focus on performance standards, the conditions that differentiate jobs and the linkages between standards, SKAs and qualifications. In so doing, they resolve many of the problems associated with traditional job descriptions.

- They give the program planner a means of relating personnel inputs to organizational outputs.
- They give managers a means of orienting new employees to performance expectations, setting MBO goals and evaluating employee performance objectively.
- They give employees a clearer idea of organizational performance improvement expectations

and of the minimum qualifications for promotion and reassignment.

- They increase the impact of personnel managers on organization and employee productivity, rather than merely on position management and control.

Disadvantages of RODs
While they are useful for these purposes, RODs appear to have some serious disadvantages: (1) changes in conditions and standards require constant rewriting of RODs; (2) each position requires a different ROD; (3) some positions do not have measurable performance standards; and (4) RODs cannot be used to classify jobs for human resources planning purposes or to evaluate them for pay comparability purposes.

SOURCE: Donald E. Klinger, "When the traditional job description is not enough," *Personnel Journal* (April 1979). Reprinted by permission.

FIGURE 10.3A

Job description

Job Description

Job Title	Number
BUYER	B-8

Department	Division	Date Classified
Purchasing & Facilities Services	Business Services	1996 03 18

Title of Immediate Supervisor

Director of Purchasing & Facilities Services

Position Supervised

Provides direction to and oversees the work of Shipper/Receiver and Purchasing Clerk

Purpose

Under the general direction of the Director of Purchasing and Facilities Services, ensures that the material, supply and equipment requirements are adequately met through the application of established purchasing policies and procedures.

Duties and Responsibilities

— Communicates with personnel in other departments as required to determine the nature, quality and quantities of a wide variety of items to be purchased.

— Prepares and processes purchase requisitions for goods to be purchased.

— Issues purchase orders for stationery, supplies, books, equipment, and for some capital expenditures.

— Investigates and researches products and sources of supply.

— Prepares tender calls, reviews quotations and makes recommendations regarding goods to be purchased.

— Resolves any discrepancies that may occur on packing slips and invoices.

— Corresponds with suppliers, dealers, manufacturers and others as required on any matter related to the supply, shipment, status or condition of any commodity.

— Reconciles outstanding purchase commitments records, using EDP equipment.

— Sets up payment schedules of monthly leases and equipment contracts and forwards necessary documentation to Accounting.

— Maintains contact with customs brokers and supplies necessary documentation to ensure that goods can be cleared through customs.

— Maintains equipment inventory records for all capital goods purchased.

— Organizes and directs annual capital inventory count, using EDP equipment.

— Maintains contact with tax officials, interprets and applies regulations as they apply to the tax status of the company; reviews and applies for payback to taxes.

FIGURE 10.3B

Job specification

Job Title: Buyer			Page 2

Rating

Dgr.	Pts.	Factor	
3	75	Problem Solving	Incumbent is required to evaluate supplies, material quality and prices to ensure the best materials are purchased at the lowest possible cost. Must also have the ability to judge whether materials of lower quality can be substituted if there is a substantial savings cost. For complex materials, this substitution must be done in consultation with various technical departments.
			Considerable responsibility for loss from incomplete shipments, poor-quality products, out-of-stock conditions because of late shipments from suppliers.
			Loss can also occur from incomplete knowledge of products and prices.
			Incumbent provides direction to and oversees the work of two junior employees.
3	60	Qualifications	Education/Training: High School Graduation, supplemented by relevant course(s) in purchasing. Some data processing skills required.
			Experience: Minimum three years' related purchasing experience, preferably in institutional buying.
1	15	Effort	Considerable mental demand to evaluate supply orders and compare supplier price quotations.
1	10	Contacts	Incumbent must have the ability to communicate with suppliers and various company executives. Must seek out new sources of supply, and constantly evaluate materials and pricese
1	5	Working Conditions	Normal office conditions; no hazards or probable injury.

Score Range: 155–185   Grade: C

Rating	P	Q	E	C	W	Total
Degree	3	3	1	1	1	—
Points	75	60	15	10	5	165

Approved: _____   _____   _____

Department Head   Divisional Manager   Industrial Relations Mgr.

Since your firm has no personnel department, you will have to place the job ad in the various newspapers, review the applications as they come in and interview the most promising candidates yourself before making the final choice. While this process will add extra work to your already busy schedule, you are not overly concerned, because you do not expect many problems. So you write the ad next morning and have it placed in the local newspaper; as a precaution, you also contact the Human Resources Development Canada (HRDC) office.

A few days later, the applications start to come in. You arrange to spend an evening going through them to choose the most promising applicants. You soon realize that few have the qualifications specified, and at the end of the evening you are left with only a few barely qualified candidates. You begin to think that you may not find anyone suitable this time and that the entire process may have to be repeated. Even if you do find someone, there is no guarantee that the person chosen will be good at the job, or will stay for any length of time.

Finding qualified people who are prepared to stay with a firm is a difficult task for any company, large or small, with or without a personnel department and trained personnel specialists. We now examine some of the methods used to recruit and select employees in more detail.

Recruiting Job Candidates

Larger organizations with a human resource department can expect to receive a considerable number of applications for jobs. However, when people are needed to fill specific positions, an active search is usually required to attract qualified employees. This is known as **recruiting**, which is the process of informing, searching for and attracting applicants with the necessary abilities, attitudes and motivation, in order to offset shortages identified in human resource planning.

> **Recruiting** is the process of informing, searching for and attracting applicants with the necessary abilities, attitudes and motivation to offset shortages identified in human resource planning.

Recruiting from Within the Organization

Before actively searching outside the organization, the firm often first considers its own employees. There are many advantages to having people currently working in the business fill positions of responsibility and higher pay. The appointments often raise morale and reduce employee turnover. Training costs are also reduced because employees are already knowledgeable about the firm and its policies. Larger organizations often use existing employees to fill higher-level positions, which is the goal of career development and training programs. However, an organization may be a relatively limited source of new employees and promotions may create additional work because lower-level positions become vacant. But even if present employees are unsuitable for the new position, they may know other qualified people who would be interested in working for the firm.

Recruiting from Outside the Organization

If an experienced individual is needed to fill a vacant position, recruiting from the outside may be required. The most common method of recruiting employees outside the organization is through *media advertising*. Local newspapers reach a large number of people, and advertising in them increases the firm's chances of finding qualified candidates. Other recruiting methods include radio and television advertising, job fairs and summer internships. These methods usually attract a large number of unqualified candidates, who may, however, be useful in specific instances.

More than 800 HRDC offices operated by the federal government attempt to match workers and employers as well as offer advice on labour market trends and conditions. However, these centres generally serve to place unskilled labourers, technicians, clerical sales and service workers, and lower-level supervisory positions.

Private placement agencies specialize in certain types of applicants, from computer specialists to executives and accountants. These agencies have been well received by industry and are often able to meet the employer's requirements quickly because they have a list of potential candidates already screened and classified according to their skills and qualifications. Private agencies send the employer only those candidates with the specific qualifications requested. One disadvantage of private employment agencies is that employers often pay a high fee for the service, although occasionally the employee pays the fee.

For unionized firms, the main source of skilled workers is the *local union head-quarters*. However, the company may have a limited choice of employees because the candidates with priority for the job, and who are highest on the union seniority list, may lack the specific skills required. Nevertheless, except under a closed-shop situation, the employer may hire whom he or she pleases, whether or not the candidate belongs to the union.

Schools, colleges and universities are also major sources of employees. Employers first choose the schools at which to recruit. This often depends on the type of positions to be filled. Professionals such as engineers and accountants may be recruited nationally, while sales personnel may be recruited only on a regional basis. Employers then visit the chosen campuses to interview selected students. Those candidates who survive the campus interview may then be invited to visit the organization to be evaluated further by the department where the vacancy exists.

Firms may also recruit employees from other organizations or businesses. Enticing skilled personnel away from other firms is known as *pirating*. Firms in "Silicon Valley" (located outside San Francisco) that develop microchips and other computer products are legendary for using this tactic. Technicians and scientists often leave one firm in the evening, and the next morning start at another firm that may be situated just across the street. These people are enticed away from their employer by higher salaries, better working conditions and perquisites. Thus, qualified candidates may be easily obtained by pirating at a relatively low recruitment cost, but the possibility naturally remains that another company will entice them away again by offering greater rewards or opportunities. Thus, pirating is not always advantageous.

Recruiting online, unlike most traditional forms of recruitment, can attract not only active job seekers but also skilled personnel employed elsewhere. Internet surfers often browse Web sites for casual interest and are not necessarily seeking to change employers. If companies wish to attract these people, they must "sell" the advantages of working for their organization.[2] PricewaterhouseCoopers offers the following suggestions for recruiters in the hiring process:

1. ***Web-site listings of all open positions.*** An interesting interactive Web site with links to a variety of recruitment information is critical. Information on all aspects of the company must be available to entice potential candidates; not only specific details concerning the job requirements and duties, but also a discussion of the advantages of working for the organization.

2. ***Use of E-mail.*** Resumes can be received, reviewed and forwarded at amazing speed.

3. *Alliances with external sites.* Job listings can be posted with online job banks to increase exposure.

By using 21st-century technology in recruiting, employers can meet the challenges of a fast-paced, ever-changing job market more efficiently and effectively.[3]

Selecting the New Employee

Selection involves deciding who from the pool of applicants would perform the job best. When selecting a new employee, it is essential to match an individual's skills with the tasks to be performed. As discussed earlier, the job analysis identifies the duties and responsibilities of a position and the skills required to perform them well. The job specification describes the person best suited for the job in terms of skills, education and previous experience. Unless some attempt is made to match the person with the job, problems may develop. Individuals who are too highly qualified, for example, may become bored with the job and leave soon after being hired. Those candidates who lack the necessary skills and education may be unable to perform the job adequately, and the firm may be forced to let them go. In either case, the costly and time-consuming process of recruitment and selection must then be repeated.

Selection involves choosing from the pool of applicants those expected to be the best job performers.

Human-Rights Legislation and Employment Discrimination

Personnel managers must ensure that any rejection of candidates is based on lack of qualifications rather than on any discrimination, which could result in charges and a hearing before the Human Rights Commission. According to the **Canadian Human Rights Act** (1977), an individual cannot be discriminated against because of race, national or ethnic origin, colour, religion, age, sex, marital status, conviction for an offence that has been pardoned or physical handicaps. According to the legislation, every individual should have equal access to employment opportunities and fair treatment in the workplace. The Human Rights Commission was established in 1977 to oversee employment practices for employees in the federal government, Crown corporations and all business firms that operate in more than one province. This would include banks, Air Canada and private and public corporations that conduct business across Canada. Those employees not covered under the federal legislation are covered under the various provincial human-rights acts.

Canadian Human Rights Act— designed to ensure that every individual should have equal access to employment opportunities and fair treatment in the workplace

Employment Discrimination

Adverse Intent vs. Adverse Effect If an employer refused to promote women to management positions because he or she believed that women are unable to be good managers, a complaint of discrimination may be brought against the employer based on adverse intent. However, intentional discrimination may be difficult to prove because it is easily hidden or denied. More often, employers may be unaware of the adverse effect their employment policies have on certain groups of people. A decision not to install elevators in a building because of high costs may prevent individuals with disabilities from working in this company. Certain dress regulations may prevent people from gaining employment because of their religious affiliation. Today, adverse effect is the major principle on which discrimination is decided.

Bona-Fide Occupational Qualification (BFOQ) Any employment practice established must apply to the job or occupational requirements, not to the

Canadian Human Rights Commission

www.chrc-ccdp.ca

characteristics of a certain group of individuals. For example, certain work gear, such as hard hats in construction areas, may be considered a BFOQ because of job safety. This rule is therefore not considered to be directed at any particular group.

Reasonable Accommodation An employer must be prepared to alter the conditions of work to meet the special needs of otherwise qualified people. This concept applies particularly to persons with disabilities who may require special layouts of the work area, special safety devices, wider aisles and wheelchair ramps. It may also mean that the job may have to be altered in some ways so that a person who has a disability can perform it.

Sexual and Other Harassment Discrimination on the basis of harassment is a major employment problem. Although discrimination from harassment may pertain to race, religion, age or disability, most cases are sexually based. The Canadian Human Rights Commission includes under harassment any verbal abuse or threats; unwelcome invitations or requests; unwelcome statements about a person's body, attire, age, race and the like; leering or related gestures; unnecessary physical contact; and physical assault.

Mandatory Retirement Mandatory retirement has been abolished in Quebec, Manitoba and within the federal government. There are two views of mandatory retirement: it can be looked at as a method of opening positions to hire and promote younger people, or it can be viewed as a waste of talent because it excludes people from the workforce based on an arbitrary age rather than on the ability to perform a particular job. Some courts have stated that the mandatory retirement issue should be resolved through legislation rather than through judicial interpretation of human-rights statutes that do not specifically mention this issue.

Employer Actions

Canadian employers are examining their recruitment and hiring practices. Some companies openly state that they are equal-opportunity employers, and that they are replacing the traditional résumé with employment and education histories. Many companies are also looking at their job descriptions to ensure they do not contain discriminatory requirements. In the recruitment and selection process, managers must ensure that candidates are screened out only for job-related reasons. Interviews should be highly structured and only questions of direct relevance to the job should be asked. Special training and entry requirements have to be shown as necessary. Performance evaluations and compensation plans must reward performance and not other characteristics that may preclude certain individuals.

Some large companies have established programs through which employees can voice complaints and concerns when normal channels to management are not adequate. For example, the Royal Bank's current initiatives include "making staff aware of legislative requirements; recruitment and outreach activities; retention of designated group members through the forming of support groups; and providing reasonable accommodation."[4]

Most companies publicize their equal employment opportunity practices. However, companies often do not include affirmative-action programs that would give preference to disadvantaged and minority groups. The Canadian Human Rights Act encourages affirmative-action programs as a means of improving opportunities for groups that have been discriminated against in the past.

The Selection Process

The process for selecting new employees varies among organizations, but it usually includes a number of procedures for gathering information about individuals. How these procedures are used depends on the selection process chosen.

There are two basic methods used to select applicants. With the **multiple hurdles method**, each selection procedure serves as a screen. A person must successfully pass this screen before proceeding to the next step of the procedure. This method is useful for jobs where a minimum level of competence is required and where a strength in one area is not considered to offset a weakness in another area. A person who cannot pass a particular screen will be rejected. For example, the employment manager will look for basic qualifications in education and experience on the applications form. Unless these qualifications are present, the person will be disqualified from further consideration.

Under the **compensatory method**, a person's strength in one area may be used to offset shortcomings in another area. Although basic qualifications are still considered, a higher level of education may be used to offset less job experience. Furthermore, a person is not rejected or hired until he or she has completed all of the selection procedures. Managers base their final decision about which candidate(s) to hire on all the information gathered about the applicants.

A third method is a combination of the above two methods. Certain basic qualifications are required for successful job performance. Those candidates that lack such qualifications are rejected. Beyond these minimums, individual qualifications and specific talents in some areas may be used to compensate for lack of talents in others. It is important to remember that any hurdles established must comply with human-rights regulations.

Selection Procedures

Most employers use the following procedures:

Application Almost all employers use an application form. It provides the company with background information including the applicant's education, skills and experience. Because of anti-discrimination legislation, there are no longer requirements

Multiple hurdles method—a person must successfully pass each screen before proceeding to the next step of the procedure.

Compensatory method—a person's strength in one area may be used to offset shortcomings in another area.

The Defensive Approach to Hiring

Firing an employee is always difficult, but in today's climate, a wrongful dismissal suit can be both costly and time consuming, not to mention the psychological stress borne by both the employer and the employee. Being more careful in their hiring and in their recruitment can protect employers from the problems inherent in firing an employee down the road. Increasingly, lower-level employees are required to sign formal employment contracts that spell out salary, job responsibilities, and even termination terms. In addition, employers are spending more time defining job descriptions, and involving more people in the hiring process and decision making. Also increasingly more employers are hiring people as contract workers for a specified period of time.

Increasingly, employers are setting out formal company policies and codes of conduct and communicating them to their employees. Clearly identifying the offences for which firing might occur are more likely to be upheld by the courts.

Employers are also encouraged to create a more extensive paper trail when documenting an employee's performance problems over a period of time. For example, if a person is being fired for absenteeism or incompetence, there should be a policy in place and the employee should have been warned that future action will be taken. And all discussions with the employee relating to their conduct on the job must be documented. Nevertheless, many employers are still lax in their annual reviews of employees. Often an employee is set to be fired for incompetence or a bad attitude, yet their employee files only show yearly salary increases.[5]

for listing a person's age, sex, religious affiliation, colour, race or nationality. An application form is usually the first step for a walk-in applicant. A person answering a job advertisement may be required to complete an application form and mail it to the company, or be required to submit a letter of application. Individuals applying for a management position usually must send in a detailed résumé that employers use to screen out unsuitable applicants. Sometimes this step is followed by a pre-screening interview to further reduce the number of candidates to a manageable level by selecting only those who are most suitable for the job. Regardless of how an applicant initially contacts an employer, at some point an application form is usually required to ensure that the potential employer has consistent information about all the applicants.

Employment Interview   Most personnel managers consider the employment interview to be the most important step in the selection procedure, and as a result it is used by almost all organizations. Yet according to studies conducted over 20 years, the interview is rarely a valid predictor of job success.[6] Before a person is chosen for a job, he or she may be required to participate in a number of interviews, including a preliminary and final-selection interview. As in other selection procedures, discrimination is a key concern in the interview. Only questions that refer to the applicant's ability to perform the job should be asked.

Many types of interviews may be used to gather information about an applicant. A skilled interviewer can ask questions that will reveal a candidate's aptitudes and abilities, including speaking ability and personal goals. This will provide the interviewer with an indication of how each individual might fit into the job and the organization.

A preliminary interview is used to get a general idea of the applicant's suitability for the job and for the organization. The applicant has an opportunity to ask questions about the job and the firm, and there is an opportunity to discuss job skills, education and experience as well as career plans. The final interview is usually the last stage in the selection process. By this time, considerable information is available about each candidate, including the results of any employment and medical tests and reference checks. Often the selection of individuals for public or non-profit institutions is done by a committee. In this instance, the final interview may include all of the people who have been involved in the selection procedure to date. Although the final selection decision may be a joint decision, in most cases the final selection is left to the manager to whom the individual will be reporting directly.

Testing   One of the selection procedures usually involves testing. Intelligence, personality, aptitude and skills tests are all commonly used to assess the candidates and their skills. A controversial test is the polygraph, which has been used lately in checking data during personnel selection. The polygraph tests a person's physiological reaction to stress, which may be caused by lying. However, there is no evidence that this test is either reliable or valid. Another controversial test, handwriting analysis—graphology—is used to study an individual's personality. According to studies, graphology does indicate some things about a person's personality, but it is not a predictor of job success. While general medical tests were commonplace at one time, most medical tests today are used for screening for drug abuse. If more reliable tests are ever developed, applicants in the future might also be screened for the AIDS virus. Future screening might also be used to screen out individuals who because of their genetic makeup are susceptible to certain types of occupational diseases that might be related to particular jobs.

Reference Checks   Once testing has further narrowed the field of applicants, reference checks are usually conducted, in which previous employers are questioned about the candidate's job performance. However, information obtained from previous employers is often questionable because they are often reluctant to state why an employee was let go or to discuss the employee's specific conduct in his or her previous position.

It is important to remember that the selection process as discussed above and as shown in Figure 10.4 may vary among organizations; additional steps may be included depending on the type of position to be filled. For example, a candidate for a high-level management position may be asked to attend three or more interviews before the final selection is made.

Employee Orientation

Once applicants have been chosen for the job, they must be introduced to the organization as a whole, to their new tasks, superiors and workgroups and to the immediate work environment. This is called **orientation**. A comprehensive orientation program would cover the following: an overview of the company, key policies and

Orientation occurs when a person chosen for a job is introduced to the organization as a whole, to his or her new tasks, to superiors and workgroups and to the immediate work environment.

FIGURE 10.4

The selection process

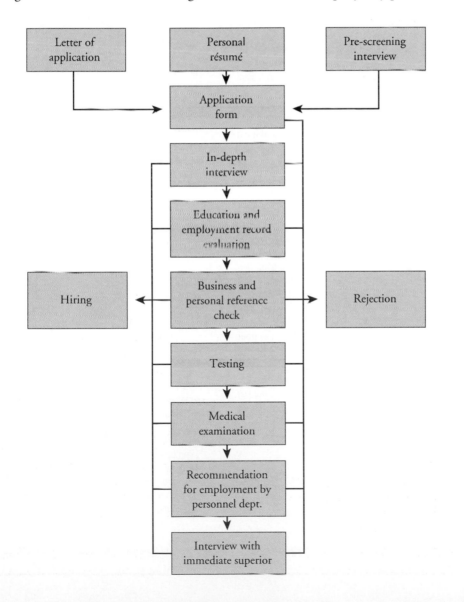

Do's and Don'ts at the Job Interview

Do's

- Be punctual. The first five minutes are critical. No matter how legitimate your excuse, a busy interviewer will not feel charitable if kept waiting.

- Pay careful attention to your appearance. Get your clothes pressed and your shoes shined; get a haircut. Don't drink beforehand. Go early, find the washroom, and check yourself in a mirror.

- Dress conservatively. If in doubt, pick up a copy of John T. Molloy's *Dress for Success* or *The Woman's Dress for Success Book*, the sartorial bibles of upwardly mobile executives. Don't show up in a T-shirt and Bermuda shorts, as one senior executive did in Miami; he took the advice to "dress comfortably" too literally. No matter how hot the weather, wear a suit (for women, Molloy suggests a skirted suit). And make sure it's appropriate to your role. One highly qualified applicant for a financial controller's job was turned down because he wore a dark shirt with a light-coloured suit and tie. The prospective employer thought he looked like Al Capone.

- Know your strengths and be sure to communicate them. Don't rely on the interviewer to draw this information out; he or she may not have good interviewing skills.

- Be enthusiastic. Tell the employer you want the position. One executive was turned down because he just didn't seem interested. He was, but he hadn't let it show. He was crushed when he didn't get the job.

- Answer all questions in a business-like manner. Never volunteer negative information about yourself, but never lie when asked. It's a good idea to think of the worst possible questions you can be asked, and have your answers—*positive* ones—ready. And be prepared when the interviewer asks you what questions you have. If you've done your research, you won't appear uninformed or uninterested in the company.

- At the end of the meeting, tell the interviewer that you can handle the job and that it interests you. Confirm it in a brief thank-you letter. If the job doesn't interest you but the company does, send a note as well.

Don'ts

- Don't talk too much. That may seem obvious, but stress plays peculiar games with perfectly normal people. One applicant for a vice-president's job with a major multinational talked non-stop for an hour and a quarter answering a single question.

- Watch your language. Vulgarity and colloquialisms show a lack of professionalism in communicating.

- Don't ignore the person who takes you into the interview. Many senior people ask their secretary or receptionist what they thought of the applicant.

- Don't raise the question of money. Many applicants price themselves out of the market. Wait until you get the job offer, and negotiate from strength. If you're asked how much you want, give a range rather than an absolute figure.

- Don't lose interest if the job isn't what it appeared to be. If the company is sufficiently impressed with you, it may change the position to suit you, or it may make something else available later.

- Don't talk about what the company can do for you; talk about what you can do for the company. One Toronto tax manager was more interested in the benefits than the job. He wanted a large salary, stock options, a company car, a month's vacation and a five-year employment contract. Needless to say, he not only didn't get the perks, he didn't even get considered for the job.

- Don't criticize your previous employers. No matter how sour the grapes, don't make the interview an exercise in self-justification. The new employer will only think you'll badmouth him [or her] someday. And don't reveal confidential information about previous employers, such as sales trends, financial situation or office immoralities. There's no need to give specific information, even if you're selling yourself. You can say, "I was responsible for a $2-million turnaround," without revealing how much your former company was earning.

- Finally, if you're applying through an executive search firm, remember that it's paid to be safe. You'll have to convince [it] that you're indisputably what they want. And if you're seeing the person who may someday be your boss, remember that although he [she] may be a superb executive, he [she] may be a lousy interviewer. He [she] might even be more nervous than you are. If that's the case, take a few minutes to relax him [her] before launching into an account of your exploits or a barrage of questions. Being interviewed can be as much an art as interviewing.

SOURCE: Mike MacBeth, "The job interview: how not to blow it," *Canadian Business Magazine* (November 1979).

procedures, compensation, fringe benefits, safety and accident prevention, employee and union relations, physical facilities and economic factors affecting the company that have to do with employees.

A major function is to enter the employee's name on all company records and establish his or her right to benefits such as employment insurance, the Canada Pension Plan, company pensions, special bonus and profit sharing plans and, of course, the payroll.

Another major function is to introduce the new employee to the organization. Many large firms conduct a formal orientation program. While some last only a few hours, longer programs may offer an introduction to the firm's operating philosophy, internal procedures, compensation and fringe benefit programs and methods of promotion. In addition, new employees may be required to become familiar with company procedures and policies outside of their immediate area of concern in order to acquire a better understanding of how the company operates as a whole. Orientation also helps the new employee to establish relationships with co-workers, subordinates and superiors, and helps to reduce the individual's anxiety.

Employee Training and Development

With the increasing pressure of international competition, it is critically important that the workforce become more skilled and productive. At the same time, there is widespread concern that training in Canada is deficient. Fortunately, this concern on the part of business, labour and government resulted in the establishment of the Canadian Labour Force Development Board. This board is charged with overseeing national worker skills development and retraining programs. A proposed national training survey will assess training now provided in the private sector and will identify opportunities for, and barriers to, training.

Despite the knowledge that employees who have been well trained are generally more productive and satisfied because they know how to perform their jobs effectively, many firms invest little in training. Studies by the Canadian Labour Market and Productivity Centre have shown that 41% of all full-time employees surveyed received no training in the preceding two years, while an additional 18% received one week or less. More than half (53%) of unskilled workers received no training. Of full-time employees, 30% believe they lack the proper education, training and experience to find another job if they had to. Yet 50% of those surveyed said training is carried out most effectively in the workplace.[7]

A recent survey conducted by Interim Services Inc., a staffing and recruiting company, revealed that 62% of employees who had received mentoring, training or education were more likely to stay with their current employer.[8] However, another study by researchers Knoke and Ishio identified a gender gap in company job training. This study defined company job training as "any program of employee skill and improvement provided by private business that is planned in advance and involves workers participating in off-production instructional activity."[9] The results revealed substantial gender differences in participation in company-provided training programs. One explanation for this gender disparity relates to the industries in which each group is concentrated—in general, men were concentrated in the manufacturing, wholesale and transportation sectors, while women were in the retail sector where training is less common. Furthermore, more training is typically provided for full-time employees than part-time workers, and men average more hours per week at work than do women. Finally, employers are less willing to invest company resources in training employees whom they believe may not remain with the organization for the long term; due to marital and child-care obligations, women often fall into this category. The researchers concluded that there is a need to examine how employees' career preferences and employers' human resource policies together contribute to creating and sustaining such a gender gap.[10]

The various levels of government often institute job training programs. For example, in 1985 the federal government announced the Canadian Jobs Strategy, a $2-billion program aimed at specific unemployed groups, including the young, native peoples, women, the unskilled and the elderly. Under some of these programs, companies receive funds to take on unskilled workers and provide training. The Canadian Labour Congress (CLC) has called this a "wage-subsidy program dressed up as a training program." The CLC believes that companies should contribute money to a common fund and then receive a grant for any training conducted. The Canadian Federation of Independent Business, on the other hand, is strongly opposed to a grant-levy system. They do, however, agree that small businesses often train new workers, who are then lost to other, often larger companies.[11]

Many believe that business should take more initiative in training its employees. It would require more funds and a commitment by employers to continuously upgrade the skills of their employees beyond those strictly required for their current job. While initial training must focus on technical skills, business skills are equally important. Employees who are provided with multiple skills are better able to adjust to changing job requirements both in and out of the organization.

Employee Training

On-the-job training means that a new employee learns the job by doing it, usually under the direct supervision of an experienced employee or the department supervisor.

Job training programs are established to make new employees as productive as possible in the shortest period of time. For relatively simple jobs, **on-the-job training** may be all that is required. The new employee is placed on the job under the direct supervision of an experienced employee or the department supervisor, who provides guidance, advice and assistance as required until the trainee has gained sufficient experience to perform the job without supervision.

> Job training helps to make employees as productive as possible in the shortest period of time

In the case of trades, on-the-job training may be combined with classroom instruction in an **apprenticeship program** designed to give the inexperienced worker both practical and theoretical knowledge. These programs may range from two to four years in length, and are generally used to teach skilled trades such as carpentry, welding, electrical work and plumbing. Apprenticeship programs are often established jointly with a union to ensure that skills and training are uniform.

If on-the-job training is not possible or is too costly or dangerous, a technique known as **vestibule training** is often employed. In simple vestibule training, workers learn to perform their jobs outside the regular work process. They thus gain the necessary skills while the cost of mistakes is reduced. For example, airline pilots are trained in a simulator where they can perform the actual operations of flying an airplane, encountering realistic flight conditions and problems to test their reactions, without the dangers and risks of a real flight. Vestibule training may also be employed in conjunction with classroom training. The employee then learns the theoretical aspects of a particular operation and gains some degree of competence before performing the actual job.

> **Apprenticeship program**— designed to give the inexperienced worker both practical and theoretical knowledge.

> **Vestibule training** allows individuals to learn their jobs outside the regular work process.

Management Development

The problems involved in management training and development are different from those encountered in training employees to perform specific jobs. While it may be relatively simple for colleges and universities to establish management programs to teach the functions of management—planning, directing people, organizing and controlling performance—it is difficult to teach logical thinking and decision making, human relations skills, the ability to analyze the future and good business sense. Yet these are precisely the skills required in management positions.

The objective of **management development** is to improve the skills and advancement potential of employees and thereby enlarge their future contribution to the organization. Candidates for development fall into two groups, each of which presents different training problems. The first group consists of new management recruits who may have the necessary theoretical background, but lack practical experience. In addition to gaining actual management experience, they must learn how the company operates. The second group consists of experienced managers who have been in their positions for a number of years, but who may require development of particular management skills. They may also lack basic theoretical knowledge in new management principles and practices.

> **Management development** is an attempt to improve the skills and advancement potential of employees and thereby enlarge their future contribution to the organization.

Large companies usually operate in-house training programs. The new manager spends a few days or weeks in a variety of departments to gain an understanding of how the company operates as a whole. The trainee may then receive on-the-job training by assisting an experienced manager while continuing classroom instruction in company procedures, policies and management skills. At the end of the training period, which may last from six months to two years, the trainee should have gained sufficient practical experience to assume a regular management position when the opportunity arises.

Development of the experienced manager presents a different problem. While these individuals are usually enthusiastic about learning new theoretical concepts of management, it is not easy to change habits. It may be difficult to persuade a manager to use a new leadership approach or to take a less authoritarian stance with employees. While short seminars may alert managers to some of their managerial problems, their regular work environments will not have changed, and when they return they may find it difficult not to revert to their previous managerial styles. Nevertheless, management development programs identify problems and new concepts.

Training Supervisors— On and Off the Job

Whether or not a person has had formal education in business and management, most practical training occurs on the job. On-the-job training provides direct, practical experience, but a new supervisor may also learn faulty methods from the training. A carefully designed plan will ensure that the right information is acquired.

On the Job

On-the-job programs require extensive development and include stated objectives, experienced trainers, scheduled performance reviews and a schedule of specific experiences that the employee should acquire. The programs may involve grievance handling, training workers and reviewing employee performance.

Observation and guided practice are other key methods for learning on the job. In addition to observing other department heads and supervisors, the trainee may be given a temporary assignment as assistant supervisor during a regular manager's absence.

Off the Job

The classroom lends itself to a more structured learning process, in that information can be presented in a logical sequence. Various training devices, including visual aids, can be used to clarify difficult concepts and situations. Role-playing and business games can simulate real-life experiences and provide practice in handling such situations. Other areas covered in the classroom include leadership skills, employee motivation, management principles, and company policies and practices.

Wage and Salary Administration

Compensation administration, also known as wage and salary administration, is concerned with the establishment and implementation of sound policies and methods of employee compensation. It includes job evaluation to establish wage and salary rates; development and maintenance of wage structures, surveys, incentives, changes, supplementary payments and profit-sharing plans; and control of compensation costs.

Employees must be paid competitive wages and salaries that adequately compensate them for their skills, experience and education, or they will go elsewhere. A **compensation system** should achieve the following three objectives:

> **Compensation system**—the establishment and implementation of sound policies and methods of employee compensation.

1. It should attract qualified workers to the firm by offering wages and salaries that are at least equal to those paid by similar firms in the same industry or area.

2. It should be fair to all workers, and should take into account the difficulty of the job as well as the education, special qualifications and experience required to perform it.

3. It should encourage production by rewarding employees' productivity through wage incentives, stock options and profit-sharing plans.

Establishing Wages and Salaries

Wages and salaries are based on the following seven factors:

1. *Federal and provincial laws.* Almost all employees are covered by minimum-wage laws established by either the federal or provincial governments. There are also laws that prohibit discrimination in pay based on sex, age, race and so on.

2. *Ability to pay.* The financial health of the firm may also determine the wages paid. Profitable firms tend to pay higher wages than firms that make only marginal profits.

3. *Prevailing wages.* Wages are often based on rates other firms are paying for the same class of work in the same labour market or industry. This prevailing wage rate may rise or fall as supply and demand for particular skills fluctuates.

4. *Job requirements.* Pay rates for jobs are based on the difficulty of the job, the amount of skill and effort required and the responsibilities involved in relation to other jobs in the organization.

5. *Cost of living.* Wages tend to rise as the cost of living rises so that purchasing power remains constant. Many union agreements now contain a cost-of-living adjustment clause specifying that wage rates rise according to the consumer price index.

6. *Productivity.* Increased productivity leads to a rise in the standard of living. Increased productivity is generally measured in increased output of goods and services, which may be the result of technological improvements, greater capital investment, more efficient methods of production, better education and job skills, and more effective management. Generally, a productive firm can pay higher wages than can less productive firms.

7. *Bargaining power.* Unionized workers have the power to bargain for higher wages. Non-unionized workers do not have that power and must accept what the employer is willing to pay. During times of inflation, the wages of unionized workers are more likely to keep up with the rate of inflation than the wages of non-unionized workers.

Equal Pay for Equal Work vs. Equal Pay for Work of Equal Value

For some time, employers have had to ensure that compensation plans do not discriminate against people or groups doing similar jobs. The concept of **equal pay for equal work**— all people who perform similar jobs should be paid equally— is firmly entrenched in Canadian employment legislation. Generally, jobs are compared according to four categories: skill, effort, responsibility and working conditions. If the jobs are shown to be equal in each category, then they require equal pay.

Another concept—**pay equity** or **equal pay for work of equal value**—requires that the relative worth of two different jobs be determined, as for example a receptionist and junior accountant. Once the relationship between the jobs is established, pay scales are adjusted accordingly.

Pay equity is based on the principle that jobs that are similar in terms of skill, responsibility, effort and working conditions can be compared. Each job is evaluated according to a gender-neutral system and awarded points. If two different jobs add up to the same points then they should receive the same pay regardless of what type of job it is or what the market is willing to pay for performing that job.

The drive behind pay equity was the difference between the average earnings of men and women. In Ontario, for example, the two million women who worked outside the home earned, on average, 36% less than men.[12] Advocates of pay equity insisted that the market rates of pay for jobs traditionally performed by women were unfair. They were set at a time when men were expected to earn a family income, while women worked to supplement the family income to acquire some luxury items.

In 1988, Ontario's pay-equity law set out to return fairness to wage payment. All Ontario employers in the public and private sector with 10 or more workers have had to pay the same wages to women performing jobs judged to be equal in value to those performed by men in the same workplace. For example, a college-educated

Equal pay for equal work means that men and women in jobs with the same or similar duties receive similar levels of pay.

Pay equity or **equal pay for work of equal value** means that men and women in jobs with the same or similar value receive similar levels of pay.

Implementing Pay Equity in the Public Service

www.chrc-ccdp.ca/pe-ps/default.asp?1=e

single mother worked as second-in-command at a daycare for nearly 80 youngsters, but she earned less than the man who swept the floors. When Ontario's pay-equity law came into effect, her salary increased from $23,840 to nearly $40,000, equivalent to the pay of a senior building inspector. A large number of the female workers won raises averaging $4000 a year.

In both the private and the public sector, a firm that employed 10 or more workers had to do the complicated task of comparing men's and women's jobs and awarding pay raises where necessary. If a company had fewer than 100 employees, it had to decide how to achieve pay equity. For organizations with more than 100 employees, pay equity had to be achieved in consultation with the unions.

Needless to say, Ontario business groups, and even some pay-equity advocates, complained that comparing jobs was far too complex for many employees and many managers in smaller firms. Neither did the information package, nearly 10 centimetres thick and published by Ontario's Pay Equity Commission, employers.

In many unionized companies, disputes between employers and unions erupted over every step. A major stumbling-block was deciding whether a job was a "female" job. According to the Commission the process was easy to learn, but many companies employed consultants or lawyers. Often they were hired to determine how to minimize or avoid big payouts to women. Any disputes had to go to the pay-equity tribunal, which often took two years to resolve cases. Often businesses spent more to apply or resist the law than they did in payouts.

The pay-equity law in Ontario has created a host of onerous new rules for businesses, but has not significantly closed the gap between men's and women's salaries, according to Judith Andrew of the Canadian Federation of Independent Business in Toronto. She says that something is wrong when it costs a business more in consulting fees than in pay adjustments. Jean Read, former director of Ontario's arbitration office, who was assigned by the government to study the law, advised the government in 1996 to replace the pay-equity scheme with a simpler system in which women could complain if they felt they were underpaid.

The Ontario pay-equity model was a complicated and time-consuming task, and no other province has copied it. But pay equity in some form has been in force in Quebec since 1975 and in the federal public service since 1978 and is included in the 1977 Canadian Human Rights Act. Pay-equity legislation was also introduced in Manitoba, in 1985, for public-sector organizations, and in 1991 in British Columbia.

On May 15, 1995, the Quebec government tabled Bill 35, which sought to eliminate disparities in pay between employees in predominantly "female" jobs and those in predominantly "male" jobs who perform work of equal value. However, the province decided to postpone adoption of the bill until late 1997.[13]

On the federal level, in 1984 a group of clerical and regulatory workers registered a pay-equity complaint with the Human Rights Commission, a complaint that took 15 years to resolve and resulted in a possible $5 billion pay-equity settlement by the federal government. Approximately 200 000 federal civil servants (mostly women) were awarded an average of nearly $2000 for each year of government service. The latest ruling on the complaint, a 92-page document, was tabled in October 1999, seemingly ending the protracted battle.

Methods of Compensation

There are three main methods of compensating people for their work. Some receive a monthly salary, while others are paid for the specific number of hours they have

Without the resources to hire personnel specialists, the owner-manager of a small business may find it difficult to establish wages and salaries for employees and to compensate them for their performance. The three primary factors to keep in mind when setting or revising wages and salaries are federal and provincial legislation regarding minimum pay, vacation pay and termination pay; the firm's ability to pay; and prevailing wages in the industry.

Wage Legislation

Provincial and federal legislation specifies minimum wages, and vacation and termination pay rates for all employees. Labour Canada periodically publishes minimum pay rates for all provinces and territories, and notes any changes.

Ability to Pay

The financial health of the firm is an important consideration in setting pay scales. A profitable company can pay relatively high wages and thereby attract good employees. A firm with financial problems may lose employees to competitors who can provide better pay and benefits.

Prevailing Wages

Most firms pay their employees according to prevailing wages and salaries in the community and/or industry. Wage rates can be determined by conducting a wage survey. The local board of trade, provincial Department of Industry and other local employers can usually supply average wage rates and ranges for similar jobs. The survey must be based on job descriptions and specifications, so that accurate comparisons can be made.

Once wage rates for employees have been established, an ongoing system of performance appraisal must be set up. Appraisals should be performed once a year and should include a written review. The larger the firm, the more formalized the appraisal process. The main concern is the objectivity of the owner or manager doing the performance appraisal. An employee must believe that the appraisal is objective if there is to be a meaningful discussion about what the employee is doing well, where improvement is required and how it can be accomplished. Once the performance appraisal is complete, a wage revision can be implemented.

Setting Wage Rates— A Problem for Small Business

---

worked, or for actual production—for the number of units produced or the amount sold. Each method has its advantages and disadvantages, but the one chosen must be appropriate to the situation.

Wages

Wages—the most common method of compensation—are payment for the number of hours worked. Sometimes hourly workers can increase their earnings by working overtime—working more hours per day or week than what provincial legislation specifies as a normal workday. Overtime usually means that a person gets paid either time-and-a-half or twice the normal hourly rate.

Wages are payment for the number of hours worked.

Piecework and Incentive Pay

A straight hourly wage does not provide incentives to produce more than the basic minimum for an average workday. To entice employees to work faster and therefore earn more money, some companies offer a direct incentive by paying more when more items are produced. This is called a **piecework incentive**. A sewing machine operator, for example, may receive a basic hourly wage rate of $7.50 per hour, based on the fact that a person can sew on average five pairs of jeans in that time. Thus, each unit is worth $1.50. If the output is greater, then the employee earns more money, but in any case the person earns no less than the standard rate of $7.50 per hour.

Piecework incentive—a payment in addition to regular wages or salary that is intended to encourage higher performance.

Salary

The other major method of payment is **salary**—a fixed sum paid weekly, biweekly or monthly. This system is used primarily in jobs where output cannot be easily measured. Salaried employees usually do not receive overtime pay, but they are also

Salary—a fixed sum paid weekly, biweekly or monthly.

seldom penalized for absences due to illness or other reasons. Salaried employees may also have some flexibility in their work hours; most are paid their full salary for statutory holidays and exceptional occasions when the firm may be closed due to a strike or major equipment breakdown.

Bonus Plans

Bonus—a sum paid to employees in addition to their regular wages or salaries.

To provide extra incentive for both hourly and salaried employees, many companies have instituted bonus plans. A **bonus**—a sum paid to employees in addition to their regular wages or salaries—may be based on seniority, production or various other factors. Bonus plans can be an effective incentive, provided employees believe their effort will have some effect on the size of the bonus. However, if the bonus is based on arbitrary criteria (e.g., how employees fit in with the organization), it may provide little incentive, since an increase in actual productivity will not necessarily increase the bonus.

The most common bonuses are productivity sharing, commissions, profit sharing and employee stock ownership plans.

Productivity sharing rewards employees on the basis of their increased productivity according to a predetermined formula.

Productivity Sharing   The most direct method of distributing a bonus is **productivity sharing**, which rewards employees on the basis of cost savings rather than on an overall profit increase according to a predetermined formula. If employees work harder and produce more, or reduce the production costs per item, then a portion of the savings is returned to them.

Commission—a percentage based on the total value of the sale that is paid to salespeople either as total compensation or as an incentive.

Commissions   A **commission** plan may operate in conjunction with a guaranteed monthly salary or it may be the sole method of compensation; sometimes salespeople are paid straight commission according to a percentage based on their total sales volume. Commissions for salespeople are similar to piecework incentive systems for production workers—the salesperson is usually required to achieve a basic dollar volume of sales, and receives a commission either for all sales made or for any sales above the basic amount.

Profit sharing means that a portion of the increase in total profit is paid to the employees, and may take the form of a direct cash payment or as shares in the company.

Profit Sharing   **Profit sharing** encourages employees to work harder in the hope that their increased productivity will result in greater profits for the company at the end of a specified period. A portion of the increase in total profit then flows directly back to the employees. Profit sharing may take the form of a direct cash payment or of shares in the company. The major problem with a profit-sharing plan is that factors over which employees have no control could interfere with achieving an increase.

The article "Profit Sharing, Productivity and More" outlines some of the benefits of establishing profit-sharing plans.

Employee Stock Ownership Plans (ESOPs)   Making employees owners in the company is a relatively new method of encouraging higher productivity and higher profits. The company usually offers its shares to employees at a discount from their market value. Employees typically do not have to pay commissions, and they can pay for their share purchases in monthly instalments. In some instances, the company may even guarantee that for a specific period any drop in share prices will be absorbed by the company. By having some ownership in the company, employees often feel as if they are working for themselves, and are motivated to perform better and need less supervision. A Toronto Stock Exchange study showed that firms with an employee stock ownership plan were 123% higher than firms without such plans; net profit was 95% higher and productivity in terms of revenue per employee was almost 25% higher.[14]

Profit Sharing, Productivity and More

Profit sharing has long been proposed as an incentive program to enhance productivity. However, the benefits seem to go far beyond this. In a study conducted in 1999, researchers examined the impact of profit sharing on grievance rates and absenteeism in an attempt to better understand the effect of profit sharing on labour management relations. Researchers examined the total number of employee grievances filed per month, total employee absences per month and monthly employment levels. The results indicated that the introduction of a profit-sharing program can lead to changes in labour management relations, as illustrated by a decline in both the grievance rate and abseeism rate. The rates continued to decline over time, which suggests that they are not simply a short-term effect. These findings, combined with the widely accepted view that improved firm performance is the ultimate goal of most profit-sharing programs, reinforce the need for companies to support such initiatives, including a strong commitment by union and management to the success of the program. Such a commitment can contribute to an organizational culture of mutual respect and fairness that is critical to both the success of the profit-sharing program and to the continuation of employee performance participation.

Share ownership also creates a better climate for relations between workers and management, and promotes the sharing of results, knowledge and problems. It also encourages loyalty to the organization and reduces employee turnover. ESOP plans are becoming commonplace in Europe, Japan and the United States.

A major problem with **employee stock ownership plans (ESOPs)** is that only a few people in a company have a direct impact on the price of the firm's stock. Lower-level managers and regular employees have no control over management decisions that affect corporate performance, or over market forces. Furthermore, in a multiple-division firm, the problems of one division may be so overwhelming that they affect the stock of the total company and thus employees in other divisions.

Another major problem is that general economic problems can affect the stock market and reduce share prices even though the company may be performing well. For example, managers and employees at Vancouver-based MacMillan Bloedel Ltd. increased their share purchases of the company's stock in August 1987, shortly before the stock market crash, through monthly payroll deductions. They paid $24 to $29 per share, but after the 1987 stock market crash their shares were worth just over $16. While stock prices generally increase in the long run, which makes ESOPs a good investment, a sudden significant drop in share values can be a demoralizing experience for many employees, particularly if they must continue to make monthly payments for devalued shares.[16]

Nevertheless, many employees benefit from stock ownership plans. Canadian Tire Corp. is just one stock ownership success story. In the years between 1944 (when shares were first offered to some employees) and 1971, this company's value increased 225 times. Even though broad-coverage profit sharing was not introduced at the parent company until 1957, an office clerk was able to retire with $324 000 after 14 years' service, while a maintenance worker pocketed $300 000.

According to the owner of an independently owned Canadian Tire dealership, small businesses have the most to gain by selling shares and sharing profits with employees. If a stock ownership plan has been set up, employees can buy shares in the business. Once the owner is ready to retire, he or she can withdraw the money by allowing employees to go to the bank and use the shares as collateral to pay him or her off. Through employee stock ownership, the perpetuation of a small busi-

Employee stock ownership plans (ESOPs) allow employees to take some ownership in the company through the purchase of shares, usually at a discount from their market value.

ness can be assured. The dealership owner nevertheless stresses that a person should not go into profit sharing unless he or she really believes in the philosophy.[17]

Although incentive plans are becoming more prevalent, they are a controversial issue in unionized firms. Many union leaders view incentive pay programs as a way of manipulating workers to do more with no guarantee of any reward. Nevertheless, union leaders can't simply reject these plans out of hand, as their members would not want to give up a potentially rewarding payback. To make incentive plans work in unionized companies, management must consult and share information with the union, and with the employees. Employees must be involved in defining what can be done to improve performance from which incentive programs will be financed. And without union involvement, the incentive program may not get off the ground or may be plagued by endless grievances.[18]

Employee Benefits

Employee benefits are the part of total compensation that is not directly paid to employees.

Employee benefits are the part of total compensation that is not directly paid to employees. They may include financial and non-monetary benefits such as life, health and accident insurance plans, unemployment benefits, medical and dental plans, pensions, paid holidays and sick pay. Specific benefits and the ways in which they are administered vary among companies. Basically, all benefit plans are designed to protect employees from loss of income due to factors beyond their control. However, they are also used as incentives to attract qualified people and encourage current employees to be more productive. While they may have been fringe benefits at one time, today they are expensive for employers, currently amounting to approximately 36% of annual payroll of the firms involved in the annual survey.

Insurance Plans

Insurance plans—life, health and accident—are usually established on a group basis and cover all the firm's employees. Sometimes the premium is paid by the employer, and sometimes it is shared with employees. Life insurance coverage is usually two or two-and-a-half times the employee's gross annual salary, with varying benefits for those unable to work because of serious health problems or accidents.

Often medical and dental plans are also established on a group basis, with the premium paid either entirely by the employer or split on a percentage basis with employees.

Canada Pension Plan

www.hrdc-drhc.gc.ca/isp/common/cpptoc_e.shtml

Pension Plans

All individuals between the ages of 18 and 70 employed in Canada are covered under the Canada Pension Plan (CPP), which was established in 1965. The benefits to be paid on retirement are based on an individual's earnings during his or her working life, and contribution to the plan is compulsory. Both employer and employee contribute equally; self-employed individuals must pay the entire amount themselves.

In addition to the Canada Pension Plan, many large companies offer private pension plans. Usually, both the employer and the employee contribute to the plan over the employee's working life with the firm. The money is invested in securities of various kinds. This is usually done by an outside pension fund manager who chooses the particular investments, which may be common stock, preferred stock, bonds or other investments. The return on these investments provides a large part of the pension that an individual eventually receives. Depending on the type of pension plan, the management of the fund and conditions that affect the securities market, it could have a big impact on the pension a person receives at retirement.

There are two basic kinds of pension plans:

1. The *defined benefit plan* guarantees a pension at retirement, based on salary and years of service. If there is not enough money in the fund to cover the promised pension, the employer must make up the shortfall. Only a small percentage of workers in Canada (6%) belong to such a plan.

2. The *defined contribution plan* specifies how much the employer and/or employee will contribute each year. The amount of pension a person will receive is unknown until the retirement date, when accumulated funds are used to buy an annuity. (Annuities are purchased from an insurance company that guarantees the owner a certain payment per month over a stated number of years. The amount paid out per month depends on the principal and the existing rate of interest.)

For many years the federal and provincial governments have discussed pension reform. One major problem is the lack of portability between private pension plans. One recommendation is to have a person's private pension vested after five years. If the employee subsequently leaves that employer, he or she should be able to carry the pension to another employee or transfer it into a registered retirement savings plan (RRSP). Another major concern is the single pensioner who is often unable to cope with living expenses on current pension rates. A large proportion of single pensioners are women whose benefits were curtailed when their spouses died. To end this inequitable treatment of women in pension arrangements, it is proposed that a pension be treated as a family asset, to be shared equally either on retirement or in the event of marital breakdown.

A final controversial proposal is the indexing of pension plans. Employers have generally opposed this move because the cost of indexing cannot be precisely computed. Workers who belong to pulp and paper, automobile and airlines unions have won indexed pensions in their negotiations in the past, but these contracts will eventually expire. Indexing can be a potentially costly venture for employers, and no government legislation has been proposed. The indexing factor would be based on the consumer price index and would not apply to pensions accrued to date or to existing pensioners.

Pensions come under provincial jurisdiction, and while rules are essentially similar there are variations. Generally, pension reform has improved coverage for part-timers and women and has ensured that the employer's contribution becomes the property of the employee much sooner.

Employment Insurance Benefits

While the Unemployment Insurance Commission (UIC), established in 1940, has insured most workers against loss of wages from unemployment, the Unemployment Insurance Act of 1971 made contributions to the fund compulsory for all workers. In 1996 the federal government brought in the **Employment Insurance (EI) system**. This system will continue to provide Canadians with basic income protection, as did the previous UI system. It would also include a range of new employment measures to help people get jobs.

Under the new Employment Insurance Act, income benefits will be more closely linked to work effort. About 14 million Canadians per year will be covered by temporary income protection in the event of a job loss. Under EI, income benefits will be based on hours rather than weeks worked—a better measurement of work effort. For the first time, 500 000 part-time workers will be able to insure their income.

Employment Insurance

www.hrdc-drhc.gc.ca/ei/
common/home.shtml

Employment Insurance (EI) insures most workers against loss of wages from unemployment.

Also available are information and advisory services through a modernized **National Employment Service**. A stronger, automated labour market information network will help unemployed Canadians conduct and complete their job search nationwide.

The federal government recognizes provincial responsibilities for labour market training. It will work with the provinces to implement EI's new employment measures. With the provincial governments, it will focus on what works, reducing overlap and duplication.

Other Benefits

Along with the benefits directly related to salary and income protection, companies also offer their employees paid annual vacations and statutory holidays in excess of what is required by law; sick pay; premiums for overtime and for unusual hours; legal aid; training and development at educational institutions; low-interest loans; and maternity and parental leave. The list is long, and new benefits and services are constantly being introduced. Some new types of benefits are employee assistance programs, home computer programs, fitness-club memberships and group mortgage plans.

The Cost of Employee Benefits

In 1991, the cost of employee benefits amounted to 34.1% of gross payroll or $13 573 per employee, more than double the percentage 30 years ago. The cost of major employee benefits as a percentage of gross payroll cost is shown in Table 10.1.

Many employers have found that a large percentage of their employees do not realize how high their benefit costs are. In one survey of a Toronto firm, out of 850 employees surveyed only 5% knew their benefit costs. Other surveys have shown that the larger the company, the better employees understood their benefits because larger companies had the resources to provide information sessions and printed brochures.

Keeping employees informed of benefits and their cost to the company is important to counteract employee dissatisfaction. A more flexible approach in distributing benefits is also effective. Allowing employees to choose the types of benefits they want cafeteria-style and adding them to a core program is popular in the United States. Employees choose benefits up to a particular cost. U.S. employers tend to offer a lump sum, which is most appropriate for this type of plan. Thus, two individuals could have widely different benefits for the same cost. Younger workers and women would have lower costs for pension benefits and life insurance coverage, for example.

In the past, companies added individual benefits based on popularity, union demands or the personal interest of the benefits manager. As a result, there were gaps in some benefits and duplications in others. Managers did not consider a total package that was flexible enough to appeal to employees of different ages. Today, employees are more concerned about benefits; they want plans that meet their needs.

Health and Safety

Canadian Centre for Occupational Health and Safety

www.ccohs.ca/

In 1886, the Ontario Factories Act came into effect in response to the growing opposition to child labour, the unsanitary conditions that existed in the factories and the dangerous working conditions that caused disease and injuries. This act, which underwent several changes and revisions over the past hundred years, was the forerunner of the Ontario Occupational Health and Safety Act.

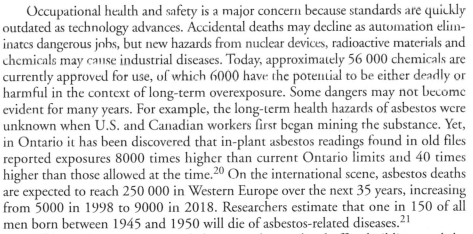

The salary that a person gets paid for a job is really only the tip of the iceberg. Assume, for example, that the basic hourly wage is $7. Add up the cost of employee benefits—Canada Pension Plan, employment insurance, workers' compensation and all the rest—and the cost amounts to 41% of the basic wage.

Now add in the costs of providing that employee with the tools required to do the job. This could be a desk, a computer and a place on the assembly line with all of the safety equipment and tools. Also add in the cost of providing the services that employees require such as a cafeteria, employee lounge, daycare services, health facilities and so on.

For some businesses there are the costs of unionization, which include management and employee time off for union activities, such as bargaining for the contract, grievance procedures, and the costs of complying with the union agreement. When a union goes on strike, there are the costs of strike action, which can be devastating for some businesses.

Then there are the intangible costs of having employees. This includes the costs of office politics, family problems, substance abuse, using the company's long-distance line for personal matters, playing solitaire or other games on the computer during work hours, surfing the Internet and a host of other activities that do not get the work done or cause it to be done badly.

Last, but not least, there is the cost of employee attitude. An employee with a good attitude is one of the most important assets a business can have. Equally, a bad-attitude employee—a rude waiter, a sales clerk who does not take the customer's interests to heart—can cost the company business.

It follows that whenever possible, a firm should attempt to minimize all these costs by treating employees like the important resource they are. Proper training can make an employee more productive and reduce any attitude problems. Good equipment can reduce fatigue and accidents as well as sick days. Clear policy manuals as to the firm's stand on sensitive issues can reduce lawsuits and make it easier to terminate those employees not willing to be productive. A good benefits package, while not necessarily a motivating factor, will make employees more satisfied with their place of work. Finally, well-trained managers who can provide good supervision can go a long way toward creating an effective employee atmosphere.[19]

What Is the True Cost of an Employee?

Occupational health and safety is a major concern because standards are quickly outdated as technology advances. Accidental deaths may decline as automation eliminates dangerous jobs, but new hazards from nuclear devices, radioactive materials and chemicals may cause industrial diseases. Today, approximately 56 000 chemicals are currently approved for use, of which 6000 have the potential to be either deadly or harmful in the context of long-term overexposure. Some dangers may not become evident for many years. For example, the long-term health hazards of asbestos were unknown when U.S. and Canadian workers first began mining the substance. Yet, in Ontario it has been discovered that in-plant asbestos readings found in old files reported exposures 8000 times higher than current Ontario limits and 40 times higher than those allowed at the time.[20] On the international scene, asbestos deaths are expected to reach 250 000 in Western Europe over the next 35 years, increasing from 5000 in 1998 to 9000 in 2018. Researchers estimate that one in 150 of all men born between 1945 and 1950 will die of asbestos-related diseases.[21]

Office workers are concerned about poorly ventilated office buildings and the potential hazards from computer video screens. They are also seeking widespread use of office equipment designed to promote comfort and efficiency. **Ergonomics** refers to arranging and designing the workplace environment in order to reduce fatigue, physical strain and injuries associated with the performance of repetitive tasks.

Federal and provincial regulations aim to prevent accidents and occupational diseases. Regulations are concerned with noise, lighting, dangerous substances, the handling of materials and personal protective equipment. In 1982, a federal government task force established the Workplace Hazardous Materials Information System (WHMIS), a joint federal-provincial project that includes representation from

Ergonomics refers to arranging and designing the workplace environment in order to reduce fatigue, physical strain and injuries associated with the performance of repetitive tasks.

TABLE   10.1   **Cost of individual employee benefits**
(expressed as a percentage of gross annual payroll)

	Percentage of Total Payroll
Benefit	
Statutory holidays	2.3
Vacations pay	5.0
Incentive bonus	0.5
Bereavement, Military leave	0.1
Rest periods, coffee breaks	2.3
Sick leave	1.9
Maternity	0.2
Other	0.2
Pay for Time Not Worked	**12.4**
Employment Insurance	4.5
Workers' Compensation	0.9
CPP/QPP	3.2
Provincial medicare	0.7
Statutory Benefits	**9.3**
Group life	0.4
Survivor benefits	0.0
Accident	0.0
Business travel accident	0.0
Hospital and health care	1.5
Employee assistance	0.0
Dental care	1.2
Long-term disability	1.0
Short-term disability	0.1
Pension plans	7.2
Health care spending account	0.0
Savings plan	0.0
Share purchase plan	0.0
Employer-Sponsored Benefits	**11.5**
Severance payouts	0.5
Bonuses	0.0
Profit sharing	3.0
Additional Compensation	**3.5**
Total	**36.7**

SOURCE: Data taken from *KPMG Survey of Employee Benefits Costs in Canada—1998* (Toronto: KPMG Actuarial, Benefits & Compensation Inc.).

industry, organized labour and the federal and provincial governments. The project's aim was to determine the criteria by which to evaluate and classify hazardous materials and to distribute this information to all concerned while still protecting trade secrets. The committee's work resulted in the amendment of the Hazardous Products Act in 1987, a significant step in informing workers about the hazards of certain products. Provincial legislation is also being brought in line with federal regulations.

Organizations Concerned with Health and Safety

There are two major organizations concerned with health and safety. The Canadian Centre for Occupational Health and Safety, established in 1978, reports to Parliament through the Minister of Labour. The Centre's tasks are to advise on occupational and safety matters; collect data to develop codes of practice and standards; provide technical advisory services; deal with hazardous substances; and maintain contact with national and international organizations.

The Industrial Accident Prevention Association (IAPA) is a federation of 10 safety associations, including approximately 65 000 firms and more than 1.5 million workers. The IAPA is funded by the Ontario manufacturing and retailing industry, and its staff provides consulting and educational services throughout Ontario. The association also studies company safety programs and the cause of accidents, and suggests training courses and preventive measures.

Industrial Accident Prevention Association

www.iapa.on.ca/

When employees are injured at work, they receive the major portion of their salary from the Workers' Compensation Board until they are able to return to work. Contributions for this benefit are made entirely by employers, and companies are concerned with preventing accidents in their plants. Hence, many firms mount extensive health and safety programs designed to prevent accidents.

Employee Evaluation

Performance evaluation is the systematic process of assessing an employee's job performance. A periodic evaluation of employees is essential both to companies and their employees. For the company, it provides proof of job performance or non-performance; employee evaluations are necessary both to terminate employment and to identify candidates for promotion. For employees, evaluations are also important factors in motivation and morale—all employees like to know how they are doing, and whether they are meeting the expectations of the job and of their superiors.

Performance evaluation is a systematic process of assessing an employee's job performance.

Choosing the proper method for performance evaluation, however, can be a problem. While productivity and performance can be evaluated on the basis of an objective standard, such as the number of units produced, objective evaluation of a worker's relationship with other employees and of his or her contribution to company morale is more difficult. A salesperson, for example, can be judged directly on the number of sales made, but it is not easy to evaluate his or her contribution to future sales or customer goodwill.

There are many other jobs for which objective standards cannot be established, despite constant efforts to quantify information that is essentially qualitative. How can a manager's job be evaluated? Can a teacher's contribution to student learning be measured objectively?

One method of evaluating employees is to judge their performance on the basis of the objectives established in a results-oriented job description. Objectives set by employees, together with their immediate superiors, can also serve as a standard. This variation of management by objectives (MBO) (discussed in Chapter 6) is known as *appraisal by results.*

Once an employee's job performance has been evaluated, the manager discusses the results with the employee, who then signs the evaluation to indicate awareness of the comments. Thus, the employee has the opportunity to read and discuss the evaluation. If the assessment seems unjust, the employee may go to higher levels of management for recourse; union members may file a grievance.

Career Development

Many individuals join an organization in the hope that they can earn their living in a meaningful job and advance in the organization according to their capabilities. On the other hand, if an organization wants to ensure that it has talented and motivated people it must not leave career planning solely to the individual. By offering career development, organizations can provide their employees with advice and guidance in career planning. By identifying opportunities for job advancement, the company will not lose valuable individuals to other employers who may offer more attractive opportunities.

Career development is a formal activity by which members of an organization increase their awareness, knowledge or capabilities such that the direction and progression of their career is affected. Although the individual is heavily involved in developing a career, there is considerable input from the organization as to what it expects from, and anticipates for, the employee.

Career development does not mean that an organization maps out a plan of how to reach the top. Indeed, most individuals will find satisfying careers at any level of an organization. Nevertheless, all the opportunities should be made clear to individuals. Beyond that, an organization must make every effort to ensure that individuals have interesting jobs and that they have clear knowledge of how they can advance in the organization if they perform well in their present job. Rotating individuals through different jobs, meaningful performance appraisals that are career-oriented, and appropriate training and development are important factors in career management.

> **Career development** is a formal activity by which members of an organization increase their awareness, knowledge or capabilities such that the direction and progression of their career is affected.

Promotion, Transfer and Separation

Virtually all firms experience employee turnover. Some employees leave the company; others are promoted to higher positions; still others are transferred laterally to positions where responsibility and duties, though similar, pertain to a different area of the firm's activities. As positions become vacant, new employees must be recruited, hired and trained to fill them.

Promotion

Promotion usually refers to upward movement, within a particular organization, into a position with greater responsibility, increased authority and (usually) higher pay. As managers move up in the company hierarchy, positions in the lower levels are often filled through promotion of operating personnel. Individuals who started at the lowest level have been known to rise to the position of president.

Promotions for management are almost always based on **merit**, which refers to employees' performance and the quality of their work in previous positions. However, when a worker is promoted to supervisor in a unionized firm, problems may develop if the union insists that seniority be used as the basis for the promotion decision. **Seniority** refers to the length of the employee's service with the company. Promotion based on seniority alone does not always provide the company with the best-qualified supervisor. To resolve the problem of merit versus seniority, a compromise is usually reached whereby length of service is used as a basis for promotion only when there are two or more candidates with equal qualifications.

> **Promotion** refers to upward movement within a particular organization, into a position with greater responsibility, increased authority and (usually) higher pay.

> **Merit** refers to a person's qualifications and performance, and is generally used when selecting individuals for promotion.

> **Seniority** refers to an employee's length of service relative to others in the organization, and is sometimes used to promote individuals to higher positions in an organization.

Transfer

The horizontal movement of workers or managers from one position to another of equal responsibility or authority is known as a **transfer**. Generally, transfers are used to give individuals a wider range of experience within the company, but they can also provide an employee with new challenges and interests. Often transfers require movements between geographical regions; many companies have established various compensation plans to cover the expenses incurred in transfers. In some instances, a transfer also means an increase in salary.

Transfer—the horizontal movement of workers or managers from one position to another of equal responsibility, increased authority and (usually) higher pay.

Separation

Separation occurs when employees resign, retire, are dismissed or are laid off. Some workers resign because they have found other employment. Often an employer has to reduce the work force because of economic downturns in business or because of strong international competition that has hurt sales and profits. These dismissals or **layoffs** may be temporary or permanent depending on the nature of the downturn. Sometimes early retirement is offered to older workers. For example, Dofasco, Canada's largest steelmaker, offered early retirement to 1450 workers in 1991 in order to reduce its workforce, improve competitiveness, and lower overall production costs. Companies usually provide some form of severance pay to the employees who are laid off. Many of these workers may be covered by union contracts that state how layoffs are to be handled and what compensation the employer must provide. Laid-off employees may also be eligible for employment insurance benefits.

Separation occurs when employees resign, retire, are fired or are laid off.

Layoff—when a company lets employees go because they are no longer needed.

Some employees are dismissed because they are unable to perform their job properly, or because they have engaged in misconduct such as theft. The employer must be careful in these instances to prove cause for dismissal, which means that the employee has violated a fundamental aspect of the contract of employment. According to common law, every employee has an implied contract of employment if no written contract exists. Either party may terminate this contract by giving reasonable notice. The employee, however, can be dismissed immediately if given an appropriate amount of severance pay. The courts may decide that an employee was wrongfully dismissed if the severance pay was insufficient. If an employee is dismissed for just cause, however, the employer is not obliged to provide severance pay.

A common form of separation is **retirement**. When mandatory retirement at age 65 was still standard practice, many productive employees were forced to give up their job and retire, while employees who had performance problems due to advancing age were kept until they were 65. Today, with mandatory retirement no longer legal in some provinces and within the federal government, many companies are attempting to be more flexible by offering employees early retirement with full benefits. Those who want to continue working are able to do so.

Retirement occurs when a person has reached a particular age, or length of service with a company, and decides to give up his or her employment in order to draw company or legislated retirement benefits.

For many individuals, retirement can be a traumatic experience. They may feel helpless, discarded and no longer productive. Financial worries may add to their retirement anxieties if they feel they will not have enough income, even with their pensions, to retire with a decent lifestyle.

To ease retirement anxieties, many companies offer pre-retirement counselling to make their employees aware of their company benefits as well as government social security programs. Other help may take the form of educational programs that outline the benefits of retirement, and explain the types of activities in which an individual can become involved. For some individuals, a second career may be appropriate. Many companies are finding that older workers are highly motivated and have considerable experience that should not be wasted. This is particularly true for management personnel who can acquire successful second careers in business consulting. For example, the Federal Business Development Bank, through its CASE counselling department, uses retired managers to help individuals start their own business.

Chapter Summary

1. People are the most important resource of an organization, and managing these human resources is a basic task of every manager. However, as organizations grow and personnel matters become increasingly complex, human resource or personnel management is becoming increasingly time-consuming and complex. Whenever possible, firms hire specialists in personnel planning, recruiting, hiring, training, compensation and evaluation. With the growth of unions, personnel specialists have also become involved in contract negotiations and liaison activities between the parties involved.

2. Personnel planning is an attempt to forecast future personnel needs in conjunction with long- and short-range organizational plans, while keeping present personnel resources in mind. Planning also involves job analysis, from which job descriptions and job specifications can be developed.

3. One major task of the personnel department is to hire competent employees. Employees can be recruited through advertising, government and private employment agencies, union headquarters and schools. Whenever possible, however, firms fill job vacancies from within by promoting employees. Since the passage of the Canadian Human Rights Act in 1977, personnel managers have become particularly concerned about their recruitment and hiring processes that may discriminate against particular groups of people.

4. The selection process involves obtaining information on applicants to ensure that they can perform the job and fit in with the organization. The selection process involves any or all of the following: filling in application blanks, prescreening interviews, testing, in-depth interviews and reference checks. Once hired, workers usually undergo a formal orientation program through which they are introduced to the company, their boss, co-workers and work environment.

5. Lack of employee training has become a major issue in Canada. Government does not have the resources to engage in more training. The onus is now on business to provide more money and a commitment to employee training to ensure that Canada's workforce can meet the increasing international competition.

6. Most employees receive their training on the job. When potential dangers and costs make on-the-job training impractical, vestibule training or a combination of the two may be used. When the training required is extensive, apprenticeship programs are common. Managers, both new and practising, may also engage in management development through special in-house training programs or a variety of seminars and outside courses. College and university courses are often paid for by employers after successful completion by employees.

7. Compensation is also of prime importance to employees. A compensation plan should attract qualified employees, treat them fairly and encourage increased production. Wages and salaries are based on minimum-wage legislation, the firm's ability to pay, the prevailing wages paid in the community and/or industry, cost-of-living clauses and union bargaining power. Direct monetary compensation may take the form of wages and salaries, bonuses, profit sharing or commissions. Indirect forms of compensation, or fringe benefits, include life insurance, pension plans, medical and health insurance, holiday, vacation and sick pay.

8. Profit sharing and employee stock ownership plans are becoming popular among companies and employees. Some plans provide employees with large payouts at retirement. Companies that have instituted these plans have found that they decrease labour strife and increase productivity. Nevertheless, the programs must be properly administered, and employees must be educated to understand how profit works and what they can expect if profits for the company should increase or decrease. Nor should the programs be used in lieu of adequate compensation.

9. A difficult task faced by managers is employee performance evaluation. The personnel manager can help by developing performance evaluation systems. The evaluation system chosen should be as objective as possible and based on criteria established with the employee at the beginning of the evaluation period. Performance evaluation is particularly important for employees who are either in line for promotion or to be dismissed for poor performance.

10. Promotion, dismissal and retirement are important matters. Promotion may be based on seniority or merit, although a combination is often used. Transfers are often given to individuals to expose them to different aspects of the organization. Dismissal of employees may occur because a firm has to lower its operating costs by reducing the size of its work force. Layoffs are common and may be temporary or permanent. Early retirement is another method of reducing the workforce. Since retirement is no longer mandatory at age 65, organizations have become more flexible in allowing workers to retire earlier, or later, depending on their ability to perform.

KEY TERMS

Human resource management 365

Human resource or
     personnel planning 368

Job analysis 368

Job description 369

Results-oriented job description 369

Job specification 370

Recruiting 373

Selection 375

Canadian Human Rights Act 375

Multiple hurdles method 377

Compensatory method 377

Orientation 379

On-the-job training 382

Apprenticeship program 383

Vestibule training 383

Management development 383

Compensation system 384

Equal pay for equal work 385

Pay equity/Equal pay for
    work of equal value 385

Wages 387

Piecework incentive 387

Salary 387

Bonus 388

Productivity sharing 388

Commission 388

Profit sharing 388

Employee stock ownership plans
    (ESOPs) 389

Employee benefits 390

Employment Insurance
    (EI) system 391

National Employment Service 392

Ergonomics 393

Performance evaluation 395

Career development 396

Promotion 396

Merit 396

Seniority......................396

Transfer 397

Separation 397

Layoff 397

Retirement 397

REVIEW QUESTIONS

1 Why is the human resources department so important today?

2 Why is the human resources or personnel department a staff department?

3 What are some of the major activities of the human resources department?

4 Outline the steps in the personnel planning process.

5 What is job analysis? What are some of the major uses for the information gained from job analysis?

6 Distinguish between a job description and a job specification.

7 What is the main shortcoming of a traditional job description?

8 List the major sources of job candidates that are available to the personnel manager.

9 What are the key areas concerning employment discrimination?

10 What are the major steps undertaken by personnel departments to ensure they are not discriminatory in their hiring practices?

11 Outline the steps that make up the employee selection process. Which step is considered to be one of the most important?

12 Describe the various types of worker training and management development programs.

13 Name the three major objectives of a good compensation program.

14 List the major factors that determine wages and salaries. What are the most important factors for the owner-manager of a small business to consider in setting wages and salaries?

15 Distinguish between equal pay for equal work and pay for work of equal value.

16 Give an example of jobs for which each of the following would be an appropriate method of payment: (a) hourly wages; (b) monthly salary; (c) straight commission; (d) piecework.

17 What are the major considerations that companies should consider when establishing a profit-sharing plan? What potential benefits does a firm get from a profit-sharing plan?

18 Describe some of the major employee benefits.

19 Why should employees undergo periodic formal performance evaluations by their managers?

20 Distinguish between promotion and transfer. When do companies promote on the basis of seniority? When do they promote on the basis of merit?

DISCUSSION QUESTIONS

1 Should employers be responsible for providing employment insurance benefits? What is their responsibility for employees' health and safety?

2 Discuss the pros and cons of mandatory retirement.

3 How can one reconcile the problem of discrimination in employment versus freedom of a business owner to hire whomever he or she wants?

4 What is your view of affirmative action and equal pay for work of equal value?

5 Under what circumstances might employee stock ownership plans and profit-sharing plans become more important in the future as an incentive for employees? Give reasons for your answer.

CASE

10-1

Trees and Leaves

Trees and Leaves, a company specializing in commercial landscaping and maintenance, was founded by Harvey Jones, the current owner and president, in 1975. Harvey had taken out a small government "start your own student summer business" grant after his second year in the business program at the University of New Brunswick. He made so much money that summer that he dropped out to work at the business full time.

Over time, the company expanded. Now it has more than 75 contracts with both large and small businesses in the Fredericton area, and employs 35 landscape maintenance employees. This service-oriented business specializes in the care and maintenance of lawns and shrubbery.

Jones wants to expand the operation to both Moncton and Saint John, but certain problems have arisen that must be resolved. As the local consultant specializing in human resources management, you have been called in.

Harvey employs three key people in accounting, operations and sales. Janice Hope, the accountant, holds a CGA, which she got the hard way—through seven years of night school. A single parent with two small children, she has been with the company for eight years. She and Harvey are good friends. She's extremely loyal, as Harvey stood by her when her work deteriorated during a very bitter divorce.

Edward Long, the salesperson, is the nephew of Harvey's wife. Harvey felt obliged to "give him a chance" after a little family pressure was applied. Edward is not particularly good at the job and motivation tends to be a problem.

Mike Flatbush, a Micmac, was Harvey's first employee. Mike worked his way up from labourer to operations manager. After 14 years with the company, he is fiercely protective of his "turf." He knows that should he lose this job, it would be difficult to find another at a comparable level.

Lately, instead of expanding, Trees and Leaves has been losing customers. The trouble seems to be in the operations area, but other problems have also arisen. Customers have been complaining that the work is sloppily done and that crews are late arriving. Edward is supposed to look after customer service, but when Harvey questions him, Edward blames the problems on operations.

Mike Flatbush, on the other hand, says that the new Human Rights Commission ruling forcing him to integrate whites into his previously all-Micmac crews is causing untold problems, because "these new guys are a bunch of racists." In fact, the grounds supervisor, also a Micmac, just quit and no replacement has been found.

To complicate the situation, both Mike and Edward are complaining that they're not getting enough financial information from Janice. She says that she's the accountant and they're just nosy and don't need to know "all that stuff anyway."

As a consultant, your reputation has been made on getting clients to face reality and make those "hard" decisions. You hold a meeting with Harvey during which you try to pin him down about his future and where the company should be headed. You try to get him to recognize his problems, but Harvey doesn't want to grapple with the people side of his operation. "Look, I know where I want to be in five years—in Moncton and Saint John—but this people thing keeps getting in the way. Make some recommendations to help me out—that's what you're paid for!"

SOURCE: Dr. P. C. Wright, Faculty of Administration, University of New Brunswick. Reprinted by permission of the author.

1 Develop a human resource strategy for your client.

2 What is likely to happen if Harvey doesn't solve his "people" problems?

3 How important are human resources to the successful, long-term functioning of an organization?

Temglow

CASE
10-2

Temglow Corporation is a mid-size Canadian firm with extensive contacts in the Far East—Hong Kong, Singapore, Malaysia, Thailand, and so on. The firm has managed to build a solid business base, mainly by making an extensive study of each culture and training the marketing staff thoroughly. Temglow also ensures that its overseas partners make more money than the Canadian operation. In short, these people know what they're doing, and they are successful at the cross-cultural aspects of international management.

Recently, the opportunity has arisen to expand operations to the Middle East—Saudi Arabia, Kuwait, Oman and the United Arab Emirates. A new marketing manager is needed, and management is searching for the right person. At present, there are three candidates:

Angela Lam: Assistant marketing manager for the Eastern Region, and long overdue for a promotion. Management would like to reward her for almost 10 years of success. She is a good people person, a skilled negotiator and seems to be able to deal with some of the chauvinism so prevalent in Eastern business circles. Breaking into the Middle Eastern market, however, with the many prohibitions on what women can and cannot do, may be a different matter.

Mohamed Aboud: Relatively new with the company, Mohamed certainly understands Middle Eastern culture and ways of doing business. He has no management experience, however, and Temglow's management is concerned that his authoritarian attitude toward the support staff might be carried over to the sales team.

Joe Henry: Joe is an outsider. He has been roaming the Middle East for years in charge of a three-person sales team. He knows nothing about Temglow's product, and management is concerned that his expressed desire to "come home and settle down" might translate into "I don't want to travel at all anymore!" Still, Joe has the field knowledge, the aptitude and at least some supervisory experience. He is 58 years old.

SOURCE: Dr. P. C. Wright, Faculty of Administration, University of New Brunswick. Reprinted by permission of the author.

1 If you were the president of Temglow, which of the three candidates would you promote to the position of marketing manager? Why? To remain strictly within Canadian law what factors would you ignore in making this decision?

2 After making your choice, how would you deal with the other two candidates?

COMPREHENSIVE CASE 10-3

SOMERSET OPTICAL

With its continued growth, Somerset Optical soon found itself a major player in the small business employer market. Sales volume continued to increase almost weekly and it soon became apparent that more staff would be required. Fowler and Dewar decided that it was necessary to hire four additional full-time sales clerks. A one-time advertisement placed in the local newspaper produced 86 applicants. After the initial screening, five candidates were to be interviewed for four positions.

To save time, Dewar suggested that all candidates be interviewed simultaneously in a "boardroom-style" interview. Fowler, Dewar and a friend of Dewar's (a personnel specialist from a close but unrelated firm) would sit on one side of the interview table with the five candidates sitting across from them. They would ask questions of each candidate from a prepared list of questions. In addition to recording each candidate's response, they would also observe how the candidates interacted. Fowler and Dewar were particularly interested in the interactions among the candidates, each of whom would be aware that there were only four positions.

The interview would last two hours. Each candidate would be asked the following questions (among others):

1. Why they felt qualified for the job.

2. What they saw as being their major strength and weakness.

3. The one thing they would change about their present job.

Each candidate's résumé would also be discussed in the interview.

SOURCE: By David H. Jones-Delcourt. Reprinted by permission of the author.

Questions

1 Evaluate the interview method that has been suggested by Dewar. Identify the advantages and disadvantages of this interviewing method.

2 Does Dewar's interviewing method violate human-rights legislation? Give reasons for your answer.

VIDEO CASE—PART 3

OVERBRANDING

Regardless of how good a product or service is, much of a company's success depends on how well it exposes its products or services to the public. This is where branding plays a critical role—once established, a successful brand is a valuable resource for a company.

Making sure a company's brand name is well known to the public has been a primary marketing strategy of the 1990s. The first objective is to get the brand out to the public, so that as many potential consumers as possible know what to associate the brand with. Once that objective has been accomplished, the second goal is to ensure that the brand *means* something to the potential market. But too many brands, or one brand representing too many products, could turn off consumers. It's at this point that problems can arise. Companies that go overboard in their branding may cause themselves more harm than good.

SOURCE: Based on "Overbranding," *Venture* 705 (November 24, 1998)

Questions

1 The video looks at three companies and the ways they try to manoeuver through today's complicated brand situations. Two of these companies, in particular, are Roots and Nike. How do you feel about wearing a piece of clothing that carries a particular company's brand name?

2 Can you suggest other products that might have a problem with overbranding?

3 One common view maintains that creating a strong brand is the ultimate weapon that takes a company through the peaks and valleys of the business cycle. Another view contends that it is a vicious cycle—there is so much of it, you need *more* branding to break through it. Which of these two views do you subscribe to?

4

Business and Its Environment

Businesses today operate not in isolation but in constant interaction with consumers and labour unions; with government on the federal, provincial and municipal levels; and, increasingly, with other countries. Part Four examines these relationships in detail.

In Chapter 11, we look at labour unions—their goals and aims—and describe the collective-bargaining process between management and labour. We also briefly examine the history of unions before focusing on some of the traditional conflicts that characterize the relationship between management and labour, and how these conflicts might be resolved in the future.

In Chapter 12, we examine the relationship between business and government—how government promotes business as a vehicle for increased economic growth and prosperity while at the same time it attempts to control it, sometimes stringently, through legislation, rules and regulations.

In Chapter 13, we look at international trade and its benefits for all countries. We discuss both the factors that hinder trade between nations and the steps that have been taken to remove international trade barriers. We also look at international finance and the multinational corporation.

In Chapter 14, we examine the relationship between business and society. The specific ethics of business behaviour and the broader question of the responsibility of business toward society are two issues of major concern today.

11

Business and Labour

Learning Objectives

After reading this chapter, you will be able to

1 Explain why workers join unions.

2 Describe what a union is.

3 Explain why management is often reluctant to deal with unions.

4 Outline the history of the labour movement in Canada and the problems facing it today.

5 Outline the process required for certification of a union as the sole bargaining agent for a group of workers.

6 List the major issues at stake in negotiations between labour and management, and explain how the collective-bargaining process works.

7 List the weapons, or tools, that both labour and management can use to back up their demands.

8 Describe the roles of mediation, conciliation and arbitration and explain how each of these is used when the negotiation process does not lead to an agreement.

9 Describe the current climate of labour-management relations.

Aims of Management and Labour

Imagine for a moment that you are the owner of a small manufacturing company. For the past 10 years, you have struggled to make it successful through tireless effort, taking extraordinary risks and often spending sleepless nights worrying about your financial obligations. One day your employees announce that they now belong to a union and present you with a list of demands for their first contract. As you review the proposal, you realize that the company cannot meet the demands. You are both outraged and hurt—you have always treated them well, paid good wages and endeavoured to build a good relationship with them. "Why are they doing this to me?" you ask. A strike begins and you see your revenues dwindle as your customers, whom you have worked so hard to win over, take their business elsewhere. If you were this owner, how would you feel about labour unions?

Now put yourself in the position of the worker. You do not feel that you are participating in the success of the business. Although you have been treated reasonably well and have received regular wage increases, your raises have not kept pace with inflation. When you talk to your friends who are unionized, they appear to have fared much better. In addition to large wage increases, often tied to the cost of living, they have also received many other benefits, including job security and shorter working hours. Obviously, there appear to be advantages in belonging to a union, and so you decide to join.

This general scenario has been repeated many times in the past. In Canada today, many small and medium-sized businesses deal with unionized workers. In addition, public employees on all levels—federal, provincial and municipal—have been eligible to join unions and have held the right to strike since 1967.

The foregoing example indicates why management and labour are at odds. Both the owner (management) and the workers have different goals that influence their philosophy and their actions. Management and owners generally believe that only a profitable firm can offer competitive wages and benefits. If workers demand wages beyond what the firm can afford, its financial stability is jeopardized and the result could be bankruptcy. Workers, on the other hand, often believe that firms make large profits at their expense and that they do not receive enough of the firm's profits in return for their efforts. These opposing views cause conflicts between labour and management.

The conflict, however, is not always noticeable. Today, workers of many small and medium-sized firms and public employees on all levels are unionized, but for the most part workers and management appear to work well together. We hear of strikes, but almost 90% of collective agreements are concluded without a strike. Only a small number of labour disputes turn into lengthier strikes. Clearly, then, while there are differences between management and labour, they share a common aim: to ensure that the business provides income for both the workers and its owners. We now examine the aims of management and labour more closely.

Aims of Management

Management represents the owners or stockholders of the business, who want both a reasonable return on their investment and some assurance that it will be protected in the future. It is management's responsibility to ensure that the firm survives. Ideally, management would like to maintain high revenues while keeping the costs of operating the firm as low as possible. Since labour is a major cost factor in most businesses, keeping wages down is a central concern. At the same time, however, it is in management's interest that workers are productive, skilled, educated and, above all, loyal to management and the firm.

Aims of Labour

In general, the major aim of labour is to improve its material well-being through increased wages and salaries, improved fringe benefits, better working conditions and job security. Workers realize that, without a union, they have little bargaining power with management—they can either accept what management is prepared to give them, or do without work. As an organized group, however, workers have more power—if they withhold their services, they may bring a giant corporation to a standstill. Although some companies use management to fill in for striking workers, the output in goods and services is usually reduced and the firm's action often merely delays the inevitable shutdown.

Labour's aims are not limited to economic benefits, however. Traditionally, organized labour has played a major role in furthering social issues through political action. In Great Britain, for example, one of the two major political parties specifically represents labour and periodically forms the government. Although it has not established a political party in the United States, labour there has a history of lobbying for its interests. In Canada, labour has generally not been directly involved in politics. However, the New Democratic Party has made a significant effort to represent labour's interests, which has brought labour and politics much closer. The Canadian Labour Congress has endorsed the NDP, and local unions often support the party financially.[1]

What Is a Labour Union?

Unions are groups of workers who have joined together to negotiate with employers about wages and working conditions. Because a union speaks for many employees, it can get a better deal for its members than individuals could for themselves. Before the formation of unions, workers had to take the wages and working conditions offered. Workers could be fired for no apparent reason.

A **craft union** consists of workers with a particular skill or trade, such as carpenters, painters or printers. An **industrial union** includes all workers in a particular industry regardless of their skills or trades—the Canadian Auto Workers, for example, or the United Steel Workers. In actual practice today, many craft unions also take in workers outside of the craft field, giving them the appearance of industrial unions. Unions in Canada with more than 50 000 members in 2000 are shown in Table 11.1, while Figure 11.1 shows the percentage distribution of union membership throughout Canadian industry. (Statistics Canada kept no figures after 1992.)

Union—a group of workers who have joined forces to achieve common goals.

Craft union—consists of workers with a particular skill or trade, such as carpenters, painters or printers.

Industrial union—includes all workers in a particular industry regardless of their skills or trades.

Looking Back: The Canadian Labour Movement

Unions were first organized in Canada in the early decades of the nineteenth century, though various economic downturns meant that most were relatively short-lived. While some of these unions originated locally, most were international, with British unions dominating in the 1840s and 1850s and American unions from the 1860s on.

In 1871, five Toronto craft unions established the *Toronto Trades Assembly*, and similar trades councils were subsequently formed in other major Ontario cities. In 1873, the Toronto group called a convention of unions, and a national central organization, called the *Canadian Labour Union*, emerged. This body held meetings for four consecutive years starting in 1874, but ceased meeting thereafter because of the depression of 1878–82. See Figure 11.2 for a breakdown of the history and development of the Canadian labour movement.

TABLE 11.1

Some of the largest Canadian unions

Canadian Union of Public Employees	474 400
Canadian Autoworkers	238 000
United Food and Commercial Workers	205 000
Public Service Alliance of Canada	150 000
United Steelworkers Figure America	190 000
Communication, Energy and Paper Workers	150 000
Teamsters Canada	95 000
Service Employees International Union	85 500
Ontario Public Service Employees	100 000
International Brotherhood of Electrical Workers	71 000
International Association of Machinists and Aerospace Workers	50 000
Nurses Association of Ontario	45 000
United Brotherhood of Carpenters and Joiners	51 000

SOURCE: Internet Home pages of various unions. Please note that these figures represent approximate memberships in April 2000. See www.clc-ctc.ca/links/index.html for information about unions.

FIGURE 11.1

Percentage of distribution of union membership

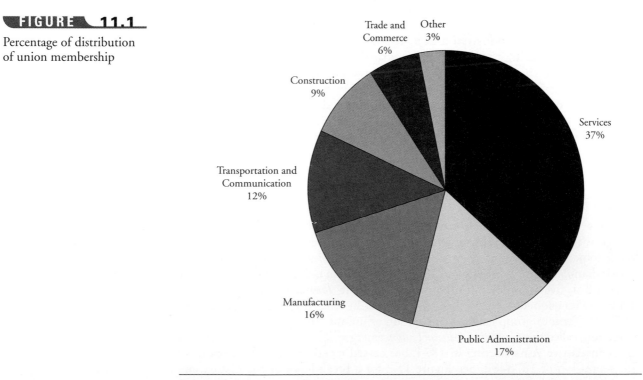

SOURCE: Data adapted from CALURA 1992, *Labour Unions* (Ottawa: Statistics Canada), Cat. no. 71-202.

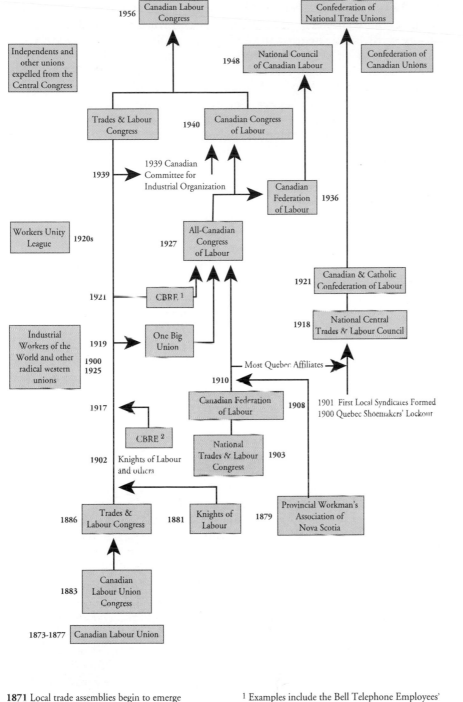

FIGURE 11.2

History and development
of the Canadian labour
movement

1871 Local trade assemblies begin to emerge
1867 Knights of St. Crispin
1825–1860 Numerous weak and isolated locals
1800–1825 Scattered Friendly Societies and labour circles

[1] Examples include the Bell Telephone Employees'
and the Teamsters' Union
[2] Canadian Brotherhood of Railroad Employees

SOURCE: John Crispo, *The Canadian Industrial Relations System* (Toronto: McGraw-Hill Ryerson, 1978): 158.
Reprinted by permission. © by McGraw-Hill Ryerson

In the last two decades of the 19th century, union membership increased, particularly in the West, mainly as a result of the construction of the Canadian Pacific Railway (CPR) and the growth of Canadian industry encouraged by federal government tariff protection. The first industrial union, established in 1878 by the Nova Scotia coal miners, included all workers in that industry. In 1881, an industrial organization called the *Knights of Labour* entered Canada from the United States. In all, more than 100 new locals were established during the 1880s, almost half of them in Ontario, with 21 in the Maritimes, 19 in Quebec and 18 in the West.

Labour councils and assemblies were also revived in the 1880s following the depression. In 1883, delegates from various Ontario unions and the Knights of Labour assemblies in that province formed the *Canadian Labour Union Congress.* This body underwent various name changes at subsequent meetings until 1892, when it became the *Trades and Labour Congress of Canada (TLC).* Although the Knights of Labour initially had the majority of delegates in the congress, membership declined rapidly after 1894 because of internal organizational disputes, and the group was eventually expelled from the Congress.

The early decades of the 20th century were characterized by upheavals in the labour movement, as unions broke away from existing congresses and formed new groups. In 1902, various unions expelled from the Trades and Labour Congress formed the National Trades and Labour Congress, which became the *Canadian Federation of Labour* in 1908. In 1919, the *One Big Union* was established by western unions that had broken away from the *Trades and Labour Congress.* In 1921, a number of local unions in Quebec formed the *Canadian Catholic Confederation of Labour,* and in 1927 the *All-Canadian Congress of Labour,* comprising the *Canadian Federation of Labour* and other national unions, was established.

In the United States, the *American Federation of Labour (AFL)* expelled the industrial unions because of continuing conflict over the right of member unions to organize on an industrial basis rather than on a craft basis alone. These expelled unions then established the *Congress of Industrial Organizations (CIO)* in 1935. The AFL demanded that the Trades and Labour Congress in Canada also expel the affiliated CIO unions. Although the TLC initially refused the request, eventually it did comply, expelling a total of 11 international unions representing 22 000 members.

In 1940, the expelled CIO unions joined the All-Canadian Congress of Labour, which up to this time had been a relatively insignificant rival to the TLC. At a convention held that year, however, the constitution of the All-Canadian Congress was revised and the organization's name changed to the *Canadian Congress of Labour (CCL).* This Canadian counterpart to the CIO experienced tremendous growth and became the second-largest labour organization in Canada, next to the TLC.

Following the 1955 merger of the AFL and CIO in the United States, the two major Canadian labour federations—the TLC and the CCL—also merged to form the *Canadian Labour Congress (CLC).* Altogether, these mergers united 111 international unions and 32 million members. Approximately 300 000 workers remained outside the congress; of these, 200 000 belonged to independent, non-affiliated locals, and the remainder to the *Confédération des travailleurs catholiques du Canada (CTCC),* which, in 1956, voted to join the CLC.

The merger of the various congresses in Canada and the United States brought peace to the labour movement in North America. Unions were able to concentrate their efforts on the improvement of wages and working conditions for their members until the late 1960s and early 1970s, when the movement once again became active in its drive to organize white-collar workers, government employees and professional groups.[2]

A dark period in Canada's labour history began on May 15, 1919, when several unions went on strike in Winnipeg. The strike was in response to the refusal of a number of Winnipeg employers to negotiate with the newly established metal trades council. The metal trades workers, who earned from $12 to $15 a week, had seen their purchasing power drop drastically as a result of high inflation, while the employers had enjoyed high profits throughout the war. The modest demands of the strikers found sympathy with the general public, which was generally dissatisfied with Canada's social and economic system as well as with the high rates of inflation and unemployment. The metal workers were joined in their strike by workers from both the public and the private sector, including postal workers and the police. This concerted effort was to bring to a standstill all production, construction, transportation and communications in Winnipeg and the surrounding areas. It also succeeded in closing hotels, banks and other main buildings.

Prime Minister Robert Borden, argued that public servants had no right to strike and sent the RCMP to Winnipeg, followed by a battalion of soldiers and two machine guns. The federal, provincial and municipal governments ordered all government workers back to work, but the postal workers and police refused to return, and most were dismissed.

The principal leaders of the strike were arrested on June 17 and held in jail for 72 hours. On that same day, a large crowd assembled in front of the Winnipeg town hall, only to have the Riot Act read to them by the mayor. In the resulting confrontation with 50 mounted RCMP and "special" police, one person was killed and 29 injured. The federal government then placed the city under military rule, and many arrests were made. The strike was effectively broken on June 26, and people returned to work. However, many were locked out, blacklisted, dismissed or otherwise discriminated against.

The Winnipeg General Strike

The Canadian Labour Congress

The **Canadian Labour Congress (CLC)** is the major labour organization in Canada, uniting **national**, **international, local unions**, **labour councils** and other union federations. The purpose of the CLC is to act as a liaison among the various labour organizations, and tries to increase solidarity between workers in Canada and other countries. It also has a political function. It presents a common front to the federal and provincial governments for all organized labour in Canada. According to the CLC it promotes decent wages and working conditions, and improved health and safety laws. It also lobbies for fair taxes and strong social programs, including childcare, medicare and pensions, to develop job training and job creation programs, and work for social equality, and to end racism and discrimination. From a founding membership of about one million, the CLC has grown to over 2.3 million in 2000, and represents 12 provincial and territorial federations, and 125 district labour councils. CLC membership increased significantly in the early 1970s with the addition of many public service unions. Figure 11.4 outlines the structure of the CLC. A list of all of the unions that belong to the CLC is available from the CLC Web site at http://www.clc-ctc.ca/about/affiliates.html

In 1993, the Teamsters rejoined the CLC after they rejoined the American labour congress, the AFL-CIO, in 1987. They were originally expelled from the AFL-CIO for allegations of underworld affiliations. In Canada, they were expelled from the CLC in 1961 for raiding Canadian unions. The Teamsters added 95 000 members to the CLC, strengthening the federation and increasing annual dues by $500 000.

Perhaps the major problem facing the CLC is diffusing the growing antagonism between Canadian- and U.S.-controlled unions. Canadian unions generally feel that they are being treated unfairly by the American-controlled international unions. For this reason, the Canadian Auto Workers pulled out of the United Auto Workers (CAW) union and became an independent Canadian union under the

Canadian Labour Congress (CLC)—Canada's national labour body, which represents over 60% of organized labour in the country.

National union—a union whose membership is confined to Canada

International union—a union with members in both Canada and the United States.

Local union—the basic unit of union organization. It elects its own officers and has its own constitution, and is usually responsible for the negotiation and day-to-day administration of the collective agreement.

Labour council—an organization composed of locals of CLC-affiliated unions in a given community or district.

Canadian Labour Congress

www.clc-ctc.ca

FIGURE 11.3

Structure of the Canadian
Labour Congress

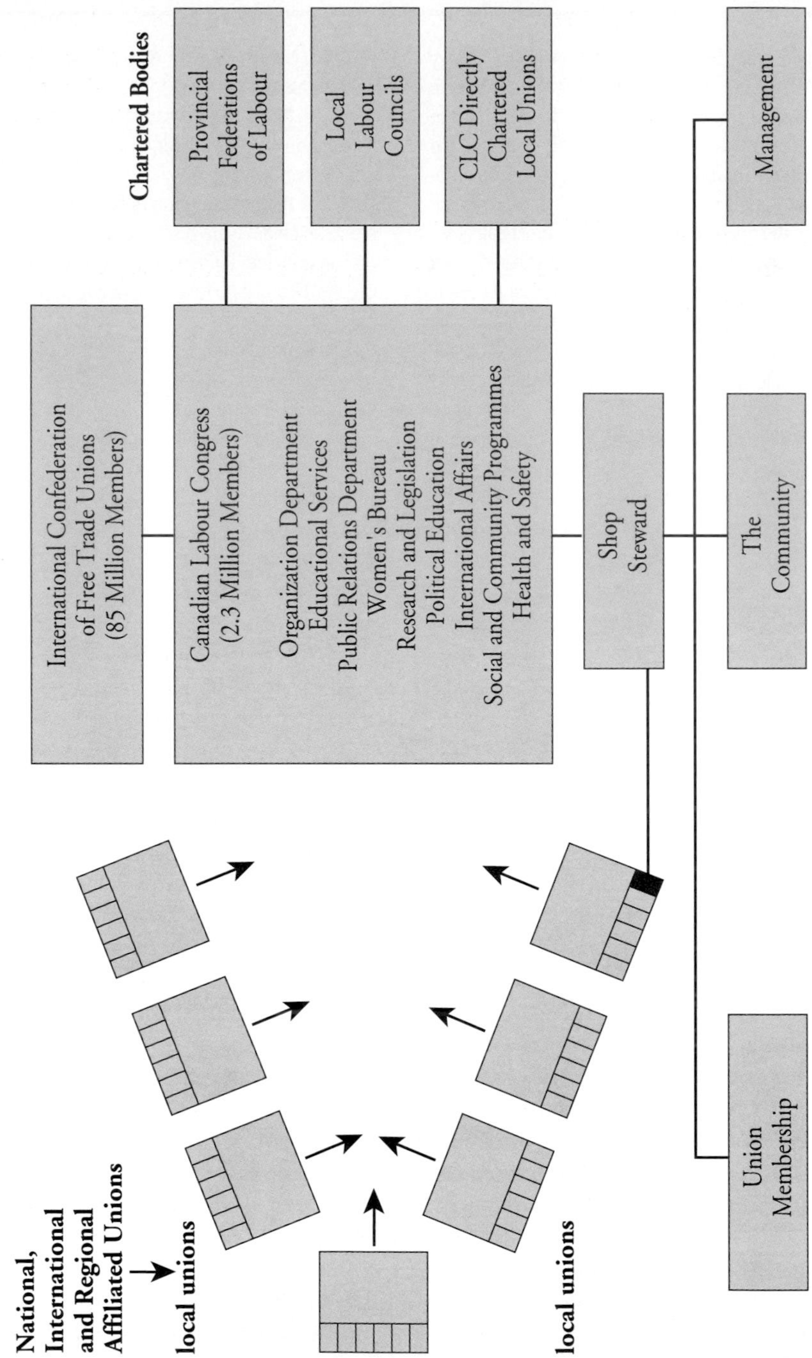

leadership of Bob White, who became president of the CLC in 1992. This same
union has recruited Newfoundland fishers and fish-plant workers, an action not
taken lightly by the U.S.-based United Food & Commercial Workers, which represented these workers in the past. In May 2000, the CLC threatened to expel the
CAW union for raiding 30 000 members of the Service Employees International
Union. A number of other union affiliates are urging that the ouster proceed. The

CAW, with its 240 000 members, comprises about 10% of the total membership of the CLC. Union democracy is another issue with the Canadian longshore workers, who are trying to set up a Canadian district within the International Longshoremen's Association. This proposal was overwhelmingly rejected by the international union.[3]

Major Labour Legislation in Canada

In the early 1800s, unions were illegal, and any attempt to unionize was considered a criminal act. However, the designation was soon changed from a violation of criminal law to a violation of civil law, and when the *Trade Union Act* was passed in 1872, unions were given the right to organize and to exist legally without being subject to criminal or civil conspiracy charges. Since that time, the body of labour legislation has grown considerably.[4]

In 1900, the federal government passed the *Conciliation Act*, under which the Minister of Labour could provide voluntary conciliation services upon request. The *Railway Disputes Act* of 1903 eliminated the voluntary aspect of conciliation for CPR trackmen by requiring the use of a mediation board and voluntary non-binding arbitration if conciliation was unsuccessful.

The *Conciliation and Labour Act* (passed in 1906) combined the acts of 1900 and 1903 and extended the provisions of the Railway Disputes Act to other industries. When this act proved to be inadequate, it was succeeded in 1907 by the *Industrial Disputes Investigations Act*, which applied to workers in the areas of mining, transport, communications and public utilities, but could also be used by other industries if they consented. The act—which was passed because a series of strikes during the previous decade had been harmful to the general public—provided for a three-person conciliation board with the power to investigate disputes and request testimony and evidence. Furthermore, no strike could be called while these hearings were in progress. While the board was mainly restricted to the role of conciliator, it did have the power to make recommendations if conciliation failed.

No other major legislation affecting labour was passed for many years, with the exception of the *War Measures Acts* of 1914 and 1939, which were intended to ensure that wartime production would not be disrupted. Then, in 1944, an order-in-council was passed that specifically defined the rights of unions and outlined the process for union certification and the workers' right to strike. In addition, the order made it compulsory for employers to bargain with duly certified unions, prevented employers from interfering with any union activity and required unions to expose their activities to union members and to the general public. It also required compulsory conciliation, designed as a "cooling-off" period when negotiations broke down, before a strike could be called.

Finally, in 1948, the passing of the *Industrial Disputes Investigations Act* incorporated the 1907 act and the order-in-council of 1944, and rescinded the War Measures Act. In 1971, previous federal legislation governing employment practices and labour standards was consolidated in the *Canada Labour Code*, which has since been split into three sections: (1) Mediation and Conciliation Services; (2) Occupational Health and Safety; and (3) Labour Standards.

Federal Labour Legislation

Most Canadian labour legislation is provincial, because it is considered law pertaining to property and civil rights over which provincial legislatures have authority. The

Human Resource Development Canada Labour

labour-travail.hrdc-drhc.gc.ca /doc/lab-trav/eng/

Human Resource Development Canada Labour Standards

http://info.load-otea.hrdc-drhc.gc. ca/~lsweb/homeen.shtml

federal government has authority only over industries under its jurisdiction, federal government employees and those matters delegated to the federal government by the provinces. These laws are embodied in the Canada Labour Code, which, as mentioned above, came into force in 1971.

The federal Department of Labour (Labour Canada) was established in 1900. The Minister of Labour is responsible for the **Canada Labour Code**, which outlines employment standards such as hours of work, minimum wages and annual vacations; it also provides for fair employment practices, equal pay for women and employee safety and industrial relations.

Matters delegated to the federal government by the provinces include the payment of unemployment insurance (now called employment insurance), benefits and pensions. Under the new *Employment Insurance Act* of 1996, all full- or part-time employees are covered against loss of wages caused by unemployment. The *Canada Pension Plan*, which came into effect in 1965, also requires contributions from both employer and employee in order to provide retirement pensions for all employees.

The administration of labour legislation rests primarily with the **Labour Relations Boards**, which are quasi-judicial tribunals composed of representatives from labour, management and the public. There are 11 such boards in Canada, one under the jurisdiction of the federal government and one for each of the 10 provinces. The boards are an alternative to the courts of law, which may be unable to respond adequately to labour problems. Although the boards are a subject of ongoing debate, they do offer a number of advantages. Their small size allows them to handle disputes more quickly than the courts. They are informal and cost relatively little to operate. Moreover, because they are specialized, members can develop expertise in labour matters. The boards' mixed composition—labour, management and the public—means that their decisions are more readily accepted by both sides. They also have flexibility in settling disputes, as they are not constrained by common-law precedents.[5]

Provincial Labour Legislation

All provinces have legislation designed to establish harmonious relations between employers and employees and to facilitate settlement of industrial disputes. These laws guarantee freedom of association and the right to organize. They also provide for labour relations boards or other bodies to certify trade unions as bargaining agents, and require that employers bargain with the certified union representing its employees. Other legislation establishes minimum wages, working hours, general holidays, vacations with pay, minimum-age restrictions, fair employment practices, equal pay for men and women, apprenticeship legislation, termination and workers' compensation. All provinces have passed labour relations acts to provide a framework for conciliation, mediation and arbitration services as required. The 1980s were characterized by new labour legislation, passed in many provinces, which curbed the power of unions. In British Columbia, for example, under a labour law passed in 1987, an Industrial Relations Council can recommend an end to strikes that are against "the public interest."

The Union Process

It is important to understand that the entire union process—indeed, Canada's entire industrial relations system—is bound by federal and provincial government regulations. The government specifies what a union must do to become the bargaining agent for a group of workers; how both sides must conduct themselves during

---

Canada Labour Code—sets out employment standards (e.g., hours of work, minimum wages and annual vacations) and provides for fair employment practices, equal pay for women, and employee safety and industrial relations.

Labour Relations Board—a board established under federal or provincial labour legislation to administer labour law, certify bargaining units, investigate unfair labour practices and perform other functions prescribed under the legislation.

negotiations; and what both sides must do before a strike or lockout can be called. Within this legal framework, both union and management are free to bargain for as much as each can obtain from the other.

Before workers can bargain as a group with management, they must become a legally recognized body; otherwise any contract negotiated would not be binding on management. Union certification alone does not ensure that negotiations will result in a contract. Even after exhaustive bargaining, management and unions may remain far apart on many issues, in which case conciliation, mediation and arbitration may be used to arrive at a contract. For workers who are engaged in essential services and are therefore forbidden to strike, compulsory arbitration is required. In compulsory arbitration, an outside party imposes a settlement. Should problems arise during the term of a contract, they can be resolved through a grievance procedure established during negotiations. We now examine each of the steps in the negotiation process in more detail.

Certification

Union **certification** ensures that a particular group of employees is legally recognized as a **bargaining unit**, so that a collective agreement concerning wages and working conditions can be negotiated and later enforced. Certification also indicates to the employer that a majority of employees wish to belong to the union.

The certification process begins when a group of workers either approaches a union or is invited by a union to become members. Those wishing to join complete an application and pay an initial fee to indicate their commitment.

Federal and provincial labour laws specify that a union must have a majority of employees before it is certified. Once this minimum has been obtained, an application is made to the appropriate labour relations board for certification. The Canada Labour Relations Board, which we discuss in more detail later, is responsible for the certification of bargaining units for employees that fall under federal jurisdiction. In addition, each province has a labour relations board that performs a similar function for workers under provincial jurisdiction. These boards ensure that voting for certification is properly conducted; that the proposed bargaining unit is appropriate for both the workers and the firm; and that the trade union in question is legally constituted and recognized.

The members of a new local union elect their own officers—president, vice-president, secretary, treasurer—to look after the local's affairs. Part of the dues paid by the members remain in the local union; the remainder goes to the national and/or international union. In return, the local receives a wide variety of services to help it in its negotiations with employers, including research, education and publications.

The local union, for its part, must maintain the support of a majority of the workers. Otherwise, the members or the firm's management may apply for **decertification**. In practice, however, management generally does not seek decertification when members are dissatisfied, since this action might lead to the formation of a new and stronger union, which would not be in management's interest.

Negotiation: Collective Bargaining

Once a union has been certified as the bargaining agent for a group of workers, negotiations between the union and management may begin for the purpose of establishing a contract. Each side is obliged to **bargain in good faith** with the other, which means that both parties must make every reasonable effort to develop a

Certification by the labour relations board ensures that a particular group of employees is legally recognized as a bargaining unit, so that a collective agreement concerning wages and working conditions can be negotiated and later enforced.

Bargaining unit—a group of workers in a craft, department, plant, firm, industry or occupation that a labour relations board deems appropriate for representation by a union for purposes of collective bargaining.

Decertification occurs when the labour relations board withdraws its certification of the union as the exclusive bargaining representative.

Bargaining in good faith means that both parties must make every reasonable effort to establish a collective agreement.

Collective agreement—a contract between one or more unions and one or more employers covering wages, hours, working conditions, benefits, rights of workers and unions, and the procedures to be followed in settling disputes and grievances.

Collective bargaining is a method of determining wages and other conditions of employment, through direct negotiations between the union and employer, that usually results in a written contract covering all employees in the bargaining unit.

collective agreement. However, the two sides often differ on what is reasonable. Attempts to reach a precise definition of "good faith" in collective bargaining have so far been unsuccessful, and except when one side or the other shows a clear unwillingness to negotiate, there is little recourse other than a strike or lockout. British Columbia and Quebec are exceptions, in that their laws allow either party to have outstanding issues in a first contract settled by an outside party.

The process of **collective bargaining** begins when the local union holds a series of meetings to discuss proposals that will be made to management and to select members who will act as the negotiations committee. The committee may also ask an affiliated union to provide experienced negotiators who can help with technical subjects such as pensions, technological change or health and safety. The contract proposals may address a wide variety of issues, the most common of which are listed in Table 11.2.

In collective bargaining, management and union are adversaries. Proposals advanced by the union are met with counter-proposals by management. Sometimes proposals are discussed at length and amended, or concessions are made by either side. Sometimes a strike vote is held early in the bargaining process to impress upon management the fact that the workers are prepared to back up union demands. Periodically, the bargaining committee reports to the union members, the management group to its superiors.

While the negotiation process may be lengthy, minor issues such as job posting and hiring procedures are often settled relatively quickly. Major issues such as wages and job security may also eventually be settled voluntarily. The concessions made depend on the relative strength of each group. Management is in a strong position during a recession or when the company is performing poorly since it may threaten to lay off employees or even shut down. On the other hand, when the company is doing well and is profitable, the union has the advantage because management does not want to jeopardize its operation with a lengthy strike. But regardless of how

TABLE   11.2   **Items usually included in a union contract**

Union Rights and Management Rights	Overtime pay regulations
Union activities and responsibilities	Leaves of absence and sick pay
Collection of union dues	Rest periods and lunch periods
Union officers and ship stewards	
Union bulletin boards	**Job rights and seniority**
Strikes and slowdowns	Seniority regulations
	Transfers
Wages and salaries	Promotions
Wage structure	Layoffs and recalls
General wage adjustments	Job posting and hiring procedures
Job evaluation	
Wage incentives	**Insurance and benefit programs**
Time studies	Group life insurance
Pay for reporting and call-in	Medical insurance
Shift differentials, bonuses, profit sharing	Pension program
	Supplemental unemployment benefits
Hours of work and time off	
Regular hours of work	**Health and safety**
Holidays	
Vacations	**Discipline, suspension and discharge**
	Grievance handling and arbitration

much power either side has at any given time, both sides generally have a common interest—to see that the organization survives and continues to provide income for all concerned. In most instances, this common interest is sufficient incentive for the two sides to reach an agreement and sign a contract.

When an agreement has been reached, union members must vote to accept the contract—**ratification**. If the contract is accepted by the union membership, it becomes a legal agreement binding on both sides for the duration of the period specified. If problems arise in the interpretation of the contract at a future date, a grievance procedure can be used to resolve them, whether they involve a particular individual or the entire union.

If the contract is rejected, bargaining may be resumed by both parties. If further bargaining is not possible, federal and provincial labour laws provide other methods to help the two sides reach an agreement.

Ratification of a contract means that once an agreement has been reached, union members must vote to accept the contract before it becomes a legal agreement.

Conciliation and Mediation

When contract negotiations reach an impasse, relations between union and management can become strained and deteriorate. Neither side may be willing to concede on any issue lest concession be interpreted as weakness. To bring the two sides together, a conciliation officer is appointed to encourage and focus discussion. If the talks fail, the conciliation officer will write a "no board report" that will allow a local union, after a number of specified days, to be in a legal strike position.

Conciliation is a requirement for both parties before a legal strike or lockout can occur. Both the federal and provincial governments employ full-time mediators to help settle disputes. Alternatively, judges, lawyers, priests, university professors or people from other occupations may be appointed as mediators.

It is during this cooling-off period, after the no board report has been issued, that a mediator is either requested by the two parties or appointed by the government in a last-ditch effort to try to get the two parties to make a deal. The mediator's first task is to meet with both sides to determine whether they are serious about reaching a settlement, or whether they are simply going through the process of mediation as a legal requirement before calling a strike or lockout. Mediators explain their role in the **mediation** process and indicate how they expect to facilitate an agreement, whether by recommending a possible settlement or by acting as spokespersons for each side. Since mediators hold no special powers, the success of their efforts depends entirely on the trust and respect the two parties have for them.

If the mediator finds the parties want a settlement, he or she determines the issues to be resolved and the positions of both parties. The mediator then meets with each side separately to determine what concessions each may be prepared to make in arriving at a settlement. At this point, the mediator's skill and experience is important; he or she must convey to each side the extent to which the other is prepared to compromise. The mediator then tries to lead the two parties toward an agreement without letting either side feel it has capitulated.

If the mediator is able to bring the two parties to an agreement, then a contract is signed. If the talks fail, the union will be in a legal strike position according to the no board report. A union may not strike until members have voted, by secret ballot, to do so. In some provinces, an employer has the right to ask for a supervised vote by the employees in the bargaining unit on their employer's final offer. In all provinces, both parties have the option to submit their outstanding issues to voluntary arbitration.

Conciliation is the first stage in the mediation process intended to bring the two sides together to resume talks.

Mediation is a method of settling disputes by bringing in a neutral third party (mediator).

"Another setback — the mediators just went out on strike."

SOURCE: Artist—Al Kaufman. Reproduced by permission of the Masters Agency, Capitola, California.

Arbitration

Both sides may agree to the appointment of an arbitrator or to the establishment of an arbitration board. The latter is composed of three people, one nominated by the company, one by the union, and the third—the chair—by the two board members. If there is a disagreement over the selection of the chair, the Minister of Labour may make the appointment. Increasingly today, single arbitrators are being used instead of arbitration boards to reduce the cost of this process for both sides.

The arbitrator or the board listens to both sides and includes its findings and recommendations in a report. Although the recommendations of the arbitrator are not binding on either side, the fact that both sides have agreed to **arbitration** means that there is considerable pressure on both sides to accept them. This means that by agreeing to **voluntary arbitration** both sides take some risks, since they may be obliged to concede more than they would have in the event of a strike. If an agreement is reached, then a contract is signed. If no agreement is reached after a period specified in the federal and provincial labour laws, workers may strike or management may institute a lockout. The decision to strike depends on the outcome of the strike vote.

For employees in essential services (e.g., hospital workers or police), legislation may prohibit strikes and lockouts, and thus compulsory arbitration is required. Under **compulsory arbitration**, both management and union are compelled to submit unresolved issues to the arbitration board, whose decision is binding on both parties. Although compulsory arbitration may be less effective than strike action, it can prevent the loss of income and profits that might result from a prolonged strike or lockout. Arbitration thus maintains union-management relations since both parties are interested in securing their incomes. Arbitration may also save face for both sides, as neither is seen to concede to the other and both may claim that the settlement was imposed on them by an outside party.

Arbitration is a method of settling disputes through a third party, usually a board of three people, whose decision is final and binding.

Voluntary arbitration occurs when both union and management agree to be bound by the arbitrator's decision.

Compulsory arbitration occurs when both parties must subject outstanding issues to an arbitrator or board because of legislation that forbids a strike.

Grievances

Even when a contract exists between management and the union, problems may arise in the interpretation of its terms. For example, a worker may believe that she is not receiving the rate specified in the contract for the job she is doing. In another instance, a worker who has been laid off may claim seniority over another worker who has not been laid off. Workers who believe they have been unfairly treated according to the terms of the contract may file a **grievance** that will then be processed according to the procedure established during collective bargaining.

When a grievance is filed, management and the union first try to resolve it within the worker's department. If the problem cannot be solved at that stage, progressively higher levels of union and management personnel become involved. If still no settlement results, the grievance may be submitted to an impartial third party known as an arbitrator, or to an arbitration board, whose decision will be final and binding on both the union and the company.

Occasionally, a grievance may lead to a wildcat strike—an illegal and unauthorized strike by workers to show that they are not satisfied with the handling of the grievance by either management or the union, or both.

Grievance—a complaint against management, filed by one or more employees or a union, concerning an alleged injustice or breach of the collective agreement.

When All Else Fails

Though management and union are put into adversarial positions because of the nature of the collective-bargaining process, in 95% of all contract negotiations a collective agreement is reached and a contract signed in the absence of any strike action. However, when it appears that an agreement will not be reached, one side may resort to the use of certain "weapons" to force the other to an agreement. Table 11.3 lists the weapons commonly available to each side.

Weapons of labour and management

TABLE 11.3

LABOUR

Weapon	Effect
Strike	Union members refuse to work.
Picketing	Discourages customers and suppliers from dealing with the firm; spreads information about the strike.
Boycott	Members of other unions and/or the public refuse to do business with the firm.

MANAGEMENT

Weapon	Effect
Lockout	Workers are prevented from entering the firm's premises to work.
Injunction	Legal means are used to stop union activities such as strikes and picketing. Though used more often by management, the injunction may also be requested by the union to stop illegal actions on the part of management.
Employers' Associations	A number of firms make a cooperative effort to deal with unions, particularly in contract negotiations.

By picketing, strikers attempt to publicize their dispute and try to persuade others not to enter the premises to work

Strike action—the total withdrawal of labour's services, which is intended to put pressure on the employer to agree to terms and conditions of employment.

Rotating strike—a strike organized in such a way that only some groups of employees stop work at a given time, with each group taking a turn.

Sympathy strike—a strike by employees who are not directly involved in a labour dispute, but who want to demonstrate their support for another union.

Wildcat strike—a strike in violation of the collective agreement and not authorized by the union.

Work-to-rule—a concerted effort by employees to slow down work activity by obeying all laws and rules applying to their work.

Picketing—occurs when striking workers patrol the outside of an employer's premises to publicize the existence of the labour dispute and to persuade employees of other firms not to cross the picket line.

Weapons of Labour

A union's most effective weapon is **strike action**—the total withdrawal of labour's services in order to halt production. A strike is costly to the union since it does not receive regular dues from members while they are on strike, but instead pays them a token amount each week from the union strike fund. Unless it has adequate funds, therefore, the union will not usually resort to a strike. Nor are workers generally willing to forgo regular wages in a protracted strike, since the loss is seldom recovered. Hence, when a union decides on strike action it usually means that the issues at stake are of great importance.

On the other hand, the mere threat of a strike is often equally effective in achieving a settlement with management, particularly if a strike would disrupt an otherwise profitable operation. Unions thus often ask their members for a strike vote early in the bargaining sessions to show management that its members are prepared to strike to back up their demands.

The strike is usually the last act a union considers after all avenues of negotiation have been exhausted and after the mediation step has been concluded. A union may decide to use a **rotating strike** in which only some groups of employees strike at any one time. A **sympathy strike** is a strike by workers who are not directly involved in a labour dispute but who want to show their support for another union. Sometimes a union's members may go on an illegal strike—a **wildcat strike**—which is not supported by the union. Although not a strike in the strict sense of the word, **work-to-rule** is a concerted effort by employees to slow down work activity by simply obeying all laws and rules applying to their work.

Picketing during a strike serves two major purposes. First, the signs and placards carried by union members outside the firm's premises let the public know that a labour dispute exists, and often provide information about it. Second, picketing attempts to discourage other firms from dealing with the firm engaged in the strike. Strikers attempt to persuade employees of other firms not to cross the picket line. While this action is often successful, on occasion it has led to violence and property damage.

A **boycott** is an appeal to customers not to buy the firm's products, especially if the company has been able to operate using managerial staff. A **primary boycott** attempts to prevent other union members from dealing with the firm. A **secondary boycott** attempts to discourage other unionized businesses from patronizing the firm through threats that the business's own employees may resort to a work stoppage. For example, if a steel mill that is engaged in a strike is able to continue selling the products in its inventory to manufacturing firms, employees of those firms could threaten work stoppages if the firms continue to purchase from the mill.

Weapons of Management

The **lockout** is one of management's chief means of forcing labour to accept its demands. The employer closes the plant, thus cutting employees off from their source of income. Management seldom initiates a work stoppage since it would reduce the firm's production. However, a lockout might be used if, for example, production has been curtailed because one union is on strike, while other employees belonging to non-striking unions are still working. A lockout of all employees would then reduce costs and possibly put pressure on the striking union to work toward a settlement.

An **injunction** is a court order prohibiting an illegal practice by either the union or management. For example, if a union has too many picketers in front of the employer's place of business, management or customers may be prevented from entering the premises. This practice is illegal, and management may apply for a court injunction to have it stopped. Similarly, if management is engaged in an illegal practice with respect to the union, the union may apply for an injunction. While today the injunction can be used by both parties, in the past unfair legislation allowed employers to use the injunction to prohibit strikes. This practice is no longer permitted, and today the injunction is used mainly to prevent excessive picketing and deter violence and damage to company property.

The formation of **employers' associations** is another tool management uses to deal with labour. Employers may join together as a group to lobby government and bargain with unions for an industry wide settlement. Examples are the Canadian Manufacturers' Association, Forest Industrial Relations Bureau in British Columbia and Ontario Trucking Association. In the past, employers were reluctant to join together and bargain with labour because of their traditional concern about competition for customers. However, when there are many small firms in an industry and only one or a few large unions, employers have found it advantageous to be represented by a single bargaining group, so that all firms face the same labour costs.

Basic Issues in Collective Bargaining

As Table 11.2 indicated, a typical union contract may include a wide range of issues to be negotiated. Some issues are of major importance in any agreement, however. These include union security, wages and fringe benefits, hours of work, job security and promotion.

Union Security

It is not easy for a union to gain legal recognition as the sole bargaining agent for a group of workers in a given firm or industry. Certification is costly and requires considerable effort on the part of the organizers. Certification also does not guarantee security. If union members become dissatisfied with their present organization, they

---

Boycott—an appeal to customers not to buy the firm's products if the employees are out on strike and/or the company has been able to operate using managerial staff.

Primary boycott—attempts to prevent other union members from dealing with the firm.

Secondary boycott—attempts to discourage other unionized businesses from patronizing the firm through threats that the business's own employees may resort to a work stoppage.

Lockout—a labour dispute in which management refuses to allow employees to enter the work premises.

Injunction—a court order restraining an employer or union from committing or engaging in certain practices.

Employers' association—composed of a number of employers who join together as a group to lobby government and bargain with unions for an industry-wide settlement.

Closed shop—all employees in a bargaining unit must be union members in good standing before being hired; all new employees are hired through the union.

Union shop—a place of work where every worker covered by a collective agreement must become and remain a member of the union. New workers need not be union members but must become members after a certain number of days.

Union shop with preferential hiring means that employers are obliged to hire union members if any are available; if non-union workers are hired, they must subsequently become union members.

Preferential hiring is an arrangement whereby an employer agrees to hire only union workers so long as there are union workers available.

Rand Formula/agency shop refers to a clause in the collective agreement that states that the employer agrees to deduct an amount equal to the union dues from all members of the bargaining unit, whether or not they are members of the union.

Open shop—a place of work where union membership is not required for an individual to secure or retain employment.

Dues check-off—the employer deducts union dues directly from the employee's paycheque and remits it to the union.

Cost-of-living allowance (COLA)—refers to periodic pay increases based on upward changes in the consumer price index.

may ask for decertification in order to have another union represent them. And if a rival union, or even management, senses dissatisfaction among members of a union, they too may seek decertification. Thus, security is usually one of the first issues negotiated in any new contract.

Security, to a union, means members. The more members it has, the stronger it is, both financially and in the eyes of management. The ideal situation for a union is a **closed shop**—only union members are permitted to work in a particular firm or industry. If a closed shop cannot be negotiated, the next best alternative is the **union shop**—employers are free to hire as they please, but the new workers are required to join the union after a probationary period (usually 30 days). A modified version of the latter, the **union shop with preferential hiring**, means that employers are obliged to hire union members if any are available; if there are none, and non-union workers are hired, they must subsequently become union members.

Under simple **preferential hiring rules**, employers must hire union members if available, but no one need become or remain a union member unless he or she so wishes. Another situation, known as the **Rand Formula** or **agency shop**, leaves the worker the choice of joining or not joining the union; however, all workers must pay union dues. Finally, the **open shop** allows workers to join a union if they wish, but non-union workers are not required to pay dues. In any of the last three situations, the union is not particularly secure.

By maintaining its membership, a union also strengthens its financial security through members' dues. The union will usually negotiate to have the employer deduct union dues from the workers' paycheques, a practice known as **dues check-off**.

Wages and Employee Benefits

Wages are always a key issue in any contract. The union attempts to obtain an increase in real income for its members, which means an increase over and above the rate of inflation. Since this may be difficult to obtain, especially when inflation is high, unions often negotiate for a **cost-of-living allowance (COLA)** clause, which allows wages to rise automatically in direct proportion to the consumer price index. COLA arrangements were popular in Canada while inflation was high. In 1977, more than one-fifth of Canadian workers were covered by a cost-of-living allowance clause in their contracts. However, this trend peaked in 1980 when 42.6% of workers were covered by new contracts with COLA clauses. By 1986, only 12.7% of new contracts were so covered.

The cost of employee benefits is also rising. As noted in the preceding chapter, typical non-wage benefits include holidays, paid medical and dental plans and pensions. However, the list is becoming longer as unions continue to seek new benefits such as paid legal services, daycare cost sharing for working mothers and subsidies for cafeteria lunches. Employee benefits amount to approximately one-third of the average Canadian worker's total wages.

Hours of Work

One hundred and fifty years ago, standard working hours stretched from dawn till dusk, six days a week. Even at the turn of the century, 60- to 72-hour weeks were not uncommon. Today, the legal workweek is 40 hours, and many people work only 30 or 35 hours per week. This reduction in the length of the workweek was accomplished primarily by unions in the early part of the 20th century, and was aided by government legislation.

In addition to regulating the length of the workweek, unions negotiate for overtime and shift differential pay if their members are required to work hours that differ from the norm. Workers usually receive time-and-a-half, or double time, if they are required to work longer than the regular quota of hours per day or week, or on weekends or holidays.

Job Security and Promotion

People generally want to be assured of a job and a steady income. Sudden loss of employment can cause tremendous hardship for individuals and their families. Unions are therefore often forceful in their attempts to gain job security for their members. For example, they have insisted that if layoffs are necessary, they should be done on the basis of seniority. Certainly, from the union's point of view, letting the last person hired be the first to leave is a fair method of solving the problem. However, employers would naturally prefer to retain the most productive workers, laying off those who are not performing as well. Management claims that a layoff system based on seniority tends to lower the productivity of workers who have been with the firm for a long period, as their jobs are virtually assured regardless of performance.

In protecting their members' jobs, unions sometimes contribute to inefficiency through the practice known as **featherbedding**— keeping workers in jobs that are no longer necessary. Railway unions, for example, insisted that engine firefighters be retained, even though they were no longer required once all railways had converted to diesel engines. Nevertheless, it took 13 years to resolve the issue. Job security was also at the heart of the eight-month newspaper strike in Vancouver in 1978–79, when computer typesetting threatened to make the jobs of some workers obsolete. The question became a major strike issue when the union insisted the jobs be retained. To resolve such issues, management generally resorts either to early retirement of workers whose jobs have become obsolete or to payment of a healthy separation allowance.

When workers are to be promoted to better-paid jobs or supervisory positions, unions also insist that management proceed according to seniority. Employers, however, generally do not readily accept the seniority rule, since not everyone is capable of performing all jobs equally well, or of being a good manager or supervisor. Management therefore often compromises, taking both merit and seniority into consideration. If two employees with equivalent qualifications are considered suitable for promotion, the one with the longer service record is promoted first.

Featherbedding—union practice that involves keeping workers in jobs that are no longer necessary.

Labour Unions in Canada Today

With the 1982 recession, labour's woes began. The federal government (followed by British Columbia) introduced a wage restraint bill that, in effect, suspended collective-bargaining rights for two years. Similar curbs were later adopted by most provinces. Both the federal and provincial governments have been especially tough on public service unions, legislating them back to work and declaring many public service employees essential to public health and safety, thereby effectively removing their right to strike.

Labour's ability to fight back depends on the economy. When the economy slows down and unemployment rises, as in the early 1980s and 1990s, job security and working conditions are at the top of a union's bargaining list. Wage increases are only possible when the economy improves and companies declare profits.

Although the labour movement experienced problems associated with the poor economic climate in the early 1980s and 1990s, it is unlikely that it will decline in importance. In a survey, some 69% of the general public support a role for unions in public policy; 57% support close consultation with labour groups by the government; and 31% support some consultation with government. Nevertheless, as shown in Figure 11.4, the percentage of the labour force affiliated with the union movement has not grown appreciably in the past few decades.

A major reason for the slowdown in the growth of union membership is the lack of a clear-cut cause. In the past, low wages and poor working conditions provided workers with ample reason for joining a union. Today, the gains already achieved in these areas make organization less of a necessity. Moreover, it is unlikely that current economic conditions will allow either substantial reductions in hours of work or large increases in wages.

Another major reason is due to the decline in manufacturing industries and a rise in employment in the service industry where the average size of the firm is small and there is a great reliance on part-time workers. This makes it difficult and costly for unions to organize workers in these firms.

Other problems facing unions are technological advances in the automation of factories, cutbacks in government-funded programs and the trend toward self-employment as communication and computerization continue to expand.

Particularly threatening to unions is the North American Free Trade Agreement. As Canadian companies face increased competition from U.S. and Mexican companies, they will have to look hard at the costs of doing business in Canada. Mexico's low-cost labour may make it difficult for Canadian companies not to relocate their plants to countries with lower minimum wages, higher unemployment, weaker unions and more stringent anti-labour legislation.

FIGURE 11.4

Union membership;
1921–1992

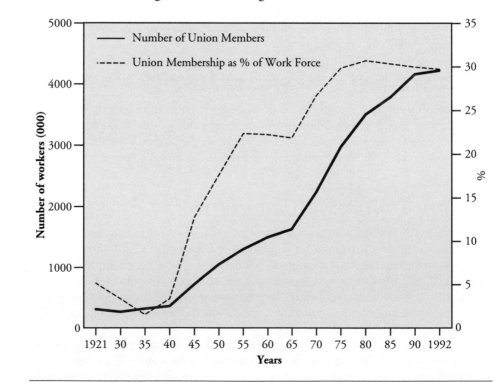

SOURCE: Adapted from *Labour Organization in Canada* (Ottawa: Supply and Services, Canada, 1993).

Unions are now turning to other concerns such as social reform, environmental problems and politics. This shift is due partly to the retirement of older workers and the influx of many young workers who grew up during a period of affluence. With over half of their members today under 35 years of age, and their basic concerns largely taken care of, unions can turn their attention to a wider range of issues.

Regardless of how the public views unions and their role in society, unions have always struggled to maintain their membership. Unions have been especially frustrated and continue to lose ground in their efforts to unionize the white-collar sector in financial institutions and retail stores. The number of unionized bank branch workers, for instance, has slipped considerably.

Labour-Management Relations— Some Critical Issues

Labour unions came into existence to strengthen the bargaining power of workers and improve working conditions. It has not been easy for unions to get owners/ management to accept collective bargaining. Even when it is finally accepted, management still often holds the upper hand because it ultimately controls the union members' jobs. Often the unions are forced to accept lower settlements, or even to lose benefits when the economy is performing poorly and the company is not earning a profit.

Labour-management relations in North America have at times been stormy. This is particularly true of times when many agreements come up for renewal during a particular year and strikes occur more frequently than normal. The general public also takes notice when public service unions go on strike and cause major disruption in services. During such times, the effectiveness of the whole process of collective bargaining is questioned with cries of "There must be a better way," particularly when long strikes affect many innocent people. Let us look at some of the major issues affecting labour management relations.

The Adversarial Nature of Collective Bargaining

Collective bargaining between labour and management is still considered the best method of sharing the surplus produced by the firm. The strike, or threat of it, is the weapon that backs up the union's demands, while the lockout and loss of jobs are the weapons behind management's attempts to keep union demands in line. Most labour agreements are settled peacefully. When we look at the years 1967 to 1975, considered a stormy period in Canada's labour scene, almost 80% of all major collective agreements covering 500 or more persons in the private sector, and nearly 90% in the public sector, were concluded without any disruption; half of these did not even require third-party intervention. If smaller bargaining units were included, the percentage of peaceful settlements would be even higher.[6]

Nevertheless, collective bargaining is an adversarial process. Unions make their demands, management tries its best to minimize those demands— and conflict develops. During good economic times, management will give in to union demands more readily because it does not want to risk a strike. On the other hand, when times are bad, management has the upper hand because it can threaten the union with layoffs or, in extreme cases, with plant closure. Sometimes both sides simply dig in their heels, particularly on issues that threaten the authority of management or the survival of the union. If mediation cannot resolve the issues, a strike or a lockout is the final step.

The Effectiveness of the Strike

An increasing number of people are now convinced that a strike is not the best way to resolve issues that cannot be settled in the normal collective-bargaining process. Halting production reduces the total amount of wealth available for distribution to both parties. More significantly, it seems that the strike, or threat of it, no longer effectively generates pressure for a settlement. The economic impact of the open-ended strike is lessening because, in many instances, the employer can continue to operate; at the same time, the availability of alternative economic benefits such as strike pay or employment elsewhere during a strike makes settlement less urgent for strikers.

Though strikes may be out of date from an economic point of view, they may be used by workers for other reasons. Some employees take strike action for ideological reasons; others regard it simply as a break in routine. But research should be done to learn more about the modern strike before considering any alternatives.

Labour Disputes in Canada

Canadians have been accused in the past of having an unsettled labour scene. For example, in 1977 Canada shared first place with Italy in having the greatest total number of workdays lost among the reporting industrialized countries.[7] One reason for this is that when strikes occur in North America, they usually last much longer than those in most other industrialized countries. In Italy, for example, general strikes involving many workers occur much more frequently than in North America. In the late 1990s, however, work stoppages in Canada have fallen dramatically.

There are several reasons for this relative labour peace. First, the inflation rate is very low and unemployment very high, which has made labour more concerned about job security. Consequently, unions focus on items such as early retirement incentives, pension indexing and job sharing to keep more members employed. But there is also a major change going on in labour-management relations. More and more companies are involving workers in both day-to-day and longer-term decision making, employee ownership and profit sharing. Companies are doing this in return for various agreements with unions that will allow the companies to react more quickly to global competition.[8]

Compulsory Arbitration

Compulsory arbitration must lead to an agreement between union and management, but it often leaves many problems unsolved.

Regardless of the cost of a strike, it remains the main weapon by which labour can back up its demands. While **compulsory arbitration** has been cited as an alternative to strike action, it is often an unacceptable alternative for both unions and management. In many cases, both sides entrench themselves in extreme positions, knowing that compulsory arbitration is likely to bring about a settlement that reflects a middle position. Nevertheless, some of the pressure to resolve disputes is relieved when an outside party works out a solution.

Labour in the Boardroom

Mitbestimmung (co-determination) grants workers a larger part in major management decisions, particularly those that affect their jobs and working conditions.

As previously mentioned, labour-management relations have started to go through a transition period as more decision making, both day-to-day and longer term, is passed on to labour. Workers are being granted a larger say in major management decisions, particularly those that affect their jobs and working conditions. The practice known as **mitbestimmung**—roughly translated as "joint decision making"—has helped to maintain good relations between management and unions in West Germany for many years. However, in order for this practice to work in North America, a fundamental change would be required in the attitudes of management and labour toward one another. Management has traditionally claimed the sole right to make decisions. Labour in both the United States and Canada has also been reluctant to become more involved in management decision making. Since unions would be required to show more restraint in their contract demands and more responsibility for the successful operation of the firm, leaders believe such a move would prevent unions from bargaining effectively for their members.

The first step was taken in 1980, when Douglas A. Fraser, president of the United Auto Workers union, joined the Chrysler board of directors as part of the deal in which workers were to assist the ailing company by deferring wages and other benefits. Chrysler was thus the first major U.S. corporation to allow a labour representative to sit on the board of directors. After three one-year terms, Fraser resigned in 1984. Upon his departure, the new president of the United Auto Workers union, Owen F. Bieber, was elected to the Chrysler board of directors. Although viewed as "unwilling to hold hands with management," Bieber had by 1989 acquired a reputation for having significantly reduced labour-management confrontation in collective bargaining.

According to Fraser, workers have benefited from labour's position on the board by knowing about plant closing and economic dislocations beforehand so that they can be prepared. In one instance, Fraser was able to prevent 119 Chrysler workers in the tank division from losing their seniority rights. From management's point of view, communications between union and management have improved considerably. According to another labour leader, however, this practice has not won widespread acceptance, since one representative on the board cannot change a corporation.[9] As of the time of writing, Chrysler has no union leader on the board. However, it may be too early to call the experiment a failure. As global competition increases, management and labour in North America may be forced to act more harmoniously in order to survive.

Sharing Information and Management Credibility

Another potential method of resolving conflicts between labour and management is increased sharing of information between the two factions regarding the firm's financial condition and future plans, especially as they affect the worker.

A survey conducted by Hay Management Consultants Ltd. of Toronto questioned employees of about 1900 organizations each year for the past 10 years. The results indicated that most employees of better-performing companies feel that senior management is open and frank with them. In general, the survey found that most workers considered their managers credible, even though the believability rate has slipped.[10]

Data drawn from the survey compared employees' opinions and corporate performances of 500 firms over the past four years. Employees at all levels in companies that were performing well viewed information from executives as more credible than did those in poorly performing firms. They were satisfied with the amount of information the company provided to them. On questions about satisfaction with pay, opportunities to learn new skills, how the company is perceived as a place to work and so on, in each case senior management in the better-performing companies received high marks from their employees.[11]

In contrast, poorly performing companies generally keep their employees in the dark about what is happening with the company. Companies that fail to involve their workers will quickly see the results emerge on their financial statements.

A key factor in getting employees on side with management is the latter's credibility. Management cannot expect their employees to be concerned about competitiveness in the market, productivity, financial structure, budget, staff costs, research and so, if management does not communicate to them the financial state of the company. Furthermore, most employees want to be involved in decisions about issues that affect their working lives. Strikes are not primarily caused by money disputes, contrary to what many executives seem to believe, but more by poor communication and the poor credibility thus generated.

Management's credibility with its employees takes time to establish. It comes from effective and consistent two-way communications over time. Management must sit down in face-to-face interviews with groups of employees to find out directly from the employees how they feel about their company, their jobs, their working environment, their management and their future. Managers who use this strategy often gain enormously in credibility—which is the secret of harmonious labour-management relations.

One company that tried this approach in Canada was Timken Co., the world's largest tapered roller bearings manufacturer, with plants in St. Thomas, Ontario, the United States, Europe and South America. The company started a worldwide two-way communications effort designed to obtain comments from Timken employees to get their cooperation to meet the challenge of the changing nature of competition.

The company held face-to-face group meetings with employees and obtained thousands of comments, complaints, ideas and suggestions for lowering costs and improving efficiencies.

Timken did this 18 months before contract negotiations were due, so, when the steelworker negotiations concluded, Timken members in U.S. plants overwhelmingly approved a deeply concessionary contract without a strike, and without rancor. Timken has continued its two-way communications policy since the contract settlement, inviting employee ideas during group meetings with management. The company has adopted many of these ideas; the result has been a 10% cost reduction.[12]

Chapter Summary

1. While there are differences between the aims of labour and the aims of management, both sides are generally interested in ensuring that the business provides income for both the workers and its owners. A union is a group of workers who have joined together to achieve common goals. Although distinctions are becoming blurred, there are two types of unions: craft unions and industrial unions.

2. Early in the 19th century, workers first attempted to increase their bargaining power with employers by joining together into labour unions aimed at improving their income and working conditions. However, unions could not legally organize until the Trade Union Act was passed in 1872. Thereafter, the union movement experienced tremendous growth, even though economic conditions and internal union disagreements caused periodic disruptions.

3. A major upheaval occurred in 1935 when the industrial unions in the United States split away from the craft unions to form the Congress of Industrial Organizations; a similar split followed shortly in Canada. Thereafter, the industrial

unions in both countries grew rapidly until 1955, when the CIO in the United States merged again with the craft unions represented by the American Federation of Labour. There followed in Canada a similar merger between the Trades and Labour Congress, which acted for the craft unions, and the Canadian Congress of Labour, which represented the industrial unions. The merger brought peace to the labour movement and enabled it to concentrate once again on union growth and improving wages and working conditions for members.

4. Before a union can become the legal bargaining agent for a group of workers, it must be certified by the appropriate Labour Relations Board. For certification to occur, a majority of the workers must indicate their desire to belong to that particular union. Once certified, the union can begin negotiations with management on issues affecting the workers, such as wages and fringe benefits, working conditions, hours of work, job security and promotion.

5. If management and the union cannot reach agreement on work-related issues and establish a contract, then both must go through a process of conciliation and mediation. If this step fails to produce a settlement, the two parties may voluntarily put the unresolved issues to an arbitration board for settlement. If the union and management cannot agree to voluntary arbitration, then the union is free to strike, just as management is free to lock out employees. In some instances, particularly if essential services are involved, a strike or lockout is illegal; all issues are then subject to binding arbitration. The entire collective-bargaining process must be carried out according to federal or provincial government labour legislation.

6. The strike is a union's major weapon. Unions may also resort to picketing to get their message across, and may prevent non-union labour from crossing the picket lines. Boycotts, both primary and secondary, are used to persuade customers and union workers not to deal with the struck firm. Labour is making increasing use of its financial influence (through their pension funds, unions are often major investors in companies) to gain concessions. Management for its part is turning to employer associations for industry-wide bargaining.

7. With completion of the unionization of public employees, union growth has once again stabilized. Future growth may only come from organizing agricultural and white-collar workers. Unions today are often accused of having too much power and of using it unwisely; calls for limiting union power and curtailing their ability to strike are not uncommon.

8. Although collective bargaining is still considered an effective method of distributing a firm's surplus between owners and labour, there is evidence that the strike is becoming outmoded. As companies face more global competition, unemployment has soared in Canada, resulting in changes for labour negotiations. In response to global pressures, management has negotiated with labour agreements that allow workers to be involved in both day-to-day and long-term decision making. Increased sharing of information between management and labour will give the latter a better understanding of the financial situation of the firm and the problems facing it.

KEY TERMS

Union 409

Craft union 409

Industrial union 409

Canadian Labour Congress (CLC) . . .413

National union 413

International union 413

Local union 413

Labour council 413

Canada Labour Code 416

Labour Relations Board 416

Certification .417

Bargaining unit 417

Decertification 417

Bargain in good faith 417

Collective agreement 418

Collective bargaining 418

Ratification 419

Conciliation .419

Mediation 419

Arbitration 420

Voluntary arbitration 420

Compulsory arbitration 420

Grievance 421

Strike action .422

Rotating strike 422

Sympathy strike 422

Wildcat strike 422

Work-to-rule .422

Picketing 422

Boycott 423

Primary boycott 423

Secondary boycott 423

Lockout 423

Injunction 423

Employers' association 423

Closed shop .424

Union shop 424

Union shop with preferential hiring . . .424

Preferential hiring 424

Rand formula/agency shop 424

Open shop 424

Dues check-off 424

Cost-of-living allowance (COLA) 424

Featherbedding 425

Compulsory arbitration 428

Mitbestimmung 428

REVIEW QUESTIONS

1 Describe the aims of labour and those of management.

2 What is a labour union? Explain the difference between a craft union and an industrial union.

3 Briefly outline the history of the labour movement in Canada.

4 What is the purpose of the Canadian Labour Congress (CLC)?

5 Briefly outline the major federal labour legislation.

6 What advantages do labour relations boards have over labour courts?

7 Explain the following steps in the union process: certification, collective bargaining, conciliation, mediation, arbitration and grievance.

8 List and describe the weapons used by both labour and management to back up their demands.

9 Why is the strike weapon important to unions?

10 Briefly describe the four major issues involved in collective bargaining. Why are they important?

11 Why is collective bargaining described as an adversarial process?

12 Why is the strike no longer considered an effective weapon in settling disputes?

13 How could a union representative on a firm's board of directors facilitate union-management relations? Why has management in North America not accepted union representation on the board of directors?

14 How can better sharing of information between management and labour improve relations between the two groups?

DISCUSSION QUESTIONS

1   "Government employees should be allowed to strike." Discuss.

2   What would be the repercussions if lower and middle managers belonged to unions?

3   "Unions have become too powerful." Discuss both sides of this issue.

4   Will labour unions always be necessary? Give reasons for your answer.

5   Is the collective-bargaining process the best means by which labour can ensure its share of the economic pie? Give reasons for your answer.

6   Should management share more information with unions? How could this solve some labour-management problems?

Stresses and Strains on the Way to Glory

When her father had left her the clothing factory, little did Marie expect she would have to devote her entire existence to keeping the place afloat. Making and selling baby clothes in a competitive market is a cut-throat business, especially since offshore factories pay a fraction of the cost for labour. In fact, there weren't many baby clothes being made in Canada anymore! If Marie's factory closed, jobs would be pretty hard to find in her rural neighbourhood.

With the long hours, the pressure and squeezed profit margins, Marie wasn't sure she wanted to be an entrepreneur for the rest of her life. Still, she derived a certain satisfaction from knowing that her company's payroll put food on the table for 50 families, even if she wasn't getting rich in the process.

The problem was, her employees sometimes acted as if the firm were a bottomless pit. There seemed to be constant agitation for more money. Even though the cost of living wasn't all that high around these parts, and a young couple could buy a building lot for under $5000, everybody seemed to constantly want more. Didn't these people understand economics?

So far, Marie had resisted. In fact, she had put her foot down—hard! There would be no raises until she had a firmer sense of what her profit (or loss) was going to be at year-end.

Well, you'd think she was the reincarnation of Attila the Hun! There were even mutterings about joining a union. Her employees were saying that she didn't understand what it was like to be a working person—that she was insensitive to their needs! What was she to do? A raise now might really put the company in financial difficulties. No matter what happened, she couldn't give in.

There was this other thing. Only about half of Marie's employees stayed on the job for any length of time (and even this lot might be absent during deer-hunting season). The rest would work for 10 weeks, then draw unemployment insurance for the rest of the year. This was a way of life. In some parts of rural Canada, it's called the 10/42 syndrome.

Anyway, these work habits were driving Marie crazy! She wondered how much the constant retraining and new-employee inefficiency was costing her. Some days, she hardly recognized anyone on the production floor! It seemed that she was being held hostage by her own employees—"Give us more money or we'll join the 10/42 crowd."

SOURCE: Dr. P. C. Wright, Faculty of Administration, University of New Brunswick. Reprinted by permission of the author.

Questions

1 How should Marie handle her employees' threats about joining a union?

2 Does she have the right to refuse employees' demands for more money, even if the 10/42 threat is real? Why do employees ask for more money?

3 In terms of shop-floor labour relations, how does Marie handle the charge that she is insensitive to her employees' needs?

Should Government Employees Be Allowed to Strike?

The right to strike was given to public service workers in the federal government and in Quebec and New Brunswick in the late 1960s, and in British Columbia and Newfoundland in the early 1970s. However, this right was soon circumscribed when many governments began to order employees back to work. In 1978, acts of Parliament ended the walkout of 375 marine engineers who worked on Canada's Great Lakes fleet, and a strike by 23 000 inside postal workers, whose service was considered essential to the public. In October 1987, the same 23 000 postal workers were ordered back to work by the federal government, which two months previously had passed legislation to end a national rail strike. Public service employees in both Quebec and Saskatchewan, and nurses in Alberta, were also forced back to work by government-imposed contracts.

In 1991, the Vancouver grain handlers were ordered back to work, as was the Public Service Alliance of Canada. The Union of Postal Workers also returned to the bargaining table with a mediator following a two-week period of rotating strikes that caused hardship for many small businesses. A prolonged strike by CUPW would certainly result in back-to-work legislation.

The right to strike by public service employees has never been popular with the Canadian public. In April 1987, the Supreme Court of Canada ruled that unions do not have a right to strike simply on the grounds that the 1982 Constitution guarantees freedom of association.

The federal government, along with the governments of Newfoundland and Quebec, has limited the number of union members in a bargaining unit who are eligible to strike by designating a greater number of workers as essential for ensuring public safety and health. In British Columbia, industrial labour reforms gave independent commissioners the right to order a 40-day cooling-off period whenever they think the public interest is not being served.

Would outlawing public service strikes put an end to them? Organized labour argues that such an action would not end strikes, but instead result in defiance of the law. This was true in the 1978 postal walkout when employees continued to maintain picket lines even after the legislation was passed. The legislation was also defied in 1988 by the Alberta nurses who continued to strike, accepting a court-imposed fine for each day that they remained on strike. Furthermore, if the right to strike is denied, unions ask, what guarantee do employees have that their rights will be upheld? It is the option to strike that gives negotiators bargaining power. Without it, the power of the employer would be increased. Obviously, if the right to strike is denied, adequate compensation would have to be made for the loss of that right.

Arguments for denying the right to strike to public-sector employees are based on the fact that differences exist between collective bargaining in the private, profit-oriented sector, and in the public sector, which is directly supported by taxes.

A strike or lockout is supposed to hurt both sides in a dispute, and thus bring about the motivation for a settlement. If a strike occurs in the private sector, the public can usually obtain the goods from other sources, therefore suffering minimal inconvenience. When a strike occurs in the public sector (e.g., the post office or hospitals), the public is directly affected because alternative services are not readily available. Instead of hurting the employer, the strike hurts the public.

>>

It is also argued that private employers have more incentive to hold out against high wage demands because they would affect the company's prices and hence its ability to compete. Governments, on the other hand, are likely to settle a strike more quickly and be more generous in their settlement because they can raise taxes to cover the higher costs.

Another consideration is the value of public services. The public becomes accustomed to certain services and expects them to continue. When they are suddenly discontinued because of a strike, it reminds people dramatically of the value of such services. It brings to the forefront the fact that public services must be paid for, and that the public payroll is part of the cost. This reminder to the taxpayer contributes to the unpopularity of public service strikes.

When governments threaten legislation, however, what incentive is there for management to continue to bargain in good faith? One official with the Canadian Union of Postal Workers has said that Canada Post stopped negotiating the moment the labour minister started talking about back-to-work legislation. The best collective agreements are those agreed upon jointly by workers and management, the two parties that have to live with a labour contract. If a stalemate develops, a mutually agreeable settlement usually results because the threat of a strike or lockout produces movement at the bargaining table.[13]

Question

1 Should government employees be allowed to strike? List arguments for and against this statement.

COMPREHENSIVE CASE 11-3

SOMERSET OPTICAL

In September 1999, Dewar and Fowler were surprised to learn from one of their employees that a meeting had been held on the previous Sunday evening. All of Ottawa's optical workers, including Somerset Optical employees, had been invited to a presentation given by Luc Bélanger. His intention was to drum up sufficient support to start what he dubbed the United Union of Optical Workers (UUOW)—an organization that would represent all eyewear employees (except physicians) in Ottawa.

At the meeting, Bélanger explained that there were approximately 500 persons employed in the eyewear business in Ottawa. To date, more than 225 had prepared application forms and paid the $250 annual dues. Bélanger also explained that an application to the Labour Relations Board had been prepared and was now under consideration.

Bélanger stated that the purpose of his union was "to support employees in collective-bargaining activities and ensure that management treated them fairly." He briefly outlined the demands that the UUOW intended to present to management:

1. A minimum-wage rate for the industry equivalent to $55 000 per year for opticians, $40 000 for laboratory technicians and $30 000 for full-time sales personnel; any part-time workers would receive a prorated amount of these salaries based on the actual number of hours worked and overtime at twice the computed hourly rate for any time worked over 40 hours per week.

2. An annual wage increase of not less than eight percent per year.

3. Mandatory profit-sharing plans, a defined benefit pension plan, life insurance coverage and medical insurance.

4. Job security guarantees requiring that the management of any optical retail outlet that released an employee, for whatever cause, make every reasonable attempt (by calling every other manager) to place the employee before dismissal. All dismissed employees were to receive severance of not less than five weeks pay plus accrued vacation pay at nine percent, plus an amount equivalent to 10 percent of the employee's salary representing lost benefits and insurance, as well as a refund of any contributions to the pension plan made by the employee.

5. Leaves of absences with full pay for a period of 12 months for any employee who works continuously for 10 years within the industry, and who has been a member of the union for 10 years.

6. Paid vacation leave amounting to five weeks per year initially, and climbing to eight weeks per year in increments of one extra week for every five years of continuous employment.

7. Positions that became available in any store were to be offered first to union employees on the basis of seniority; only after all union employees had refused the job would management be able to recruit from outside.

"This is just the beginning!" Bélanger had exclaimed triumphantly at the meeting.

"Management will have no other choice but to bow to our demands. This union will make the eyewear industry a role model for workers across the country!"

Paul Stone, a longtime friend of Fowler and Dewar and an employee of Somerset Optical, asked Bélanger how he expected to persuade management to meet these somewhat outrageous union demands. Bélanger replied that management would have no choice because of the weapons the union had at its disposal, including "strike, picketing and boycott."

>>

At the end of the meeting, the employees filed out quietly. Not a single Somerset Optical employee filled out an application. It was decided at the meeting that Bélanger would return in two weeks to chair another meeting and obtain employee feedback.

SOURCE: By David H. Jones-Delcourt. Reprinted by permission of the author.

Questions

1 Why would Dewar and Fowler be concerned about this development? Evaluate Bélanger's proposed union demands and assess their impact on operations.

2 In general terms, how could unionization assist employees in the eyewear industry? How could unionization harm otherwise good relationships with management? In situations where the relationship between management and employees is very good, as is the case with Somerset Optical and its employees, does a union have any place in the relationship?

3 Discuss the pros and cons of each of the "union weapons" proposed by Bélanger. How would you expect management to respond to these tactics?

4 Why do you think the Somerset employees declined to apply to the union?

5 What stance should Fowler and Dewar take with respect to the next meeting between Somerset employees and Bélanger?

12

Business and Government

Learning Objectives

After reading this chapter, you will be able to

1 Explain why government helps to promote business and economic activity in Canada.

2 Explain how tariff and non-tariff barriers to international trade help to promote business.

3 Recognize why the various levels of government provide incentives for both industrial and natural resource development.

4 List some of the major services provided by government to assist business.

5 Discuss the reasons for competition legislation and list the major changes in competition legislation.

6 Identify some of the controls imposed on retailers and the consumer protection provided.

7 Explain the purpose of Canada's transportation legislation and how it is expected to help deregulate the transportation industry.

8 Identify why deregulation has become such an important objective of federal and provincial governments.

9 Explain why the federal government wants control of communication.

10 Explain why and how public utilities are controlled.

11 Describe the purpose of Crown corporations.

12 Explain why foreign investment was controlled in the past and how the mandate has changed for Investment Canada.

13 Describe some of the major taxes levied by government to finance its operation.

14 Explain the meaning of fiscal policy and how it can be used to stabilize economic activity.

15 Describe the role of the Bank of Canada, and explain how it can use monetary policy to stabilize economic activity.

16 Discuss how government has grown, and how this growth has affected business and private individuals.

17 Explain the meaning of industrial strategy.

Government Involvement in the Canadian Economy: A Historical Perspective

When Adam Smith published his book *An Inquiry into the Nature and Causes of the Wealth of Nations*, in 1776, he did not know that it would have such significant effects on the world that today it is considered one of the most important books ever written.

The Wealth of Nations, which had taken Smith about 10 years to write, basically stated that labour is the only source of a nation's wealth. Smith advocated division of labour in the productive process, stressed the importance of individual enterprise and argued the benefits of free trade. The true wealth of a nation, he believed, lay not in accumulating gold but rather in achieving an abundance of the necessities of life. He warned against unnecessary intervention by the state in this process.

Smith believed that government played a minor role in supporting the operation of the market system. According to him, government should provide a system of currency, protect and defend the country from foreign attack. Any other government involvement would result in a breakdown of the system because it would disrupt the orderly workings of the market. As we noted in Chapter 1, a key force in the market system, as Smith saw it, was the individual. By striving to satisfy the individual's needs, the market system through the force of competition would ensure the orderly distribution and allocation of resources among individuals.

Smith's concept of the market system and advocacy of non-intervention by government received wide support. The system worked well as long as business firms were relatively small and operated to serve their own communities. Under these circumstances, no single person or group could significantly influence wages, the supply of labour or the prices of goods produced.

However, as business firms became giant corporations and labour unions grew more powerful, they could influence the operation of the market. The Great Depression of the 1930s, which affected so many individuals through no fault of their own, forced government to reverse its position of non-intervention and provide direct aid to individuals and businesses. Gradually, government became more involved in the economy, providing legislation to regulate business conduct and protect individuals in society. Government also became increasingly involved in the general management of the economy, controlling business cycles through fiscal and monetary intervention. Government has addressed in particular the welfare of individuals by providing benefits for people who are ill, out of work or unable to care for themselves.

It is the relationship between government and business in Canada that we want to examine more closely in this chapter, taking particular note of how government promotes business while simultaneously controlling and regulating it.

Cooperation between business and government began early in Canada's history with the building of the Canadian Pacific Railway. The money to build the railway came from English and American investors for the most part, with the Canadian government guaranteeing many of the loans. The government also granted the CPR approximately 10 million hectares of land and $25 million, as well as those sections of railway in the east-west link that it had already built.

Although the building of the CPR created a massive national debt, many believed it was crucial to strengthen east-west ties within Canada and thus counteract the strong social and economic link between Canada and the United States. In an effort to strengthen the east-west bond further, and help industry become established in Canada, in the 1870s the government imposed tariffs on American goods. The tariffs forced Canadians to buy goods manufactured in eastern Canada where industry was starting to become established. Because of the smaller market available to Canadian industry and the monopolistic freight rates established by railways that transported goods west from Ontario, the prices of manufactured goods for western Canadians increased significantly.

Since Confederation, the Canadian government has sought to even out regional economic differences with subsidies to the poorer provinces and regions. In the last half-century, it has established various agencies to foster economic development, and has provided grants and loans to finance businesses that might otherwise have difficulty raising capital. The federal government has also invested in commercial enterprises and joint ventures to provide services that private firms might be hesitant to provide because of the widely distributed population and the poor prospects for profit.

To get a better idea of how government has affected the Canadian economy and its relationship with business, we can look at how the federal government, and to some extent the provincial governments, have both promoted and controlled business.

Government Promotion of Business

Initially, the federal government promoted business by protecting it from foreign competition through tariff and non-tariff barriers. Eventually, government began to provide direct incentives for industrial and resource development. Other government services offered include the provision of information, financing and the granting of copyrights, patents and trademarks.

Protection from Foreign Competition

Throughout Canada's history, the federal government has protected businesses by imposing tariff and non-tariff barriers on goods imported from other countries. These measures were designed to ease pressure on domestic producers by making goods from other countries as expensive to Canadians as those produced domestically. In some instances, however, imports have been severely restricted in quantity, and some have been completely banned. The various tariff and non-tariff barriers are examined below.

Tariff Barriers to Trade

A **tariff** is a special tax on imported goods designed to make their prices equal to those charged for similar domestic goods. However, the use of tariffs is controversial. While some believe that the government has a duty to protect newly established industries within the country from foreign competition, others point out that tariffs tend to remain long after the business or industry is established, while the lack of foreign competition may result in either high prices or poor quality (or both) for domestic goods.

Others, following 19th-century economist David Ricardo, believe that tariffs create industries or manufacturing activities that would not be established if foreign goods were allowed into the country tariff-free. In other words, the artificially high prices charged for some foreign goods because of tariffs lead some entrepreneurs to seek easy profits by producing these goods domestically—in the process using financial and other resources that might be better used to produce goods that cannot be imported.

Nevertheless, tariffs have in the past been widely imposed by most countries, and their use continues today. Most of Canada's industrial development can be attributed

Tariff—a special tax on imported goods designed to make their prices equal to those charged for similar domestic goods.

to protectionism through the tariffs imposed in 1879 by Sir John A. Macdonald's National Policy. While the use of tariffs was often the cause of heated debate in Parliament, with free trade (especially with the United States) frequently proposed, no substantial reductions in tariffs were achieved. In fact, the protection of industry through tariffs increased after 1930 as a worldwide trend to protectionism spread, even though most countries realized that, in the end, they gained no advantage from this action. As one country raised tariff barriers, so did another. Countries such as Canada were particularly hurt because they relied on world markets to sell their raw materials.

Since the introduction of the General Agreement on Tariffs and Trade (GATT) in 1947, significant reductions of tariffs on a worldwide basis have been achieved. Many countries have banded together to create customs unions and free trade agreements to reduce tariffs. The Canada-U.S. Free Trade Agreement would eliminate all tariffs between Canada and the United States by 1999. Its successor, the North American Free Trade Agreement (NAFTA), which came into force in 1994, would also eliminate most continental duties among Canada, the United States and Mexico in stages over 15 years as well as cut investment barriers among the three countries. Ultimately, NAFTA could include central and south American countries as well. We will discuss these free trade agreements in more detail in Chapter 13.

Non-tariff Barriers to Trade

Tariffs are not the only means used by the federal government to protect domestic industry from foreign competition. A variety of **non-tariff barriers** are also employed, including quantity restrictions on imports, selective use of government purchasing power and subsidies to Canadian manufacturers for producing goods that might otherwise be imported.

Quantity restrictions on imports, or import quotas, allow only a certain amount of a particular type of product into the country. They are a favourite tool of government for two reasons. First, their effect is immediate, as only a limited quantity of products is allowed into the country. Tariffs, on the other hand, only raise the price of the product, and anyone who prefers the imported product to a similar domestic product may continue to buy the former at the higher price. Second, it is easier to apply import quotas selectively, that is, against particular exporting countries; from an administrative point of view, they are thus more flexible than tariffs.

Import quotas have been applied on textiles, shoes, Japanese automobiles and some agricultural products. The quotas, however, may cause shortages, since the supply of imports is limited and domestic manufacturers often cannot expand their productive capacity quickly enough to meet the increased demand. As a result, prices rise and consumers suffer from both higher prices and a shortage of the product they want to buy. Even if domestic manufacturers increase production, they may not provide the product, quality or style that consumers want.

Another method of protecting specific industries is through the **selective use of government suppliers**. As the largest single purchaser of goods and services from the private sector, the federal government can give its business to Canadian firms rather than foreign-owned or -controlled companies, or to particular regions and businesses that may require economic stimulus. When the government uses this method to aid businesses or industries, the prices it pays for the products or services are not a prime consideration.

A third method of protection is direct aid. The federal government may provide **production subsidies** to domestic industries that have difficulty competing with imported goods. It may also provide temporary employment support programs to industries facing a drop in exports when foreign countries impose tariffs on their

---

Non-tariff barriers protect Canadian industries from foreign competition by restricting imports or providing direct aid and subsidies to Canadian firms that must compete against imports.

Quantity restrictions on imports, or import quotas, allow only a certain amount of a particular type of product into the country.

Selective us of government suppliers may provide domestic companies with an advantage in selling their products or services to the federal government, which may exclude foreign companies.

Production subsidies may be paid to Canadian manufacturers that have difficulty competing with imports.

products. Finally, the government may provide **temporary adjustment assistance** to domestic industries that face large drops in revenue because of the elimination of tariffs on competing imports.

Temporary adjustment assistance is provided to domestic industries that face large drops in revenue because of the elimination of tariffs on competing imports.

Federal Industrial Development Incentives

The 21-volume *Report of the Federal Task Force on Program Review* found that, in 1985, there were no fewer than 989 different federal programs costing $92 billion per year. This included 24 housing-related programs ($2 billion per year), 109 education-related programs ($6 billion per year), 90 arts- and culture-related programs ($2.5 billion), 60-plus job creation programs ($1.7 billion) and 218 federal or federal-provincial programs to service and subsidize business ($16.4 billion).

The four main types of government assistance are grants and contributions, loans, insurance and tax credits. In addition to making grants and contributions to businesses, government also supports business through its own procurement activities. Canadian government expenditure on current goods and services as a percentage of GDP increased from an average of 15.1% in the 1960-67 period to 19.5% in 1987.

Atlantic Canada Opportunities Agency

A major aim of the Atlantic Canada Opportunities Agency (ACOA) is to reduce the economic disparity between Atlantic Canada and the rest of the country. The program has four main components:

Atlantic Canada Opportunities Agency

www.acoa.ca/

1. *Cooperation.* ACOA wants to cooperate with the private sector, provincial and municipal governments, and institutions such as universities and industrial commissions.

2. *Coordination.* ACOA coordinates the activities of other federal departments in the region that share the same objectives for economic renewal.

3. *Advocacy.* ACOA works to ensure that federal programs have a positive impact on Atlantic Canada's economic development.

4. *Action.* Small and medium-sized businesses can obtain direct financial assistance, loan guarantees and interest buy-downs to modernize, expand, design a product, develop a new technology or carry out needed feasibility and marketing studies.

Western Economic Diversification Canada

When the Western Economic Diversification program was established in 1987, its mandate was to promote the development and diversification of the economy of Western Canada and to advance the interests of the West in national economic policy.

Western Economic Diversification Canada

www.wd.gc.ca/

Aboriginal Business Canada

abc.gc.ca/

Instead of providing direct financial assistance to individual companies, Western Diversification is working in cooperation with industry associations, financial institutions and the four western provinces, to address the needs of small business and business services. Resources are strategically targeted to industries having the greatest potential for growth and that support the federal government's *Jobs and Growth Strategy.*

Western Economic Diversification Canada

http://www.wd.gc.ca/eng/

The Western Economic Diversification program is intended to make the economies of the four western provinces less dependent on primary resources. The prices of products in agriculture, forestry, energy, mining and fisheries tend to rise and

How to Get Government Money

Dr. Hawley Black, in his book *Easy Money: Your Guide to Government Giveaways*,[1] suggests 10 rules to follow when obtaining government assistance.

1. Find an appropriate program, and then continue to look for more programs.

2. Look in more than one area; many department-specific training programs are offered by Employment and Immigration Commission Canada.

3. If your submission is not successful, try to repackage it.

4. Prepare a good proposal.

5. Speak to the government officers who actually give the money away.

6. Read government publications that concern the programs or agencies from which you seek funding.

7. Try to obtain a copy of any government publication or directory that lists all programs administered by your target agency.

8. Start small in your requests for assistance while you develop your grant-applying skills.

9. Improvise—when speaking with government officers, be open to their ideas on projects that need to be done or planned.

10. Lobby the government.

fall drastically over relatively short periods of time, causing "boom and bust" cycles. Diversification into other industries could smooth out these cycles and thus bring about more stable economic growth.

Provincial Industrial Incentive Programs

Every province has some government agency or ministry with a mandate to foster economic development provincial and municipal governments also help to create new employment opportunities by offering incentives for industry to locate in their areas. Municipal governments may provide property tax incentives or establish low-cost industrial parks to attract industry to their jurisdictions. To encourage the establishment of large-scale industry, a provincial government may provide either special tax incentives or outright grants.

Agriculture and Natural Resource Development Incentives

The importance of natural resources to Canada's economy makes agriculture and natural resource development prime candidates for government aid programs. Programs to help agriculture range from support for 4-H clubs to agricultural product marketing, and from financial assistance to farmers to racetrack supervision and the promotion and financing of farm fairs.

The mining industry has also received incentives through specific tax provisions, depletion allowances and the opportunity to write off exploration and development costs rapidly. In the past, the government has protected the petroleum and natural gas industry from foreign competition and helped to open the U.S. market to domestic producers, in addition to providing various tax incentives.

Other Federal Government Assistance

The federal government has a number of departments and many agencies that provide a wide variety of services to consumers and businesses. Let us look at a few of the federal departments for a brief overview of their services.

Industry Canada

In 1993, **Industry Canada** was created through an amalgamation of the Department

Industry Canada—federal government department whose primary mandate is to encourage international competitiveness and growth of Canadian business.

Two of the major government assistance programs are the Atlantic Canada Opportunities Agency and the Western Economic Diversification Canada.

Business Opportunities Sourcing System (BOSS) is an authoritative database on Canadian companies, their products and the markets they serve.

Cape Breton Development Corporation (DEVCO) aims to promote and assist the financing and development of industry on Cape Breton Island; to provide employment outside the coal-producing industry and broaden the base of the economy of the Island; and to contribute to the rehabilitation and modernization of mines in the Sydney coal field.

Defence Industry Productivity Program (DIPP) is designed to enhance economic growth through the promotion of viable defence or defence-related exports; to provide a defence industrial base; and to maintain a defence technological capability.

Native Economic Development Program assists native peoples in the development of economic self-reliance.

Small Business Office provides general information and help with problems relating to government regulations, paperwork and red tape. A telephone hotline provides information or help in overcoming a particular difficulty. The office also provides information on how to establish a business and on programs and services offered by provincial and municipal governments, associations, small business groups and so forth.

Special ARDA (Agricultural and Rural Development Act) is designed to assist residents of remote and northern areas (in particular, native peoples) to improve their economic circumstances.

Tourism Canada provides a number of useful services that help to ensure the continued success of Canada's tourism industry.

Other Federal Industrial Assistance Programs

of Communication, the Department of Industry, Science and Technology, the Department of Consumer and Corporate Affairs, and Investment Canada. Industry Canada's mandate is to encourage international competitiveness and growth of Canadian business (especially small and medium-sized firms), to promote a fair and efficient Canadian marketplace and to protect, assist and advocate consumer interest.

Industry Canada addresses a wide range of business needs and concerns, including the following:

1. Policy leadership in the development of key industry sectors.

2. Vital business intelligence on industry sectors, markets, new technologies and best business practices.

3. Administration and enforcement of consumer legislation for the accurate identification and safe usage of a variety of products.

4. Access to federal trade development services and programs, plus information and guidance in new export markets and joint ventures.

5. Continuing assurance of the free flow of goods and services within Canada.

6. Policies, programs and services that promote the advantages of a fair and efficient marketplace for both businesses and consumers.

7. Ongoing reviews of, and appropriate changes to, regulations dealing with trade and competitiveness.

8. Enforcement of the Competition Act, which promotes marketplace competition and efficiency.

9. Administration of Canada's intellectual property laws, and the development of strategic information derived from such products.

10. Federal business incorporation and related services.

11. Investment policy, evaluation of investment opportunities and review of in-Canada investment proposals.

12. Help in developing new technologies and techniques for new products, processes and services.

13. Programs and services that address the requirements of the growing number of Aboriginal entrepreneurs in Canada.

14. Spectrum management that ensures high-quality, reliable radio communications services throughout Canada and helps coordinate the international radio frequency spectrum.

15. Technical regulation of broadcasting and the issuance of new, advanced broadcasting technologies such as digital radio, high-definition television and direct broadcasting satellites.[2]

Statistics Canada

www.statcan.ca

Statistics Canada

Statistics Canada, under the Department of Supply and Services, gathers information and statistics on all aspects of Canada's population and economic life, and makes the data available to businesses free of charge or at a nominal cost. It has advisory services staff, active in centres across Canada, who offer statistical consultative services and business-oriented seminars.

Canada Employment and Immigration Commission

The Canada Employment and Immigration Commission provides a variety of programs to encourage the unemployed to find work. It provides public works projects for temporary employment, helps employers hire people who have faced severe difficulties in finding work, helps foreign entrepreneurs to establish businesses in Canada, operates a host of training programs for workers and provides counselling services for employees experiencing problems because of technological change.

Labour Canada

Labour Canada provides mediation and conciliation services for unions and employers engaged in collective bargaining. The department also collects, processes and analyzes data on labour-related matters, for use by both business and the public, and provides financial assistance for labour education. In addition, it handles the Women's Bureau, Occupational Health and Safety Program and Employment Relations and Conditions of Work.

The Business Development Bank of Canada

Established in 1944, the Industrial Development Bank became the Federal Business Development Bank (FBDB) in 1975. In 1996 it was renamed the Business Development Bank of Canada (BDC). It is a Crown corporation with assets of $2.7 billion and with 78 branches across Canada. It is set up to promote and assist most types of businesses in Canada at various stages in their development. It pays particular attention to small and medium-size businesses.

The BDC offers financial services that address the unique needs of small and medium-sized businesses. The Bank can provide a regular term loan of up to $5 million as well as venture capital through its "Just-in-Time Development Capital" line. BDC can structure a wide variety of alternative financing schemes and adjust re-

< The BDC is a Crown corporation with assets of $2.7 billion and 78 branches across Canada

payments according to the client's ability to pay. It complements the services offered by private financial institutions by providing worthwhile projects with funding that might not be available elsewhere on reasonable terms and conditions. The bank's mandate is to take more risks than other private lending institutions. It requires less collateral, lends at one percent above the market rate and will finance businesses in higher-risk areas in the country. The BDC often works with commercial banks to undertake shared financing for small business.

Although the BDC may provide equity financing by purchasing a business's shares, the bank's policy is to remain a minority shareholder. Its prime goal is to increase the amount of venture capital available to small and medium-size businesses by using its own capital or by serving as a catalyst to attract more equity financing from the private sector. Equity investment might be necessary for companies with high growth potential but little access to capital markets.

The function of BDC's management services is to provide the most complete source of business counselling, training and information for small and medium-sized businesses in Canada. In fact, 80% of the BDC's customers don't come to borrow money, but rather to take advantage of its management services through its counselling division.

Through **Counselling Assistance to Small Enterprises (CASE)** some 1100 small business counsellors (many of them retired businesspeople) counsel firms in all areas of business management, including strategic planning, bookkeeping, marketing, production and personnel. CASE counsellors have helped over 125 000 businesses avoid problems and improve profitability.

Government Control of Business

The concept of government control and regulation of business appears to be at odds with a private enterprise economy such as Canada's. According to the traditional theory, the force of competition alone should ensure that quality goods are available at the lowest possible price and in adequate supply. Competition generally works well when a number of firms produce a similar product or service. When that is not the case, however, some businesses could restrict output, charge higher prices or let the quality of the products and services deteriorate, in order to make a higher profit.

For example, services such as transportation, utilities and telephones in Canada are often provided by only a single firm—first, because of the tremendous capital

Business Development Bank of Canada

www.bdc.ca/

Canadian Intellectual Property Office

www.cipo.gc.ca

Counselling Assistance to Small Enterprises (CASE) uses some 1500 retired businesspeople to counsel firms in all areas of business management, including bookkeeping, marketing, production and personnel.

investment required, and second, because inconvenience and cost to the customer would both increase if these services were provided by a number of competing firms. Under these circumstances, nothing would prevent a private firm from charging excessive rates or allowing its service to deteriorate if government did not exercise some control over service and rates.

Sometimes the federal government or one of the provincial governments establishes a Crown corporation that provides a required service or product. Examples are Ontario Power Generation, Canada Mortgage and Housing and the New Brunswick Electric Power Commission. If the government believes there is not enough competition, or that some areas are not served as they should be, it can establish a competing service. For example, Canadian National Railway competes with Canadian Pacific Railway, and Air Canada competed with Canadian Airlines until the latter was bought out by Air Canada. Sometimes government is required to be a partner with one or more private firms because of the cost of the venture and the expectation of low profit.

Regulation of Competition

Without competition, businesses have little incentive to produce goods and services at the lowest possible cost. When there is no other seller, a company is free to charge whatever price the public is prepared to pay, often with little concern for the quality of the product. In a monopoly situation, the consumer is at the mercy of the producer, especially if the product or service is a necessity. To protect the consumer, government can enact legislation designed to promote and maintain competition among business firms.

Anti-combines Legislation: A Historical Perspective

As late as the 1880s, businesspeople were relatively free to conduct their activities as they saw fit. Monopolies and cartels took advantage of consumers with little interference, and fraudulent practices, swindles and misleading advertising were common. Through such practices some individuals built huge business empires and personal fortunes. Consumers had little recourse when products were unsatisfactory, and could rely only on the Roman principle of *caveat emptor* "Let the buyer beware." For example, to curb the discrimination in rates and services perpetrated by the railways in the United States, which eventually resulted in public outcry, the U.S. government introduced the Interstate Commerce Act in 1887. Soon afterward, the Canadian government appointed a House of Commons committee to examine similar practices in Canada, as well as monopoly situations, combinations and trusts. In 1889, the committee's findings resulted in the passage of legislation under the Criminal Code that made it a misdemeanour to conspire, combine, agree or arrange unlawfully so as to restrict competition and fix prices in various activities, including transportation, production and storage of commodities. Although some convictions were made, the Act was vague and difficult to enforce; it was subsequently revised a number of times to facilitate prosecution of individuals and companies that persisted in undermining competition.

The Combines Investigations Act, passed in 1923, clarified the procedure for administering the legislation and specified the penalties for knowingly assisting in the formation of, or being party to, a combine. Further changes were made to the legislation in 1952 and 1960. In 1966, the federal government asked the Economic Council of Canada to study the whole field of combines, mergers, monopolies and restraint of trade, together with the system of granting patents, trademarks, copyrights and industrial designs. The council was subsequently asked to include in its study the need for consumer legislation, and to recommend appropriate government action in this area. As a result of this study, the government hoped to enact comprehensive legislation regarding competition and consumer protection.

The Combines Investigations Act (1975)

The **Combines Investigations Act, 1975** dealt with deceptive selling practices, restraint of trade in any manner, and outlawed monopolies of both consumers and producers—neither could combine to restrain competition. Discriminatory pricing, other than for quantity discounts, was made illegal, and differences in prices to customers had to be accounted for. Advertising and display allowances were regulated, and misleading advertising was outlawed, as were misleading selling practices such as "bait and switch," referral selling and selling at prices higher than those advertised. Specific conditions were established for performance and other tests used in advertising, as well as for testimonials, games and lotteries. Finally, suppliers could only recommend minimum prices; they could not set them.

Stage II of the Act, dealing with mergers and monopolies, was proposed but never passed. After extensive lobbying by the business community, the Conservative government reviewed some of the more onerous provisions of the proposed legislation.[3] After extensive review, the government finally passed the **Competition Act** in **1986** along with the Competition Tribunal Act (CTA), which created the Competition Tribunal. The Tribunal is a specialized court combining expertise in economics and business with legal expertise. It is composed of both judicial and non-judicial members. The judicial members are judges of the Federal Court, Trial Division. The non-judicial members have backgrounds in economics, business, accounting, marketing and other relevant fields. The tribunal has exclusive jurisdiction to hear and determine applications concerning non-criminal matters such as refusal to deal, exclusive dealing, tied selling, market restriction, abuse of dominant position in the market, specialization agreements and mergers. Over non-criminal matters, the tribunal has broad remedial powers, including prohibition orders, interim injunctions, dissolution of a merger transaction and divestiture of assets.

Offences falling under criminal jurisdiction include agreements made to restrain trade, discriminatory and predatory practices such as price discrimination, predatory pricing and promotional allowances, price maintenance and refusal to supply, and misleading advertising and deceptive selling practices. To commit a criminal offence is cause for severe penalties—fine or imprisonment, or both.

The Competition Act was updated in 1996 to allow more liaison with regulators in other countries; decriminalize provisions on misleading advertising; and introduce new rules for telemarketing to curb abuse. Some of the changes are designed to ease the regulatory burden on business in complying with the Act.

Since its creation, the Tribunal has heard cases relating to mergers, abuse of dominant position and various trade practices that involved key players in a number of industries. Some of the products and services dealt with include airline computer-reservations systems, oil refining and gasoline retailing, power transformers, community newspapers, aspartame, waste disposal, car parts, photocopier parts, marketing research services and shared electronic-network services. Most of the cases brought before the Tribunal by the Commissioner were contested, and the claims made were vigorously disputed by the firms involved. Others proceeded on a consent basis where the parties agreed on the terms of an order to solve the problem and brought it to the Tribunal for approval.

Combines Investigations Act— designed to maintain competition by making certain business activities—to conspire, combine, agree or arrange unlawfully so as to restrict competition and fix prices in various activities—illegal under the Criminal Code.

Competition Act (1986)— created the Competition Tribunal, which has jurisdiction to deal with non-criminal matters as well as offences falling under criminal jurisdiction, including agreements made to restrain trade.

Competition Tribunal

www.ct-tc.gc.ca

ISSUE

What Does Business Want—Competition Legislation or Government Regulation?[4]

Canada's economic system rests on the principles of competition. It allows individuals to enter the market and, by providing goods and services, to compete freely with other firms for the consumer dollar. All individuals are free to use their talents and abilities to their best advantage without government interference or constraints. And this is exactly the purpose of competition legislation: to ensure a proper and efficient functioning of the market system, and to ensure that artificial restraints to market forces are removed or never become established. Many businesspeople view competition legislation as government interference in the orderly workings of the market. In fact, the market system in Canada today is far from orderly or ideal. It is characterized by giant corporations and big labour unions, which operate as virtual monopolies. "Atomistic" competition (many sellers, each having little power to affect price), as it may have existed 200 years ago and as it was envisioned by Adam Smith, seldom exists today.

Thus, Canadian businesspeople have two choices: they can either support competition legislation that establishes the ground rules to allow private individuals to decide how resources should be allocated and used, or they can let government carry out this task through a multitude of rules and regulations. Effective competition legislation is perhaps the best safeguard against greater direct government intervention in our current market structure.

Control of Retailing and Consumer Protection

Although retailing in Canada is of major importance to the Canadian economy, no overall policy to regulate or control the retail sector has been advanced by either the federal government or the provincial governments. Nevertheless, retailers are affected by other government legislation, regulations and controls. Excise taxes and tariffs affect their product mix of imported and domestic products.

Consumer legislation on both the federal and the provincial level specifies the types of products retailers may sell, the warranties they must give and the information they must provide to credit customers. Provincial legislation regulates working hours for employees, minimum wages and fringe benefits such as holidays and workers' compensation. At the municipal level, retailers are subject to zoning laws specifying where they may locate, the size and shape of their buildings and the facilities they must provide. The municipal government also regulates store hours and days when businesses must be closed (e.g., Sundays and holidays). In addition, federal inspectors ensure that product quality meets acceptable standards. Finally, retailers are required to comply with various acts and regulations passed by the federal government and administered by the Department of Consumer and Corporate Affairs.

Control of Transportation

Government control over transportation began in 1895 with the historic deal made between the Canadian Pacific Railway and Prime Minister Wilfrid Laurier. The government promised the CPR the money it needed to build a transcontinental line if the CPR would promise to carry the wheat produced by western farmers to the sea or lake ports, and do so on a permanent basis and at the rate then negotiated. The Crow rate, as it has become known, was finally revised in 1982 after much debate. In 1970, the National Transportation Act established the Canadian Transport Commission (CTC) to regulate and control the various modes of transportation in Canada. Included were motor, air and water transport; railways; and transport of commodities other than oil and gas through pipelines.

The CTC era officially ended on January 1, 1988, when the new **National Transportation Act** came into force and officially ushered in a new era of deregulation of transportation. The new legislation contains a revised, comprehensive declaration of national transportation policy, a statement that establishes the focus of transportation in the future. These key elements are:

1. The safety of the transportation system is the top priority.
2. The transportation system exists to serve shippers and travellers.
3. Competition and market forces are to be the prime agents in providing economic, efficient and adequate transportation services at lowest total cost.
4. To encourage competition both within and among the transportation modes, economic regulation of carriers will be minimized.
5. Carriers should, so far as practical, bear a fair share of the costs of facilities and services provided at public expense, and be compensated for publicly imposed duties.
6. Transportation is a key to regional development.
7. Undue obstacles to the mobility of all, including persons with disabilities, should not be created by carriers.[5]

The Canada Transportation Act (1996)

In 1996, the transportation legislation was introduced by the Minister of Transport, to ensure that the new Canadian transportation system be dynamic and as unrestricted as possible to meet the demands of Canada's changing economy. The **Canada Transportation Act (1996)** is designed to streamline the process for rail line abandonment, and eliminate the requirement for firms or individuals to obtain approval from the transport regulator for mergers and acquisitions of transportation undertakings. It also establishes a single regulatory regime in the domestic air sector by reducing regulation of northern air services. Finally it provides some important new consumer protection such as prohibiting airlines from advertising or selling tickets prior to obtaining a licence. This happened in 1996 when Greyhound Air had full service in place and had airline tickets sold to the public but did not have the actual licence to operate an airline.

The Canadian Transportation Agency

The **Canadian Transportation Agency (CTA)** is a quasi-judicial tribunal that replaces the National Transportation Agency. The agency has the mandate to issue licences to carriers who wish to enter into the rail and air modes, and includes a dispute-resolution power over various transportation rate and service matters. The CTA has the power to remove undue obstacles to the mobility of persons with disabilities in the federally regulated transportation network.

To carry out these duties, the CTA has the power to inquire into air licensing matters and to conduct inquiries necessary to determine complaints before it on

Canada Transportation Act (1996) is designed to make Canada's transportation system dynamic and as unrestricted as possible to meet the demands of Canada's changing economy.

Canadian Transportation Agency (CTA) is a quasi-judicial tribunal that issues licences and can resolve disputes over transportation rates and service.

Canadian Transportation Agency

www.cta-otc.gc.ca/

other matters. The CTA may also inquire into other federal transportation matters at the request of the Minister of Transport. It can also enforce the decisions under its jurisdiction, levy fines for non-compliance and wield broad cost-recovery powers allowing it to charge for services such as the issuance of licences and permits.

Deregulation of the Trucking and Airline Industries

The objective of government regulation is to protect the public interest. The railways were the first to have controls applied since it was believed that 'the public convenience and necessity' could not be served by the free market. As trucking and airlines became more important, control over these carriers was also exercised. Truckers, for example, were prevented from attracting off-peak loads or filling up empty vehicles for back hauls, which in effect restricted them from optimizing their economic productivity.

A 1976 U.S. study estimated that costs of regulations amounted to US$66 billion, $63 billion of which should have been borne by business, but which was naturally passed on to consumers. This amounted to a hidden tax for every man, woman and child in the United States of US$307. By 1980 the costs of regulations were more than US$100 billion.[6]

Motor Vehicle Transport Act
(1988)—promotes competition in the trucking industry by making it easy to get a licence to operate a truck for commercial purposes.

The Trucking Industry   The passage of the new National Transportation Act also brought the passage of the new **Motor Vehicle Transport Act** (1988). The new legislation has helped to reduce costs to truckers and has benefited shippers through more competitive rates and a wider choice of trucking services. At the same time, **deregulation** of the trucking industry also resulted in many trucking companies becoming bankrupt, which led to hundreds of lost jobs.[7]

Deregulation is designed to reduce regulations, particularly in transportation industries, in order to increase competition and reduce costs for the consumer.

The Airline Industry   Deregulation of the airline industry in Canada began slowly in 1984. The government made the initial move toward deregulation because it felt that Canadian carriers had to learn how to compete internationally. One of the major forces behind this move was the large number of Canadians taking advantage of the low airfares in the United States. With the passage of the new National Transportation Act in 1988, many other restrictions—of routes, frequency and type of aircraft (as well as the distinction between national and regional carriers)—were eliminated. Airlines were able to offer any combination of scheduled and charter services on their current routes, and were no longer restricted in offering discounts.

Steps to remove the remaining Canada-U.S. government-imposed restrictions (except those that pertain to safety on North American airlines) were undertaken in October 1990. The **open skies agreement** that was finally concluded in 1995 allowed Canadian and U.S. airlines to fly across the border on any routes they thought profitable, and created a single North American market for air travel. The agreement benefited consumers with lower prices and much-improved access to American cities.

Open skies agreement allows airlines to fly across borders on any routes they think will be profitable and will create a single North American market for air travel.

The trucking and the airline industry are only two examples of how Canadian industries must adjust in order to be competitive with the rest of the world. As difficult as the adjusting process may be, Canada's future prosperity depends on it. And Canadian consumers will ultimately gain because of lower prices and, perhaps, better products and services.

Control of Communications

Department of Communications—established in 1969 to provide Canada with the best possible communication services and to control international broadcasting, particularly from the United States

The federal government established the **Department of Communications** in 1969 to provide Canada with the best possible communication services and to control

FIGURE 12.1

How the Canada Transportation Act affects the carriers

Many regulations were done away with in the airline industry in 1984. Under the new act, it is easier to start an airline, and existing air carriers can begin

services anywhere as long as they can show that they are fit to operate safe air service. They can also drop unprofitable routes or reduce service simply by giving 120 days' notice. They can increase or cut fares if they wish without regulatory approval. Furthermore, they can negotiate confidential contracts with their customers. However, air carriers in northern and remote areas may not have the same freedom as in the rest of Canada if essential air services to these areas remain necessary. The government hopes that the removal of previously restrictive economic regulatory controls will produce a more competitive, market-oriented industry that is more cost-conscious, more productive and more flexible.

For railways and their customers, reform has been even more dramatic. The CNR and CP Rail can no longer jointly set freight rates, which reduced competition, as they had since 1967. Shippers can now negotiate confidential contracts and shop for the rates and conditions that best suit their needs. All rates must cover the variable cost of carrying the particular shipment, which rules out railways' adopting predatory rates designed to drive competitors out of the market. The new legislation also makes it easier to sell a rail line to an independent operator who will run it as a smaller, short-line service. This is necessary because these short, sparsely used branch lines are costly to operate. If a rail line has economic potential, the Canadian Transportation Agency may order the railway to operate it on a subsidized basis. Otherwise it may be abandoned, with or without a delay of up to two years, to allow a smooth transition to an alternative service. Although the railways do not expect severe freight rate cutting, they are nevertheless moving quickly to make their operations as lean as possible. While the railways will be allowed to compete fairly with American carriers, the concern is that U.S. transportation companies will have equal access to about $2 billion in Canadian shipments. Both CN and CP are stating that if competition dramatically cuts revenues, the companies may have to delay investments in new equipment, facilities and new technology. This could mean that the railway will not be able to provide adequate levels of service to customers.

In marine shipping, competition has been boosted with changes in the Shipping Conferences Exemptions Act, the legislation that controls the price-fixing shipping cartels known as "conferences." Although conferences are still exempt from federal competition regulations, the conference members can offer rates lower than those set by the conference as a whole. Customers can now negotiate confidential service contracts, and it is illegal for conferences to force customers to ship all their goods with one carrier.

In the trucking sector, deregulation is designed to make it easier for new firms to enter the interprovincial or international market, and for existing firms to expand operations. Applicants must show that they can conduct operations safely and have proper insurance coverage. The new law allows confidential contracts to be negotiated between truckers and their customers instead of the standard rates that existed in the past. Shippers hope the private deal making will drive prices down.

Regulations affecting short-distance commodity pipelines will focus exclusively on safety and environmental protection.

international broadcasting, particularly from the United States. In 1976, the Canadian Radio-television and Telecommunications Act was passed, and the **Canadian Radio-television and Telecommunications Commission (CRTC)** was established to regulate broadcast operations. This body is responsible for licensing all radio stations and television broadcasting stations, including cable companies, in addition to regulating

Canadian Radio-television and Telecommunications Commission (CRTC)—responsible for regulating broadcasting in Canada and oversees the rates charged by federally incorporated telephone and telegraph companies.

types of broadcasts and the amount of Canadian content. The CRTC also oversees the rates charged by federally incorporated telephone and telegraph companies.

In addition to the federal government regulations, the provinces have control over some telecommunications companies that operate within their borders. This shared responsibility has resulted in an exceedingly complex regulatory system that many feel hinders competition and ties up the telecommunications industry in federal and provincial politics more than any other sector of Canadian business.

However, the CRTC has been more willing than it has in the past to accept competition in the telecommunications market. The consortium of nine telephone companies dominated by Bell Canada traditionally had a monopoly on long-distance telephone rates and charged higher than necessary rates, using the excess to subsidize their money-losing local rates. But all that changed on June 12, 1992, when the CRTC opened up long-distance to competition. Other companies were now allowed to set up cross-Canada calling services. To keep customers, the major telephone companies cut prices quickly to keep their customers. Both Bell Canada and BC Tel saw drastic drops in their profit margins. Then in 1995, the CRTC allowed phone companies to raise their local rates, but they had to pass on any savings to users by lowering long-distance charges.

Control of Public Utilities

Competition is clearly instrumental in increasing products and services, and lowering prices in many instances. Nevertheless, when competition is clearly not beneficial, then the public interest must be protected against monopoly power through regulations of service and rates. This may be the case for services such as cable television, gas, electricity, water, as well as rail, bus, subway, pipeline, air, water and motor transport companies.

Regulation of Service and Rates

Most public utilities are operated by either the municipality or the province. When a private firm provides the service, however, the rates it may charge are government-controlled. Rates are generally based on the level of service required of the company, while allowing for a fair rate of return. The latter is determined by the value of the utility company's property, the calculation of which may be based either on the original cost or on replacement cost.

Hence, a regulatory agency must make two critical decisions—establishing a fair rate of return and determining the value of the company's property. Both of these decisions are particularly difficult during inflationary periods when costs increase rapidly. For example, to renew or upgrade their plants and equipment, public utilities require increasingly larger investments, which must come from company earnings or from outside borrowings. In either case, the companies require greater returns on investments; therefore, rates must increase.

A regulatory agency is always placed in a difficult position. The utility must be allowed to increase its rates to finance future capital investment and ensure that it can operate effectively, while the consumer, who is subject to a monopoly situation in an essential service, must be protected.

Government Ownership

Crown corporations are owned by federal, provincial and municipal governments, and are generally used to provide special functions for the public. The Bank of

Crown corporations are government-owned corporations designed to compete with private firms or to provide services not available through private companies.

Canada, for example, is responsible for regulating credit and currency, while the Canada Mortgage and Housing Corporation provides financial capital for private housing. In some cases, federal or provincial governments may create a Crown corporation to take over a private firm that has decided to close its operation, if this closure significantly threatens to harm the region economically.

Sometimes Crown corporations are established to compete with private companies. When government competes with private companies, however, a fundamental question must be answered: Should a public company be concerned primarily with providing service to the public, or should it compete with private companies in all respects, including the making of profit?

If service is of primary concern, the government must be prepared to make up operating deficits incurred by the public company. A private company receives no such assistance, and losses are borne by the shareholders. In effect, shareholders pay twice—first, when they absorb their own losses, and again when they pay taxes, some of which go to support public corporations. If service to the public comes before profits, how can we tell whether a public company is effective and efficient in its operation? How can we compare the operations of public and private companies? Valid arguments can be made on both sides of this issue, which is far from being resolved.

Crown corporations may also be established to assist in the economic development of particular regions of the country, to undertake basic research, to prevent a

Largest Crown corporations, federal and provincial, 1999

TABLE 12.1

	Revenue ($ 000)	Profit ($ 000)	Assets ($ 000)
Federal			
Canada Post Corp.	5 088 000	36 000	2 919 000
Canada Mortgage & Housing	2 140 000	316 000	22 046 000
Export Development Corp.	153 000	110 000	19 423 000
Canadian Broadcasting Corp.	1 444 786	(35 510)	1 513 103
Atomic Energy of Canada	552 582	(10 308)	916 509
Farm Credit Corp.	498 365	42 559	6 125 061
Business Development Bank	476 790	32 784	5 098 461
Via Rail Canada	426 875	(40 277)	623 835
St. Lawrence Seaway Mngt. Corp.	49 335	1 190	65 973
Marine Atlantic	94 552	(2 563)	228 219
Provincial			
Hydro-Quebec	9 624 000	906 000	56 785 000
Ontario Power Generation	6 123 000	227 000	15 610 000
Caisse de Depot et Placement	3 240 000	3 027 000	100 263 000
B.C. Hydro and Power	3 017 000	395 000	11 685 000
Insurance Corp. of B.C.	2 834 864	95 723	5 945 610
Manitoba Hydro-Electric Board	1 166 100	100 100	7 865 900
Societé de l'assur automobile	1 127 463	33 479	5 428 014
Saskatchewan Power Corp.	1 004 000	114 000	3 203 000
Epcor Utilities	1 002 730	116 561	2 357 019
Alberta Heritage Savings	933 662	932 011	12 097 526

Canadian company from being taken over by a foreign firm, to ensure competition or to provide a service that otherwise might not be available. Table 12.1 shows the 20 largest federal and provincial Crown corporations.

Control of Foreign Investment

Foreign capital has played a major role in Canada's industrial development. Foreign investment has benefited Canadians by providing jobs, capital, technology and access to foreign markets. Initially, much of the foreign investment in Canada came from England, but after World War II most came from the United States, which has remained the major foreign investor in Canada.

The Canadian government was concerned that foreign ownership of Canadian companies and assets could affect Canada in a number of ways. First, there is the fear about preserving the Canadian culture, particularly with the United States having such a dominant investment position. Can the Canadian identity be maintained in the face of the powerful social, economic and political influence from the United States? Second, there is the fear about the economic influence of foreign firms on Canada. A financially troubled company is more likely to close a Canadian subsidiary plant than one in its home country. This could affect the jobs of Canadians. When it comes to increased spending on research and development, will the money be spent in the home country or in Canada? Foreign firms could also affect the Canadian balance of payments by taking profits and other fees out of Canada. Finally, when foreign governments impose controls on their corporations, these controls would also apply to Canadian subsidiaries - Canada could thereby lose some control over national affairs. We will discuss foreign ownership and its associated problems in greater detail in Chapter 13.

The Foreign Investment Review Agency

To retain some control over foreign ownership and investment in Canada, the federal government in the early 1970s established the Foreign Investment Review Agency (FIRA) to screen takeovers and the establishment of new businesses in Canada by foreign-controlled corporations, or foreign individuals or governments. The first part of the Foreign Investment Review Act was instituted in 1974 to investigate all foreign takeovers of Canadian businesses by non-Canadians. The second part, which came into effect in 1975, covered the establishment of new businesses in Canada by foreigners.

When assessing foreign takeovers or the establishment of new companies in Canada by foreign investors, the Agency was primarily interested in the benefits that would accrue to Canada. However, FIRA quickly drew criticism from foreign investors. While few objected to an agency to screen foreign investment to ensure that it met the needs of Canadians, many objected to FIRA's tactics and procedures. They claimed that its policies were often arbitrary and poorly communicated; that foreign investors were unable to determine in advance what kinds of investments might be approved; and that the screening process was conducted in total secrecy, with no right of appeal. Critics also stressed that foreign investors had no way of knowing what FIRA might do in the future.

Investment Canada

The Progressive Conservative government elected in 1984 changed the Agency's mandate. In 1985, FIRA was renamed **Investment Canada**, and its new function was

Investment Canada is a monitoring agency designed to uncover abuses by outside investors, particularly in areas where some measure of domestic ownership is considered essential to Canada.

For years, the federal and provincial governments purchased private companies and turned them into Crown corporations, until the late 1970s when a turning point occurred. In 1979, Premier Bill Bennett of British Columbia returned a number of government-owned companies to private ownership by establishing the B.C. Resources Investment Corporation and giving each B.C. resident five free shares in the company. Prime Minister Joe Clark's plan to sell a part of Petro-Canada, and give away five free shares to every adult Canadian, was never implemented because his government fell.

Spurred by Britain's drive to revitalize a stagnant economy, privatization of government-owned enterprises took on a new meaning as the British government sold off numerous Crown companies, some at fire-sale prices. Government-owned housing was sold to its renters, and the sale of well-known companies, including British Airways PLC, Jaguar PLC, British Telecommunications PLC and Rolls-Royce, has shifted more than 600 000 workers into the private sector.

Privatization means selling Crown corporations, either in whole or in part, to the private sector. It is based on the belief that, under private ownership, these enterprises would be managed more efficiently because they must show a profit and compete with other firms.

In 1984, the Progressive Conservative government that came to power made plans to sell off some of its $60 billion of government enterprises. De Havilland Aircraft of Canada Ltd. and Canadair Ltd. were both sold in 1986. In early 1988, the government sold Teleglobe Canada Inc. (which handles overseas satellite calls for the telephone and telecommunications companies) for $488 million to Memotec Data Inc., a small Montreal firm. By 1988, Ottawa had sold $2.1 billion of assets to the private sector. The federal government had divested itself of 13 companies and announced the sale of five others, including a share issue for Air Canada and Eldorado Nuclear Ltd. In 1991, Petro Canada began its privatization program by offering 39.5 million shares to the general public, representing 19% of the company's total shares outstanding.

In the case of Air Canada, its president predicted that the privatized company, free from government control and with the injection of new equity, would be able to take advantage of new opportunities more quickly in the deregulated and competitive environment. In the past, the budget of the airline had to be approved by the Minister of Transport, the Department of Finance and the Treasury Board. Because these departments were not market-driven, there were delays before funds

were approved for the airline. Air Canada's president stated further that in the future the market would decide whether the company should receive new funds through equity issues; the company would not have to depend on government whims or priorities. Being government-owned was also psychologically damaging to the company's employees, who were perceived by the public as inefficient government employees. Now employees would get the chance to demonstrate their worth.

A very successful privatization plan was the 1983 share offering of Pacific Western Airlines, which raised a large amount of money for PWA and allowed it to take over CP Air three years later to form Canadian Airlines International Ltd. The Alberta government bought PWA for $38 million in 1973 to prevent its head office from moving to British Columbia. Saskatchewan and British Columbia have also privatized a number of Crown corporations amounting to $430 million and $1.1 billion respectively.

In 1986, the Ontario government sold 85% of UTDC Inc., a company that manufactures trains, for $30 million to Lavalin Industries Inc. of Montreal. The new UTDC has since become a significant federal defence contractor, and has overcome the loss of a $380 million Via Rail contract it expected to get. According to a spokesperson for the old company, privatization made UTDC much more dynamic than its predecessor. It reduced a bureaucratic management structure from 33 vice presidents to six, and operated in a much more businesslike manner.[8] A major privatization venture will be Canadian National Railway Co., with which the federal government is expected to proceed in the near future.

Not everyone is happy with the privatization drive, however, especially public-sector labour unions. Labour's resistance is part economic, part ideological. In concert with the New Democratic Party, labour has traditionally favoured a balanced mix of public and private business ownership similar to that promoted in many of the Social Democratic countries of Western Europe. Labour points out that there is little evidence that the result of most privatization efforts has shifted the costs from taxpayers to the specific user of the service. Another one of Labour's main arguments is based on quality of service. Labour claims that the service and cost benefits one might associate in the dismantling of state-run services are illusory; since the break-up of AT&T and deregulation of the airline industry in the United States, telephone service complaints and flight delays have increased significantly.[9]

Privatization

Privatization means selling Crown corporations, either in whole or in part, to the private sector.

to act as a monitoring device to uncover abuses by outside investors, particularly in areas where some measure of domestic ownership is considered essential to Canada. Since that time, Investment Canada has not turned down a single foreign takeover. When the free trade agreement with the United States came into force, the federal government relaxed the rules for American takeovers of Canadian companies. Initially, foreign takeovers of Canadian firms with less than $5 million in annual sales or assets escaped the screening process. In 1993, this limit rose to $150 million. However, even under the new rules, Investment Canada can still require a U.S. company to retain research and development in Canada, or to transfer technology to Canada, as a condition for approval of a takeover that falls within the reviewable category.

**Canada Customs
and Revenue Agency**

www.ccra-adrc.gc.ca

How Government Is Financed

While it might be difficult for some individuals to state accurately their gross earnings each month, most know what their net pay is—the amount of money they receive when they cash their paycheques. The difference between net and gross pay is often quite substantial, and most of it goes directly to the government tax department. Approximately 20% of the average Canadian's gross pay goes to Revenue Canada. But taxes affect more than the amount of money that individuals or businesses have left to spend—they also affect the overall economy in various ways. In the remainder of this chapter, we examine the means by which government raises revenue for its operation, and how it can influence business cycles and economic growth through fiscal and monetary policy. Finally, we look at the growth of government and its effects on Canada.

Types of Taxes

With three levels of government and a relatively small population, Canadians are sometimes referred to as the most overgoverned people in the world. Electing representatives on the federal, provincial and municipal levels, the citizens of Canada also pay the cost of operating all three levels of government through taxes.

The Fraser Institute in British Columbia calculates an annual "Tax Freedom Day" at which time the average family in Canada has fulfilled its tax obligations and begins to work for itself. In 1999 Tax Freedom Day corresponded to Canada Day, July 1. Since provincial taxes vary throughout Canada, the Day is different in all provinces. The earliest 1999 provincial Tax Freedom Day fell on May 28 in

TABLE 12.2

Taxes of the average family (with two or more individuals), 1999, preliminary estimates (in Canadian dollars)

Cash income	**$ 61 825**
Income tax	**11 357**
Sales taxes	**4 900**
Liquor, tobacco, amusement and other excise taxes	**1 962**
Auto, fuel and motor-vehicle licence taxes	**929**
Social security, pension, medical and hospital taxes	**5 733**
Property taxes	**2 235**
Import duties	**256**
Profits tax	**2 304**
Natural resource levies	**250**
Other taxes	**660**
Total tax bill	**30 585**

Newfoundland. The latest date is July 13 in Quebec. The Atlantic provinces historically have the earliest Tax Freedom Days due, in part, to the large share of their total revenue that comes from other provinces through the federal government. Table 12.2 shows an estimate of the total taxes paid by the average Canadian as compiled by the Fraser Institute.

Tax Freedom Day in 1999 was 59 days later than it was 38 years ago. In 1961, the earliest year for which the calculation has been made, Canadian Tax Freedom Day was May 3. By 1974, the date had advanced to June 8.[10] You can calculate your own Tax Freedom Day using the Fraser Institute's calculator found on their Web site.

Table 12.3 shows the share of revenue each government received from specific taxes in 1999.

Fraser Institute

www.fraserinstitute.ca

Revenue Taxes

Revenue taxes include individual and corporate income taxes, property taxes and sales taxes; together they provide most of the revenue for the three levels of government.

Individual **income taxes** are the largest source of revenue for both the federal government and the provincial governments. Table 12.3 shows the revenue the federal and provincial governments received from personal income taxes. Personal income taxes are levied on the incomes of private individuals and on the net profits of proprietorships and partnerships. The amount of income tax that individuals pay depends on their level of income. Under the new tax system there are only three brackets, 17%, 26% and 29%, as compared to the 10 brackets that existed under the

Revenue taxes include individual and corporate income taxes, property taxes and sales taxes.

Income taxes are levied on the incomes of private individuals and on the net profits of proprietorships and partnerships.

Revenue of federal, provincial and local governments, fiscal year ended March 31, 1999

TABLE 12.3

Source of Revenue	All Governments Consolidated	Federal Government		Provincial Governments		Local Governments	
		Amount	Share of Total Revenue	Amount	Share of Total Revenue	Amount	Share of Total Revenue
	$'000 000	$'000 000	%	$'000 000	%	$'000 000	%
Income taxes	231 051	169 860	71.5	61 191	30.3	0	0.0
Property and related taxes	30 606	0	0.0	7 354	3.6	23 252	40.4
Consumption taxes	76 373	34 379	14.5	41 936	20.8	58	0.1
Contributions to social insurance plans	21 265	19 283	8.1	1 982	1.0	0	0.0
Other taxes	14 859	1 535	0.6	12 884	6.4	440	0.8
Sales of goods & services	18 238	5 471	2.3	4 260	2.1	8 507	14.8
Return on investments	23 512	5 000	2.1	16 492	8.2	2 020	3.5
Other revenue from own sources	1 974	908	0.4	615	0.3	451	0.8
Transfers							
General purpose transfers	24 724	498	0.2	23 024	11.4	1 202	2.1
Specific purpose transfers	9 744	59	0.0	4 584	2.3	5 101	8.9
From federal government						272	
From provincial government						4 829	
Total transfers	39 569	557	0.2	27 608	13.7	11 404	19.8
Total revenue	491 915	237 550	100.0	201 930	100.0	57 536	100.0

SOURCE: Adapted from Statistics Canada Web site http://statcan/english/Pgdb/State/Government/govt02a.htm5/23/2000

system in effect until 1987. In all provinces, with the exception of Quebec, the federal government collects provincial income taxes along with the federal tax, and then distributes the appropriate amount to the provinces.

Corporate income taxes represent the second-largest source of revenue for the federal government, though not for the provinces, where they rank after natural resource, general sales and health and social insurance levies. Corporations are taxed on their net profit at a combined federal-provincial rate that can range from 45% to 58%, depending on the province. These rates are subject to change according to government policy, which may use taxation to stimulate corporate investment or raise additional revenue. The federal government has in the past imposed a surtax for individuals or corporations, or both, to raise extra revenue. The surtax may be added for one year, but often remains indefinitely.

Unlike individual income taxes, corporate taxes are not progressive—a corporation does not have to pay a proportionately greater amount of tax the higher its income. Corporations operating in a foreign country must, of course, pay corporation taxes in that country. The federal government thus allows the company a tax credit deductible from the taxes it would normally be required to pay in Canada if all its income had been earned here.

Sales taxes are levied on the retail price of goods when they are sold to consumers. A sales tax is known as "selective" if only certain items are taxed, and "general" if most items are taxed. As Table 12.3 shows, sales taxes provide substantial revenue for both the federal government and all provincial governments. The provincial sales tax rate ranges from 7% to 10% among provinces; some provinces allow exemptions for various types of goods. Alberta is the only province that does not levy a retail sales tax. Until recently, royalty revenues from its huge oil and natural gas reserves provided the Alberta government with the required revenue.

The federal **Goods and Services Tax (GST)** came into effect at the beginning of 1991. It replaced the Manufacturers' Sales Tax (MST) of 13.5%, which was charged only on manufactured goods produced in Canada. Because it was not charged on imports, the tax was blamed for making Canadian goods uncompetitive internationally.

The GST is a **value-added tax**—in other words, a tax that is paid at each stage of the manufacturing process. For example, when a producer buys raw materials, GST is charged by the supplier. The producer then uses the raw materials to make a product and sells it to a consumer goods manufacturer, charging GST on the sale. The difference (usually positive) between what the producer pays in GST and receives in GST from sales is then sent to the federal government revenue department. Everybody involved in the goods or services production pays GST, but only the final consumer cannot pass the tax on.

Property taxes provide no revenue to either the federal or the provincial governments but, as shown in Table 12.3, they are the largest source of revenue for municipal governments—counties, cities, villages and municipalities. In some provinces, the tax rate is based on an appraisal of the current market value of real property; in others the rate is based on the historical cost of the property. The tax rate, often termed the "mill rate," is then set at a given number of dollars per thousand of the appraised value of real property. The revenue derived from property taxes is intended to cover the operating costs of the municipal government and the services that it provides.

Estate (succession duties) and **gift taxes** were levied by the federal government until 1971. An estate tax is a tax on the wealth of a deceased person. Between 1971 and 1977, most provinces (except Quebec, Ontario and Manitoba) did away with collection of succession duties. A succession duty is levied on the deceased's property

Corporate income taxes are levied on a corporation's net profit at a combined federal-provincial rate that can range from 45% to 55%, depending on the province.

Sales taxes are levied on the retail price of goods when they are sold to consumers.

Goods and Services Tax (GST) is a value-added tax that is paid only by the final consumer.

Value-added tax—a tax levied at each stage of the manufacturing process.

Property taxes are levied on real property and the revenue derived is intended to cover the operating costs of the municipal government and the services that it provides.

Estate/gift taxes—an estate tax is a tax on the wealth of a deceased person; a gift tax is levied on monetary gifts to individuals.

located in the province and on the value of property passing to inheritors. Individuals can easily circumvent the payment of such taxes by transferring their holdings to provinces with no succession duties, or to countries such as Bermuda where these taxes do not apply. Another alternative is to transfer, while still living, part of one's wealth to other people; however, such transfers may be subject to gift taxes. By 1977, gift taxes were levied only in Quebec, Ontario and Manitoba, where rates range from 15% to 50% depending on the value of the gift.

Regulatory Taxes

Although **regulatory taxes** produce some revenue for the governments that levy them, they are primarily designed to curb the use of certain commodities or services that are potentially harmful to the individual or to the economy of the country. The two major types of regulatory taxes are excise taxes and customs duties.

Excise taxes, also known as selective sales taxes, curb potentially harmful practices by making products such as tobacco and liquor much more expensive than would otherwise be the case. Excise taxes are also levied on non-essential or luxury goods and services such as gasoline, airline travel, movie tickets, telephone calls, fine furs and jewellery. The gasoline tax, for example, is used by provincial governments to finance the building and maintenance of highways. As a conservation measure, however, in 1976 the federal government levied an additional tax on gasoline to discourage excessive use. Taxes on cigarettes and liquor, on the other hand, are strictly regulatory.

Customs duties or **tariffs** are levied on many goods imported from other countries to make them more expensive than similar domestically produced goods. As discussed earlier in this chapter, customs and tariffs are intended to protect Canadian industry, and therefore jobs, from foreign competition. The customs duties imposed vary according to the product and the country of origin.

Fiscal Policy

Many years ago, when the federal government budget represented only six or eight percent of national income, relatively large changes in the various budget balances of revenues or expenditures had relatively little impact on the economy. However, as the federal budget began to increase to 20%, 30% and—today—50% of national income, changes in either the revenue or the expenditure side of the budget had significant impact on the levels of economic activity. The careful choosing of how revenue is raised, and how this revenue is dispersed, can affect various economic sectors. A **fiscal program** constitutes a carefully chosen plan for raising revenue through various tax measures, together with a carefully chosen program of expenditures to combat a specific economic problem such as a recession. **Fiscal policy** is the choice of a fiscal program.

For example, when a business recession threatens the existing level of economic activity, taking less money from individuals and business in income taxes and leaving it in their hands to spend as they see fit may be enough to stimulate consumer and business demand and neutralize the recession. A more serious recession may require additional government expenditures—new roads or public building construction, or specific job creation programs—to augment private investment and thereby ensure that employment is kept as close to pre-recession levels as possible. If fiscal policy is applied at the appropriate time, there should be little fluctuation in the level of economic activity because employment and the demand for goods and services will remain fairly steady.

Timing is a major problem with fiscal policy. It is difficult for the government

Regulatory taxes are primarily designed to curb the use of certain commodities or services that are potentially harmful to the individual or to the economy of the country.

Excise taxes are levied to curb potentially harmful practices to individuals or to the environment such as smoking or air pollution. They may also be levied on luxury items such as jewelry and airline and movie tickets.

Custom duties/tariffs are levied on imported goods to make domestic goods competitive with imports that are usually lower-priced because of lower labour costs in other countries.

Fiscal program—a carefully chosen plan for raising revenue through various tax measures, together with a carefully chosen program of expenditures to combat a specific economic problem such as a recession.

Fiscal policy—the choice of a fiscal program.

Taxation in Canada

Canadians generally agree that a tax system is necessary to finance the operation and expenditures of government. When questioned, people favour the income tax as the fairest form of taxation, followed by sales tax and property tax. Some individuals suggest abolishing income tax altogether and replacing it with a consumption tax such as Canada's GST. Many economists in particular believe that individuals should be taxed on what they take out of the economy as consumption rather than on their effort to create the country's future wealth. They also point out that if income were not taxed, there would be no tax avoidance via the "underground economy" (see discussion later).

The New Tax System

Tax reform was undertaken by the Progressive Conservative government in the 1980s in an attempt to reduce the amount of tax taken from income and to make the system fairer to those who work and produce. With more money left in their hands, individuals have more incentive to work hard and invest their money in new ventures. The result is increased individual effort and entrepreneurial risk-taking, which are necessary if Canada is to adapt to rapidly changing economic conditions. Tax reform was also expected to fuel economic growth and raise the standard of living in Canada. Despite the evidence collected to the contrary, it was also hoped that tax reform would reduce underground economic activity and thus increase government revenues and reduce deficits.

The income tax system that came into effect in 1988 had only three tax brackets: 17% on income under $27 500; 26% on income from $27 501 to $55 000; and 29% on income over $55 000. The old system had ten brackets ranging from 6% on the first $1320 to 34% on taxable income over $63 347. What used to be exemptions that would be deducted from income before tax was calculated are now tax credits. Many tax shelters were eliminated and some deductible business expenses cut altogether, while others were substantially reduced. The new tax system was expected to take some 850 000 people off the tax rolls, while reducing the tax paid by top earners. The result was to have a fairer income tax system, but one that would also reduce total federal tax revenue significantly.

The Goods and Services Tax

To recoup this loss in revenue, the federal government introduced the seven percent Goods and Services Tax in January 1991. The GST replaced the existing 13.5% Manufacturers' Sales Tax, which was applied only to goods manufactured in Canada and not to services. The MST was criticized for being inefficient and for distorting trade. The GST was said to be revenue-neutral, meaning that it would not raise new taxes but only replace the tax revenue lost from the changes to the income tax system and the removal of the MST.

In 1991, indications were that the GST would produce 25% more revenue than the Manufacturers' Sales Tax had generated. Some also believed that it would bring in an extra $5 billion by discouraging the underground economy, which at the time was estimated at $18 to $25 billion per annum.

The underground economy represents all of the transactions between individuals and/or businesses who pay for goods or services either in kind or in cash. With no receipts to indicate services rendered, participants can avoid paying income tax. It was expected that the GST, with its system of tax credits and the documentation required, would help reduce this underground activity. Unfortunately, the underground economy has not been reined in. Instead, it has grown and is pegged at approximately 15% of GDP or $105 billion. The revenue from the GST dropped as individuals and some businesses learned how to circumvent the tax by offering services and goods for cash.

While some blame the GST itself for being an unwieldy tax to administer and collect, most blame the high level of taxation that exists in Canada for the growth in the underground economy, not to mention a number of other economic woes. The Paris-based Organization for Economic Co-operation puts Canada out in front of 21 other countries in terms of tax increases.[11]

Since the day it was implemented, Canadians have been adamant about getting rid of the GST. Indeed, the Liberal government promised to do just that before it was elected in 1993. Some individuals suggest that the GST should be replaced with higher income and corporate taxes. But that would simply aggravate the existing problem of high taxation. Furthermore, increasing income taxes reduces the incentive to work and results in lower economic activity or an increase in underground economic activities for which no taxes are collected. Sales taxes or the GST are appropriate because they shift the tax burden from income to expenditures; in other words, people are taxed not on what they earn but on what they consume. This means that those individuals who consume less do not pay as much in taxes. Therefore an expenditure tax encourages saving which in turn helps investment and creating jobs.

One alternative is a business transfer tax, which would be paid by business on the difference between sales to customers and purchases from registered business. Since tax would not be collected on each invoice, the business transfer tax would be simpler to administer. Another alternative is to institute a >>

consumption tax levied on the difference between the income of individuals and their savings for the year. A third alternative is to institute a single-stage retail sales tax on consumer purchases of goods and services, with business purchases exempted. This tax would be similar to the existing provincial sales taxes. A final alternative is to overhaul the GST. This could mean reducing the overall rate by two or three percent and taxing all items, including food.

The GST has a number of strong points. First, unlike its predecessor—the Manufacturers' Sales Tax—it is visible. While this may be a sore point with Canadian consumers, it does make it more difficult for government to increase the tax. Second, the fact that all but final purchasers get a credit for GST inputs means that business costs don't get taxed, which is good for economic efficiency. Third, low-income earners get a GST credit, which makes the GST less regressive as a real consumption tax. Finally, it would cost the government several billion dollars to revamp the GST and educate Canadians about the new version.

A solution is to fix the GST and harmonize it with provincial sales taxes - charge the same percentage of tax on the same goods. Quebec took this step in 1991 and the four Maritime provinces followed suit in 1997. In the case of the Maritimes, the federal government insisted that the tax be included in the final price. Harmonization was expected to reduce costs for both businesses and individuals and reduce collection costs for the various levels of government, but it would mean that the same bundle of goods would have to be taxed both federally and provincially. Since each province has a different set of goods subject to provincial sales taxes, it would eliminate provincial autonomy in one taxation area.

For national retailers, hiding the tax meant that their computerized inventory systems had to be changed to separately price goods that are shipped to the Atlantic provinces at significant cost to the manufacturer and/or retailer. Furthermore, prices advertised for Atlantic Canada are different from those in other provinces. Even if harmonization eventually spreads to the rest of the provinces, none of them are likely to have the same total tax percentage. This could mean that different prices would have to be advertised for each province. The savings from harmonization could easily be outweighed due to the inclusion of the tax in the final price.

But perhaps a fundamental problem with hiding the tax in the final price is that it deceives the Canadian consumer; when the tax is always visible to consumers, it is much more difficult to change the rate. Consider that in the years between 1985 and 1989, the then-existing Manufacturers' Sales Tax increased from 9% to 13.5% with virtually no outcry, since the tax was hidden in the final price.

Reducing Taxes

From economists to small business owners to the average Canadian, all are adamant that taxes in Canada are much too high. High taxes discourage consumer spending and business investment. The federal government is adamant that it cannot reduce taxes until the deficit is brought under control. However, supply-side economists argue that when taxes are reduced, consumers spend more and businesses create more jobs. Since economic activity increases, so will overall tax revenues. Some point to Alberta, where economic activity has risen dramatically due to the deficit-fighting policies of the Conservative government. With the elimination of the deficit in 1996, some of the surplus will be returned to Alberta's residents through tax cuts.

The *flat tax* briefly achieved prominence prior to the U.S. elections in 1996 and has been revived lately by the new Canadian Alliance Party. The argument for it is that the existing graduated tax system is complicated, penalizes savings and rewards consumption and inhibits economic growth. A flat tax rate in the range of 15% to 20% charged on income would simplify tax preparation for individuals and reduce many of the costs associated with tax collection. The loss of government revenue due to a lower tax rate would be more than offset by the tax revenue generated because of new economic stimulus. When tax rates were cut in the United States at various times, tax revenue actually rose and the share of taxes paid by higher-income earners also rose.

But in Canada as elsewhere, there are practical problems with introducing a flat-tax system. Since Canada's economy is based on the existing tax system, it would create havoc in some of these sectors. For example, a significant financial industry has developed because contributions to an RRSP are deductible. A flat tax would have to be phased in over many years, so that existing institutions could stabilize under the new system.

to react quickly when economic activity is threatened by a recession. Thus, a fiscal program is often applied either too early or too late. For example, if tax reductions are provided while the economy is still strong, then the extra money injected may simply fuel inflation; on the other hand, if the recession has already started before action is taken, then the recession will continue on its course, although it will probably not be as severe as it might otherwise have been.

Fiscal policy can also be used to curb spending during inflationary periods. Inflation—a general rise in the prices of all goods—stems from excessive demand on the producing sector of the economy. By raising taxes, the government can siphon off the excess money available to individuals, which may reduce consumer demand sufficiently to ease inflationary pressure.

Fiscal policy can be shaped so that it affects different sectors in society. For example, federal tax policies can be designed to influence a firm's investment decisions. If businesses are allowed to depreciate new investments in plant and equipment more rapidly, they will be able to write off a greater part of their investments against current profits and thus reduce the amount of current taxes payable. The reduction in taxes may be enough to entice firms into making new business investments that will create employment.

Fiscal policy is not limited to the federal government; it is also practised by provincial and local governments, since both of these levels collect taxes and spend money for various projects. Tax incentives from all levels of government can induce companies to locate in specific regions where unemployment may be high. Federal, provincial and municipal governments alike may be prepared to offer tax concessions in anticipation of higher tax revenue from these businesses and from the jobs created. Provinces and municipalities can spend money to upgrade highways and public projects during recessions or when employment drops.

A stable economic climate is good for everyone. Since uncertainty about the future and risk of loss from a deep recession is reduced, businesses are better able to plan for inventory levels, for hiring and training of people and for investing in new ventures. Economic stability also allows businesses to concentrate on production efficiency and expansion. For individuals, it reduces concerns about job loss and allows them to spend more on discretionary goods and services, as well as to plan for major expenditures, such as cars, furniture, housing, vacations and so on.

Monetary Policy and Its Effect on the Economy

Monetary policy—controlling the money supply in order to effect specific economic results.

Fiscal policy—the judicious use of government tax revenues and expenditures to affect economic activity—is one tool government can use to alleviate the severe effects of business cycles. **Monetary policy**—controlling the money supply in order to affect specific economic results—is another. In Chapter 9, we discussed how businesses acquire loans from banks and other financial institutions when necessary so they can carry on their operations. We now look at how the government can use the banking system and the Bank of Canada to regulate the economy.

Chartered banks and most of the other financial institutions in Canada are privately owned. They take deposits from private individuals and businesses in the form of chequing and savings accounts and in turn lend this money to individuals and businesses requiring it. The borrowers pay interest, while the lenders receive interest from the bank. The bank's income is derived primarily from the difference between what they receive from borrowers and what they pay out to lenders. They also offer other services for which they charge various fees.

Bank of Canada—acts as a control agent for the chartered banks, formulating monetary policy and regulating monetary operations in Canada.

Prior to the Great Depression, banks and other financial institutions could easily become bankrupt. To ensure confidence in the Canadian banking system, Parliament passed the Bank of Canada Act on March 11, 1935, creating a central bank—the **Bank of Canada**. The Bank has two major purposes. First, it acts as a control agent for the chartered banks. It requires them to provide regular reports about their operations, and to deposit reserves with it. Second, it is responsible for formulating monetary policy and regulating monetary operations in Canada.

< The Bank of Canada regulates the Canadian money operations and acts as a control agent for the chartered banks

Although the government in power has ultimate control over the Bank and its actions, it generally does not intervene, leaving the governor and the board of the Bank relative independence in setting monetary policy. Nevertheless, there is close consultation between the Minister of Finance and the governor of the Bank. In the event that the Bank's policy is in serious disagreement with the government's economic policy, the actions of the latter prevail.

Controlling the Money Supply

Monetary policy is primarily concerned with regulating the money supply to best serve the needs of the economy. The major tools used to control the money supply are cash reserves, open market operations and the bank rate. Monetary policy is most effective in combatting inflation because raising interest rates and restricting the money supply is an effective way of reducing demand for goods and services. With reduced demand, the upward pressure on prices is diminished, which tends to reduce inflation. During a recession, on the other hand, the Bank of Canada can act to increase the money supply, reduce interest rates and generally establish an attractive climate for borrowing. Unfortunately, it cannot directly affect the will of individuals to borrow. As long as the business outlook is poor, individuals will hold off on major purchases even if interest rates are attractive. Therefore, the desired increase in bank loans (and, consequently, consumer spending) may not happen.

To control the money supply the Bank of Canada relies primarily on buying or selling government securities in the open market and setting the bank rate. Increasing or decreasing the cash reserves of the chartered banks is not used today as a tool for monetary policy but is an important factor in controlling the money supply.

Bank of Canada Services

The Bank of Canada provides a number of services.

1. Every day Canadians write large numbers of cheques on accounts with Canadian financial institutions. The Bank of Canada acts as the central clearing house. It calculates the amount each financial institution owes to the other and then transfers the funds to the appropriate accounts on the books of the Bank of Canada. This is called the payments clearing and settlement process. By controlling the total supply of funds for these accounts (usually by moving government deposits), the Bank can influence very short-term (overnight) interest rates. This daily cash-settling process is, in fact, the Bank's primary technique for implementing monetary policy on a day-to-day basis. Thus the Bank of Canada's involvement in the clearing and settlement process is an integral part of the implementation of monetary policy as well as a vital banking service which the Bank provides to the financial system.

2. The Bank of Canada is also the federal government's banker and financial adviser. It handles the accounts of the Receiver General, which keeps track of all the money collected and spent by the federal government. The Bank also acts as adviser and agent for the Government of Canada in the management of the nation's foreign exchange reserves, including gold reserves, held in the government's Exchange Fund Account.

3. The government's activities on the foreign exchange market (including investment of foreign exchange reserves) are carried out by the Bank. When the Canadian dollar is under excessive upward or downward pressure, the Bank will buy or sell foreign currencies (usually U.S. dollars) from reserves in exchange for Canadian dollars. For example, when the Bank responds to a rising Canadian dollar, it adds to foreign reserves by selling Canadian currency and acquiring U.S. dollars. By intervening in the foreign exchange market in this manner, the Bank of Canada tends to smooth out the rise and fall of the Canadian dollar (a technique called "leaning against the wind"). This is done to maintain confidence in the Canadian currency and reduce rapid changes in the value of the currency, which could otherwise have an undesirable impact on Canada's economy.

4. The Bank of Canada maintains deposit accounts for many foreign central banks, thereby facilitating the official transactions that these banks or their governments may have in Canadian dollars.

5. The Bank also has sole responsibility for the issue of bank notes in Canada, a role it assumed in 1935. It is involved in every phase of note design, production and distribution. The Bank does not create currency at will, however; it responds to the demand of financial institutions, which respond to public demand.

6. The Bank advises on the size, timing and makeup of the borrowing program and on the management of the government's cash balances. The government can raise funds in two ways: through taxation and by borrowing money from the public through treasury bills and bond issues. The Bank of Canada, as the government's fiscal agent, assists the Department of Finance in carrying out the government's borrowing program. The Bank works closely with many members of the financial community. Its representatives in regional offices in major financial centres consult regularly with market participants, who provide valuable insight into current market developments and the market outlook. The Bank of Canada also makes the arrangements for issuing new government securities, acts as the registrar for the outstanding debt, makes interest payments, executes transfers of ownership and redeems securities at maturity.

7. The Bank of Canada issues, services and redeems three major types of securities on behalf of the government: Canada Savings Bonds (CSBs), Government of Canada marketable bonds (referred to as Canada bonds) and treasury bills. This range of instruments provides government with options for responding to changing market conditions and investors' needs.

Cash Reserves

Cash reserves determine the amount of money the chartered banks can lend on the basis of their deposits.

Each chartered bank is required to hold primary and secondary **cash reserves** in the form of deposits and notes with the Bank of Canada. These reserves in effect limit the amount the banks can lend to individuals or businesses. For example, if a 10% reserve is required, then for every $1000 of deposits a chartered bank can lend $9000. Changing this reserve requirement would have an immediate effect on how much the chartered banks could lend out. If the reserve requirement were to increase, for example, the banks would have to curtail the amount of money lent out or attempt to get more deposits from customers.

Although the Bank of Canada occasionally does change the reserve requirements of the chartered banks, this action is generally not used as an instrument of monetary policy. Instead, the Bank of Canada exerts its influence by managing the cash reserves of the banking system. For example, a chartered bank can borrow money from the Bank of Canada if its lending needs for customers become greater. The cost of the loan to the chartered bank is called the bank rate, which we will discuss shortly. If the Bank of Canada wants to reduce the amount of money in circulation, it raises the bank rate; the chartered banks, in turn, raise the interest rate they charge their clients. Conversely, a lower bank rate would act to expand the amount of money in the economy because the price of borrowing money—the interest rate—would go down. This drop might encourage business investment and consumer spending, which creates jobs and stimulates economic activity.

Open Market Operations

The Bank of Canada, in its **open market operations**, can also control the money supply by buying or selling government securities of various kinds in the money market. If the Bank sells its government securities on the open market, the increased supply of securities would lower their price, just as the price of any commodity is reduced if its supply increases. As the price of a fixed security falls, its yield—return to investors—rises. For example, a newly issued $100 bond with a yield of 10% at issue would yield 10.2% if the price of the bond dropped to $98. The market would probably interpret the sale of a large amount of securities to mean that the Bank of Canada wants to increase interest rates.

The sale of securities changes the reserves of the chartered banks and hence the money supply. To understand how this works, remember that when individuals and institutions buy securities from the Bank of Canada, they issue cheques on their accounts with the chartered banks. Since the amount of money these banks have available as deposits is reduced, they must increase their cash reserves with the Bank of Canada. To bring their reserves into line, the chartered banks can either borrow from the Bank of Canada at the existing bank rate or reduce the amount of money they lend. In either case, the result could be higher interest rates for borrowers, which in turn would reduce the demand for loans. Similarly, if the Bank buys securities in the open market, individuals selling their securities would deposit their cheques into their bank accounts. This action would increase chartered bank deposits, allowing the banks to lend more money. An expanded money supply and lower interest rates might lead to an increase in economic activity.

Open market operations— refers to the Bank of Canada controlling the money supply by buying or selling government securities—treasury bills—in the money market.

Setting the Bank Rate

Until 1996 the bank rate was set 25 basis points above the average yield of new three-month treasury bills which were auctioned off each Thursday to borrow money to finance the federal government's operation. The Bank of Canada also put in a bid, and this bid—high or low—gave some indication as to the Bank's intention about future interest rates.

In February 1996, as part of a package of changes, the Bank of Canada also redefined the setting of the bank rate. Under the new system, the bank rate will no longer be tied directly to the market rate of treasury bills, but to the rate at which major participants in the money market borrow and lend one-day funds. Part of the new electronic payments system, to be fully implemented in 1997, this "overnight operating band" (now ranging from 5% to 5.5%) has three components. The bank rate, which is the rate charged to financial institutions that need to borrow money, is the top of the range. The bottom of the range is the rate that the Bank of Canada pays to financial institutions if they have uninvested funds with the central bank. Between these two levels is the "target rate" that is used by the Bank of Canada as a signal of its monetary policy.

Normally the target rate would be the mid-point of the range. But if the Bank of Canada wanted to indicate that it intends to raise interest rates it could advance the target rate by 12.5 basis points (0.125%) off the mid-point and consequently raise the bank rate. Similarly, lowering the target rate would signal that the central bank wants to move toward lower interest rates.

The **bank rate** is the basis for which the prime rate is determined. The **prime rate**—the rate of interest charged to a financial institution's best customers—is usually one percentage point above the bank rate. **Consumer interest rates** are derived from the prime rate, which varies among institutions depending on the competition between them for deposits and loans.

How the Bank of Canada Can Affect the Economy

Its power to affect the money supply, and thus interest rates, gives the Bank of Canada significant influence over economic activity. If it wants to stimulate the economy, it can reduce the bank rate and make more money available. A lower bank rate means lower interest rates for businesses and consumers. Businesses are more liable to invest in new ventures because there is a better chance of a return on the investment. This leads to job creation. Borrowing for consumers also becomes less expensive, encouraging demand for goods and services. The overall effect of an increased money supply means more employment, increased production and, consequently, more income for both businesses and consumers. For government, it means higher tax revenues.

Should the Bank decide that the economy is being subjected to inflationary pressure because the demand for goods is becoming too great for the existing productive capacity, then it can attempt to reduce the money supply. The reduction would raise interest rates and make borrowing money more expensive, eventually reducing economic activity.

Obviously, monetary control is a delicate process because there is always a lag between the time action is taken by the Bank and the time results are achieved. Another problem is that low interest rates may have no effect on economic activity if consumers and business owners are pessimistic about the future economic outlook and hold off on purchases. In addition, events outside of the Bank's power may influence economic activity. For example, in the late 1980s and early 1990s inflationary pressure forced the Bank to institute high interest rates while at the same time the federal government and the provinces were spending far more than they received in tax revenue; government fiscal policy was, therefore, in direct conflict with the monetary policy instituted by the Bank of Canada. Finally, the actions of other nations, particularly the United States, can have a strong effect on Canada. A recession in the United States inevitably has a severe effect on Canada, because of Canada's huge amount of exports to that country. Interest rates in the United States will invariably affect Canada's interest rates, which are usually higher to attract foreign investment.

Growth of Government

The Canadian government has always played a major part in developing Canada's economy. However, government's main entry into the direct management of the

Bank rate—the rate derived from the average yield on the 91-day treasury bills plus one-quarter of a percentage point.

Prime rate—the rate of interest charged to a bank's best customers; usually one percentage point above the bank rate.

Consumer interest rates are derived from the prime rate, which varies among institutions depending on the competition between them for deposits and loans.

Bank of Canada

www.bankofcanada.ca

Canadian economy was largely in response to the tremendous unemployment caused by the Great Depression. Government's first major task was to check the high level of unemployment and provide relief to those in dire need. Thereafter, it instituted programs that were designed to prevent the recurrence of another serious depression. World War II, along with some hastily developed economic and social programs, brought Canada and the United States out of the Great Depression. After the war, the work of John Maynard Keynes found many followers and government began to apply his revolutionary economic teachings. Fiscal and monetary programs were employed to maintain full employment. Thus, government came to accept responsibility for creating jobs and maintaining full employment. Soon everyone looked to government if unemployment increased; of course, government was also quick to take credit for any decrease in unemployment.

To achieve full employment, there had to be constant economic growth, which in turn required high investment by business and high consumption by consumers. Whenever demand for goods and services appeared to slacken, threatening a recession, government intervened with fiscal and monetary programs to ensure that the level of economic activity remained high. As Canadians became more affluent, they also demanded more government services; most came to believe that government could cure all economic ills.

However, the federal government was not satisfied with only economic management. There was a strong push, particularly during the Liberal governments from 1968 to 1984, to mould Canada into a more social democratic society with power centralized in Ottawa. In recognition of the French-speaking minority in Canada, bilingualism was promoted. There were also efforts to make Canada more self-sufficient in energy and to reduce foreign ownership of Canada's manufacturing, petroleum and mining industries. There was a fear that too many decisions affecting Canada were being made abroad, particularly in the boardrooms of American companies.

Although some of the social and economic programs and policies were good for Canada, the appropriateness and cost of others were greatly disputed. Not only did the programs cost money to implement, but their administration required an increase in the number of civil servants, which required new layers of management, support services, office space and so on. Furthermore, new programs require rules and regulations that must be written and enforced. Needless to say, the expanding government sector became more expensive to operate; the major problem was to finance the economic and social programs the government developed and the policies that it embraced.

Financing Government Programs

Government can finance its programs and services by increasing taxes or by borrowing, either from its citizens or from other countries. If new programs are financed through tax increases, the spending power of the private sector is reduced, leaving less money in the hands of individuals to spend as they see fit. On the other hand, if government chooses to finance its spending by borrowing, it is considerably easier to implement new services and programs since it does not directly affect the pocketbooks of Canadians.

Unfortunately, in the mid-1970s the federal government chose to borrow the money needed to finance the maintenance of Canada's economy, the various programs and services offered and most of the social programs established. The result has been a huge increase in the national debt. By 1998, the **net public debt**, which represents

Net public debt—represents the accumulated deficit since Confederation.

the accumulated deficit since Confederation, stood at $578 billion. Table 12.4 shows **federal government deficits** from 1968 to 1999, along with various dollar amounts pertaining to Canada's debt problem. The **Consumer Price Index (CPI)** is also shown, as well as the percentage of GNP represented by debt. (The CPI measures the increase in prices of a selected number of consumer goods over a period of time.) Figure 12.2 is a graphical representation of some of the information in the table.

This uncontrolled spending of unearned money was the major factor leading to the high rate of inflation in the late 1970s and early 1980s. As this "unearned" money flowed into the economy and was used to purchase goods and services, prices rose because total national income on aggregate was greater than total national

TABLE 12.4 Federal expenditures (surplus or deficit), public debt, interest charges on public debt and consumer price index

Year	Federal Revenues Expenditures (surplus or deficit) ($000 000)	Gross Public Debt ($000 000)	Net Debt ($000 000)	Debt Per Capita	Net Debt as % of GNP	Interest Paid on Debt Gross ($000 000)	Interest Paid on Debt Per Capita $	CPI 1986 Base
1968	-711	29 810	17 508	846	25.4	1 409	62	22.4
1969	-400	32 020	17 908	853	23.7	1 589	69	23.4
1970	332	33 260	17 576	825	21.2	1 862	79	24.2
1971	-780	37 114	18 356	851	20.6	1 974	83	24.9
1972	-1 542	41 169	19 898	913	20.5	2 253	90	26.1
1973	-1 675	44 693	21 573	979	19.9	2 518	96	28.1
1974	-1 999	47 542	23 572	1 054	18.5	2 961	115	31.0
1975	-2 009	52 866	25 581	1 127	16.8	3 705	139	34.5
1976	-5 737	59 612	31 318	1 362	18.3	4 579	170	37.1
1977	-6 297	67 323	37 615	1 616	19.0	5 101	200	40.0
1978	-10 426	79 879	48 041	2 043	22.0	6 410	273	43.6
1979	-12 617	96 957	60 658	2 554	25.1	8 080	341	47.6
1980	-11 501	104 862	72 159	3 001	26.1	9 897	355	52.4
1981	-14 303	120 446	85 681	3 520	27.6	13 739	438	58.9
1982	-15 541	137 573	100 553	4 082	28.2	16 675	615	65.3
1983	-29 029	166 203	134 918	5 158	36.0	17 463	680	69.1
1984	-32 917	199 497	167 835	6 394	41.4	21 006	720	72.1
1985	-38 512	237 112	206 347	7 845	46.4	24 738	885	75.0
1986	-34 583	269 286	240 930	9 118	50.4	26 216	1 013	78.1
1987	-30 733	302 744	271 663	10 235	53.7	27 883	1 030	81.5
1988	-28 201	333 521	299 864	11 260	54.4	31 711	1 107	84.8
1989	-28 951	373 547	328 815	12 537	54.3	37 424	1 252	89.0
1990	-28 996	398 036	357 811	13 456	55.0	41 880	1 482	93.0
1991	-30 618	433 932	388 429	14 230	58.2	41 053	1 465	98.5
1992	-34 643	466 690	423 072	15 436	62.7	39 558	1 394	100.0
1993	-35 500	515 749	458 572	16 566	65.7	39 219	1 366	101.8
1994	-39 000	558 701	501 000	17 657	71.2	40 157	1 383	102.0
1995	-33 211	595 877	550 685	18 323	72.2	46 254	1 576	104.2
1996	-13 499	634 939	578 718	19 504	69.5	45 352	1 528	105.9
1997	4 508	651 124	588 402	19 611	67.0	43 775	1 459	107.6
1998	2 591	646 075	581 931	19 205	64.5	43 958	1 451	108.6
1999	2 566	651 888	578 323	18 899	60.4	43 507	1 422	110.5

Note: Gross Public Debt includes total liabilities of the federal government. The Net Debt is the Gross Public Debt minus recorded assets but excluding physical assets such as public buildings. The Net Debt represents the accumulated overall deficit since Confederation. Recorded assets represent cash, investments, sinking funds, advances to exchange fund account, securities held in trust, deferred charges, miscellaneous loans, and sundry expense account. All physical assets such as public buildings are not recorded on the balance sheet but charged as expenditures when required.

SOURCE: Adapted from various sources including National Finances, Canadian Tax Foundation Publication and Statistics Canada.

A

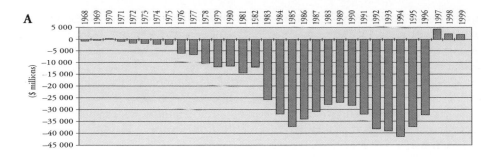

FIGURE 12.2

Federal revenues/
expenditures (A), net debt
(B), net debt as percentage
of GNP (C) and interest
paid on debt (gross) (D)

B

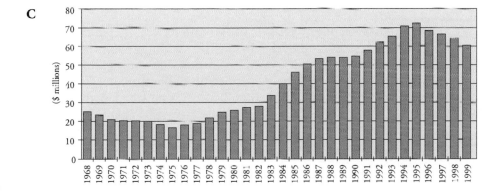

C

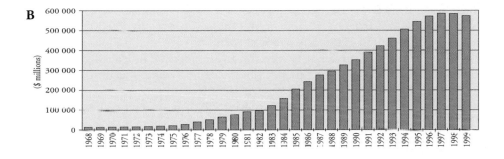

D

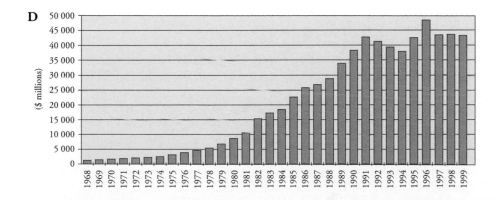

production. Other factors that contributed to high inflation were the increases in the price of oil due to OPEC, and structural changes in the economy. Once started, inflation can quickly spiral out of control unless drastic action is taken to reduce demand for goods and services by raising interest rates. If inflation is not brought under control, it will quickly result in the devaluation of money, high unemployment and, eventually, a drop in the standard of living. At its extreme, it may have severe social consequences, leading to disorder throughout the country. For example, inflation contributed to the rise of totalitarianism and dictatorship in Germany following World War I.

The federal government's financial policies have been the subject of considerable debate. Politicians, economists and business leaders are among critics who have charged that the growth of government expenditures is out of control. Government expenditures increased from $10.5 billion in 1967 to $55 billion in 1980. At the same time, the size of the federal government bureaucracy went from 369 000 employees in 1967 to 494 000 in 1980. Thus, federal spending increased fivefold in 13 years, while the civil service increased by one-third. The increase in federal government employees was even more pronounced from the end of World War II to 1975. Over these 30 years, the number of federal civil servants multiplied seven times, while the Canadian population only doubled.[12] By 1993 the federal employment (excluding Crown corporations), stood at 406 000, even though the Conservative government embarked on an ambitious plan to reform the civil service in 1989.

Although government spending was not really reduced until the mid-1990s, the federal government realized in the early 1980s, when inflation was in the double-digit range, that its policies were responsible for inflation. It capped wage increases in Canada at six percent and put a hiring freeze on the federal civil service. Along with the Bank of Canada, which kept a tight rein on the money supply, inflation dropped from a high of 12.5% in 1981 to 5.8% in 1983. From there, it decreased further to around the 4% level by the end of the decade. By the mid-1990s, inflation had been beaten down to the 1% to 2% range. Unfortunately, the high interest rates that resulted from reining in inflation are blamed for business failures and high unemployment. Debate continues on whether the fight against inflation was worth the cost.

Government Rules and Regulations

Another major issue is the increasing government control over private individuals and businesses. In order to provide more services, government is constantly seeking to learn more about people—their wants and needs; in the process, it requires more information about people's private lives. Similarly, businesses must be prepared to disclose their operations to government representatives and adhere to the ever-increasing number of often-questionable regulations.

Coping with the rules and regulations of federal, provincial and municipal governments may be one of the greatest difficulties faced by business. In 1977, the government began to compile a list of all existing regulations. In all, 12 000 computer printout sheets were used; when bound, they made up 15 volumes of 800 pages each. And these were only federal regulations—they did not include the regulations issued by provincial and municipal governments.[13] A 1996 study by the Fraser Institute found that, on average, federal and provincial governments had passed 4549 regulations each year for the past 20 years. The Institute estimated that in real dollars the cost of dispensing these regulations cost governments $4.9 billion in 1993-94, in contrast to $2.9 billion in 1973-74.

Although inflation has been beaten to the ground, and yearly deficits have been changed to surpluses, Canada's national debt has continued to increase. As was pointed out earlier, by 1998, the consolidated net public debt (includes all governments) stood at $847 billion. Interest payments on that debt amount to approximately $42 billion per year—about 40 cents out of every tax dollar received. In round figures, this means that every person in Canada owes approximately $30 000. The interest payment on the national debt is now the greatest single expenditure for the federal government. Furthermore, the government has virtually no resources to establish large-scale training and employment programs unless it withdraws the funds from other programs.

Canada is today the second-largest international debtor, behind the United States. For the past three decades, Canadians have increased their standard of living by borrowing from themselves and from outsiders. The big annual interest payment severely limits the federal government's ability to meet the costs of existing social programs or to finance new ones. Yet there is virtually nothing that can be trimmed from current expenditures without affecting existing social programs.

The following may begin to happen during the next 10 years (or sooner) if the situation is not brought under control:

- The health care system, already in financial crisis, will deteriorate further. Canadians may be faced with a health care system similar to that currently in the United States, where the user pays most of the fees.

- Less money will be available for higher education.

- There may need to be large tax increases or big spending cuts in social programs at both the federal and the provincial level.

- A big increase may be necessary in Canada Pension Plan premiums and/or a reduction in benefits for people not yet retired.

Much depends on Canada's economic growth over the next few years, as well as on the government's ability to curtail its spending and readjust social programs. If the government can show that it is serious about reducing spending and if Canada has a healthy economy, there will be less downward pressure on the Canadian dollar, because investors will have more confidence in Canada's management of the economy. The Bank of Canada could then keep interest rates low, which would mean lower service charges on the national debt. With prudent economic management, the annual deficit could be reduced to zero at some point in the future. Further economic growth would then generate greater revenue that could be used to reduce the outstanding debt.[14]

On the other hand, if economic growth is slow, then the deficit is likely to increase, with the resultant increase in the national debt. At some point, foreign lenders would begin to worry about Canada's ability to pay its interest costs or repay the debt. They may want higher interest rates on new lending, which would aggravate the problem for Canada. At some point, heavy cuts in expenditure would become a necessity along with large tax increases. This would affect Canada's ability to remain competitive on the world scene. It would cause greater unemployment, putting more strain on the employment insurance fund and necessitating a reduction in benefits.

If foreign investors should stampede to reduce their holdings of Canadian debt, severe consequences could ensue for Canada. As foreign money left Canada, the dollar would decline, perhaps very rapidly depending on how quickly investors wanted to leave Canada. To offset the drop in the value of the Canadian dollar, the Bank of Canada would have to raise interest rates. But the stampede might be hard to stop and the value of the Canadian dollar could go into freefall. Then the only choice would be to ask the International Monetary Fund to help out. They would insist on drastic action to eliminate the federal deficit and reduce the debt. Other countries whose help could be needed might also make demands. The end result would be high interest rates, high unemployment, sky-high prices for imported goods, a greatly devalued dollar and a sharp drop in foreign investment. Above all, Canada's domestic economic and social policies could be dictated by outsiders for years to come.

Coming to Grips with Canada's National Debt

Surveys indicate that Canadian businesspeople spend 35% of their time complying with government regulations. Although no study has been done in Canada as to how much it costs to comply with these regulations, it was estimated in 1980, in the United States, that government regulations cost business in excess of $100 billion per year. If we assume that regulations are similar in Canada, then judging from Canada's population the cost to the Canadian economy at that time was approximately $10 to $11 billion annually.[15]

Regulations hit small and medium-sized businesses especially hard, and are a major deterrent to job creation among such firms. But they also tend to retard economic growth, according to a Dutch study performed in 1996. Of the 11 member countries of the European Union, those countries with the fewest regulations had the highest growth rates.[16]

Since the rules and regulations issued by the government are not subjected to regular review, they tend to remain long after they have served their purpose. Nevertheless, businesses must adhere to them. Staff are required to keep track of regulations and do the paperwork, while a business that overlooks regulations may face fines as well as court costs and associated legal fees. This increases business operating costs.

In 1992, Newfoundland started to eliminate up to 50% of all existing regulations and paper burdens on small business. Its initial cost of $2 million was offset by its saving of $3 million on administration and collection fees. Business people across Canada hope that Newfoundland's example will make an impression on other governments to remove three of the major barriers to the growth of small business—excessive regulations, taxation and paperwork.

What Should Government's Role Be?

In 1991, the Group of 22, a panel of Canadian representatives from business, politics, the public service and academia, published a report suggesting that Canada must have a strong federal government, although one not necessarily as large as the current one. The federal government should retain power over foreign policy, defence, and trade and commerce, regulate competition and intellectual property, and take over from the provinces the regulation of securities markets.

According to the Group, the Bank of Canada should have a statutory obligation to pursue a policy of curbing domestic inflation, along the lines of Germany's central bank, in order to ensure price stability. The provinces should appoint the Bank's board, thereby ensuring better regional representation, with the federal government continuing to appoint the Bank's governor.

Under the Group's recommendations, the provinces would gain some new powers. They would run culture, energy and natural resources, and regulate the environment within provincial borders. Responsibility for regional development would also go to the provinces, as would worker training, with national standards outlined by Ottawa to ensure international competitiveness. It is also suggested that health care become the responsibility of the provinces on the basis of clearly defined standards and principles.

While it is doubtful that the Group of 22 has all of the answers to Canada's economic, political and social problems, the current situation of high welfare, record bankruptcies, 10% unemployment, record debt and record taxes is clearly untenable.[17]

The evidence seems to indicate that a market system with competition is the most effective method for creating employment and increasing a country's wealth. Governments should facilitate the private-sector function by providing a stable economic and social environment. It must control inflation by curbing its own spending and by implementing appropriate monetary and fiscal policies. It must also ensure that the private sector is given the necessary incentives to invest in the productive capacity of the country; in other words, it must allow business to make adequate profits. Government should remove unnecessary rules and regulations, and reduce its involvement in areas where private firms could be more effective. It

An *industrial strategy* is a set of government policies that directly affect the pattern of industrial development in the country. This may include joint funding between government and industry for research and development, programs to stimulate high-risk investments through low-interest loans or other means of funding, help in developing overseas markets and in modernizing facilities at home. It may include the encouragement of mergers to enable the industry to compete internationally because of economies of scale. It may also include retraining of workers affected by restructuring specific industries, or establishing training programs to correct skill shortages. It almost always includes the subsidization of exports or protection of selective imports to protect domestic industries.

In Japan, for example, industrial policy has been carefully developed over the long term, while in Canada and in the United States, policies have been implemented on an ad-hoc basis, or as a response to a particular crisis. In either case, it appears that the marketplace alone cannot be relied upon to establish a competitive national industrial structure because of market imperfections. Although individual investors may be successful in maximizing the return on their investment, this action may not yield the best return for a country as a whole. Individual investors are generally more interested in short-term returns, while a country must plan its industrial structure for the long run.

Debate has been ongoing as to who should develop an industrial strategy for Canada. Should it be left to private business according to the dictates of the marketplace, or should it involve the hand of government?

Whether Canada should establish a formal industrial strategy is an ongoing debate. Canada must deal with the impact of international trade and with the competitiveness of industries within Canada. Ad-hoc policies and special aid to industries that have little chance of becoming competitive without government assistance can be detrimental to the economy. This special aid not only raises prices for Canadian consumers, but it also uses up capital for development and expansion of new industries that may have a competitive advantage in trading with other countries.

How can a successful industrial strategy be developed? Countries that have developed successful strategies have adhered to the following principles:

1. The market and not government should dictate investment initiatives. Government should take the public perspective to ensure that certain important areas receive the proper funds such as research and development, development of high-risk projects, skill development, and so on.

2. Public money should not be used to bail out dying companies or companies near bankruptcy unless they are necessary for the country in the long run and they can be restructured and become competitive.

3. Industrial policy agencies should have a small staff who consult boards of experts from universities, industry, professions, unions and the financial community.

4. Initiatives for investment projects and most of the funds should come from industry. Government agencies do not have, nor should they try to have, the expertise to initiate investment ideas. Only in developing the infrastructure - transportation systems, for example - should government be the primary investor.

5. Policies should be set so they are flexible when applied to different types of businesses. The competitiveness of each business depends on different factors that should be taken into account by government policies. While costs may be a problem for manufacturing industries, for example, it may be marketing or distribution for other firms.

6. The government's role should vary depending on the strength of private firms in a particular industry. In the case of a strong private sector, government should provide only secondary support, as compared to an industrial sector where the private firms are weak. In either case, government action should be in line with market forces instead of acting counter to them.

There are political risks in establishing an industrial strategy because some funds will be wasted and misused and various political pressure groups will force funds to be directed to unworthy projects or to serve special interests. Nevertheless, the risk of not developing an effective industrial strategy, resulting in economic stagnation, is far greater.

An Industrial Strategy for Canada?

Industrial strategy—a set of government policies that directly affect the pattern of industrial development in the country.

SOURCE: Ira C. Magaziner, "Troubled times demand an industrial strategy," *Canadian Business Review* (Spring 1983): 28. Reprinted by permission.

must also take a leadership role in making Canada globally competitive. At the same time, it must ensure that the economy works for the benefit of all. It must protect individuals from adverse economic conditions when necessary and take measures to guarantee a minimum level of health care, education and social welfare to all citizens.

Chapter Summary

1. Throughout Canada's history, government has been a major force in stimulating industrial development through tariff and non-tariff barriers against foreign imports, together with various industrial agricultural and natural resource development incentives. Today, government provides services ranging from mediation and arbitration in labour disputes to bank loans and consulting services for small businesses.

2. Government also tries to protect the public from monopoly businesses, and from unscrupulous business practices, through competition legislation and rules regulating the conduct of business in society. Government has also established various commissions designed to oversee business activities, such as transportation and communication, and to review all investments made in Canadian companies by foreign operations. In addition, where private business is unwilling or unable to supply essential services, various levels of government have established Crown corporations to provide them.

3. To finance their operations, the various levels of government depend mainly on personal and corporate income taxes, sales taxes and property taxes. In addition to providing revenue, taxes play an important role in fiscal policy. Fiscal policy refers to the particular fiscal program that constitutes a carefully chosen combination of adjustment of tax and expenditure levels relative to each other to combat a specific economic problem.

4. Another tool that government uses to manage the economy is monetary policy, which means controlling the money supply to achieve specific economic results. When the economy is in recession, an increase in the money supply lowers interest rates and makes borrowing less expensive both for businesses and private individuals. This is intended to increase business investment and the demand for consumer goods and services, which in turn should increase employment. As business profits improve and employment increases, government revenue also increases because of higher tax revenue. Conversely, when inflation threatens, reducing the money supply by raising interest rates makes the cost of borrowing more expensive, thereby reducing investment and the demand for consumer goods and services. With less pressure on the existing productive capacity of the economy, prices are less likely to rise and inflation may be reduced. Monetary policy is more effective in combating inflation than in lifting an economy out of a recession.

5. In the past two decades, government expenditures at all levels have increased dramatically, far exceeding government revenues, particularly in the late 1970s and 1980s. A large part of these expenditures were due to the establishment of social programs and programs designed to support government economic policy. Excessive government spending contributed greatly to high inflation in the latter half of the 1970s and the early part of the 1980s. It also increased the

government bureaucracy and confronted business with many rules and regulations about its conduct. Perhaps the most dangerous potential problem is Canada's national debt, which continues to rise at an alarming rate, threatening the standard of living of Canadians and the maintenance of Canada's social programs.

6. The greatest challenges facing the federal and provincial governments include keeping inflation in check, reducing excessive government spending, reducing the deficit and restoring confidence in the Canadian economy. Deregulation and privatization are attempts to reduce regulations and red tape for business and revitalize business performance. Income tax reform was intended to make the tax system fairer and encourage individual effort and the entrepreneurial spirit, which should ultimately result in greater employment and more revenue for the government to reduce its deficits. The implementation of the Goods and Services Tax in 1991 was intended to make Canadian manufacturers more internationally competitive, and eliminating the Manufacturers' Sales Tax was intended to reduce the prices of exports. The North American Free Trade Agreement should open up new markets for many Canadian firms and reduce prices of some consumer products. The above measures (and other measures yet to be implemented) should allow Canada to continue to compete in international markets. However, some believe that Canada can overcome its economic problems only by implementing a carefully designed industrial strategy.

KEY TERMS

Tariff 441

Non-tariff barriers 442

Quantity restrictions 442

Temporary adjustment
    assistance 443

Industry Canada 444

Counselling Assistance to
    Small Enterprises (CASE) 447

Combines Investigations Act 449

Competition Act 449

Canada Transportation Act 451

Canadian Transportation Agency . . .451

Motor Vehicle Transport Act 452

Deregulation 452

Open skies agreement 452

Department of Communications 452

Canadian Radio-television and
    Telecommunications
    Commission (CRTC) 453

Crown corporations 454

Investment Canada 456

Privatization 457

Revenue taxes 459

Income taxes 459

Corporate income taxes 460

Sales taxes .460

Goods and Services Tax (GST) 460

Value-added tax 460

Property taxes 460

Estate/gift taxes 460

Regulatory taxes 461

Excise taxes 461

Customs duties/tariffs 461

Fiscal program 461

Fiscal policy .461

Monetary policy 464

Bank of Canada 464

Cash reserves 466

Open market operations 467

Bank rate 468

Prime rate 468

Consumer interest rates 468

Net public debt 469

Federal government deficits 470

Consumer Price Index (CPI) 470

Industrial strategy 475

REVIEW QUESTIONS

1 Why is government involvement in a capitalistic economy more necessary today than it was in Adam Smith's time?

2 Why has the federal government been so heavily involved in the economy since Confederation?

3 How can government promote business by placing a tariff on imported goods? What is the major drawback to imposing tariffs on imported goods?

4 What are some of the major non-tariff barriers? How do they operate?

5 Why does the federal government provide industrial development incentives to private firms?

6 Distinguish between industrial designs, copyrights, trademarks and patents.

7 Why does government believe that it must control business?

8 How can government ensure competition between firms through anti-combines legislation? What are the major provisions of the 1986 competition act? What are the powers of the competition tribunal?

9 What are the functions of the National Transportation Agency, the CRTC and Investment Canada?

10 What is meant by privatization? Why is the government interested in privatizing Crown corporations?

11 What is the purpose of deregulation?

12 What are the major revenue taxes for each of the three levels of government?

13 How has the federal government reformed the tax system? What was the purpose of tax reform?

14 What is fiscal policy? How can government help to level out business cycles through manipulation of tax rates and government expenditures?

15 Why was the Bank of Canada established? What is monetary policy? How can the Bank of Canada control the money supply?

16 What does the expression "growth of government" refer to? How has government growth in Canada affected business, private individuals and Canada's financial position?

17 What is meant by industrial strategy? How can it help a country's economy?

DISCUSSION QUESTIONS

1 "Competition legislation is preferable to government regulation." Discuss.

2 Do you think that government should extend its aid to private business? Give reasons for your answer.

3 In what ways are government regulations beneficial to business?

4 Identify some specific cases in which large-scale government involvement has been beneficial to business and society in Canada, and others in which it has been detrimental.

5 What should the Canadian government take into account when developing an industrial strategy?

6 What services should be operated by government and what should be left to the private sector?

Canada Post Report Doesn't Deliver

George Radwanski's mandate review report on Canada Post is a disappointing jumble of recommendations—31 of them—that simply don't hold together as a coherent whole. His criticisms of its shift to a private-sector corporate culture are also overly savage.

True, Canada Post's jerky financial performance has not been what was hoped for after, in 1982, it became a more autonomous, commercially minded Crown corporation rather than a bureaucratically riddled government department. It has lost money in two-thirds of the years since, including some hefty losses in the 1990s.

However, in recent years it has improved productivity, cut a lot of unnecessary costs, improved delivery service, and introduced such efficiencies as franchising post office outlets to the private sector. Hours of access are longer. Labour-management relations are better. It has pioneered performance measurement and tracking systems now used by other postal services. It moves 30 million pieces of mail a day across a vast geographic area. Its challenges are quite unlike those facing postal services in other countries, and its achievements impressive. Canada Post expects to make more than $100 million in fiscal 1996—97, and predicts increasing profitability. Radwanski is skeptical, but, with big structuring costs behind it, the corporation should be able to be self-sufficient in the years ahead.

Rightly, Radwanski wants Canada Post out of activities that compete directly—and sometimes unfairly—with the private sector. But he shouldn't have stopped at partial privatization, such as selling subsidiary Purolator Courier and getting out of junk mail delivery. The government agrees on withdrawing from the major category of flyer delivery, won't put the courier business on the block for now, but left the door slightly open by commissioning further analysis. However, full privatization, which management is ready for, is the real answer to what ails the corporation.

The mandate review recognizes the huge changes that have taken place in the business environment in which postal services in Canada and other countries now compete. Yet Radwanski still plumps for a back-to-the-core Canada Post that would be government-owned and -directed and retain its letter mail monopoly—at higher prices.

Reminiscent of proposals to put a special tax on private-sector cable and telecom services to support the CBC, he wants to impose a levy on private courier services and the private delivery of unaddressed ad mail. The intention is to compensate Canada Post for withdrawing from competition and forgoing revenue. The argument is even thrown in that tax on junk mail will "counterbalance" the negative environmental implications of all those flyers. Fortunately this kind of woolly thinking has not been accepted by the government. Some of the report's other ideas would turn back the clock by creating more layers of bureaucracy, such as a proposed secretariat in the office of Public Works Minister Diane Marleau to monitor Canada Post's directions, advise the government, and ensure ministerial instructions to the corporation "are carried out promptly and faithfully."

The point of the corporation's restructuring has been to give it more management flexibility to be financially self-sufficient. Directions from big brother would stifle this. Accountability is needed, but this best comes from requiring more detailed, public disclosure on finances and activities and scrutiny by Parliament.

The report noted that attempts to become more efficient, downsize, and cut costs have been hampered by the collective agreement with the Canadian Union of >>

Postal Workers. While relations with the union have improved, management has been unable to get the flexibility to do all that's necessary. This is another argument for a no-strings-attached, full privatization of the corporation.

As the Fraser Institute and some others argued in their submissions, the corporation's exclusive privilege over the collection and delivery of letters should be revoked and its entire letter mail operation put up for sale to the private sector (giving postal workers themselves an opportunity to participate). As integral parts of letter-mail operations, Canada Post's retail operations and addressed ad mail would have to be included. Successful privatizations need something of real value to manage and develop.

There are other faster, convenient, cheaper alternatives to the postal system, such as electronic deposits and payments, faxes, e-mail, and the Internet. More delivery services would emerge, including in rural areas, if letter mail monopoly were ended and the system run privately.

SOURCE: Neville Nankivell, "Canada Post doesn't deliver," *The Financial Post* (October 10, 1996): p. 15.

Questions

1 Should Canada Post retain its monopoly on mail delivery? Why or why not? If Canada Post remains a Crown corporation, under what rules vis-a-vis the private sector should it operate?

2 Do you agree that full privatization is the cure for what ails the corporation? Why or why not?

3 How might alternatives to the postal system affect Canada Post in the future?

COMPREHENSIVE CASE 12-2

SOMERSET OPTICAL

As Somerset Optical continued to grow, it soon became obvious that the company would have to consider purchasing a location to house its optical laboratory. Demand was so high that Somerset added three more lens-grinding machines and two additional laboratory technicians. As well, the company's product quality was so high that a number of competing retail outlets had their lab work done by Somerset Optical.

Like any business in the growth stage, Somerset lacked the $300 000 cash necessary to purchase the building they selected as being the most appropriate due to location and layout.

In December 1999, Dewar and Fowler met with a government relations consultant who told them that funds might be available from government sources. The partners immediately jumped at the idea. They asked the consultant to suggest a number of programs that they could pursue to obtain government funds.

The consultant cautioned that it wasn't quite as simple as that. Somerset Optical would have to carefully outline its requirements and show, among other things, how the government would benefit from making this type of investment. For example, Dewar and Fowler would have to consider such things as job creation, research and development, manufacturing objectives, if any, and the economic spinoffs of their activities. Further, they would have to consider not only federal sources of funds, but also provincial (and, to a lesser extent, municipal) sources of funds.

In addition to a set of recent financial statements, they would require a top-notch business plan. After all the necessary documents were ready, they would need the proper contacts to work their way through the hundreds of government assistance programs available.

The consultant suggested that, for an agreed-upon price, she would be happy to undertake the search for government money on their behalf. Terms of the agreement would call for an initial payment by Somerset Optical of $5000 and a finder's fee of 10% of the amount of any government assistance obtained on behalf of Somerset. While there would be no guarantees, the consultant pointed out that having worked as a government relations specialist for a number of years, she had all the contacts needed to obtain funds for the company.

SOURCE: By David H. Jones-Delcourt. Reprinted by permission of the author.

Questions

1 Should Somerset make the deal?

2 Is dealing with a government relations consultant ethically acceptable?

3 Does the need for a small company to engage the services of a private government relations consultant suggest that government is not really committed to assisting firms?

13

International Business

Learning Objectives

After reading this chapter, you will be able to

1 Explain why countries trade with one another.

2 List and describe some of the major barriers to international trade.

3 Identify the efforts that have been made to facilitate international trade and list the major services provided by the Canadian government to help and encourage Canadian firms to trade internationally.

4 Discuss some of the arguments for and against free trade between Canada, the United States and Mexico.

5 Recognize why trade with Pacific Rim countries is becoming more important.

6 Describe the function of the World Bank and the International Monetary Fund.

7 Explain the basic concepts underlying international finance—balance of trade and balance of payments.

8 Explain how currency fluctuations can cause problems for a country's economy.

9 List the characteristics of multinational corporations, and discuss how they present both benefits and disadvantages for both host and home country.

10 Explain how foreign investment has brought benefits and disadvantages for Canadians.

Why Countries Trade with Each Other ✓ ∫

Canada's International Business Strategy

strategis.ic.gc.ca/sc_mrkti/ibin/engdoc/1c1.html

Foreign trade is not new. The earliest tales tell of adventurers setting off with their wares across the oceans of the world, despite fears that they might drop off the edge at any time. Throughout the Middle Ages, itinerant merchants struggled along muddy roads to sell their goods in town markets, while traders in the medieval capitals of Venice and Florence conducted their foreign trade with a flair perhaps unrivalled even today.

Although foreign trade has occasionally been restrained because of war, trade restrictions or tariff barriers, the desire for foreign goods has never abated. The reasons are varied. Goods from other countries may be less costly; some are perceived to be of better quality, while some are not otherwise available. Moreover, with the improvement in communication and transportation systems, we are more aware of the products available in other countries, and are able to obtain them more readily.

International trade is big business and growing faster every year. According to the World Trade Organization (WTO), world trade in 1998 in goods and services amounted to US$6.5 trillion—merchandise in goods US$5.2 trillion and trade in commercial services $1.3 trillion. The rate of growth in the volume of world merchandise exports slowed to 2% in 1998, from over 3% in 1997, due largely to continuing economic contraction in much of Asia.

Canada's total merchandise trade exports reached $214 billion in 1998, up from $148.9 billion in 1990, while imports amounted to $205 billion. Canada's share amounted to 4.0% of world exports and 3.7% of imports. In fact, exports of goods and services were equivalent to more than 40% of gross domestic product in 1995.

International trade is now recognized as the engine of global economic growth—largely thanks to the multilateral trading system. Over the 50-year lifespan of the General Agreement on Tariffs and Trade (GATT) and the World Trade Organization (WTO), global trade has grown 17-fold, production has quadrupled and per-capita income has doubled. Almost half of all international trade stems from a small group of nations including the United States, West Germany, Japan, the United Kingdom, France, Italy and Canada. The United States accounts for over 70% of Canada's trade, and Canada is, in turn, its main customer. Unfortunately for Canada, two-thirds of total imports are manufactured goods, while two-thirds of exports are products of primary industries, which employ only about 10% of the labour force.

As noted above, some goods are imported because they are less expensive and consequently can be sold at lower prices than similarly produced goods in Canada. Many garments and other textile products sold in Canada, for example, come from countries in the Far East. With lower labour costs than in the West, China, Hong Kong and Taiwan can produce garments much more cheaply, and thus sell them at lower prices.

However, a more fundamental reason for trade is the fact that virtually no country in the world can produce all the products that its people want. Canada cannot grow coffee or bananas, so those products must be imported from other countries. Other nations such as Japan and West Germany have developed superior technology in certain areas, making them leaders in the production of industrial machinery, cameras and electronic products. However, these countries lack raw materials, which they must import from countries such as Canada.

Thus, virtually every country enjoys some advantage in the production of certain products that can be traded to other countries for the goods that they, in turn, have an advantage in producing. The fact that international trade makes some goods available at lower prices than if they were produced in the home country is central to the concept of absolute and comparative advantage.

Absolute and Comparative Advantage

To clarify the concepts of absolute and comparative advantage, suppose that all industrialized nations depended on a specific raw material that only one particular country could supply. That country would have an **absolute advantage** in the production of the material. Now let us suppose that one of the industrialized countries makes a technological breakthrough in extracting the raw material from sea water. Suddenly, our hypothetical supplier nation loses its absolute advantage. However, if it can continue to produce the material at a lower cost than its new competitor can, it may still have a comparative advantage.

As this example shows, an absolute advantage in the production of a particular good can disappear quickly as technological and economic conditions change. Rather than relying on an absolute advantage, therefore, it makes sense for a nation to concentrate on maintaining a **comparative advantage**. Accordingly, it should produce and export those goods that it can produce at low cost, and import those goods that it can produce only at high cost. For example, although both Canada and Taiwan are able to produce shirts, lower labour costs in Taiwan mean that a shirt made there can be sold in Canada at a much lower price than a shirt produced in Canada. In turn, Taiwan may need certain raw materials or agricultural products that Canada can produce at relatively low cost. Trading these goods with one another would benefit both countries. It follows that if all nations adhered to the principle of comparative advantage, more goods would be available for everyone at lower prices.

However, the principle of comparative advantage is not always applied in international trade, and sometimes political considerations enter the picture. Particular domestic industries may, for political reasons, be protected from foreign competition through tariffs on imports. A country might choose to produce some goods, despite a low comparative advantage, in the interest of military or technological secrecy. In other instances, economic considerations influence trade. For example, eastern Canada imports foreign crude oil from Venezuela and the Middle East, while western Canada exports crude oil to the United States, because at present no facilities exist to transport western crude oil to Quebec and the Maritimes.

Nevertheless, comparative advantage remains the prime consideration in foreign trade. Some highly industrialized nations such as West Germany and Japan import raw materials and foodstuffs, and export manufactured goods. Countries with large populations, such as China and Taiwan, tend to specialize in the production of labour-intensive products for export to industrialized countries where labour rates are much higher. Most of their imports consist of food products and capital goods, in contrast to countries such as Canada that export raw materials and food commodities, and import manufactured goods.

Table 13.1 lists the major categories of Canadian exports and imports and some of the major commodities or products within each category. By comparing the amount of **imports** and **exports** in various categories of goods, we can see how the principle of comparative advantage works for Canada. Figure 13.1 shows imports and exports in the major commodity categories. In the first three categories, Canada exports significantly more than it imports. In the fourth category, end products (meaning manufactured goods), Canada's imports are significantly greater than its exports.

Canadian Foreign Trade

If a country consistently imports more than it exports, which means that it has a negative trade balance, it will eventually encounter financial difficulties in terms of its

---

Absolute advantage exists when only one particular country can supply a particular product or service.

Comparative advantage exists when a country produces and exports those goods that it can produce at low cost, and imports those goods that it can produce only at high cost.

Imports are products or services brought into one country from another country.

Exports are products or services that a country sells to other countries.

Selected exports and imports, 1999, by commodity grouping

TABLE   13.1

Exports by Category ($000 000)		Imports by Category ($000 000)	
Agricultural and Fishing Products	25 568		17 643
Meat & fish		Fruits & vegetables	
Alcoholic beverages		Coffee, cocoa, tea	
Wheat		Fish & marine animals	
Energy Products	29 723		10 708
Crude petroleum		Crude petroleum	
Natural gas		Coal	
Coal		Petroleum & coal products	
Forestry Products	39 117		2 740
Lumber		Crude wood products	
Wood pulp		Wood-fabricated materials	
Newsprint			
Industrial Goods and Materials	57 430		62 131
Metal ores		Metals & metal ores	
Chemical, plastics, fertilizers		Chemicals & plastics	
Metals & alloys		Metal-fabricated basic products	
Other industrial goods		Textile-fabricated materials	
Machinery & Equipment	85 985		108 168
Industrial & agricultural		Industrial and agricultural	
Aircraft & transportation equip.		Aircraft & transportation equip.	
Other machinery & equipment		Other machinery & equipment	
Automotive Products	95 493		75 916
Passenger autos & chassis		Passenger autos & chassis	
Trucks & other motor vehicles		Trucks & other motor vehicles	
Motor vehicle parts		Motor vehicle parts	
Other Consumer Goods	13 471		36 954
Special Transaction Trade	7 349		6 326
Other Balance of Payment Adjustments	6 474		6 234
Services	53 681		59 121
Total Merchandise Exports, 1999	414 291	**Total Merchandise Imports, 1999**	385 941

SOURCE: Data adapted from Statistics Canada, *Canadian International Merchandise Trade* (Ottawa: 2000), cat. no. 65-001.

balance of payments as money flows out of the country. Conversely, if a country consistently sells more to another country than it buys from that country, it will have a positive merchandise trade balance as money flows into the country. For example, Japan for many years has had a positive merchandise trade balance with the United States, meaning that it has consistently been able to sell more to the Americans than the Americans have been able to sell in Japan.

Department of Foreign Affairs and International Trade

www.dfait-maeci.gc.ca

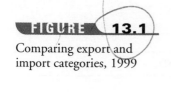

Comparing export and import categories, 1999

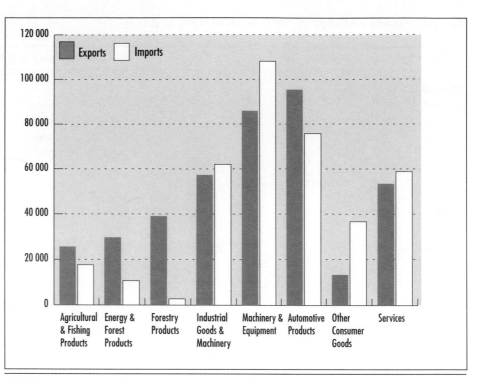

SOURCE: Data adapted from Statistics Canada, *Summary of Canadian International Merchandise Trade* (Ottawa: July 2000), cat. no. 65-001.

The U.S.-Japan trade imbalance has created tension between the two countries. When people buy more import products than domestically produced products, the result is lower domestic production and a loss of jobs. In the United States, the unemployed, unions and other affected groups have pressured politicians to put restrictions on imports to protect domestic jobs. Japan has retaliated with similar import restrictions. When this happens, people in both countries are deprived of imported products and must buy locally produced products, which may not be as good or may be more costly. Such "trade wars" are detrimental to both sides in the conflict and should be avoided at all costs.

Even though individual countries may have a positive or negative trade balance, on a worldwide scale the value of exports and imports between all countries must balance. Canada has been fortunate in that exports have generally exceeded imports, particularly in trade between Canada and the United States. Figure 13.2 shows Canada's generally positive balance of trade for the years 1955 to 1999.

Principal Trading Countries

Although Canada trades with most nations of the world, two of its customers account for 84% of exports, with the United States alone taking over 79%. In the case of imports, Canada buys almost 67% of its products from the United States. Canada's leading trade partners are listed in Table 13.2.

Canada's Leading Exports and Imports

In the list of Canada's leading exports and imports shown in Table 13.3, motor vehicles and parts are prominent in both export and import categories. This is largely

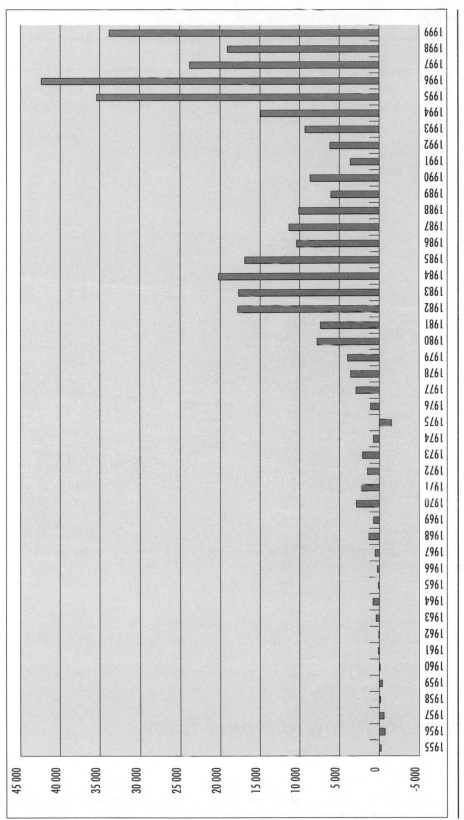

SOURCE: Data adapted from Statistics Canada, *Summary of Canadian International Merchandise Trade* (Ottawa: 2000), cat. no. 65-001.

FIGURE 13.2

Canada's balance of trade,
1955–1999

TABLE 13.2

Canada's principal trading partners, 1999

Top Sellers	%	(000 000)	Top Buyers	%	(000 000)
Imports			**Exports**		
United States	67.2%	215 111	United States	86.6%	286 761
Japan	4.7%	15 031	Japan	2.5%	8 250
Mexico	3.0%	9 520	United Kingdom	1.3%	4 412
China, People's Republic	2.8%	8 914	China, People's Republic	0.7%	2 482
United Kingdom	2.5%	8 150	Germany	0.7%	2 250
Germany	2.2%	7 005	Korea, South	0.6%	1 934
Canada	1.7%	5 546	France	0.5%	1 763
France	1.7%	5 311	Mexico	0.5%	1 522
Taiwan	1.4%	4 583	Netherlands	0.4%	1 463
Italy	1.1%	3 645	Italy	0.4%	1 382
Korea, South	1.1%	3 573	Belgium	0.4%	1 313
Norway	0.8%	2 547	Taiwan	0.3%	1 081
Malaysia	0.6%	2 056	Hong Kong	0.3%	919
Thailand	0.5%	1 508	Australia	0.3%	914
Sweden	0.5%	1 488	Brazil	0.2%	825
Brazil	0.4%	1 358	Norway	0.2%	715
Hong Kong	0.4%	1 303	Spain	0.2%	613
Switzerland	0.4%	1 265	Iran	0.2%	537
Singapore	0.4%	1 252	Indonesia	0.2%	528
Netherlands	0.4%	1 223	Algeria	0.1%	472
Australia	0.4%	1 210	Switzerland	0.1%	462
Ireland	0.3%	1 078	Venezuela	0.1%	431
Phillippines	0.3%	1 044	Malaysia	0.1%	409
India	0.3%	1 015	Ireland	0.1%	388
Venezuela	0.3%	1 013	Sweden	0.1%	369
Belgium	0.3%	932	Cuba	0.1%	355
Spain	0.3%	854	Chile	0.1%	346
Algeria	0.2%	653	Singapore	0.1%	339
Russia	0.2%	606	Thailand	0.1%	291
Total Imports	100.0%	320 159	Total Exports	100.0%	331 222

SOURCE: Data adapted from Statistics Canada, *Canadian International Merchandise Trade* (Ottawa: December 1999), cat. no. 65-001.

a result of the Canada-U.S. Auto Agreement, which allows Canada to produce a share of automobiles and parts for the United States market; in turn, many of the cars purchased by Canadians are made in the United States. Crude petroleum also appears in both columns since eastern Canada imports crude petroleum from the Middle East and Venezuela, but exports crude oil to the United States in the west.

Barriers to International Trade

There are always some barriers to be overcome when Canadian companies attempt to sell their products in other countries. Some problems are due simply to lack of experience, and may be easily resolved as firms become more accustomed to dealing in foreign markets. However, others may in fact prove insurmountable. Some typical problems of both kinds are discussed below.

Canada's leading exports and imports, 1999

TABLE 13.3

Exports	($000 000)	Imports	($000 000)
Passenger automobiles	35 590	Motor vehicles and parts including engines	30 264
Motor-vehicle parts including engines	15 338	Motor vehicles & parts and accessories	15 923
Lumber	12 656	Crude petroleum	6 916
Trucks and other motor vehicles	12 198	Digital integrated circuits	6 870
Natural gas	10 951	Engines for off-road vehicles	6 710
Crude petroleum	10 121	Gear boxes for motor vehicles	4 131
Newsprint	6 441	Data processing machines, parts and accessories	3 906
Chemical, woodpulp	5 032	Trucks	3 887
Engines for off road vehicles	4 154	Auto engine parts	3 053
Airplanes	3 828	Airplane parts	2 880
Parts and accessories of motor vehicles	3 690	Medicines	2 802
Data processing machines, parts and accessories	3 596	Data processing input output units	2 177
Telephone electrical apparatus	3 596	Digital processing units	2 172
Non-crude petroleum preparations	3 336	Road tractors for semi-trailers	2 128
Total exports	331 222	Total imports	320 159

SOURCE: Industry Canada, Trade Data Online, Strategis http://strategis.ic.gc.ca/cgi-bin/tdst-bin/wow/wow.codeCountrySelectionPage

Economic, Social and Cultural Barriers

Fortunately, Canada shares with its largest trading partner similar cultural backgrounds and social values. Trade with the United States is particularly easy since our main exports there are primary products and specialty capital goods. Even if we were selling consumer goods, however, we could safely assume that most products suitable for Canadians would also appeal to Americans. With the appropriate product, sales would almost certainly be assured.

Other countries, however, may present problems. Cultural and social customs in France, Venezuela and Italy, for example, differ markedly from our own, and these differences could seriously hamper sales of some manufactured products. The promotional approach usually used in Canada may not work in these countries. On the other hand, these countries may have similar problems when they to try to sell their products in Canada.

In some cases, even the name of the product must be changed, since a term accepted in North America may have an entirely different connotation or meaning elsewhere. For example, General Motors was puzzled when its Chevrolet Nova failed to sell in Puerto Rico. After some probing, the company discovered that the name Nova sounds like "no va"—"it does not run." Sales improved noticeably once the car was renamed Caribe. In another instance, the reason sales of Colgate-Palmolive's new Cue toothpaste were low in French-speaking countries was that "Cue" was also the name of a well-known pornographic magazine.[1] On the other hand, Volkswagen gave careful consideration to the problem of names before introducing to the North American market the successor to the "Beetle." By calling it "Rabbit," Volkswagen hoped the name would suggest exceptional handling qualities. In Germany and other European countries, however, a similar car was sold under the name of "Golf," while a less luxurious model not available in North America was called the "Polo"

The export of primary products is important to Canada's economic health >

(both names suggest well-known sporting activities). The sound of a name, as well as its meaning to people in a particular country, can be extremely important considerations when it comes to product names, particularly for automobiles.

Economic conditions may also influence the purchase of an imported product. A convenience good in Canada may be a luxury item in a foreign country. An electrical appliance common in Canada may be too expensive to operate where energy is costly and in short supply, while many disposable products popular in North America are far too wasteful for less affluent nations.

Moreover, the imported product may not meet the needs of foreign customers. For example, North American cars were cherished in Europe in the 1950s and 1960s, but few could afford to drive them because they used too much gasoline; the cars were also too large to manoeuvre in the narrow streets of many European towns.

Exporters of manufactured goods to countries with entirely different cultural backgrounds and economic conditions may find the barriers to trade insurmountable at times. However, since Canada's major exports are primary products, we encounter few of these particular problems.

Legal and Political Barriers

When a firm conducts business in a foreign country it must be familiar with both the laws of the buyer nation and the international laws regulating trade between countries. In some areas, laws may be more stringent than those in Canada; in other areas, they may be more lax. For example, while bribery is considered unethical in North America, it is common practice elsewhere. Property ownership, on the other hand, may be subject to much stricter regulations in other countries than in Canada. **Cartels** such as OPEC, which combine to fix a common price for their product,

Cartels—a group of nations or businesses that act as a monopoly by restricting prices or quantities produced.

are prohibited in Canada but accepted in some countries. Moreover, various aspects of business may not have the same protection elsewhere that they have in North America. In the case of patents, for example, a foreign corporation may be legally able to copy a product and sell it at a lower price, thereby undercutting the import without paying royalties to the company that owns the patent. In addition, each nation has its own trade restrictions, tax laws and requirements for imports and exports.

Most legal problems in international trade can be avoided because Canadian government agencies and services can provide exporters with the necessary legal information. On the other hand, a business has little control over political problems; it must accept the risk of loss from expropriation or destruction of property as one of the hazards of operating in a foreign country.

Tariff and Trade Restrictions

Tariffs were used by Canada in the late 1800s to almost force Canadians to buy Canadian instead of from foreign countries. Tariffs were reduced with the establishment of the General Agreement on Tariffs and Trade and eliminated between Canada and the U.S. and Mexico when the North American Free Trade Agreement came into force in 1994.

Foreign trade offers many benefits, but it can also be detrimental to a country's economy. Low-priced foreign-made goods can harm domestic industries that have higher labour costs, and people employed in those industries may lose their jobs. Another serious problem is the negative balance of trade that results when people are buying too many imports and the country is not exporting enough. To remedy these problems, the federal government used tariffs and import restrictions. The imposition of a **tariff** makes imported goods as expensive as similar goods produced in Canada; an **import quota** limits the amount of a certain product that may be imported, to ensure that domestic industry retains an adequate share of the total demand for particular goods.

While tariffs and import quotas can be defended in cases where a domestic industry is struggling to become established, or where an existing industry needs help in adjusting to international competition, they are nevertheless barriers to trade. Unless they are monitored constantly as to their usefulness in particular cases, they tend to become permanent. Then consumers suffer, since they are forced to pay higher prices. Moreover, tariffs and import restrictions may have negative consequences for domestic industries, since the incentive to improve efficiency in production and service to consumers is reduced when producers are sheltered from competition.

Although tariffs and import quotas are the major means of restricting trade, other methods also exist. Occasionally, some goods are banned from import completely under an **embargo**, a type of restriction often used as a political weapon against another nation. To prevent another country from selling its products in Canada at prices well below cost—a practice known as **dumping**—the federal government has enacted anti-dumping laws. These laws allow the government to impose an anti-dumping duty on such imports equal to the difference between the price of the product dumped and the regular price of similar Canadian goods.

Tariff—a special tax on imported goods designed to make their prices equal to those charged for similar domestic goods.

Import quotas allow only a certain amount of a particular type of product into the country.

Embargo—exists when some goods are banned from import completely.

Dumping occurs when a country sells its goods in another country at less than cost.

Efforts to Facilitate International Trade

It is a paradox in international trade that the same countries that put barriers in the way of imports also attempt to encourage their own exports. Most countries realize that barriers to trade are self-defeating because other countries can retaliate. This is particularly true in the case of Canada, which depends heavily on the export of raw materials to other countries. Thus, government is torn between two competing objectives. On the one hand, it should protect domestic industries and jobs against lower-priced imports; on the other hand, it realizes the necessity of exports and the benefits of trade to a country's standard of living.

Nevertheless, there is a worldwide effort to reduce trade barriers. Various international agencies and agreements have been created to encourage international trade. Some countries have established free trade areas to facilitate the free movement of goods between countries. And the federal government sponsors a number of agencies designed to help Canadian companies establish international markets and export their products.

International Agreements and Agencies

Among the best-known international agreements designed to promote freer trade are GATT, now known as the World Trade Organization, the World Bank, the International Monetary Fund and various multinational trade communities. The North American Free Trade Agreement (NAFTA) and the Canada-U.S. Auto Agreement (Autopact) are two significant trade agreements for Canada and the United States.

The General Agreement on Tariffs and Trade (GATT)

General Agreement on Tariffs and Trade (GATT)—designed to reduce the level of tariffs on a worldwide basis.

Perhaps the most ambitious program established to encourage free trade was the **General Agreement on Tariffs and Trade (GATT)**, which was signed in 1947. To reduce the level of tariffs on a worldwide basis, approximately 100 countries signed the agreement. Canada was one of the major forces behind GATT, despite its strong ties to the Commonwealth and preferential tariff arrangements between Commonwealth nations. Canada pledged not to initiate any new tariff arrangements with Commonwealth countries beyond those already existing.

A major provision, the "most favoured nation" clause, stated that any reduction in tariffs between any two member nations must be extended to all other participants in the agreement. Subsequent negotiations have led to further agreements, reducing tariffs in the industrialized countries from an average of 40%, when GATT was signed, to about 4% to 5% today. Trade in manufactured goods multiplied twentyfold.

As economic growth slowed in the mid-1970s, unemployment climbed and the West faced stiff competition from developing countries and Japan. To keep out imports, nations turned increasingly to non-tariff barriers, such as subsidies, and sometimes-dubious government regulations. In other instances, voluntary bilateral deals were made to restrict exports of certain products (e.g., Japanese cars to the U.S. market). In the agricultural area, subsidies on exports of grain and other products by the United States and EC countries hurt the efficient, non-subsidized farmers in countries such as Canada and Australia. The rules also did not include services, which account for a quarter of world trade, or investment in intellectual property (patents, copyrights), which increasingly have figured in trade disputes.

In 1986, the Uruguay round of GATT talks began by focusing on some of the above-mentioned problems. After nearly failing a number of times, these talks were finally concluded on December 15, 1993. Even before the provisions came into effect mid-1995, most studies concluded that, over the medium and long term, the treaty will add hundreds of billions of dollars to world income.[2] According to official estimates, the new GATT treaty will boost global income by between US$200 billion and US$300 billion a year—more than 1% of world GNP—over 10 years, starting in 1995.[3]

Canada particularly stood to benefit because it is a net exporter, and because the tariffs on many of its most important exports will drop to zero. Highlights of the new agreement were as follows:

1. *Tariffs.* Canada, along with the United States, Japan and the 12-nation European Community are to drop tariffs to about 0% to 3% on products in a broad range of sectors, including paper products, chemicals, pharmaceuticals, construction equipment, medical equipment, steel and aluminum. This should benefit Canada because it is a major producer in most of these areas.

2. *Agriculture.* The volume of subsidized wheat exports by EC nations will be reduced 21% over the next six years, which will be of great benefit to Canada. On the other hand, Canada's marketing boards, which protect poultry and dairy farmers, will eventually have to be disbanded. Import quotas that have existed under the marketing boards will be turned into tariffs of up to 351% on basic farm products, which will then be reduced progressively by an average of 36% over six years. Some access to the Canadian market must be allowed. Even with this arrangement, it is unlikely that prices to Canadian consumers on these products will drop appreciably in the near future.

3. *Anti-dumping.* A country that sells its products in another country at prices below cost is engaged in dumping. Anti-dumping laws are designed to prevent this practice through duties placed on these products. Anti-dumping tariffs, while still allowed, require a stricter definition of damage. An industry will now have to prove that it has been hurt by cheap imports before anti-dumping can be considered, and these measures will expire after five years.

4. *Subsidies.* Some of Canada's provinces will still be able to make industrial development grants to economically deprived regions. Originally, these grants were not to be allowed.

5. *Textiles and apparel.* The quotas that have protected trade in these areas are to be phased out over 10 years; existing tariffs will drop by 25%.

6. *Intellectual property.* Broad agreements will ensure that, among many other things, computer programs will receive the same protection as literary works. Almost all industrial inventions will receive 20-year patent protection.

7. *Dispute resolution.* The process has been changed to resemble more a Western-type court, with right of appeal by the guilty party. The World Trade Organization now administers the GATT rules.

8. *Food safety measures.* An important section for Canada. Some countries have in the past used the excuse of allegedly unsafe foods (e.g., hormone traces found in meat) to block imports and protect domestic producers. GATT will set international standards on food safety to reduce these abuses.

The World Trade Organization

On January 1, 1995, the **World Trade Organization (WTO)** representing 120 governments took over from the GATT secretariat to manage the global trade system. It has a broader mandate and stronger procedures to speed up trade liberalization among countries. But like GATT, the WTO will not have any powers to enforce decisions and will have to rely on consensus to achieve its goals. Ultimately,

World Trade Organization (WTO) is the organization that took over from the GATT secretariat to manage global trade with a broader mandate and stronger procedures to speed up trade liberalization among countries.

its effectiveness will depend on how readily members cooperate in advancing liberalization by making reciprocal concessions based on self-interest.

The major objectives of the WTO are:

1. *Predictable and growing access to markets.* While quotas are generally outlawed, tariffs or customs duties are legal in the WTO. Tariff reductions made by over 120 countries in the Uruguay Round are contained in some 22 500 pages of national tariff schedules, which are considered an integral part of the WTO. Tariff reductions, for the most part phased in over five years, will result in a 40% cut in industrial countries' tariffs in industrial products from an average of 6.3% to 3.8%.

2. *Promoting fair competition. Promoting fair competition.* The WTO extends and clarifies previous GATT rules that laid down the basis on which governments could impose compensating duties on two forms of "unfair" competition: dumping and subsidies. The WTO agreement on agriculture is also designed to provide increased fairness in farm trade. For intellectual property, where ideas and inventions are involved, the agreement will improve conditions of competition. The agreement also provides rules to make trade in services fairer.

3. *Encouraging development and economic reform.* GATT provisions intended to favour developing countries are maintained in the WTO, in particular those encouraging industrial countries to assist trade of developing nations. Developing countries are given transition periods to adjust to the more difficult WTO provisions. Least-developed countries are given even more flexibility and benefit from accelerated implementation of market access concessions for their goods. The main functions of the WTO are:

- administering and implementing the multilateral and plurilateral trade agreements that together make up the WTO;

- acting as a forum for multilateral trade negotiations;

- seeking to resolve trade disputes;

- overseeing national trade policies; and

- cooperating with other international institutions involved in global economic policy making.

With freer trade, farmers and businesses can sell to wider markets, creating economies of scale that promote investment and research. Imports raise living standards by giving consumers better prices and wider choice, and they also make businesses more efficient and competitive. The effects are clear in the unprecedented growth of the past 50 years, as world economic production has grown sixfold and per-capita income has nearly tripled. Still more important, as the GATT founders predicted, the trading system has helped to build the foundation of a stronger peace, by increasing the interest of nations in one another's prosperity and stability

For more information about the World Trade Organization, check its Web site.

World Trade Organization

www.wto.org

The North American Free Trade Agreement (NAFTA)

On January 1, 1994, the Canada-U.S. Free Trade Agreement (FTA), which came into force on January 1, 1989, was superseded by the North American Free Trade Agreement.

The Canada-U.S. Free Trade Agreement had the following objectives:

1. to eliminate barriers to trade in goods and services;

2. to establish predictable rules, secure access and fair competition;

3. to significantly reduce impediments to cross-border investment;

4. to establish effective procedures and institutions for the joint administration of the agreement and the resolution of disputes;

5. to lay the foundation for further bilateral and multilateral cooperation that would expand and enhance the benefits of the agreement.

When the FTA came into force, some tariffs were eliminated immediately. Further tariffs were to be eliminated over 10 years. Goods that originated in Canada and in the United States qualified for the new tariff treatment. For goods incorporating offshore raw materials or components, there had to be sufficient change made in either country in order to qualify for the treatment. This meant that a certain percentage of the manufacturing cost would be incurred in the country of origin. Both parties agreed to maintain the basic rules of GATT and regulate quantitative restrictions on imports or exports. Any existing quantitative restrictions would be eliminated either immediately or according to an agreed-upon timetable.

With NAFTA, the world's largest single market—380 million people—was created and the beginning of free trade between Canada, the United States and Mexico.

When NAFTA was first proposed in October 1991, it was not greeted with enthusiasm. According to polls, most Canadians believed that the FTA with the United States had hurt Canada. Labour leaders in particular blamed the agreement for the loss of 105 000 manufacturing jobs since the beginning of 1989. They said that if Mexico entered the picture many more jobs would be lost because of the low wages paid to skilled labour, which average $1.60 in Mexico, compared to $12 an hour in Canada.

Mexico is the world's thirteenth-largest economy. Since NAFTA came into effect, Mexico has become Canada's main trading partner in Latin America. From 1993 to 1999, Mexican exports to Canada rose 47.33%, reaching an amount of US$2.31 billion in 1999. In the same period Mexican imports from Canada rose 150.91%. In 1999, Mexican imports from Canada were 28.76% higher than the previous year. For the first month of 2000, Mexico purchased US$97 million from Canada, 29.2% more than in the same period of 1999.[4] Mexico is now the third most important supplier of products into Canada.

Meeting the challenges of liberalized trade—particularly with countries such as Mexico that have low wage rates—will require cooperation between labour and business. In return for labour's support of trade liberalization, management must provide longer notice in advance of plant closure. In addition, both labour and management should share the cost of gathering and interpreting data about the impact of trade liberalization. Then both must develop effective worker training programs. Only worker training can mean long-term job security for workers and long-term profitability for owners in the face of international competition. Both sides must invest in training programs. Business must invest in training programs directly, while unions must invest by reducing wage demands. Otherwise already cash-strapped companies may have no choice but to relocate south of the border. Both sides must be prepared to pay now for the future.[5]

For more information about NAFTA visit the Canadian Government Web site. At the site you can review the following document: Reference Document No. 6, The Impact of FTA/NAFTA on Canada: What Does the Recent Literature Say? Also review http://www.mac.doc.gov/nafta/menu1.htm for an automated information

North American Free Trade Agreement (NAFTA)—designed to reduce, over the next 15 years, tariffs and trade barriers between Canada, the United States and Mexico.

Canada-U.S. Free Trade Agreement (FTA)—designed to eliminate barriers to trade in goods and services between the two countries.

Canada–Mexico Trade

www.mexicanshowroom.com/
industry/Paginas/canTrade.html

NAFTA

www.dfait-maeci.gc.ca/
nafta-alena

The Free Trade Debate

In 1989, Canada and the United States broke with 100 years of tradition and signed a bilateral trade agreement. Canadians were deeply divided over the agreement. Critics charged that the deal would, among other things, erode Canada's health-care system and income maintenance systems, result in a loss of jobs for Canadians, tie Canada's hands in discriminating against foreign investors and foreign buyers of our energy; that Canada would not have any say in environmental matters; that Canada would lose its culture and identity; and that the FTA would ultimately lead to annexation to the United States.

Advocates claimed that Canada's productivity and living standards would be improved, and that trade disputes would be taken out of the political arena and handled by impartial trade panels. Supporters argued that the agreement was of crucial importance to Canadians. Perhaps the major impact would be on future employment. Free access to a major market such as the United States would mean substantially increased sales of products to that country. A larger market would allow Canadian companies to increase production runs, which would lower costs per unit.

After 10 years, the facts indicate the FTA has been remarkably successful. Cross-border trade and investment have continued to expand dramatically. As tariffs have been eliminated, the volume of merchandise trade between the two countries has doubled, from under $200 billion in 1990 to more than $400 billion in 1997. The two countries are by far each other's largest trading partner, with the United States taking some 80% of Canadian exports and Canada taking, in the first 11 months of 1998, as much in U.S. exports as European Union countries combined.

The economies between the two countries have integrated to the point where there is now a single market for most tradable commodities. Production has been consolidated on a North American basis, eliminating Canadian branch-plant status in the freely traded sectors. As international competition has forced a reduction in excess capacity, many U.S. firms integrated their U.S., Canadian and even Mexican operations (post-NAFTA) on a continental scale. Downsizing was painful wherever it occurred, but the result in many industries was a marked improvement in manufacturing competitiveness during the past decade.

Instead of having Canada's social net dismantled, a new set of federal-provincial accords to increase spending on social programs was initiated. In fact there would be more danger of losing social programs if Canada is unable to compete internationally, because it would result in great unemployment and a loss of tax revenue.

The FTA failed to eliminate all bilateral trade problems particularly where cross-border trade issues have deep political as well as regional roots, as in softwood lumber, wheat or dairy products. In these areas U.S. protection is still powerful. But these irritants represent only a small share of total bilateral trade and seem not to have inhibited the emergence of an integrated North American market. More importantly, the free trade agreement made the resolution of these trade issues much easier. Instead of undergoing a long and costly process of defending themselves against all kinds of subjective trade sanctions that U.S. politicians might conjure up, Canadian companies can rely on objective rules and regulations in the FTA to resolve these issues. No more will Canadian delegations have to rush to Washington to plead exemption from a new U.S. law aimed at Europe or Japan that inadvertently hits Canada because U.S. legislators forgot about our existence.[6] By incorporating services into the agreement, on almost the same footing as trade in goods, the FTA forever changed the dimensions of protectionism. Opening services to international competition meant opening up domestic regulation to trade law and to the discipline of intense global competition. There was nothing in the agreement that tied Canada's hands over environmental issues. Indeed, it is more likely that major pollution threats to Canada from the United States could be stopped through negotiation with the agreement than without it. Canada's culture or identity would be no more threatened than without the agreement. Furthermore, the nations that make up the European Community have, with even tighter free trade associations, managed to preserve their political independence, their distinctiveness and their very different levels of spending on social policies.[7]

As far as energy is concerned, there is nothing specific in the agreement that would be injurious to Canada. However, it gives the West and Quebec secure access to the U.S. market for their oil, gas and electricity. Canada has also agreed not to sell energy in its domestic markets at a price lower than in the United States, which effectively means not below the competitive price in North American markets.

Exports to the United States are vital to Canada's prosperity, but the United States has been hit hard by its open-door trade policy. Americans believe that foreign-based producers have had easy access to the U.S. market while at the same time using various techniques to limit American penetration of their own markets. Furthermore, few restrictions limit foreigners from investing in the United States, but U.S. companies face many restrictions when they want to invest abroad. Canada, for example, established the Foreign Investment Review Agency and the National Energy Program in the >>

1970s primarily to limit American investment in Canada. Many Americans also believe that foreign governments provide support to some of their industries, which amounts to indirect subsidization of exports. Therefore, general protectionist legislation designed to curb foreign trade practices that the United States considers harmful to its own interests could have disastrous effects on Canada's economy in the absence of a free trade agreement with the United States.

With NAFTA a series of new issues came to the forefront. Critics argued that any benefits the NAFTA brings to Canada will be offset by an exodus of manufacturers to Mexico seeking lower wages. But even before the NAFTA, Canadian and U.S. companies had been moving south of the Rio Grande into Mexico's Maquiladora program, which was established to provide tax concessions to foreign-owned manufacturers and to allow duty-free imports of raw materials. By the end of 1989, more than 1800 plants had taken advantage of this program—plants employing about 500 000 workers and generating approximately $2 billion in exports. Canadian-owned companies had established only 16 Maquila plants, but other large multinational companies, such as the Ford Motor Co. and General Electric Co., have built their factories in Mexico—factories that might otherwise have been built in Canada.[8]

From Mexico's point of view, this initiative has been a success. It has provided most new jobs in recent years and accounts for about 80% of the country's manufactured exports. It has helped to raise skill levels, and has been the main contributor to Mexico's economic recovery and restored currency.[9]

Mexico regarded its low wage rates as a competitive advantage. But low Mexican productivity due to poor skills erased much of the low-wage advantage. In addition, poor roads, unreliable power delivery, high labour turnover and a host of other problems prompted a return to the United States by companies that had established plants in Mexico. But for some industries, such as apparel, the low wage rate was the overwhelming factor in relocating a factory.

What should Canada have done? Free trade between countries is ultimately beneficial, as most industrialized and Third World countries know. In the short run, when a free trade agreement is first implemented, it can cause hardship to some companies and individuals; in the long run, it will ensure the competitiveness of a country's business firms and result in lower consumer prices and a greater variety of goods. Had Canada refused to take part in the deal, it has been argued, many companies would simply have moved to the United States and thereby be guaranteed access to all three markets.

Trade-union leaders would like to see the jobs of their members preserved. But the question remains, for whom would these workers produce? Since so much of Canada's production is geared toward exports, it would not be possible for Canadian companies to compete by maintaining the status quo. The manufacturing costs of Canadian firms would remain high, while countries participating in free trade agreements would be working to lower theirs. They could capture large world markets, while Canada's international trade would decline. The end result would be a dramatic decline in Canada's GNP, high unemployment and a drop in the standard of living. The jobs that were preserved initially would be lost quickly, yet the ability to remain competitive and have access to world markets would be gone.

---

service is designed to provide you with convenient access to current trade-related documents concerning NAFTA and exporting to Mexico and Canada.

Key Facts About the North American Free Trade Agreement[10]

- **Tariffs:** To be eliminated by 2009. Levies on more than 9000 products were eliminated immediately, 65% of them within five years. U.S. tariffs on Mexican products now average less than 4%; Mexican tariffs on American products average 10%.

- **Agriculture:** Tariffs on all farm products will be phased out, but producers will be given 15 years to adjust to a duty-free status on some products (e.g., corn and dry beans for Mexico, and orange-juice concentrate, melons, sugar and asparagus for U.S. farmers). Rules governing U.S.-Canada farm trade on existing free trade agreement will remain the same.

- **Autos:** To qualify for duty-free treatment, the North American content of cars, now 50%, must reach 62.5% by 2002.

- **Financial Services:** Mexicans will allow U.S. and Canadian banks, brokerage firms and insurance companies free access after a six-year transition period during which bans on foreign ownership will be phased out.

- **Telecommunications:** U.S. and Canadian companies will be allowed to compete for contracts from Mexico's public telephone system, while investment restrictions were eliminated by 1995.

- **Textiles:** Mexico will be able to escape high duties of shipments to the United States and Canada as long as the clothing is made from yarns and fabrics from North America.

- **Trucking:** Mexico will allow foreigners to invest in its trucking firms, and U.S., Mexican and Canadian trucking companies will be allowed to do business on cross-border routes that are now prohibited.

- **Side Agreements:** Will establish tri-national commissions to oversee environmental and labour laws with the possibility of sanctions—either punitive trade tariffs in the case of the United States and Mexico or fines in the case of Canada—for failure of a country to enforce its own laws.

The Canada-U.S. Auto Agreement

Canada's auto industry, vehicle as well as parts manufacturers, has always consisted of foreign-owned companies. Therefore decisions affecting Canada's industry and jobs were made in "foreign" boardrooms. Another problem was that Canada's auto sector was protected with high tariffs of 17.5%. As a result, the industry was high cost, inefficient and produced low-quality goods.

Canada-U.S. Auto Agreement—established to remove restrictions and tariffs on the trade of automotive products between the two countries.

The **Canada-U.S. Auto Agreement** or, informally, the Autopact, was established to remove restrictions, including tariffs, on the trade of automotive products, vehicles and original equipment automotive parts, between the two countries. The Autopact gives United States manufacturers duty-free access to the Canadian market, provided that they meet two conditions: (1) they must produce at least as much as they sell here; and (2) the Canadian value-added (CVA) content of those vehicles must equal or exceed 60%. The Canadian tariff at the time the pact was signed was 17.5%. Successive reductions since then have brought it down to 9.2%. The agreement also lifted tariffs on vehicles entering the United States market so long as they contain at least 50% North American content. The United States tariff, however, is now just 3%.

The Autopact completely exposed Canada to full North American competition. Without duties on imports, the industry had to become efficient. For 20 years the industry faced difficulties in adjusting to the removal of tariffs. The companies that could not compete were forced out of business. Since 1965 over 250 Canadian parts producers have disappeared, but between 400 to 500 parts manufacturers that were able to compete form the backbone of our industry today.

Although the Autopact is not threatened by the North American Free Trade Agreement, economic conditions have changed greatly since the auto agreement was signed in 1965. The Canada-U.S. Autopact allowed companies to bring parts and vehicles from anywhere in the world into Canada without any tariff (import tax)—but there was a condition. They had to have a certain level of commitments to jobs and investments in Canada to qualify.

"He's in shock...severe job loss."

SOURCE: Rothco Cartoons

When Canada entered into the FTA (Canada-U.S. Free Trade Agreement) and NAFTA (North American Free Trade Agreement), the Autopact was eroded. The result was that any company that had a significant presence somewhere in North America could bring parts and vehicles from the United States and Mexico into Canada.

Although weakened, the Auto Pact still has some bite because the tariff still applies to parts and vehicles coming in from overseas. For example, cars from South Korea or parts from Japan currently pay a tariff of 7.3% (cars) and 0–2.3% (depending on the kind of part). However, the federal government is now considering dropping these tariffs entirely, which could eventually mean the end of the auto agreement.

Asia–Pacific Economic Cooperation (APEC)

Asia–Pacific Economic Cooperation (APEC), founded by a dozen countries in 1989, has become a forum of 21 countries that addresses economic issues in the Asia-Pacific region. Included in this group are the United States, Canada, China, Taiwan (officially Chinese Taipei), Hong Kong, Japan, Australia, New Zealand, the Philippines, Thailand, Singapore, Indonesia, Malaysia, Brunei, South Korea, Papua New Guinea, Mexico, Chile, Peru, Russia, and Vietnam. Together, the APEC countries account for over 50% of the world's merchandise trade, half the global GNP, and two-fifths of the world population. Headquartered in Singapore, APEC sponsors regular meetings and annual summits of senior government officials and heads of state. APEC operates by consensus rather than through binding agreements as in the North American Free Trade Agreement. APEC members define broad regional goals but leave the specific aspects of how these goals are implemented to each country.

Asia–Pacific Economic Cooperation (APEC) was formed to facilitate intergovernmental economic cooperation in a politically unstable region. Made up of 18 members who envision a free trade agreement sometime after the year 2000.

APEC consists of three occasionally overlapping processes. The first is economic and technical cooperation promoting economic and human resource development, or "Eco-Tech." Second is trade and investment liberalization, an agenda that emerged at its 1993 meeting when President Clinton invited the 18 APEC leaders to Blake Island, Washington, for the first-ever APEC Economic Leaders Meeting. The Bogor Declaration, adopted in 1994, proclaimed the elimination of all trade and investment barriers by 2010 for APEC's wealthiest countries and by 2020 for its poorest ones. Subsequent meetings led to a refinement of these goals in terms of Individual and Collective Action Plans that were to provide the actual liberalization commitments.

At the 1997 Vancouver meeting, APEC leaders agreed to negotiate specific, mandatory trade-liberalization targets in nine sectors on a fast-track basis covering $1.5 trillion in trade (known as Early Voluntary Sectoral Liberalization). Those sectors included chemicals, fisheries, forestry, energy goods and services, environmental goods and services, gems and jewellery, medical equipment, toys, and a telecommunications mutual-recognition agreement. Although the last was approved in June 1998, Japan's opposition to liberalization in fisheries and forestry effectively torpedoed the broader initiative.

At the 1998 meeting in Kuala Lumpur, leaders agreed to bring the proposals to the World Trade Organization's next round of negotiations in 2000, largely as a face-saving initiative. The third—and weakest—process is the sustainable development agenda, which also emerged within APEC in 1993. To date, this process has been characterized by a flurry of small-scale, capacity-building projects and little else beyond statements of principles and a meeting on marine resources earlier this year.[11]

APEC is dedicated to increasing economic cooperation and achieving freer trade and investment in the region. The organization has an active trade facilitation agenda, which includes harmonization of customs procedures, establishment of electronic data networks to speed the flow of goods and people in the region, training programs, and so on. APEC also has a full trade and investment policy agenda, which includes formulation of principles aimed at reducing trade and investment restrictions and efforts to harmonize implementation to the Uruguay Round agreements.

APEC is important to Canada because Japan is its second-largest trading partner, after the United States, with China and Southeast Asia representing its best opportunities for expanded trade. Japan, with its market of 125 million people, is one that Canadian companies have barely touched. For example, with 14 million Japanese housing starts—10 times as many as in Canada and more than in the United States—there is tremendous potential for Canada's prefabricated home industry. If Canadian companies can meet the high standards in Japan, it could mean a much greater export of finished goods rather than just raw materials. In addition, as Japanese consumers enjoy increased purchasing power—and save less—the potential for exporting is substantially increased.[12]

If Japan is a promising new market for Canada, then the APEC group as a whole is almost too vast to comprehend. British Columbia has been the leader in developing the Asian markets, partly because of its proximity to these countries, but also because of the recession in the early 1980s, when trade with the United States dropped. For small and medium-sized firms, doing business in the United States can be tough enough, but it is even more difficult to go to Pacific Rim countries, search out the markets and remain there. Cultural and language differences are a major problem, but other aspects of doing business—dealing in Asian currencies, for example—can cause further problems. Fortunately, Canada has the advantage of strong ties to Pacific Rim countries because of its immigration levels from these countries. Cities such as Vancouver are an ideal place to build Asian ties.

Pacific Rim Trade 1999

Country	Exports	Imports
Japan	$8 250.8	$15 031.3
South Korea	1 934.0	3 573.9
China	2 480.0	8 914.7
Taiwan	1 081.5	4 583.3
Australia	914.8	1 210.4
New Zealand	195.9	370.6
Chile	346.8	421.3
Colombia	242.4	280.6

The World Bank and the International Monetary Fund

In 1944, the United Nations sponsored a conference attended by 44 countries at Bretton Woods, New Hampshire, to ensure world financial order after World War II. This conference resulted in the establishment of the International Bank for Reconstruction and Development, known today as the World Bank, and the International Monetary Fund. The **World Bank** was established to make long-term loans to countries requiring aid for reconstruction as well as to Third World countries, while the **International Monetary Fund (IMF)** was intended to provide low-interest loans to member nations who were experiencing difficulties in their balance of payments (i.e., the outflow of funds to other countries is greater than the inflow).

The IMF became an important vehicle in stabilizing international trade. Members pledged to keep the value of their currencies within certain limits in relation to others; for the sake of uniformity, all member currencies were related to the price of gold. Rather than actually transferring gold from one country to the other, however, the American dollar—a strong currency that was also pegged to gold and convertible to gold—was generally used to even out the international balance of payments.

World Bank and IMF

http://www.worldbank.org/html/extdr/annmtg/

World Bank—established to make long-term loans to countries requiring aid for reconstruction as well as to Third World countries.

International Monetary Fund (IMF)—intended to provide low-interest loans to member nations who were experiencing difficulties in their balance of payments.

< The World Bank was established to make long term loans to countries requiring aid for reconstruction as well as to Third World countries

Inter-provincial Trade Barriers[13]

Agreement on Internal Trade (AIT) is designed to reduce and eliminate barriers to the free flow of people, goods, services and capital within Canada.

AIT

www.intrasec.mb.ca/

While trade barriers are dropping around the world, those between Canada's provinces are as strong as ever. These barriers include preferential government procurement policies, restrictions on labour mobility, marketing boards and many provincial standards and regulations. Most were set up years ago to support the growth of local companies and create local jobs. In most instances, this policy has worked. For example, 10 small beer factories provide many more jobs and pay more provincial taxes than two large factories. Unfortunately, such an arrangement also increases the price to consumers and makes Canadian beer companies uncompetitive internationally. Similarly, provinces will pay up to 10% more for local products. Some simply refuse to buy goods from other provinces if there are local suppliers. Eliminating these trade inefficiencies and removing trade barriers on beer, wine and agricultural products could save Canadian taxpayers an estimated $6.5 billion a year, as shown in the following breakdown:

Estimated benefits from single market	$ billions
More efficient government goods procurement	2.5
More efficient government services procurement	2.5
Removal of trade barriers affecting beer and wine	0.5
Removal of agricultural trade barriers	1.0
Total	**6.5**

A Conference Board of Canada survey of 55 Canadian firms indicated that all of them are forced to spend more on production and distribution. These higher costs have almost always been passed to their customers.

One example of how absurd these internal trade barriers can be relates to the painting of the interprovincial bridge between Ottawa and Hull. Two separate contracts were awarded, one to an Ontario firm and one to a Quebec firm. Each painted one half of the bridge. In another example, a new sidewalk of paving bricks was dismantled at significant cost and inconvenience to the town of Alymer, Quebec, because it was found that the bricks came from Ontario and not from Quebec.

In 1995 the **Agreement on Internal Trade (AIT)** came into effect. It is to reduce and eliminate barriers to the free flow of people, goods, services and capital within Canada. An open interprovincial market would allow companies to take advantage of economies of scale, develop national marketing strategies and lower administrative costs pushed up by various provincial regulations. In turn, these companies would be better able to compete with foreign producers as trade barriers between Canada and other countries come down. But the agreement has been criticized for being too slow in implementing the deal, and because the dispute settlement process is too complicated.

Although these criticisms are valid, several important steps were taken to make the agreement more effective. A new internal trade secretariat to support implementation of the agreement is now established. There are a number of other important initiatives. A key goal is to remove the occupational restrictions to make it difficult for people to move from one province to another to work. While provincial leaders recognize the benefits from freer interprovincial trade, the barriers are often subtle, complex and difficult to resolve. It almost seems that for Canada to achieve a single market within its borders may be more difficult than reaching an international agreement.

Currency exchange rate—the value of a particular currency, which is determined by world supply and demand.

Floating currencies exist where the value, or exchange rate, of a particular currency is determined by world supply and demand.

In 1968, however, IMF member countries with a balance-of-trade surplus began converting their American dollars into gold. By 1971, the run on U.S. gold stocks had become so severe that President Richard Nixon declared that the United States would no longer allow the conversion of American dollars into gold. An effort was made to set new **currency exchange rates** in 1971, but the run on the U.S. dollar continued as speculators exchanged their dollar holdings for other currencies—German marks, Swiss francs and Japanese yen. The resulting surplus of American dollars on the world money market caused the currency to drop in relation to others, particularly the mark and yen.

By 1973, with the demise of the Bretton Woods Agreement in 1971 and the failure of efforts to establish another system of fixed exchange rates, most countries had **floating currencies**, in which the value, or exchange rate, of a particular currency is determined by world supply and demand. While the IMF forbids its members to manipulate their currencies to make exports cheaper and thus create employment at home, they are allowed to intervene in the world money markets to maintain the value of their currencies against unusual market pressures. If any currency experiences too much downward pressure, which could seriously affect trade with other nations, the government usually steps in to create a demand for its own currency and to force the price up by buying it in the open market.

As an alternative to letting their currencies float, nations can set their exchange rate in terms of **Special Drawing Rights (SDRs)**. SDRs represent the market value of a collection of 16 major world currencies and thus provide a more stable measure of the value of a particular currency than, for example, the U.S. dollar. SDRs were first created in 1969 to provide reserve assets and allow the world monetary system to expand as necessary, without relying on the actual amount of gold available or on the U.S. dollar. At that time, SDRs were valued in terms of gold; one SDR was equal to one dollar and 35 SDRs were equal to one ounce of gold, which is why they are also known as "paper gold."

Special Drawing Rights (SDRs) represent the market value of a collection of 16 major world currencies.

Multinational Trade Communities

When the **European Economic Community (EEC)** was founded with the signing of the Treaty of Rome in 1957, the ultimate intent was political unity of the countries on the European continent. The **Common Market**, as it was also known, is an economic union that has eliminated tariffs and custom restrictions, such that there is free movement of goods, services, labour and investment within the EEC bloc. However, the countries involved may raise a common tariff barrier, or other trade restrictions, against non-members.

The EEC, which came into being January 1, 1958, originally included six countries: France, West Germany, Italy, Belgium, Luxembourg and the Netherlands. It was joined in 1973 by Denmark, Ireland and the United Kingdom. Greece joined in 1981, and both Portugal and Spain joined in 1986. A supranational European Commission refereed disputes and set guidelines for the removal of discriminatory practices. Most EEC states were in the European Monetary System of fixed exchange rates.

The **European Free Trade Association (EFTA)** was established on May 3, 1960, primarily to counteract the influence of the EEC. The original members of the European Free Trade Association, also known as the "outer seven," were Austria, Finland (an associate member from 1961 to 1985), Denmark, Iceland, Norway, the U.K., Sweden and Switzerland. The U.K. and Denmark left in the early 1970s to join the EEC, and Portugal left in 1986 for the same reason. The association had three objectives: to achieve free trade in industrial products between member countries; to assist in the creation of a single market embracing the countries of Western Europe; and to contribute to the expansion of world trade in general.

The EEC and EFTA have concluded many trade deals similar to the proposed deal between Canada and the United States. When the EEC was formed, there was concern that France would swallow Belgium, in view of their shared border, common language and huge population imbalance—55 million to 10 million. These fears have not been realized.

The EEC subsequently negotiated a number of bilateral free trade treaties with individual members of the EFTA. Almost all tariff and non-tariff barriers were removed. Exemptions were made for agricultural quotas, but services and investment were not included in the agreements. The adjustment to these free trade deals went smoothly and painlessly, even between unequal economic partners. Austria was

European Economic Community (EEC)—an alliance founded in 1957 with the intention of bringing about political unity of the countries on the European continent.

Common Market—an economic union that has eliminated tariffs and custom restrictions, and allows free movement of goods, services, labour and investment within the European bloc.

European Free Trade Association (EFTA)—alliance founded in 1960, primarily to counteract the influence of the EEC.

A European Free Trade Bloc

Midnight on December 31, 1992, marked a historic moment for the Europeans. On that date, the 12-member nations of the EEC became a single market. Originally, it was designed to do away with the remaining barriers to the free movement of goods, capital, and people throughout the EEC. However, with the continent-wide recession in full swing, the original dream remained unfulfilled. For example, the closing of customs stations at borders put 60 000 customs officers out of work. On the other hand, the unimpeded passage of goods between countries is expected to save $12.5 billion a year because it will eliminate 60 million forms. People will not be able to move as freely as first envisioned. Britain, Denmark and Greece objected to the elimination of passports as it would be more difficult to fight terrorism, drug trafficking, illegal immigration and, in Britain's case, rabies.

While some of these problems were discouraging, EEC officials pointed to the fact that 95% of the 282 measures needed to make Europe a single market had been implemented. Many went into effect long before January 1, 1992, including the removal of restrictions on capital transfers and a measure intended to eliminate protectionism disguised as differing health and safety standards; this latter measure meant that companies could sell products anywhere in the EEC as long as they met the specifications of any member state. Other changes included allowing banks to set up branches in any EEC state without special approval, and making job training and school degrees from EC countries valid throughout the community.

The single market was the first step toward the establishment of a political federation called the **EU (European Union)**. A parliament was founded to represent all the member states in this new community. It enacted a European constitution to govern the new entity. All laws that could cause conflicts would be resolved by the European court, located in Brussels, Belgium, whose rulings are binding on all member states. By 2002 member states whose economic situation meet specified conditions will have a common

EU (European Union)—a political federation of European countries.

currency called the EURO. Complete political union is the ultimate goal.

Before the NAFTA agreement came into effect, the EU had the largest internal market in the world—320 million people. Canadian companies wanting to do business in the new Europe will require an understanding of the consumers in that market. Although Europe may be unified economically, people in each country have their own preferences for products and services. For example, a popular orange drink called Fanta has to be tart for Italians but sweet in Germany. Washing machines must be front-loading for the British, but top-loading for the French. Economic union does not mean that EU members will speak one language. Popular TV programs will require dubbing in the local language. These variations in demand are based on regional preferences, habits, culture, language, climate and income, none of which were affected by union in 1992.

Thus, North American companies wanting to do business in the new Europe cannot plan for a homogeneous market and rely on national brands and economies of scale for their success. Instead, a company's success will likely be determined by how well it caters to smaller national or local differences and tastes. However, the new union will have other benefits, including liberalized transportation rules and regulations, as well as common product standards.

Companies that are already in Europe are well poised to take an aggressive stance because they will know the new rules and how to apply them to achieve success. Companies that are now exporting their products from North America may find intense competition eroding their market share, making it impossible to remain outside of Europe. Another problem is that European protectionism may threaten their existence altogether. The new Europe may eliminate trade barriers among member countries, but it is not necessarily making it easier for outsiders to do business there.[14]

particularly worried about its neighbour, West Germany, whose population is eight times larger than its own, and which has branch plants inside Austria to overcome the high tariff walls established to protect Austrian industry. When tariffs were removed over five years, however, as often as not Austrian industry benefited.[15]

Other Trade Organizations

Besides the new EU and NAFTA, many other trade associations exist as Table 13.4 shows. In the future, more may come into being, or existing ones may merge. The fewer trading blocs there are, the easier international trade becomes, as arrangements can be made with overall trade regions rather than with individual countries.

Multinational trade associations

TABLE 13.4

Name	Membership	Date of Origin
The Andean Group (also called the Andean Common Market)	Bolivia, Colombia, Ecuador, Peru, Venezuela	1969
Arab Common Market	Iraq, Jordan, Syria, Egypt	1965
ASEAN: Association of Southeast Asian Nations	Indonesia, Malaysia, Philippines, Singapore, Thailand, Brunei	1967
CACM: Central American Common Market	Costa Rica, El Salvador, Guatemala, Honduras, Nicaragua	1960
CARICOM: Caribbean Common Market	Antigua, Barbados, Dominica, Grenada, Guyana, Jamaica, Montserrat, St. Christopher-Nevis-Anguilla, St. Lucia, St. Vincent, Trinidad and Tobago, Belize, Bahamas	1966
EC: European Community	Belgium, France, West Germany, Italy, Luxembourg, the Netherlands, Denmark, Ireland, the United Kingdom, Greece, Spain, Portugal	1958
EFTA: European Free Trade Association	Austria, Norway, Sweden, Switzerland, Iceland, Finland	1960
LAIA: Latin American Integration Association	Argentina, Bolivia, Brazil, Chile, Colombia, Ecuador, Mexico, Paraguay, Peru, Uruguay, Venezuela	1960

SOURCE: This table was prepared using information from *The Statesman's Yearbook*, No. 131 (1994/5), edited by Brian Hunter (with permission of the publisher, Macmillan Press Ltd.).

Canadian Government Services and Programs

The Canadian government has established a number of services and programs to identify and develop export markets for Canadian products and services throughout the world and to help finance sales. (See Table 13.5.) Industry Canada has established regional headquarters office in each of the five regions of Canada: British Columbia, the Prairie provinces, Ontario, Quebec and the Atlantic provinces. Knowledgeable counsellors provide clients with business and other information. A Business Information System can provide details of relevant programs and services. Furthermore, Industry Canada is participating with other federal departments in staffing Canada Business Service Centres located in major urban centres. These offices also provide information on business-related services and programs. Further assistance to business clients is provided by International Trade Centres and International Trade Canada, both of which are also located in these regional offices. Publications on a variety of topics are available at these centres.

Trade Commissioners

Trade commissioners provide commercial representation abroad, together with locally engaged commercial officers. They provide a useful link between foreign buyers and Canadian exporters. They offer Canadian businesspeople assistance in:

- identification of export opportunities;
- assessment of market competition;

Trade commissioners have knowledge of regional, social and cultural environments, business practices and business personalities, and assist Canadian exporters with their foreign sales.

- introduction to foreign businesspeople and government officials;

- advice on terms of pay, claims assistance and after-sales service;

- assistance with tariff problems or difficulties with foreign import restrictions, including advice on labelling and marking regulations; and

- market studies for publication.

The IMF and the World Bank: How Do They Differ?

The World Bank and the IMF are intergovernmental institutions named after the remote village, Bretton Woods, in New Hampshire, where they were founded by the delegates of 44 nations in July 1944. The fundamental difference between the two agencies is that the World Bank is primarily a development institution while the IMF is a cooperative institution that seeks to maintain an orderly system of payments and receipts between nations. Each has a different purpose, has a distinct structure, receives its funding from different sources, assists different categories of members and strives to achieve distinct goals through methods peculiar to itself.

The International Bank for Reconstruction and Development (IBRD) has primary responsibility for financing economic development. The Bank's first loans were extended during the late 1940s to finance the reconstruction of the war-ravaged economies of Western Europe. After these nations returned to economic self-sufficiency, the Bank turned its attention to assisting the world's poorer nations, known as developing countries, to which it has since the 1940s loaned more than $330 billion. The World Bank has one central purpose: to promote economic and social progress in developing countries by helping to raise productivity so that their people may live a better and fuller life.

The IMF has a different purpose. In response to the Great Depression of the 1930s there were sudden, unpredictable variations in the exchange values of national currencies. As a result, national governments were not particularly willing to allow their national currency to be exchanged for foreign currency. But those nations who chose to join the IMF were prepared to relinquish some measure of national sovereignty so as to ensure the well-being of their fellow member nations.

In signing the agreement, all members subscribe to a code of conduct that requires them to allow their currency to be exchanged for foreign currencies freely and without restriction, to keep the IMF informed of changes they contemplate in financial and monetary policies that will affect fellow members' economies, and, to the extent possible, to modify these policies on the advice of the IMF to accommodate the needs of the entire membership. To help nations abide by the code, the IMF administers a pool of money from which members can borrow when they are in trouble. The IMF is convinced that a fundamental condition for international prosperity is an orderly monetary system that will encourage trade, create jobs, expand economic activity and raise living standards throughout the world.

Whatever its original purpose, the IMF has become a lender of last resort for many developing countries, and in return for these loans the IMF has imposed strict measures on the economic management of the borrowing nations. But unfortunately, many Third World nations are politically unstable. The austerity measures imposed by the IMF as conditions for loans tended to give rise to hunger, poverty and dangerous political instability. When it came to repayment of their loans, many nations have had to borrow just to make the interest payments, and some have threatened to default. As a result, critics are questioning the policies of the IMF.

Some say the IMF makes no distinction between deficits caused by government policies and those beyond its control. They further say that the IMF is more concerned with reduction of inflation than with employment, which is a wrong approach in Third World nations. Another criticism is that the IMF wants countries with a high debt load to suppress consumer demand. While this may work with a few countries, on a global basis it would severely restrict international trade, and particularly hurt developing countries that rely on exporting their products.

The IMF argues that the major problems lie not with the austerity measures it imposes, but with the countries themselves. The nations come to the IMF as a last resort when no other lenders are willing to give them loans and when imbalances in payments have reached crisis levels. By this time they have severe economic problems, partly because of economic mismanagement and partly for the reasons such as global recession and unmanageable loans repayment schedules. Officials claim that it is not the IMF that imposes austerity measures but reality, that without these restrictions the countries would have no hope of ever getting their economy in order, nor of repaying the funds, and the end result would be even worse for the nations.

>>

The International Monetary Fund and the World Bank at a Glance

International Monetary Fund

- Oversees the international monetary system
- Promotes exchange stability and orderly exchange relations among its member countries
- Assists all members—both industrial and developing countries—that find themselves in temporary balance of payments difficulties by providing short- to medium-term credits
- Supplements the currency reserves of its members through the allocation of SDRs (special drawing rights); to date SDR 21.4 billion has been issued to member countries in proportion to their quotas
- Draws its financial resources principally from the quota subscriptions of its member countries
- Has at its disposal fully-paid-in quotas now totalling SDR 145 billion (about $215 billion)
- Has a staff of 2300 drawn from 181 member countries

World Bank

- Seeks to promote economic development of the world's poorer countries
- Assists developing countries through long-term financing of development projects and programs
- Provides to the poorest developing countries— i.e., those whose per-capita GNP is less than $865 a year—special financial assistance through the International Development Association (IDA)
- Encourages private enterprises in developing countries through its affiliate, the International Finance Corporation (IFC)
- Acquires most of its financial resources by borrowing on the international bond market
- Has an authorized capital of $184 billion, of which members pay in about 10%
- Has a staff of 7000 drawn from 180 member countries

Of particular advantage to exporters is the trade commissioners' knowledge of regional, social and cultural environments, business practices and business personalities. The service has 88 posts around the world and 10 regional offices in Canada.

Export Insurance and Guarantees

The **Export Development Corporation (EDC)**, a federal Crown corporation, provides a wide range of insurance and bank guarantee services to Canadian exporters, and arranges credit for foreign buyers to facilitate and develop export trade. The EDC offers export credit insurance to protect Canadian businesses in the event that, through no fault of their own, a sale is not completed. It also provides long-term loans to foreign purchasers of Canadian goods and services, as well as a foreign investment guarantee to protect Canadian business investment abroad from changes in government policy, civil war, revolution or expropriation. When foreign buyers require advance payments or security bonds, the EDC protects the exporter through risk insurance, so as not to discourage exporters from pursuing foreign markets.

Selling to Foreign Governments

Assistance in selling to foreign governments is provided by the **Canadian Commercial Corporation (CCC)**. This Crown corporation helps Canadian firms obtain primary contracts for government projects, many of which are linked to aid for developing countries and are therefore financed by the **Canadian International Development Agency (CIDA)**. This agency administers Canada's international development assistance program, which involves over 70 countries. Many grants and loans to developing countries are tied to the purchase of Canadian goods and services. CIDA also administers the Industrial Cooperation Program, which is designed to promote and increase the involvement of the Canadian private sector in the industrial development of Third World countries.

Export Development Corporation

www.edc.ca

Export Development Corporation (EDC)—provides a wide range of insurance and bank guarantee services to Canadian exporters and arranges credit for foreign buyers to facilitate and develop export trade.

Canadian Commercial Corporation (CCC)—helps Canadian firms obtain primary contracts for government projects, many of which are linked to aid for developing countries.

Canadian International Development Agency (CIDA)—administers Canada's international development assistance program.

TABLE 13.5 Some key federal assistance programs available for marketing products and services in foreign countries

Program or Service	Purpose and Description	Form of Assistance
Exporting		
Trade Commissioner Service (TCS)	Provides liaison services in foreign markets; identifies Canadian foreign market opportunities for producers; assists with foreign rules and regulations.	Advice on markets, opportunities, access requirements
Regional Trade Offices	Provides information on foreign markets (especially the U.S.) and market access.	Advice and publications
Export Development Corporation (EDC)	Provides financial assistance to export sales through loans, loan guarantees, insurance and surety guarantees. — provided to foreign purchasers of Canadian goods and services Foreign investment guarantees — investor requires 15% co-insurance Surety and performance guarantees	Credit insurance—up to 90% of losses caused by non-payment Loans, loan guarantees
Promotional Projects Program (PPP)	Encourages export sales through trade fairs outside Canada, trade missions, trade visitors. Companies invited to participate by ITC.	Shared-cost exhibition service: travel and other cost for missions and visitors
Program for Export Market Development (PEMD)	Assists Canadian firms to enter new or existing export markets, through participation in foreign capital projects, visits to/by foreign buyers, trade fairs, export consortium assistance.	Grants of up to 50% of costs, repayable if increased export sales result

Other Assistance

- *The Duty Drawback Program.* Designed to help Canadian manufacturers compete with foreign manufacturers, both at home and abroad, by refunding customs duties and sales taxes paid on imported materials used in the manufacture of goods subsequently exported.

- *The Remission of Duty Program.* Applies to goods sent abroad for further processing that cannot be done in Canada.

- *The Carnet System.* When goods cross several borders, customs arrangements can be made in advance through the Carnet System, details of which can be obtained through the Canadian Chamber of Commerce.

- *Export Financing Services.* Competitive financing services that manage medium- and long-term export risk.

- *Export Loan Guarantee Program.* Provides loan guarantees for working capital needed in export development.

- *Export Receivables Financing.* Helps small and medium-sized companies finance their export receivables to improve their working capital position.

- *Foreign Investment Insurance.* Helps Canadian exporters manage the risk of investing overseas.

- *Industrial Cooperation Program.* Encourages Canadian private-sector involvement in the sustainable development of eligible developing countries.

- *Insurance Services.* Insures Canadian exporters against losses caused by a range of commercial and political risks.

- *International Trade Centre (ITC).* A one-stop trade service centre for new and experienced Canadian exporters.

- *New Exporters to Border States.* Assists companies new to exporting by providing practical information and a mission to border states.

- *New Exporters to Overseas (NEXOS).* Encourages small and medium-sized exporters to expand their activities to Western Europe.

- *Performance-Related Insurance and Guarantees.* Protects exporters and enterprises that issue guarantees and surety bonds to foreign buyers.

- *Program for Export Market Development.* Designed to increase export sales of Canadian products and services; contains a repayment clause.

- *Renaissance Eastern Europe (REE).* Encourages and helps financially viable Canadian companies to enter Eastern European markets.

- *Trade Information Enquiry & Retrieval Systems (TIERS).* A Statistics Canada database providing information on Canada's imports and exports.

- *World Information Network (WIN) Exports Program.* A computer database of Canadian exporters and their capabilities. Used exclusively by 1200 trade staff around the world.

International Finance

Two key concepts related to international business and finance are balance of trade and balance of payments. While any country would naturally prefer that both of these balances be positive, such is not always the case.

Balance of Trade

The **balance of trade** is the difference between a country's imports and its exports. Foreign trade is not a one-way street, where a country only exports goods to other nations; virtually every nation in the world also imports goods from other countries. If Canada were to export more during a certain period than it imported, it would have a positive or favourable balance of trade. If, on the other hand, imports were greater than exports, Canada's balance of trade during that period would be negative or unfavourable. On the whole, countries endeavour to maintain a positive balance of trade whenever possible, but this obviously cannot be the case on a world-wide basis, as exports and imports between all countries must balance.

Balance of trade is the difference between a country's imports and its exports.

Balance of Payments

The **balance of payments** refers to the flow of money into and out of the country. Canada's total balance of payments consists of two components—the current account and the capital account. Each account is further divided as follows:

Current Account

Merchandise trade balance: The difference between exports and imports.

Services trade balance: The **services trade balance** includes all monetary exchanges between countries that do not involve goods—tourism, loans, gifts, funds transferred between banks, and interest and dividends paid to other countries.

Transfer payments: Funds transferred between countries through inheritances, pensions and immigration.

Capital Account

Canadian claims on non-residents: The net flow of funds due to Canadian direct investment abroad, and purchases of foreign stocks and bonds by Canadians. Also includes international currency reserves, bank transactions with non-residents and some other claims.

Canadian liabilities to non-residents: The net flow of funds due to foreign direct investment in Canada, and the purchase of Canadian stocks, bonds and Government of Canada money market instruments by foreigners.

The balance of payments is the difference between a nation's total monetary payments to foreign countries and its total receipts from foreign countries. Figure 13.3A shows Canada's international balance of payments since 1968. It has generally been negative, due largely to interest and dividends paid out as a result of foreign investment in Canada, and government and corporate borrowing abroad. On the other hand, Canada's merchandise balance of trade has generally been positive, offsetting the negative services trade balance. Figure 13.3B shows Canada's current account balance after all monetary inflows and outflows are combined. Table 13.6 shows the components of Canada's international balance of payments.

Currency Exchange

We have already discussed the floating currencies that exist in the world today. When it is no longer tied to an absolute value such as gold, the value of a country's currency fluctuates on the world money market according to supply and demand, in much the same way as the value of corporate stocks fluctuates on the stock markets. If investors believe that a company is sound and represents a good value, demand for its stock causes the price to rise; similarly, if a country is in sound financial condition and has a healthy economy, people eager to invest in it will push up the value of its currency in relation to others.

For example, a Canadian company intending to expand its own operation into West Germany cannot simply take Canadian dollars and use them to buy assets there. Rather it must sell Canadian dollars and buy West German marks on the world's currency markets. Such demand for West German marks, provided it is sustained, would cause the value of that currency to rise in relation to others.

A stable currency is desirable because fluctuations in its value can affect a nation's overall economy. If the value of the Canadian dollar falls, for instance, our exports will become less expensive in other countries. As a result, export sales would probably

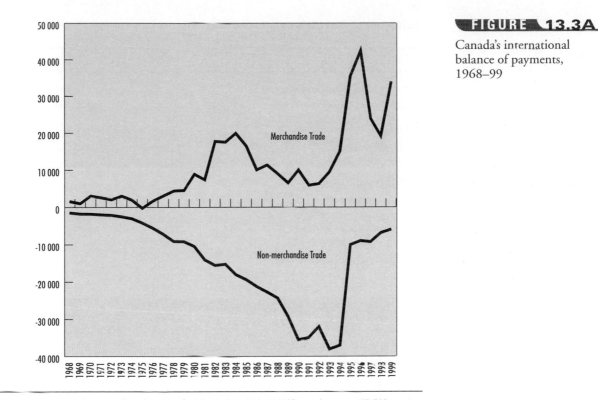

FIGURE 13.3A

Canada's international balance of payments, 1968–99

SOURCE: Data adapted from Statistics Canada, *Historical Statistics 1926–1999* (Ottawa), cat. no. 67-508.

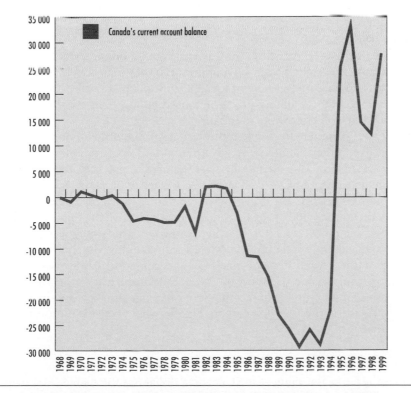

FIGURE 13.3B

Canada's current account balance, 1968–99

SOURCE: Data adapted from Statistics Canada, *Historical Statistics 1926–1999* (Ottawa), cat. no. 67-508.

TABLE   13.6   **Summary of Canada's balance of international payments**

	1998	1999
Total current account balances	−16 255	−3 447
Merchandise trade	19 097	33 788
Non-merchandise:		
Services	−6 961	−6 069
Investment income	−29 158	−32 167
Transfers	−595	−964
Capital account		
Canadian claims on non-residents, net flows:		
Canadian direct investment abroad	−46 410	−26 469
Portfolio investment abroad	−22 497	−22 898
Other Canadian Investment	7 668	−4 029
Total Canadian assets net flow	−61 239	−45 388
Canadian liabilities to non-residents, net flows:		
Foreign direct investment in Canada	32 197	37 232
Canadian portfolio investment	25 359	5 290
Other liabilities	9 968	−8 577
Total Canadian liabilities, net flows	67 524	33 946
Total capital account	4 933	5 091

Note: A minus sign denotes outflow of capital resulting from an increase in claims on non-residents or a decrease in liabilities to non-residents.

SOURCE: Data adapted from Statistics Canada, *Canadian Economic Observer* (Ottawa: January 2000), cat. no. 11-010-X.

increase, helping to create jobs in Canada. Because imports will be more expensive, Canadians may switch from buying imported products to buying more domestic products, further increasing employment in Canada. On the other hand, if people continue to buy the higher-priced imported goods, then the drop in the value of the dollar would contribute to inflation.

There are other effects when the currency value drops. The cost of money borrowed from other countries by government and corporations in Canada will increase, since more Canadian dollars are required to pay back the loans and interest. Foreign investment in Canada may also be affected as property and shares in Canadian corporations become less expensive in relation to other currencies.

A rise in the value of the Canadian dollar will have the opposite effect. Exports will become more expensive in other countries, which may lead to a drop in exports and a loss of jobs in Canada, while a corresponding drop in the price of imports may result in greater demand for them and consequent loss of sales and employment in similar domestic industries. While a rising currency value would make it less expensive for government and corporations to repay principal and interest on foreign loans, Canadian property and corporate stocks would become more expensive for foreign investors.

The Fall and Rise of the Canadian Dollar

Over the years, the value of the Canadian dollar has fluctuated, as shown in Figure 13.4. The rise in the Canadian dollar vis-à-vis the U.S. dollar in the early 1970s

At the same tin
needed technology
management and c
ideologies, MNCs i

Characteristi

A **multinational co**
although it is classifi
Ownership may be
closely held in the ho
either by the home o
lower-level managers

Evolution of tl

MNCs pass through
export products to otl
operation, the compai
of an export agent. A
company may also ent
a particular product un
tariff barriers, trade rest
with their country's sc
may also be of conside.

A more advanced s
controls a foreign sales
either the home plants
the company has reache
in the foreign country, e
firm. The major autom
international business
producing either entire
for assembly. The basic

Managing the M

In addition to the proble
a multinational corporati
tors over which it may ha
production, finance, mark
may be strongly influence

Table 13.7 shows som
must keep in mind when p
planning.

To minimize the imp
MNC management is usu
regarding daily operation:
largely recruited from the
they can readily deal with

A second level of mana
functions on a geographical
and those from the home

was due largely to trade surpluses and capital inflows. The early 1970s was a period of heavy foreign investment in Canada and heavy borrowing, primarily from the United States, by Canadian corporations and governments at all levels. As U.S. dollars were converted into Canadian funds, demand for Canadian currency caused a rise in the value of the Canadian dollar against the U.S. dollar. Once this period of borrowing had subsided, pressure on our dollar ceased, and the currency's value dropped back to its previous level. After 1975, Canada experienced a large capital outflow, which, together with poor economic performance and high inflation, caused the Canadian dollar to drop to a record low of 69.13 cents in February 1986.

From 1986 on, the Canadian dollar rose dramatically against the U.S. dollar, reaching the $0.87 level by mid-1991. The underlying reason for this rise was Canada's economic performance, one of the strongest in the industrialized world. In addition, Canada had relatively high interest rates in bond and money markets, and the Bank of Canada was always ready to fight inflation when necessary.

Canadian companies that relied on exports were unhappy about the high value because it made Canadian goods more expensive and harder to sell abroad, particularly in the United States. For every cent the dollar rose above the 80-cent level, Canada lost about $2 billion in export earnings. Many companies learned to live with this situation either by cutting costs or by limiting their currency exposure through future contracts. Companies such as CAE Industries Ltd. have a policy of keeping costs in line, instead of relying on a cheap dollar to maintain the firm's competitiveness. Many resource companies have adapted to currency fluctuations, but have also been fortunate in that the prices of their products have risen, thus offsetting the impact on their earnings of rising currency exchange rates. One economist suggested that the competitiveness of many Canadian companies would be threatened if the Canadian dollar rose above US$0.85. Particularly hard-hit would be small and medium-sized firms, which might have to spend money on new technology to remain competitive.[16] After early 1993, the value of the Canadian dollar dropped significantly. In August 1998 it set an all-time low of US $0.63; by mid-2000 it had recovered to US $0.68.

Although the low value of the Canadian dollar helps exporters of Canadian goods, it also causes other problems. First, because imports will be more expensive, living standards for all Canadians will be reduced. It also allows non-residents to buy Canadian property at a bargain basement price. This is particularly true for investments in strategic Canadian industries.

To stabilize the dollar requires an all-out attack against lower productivity in Canada. In the late 1990s, business began investing in productivity-enhancing technology and the various levels of government are upgrading Canada's education and health infrastructure and moving to reduce an uncompetitive tax burden. But the Bank of Canada also has a role to play. It is suggested that it should match prospective interest rate hikes imposed by the U.S. Federal Reserve and even increase rates above those in the U.S. to attract capital. The federal government must also make a concerted effort to reduce Canada's debt to reduce the external threat to the currency.[17]

The Multinational Corporation (MNC)

Multinational corporations (MNCs) are often simultaneously welcomed and despised. Third World nations in particular tend to see MNCs as the "imperialistic weapons" of industrialized countries, and even at home the MNC is often viewed with suspicion. The sales revenues of large MNCs may exceed the total revenues of some

◄ FIGURE 13

The Canadian dollar, monthly high, low and close in U.S. cents

What are the possible solutions to Canada's foreign investment dilemma? Rather than invite foreign corporations to establish in Canada, we could manufacture products under licence or in joint ventures. Instead of giving subsidies to foreign companies, our governments could help domestic companies finance new ventures in Canada. Financial institutions, for their part, could put more faith in Canadian entrepreneurs and make loans for business more readily available. On the other hand, tariff barriers and other forms of protection from foreign competition should be eliminated. Furthermore industries that are inefficient, such as textiles and shoe manufacturing, should not receive government aid. The onus could be put on these industries themselves to modernize their plants and equipment and thus become more productive. We should develop those skills and products that give us an international competitive advantage, and then export those products or services through our own multinational corporations.[20]

Canadian Investment Abroad

Canada has become active in foreign investment, particularly in the United States. Figure 13.6A shows Canadian direct investment abroad from 1985 to 1995. Each year shows total direct investment in all countries, as well as the portion of total investment that was made in the United States. Total Canadian direct investment abroad in 1995 exceeded $140 billion. Of the total direct investment abroad, 53% or $76.5 billion was in the United States. Figure 13.6B shows how Canadian direct investment abroad was broken down by industry group.

The flow of funds southward began with the Liberal government's energy policy in the 1970s; its struggle with the provinces regarding resource ownership and taxation contributed directly to the exodus of resource companies out of Canada. Other incentives for Canadian business to move south resembled those that first drew foreign investment to Canada—new markets, lower labour costs, fewer government regulations and business incentives in the form of lower corporate taxes and low-cost financing. Many states also had low construction costs, numerous industrial parks and a pool of labour easily trainable and under little union influence (right-to-work laws in a number of states allow workers to choose whether or not they will join a union). Also many business executives believe even today that the business climate in the United States is healthier, particularly for resource companies dealing in natural gas, petroleum and coal.[21]

Although the Progressive Conservative government virtually dismantled the National Energy Policy, other economic factors have entered the picture. The level of taxation has increased dramatically and the cost of doing business has gone up for Canadian companies. Under free trade, Canadian companies are able to move to the United States, take advantage of lower operating costs and sell into both the Canadian and American market.

Many business leaders who believe that Canada's long-term future is assured because of resources and technology also believe that, in the short run, government policies have disturbed the economic climate. Resources were used to shore up economic and social policies that drained Canada financially, creating huge deficits and a national debt that may never be reduced. Yet some social programs and policies have represented a significant improvement in the quality of life in Canada. It is important to consider the trade-off between economic growth on the one hand, and the implementation of social programs on the other.

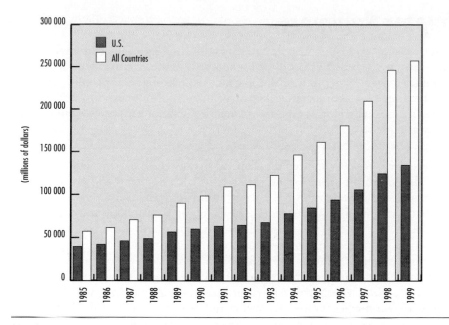

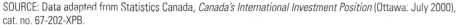

FIGURE 13.6A

Total Canadian direct
investment abroad,
1985-99

SOURCE: Data adapted from Statistics Canada, *Canada's International Investment Position* (Ottawa: July 2000), cat. no. 67-202-XPB.

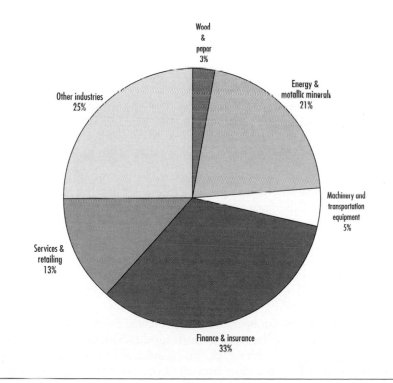

FIGURE 13.6B

Canadian direct investment
abroad, by industry

SOURCE: Data adapted from Statistics Canada, *Canada's International Investment Position* (Ottawa: 1999), cat. no. 67-202-XPB.

Chapter Summary

1. International trade is an important element in the Canadian economy—almost one-quarter of what we produce is exported. Trade is also essential to other countries, as few can produce all the goods required by their people. According to the principle of comparative advantage, nations should export what they can produce most efficiently and import what they cannot produce, or can produce only at high cost.

2. Despite the necessity for international trade, a number of barriers exist. Many governments have recognized the disadvantages of these barriers, and have combined to establish agencies and agreements such as the World Bank and the International Monetary Fund. Several countries have also joined together in trade communities of various types. The European Common Market, established in the late 1950s, has now expanded to include many more countries and is hoped to ultimately lead to political union sometime after the adoption of a common currency in 2002. The Canada-U.S. Free Trade Agreement was designed to remove tariffs on goods and services traded between the two countries over a 10-year period. The North American Free Trade Agreement, which includes Mexico, will further increase free trade and may ultimately lead to a free trade agreement covering North and South America. As well, the Canadian government offers a variety of programs and services to help Canadian manufacturers find and develop markets in other countries.

3. GATT, established in 1947, had the aim of reducing the level of worldwide tariffs. The agreement was signed by approximately 100 countries. In 1995 the World Trade Organization (WTO) took over the GATT secretariat to manage the global trade system. Representing 120 governments, it has a broader mandate and stronger procedures to speed up trade liberalization among countries. But like GATT, the WTO will not have any powers to enforce decisions and will have to rely on consensus to achieve its goals.

4. For Canada trade within the Pacific Rim is an important objective, particularly since Japan is a member with whom Canada does a lot of business. Canada is a member of APEC (Asia-Pacific Economic Cooperation), which was formed in 1989 to facilitate intergovernmental economic cooperation in a politically unstable region.

5. International trade and international finance work hand in hand, and both can affect a country's balance of payments. Although Canada has generally enjoyed a favourable balance of trade, the balance of payments since the latter part of the 1970s has been unfavourable, largely because of the outflow of funds in interest and dividend payments to foreign investors. Government and corporate borrowings abroad have also been contributing factors. An unfavourable balance of payments can affect the value of a nation's currency and its ability to borrow in world money markets.

6. International business can operate on several levels, from simply exporting products to owning facilities in other countries and producing there. Multinational corporations are those with operations in more than one country. MNCs are often resented by host countries because of their power to control markets and prices, as well as their occasional interference in a nation's internal affairs and politics. However, MNCs also offer many benefits—expanding world trade, bringing technical expertise to Third World countries, training workers and creating new jobs, foreign customers and investment opportunities.

7. Foreign investment has played an important role in Canada's economic development, helping to establish both primary and manufacturing industries. In the 1970s, many Canadians were afraid that excessive foreign ownership of industry would interfere with Canada's sovereignty and hasten its social, economic and political assimilation into the United States, Canada's major foreign investor. In response to these fears, the federal government established the Foreign Investment Review Agency to monitor and control foreign investment. In the 1980s, foreign ownership, particularly in the mining and petroleum industry, declined substantially, a decline attributable in large part to the acquisitions by Canadian-controlled companies. FIRA was also abandoned because there was increasing realization on the part of government that discouraging foreign investment was not in Canada's self-interest. In the 1980s, Canada started to become a major foreign investor in the United States, which is now the home base of many Canadian multinationals.

KEY TERMS

Absolute advantage 484

Comparative advantage 484

Imports 484

Exports 484

Cartels 490

Tariff 491

Import quotas 491

Embargo 491

Dumping 491

General Agreement on and
    Trade (GATT) 492

World Trade Organization (WTO) . . .493

North American Free Trade Agreement
    (NAFTA) .495

Canada-U.S. Free Trade Agreement
    (FTA) 495

Canada-U.S. Auto Agreement 498

Asia-Pacific Economic Cooperation
    (APEC) 499

World Bank 501

International Monetary Fund (IMF) . .501

Agreement on Internal Trade (AIT) . .502

Currency exchange rate 502

Floating currencies 502

Special Drawing Rights (SDRs) 503

European Economic Community
    (FFC) 503

Common Market 503

European Free Trade Association
    (EFTA) 503

EU (European Union) 504

Trade commissioners 505

Export Development Corporation
    (EDC) 507

Canadian Commercial Corporation
    (CCC) 507

Canadian International Development
    Agency (CIDA) 507

Balance of trade 509

Balance of payments 510

Merchandise trade balance 510

Services trade balance 510

Multinational corporation (MNC) . . .515

Foreign licensing 515

Foreign marketing 515

Foreign investment 510

Portfolio investment 518

Direct investment 518

Foreign control 518

Foreign ownership 520

REVIEW QUESTIONS

1 Why do countries trade with one another?

2 Distinguish between absolute and comparative advantage. For what goods does Canada have a comparative advantage in producing and selling to other countries?

3 Why is comparative advantage not always the basis underlying foreign trade?

4 List and describe five major barriers to international trade.

5 What is the purpose of GATT? How will the new agreement benefit Canada?

6 What was the purpose of the Canada-U.S. Auto Agreement? Why might the agreement not be very effective in the future?

7 What were the major objectives of the Canada-U.S. Free Trade Agreement? What appear to be the major advantages to Canada of free trade with the United States?

8 In general, how might the North American Free Trade Agreement affect Canada?

9 Why were the World Bank and the International Monetary Fund established? How has the IMF become entangled in the world debt crisis?

10 What is meant by a floating currency? What are SDRs?

11 Distinguish between a common market and a free trade area.

12 What are five major ways in which the federal government encourages exports of Canadian goods? Why is the government interested in expanding foreign markets?

13 Explain how it is possible for Canada to have a favourable balance of trade, but an unfavourable balance of payments.

14 Outline the major categories that make up Canada's total balance of payments. Distinguish between current account and capital account.

15 Why is a stable currency desirable?

16 Explain the effect on a country's economy if the value of its currency rises against those of others.

17 Outline the major characteristics of a multinational corporation. How do MNCs establish themselves in other countries?

18 What are some of the difficulties in managing a multinational company as compared to a domestic company?

19 Why would certain governments, particularly those in Third World countries, encourage foreign corporations to locate there?

20 What are the advantages and disadvantages of foreign investment in Canada?

DISCUSSION QUESTIONS

1 What is the responsibility of the federal government with respect to free trade? Is its foremost obligation to reduce trade barriers to ensure that the goods Canadians buy are the highest quality at the lowest cost? Or is its foremost obligation to ensure that Canadians retain their jobs?

2 Why does the government restrict trade through tariff and non-tariff barriers, while actively encouraging exports to other countries?

3 "The benefits of multinational corporations to international business and international development far outweigh their disadvantages." Discuss.

4 Should MNCs be controlled? How might this be done?

5 "We should reduce foreign ownership in Canada by buying back shares held by foreigners in Canadian corporations." Discuss.

Canada-U.S. Cross-Border Trade

Farmers on both sides of the Canadian-U.S. border are up in arms. Canadian farmers believe their very future is at stake if the border is opened up so Americans can freely sell chickens, eggs and dairy products in Canada. At the present time these products are controlled by marketing boards that attempt to manage supply. This raises the prices of these products anywhere from 30% to 50% as compared to south of the border. The objective of marketing boards is to operate in the best long-term interests of the producer and consumer by smoothing out seasonal and cyclical supply irregularities and by providing farmers with a fair return for their labour and investment. Marketing boards also attempt to promote marketing efficiency through centralized coordination of product and market research, transportation and selling.

American farmers are saying that with the signing of the free trade agreement (NAFTA) Canadians should play the game fairly. Originally, Canada had strict quotas on these products. The agreement reached under the Uruguay Round of GATT, now the World Trade Organization, changed that to tariffs as high as 350% which would fall by about one-third over a seven-year period. But under NAFTA, which forbids any new import duties, tariffs are to be eliminated by 1998. The United States maintains that Canadian tariffs on imported milk, dairy products, eggs and poultry violate NAFTA.

But Canadian farmers feel that the deck is stacked against them. Especially in the southern United States, billions of birds are processed annually and billions of cartons of eggs sent to market. If these giant American plants were to have free access to the small Canadian market, Canadian farmers would be out of business. For example, one company in Arkansas, Tyson Foods, has 48% of the U.S. market.

American farmers, on the other hand, don't feel that it would mean the end of the Canadian industry. Certain Canadian markets would be vulnerable to U.S. dairy products, but at the same time certain U.S. markets would be open to Canadian dairy products. While on balance, trade in these products would be in favour of the United States, Canadian dairy farmers should be able to compete.

A special NAFTA panel was set to rule in September 1996 on the legality of new Canadian tariffs of as much as 351% designed to keep out foreign chickens, eggs and dairy products. The panel ruled for Canada. But had the decision gone against it, it would have had a devastating effect on the Canadian dairy industry, according to a study by Ottawa-based Informetrica Ltd. It would have cost the Canadian agricultural and food processing industry $3 billion in the first year, rising to a total of $16 billion cumulatively after five years. On the average, 28 000 jobs would have been lost per year over the five years mostly in Ontario, Quebec, Alberta and British Columbia. But the result would have been even more severe in that it would hit many small towns and rural areas in Canada.

Questions

1 Ignoring the Canada-U.S. Free Trade Agreement for the moment, can you suggest reasons for and against government protection of an industry, such as the dairy or poultry industry, the wine and beer industry or the textile industry, that would otherwise not be able to compete against U.S. and European imports?

2 Make a case for and against free trade in poultry, milk and eggs.

3 The panel ruled in favour of Canada's tariffs. However, should this industry have the protection of high tariffs or should consumers benefit from free trade through substantially lower prices in these products? Discuss.

The Canadian Dollar's Roller-Coaster Ride

September 1991

The Canadian dollar rose to its highest level in more than a year, to close at US87.77 cents, even though the Bank of Canada attempted to stem its rise—to the further dismay of manufacturers and exporters, who have been calling for a lower dollar to improve their competitive edge.

The currency's strength was attributed to a variety of factors. Investors speculated that the U.S. Federal Reserve Board will allow U.S. interest rates to fall because of a disappointing unemployment report that would widen the spread between Canadian and U.S. interest rates. The Canadian dollar was also becoming increasingly attractive to investors because the Bank of Canada had maintained its tight monetary policy. However, one concern was that wage settlements for the postal workers and the federal public service workers might be too high, which would add to inflationary pressures in the economy.

March 1994

On the last day of March 1994, the Canadian dollar dropped to a seven-year low, closing at US71.87 cents. Most of the drop was attributed to fears that U.S. monetary authorities would hike interest rates due to strong job growth that could lead to higher inflation. A second major reason was Prime Minister Jean Chrétien's comments that the February budget would be the toughest in this administration. In the opinion of many investors, Ottawa is not taking the budget deficit, or the national debt, seriously enough.

June 2000

The Canadian dollar has recovered to US68 cents after hitting a record low of US63 in mid 1998. Canada's export sector was thriving, particularly in manufacturing. US residents flocked across the Canadian border in record numbers.

Questions

1   How would a lower dollar help manufacturers and exporters be more competitive?

2   Explain how higher interest rates in Canada (compared with those in the United States) would cause the value of the Canadian dollar to rise. On the other hand, why might a rise in U.S. interest rates cause the value of the Canadian dollar to drop?

3   What impact does the rise in the value of the Canadian dollar vis-à-vis the U.S. dollar have on the Canadian economy? How might it affect individual Canadians?

4   Explain how the Bank of Canada could prevent the value of the Canadian dollar from rising or falling.

COMPREHENSIVE CASE 13-3

SOMERSET OPTICAL

Somerset Optical's service and reputation for quality lenses continued to grow. In January 2000, Fowler and Dewar met Angelo Victoriosi, president of the Chicago-based Humaneye Inc., one of the largest U.S. manufacturers of designer eyewear. The meeting occurred quite by accident when Angelo stopped in to get his eyeglasses repaired. While Fowler made the necessary repairs, Dewar, after learning who Angelo was, took him on a tour of the Somerset facilities, including the new optical laboratory that had only recently been set up. Angelo was very impressed with everything he saw, and was particularly interested to learn that Somerset's volume was approaching 1700 sold frames per month.

Over lunch, Angelo suggested that perhaps Fowler and Dewar would be interested in dealing exclusively with Humaneye Inc. If Somerset could raise its demand to 1800 frames per month, Humaneye Inc. could supply the company at approximately US$29.50 per frame, including all import taxes and duties.

Angelo's proposal intrigued Fowler and Dewar because even with their volume discounts, the best price they could obtain from among all their suppliers was CDN$49.99 per frame. Their average cost price on lenses after all laboratory work and treatment was approximately CDN$40 per pair. The average selling price per frame with lenses was now CDN$145.

Angelo also indicated that the quality of Somerset's lenses was so high that he could even facilitate some export business for the firm. If Somerset carried his frames and used their own lenses, Angelo figured that the firm could supply the entire demand generated by Harley Construction Inc., also of Chicago. Harley, a huge American multinational corporation, offered annual eyeglass upgrades to all its 30 000 employees around the world as part of its employee benefit plan. Angelo estimated that the demand from Harley would be approximately 4800 frames per year and, moreover, that Harley would pay a flat rate of US$120 per frame. Angelo knew about this opportunity from his brother, the controller of Harley Construction Inc. Harley was paying its current supplier US$140 per pair of glasses, and neither the service nor the quality was acceptable. In looking for a Canadian supplier, Harley reasoned that with the U.S. dollar trading at CDN$1.37, the company would save money on foreign exchange.

SOURCE: By David H. Jones-Delcourt. Reprinted by permission of the author.

Questions

1. Should Somerset make the deal with Humaneye?

2. What programs are available to help launch Somerset into the export business? Would Somerset's deal with Humaneye harm its chances of receiving financial support from the government?

3. What is the impact of foreign exchange on import/export decisions?

4. Can you anticipate problems for Somerset, Harley and Humaneye arising from the terms of this agreement? How might these potential problems be overcome?

5. What are the advantages and disadvantages of dealing internationally?

6. Do you think this is a good opportunity for Somerset to enter into the international market? How would this decision affect Somerset's marketing plan?

14

Social Responsibility and Business

Learning Objectives

After reading this chapter, you will be able to

1 Explain the meaning of social responsibility, morals, ethics and laws.

2 Explain the arguments for and against business taking on social responsibility.

3 Explain some of the major social issues affecting employees, consumers and the community.

4 Explain some of the major ethical issues facing businesspeople today.

5 Explain the problems that business encounters in deciding how to carry out its social responsibility and measure its achievement of social objectives.

What Is Social Responsibility?

We have now reached the point in our examination of business where factual and practical matters must give way to more abstract concerns. Rather than asking how managers perform their jobs or why a particular decision is made, we will ask questions such as: "Should managers do this? Is it good or bad? Is it right or wrong?"

Questions of this nature cannot be answered by feeding information into a computer. Computers can solve many practical business problems, control production processes, compile statistical information into reports and solve mathematical problems quickly; they can even perform sophisticated logical analysis based on specific criteria. However, they cannot determine whether a management decision based (inevitably) on value judgements is good or bad, right or wrong.

What is the social responsibility of business? What is the role of business in society? These questions have not always been of concern to management. A century ago, business still subscribed to Adam Smith's principles of non-interference leave business alone, let people pursue their own interests, and society will be best served. Undoubtedly, many individuals in business today still hold the same fundamental view.

Surveying the current Canadian economic system, we find that the basic principles underlying it have not changed. We still rely on private individuals to decide what to produce; we still use the profit motive for incentive; competition is still the basic control mechanism that keeps the system in check. Nevertheless, substantial modifications have been made by government intervention in the economic system and by other groups in society, such as labour and consumers. These changes came about because an increasingly mature society demanded that business pursue social as well as economic goals. Today, business owners and managers operate in a restrictive environment. Their freedom to operate has been curtailed in many areas, and demands that business adopt a more social orientation are increasing.

But business (or, more specifically, management) faces conflicting objectives in this respect. Traditionally, it has been management's responsibility, as a hired guardian of shareholders' investment, to protect that investment and ensure the highest possible return on it. Today, while no one disputes management's duty to shareholders to strive for strong economic performance, that duty must be fulfilled with society in mind. In other words, management's responsibility extends beyond the shareholders to employees, customers, minority groups, the country as a whole and even to other nations.

Corporate social responsibility refers to a firm's role in society. Businesses generally act in such a way as to achieve the greatest economic benefit for themselves and their shareholders. This goal may or may not take into account the impact of certain business decisions on society. When a business organization is determined to act in a socially responsible manner, it will attempt to anticipate the social consequences of a proposed course of action, and, if necessary, modify it, even if the result is lower profits.

However, it is often difficult to judge how society will be affected by a course of action prior to its implementation. An example is the issue of nuclear power. Many nuclear power plants are built by private companies using private investment funds, and the shareholders of these companies want a return on their investment. Moreover, unless Canada can rely on other sources of power, the economy as a whole will continue to depend on the oil-producing countries, which can throw the economy into instant turmoil by cutting supplies or raising prices. Yet in the present stage of technology, nuclear accidents cannot be ruled out. Given the gravity of both considerations, should the management of these private companies be involved in the crucial

Corporate social responsibility means that business decisions should take into account the social consequences of a proposed course of action.

decision as to whether to build such plants at all? Or should the judgment be left to politicians? Business managers would then be responsible only for building the plants and operating them as efficiently as possible in other words, for fulfilling their responsibility to consumers by keeping the price of energy as low as possible, and to shareholders by ensuring them a reasonable return on their investment.

Business managers have a responsibility to be cost-efficient, both in operating these plants and in building them. But what if the concern for costs results in construction flaws that may ultimately contribute to a serious accident? What is management's social responsibility in this instance? Obviously, if flaws are consciously permitted, the company is not acting in the best interest of society and will pay for its negligence through heavy fines or lawsuits. But what if the accident happens inadvertently?

Social responsibility is never a clear-cut, black-and-white issue. Certainly, business must be socially responsible, but what is considered responsible behaviour hinges not only on the situation but also on society and the individuals concerned. Socially responsible behaviour is, therefore, closely tied to personal ethics, morals and laws.

Laws, Morals and Ethics

Laws of society are rules established by elected officials that generally reflect the values of society at a particular time.

Society establishes safeguards for protection against behaviour by individuals that may cause harm to other individuals or society in general. All individuals and businesses must conduct themselves according to the **laws of society** rules established by elected officials that generally reflect the values of society at a particular time or face the penalty for non-compliance. Unfortunately, the system of laws is complex and often difficult to interpret, even for judges. Thus, it is not always clear whether individuals are breaking the law when they conduct their activities.

Moral code—the standard of current acceptable personal behaviour in a society.

Ethics are a set of rules that define right or wrong conduct.

When it comes to social responsibility, businesspeople face not only the laws of society, but also moral and ethical questions. Moral and ethical rules and behaviour are generally deeply rooted in tradition and religion, and are reinforced by the family and educational institutions. A **moral code** is the standard of current acceptable personal behaviour in a society, while **ethics** is the study of moral behaviour what is morally right. In ethics, social behaviour is examined from the standpoint of what is best for society. Some organizations and professional associations in fields such as medicine and the law have thus established ethical codes that specify the behaviour expected of their members.

Business Ethics

Business ethics are the application of general rules to business behaviour.

A formal code of **business ethics** would specify how every businessperson should behave in a particular situation. Unfortunately, there is no such universally accepted code in business. What is considered acceptable varies from one individual to another, and from one society to the next. For example, while in Canada it is considered unethical to obtain a business contract through bribery, the practice is common and accepted in many other countries.

Thus, the quest for a common set of business ethics agreeable to all individuals and applicable in all situations has so far been unsuccessful. Nevertheless, most individuals do strive to maintain a high standard of behaviour, and many companies establish their own internal ethical codes. Still, the drive for profit, especially in a highly competitive situation, can put extreme pressure on executives to ignore ethics at times.

Online Ethics Center

www.onlineethics.org

Does Business Have a Social Responsibility?

There are certain cases in which few would argue against business fulfilling its social responsibility. Pollution of the environment, for example, can no longer be tolerated. Therefore, government has stepped in to legislate what organizations must do to avoid pollution (though, as we will see later, pollution control still depends for the most part on voluntary action by businesspeople).

Other issues are less clearly defined. What is a company's responsibility to long-term employees who are no longer useful to it? Should it be obliged to take care of them, or can they be let go? What is a company's social responsibility regarding the quality and possible danger of the products that it puts on the market? In both instances, ethical considerations certainly come into play. And while most managers would probably agree that they have a responsibility to employees and customers, some might indeed place business performance and profitability first.

The Case for Business Assuming Social Responsibility

The major argument for business assuming some degree of social responsibility is based on the notion that inasmuch as a firm is a "corporate citizen," its relations with society are similar to those of an individual citizen. In the eyes of the law, a corporation is an artificial person and therefore has certain rights it may produce goods and services as it sees fit and deal with the proceeds as it wishes. At the same time, the corporation also has certain responsibilities. Since it uses air, water and land, which are the joint property of society, it must ensure that its use of these resources is careful and conscientious, that it does not endanger society and that the environment is

"Before we begin this month's board meeting, does anyone want to break down and confess to any high level wrong doing, bribe taking, price fixing or what have you?"

disturbed as little as possible. If a business persistently ignores society's demands in these areas, its charter may be withdrawn.

Another persuasive reason for business to accept its social responsibility is to keep government rules and regulations to a minimum. Some businesspeople now realize that unless they assume their social responsibility voluntarily, they will be forced to accept it through increased legislation. Given that many observers believe that they are already subject to excessive government intervention, it is in their own interest to take on greater responsibility.

One factor that may facilitate an increase in social responsibility is the growing trend toward separation of ownership from management. Most large corporations today are run by professional managers who have, at most, a small share of ownership in the business. Hence, there is less pressure on managers to be concerned exclusively with economic performance, and some social costs can be included as part of the overall costs of doing business.

Moreover, as responsible private citizens, business managers should, whenever possible, use their professional expertise and power to do something about issues of concern to society.

A final major argument in favour of business accepting its social responsibility is based on the power enjoyed by large corporations. With power comes the responsibility to use it wisely. Large corporations such as General Motors and IBM have total sales revenues greater than those of many small nations; this fact alone obliges a corporation to behave responsibly toward the society that has fostered its growth.

The Case Against Business Assuming Social Responsibility

American economist Milton Friedman believes strongly that since a business is not a social organization but an economic institution, its primary responsibility is to its shareholders. According to Friedman, business should concentrate on its economic objectives. Human, material and financial resources should be used efficiently and effectively to maximize profits through the production of the goods and services that society needs and wants. Social obligations are discharged through the payment of taxes to government, which is better equipped to evaluate social needs. In fact, Friedman is not so much against the idea of social responsibility in business as he is opposed to business taking on activities that fall outside its primary function and for which it is ill-equipped to do a good job. Unfortunately, this view does not take into account two major factors. First, business uses resources such as air and water that must be shared with the rest of society; if they are improperly used, society may suffer. Second, Friedman's system also assumes that competition between firms is great enough to keep corporate behaviour in check a situation that rarely exists today.

Another argument questions the manager's right to decide unilaterally on how to dispose of shareholders' property (in this case, money) without their consent. After all, shareholders take risks when they invest in a company, and they should be adequately rewarded. Moreover, many shareholders, especially those who are retired, depend for their survival on dividends from share ownership. Even if shareholders did give managers the authority to use some profits for social purposes, are managers competent to judge which social projects are desirable?

Those who oppose business taking on social responsibility also cite the competitive disadvantage: companies that spend money for social projects must charge higher prices for their products than companies that do not. While this argument may be true in the short run if profits are adversely affected by social projects, in the long run the resulting customer goodwill would lead to increased sales. Moreover, increased acceptance of social responsibility could eventually reduce existing pressures to change the current business system because it does not meet society's needs.

Finally, some argue that firms that accept social responsibility actually take on a more powerful position in society than they should have. Social and economic power becomes concentrated in the hands of a few individuals who subscribe primarily to business values. Is business equipped to decide on the social projects to be undertaken? Or should such decisions be left to politicians with a mandate from the people? Perhaps the financing of such projects should be left to government, which can collect revenue from all citizens to carry out the programs judged essential for society.

While there are valid arguments on both sides of the issue, today business is very conscious of its social responsibility. Nevertheless, it requires a major shift in management's philosophy and its priorities. Somehow, business must achieve a balance between remaining a profitable economic institution, essential to our material well-being, and safeguarding the health and welfare of individuals in society.

Social or Public Issues

In its continuing quest for profit, business decisions and policies affect groups called **stakeholders**. The **primary stakeholders** include employees, owners/shareholders, customers, suppliers, competitors, retailers/wholesalers and creditors. These groups are affected by the firm directly through its market activities. However, a firm may also affect **secondary stakeholders** through non-market interactions. These stakeholders include local communities, federal, provincial and local governments, foreign governments, social activist groups, media, the general public and business support groups. For example, a forest-products company through its logging operations may attract the attention of environmentalists and the general public. These secondary stakeholders may shut down logging operations that affect primary stakeholders the loggers and other employees who are unable to work.

A business firm's acceptance by society depends on its performance vis-a-vis both the primary and the secondary stakeholders. Managers can no longer concentrate only on producing their goods or services and ignoring the various stakeholders. Instead, they must be sensitive to their interests and respond quickly when necessary, or a social issue could erupt.

A **social** or **public issue** is a problem that, because of its prominence or impact, attracts the attention of stakeholders. For example, when a firm pollutes the environment it attracts the attention of secondary stakeholders such as the residents in the vicinity, local government and the media. When a firm produces hazardous products, it attracts the attention of primary stakeholders the customers as well as secondary stakeholders such as the government and the media.

Business and Shareholders

Shareholders are the legal owners of a corporation, but as a group they could not possibly manage a corporation. Instead, shareholders choose a board of directors, which then hires top management to actually operate the corporation. Clearly, shareholders are an important stakeholder group. By providing the capital and by monitoring a firm's performance, they are making the business system work.

Stakeholders are groups of individuals who are affected by a business's decisions and policies.

Primary stakeholders, or groups affected by the firm directly through its market activities, include employees, owners/shareholders, customers, suppliers, competitors, retailers/wholesalers and creditors.

Secondary stakeholders are affected through non-market interactions and include local communities, federal, provincial and local governments, foreign governments, social activist groups, media, the general public and business support groups.

Social or public issues are problems that because of their prominence or impact attract the attention of stakeholders.

In return, corporate leaders have a responsibility to manage the capital entrusted to them in an efficient and effective manner, not only for the benefit of the shareholders, whose interests and needs are still central, but also for the benefit of other stakeholders such as employees, customers, suppliers and the community in which the company operates.

In terms of its shareholders, two major social issues are insider trading and mergers and takeovers. *Insider trading* occurs when a person gains access to a company's financial condition and then uses that information to buy and sell the company's stock before other shareholders or individuals have access to the information. For example, if management knows about some aspect of a firm's operation that will cause the stock price to go up when it becomes public, then it makes sense to buy stock when the price is still low. Conversely, adverse information about a company will make stock prices drop, so insiders will sell stock they own before public knowledge drives the price down. Not only is insider trading illegal, it also undermines the proper operation of the stock market, which depends on a belief on the part of stockholders that the market is essentially a level playing field.

Mergers and *takeovers* can also adversely affect shareholders. In defending itself against a takeover, a corporation can reduce the power of shareholders by staggering the election of board members and creating a variety of classes of shares, each with different voting rights.

Sometimes stock values are diluted when a company increases the total number of shares outstanding, thereby lowering the overall value and the potential earning power of each individual share. In some instances, corporate raiders are bought off by a board of directors that does not want the company to be taken over. In a process known as greenmail, the board pays a premium for the outstanding shares already owned by the raider, and often even pays for other takeover expenses incurred. Another potential abuse is the golden parachute, whereby those in top management are granted a guaranteed severance package if they lose their job because of a takeover.

Clearly, shareholders should have some control over these types of practices, for their own protection as well as for that of other stakeholders. Efforts are under way to reform some of these practices by giving common shareholders equal voting rights; requiring majority shareholder approval of greenmail, golden parachutes and other efforts to block takeovers; and allowing all shareholders to vote when another corporation proposes a share price for a takeover.

Business and Employees

The days of the Industrial Revolution, when people were often considered to be easily replaceable cogs in a machine, are over. Today, most businesses realize that people are a very important resource, and that simply handing them a paycheque is no longer adequate. Employees now desire a great deal more from their jobs. They look to the firm not only for satisfaction of their social needs, but also for self-esteem the satisfaction that comes from contributing to the operation of the business advancement and personal development. Some organizations simply cannot satisfy all these needs however hard they try; others do not even make the attempt.

For those firms that have recognized their responsibility toward their employees and can do something about it, human resource development has become a major objective. In Canada, quality-of-work-life programs have been introduced by companies seeking to shift authority, decision making and responsibility down to the lower levels of management and employees. The West German experiment in placing workers on the management boards of companies is being discussed in Canada and the United States, even though actual implementation in North America may be far in the future. Where possible, the jobs of assembly-line workers are being upgraded to make them less monotonous. Many employers are also making a serious effort to hire members of minority groups and people with disabilities.

Business is beginning to realize that employees are better motivated and more productive when they know where they are going and what their specific responsibilities are, and when they are fairly rewarded for their efforts. Even those who object to the acceptance of social responsibility by business could find little fault with the maintenance of physical resources such as plant and equipment. Today, business is acknowledging that the maintenance of human resources is equally important.

Business and Consumers

The view that "the consumer is supreme" is not always reflected in the way business treats its customers. The quality of consumer goods and services is often poor; products break down too soon and services are inadequate. In the past, the customer had little recourse against these problems. Consumers today are better educated, and demands for more information, safer products and better performance are beginning to have an effect.

The **consumer movement**, or **consumerism**, that began in the 1960s was an attempt to expand the rights and powers of consumers. It probably took its greatest impetus from Ralph Nader, whose book *Unsafe at Any Speed*, describing the safety hazards of the General Motors Corvair car, was the first major criticism aimed at a giant firm. Consumer groups formed since then have been responsible for the passage of a wide range of protective legislation in the areas of quality, packaging, labelling, advertising and warranties.

One of the major consumer-producer issues is *product safety*. Every year, millions of people in North America are injured as a result of harmful consumer products. New children's toys are withdrawn from the market because of dangerous electrical and mechanical hazards; televisions and microwave ovens are discovered to emit radiation; and drugs are found to have dangerous side effects that had gone unrecognized because of inadequate testing. One highly publicized example was the drug thalidomide, a sedative found to have caused severe birth defects. Food additives, preservatives, pesticide residues and harmful ingredients are perhaps of greatest concern today for consumers.

As products become increasingly complex, the ordinary consumer becomes more dependent on the producer for product quality. This becomes immediately clear when one goes shopping for a personal computer, a television set, stereo equipment or automobiles. The quality of these products is not readily ascertained, and users are entirely dependent on the producers to deliver the quality promised. Even more difficult to evaluate in terms of quality are specialized services. How can the ordinary consumer evaluate the services of a lawyer, doctor, dentist, college or university? Word-of-mouth recommendations, though widespread, are no guarantee that the provider of these services is competent.

Another consumer issue concerns *guarantees* and *warranties*. Some warranties contain so many exceptions that they leave buyers very little protection; in other cases, retailers and manufacturers simply refuse to meet their warranties. Each side generally blames the other for product failure, but neither party satisfies the consumer.

Perhaps the most common object of criticism is *deceptive advertising*. In one well-known case, a mouthwash that had long been advertised for its ability to kill

Consumer movement or **consumerism**—an attempt to equalize the balance of power between business and the consumer.

germs that cause colds and sore throats was found to be no more effective than salt water. A company's claims may be inflated or appeal to emotions in a manipulative fashion. Especially criticized is advertising that is woven into children's programs, since children are not generally able to differentiate between the story unfolding and commercial advertising. Many consumers automatically discount statements made in product advertising because they expect advertising claims to be inflated.

In Canada, misleading advertising is outlawed in legislation passed and administered by the Bureau of Consumer Affairs. The bureau prepares proposals for common legislation regarding packaging, labelling, weights and measures, and hazardous products, in addition to handling consumer complaints and inquiries, and promoting the consumer movement in Canada. Still, the question remains as to how much business should be forced to do through legislation, and how much it should do voluntarily.

Business and the Community

A business's community is the area in which the organization exerts its influence. A company in a large metropolitan area may exert its influence over a large surrounding area that includes smaller satellite towns and cities. Whatever its sphere of influence, there is a mutual economic and social dependence between the firm and the community.

Perhaps the two major social issues that affect a business and the community are plant closings and pollution of the environment.

Plant Closings

Many communities, including towns and cities, have grown and developed around a major company or industry. When a company decides to close a plant, for whatever reason, people are thrown out of work. The economic and social effects can be devastating to the community. The loss of wages has a ripple effect that spreads to other businesses in the area.

For individuals, a plant closure may mean long periods of unemployment, particularly if they are older, unskilled or not readily retrainable. Single-income families may have trouble meeting their mortgage payments and lose pension and various health benefits. Families worry about their future and about their ability to provide for their children's needs. Divorce rates increase, as does depression and mental illness, drug use, alcoholism, and child and spouse abuse. Moreover, as the income from wages drops, so does the local tax revenue. Often the community has to drastically curtail provision of its services. This loss further aggravates individual and family problems.

Obviously, a firm must remain profitable if it is to survive. Should a firm become bankrupt there is no recourse except for the provincial government and/or the federal government to step in to ease the suffering. Firms that have multinational operations or that operate in other parts of the country obviously must handle plant closings in a different manner. They may offer severance payments, early retirement schemes and retraining programs. A firm must plan such a closing as far in advance as possible.

Environmental Pollution

Like the consumer movement, the environmental protection movement began in the early 1960s when Rachel Carson's book *Silent Spring* revealed the uncontrolled use of pesticides and their effect on the environment. Suddenly people's eyes were opened to the smog over their cities, to polluted waters killing aquatic life, to the noxious fumes lingering in the atmosphere and to urban "noise" pollution. The public became aware of the term **ecology** the study of the fragile relationship that exists between life on earth and its environment. An ecological problem begins when wastes created by human activities cannot be readily absorbed by the environment without harmful effects to living beings.

Ecology is the branch of biology that deals with the interaction of living organisms with the environment.

Various environmental groups were formed to press for legislation enforcing pollution control. In 1971, the federal government created the Department of Fisheries and Environment (in 1978, the department was split, resulting in the formation of Environment Canada), which had a mandate to protect, preserve and enhance the quality of the environment and its renewable resources. The department was responsible for reducing existing air, water and land pollution and any new environmental hazards, as well as examining the impact on the environment of major developments on federal land. Most of the provincial governments have also introduced legislation in these areas.

While the initial legislation was passed largely in response to immediate dangers, later legislation, such as the 1988 Canadian Environmental Protection Act, is actually preventive. Under this act, industry may be asked to provide Environment Canada with information concerning contaminants; it may also be required to conduct tests on hazardous chemicals to evaluate their potential dangers. The government is empowered to ban or control the use or manufacture of hazardous contaminants.

While all provinces have some form of environmental legislation, Alberta has combined many regulatory areas under the Environmental Protection and Enhancement Act (1992). A legislated environmental assessment process is in place to balance economic development with environmental responsibility. The proposed project is examined and public notification is given. If an Environmental Impact Assessment (EIA) is required, it would include an analysis of the positive and negative impacts not only on the environment but also on the social, economic, health and cultural aspects of community life in the region of the proposed project. If a release of hazardous substances occurs or is suspected, an Environmental Protection Order (EPO) may be issued to allow investigation of the situation and enforcement of clean-up.

The Environmental Protection and Enhancement Act also covers such areas as waste disposal, groundwater conservation and conservation. At the federal level, Mayor Ted Hart of Banff, Alberta suggests that his town has become the "whipping boy" of the Canada Park System. Mayor Hart attempts to balance the economic development of Banff with the protection of its Rocky Mountain environment. Even after a careful environmental assessment, approval by council and endorsement by over two-thirds of the town's population, a recent 200 000-square-metre development was vetoed by Ottawa, amid concern about the economic impact of such rulings on an area that attracts approximately $700 million from park visitors each year. The balance between protection of the environment and economic development is an ongoing concern for those on either side of the philosophical fence.[1]

Consumer Demands for Environmentally Friendly Products Today, consumers are demanding that firms create products that are environmentally friendly, yet "green" products are increasingly difficult to find. Many observers question whether consumers are no longer interested in such products. Yet the real answer seems to be that the major manufacturers of items such as laundry detergents and cleaners are making the standard brands more environmentally sound. Now consumers can buy their traditional favourites at reasonable prices, confident that the product is effective yet

Better World Zine

www.betterworld.com/

still "green."[2] In a recent U.S. study, 87% of adults stated that they are concerned about the environment and 44% said that they were very concerned; however, consumers at either end of the environmental concern continuum, both activists and the unconcerned, do not want to pay more for "green" products. Instead, respondents reported making changes to their buying patterns; one in two respondents switched brands based on environmental friendliness in such product areas as cleaners, paper goods, beauty aids, computer products, and so on, and a similar proportion of respondents reported looking for environmental labelling on products.[3]

Business now realizes that environmentally friendly products and services are important for their profitability. Many companies have already recognized this and have invested billions of dollars in pollution abatement, recycling and alternative manufacturing techniques that use fewer harmful substances and produce less harmful waste.

While some forms of pollution can be prevented or at least reduced, in other cases the only solution is to suspend the activity responsible. However, our society cannot function without automobiles and airplanes; even though we cannot eliminate

Whether or not humankind > will exist in the future depends on how we treat the environment today

radiation pollution, we need nuclear power plants. And what would be the costs of eliminating all air and water pollution?

The answer perhaps lies in **sustainable development**, the concept that economic prosperity must go hand in hand with a healthy environment. A 1987 report prepared by the World Commission on Environment and Development proposed that societies should pass on to future generations the same amount of natural resources, or natural capital, as they inherited from their predecessors.

Recycling **Recycling** can significantly reduce the amount of resources that are used up and thereby curb the waste created by our modern society. In 1982 only about 2% of municipal waste was recycled. In 1999, 52% of Canadian households recycle through a curbside recycling program. The following summarizes some of the benefits for our environment:

- Recycling plastic uses only 5% to 10% as much energy as manufacturing new plastic.

- Every tonne of crushed waste glass used saves 1.2 tonnes of raw material and 135 litres of oil.

- Every glass bottle recycled saves enough energy to light a 100-watt bulb for four hours.

- Every tonne of newspaper recycled saves 19 trees and three cubic metres of landfill space.

- From 1988 to 1996, the volume of cardboard boxes, paper bags and cartons sent to landfills was cut by 60%.

- Every tonne of cans recycled saves 1.36 tonnes of iron ore and 3.6 barrels of oil.

- Since 1985, more than 400 000 tonnes of cans have been diverted from landfill.

- Every aluminum can recycled saves enough energy to power an average television for 108 minutes.

- Toronto spends $59 per tonne to send blue-box materials to recyclers compared to $87 per tonne to send waste to landfills.

- Recycling creates six times as many jobs as other waste-management options, including positions such as haulers and sorters of material, equipment manufacturers, importers and exporters.[4]

An analysis of 19 landfills over three years yielded the following data for one site over a four-day period: 3040 tonnes of material were received, which included 948 tonnes of municipal solid waste, 486 tonnes of construction materials, 1047 tonnes of demolition materials, 206 tonnes of industrial materials and 353 tonnes of other materials. This type of information is particularly useful to decision makers in the planning of a solid-waste management program.[5]

One study suggests that water will be the key ingredient for landfills of the future, since microorganisms that are necessary for decay need water to survive. However, too much water can lead to dangerous seepage into the groundwater; the proposed solution would be to create a water-cycling system through the waste, which has been moistened, chopped and shredded. It is estimated that 30% of treated waste will thoroughly decompose. The resulting by-product, methane, could then be used to generate electricity.[6]

Sustainable development means that economic prosperity must go hand in hand with a healthy environment.

Recycling means reusing materials.

Joint Effort Only Way to Win

Many executives realize the need to move ahead with pollution abatement and other measures designed to protect the environment. Many also agree that a coordinated effort by business, government and individuals to reverse the damage caused by environmental pollution is crucial. Some point out the need for an international effort to cure what truly is a global problem.

Hugh Eisler, General Manager, Environmental Affairs, Stelco Inc.

"The good thing about the environmental movement is it's got everybody involved. There's a general realization that we all have to do something and we are all part of the problem.

"Environmental issues are [now] being integrated into economic issues. [However], there tends to be this thinking out there that [industrial pollution] is an absolute disaster. But we have made improvements in our air and water quality.

"A lot of companies that were being targeted 20 years ago [as major polluters] were trying to reduce pollution back then. We didn't do everything, but we worked on it on a steady basis."

Dave Nichol, former President & CEO, Loblaw International Merchants Inc., Toronto

"The majority of North American business [people] think that the environment is just a passing fad, and if they just hunker down and wait it out, like so many other fads, it will just go away and they can go back to business as usual. Unfortunately, they're going to wake up and find their companies and products swept away.

"The environment and healthy eating are going to be the two major elements that are going to affect consumer buying decisions in the 1990s."

Catherine Swift, Vice-President, Research, Canadian Federation of Independent Business

"We're moving up the learning curve. This issue [has] been around for a long time, but like a lot of issues, it takes time for it to come to the forefront. Research has improved, so now we've got a lot more information of the damage we're doing, and its costs.

"Things sometimes have to become trendy to catch people's eye. It's not a bad thing if something [like the environment] becomes a bit of a trend because it [promotes] awareness. There are also many business opportunities [for small business] as a result of this heightened awareness."

Mike Supple, Executive Vice-President, Oil Sands Group, Suncor Inc.

"Sulphur dioxide emission and its contribution to acid rain have been a growing public concern for several years.

"Along with that concern is an expectation for industry to reduce emissions. Developing the ways and means to meet this expectation has certainly been a dual challenge: one of technology and one of economics.

"Both sides of this challenge must be faced by industry and governments together, should we want to ensure the future development of Alberta's heavy oil industry."

James E. Newall, Chairman & CEO, DuPont Canada Inc.

"Environmental protection is a mission not just for governments, or industry, but for everyone. It is easy to blame industry for pollution, or to claim that this or that government regulation isn't tough enough. The fact is that all of us place a burden on the environment through our lifestyles. Each one of us can and must reduce this burden.

"We all must ask ourselves what personal lifestyle changes we are prepared to make and what inconveniences we are prepared to accept to turn environmental protection into something more than just fashionable rhetoric."

Jon K. Grant, President & CEO, Quaker Oats Co. of Canada Ltd.

"We've all come a bit closer to [anthropologist and sociologist] Margaret Mead's dictum that the destruction of the environment is in itself the destruction of society. I am convinced this is the reality all of us will be forced to face in the decade ahead.

"The bottom line is this: failure to create and maintain a positive environmental record in business is penalty enough; but you're going to lose market share and dollars as well.

"Each of us is going to have to develop new skills in communication, community relations and social responsibility to make sure not only that our record is positive, but that's it's seen and understood to be so."

Adam Zimmerman, President, Noranda Forest Inc.

"Environmental issues are at the top of the agenda for major industries [that] want to play and seek the level playing field. An acknowledged common database and decision-making protocols or systems are fundamental to optimal gains."

Michael Cowpland, former President, Corel Systems Corp.

"The awareness level on the environment has gone up dramatically; we're heading in the right direction.

"Some office automation technologies will also help [the environment] because paper is one of the major sources of office waste. About one-third of land-   >>

fill waste is paper. We think, for example, optical disk technologies can help a lot because they can store hundreds of thousands of pages on one disk, which is far less damaging ecologically."

Marshall Cohen, President & CEO, The Molson Cos. Ltd.

"New value issues, such as the environment, will have a fundamental impact on the life cycle of every business product and activity, from design, manufacturing and marketing, to disposal.

"Commitment to the environment is becoming one of the measures which consumers apply to their entire shopping list. Today we need to go further [than we have in the past] in recognizing that the environment is a precious resource for us all, including corporations and their shareholders."

Howard Hart, President, Canadian Pulp & Paper Association

"Environmental considerations are getting priority from industry managers, and companies are making major investments to lessen the impact of industrial operations on land, air and water.

"Employee involvement, customer information, and the application of good science and technology are required [to reduce environmental pollution]. Furthermore, consensus on priorities is critical. Practical and financial considerations make it impossible to address all problems simultaneously."

John Thompson, Chairman & CEO, IBM Canada Ltd.

"This is an international issue because the problems are international and therefore the solutions have to be international.

"We have to work together internationally and in groups, because ... there's no one [country] that's going to solve this problem. It [requires] everybody to come to the table. However, [industrialized nations] have to set the example, because they use most of the energy and produce most of the pollutants."

Charles-Albert Poissant, Chair, Donohue Inc.

"We should, as much as possible in industry, make sure we are not polluting the water and air. We are doing that. You'd be surprised how much industry has done in the past 10 years.

"We all want pure water, pure air and pure food, but there is a limit to what we can do. We still have things to do, but it's boiling down to what will be acceptable [socially and economically] in the near future."

John Dillon, Manager, Environmental Affairs, Canadian Manufacturers' Association

"We have to look at internationally coordinated decisions.

"It's not strictly an issue for developed countries. Even if we come to an agreement in developed countries, the difficulty will be to tell the developing world they can't do the things the developed world has already done.

"The real challenge is going to be how we're going to solve the cycle of poverty so the developing countries can support a higher standard of living for their people without repeating the ... mistakes of the developed world in respect of the environment."

George Cobbe, President & CEO, Hewlett-Packard (Canada) Ltd.

"Environmental issues ... are rightly gaining attention as serious global problems. Many companies, including ours, have made significant progress toward solving these problems, including the management of unsafe substances and reducing waste and chemical emissions.

"[However], we have a challenge ahead of us: to change the perception that industry is part of the problem rather than part of the solution."

SOURCE: Bruce Gates, "Joint effort only way to win," *The Financial Post*, Special Report (June 4, 1990): 25.

Conservation of Energy and Resources

Our standard of living in the past has largely depended on the availability of cheap energy. With only 6% of the world's population, North America accounts for approximately one-third of world energy consumption. Canada has the highest per-capita rate of consumption of energy in the world, and our consumption of energy continues to increase while new sources of oil and natural gas become ever more difficult and expensive to find and develop.

However, consumers are not the only ones to blame for energy consumption. There is also a responsibility on the part of business and industry to help conserve energy. The products they offer must be made more energy-efficient (automobiles are a prime example). Houses and buildings must be better insulated. Products must be made to last longer, designed for easy repair rather than replacement at the first sign of wear. Manufacturing processes must also be redesigned to use less energy.

In 1999, Royal Dutch/Shell presented the following predictions about future worldwide energy consumption to the Offshore Europe Conference:

- Worldwide energy consumption could rise by 60% to 80% by 2020.

- Energy markets will become increasingly complex and competitive; energy prices will remain volatile and tend to decline; and society will demand more from energy companies.

- There is the potential demand in developing countries.

- Natural gas consumption could more than double by 2020.

- Renewable energy sources should become increasingly competitive.

- The major impact of renewables seems likely to come after 2020.

- Shell is building its solar and biomass power business in readiness for the blossoming of renewables.

- Shell is pursuing new competitive opportunities such as hydrogen fuel-cell engines.[7]

Types of Pollution

Air pollution: The release of gases or solid particles into the air; a contributing factor in illness and agricultural and timber losses, as well as property damage from rot and discolouration.

Water pollution: The discharge, from industrial establishments, of solid or liquid materials into lakes and streams; makes water unfit for human consumption and enjoyment, kills aquatic life and leads to losses through the destruction of fishing grounds and the cost of extraordinary water purification measures.

Land pollution: (also known as "aesthetic pollution"): Solid wastes such as bottles, tin cans and automobile bodies and operations such as strip mining in which the top soil is stripped away to expose the minerals beneath, particularly coal, deface the natural beauty of the land; in some cases, important wildlife habitats are destroyed.

Radiation pollution: The disposal of radioactive material through storage either above or below ground; a severe health hazard.

Noise pollution: Noise from industrial plants, airplanes, automobiles and so on; can cause sleep disturbances and nervous disorders.

Pesticide pollution: The use, often excessive, of pesticides to control insects in the production of food; some pesticides have been found to cause cancer, while the side effects of many others are as yet unknown.

Responsibility to Education and the Arts

If pollution control and conservation are matters of absolute necessity, business is also making voluntary contributions to the community. Corporations and individuals have poured millions of dollars into charitable organizations, educational programs, medical research, artistic endeavours and other projects of benefit to society. In addition, many businesspeople offer their time, energy, knowledge and leadership abilities to charity drives, colleges and university boards, community groups such as the Boy Scouts or Girl Guides, and other non-profit organizations.

Their motives for supporting education and the arts are many. While some obviously look for short-term business gain, others sincerely hope to make a lasting contribution. In any case, it is clear that support for education and the arts is a growing concern among many executives.

Ethical Issues

Social issues become **ethical issues** when the individuals involved make personal decisions with respect to them. Whatever the broader view of society may be, an individual's decision in a particular situation will depend on his or her values— what he or she believes is right or wrong. Some of the areas in which ethical questions most often arise are discussed in the following sections.

Ethical issues concern the behaviour of individual managers in carrying out their business functions.

Employment Discrimination

Some years ago, the person most likely to be hired for a managerial position was a white Protestant male, probably between the ages of 26 and 40. A younger individual was assumed to lack experience, while older people were considered to be resistant to change, impossible to retrain or too old to go on the company pension plan. Women were largely relegated to traditional roles, usually on the grounds that they might become pregnant and leave after expensive training; in addition, women were often considered to be too emotionally unstable to handle managerial responsibility. Finally, members of minority ethnic groups were virtually barred from managerial positions.

Today, both federal and provincial human-rights legislation prohibits discrimination in employment on the grounds of race, sex, religion, colour or national origin. But can discrimination in employment be legislated away? The young still have trouble finding jobs, because employers are reluctant to spend money on training. Women still have less chance of promotion than men, and are still paid less for performing equal work. Few companies provide maternity leave other than the minimum required by legislation, while pension and group life insurance plans often provide less protection for women than for men. Many employers are still reluctant to hire older workers, while ethnic minorities, and native people in particular, still face deep-seated prejudice.

Obviously, employment discrimination cannot be ended by passing legislation alone. Efforts must be made by employers, government and various interest groups to resolve the problem through education and incentives. But success will also hinge on the personal ethics of the employer. Is it right to pay a man more than a woman, when both are performing the same job? Should age alone restrict an experienced worker from gainful employment? In the end, the decision will be determined by the employer's own conscience.

Relations with Labour Unions

The establishment of a union is almost invariably a struggle. When management agrees to bargain, it is often with reluctance, and not always in good faith as the law prescribes. In most cases the attitude is one of mutual distrust and confrontation—"Us, versus Them."

Even if the practices employed in the struggle are not actually illegal, they are often ethically questionable. Often unions resort to strikes, and management to lockouts, when significant economic loss could be prevented through further discussion. Illegal practices are deliberately adopted in order to force the other side to seek an injunction, which costs time and money. If management hires strikebreakers people who are prepared to cross a picket line and work in place of regular employees, riots can follow. In short, little is spared by either side in attaining their objectives.

Economic hardship could often be prevented if the two sides trusted each other and shared information openly. In Europe, representatives of labour are placed in the boardroom and given voting rights; little can be hidden, and major decisions are made jointly.

However, neither labour nor management accepts the European model as being workable in North America. Unions claim they are interested only in improving wages and working conditions for their members, not in running businesses. Concerned about the amount of union influence in the decision-making process, and alarmed about the future as labour costs increase, management fears increased union encroachment on its authority.

Acceptance of Voluntary Government Restraints

From time to time, the government asks business to observe voluntary restraints, such as raising prices or discontinuing trade with another country because the Canadian government finds that country's internal policies objectionable. When the action requested conflicts with a firm's immediate interests, ethical considerations must enter into the decision. What was a firm's responsibility in a case such as South Africa, which practised apartheid for many years? Should a Canadian company that had spent considerable time and money to establish a business in, or trade relations with, South Africa have pulled out of that country at a great loss, because the prime minister asked Canadians not to deal with that country due to the way it conducted its internal affairs? Furthermore, government's reasons for supporting voluntary restraints may conflict with the personal convictions of the individual businessperson.

Responsibility to Developing Countries

What is the responsibility of Canadian businesspeople who are involved with a developing country through exporting or importing, or through the establishment of a corporation there? Should they simply consider the profit that can be made from doing business with that country, or should they be concerned with offering fair wages and good working conditions? Many foreign governments have accepted exploitative practices by multinational companies in an attempt to gain the investment as well as jobs for their people. Should a Canadian business offer the workers a better deal than their own government demands?

The Body Shop International (BSI) was founded in 1976 by Anita Roddick, with the first shop being built in Brighton, England, funded by a $7000 loan. Anita's initial objective was to make enough money to support her family by engaging in a business that was fun and was conducted with "love and a powerful force for good."[8]

Her inspiration for her products came from the observation of women in Third World countries using material products to care for their bodies. The focus of these women was on cleanliness and protection, rather than beautification. Anita believed that a market existed for such products in developed countries. Her opinion of the ethics of the cosmetics industry was very clear: "It is immoral to trade in fear. It is immoral to constantly make women feel dissatisfied with their bodies. It is immoral to deceive a customer by making miracle claims for a product. It is immoral to use a photograph of a glowing 16-year-old to sell a cream aimed at preventing wrinkles in a 40-year old."[9]

BSI provided products that created little waste and whose profits helped those in underdeveloped areas. Anita believed that business should care for its customers, work force, communities and also for the environment, with social good taking priority over the bottom line. BSI's mission statement recognizes social, environmental and political values as fundamental bases for the operation of its business.[10]

Hiring practices include an unusual employee interview that attempts to identify potential employees with values and attitudes consistent with those of BSI's. Anita's values extend beyond the walls of BSI to such endeavours as Business for Social Responsibility, an organization that she helped to establish. Maintaining an ethical position consistent with her values became very difficult when Anita moved BSI into the United States.

Historically, BSI had been opposed to mall locations and had chosen not to advertise. However, the American way of making purchasing decisions required her to change both of these positions by locating stores in malls and by using advertisements to promote her products. Although the Body Shop has not been without its critics, Anita holds firm to her values: " We will compromise on almost anything, but not on our values, or our aesthetics, or our idealism or our sense of curiosity."[11]

A Study in Ethics—The Body Shop International

Ethics is becoming a growth industry. Not only are business schools becoming aware of the importance of ethics, they are actually offering courses in ethics and ethicists are offering their expertise on the subject to corporations.

The importance of ethics came into the forefront following the insider-trading scandals of the 1980s. The green revolution brought in environmental issues that corporations are attempting to cope with in their decision-making processes. Then there are the sexist attitudes that still prevail in many businesses today. Business schools are aware of these pressures and are attempting to change their curriculums. Whether these are fleeting responses by business and education to pressing current issues is anyone's guess.

The University of British Columbia has the Centre of Applied Ethics in its Philosophy department; York University has established an endowed chair in ethical studies; and Western University teaches ethics and requires students to take a course in "sustainable growth." Most of Canada's business schools offer some courses in ethics.

But can ethics really be taught? Business schools say it is not so much a question of teaching ethics or ethical behaviour but of ethical analysis. You can present students with an ethical dilemma—for example, can a company really grow by depleting its environment? Students are taught to be prepared to ask themselves such questions and to make value choices.

So what do ethicists do? They don't tell you what is right or wrong; they lay out all of the issues that need to be looked at as well as the pros and cons of following one course of action or another.

Many companies, such as Nortel and Bell Canada, have full-time ethicists, also called "ethics officers," and employees who face ethical quandaries have access >>

A New View of Ethics

to them via a hotline. Ethical consultants offer a wide range of services, from trying to find answers to why an employee has committed fraud to why a junior executive took a bribe. They look to see if a company has a code of conduct or a statement of values and whether these have been communicated to their employees.

Companies used to think that concern for the bottom line meant finding the cheapest way to do something. But today, many executives realize that a longer-term view will be more important in maximizing shareholders' return. A lack of ethics today can be a costly mistake.

One of the most discussed ethical issues today is downsizing. How much profit should a company make by underpaying people or driving them into unemployment?

There is no ethics legislation in Canada as there is in the United States. However, a bill has been tabled to protect government whistle-blowers, and amendments are being considered that would make a company liable for criminal actions within their organizations.

According to Margaret Somerville, a Montreal ethicist, "To do good ethics, you have to have cognitive and reasoning approaches, but you also have to have what I call other ways of knowing: you have to look at your moral intuition and your examined emotions. It's really a sense of searching for the human spirit. I think that's what the euthanasia debate is all about, I think that's what the genetics debate is about, I think that's what the reproductive technology debate is about."

Source: Gordon Pitts, "Ethics move into classroom in wake of 1980s excesses," *The Financial Post* (May 31, 1990): 6; Andrew Duffy, "Ethics becomes a growth industry for the '90s," *The Weekend Sun* (September 14, 1996): D8.

Involvement in Politics

Should business contribute to political campaigns? Should it offer financial support to individual politicians? No doubt business has more money available for the purpose of influencing the political process than any other group in society, and supporting politicians who have business's interests at heart may be detrimental to other sectors of society. Is it ethically proper to exercise that power?

Management Philosophy

In our discussion of the relations between business and society so far, we have generally treated the two as if they were separate. However, the managers who make business decisions are also members of society. Since individual managers read the same books, watch the same movies, hear the same news and vote at the same polls as other people, their ethics are likely to be closely aligned with those of the majority of society.

Conflict can arise, however, when an individual works for an organization whose top management holds beliefs that differ from those of society in general. Top management's philosophy spreads throughout the organization, and individual employees who do not share those beliefs may be torn between their own principles and the demands of management. When individuals depend on the organization for their livelihood, their business behaviour may not reflect their personal ethics. Such conflicts can cause tremendous stress.

Management philosophy refers to the values and ideas that shape management decisions, whether or not managers are conscious of them in their day-to-day operations. The philosophy of top management within each firm determines how the business will respond to the social and ethical issues raised in this chapter.

Management philosophy refers to the values and ideas of top management that shape business decisions.

Measuring Social Responsibility

In general, the sequence of steps involved in fulfilling social responsibilities resembles any other business operation. Management must decide which social projects have priority; to do so, it must be in tune with the needs of society. Once particular social objectives have been chosen, managers must plan and implement the programs to achieve them. Finally, they must determine how well those objectives have been achieved.

Parameters of Social Behaviour

We cannot establish standards or parameters for socially responsible behaviour as we can for economic performance, simply by drawing up a budget. Rather, while management will obviously be guided by its own ideas and values, it must also listen to the needs and wants of other groups in society, including consumers, labour unions, government, environmental groups, educational institutions, social organizations and minority groups. Clearly, no company can meet all the demands placed upon it, but it can select those objectives considered most important by the majority.

Once the social objectives to be achieved have been clearly formulated, a business must set priorities by viewing the objectives in terms of both their importance to society and the availability of company resources. Then the firm can take steps to include those objectives in both short- and long-range operating plans.

What were once social objectives, however, are now often part of the economic objectives. Because consumers expect them, a firm must produce environmentally friendly products or services, or ultimately perish. Moreover, as legislation and government rules dictate what companies can discharge into the environment, the costs of alternative methods of disposal or redesigning products to allow recycling become an operating cost.

The Social and Environmental Audit

Just as a financial audit is required each year, a company should also make a social audit of those areas of its operation that have a social impact. The **social audit** is a self-assessment of a firm's social performance.

A number of criteria may be used to take a social audit, but two are in general use. First, a company may either list the expenditures made in implementing social programs or simply describe verbally how they were implemented. In this case, none of the benefits of the social programs are shown. The second type of social audit resembles an inventory, in which a company lists what it is doing (or not doing) in each major social program. Companies that reject the term "social audit" because it implies a virtually impossible quantification of social activities may prefer terms such as "social report" or "social statement."

Besides the social audit, companies are also now increasingly preparing an **environmental audit** that will uncover potential chemical contamination or other environmental problems that could be cause for legal action. Some of the pollution laws (such as the Ontario Environmental Protection Act) are too vague to provide companies with advance warning about what constitutes an offence, and can give enforcement officers uncontrolled discretion in charging companies with environmental pollution. Some corporate fines are as high as $500 000 per day for the duration of the offence, and may include prison terms of one year as well as fines of $25 000 a day for officers and directors.

Council for Ethics in Economics

www.businessethics.org/

Social audit — self assessment of a firm's social performance.

Environmental audit — examination of a company's impact on the environment.

New Auditors Monitor Firms' Environmental Liability

Mindful of the ever-spiralling costs and risks associated with environmental regulations, accounting firms are moving quickly to help their clients keep track of expenses and minimize liability.

"It's really in response to a perceived need of our clients—they can't pick up a newspaper these days without reading about an environmental issue," says Ann Davis, an accountant and partner with newly formed environmental auditing practice KPMG Environmental Services Inc.

"That's getting the attention of directors, who are asking what their personal liability is and how to protect themselves."

For example, last year's much-publicized case against executives of Bata Industries Ltd. has boards of directors running scared, wondering what action they can take to ensure their company is onside of the law both at home and in any jurisdiction where they do business.

In that case, the company and three senior Bata managers were charged with contravening Ontario environmental regulations. Two of the managers and the company were ultimately fined $144 000.

But legal liability is only one cause for concern, industry experts say. In addition, many companies are keenly aware that environmental issues can enhance or devastate their public image. In other words, a company still capitalizes on an environmentally friendly perception.

That's where accountants see a lucrative opportunity. A recent report issued by the Canadian Institute of Chartered Accountants recognizes companies' needs to walk the environmental straight and narrow as well as the accounting profession's chance to expand its business.

It concludes that accountants "face an unprecedented opportunity and challenge to respond to significant emerging needs and expectations arising from concerns to protect the environment for future generations."

Evidence of the growing need for such services is mounting. Recently, the Ontario Forest Industries Association tabled a code of practices for Ontario paper companies requiring independent audits of their compliance.

Banks and other major lenders are hiring environmental auditors to asses their environmental liability on properties or businesses that are used as loan collateral.

Large investors, such as pension funds, are also interested in examining a company's environmental records before taking an equity stake.

Environmental audits can take several forms, but most involve setting up a series of checks and balances to ensure that companies are meeting increasingly stringent pollution controls, Davis says.

Unlike traditional audits, accountants don't simply enter the company once a year to review the books. More often, they are involved in designing systems and reports from the ground up. Accountants use their reporting and management skills to help companies design and compile information that demonstrates environmental awareness.

Created in March 1992, KPMG's department employs 10 practitioners, including three full-time chemical engineers and an environmental scientist. Davis herself has a background in science.

"We see it as a management issue as well as a technical issue, but we're not going out there and taking soil samples we leave that to the engineers," she explains. "It's more a matter of working with the company to integrate environmental procedures and reporting into their systems."

"Everyone on the plant floor has to know exactly what to do when a dangerous substance gets spilled."

Though the chance to expand their business through environmental auditing has proved attractive for many accounting firms, the costs involved have some still standing on deck, waiting for the right opportunity to set up a full-fledged practice. Arthur Andersen & Co., for example, has yet to set up a specialized environmental auditing department.

"I think it's fair to say we're looking at it as an emerging area of practice," says Ken Vallilee, a partner in Arthur Andersen. "But there's a lot of things to consider before you jump right in with both feet."

Building up in-house expertise, hiring qualified staff and setting up strategic alliances with scientific experts will be completed before Arthur Andersen's practice becomes official, he says.

"There's no real urgency from our standpoint," Vallilee says. "But when we do set it up, we'll commit considerable resources."

Another problem for many firms is the lack of standardization for the audits an unusual state of affairs for the highly regulated accounting industry. The area's rapid growth has left some customers and service providers wondering what exactly an environmental audit is supposed to deliver.

As a result, the Canadian Standards Association is working to develop a set of standards that will spell out the general guidelines and purpose of an environmental audit.

Set for publication in August, the guidelines won't have teeth but will provide consumers and auditors with a basis for consistency in the industry.

Source: Laura Fowlie, "New auditors monitor firms' environmental liability," *The Financial Post* (June 25, 1993): 28. Reprinted by permission.

Where Do Business and Society Stand Today?

Companies have already accepted that they have a responsibility to produce, whenever possible, products and services that are recyclable. Many companies are finding that environmentally friendly products and socially responsible behaviour is not only expected of them, it is important for their profitability. Even when socially responsible behaviour does not enhance the bottom line, managers realize that unless they assume responsibility voluntarily, society will force them to do it through government legislation.

However, new evidence seems to indicate that responsible behaviour is in fact profitable in the long run. Max Clarkson, Director of the University of Toronto's Centre for Corporate and Social Performance and Ethics, devised an elaborate system for rating companies according to their performance in areas such as labour and customer relations, environmental protection and product safety. Of the 60 companies studied in Ontario and Quebec, those that received the highest marks on a series of issues related to ethics and social responsibility made the most money over the long term.[12]

According to Clarkson, those managers who are unaware of, or don't care about, highly publicized social and ethical issues are probably also unaware of other crucial business and economic factors and make poor decisions that affect their long-term profitability. He cites the case of Carling O'Keefe Breweries of Canada Ltd., a company that was unaware of the gender-equality issue. Carling did so poorly that eventually it was taken over by Molson Breweries. In his investigation of three large banks, Clarkson found that the Toronto-Dominion Bank and the Royal Bank of Canada had better employment equity records than the Bank of Montreal. The latter also had no retirement or termination counselling, while the TD had a good program in place. Additionally, the Bank of Montreal also had the worst financial performance record of the big banks throughout most of the 1980s.[13]

In Clarkson's view, it is management's job to balance the often conflicting objectives of the various stakeholders in a company—employees, customers, suppliers, governments and even competitors. If management succeeds in doing that, then healthy profits are a byproduct.

Critics of the stakeholder argument maintain that management often uses it to justify all kinds of defensive techniques. For example, selling off a money-losing division might enhance shareholder dividends, but management may argue that it needs more time in order to reduce the impact on employees and the community.

Top management's prime consideration, of course, is still the shareholders, and most social projects must still be somehow equated to profitability, rather than simply stated as a benefit to society. Nevertheless, consumers (and, to a lesser extent, government legislation) have forced greater social responsibility on business. This trend is unlikely to be reversed unless our society's material well-being takes an unforeseen drop, in which case economic objectives might once again prevail.

Chapter Summary

1. For a business firm to survive today, it must conduct itself in a socially responsible manner. Even though it is primarily an economic institution, business must take social, political and ethical considerations into account along with economic and market factors. On occasion, a course of action that might have

meant great economic benefit for the firm and its shareholders must be modified in view of possible adverse consequences for other sectors of society.

2. Some believe that a firm's duty is limited to the efficient production of goods and services, and that government should handle all other social concerns with the taxes collected from business. Others believe that since business is a part of society, it must be more responsive to the needs of that society.

3. Consumers have stated that when it comes to poorly built products, waste disposal and environmental pollution, there is no question but that a firm must act in a socially responsible manner. For consumer product firms in particular, ignoring the wishes of the consumer may lead to bankruptcy. The present interest in environmentally friendly products has resulted in efforts to recycle products; it has also provided new business opportunities for both new and established firms.

4. Major social issues today concern the relationship between business and employees, consumers and the community, particularly in terms of the environment. Some social issues also give rise to ethical questions about what is right and wrong in relation to society's interests. Major ethical issues faced by managers include the full utilization of human resources, discrimination in hiring, product safety, truthful advertising, relations with unions, adherence to government rules and regulations, political involvement and relationships with developing countries. How individual managers deal with these social and ethical issues depends largely on the firm's overall management philosophy.

5. There is new evidence that good corporate behaviour leads to long-run profits. Firms that are unaware of current social and ethical issues also appear to be unaware of economic and business factors, which leads to poor business decisions.

KEY TERMS

Corporate social responsibility 531

Laws of society 532

Moral code 532

Ethics 532

Business ethics 532

Stakeholders 535

Primary stakeholders 535

Secondary skateholders 535

Social or public issues 535

Consumer movement/consumerism .537

Ecology 539

Sustainable development 541

Recycling 541

Ethical issues 545

Management philosophy 548

Social audit 549

Environmental audit 549

REVIEW QUESTIONS

1 Why does society today demand that business assume greater social responsibility?

2 Explain the concept of social responsibility.

3 Distinguish between morals, ethics and laws.

4 Explain the meaning of business ethics.

5 What are the major arguments for and against business taking on more social responsibility?

6 What are stakeholders? Distinguish between primary and secondary stakeholders.

7 What is the responsibility of business toward its shareholders? Employees? Consumers? Community?

8 Distinguish between social and ethical issues.

9 Apart from legislation, what measures could be taken to reduce employment discrimination?

10 How does management philosophy influence an employee's business ethics and his or her reaction to social issues?

11 How should a firm decide which social issues to pursue? How can it measure its achievement of these objectives?

DISCUSSION QUESTIONS

1 Does business have a social responsibility? Give reasons for your answer.

2 How can business firms balance their need to make a profit with their responsibility to the various stakeholders?

3 What do you think is the responsibility of business to the consumer regarding product safety and quality?

4 Do you think business managers should adhere to an established ethical code in the same way that doctors and lawyers do? If so, what should be included in this code?

5 Do you think that a standard code of business ethics would be compatible with a competitive business system such as Canada's?

Waghorner Photographic Processors Inc.

Waghorner Photographic Processors Inc. (WPPI) was a manufacturer of photographic films operating in Vancouver. An employer of 50 local families, its financial condition was very weak. A chemical known as EEG was generated as a byproduct of the photographic development process.

EEG was particularly toxic to fish and other marine life. To destroy it would require that it be incinerated in industrial incinerators capable of reaching temperatures well above 3000 degrees Celsius. This limited the disposal sites to two in eastern Canada and one in the central United States. The disposal of this chemical would require the daily running of at least two tanker trucks, which would transport the chemical to the railway station to be shipped by rail to the nearest disposal incinerator.

Within 30 metres of WPPI's facilities was a river. This river was declared dead by biologists because of the amount of toxic discharge being dumped into it by a pulp and paper mill located eight kilometres upstream from WPPI. Jim Ranger, the Vice-President of Operations, felt that they would not necessarily be acting irresponsibly by discharging the EEG into the river since it was already "dead." As well, such action would save considerable resources for the company.

SOURCE: By David H. Jones-Delcourt. Reprinted by permission of the author.

Question

1 Evaluate Jim Ranger's decision. Is his argument socially responsible?

The Smell of Old Fish

Sole Food Limited was a small but extremely efficient manufacturer of men's recreation shoes and hiking boots. Its product lines had caught on well in North America and Europe because of their superior design and quality. Recently, although sales had been steady, the market appeared to be saturated and no further growth seemed possible.

Mr. Sacks, Sole Food's owner and general manager, was concerned with this situation, as he was convinced that new and different markets should be opened up in order to keep his company innovative. Thus, he was extremely interested when he met Mr. Romeniz at the Shoe Association's annual convention. It seemed that Mr. Romeniz was a "representative." When asked what or whom he represented, he was >>

vague, but confided that he had extensive "commercial contacts" in both Africa and Central America. In fact, one of these "contacts" was about to place an order for 200 000 army boots. Would Mr. Sacks care to submit a quote? There were further hints of more orders to follow.

Sensing an imminent foothold in the lucrative military market, Mr. Sacks upon his return hurriedly summoned his design staff, hand-produced several prototypes and sent them to Mr. Romeniz. At the same time, he had a credit check done on Mr. Romeniz's company. Within two days, Mr. Sacks' banker reported that Mr. Romeniz owned an export firm of good reputation and sound financial standing.

Mr. Sacks was delighted, therefore, when a letter containing a substantial advance payment and confirmation of contract terms was received. Production started immediately.

Several weeks later, Mr. Sacks held a dinner party to celebrate his good fortune. After he had told his guests about his new business venture, one of them spoke up: "I'm on the local committee for Amnesty International. We have reports that Romeniz is a prime supplier for the Republic of Rotania, one of the world's most brutal dictatorships."

This revelation shocked and embarrassed Mr. Sacks. Later in the week, he confronted Mr. Romeniz, who smiled and said softly: "You don't have to worry about who wears the boots, my friend. Besides, the name 'Republic of Rotania' never appears on any purchase order or other paperwork. You deal only with me. I sell to someone else, who sells to the Rotanians. The money is good, isn't it?"

With those words, Mr. Romeniz produced another contract, even more lucrative than the first. Mr. Sacks knew that it represented enough long-term work to keep his small company healthy for at least five years. Only this time, Mr. Romeniz was speaking in terms of "pay-offs" to certain "influential officials" in Rotania's corrupt government. He assured Mr. Sacks that these "favours" were "normal business practice." How did Mr. Sacks think he had obtained the first contract?

SOURCE: Dr. P.C. Wright, Faculty of Administration, University of New Brunswick. Reprinted by permission of the author.

Questions

1 Should Mr. Sacks continue to deal with Mr. Romeniz? Why or why not?

2 Discuss the differences between business ethics in Canada and abroad.

3 Should businesspeople be concerned about the human-rights records of their customers? Why or why not?

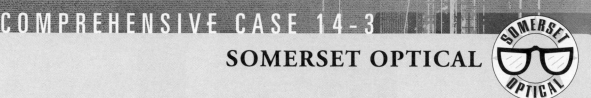

COMPREHENSIVE CASE 14-3

SOMERSET OPTICAL

Social responsibility is becoming more and more an issue for every type of business. Somerset Optical was not exempt from the desire to conduct business in a socially responsible manner. Wayne and Mike felt that one way to become more socially responsible was to become more environmentally conscious.

Somerset thus established a modest recycling project whereby any contact lens customer who returned empty bottles of contact-lens cleaning or soaking solutions would receive a 10% discount on the replacement supply

Fowler and Dewar further examined the contents of all the chemical treatment solutions used in their optical laboratory to ensure they were environmentally friendly. Those that were harmful to the ozone layer were replaced by environmentally safe substitutes. Quite often, the replacement chemicals were slightly more expensive.

For the third component of its environmental program, Somerset encouraged customers to donate their old glasses to the Somerset Recycling Program, which made these glasses available to Third World countries at no cost.

Fowler and Dewar also recognized that society had invested quite a substantial amount in their company in terms of both direct and indirect benefits. As a small token of appreciation, Somerset sponsored a local amateur football club, offering team members and families deep discounts on quality eyewear, donating money to purchase new equipment, and funding special events at which well-known guest speakers spoke on topics such as drug use and stress.

Finally, Somerset presented two $3000 scholarships to a college that offered an optician's program. In addition to maintaining the highest grades, scholarship winners were to work with youth to encourage them to stay in school.

Somerset's social responsibility program inspired four other dispensing optical locations to copy its example.

Source: By David H. Jones-Delcourt. Reprinted by permission of the author.

Questions

1 Evaluate Somerset's activities in the area of social responsibility.

2 Discuss the pros and the cons of business social responsibility.

3 Would the establishment of socially responsible programs by one business have a multiplier effect? In other words, would it cause other companies to undertake similar efforts?

PART 5

Business in Canada: The Future

It has often been said that the only constant is change. Having examined business in the Canadian environment to this point, we can be certain that it too will change. The particular twists and detours on the road ahead can be the subject of endless speculation. Nevertheless, it should be possible to make some reasonable predictions about the general direction business will take.

In Chapter 15, we attempt to forecast some of the social, economic and technological changes most likely to affect business in Canada in the next decade. We also discuss some of the challenges facing managers in the future, and offer some guidance on career planning and job search techniques.

Business, the Future and Your Career

Learning Objectives

After reading this chapter, you will be able to

1 Explain why it is necessary for businesses to make forecasts about the future even though all aspects of life are undergoing rapid change.

2 Explain some of the methods used to predict the future.

3 Explain some major changes based on current trends.

4 Explain some key factors that may affect Canada's future business system.

5 Explain the knowledge and education requirements of the manager of the future.

6 Explain the job search process.

A Word About Predicting the Future

Our examination of the present Canadian business system in the preceding chapters has shown that business works, if at times imperfectly. Some business concepts and practices are subject to debate; others are not fully developed and require further research.

We have also looked at the past, and in hindsight we realize that affairs might have been conducted better, with less hardship to the mass of society. Unfortunately, we can do nothing about the past, except to use it as a guide for the future. Executives have to make decisions today on courses of action that will often affect the organization for many years in the future. Speculating on or predicting what conditions in the future might be is, therefore, an important activity.

By "predicting the future," we do not mean gazing into a crystal ball or searching out an oracle—we mean the reasonably accurate forecasting of future events on the basis of current trends. However, trends may change direction quite suddenly: a rapidly growing economy may come to an abrupt halt when oil prices double; a single technological innovation can create an entirely new industry almost overnight. Imagine what a new source of cheap energy might do for all countries, industrialized and developing. What would it mean to the North American economy if a new battery were developed that was capable of storing and providing the energy output of a tankful of gasoline? When we base our vision of the future on current trends, any sudden developments can render our predictions null and void.

Change, Change, Change

Another reason that the future is difficult to predict is the rate of change itself. According to Alvin Toffler, author of *Future Shock* (1970), the rate of change accelerates because technology feeds on itself with each successive development. Thus, change in each future period will be much more dramatic than in the last. To illustrate this acceleration, Toffler points out that if the 50 000 years of human existence are divided into 800 lifetimes of approximately 62 years each, the first 650 of them were spent in caves. Writing has existed for only the last 70 lifetimes, and only during the last six did it ever reach the masses. The vast majority of the material goods we know today were developed in the present lifetime.[1]

With the pace of change quickening at such a rate, business and managers must learn to adapt. Resistance to change may be a common problem, but it is one no businessperson will be able to afford. Managers must be able to deal quickly with change in every aspect of the business environment—technology, economic conditions, lifestyles and society at large. While managers must have an ever-increasing store of knowledge to draw on, they must also be prepared to discard outdated information and replace it with new; they must be well trained and willing to be retrained as necessary. Above all, they must be prepared to deal with any change as it arises.

Methods of Predicting the Future

Several methods—five of which are listed below—are available for predicting the future. While different techniques can result in different predictions, that uncertainty may be useful if it prevents us from focusing on a single future possibility to the exclusion of all others.

1. *Trend analysis.* In trend analysis, we assume that what has happened in the past will continue to happen in the future, in more or less the same way.

2. *Delphi method.* In this method, a variety of experts are polled independently about a particular question. All are then shown the results of the total poll and asked to reassess their original forecasts in the light of the other opinions.

3. *Scenario.* A scenario writer chooses a single possible future situation at a given point in time, then traces the sequence of events that might lead to that future, for example, depicting what Canada may be like at the turn of the next century, and describing how Canada might arrive at these conditions based on conditions as they exist today, as well as on current trends.

4. *Model building.* This scientific approach uses computers, statistics and other data to create a model. By varying the data employed, a number of alternative futures can be postulated.

5. *Seat-of-the-pants techniques.* Science-fiction writers often create alternative futures through a combination of research and personal knowledge mixed with imagination and intuition; in many instances, their predictions have come true.

While any of these techniques can be used, futurists should also challenge the projections of others in order to clarify the terms of their own forecasts. Forecasts should be plausible; they should, in other words, describe a future that could conceivably develop out of the present. All assumptions must be clearly stated, and all aspects of the scenario must be consistent (one part must not contradict another). Above all, forecasts should cover a specific number of years, so that the direction and speed of changes affecting society can be assessed.

Major Changes Based on Current Trends

A number of future changes based on trends in population, lifestyles, economic conditions, technology and society are already evident in Canada. Perhaps the major agent for change is advancing technology. New discoveries in science are often used to develop new products or methods of operation. This can create entire new industries and shift education requirements, as occurred with the development of the computer. Advances in medicine and medical technology mean longer life spans, which has an impact on business in terms of the products demanded by senior citizens. It is essential that all managers recognize these trends and understand how they might influence the future operation of their organizations.

Using Statistics Canada numbers and computer models, John Robinson and his colleagues at the University of British Columbia drew a picture of life in 2030.

Several of Canada's largest industries shrink dramatically or die altogether. The West Coast fishery industry collapses from overfishing; pulp and paper production is cut in half; Canada's nuclear industry dies; housing starts fall through the floor and never recover.

On a more positive note, strong new industries emerge in the energy field. Canada uses biomass energy, which uses municipal and industrial waste and quick-growing trees. Marginal farmland is converted to solar energy production to drive the super-efficient public and private solar-energy vehicles.

Urban sprawl and energy-squandering homes are things of the past. Denser communities of apartments and row houses are the preferred living accommodations.

Parents are allowed three years of paid leave to care for their young children. The average work week is 27.5 hours, with lots of time off for volunteer and leisure activities. With almost half of the population over age

Canada in 2030—The Sustainable Scenario

>>

45 by 2030, Canadians are more practical and health-conscious. Clothing and footwear are selected less for fashion and more for durability. The country is virtually tobacco free and alcohol is drunk in moderation. People eat a lot less meat, milk and eggs, and more whole grains, fruits and vegetables.

Despite a more health-conscious public, the health-care system is busier than ever. Because of the aging population, more hospitals and health-care workers are required—almost double the number needed in 1990.

Education has also grown. Half the people between the ages of 19 and 25 are enrolled in some form of post-secondary education. With many older Canadians also entering the education field, the total number of Canadian students will triple.

Recreation and holidays are more modest, with people preferring inexpensive and comfortable accommodation. Superboxes that combine fax capabilities, telephones, videophones, televisions and computers allow people to transmit and receive information, news, videos and games. Public transportation is very reliable and the preferred method of transportation. Small electric cars that last 20 years or more have taken over from the fuel-driven cars of the past.

Government is less centralized and more concerned with environmental and cultural issues. Environment is a national security concern. Water consumption per capita drops as showers, dishwashers and industrial equipment become more efficient in their use of water. Agriculture no longer depends on chemical fertilizer, and there is a strong shift to natural pest control and soil enhancement.

The energy sector has experienced the greatest upheaval. Because the oil industry had to bear the environmental costs of pollution, higher oil prices reduced demand by 50%. A carbon tax virtually takes coal off the market. Cost and safety concerns kill the nuclear industry. The major fuel is alcohol made from forest and mill waste and from fast-growing hybrid poplars grown on huge plantations. Furthermore, 67 500 hectares of photovoltaic cells collect heat from the sun, which is used to drive Canada's fleet of hydrogen vehicles.

According to Robinson, the above scenario is possible but highly unlikely. The purpose of this exercise, he says, is to get people to think about the future and to start looking at alternatives.[3]

Demographic— How Does It Rate as a Forecasting Tool?

Demography is the statistical study of human population.

Perfect predictability makes some people uneasy, which is why demographics gets overlooked, according to David Foot, an economist and futurist at the University of Toronto. **Demography** is the statistical study of human population. Studying how many people were born in a given year and how many died, how many came to Canada and how many left, can provide us with knowledge of future demand for schools, housing and medical care. It can also provide us with information about shortages of workers and training needs, as well as the kinds of products and services that businesses should provide.

The most critical factor in Canada's future are the baby boomers. No one knows exactly why Canadians went on a baby-making binge from 1947 to 1966, with each year adding approximately 400 000 new Canadians to the population. These boomers have put a bulge on Canada's population graph (see Figure 15.1). As they progressed through the stages of life, they first crowded the schools. The large numbers that went on to higher education were responsible for a construction boom on university campuses, while those who went into the labour force sent the unemployment rate soaring. In the 1970s and 1980s, their need for accommodation sent house prices out of sight. Because most have homes now, house prices will start to decline after the mid-1990s.

The U.S. baby boom started in 1946 and ended in 1964, peaking at 3.5 children per family while in Canada it peaked at four. The only other countries that experienced a baby boom were Australia and New Zealand. In Australia, the boom peaked at three children but lasted 10 years longer than that in Canada.

The boom echo in the 1980s represents the offspring of the baby boomers-significant compared to the birthrate in the 1970s, but not spectacular. However, it did have an impact on elementary-school enrollments. Yet, according to Foot, no one was prepared for it. Most of the new schools being built across Canada will be empty by the end of the 1990s, yet they are not being designed with alternative uses in mind. Similarly, he anticipates a shortage of high-school teachers by 1995; again, no one is prepared.

>>

Foot further predicts that cities will stop growing. When the boomers were young, they headed for urban centres, but as they age and have families of their own they are moving to the suburbs. Unless there is a sharp reversal in the declining fertility trend or radical changes in immigration policy, city growth will slow dramatically and remain there. Foot recommends that boomers sell their homes when they no longer need them and buy themselves a comfortable retirement on the proceeds. The demand for housing will drop dramatically,

and urban real estate prices will remain flat after 1994. Meanwhile, during the 1990s, rural real estate prices will go out of sight as the boomers discover rural living and cottages. So the late boomer who is unable to buy a house now should buy a cottage instead, sell it late in the decade when cottage prices will be sky-high and buy a house with the profits. Meanwhile, the Depression babies, those now in their late 60s and early 70s, should sell their homes and live off the proceeds.

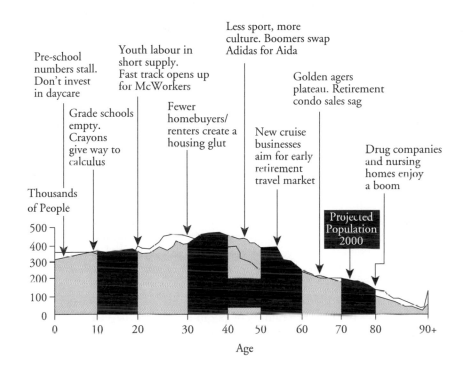

FIGURE 15.1

2000: Fade to grey—grade schools close and housing demand dips. Fortune again favours the young. Boomers face the new mortality.

SOURCE: Adapted from Daniel Stoffman, "Completely predictable people," *The Globe and Mail, Report on Business Magazine* (November 1990): 78–84.

Population Changes

How many people can this planet hold? In a book entitled *The Limits to Growth*, researchers built a computer model of the world based on five global factors: population, agriculture, production (industrial output), non-renewable resource depletion and pollution generation.[2] According to this model, if present growth trends continue, the limits to growth on this planet will be reached sometime in the next 100 years. On October 12, 1999 (approximately) the world's population reached six billion.[3] This is equivalent to 148 people being born each minute. Much of this population growth will occur in developing nations, however; the growth rate in industrialized countries will be much slower, in some instances approaching zero growth. The population projection for the year 2050 is 8.9 billion. Today 100 000 people are more than 100 years old, with this number expected to reach 2.2 million by 2050.[4]

What will happen to Canada's population in the 21st century? By 2001, using a low-growth alternative approach, Canada's population should be 31.4 million, and 34.2 million in 2016. Using a medium-growth approach these numbers become 31.9 million and 37.1 million respectively; with a high-growth approach, the numbers increase to 32.4 million and 39.9 million respectively. Statistics Canada favours the medium-growth approach.[5] Academics who study demographic trends generally predict a bleak outlook for Canada. Early in the next century, Canada's population will begin to age rapidly, and then slowly dwindle, all because of a declining birthrate. An immediate problem is the large number of senior citizens who will have to be supported by fewer and fewer workers. This will greatly affect the social welfare system and the labour market in Canada.[6]

However, on a more optimistic note, baby boomers—representing approximately one-third of Canada's population—have produced almost as many children as their parents (406 000 compared to 479 000), which will help to fund their own retirement.[7]

While some experts believe that the change will not unduly lower the standard of living, others are deeply concerned. They insist that Canada's sovereignty and ultimate survival as a nation will be at stake unless the trends are reversed. If the population shrinks, so will demand for goods and services, greatly slowing the economy. The market for new homes will be almost eliminated, and schools will have fewer students. And what effect will a shrinking population have on innovation and research and development, which are generally associated with younger age groups?

To head off this catastrophe, Canada must look to immigration for more people. Another approach is to provide more incentives to families to have more children. For example, Quebec's concern about its low fertility rate resulted in a program of cash payments to families—a $500 bonus for the first and second child and a $3000 bonus over two years for a third child. Because of the high cost of raising children, the scheme is unlikely to create a mini-baby boom in Quebec; nevertheless, it will provide some incentive to expand families.

Managers must consider how this potential change in population growth in Canada and the increasing world population will affect their business. They must ask themselves, for example, what products or services they will offer to a growing world population. Should they concentrate on providing wheat and other natural resources, or on manufacturing or information processing?

And what about the changing age structure of the population? Will the upward shift in age be beneficial or detrimental to our economy? As people age, they will require more medical and hospital services, which will be a drain on the economy. Some firms that are primarily catering to younger age groups will have to be concerned about a drop in demand for their products. On the other hand, the aging population will provide business with opportunities to offer new products and services.

Lifestyle Changes

Lifestyle refers to the way people live and work, how they spend their leisure time, what their hobbies and other interests are, including their personal philosophy. Individuals' lifestyles normally change as they grow older, leave school, take a job, marry and have children. When changes occur in the lifestyle of an entire society, the impact on the future of individual business organizations can be tremendous.

Lifestyle refers to the way people live and work, how they spend their leisure time, what their hobbies and other interests are, including their personal philosophy.

*Grim
Projections
for Canada's
Population*

- At the peak of the baby boom in 1959, the fertility rate per woman was 3.9 babies. Since then, it has dropped steadily to 1.67. A fertility rate of 2.1 is required to ensure that the population remains stable. Canada's rate has been below this rate for 17 years.

- The fertility rate is expected to drop further—to 1.4 or less. In Quebec, it is already at that level and most major cities in Canada are close to it.

- If the current trend of 1% growth per year continues, Canada's population will peak at approximately 33 million in the year 2031 and then stabilize at that level. If the fertility rate drops, the population is expected to peak at about 28 million in about 2013 and then decline. There is a possibility that Canada's population could drop to 12 to 16 million by the middle of the next century.

- There will have to be an increase in immigration, depending on the fertility rate, to about 300 000 by the turn of the century and then rising to 500 000 just to maintain the present annual population growth of 1%.

- The median age in Canada will rise from the current 31 to 43 (48 if the fertility rate drops) by 2031.

- There will be a shift from the youth population to senior citizens, the latter group almost tripling in size. If the fertility rate drops, 27% of Canadians will be over the age of 65 by 2031 compared to only 11% in 1986. Over the same period, the proportion of Canadians under age 17 will drop to 15% from 26%.

- The labour force will continue to increase in size until 2006, when the first baby boomers reach retirement age. After that it will begin to decline from 1% to 2% every five years.[8]

There has been a continuous increase in the amount of leisure time available to Canadians. Although the 40-hour workweek is still the legal standard, many people today work only 35 hours, and some even less. Furthermore, for many individuals the amount of vacation time has increased and may be supplemented with leaves of absence for various personal reasons. People also live longer than in the past, and many retire earlier. Many opportunities exist for business to provide goods and services for a leisure-oriented society.

Another essential factor in overall lifestyle is the family. Individuals are now marrying later in life and having fewer children. At the same time, the divorce rate has been rising and may rise further still as divorce becomes easier to obtain, resulting in more single-parent families. Among those families that remain intact, the proportion of women working will most likely continue to increase through the twenty-first century. Social values and behaviour can change quickly, however, and it is possible that the above trends will be reversed. In any case, business must be prepared to adjust to these lifestyle changes.

Education is another major influence on lifestyle. As people become better educated, they question the values and beliefs of the previous generation. For example, during the 1960s and 1970s many young people abhorred the emphasis on the acquisition of material goods, and instead put more emphasis on the quality of life. In the 1980s, however, as the baby-boom generation entered middle age, the trend reversed and there was renewed emphasis on economic growth and traditional values. Education also becomes more important as technology advances, since knowledge quickly becomes outdated. Old jobs disappear and new jobs are created. Many low-skilled repetitive jobs will be destroyed as well as many middle management jobs. However, new forms of employment will emerge. Thus, lifetime learning is becoming increasingly accepted.

If Canada's population continues to grow at 1% every year, it will peak at approximately 33 million in 2031

In the 1970s, the increasing cost of energy (especially gasoline) appeared to have a major impact on lifestyles and the economy. People moved closer to their place of work, or sought to find ways of working at home. Great emphasis was placed on the development of rapid transit systems. The auto industry was turned upside down as it attempted to meet the needs of commuters with smaller, more fuel-efficient cars. Energy shortages are still lurking in the background, and political events can once again make the cost of energy a major concern. But as computers and more sophisticated communications systems are developed, the need for many people to commute to their place of work at all may gradually diminish.

Lifestyle research is an attempt to identify certain lifestyle characteristics in order to compare how individuals with various characteristics behave in the marketplace.

In response to the enormous impact of lifestyle changes on many businesses, marketers of consumer products have turned to **lifestyle research** to identify clusters of homogeneous buying behaviour, allowing them better to meet the needs of their customers. Rather than simply classify consumers according to age, an attempt is made to identify certain lifestyle characteristics in order to compare how individuals with various characteristics behave in the marketplace. As lifestyle research becomes more important, it will be refined and become a major marketing research tool.

Lifestyles of The Future— Some Projections

Although many people profess to prefer country living, the lure of the city remains. Cities provide an incubator in which human culture can evolve and provide the infrastructure for growth and development in a variety of areas. On the negative side, problems of pollution, over crowding, poverty, homelessness and crime abound. The Organization for Economic Cooperation and Development (OECD) suggests that over the next few decades, the world's urban population could double from 2.6 billion in 1995 to 5.2 billion in 2025. Much of this growth is expected to occur in cities in developing countries, with populations swelling from 1.5 billion to 4 billion urban dwellers.[9] This will lead to an increase in the social problems associated with city life and hence necessitate the development and implementation of social programs to help alleviate these problems. Other projections for the future include the re-emergence of company towns to attract highly skilled, highly specialized workers.[10]

>>

These workers are not attracted by high salaries, as many employees in high-tech industries can basically write their own employment contracts due to the demand for their services. Therefore employers must be creative in luring potential employees. The freedom offered by such workplace configurations as office-to-home links, allowing the specialist to work wherever and whenever he or she chooses, have been recognized as a valuable recruiting tool. By combining such flexibility with subsidized housing and by providing basic social services such as education, healthcare and child care, employers can create their own company towns.

These all-inclusive packages may be viewed as a valuable perquisite by the target employee group. Whether we will be in mega-cities or company towns, or any other configuration of workers and work, the availability of information will enable us to engage in activities previously relegated to "Star Trek" episodes. Trend watcher Marion Salzman believes that we are now able to" think globally and act globally."[11] An illustration of this ability can be shown by accessing www.feedthehungry.com. This site enables the use to click on an icon and food will be donated to someone in a Third World country by a sponsor organization.

Economic Changes

The growing interdependence of world nations can have severe effects on the economies of many countries—as witness the 1973 Arab oil embargo that shocked the industrial world, contributed to high inflation, unemployment and subsequently slow economic growth. Then came the 1981-82 recession, which had a severe impact on many small firms and caused an unusually high number of bankruptcies. The recession also created considerable unemployment, which affected many individuals and families. The 1990-92 recession brought similar results.

As much as our governments attempt economic management, we will likely not escape recessions, although deep depressions, such as the Great Depression of the 1930s, are unlikely to recur. On the other hand, structural changes in the economy will affect many individuals over the next few decades. International competition will be the major factor. Canadian industry must change, expanding in areas where Canada has a competitive advantage and phasing out industries that are uncompetitive. Given our present economic interdependence with many nations, as currency values rise and fall inflation and interest rates in Canada can be affected.

< Lifestyle means different things to different people. Therefore, marketers have turned to lifestyle research to better meet the needs of consumers

Will the future bring us renewed high inflation, perhaps in double digits? Or will our huge national debt affect our well-being as governments scramble to raise more tax revenue? Will we be able to maintain our exports upon which so many Canadians depend for their livelihood? Will there be other energy shortages?

These questions are not easy to answer because world events that affect economies are difficult to forecast, but they underline the need for businesspeople to have a good understanding of our business system, of economics and particularly of how world events can affect Canadian businesses and individuals. No business firm can isolate itself from economic forces. Managers must be aware of them and plan accordingly.

Technological Changes

We can expect technological change to continue to accelerate in the remainder of the century. In Chapter 7, we discussed the automated factory and its potential to produce any kind of product almost immediately. Powerful computers will guide robots through dangerous or monotonous operations. Although new production methods and other advances in technology can cause great unemployment in the short term, greater employment should result in the long run. However, retraining will require money, and large pockets of unemployment may be with us for long periods of time. Furthermore, with rapid technological change, knowledge becomes outdated quickly, making education in itself a lifetime occupation.

As it has in the past, the introduction of new technology will give rise to other changes and perhaps entirely new industries. Some of these changes will become evident in new and more efficient production techniques. The greatest boon to Canada (provided we seize the opportunities as they arise) will be the creation of new jobs from new industries. A prime example is the field of communications. With the development of the Telesat telecommunications satellite, Canada became a leader in the communications industry. Today, communications is a $10-billion industry, with various sectors expected to grow by 8% to 25% per year. The job creation potential of this industry is tremendous, judging by the United States, where half of all jobs are classified as information jobs. Even though many of the job-holders are not directly involved in producing communications equipment, the potential of this industry is evident.

Although Canada obviously lacks the resources to challenge the United States in areas such as space technology, we can make a significant contribution to various technological advancements provided we have the necessary entrepreneurial spirit and moderate financial resources. One of our greatest achievements in space technology is the Canadarm, which is used in the U.S. space shuttle. However, the Canadian government's decision not to participate in the building of the space platform in the 1990s will certainly affect our expertise in space technology.

Canadians are among the most computer-literate populations of the world, ranking sixth in a recent survey of PC users, with 11.7 million people owning personal computers, and ranking fifth in Internet usage with 27.69% of the overall population being connected.[12] Canada's Internet customers are most concerned with factors such as customer support, no busy signals and no dropped lines, with value-added services and quality of the content being of lesser importance.[13] This demanding and computer-literate group of consumers has not gone unnoticed by Canadian retailers. Sixty-seven percent of large retailers report that the Internet will be their primary non-store channel, followed by catalogue and mail order/direct mail.[14]

Our Future Canadian Business System

Although the trend is toward less government involvement in the private sector, the size of government will not diminish significantly, if at all, and its influence on the economy will likely grow. Canada is blessed with abundant natural resources and an educated labour force. Under normal circumstances, we should enjoy one of the highest standards of living in the world, but we are also faced with some towering problems. The federal and provincial government deficits are enormous. The federal deficit alone requires one-third of every tax dollar to meet interest charges. Unless this deficit is reduced, funds may not be available to continue with the major government programs—unless taxes are increased. This in turn could cause an economic slowdown and further aggravate unemployment. Furthermore, structural unemployment from continued automation could increase, necessitating large amounts of money for re-training and assistance of the unemployed.

What will business do? An overriding concern for many Canadian firms is increasing productivity in order to retain our competitive position in the world. Canadian managers are studying Japanese management techniques, but, as we found in Chapter 6, these techniques are unlikely to work the same in Canada as they do in Japan. Perhaps the emphasis will have to be on quality, satisfying customers and placing renewed value on the employee. George S. Day, in a recent article in the *Academy of Marketing Science,* suggests that one strategy to maintain a competitive advantage is for a firm to manage their marketing relationships. He suggests three steps to achieve this goal: 1) The culture of the organization must support the customer relationship orientation, 2) The knowledge and understanding of this customer base must be an ongoing activity on the organization, 3) The processes of the organization must exhibit an understanding of and a response to the processes of the firm's customers.[15] This approach puts the emphasis on customer satisfaction and response, a view echoed in another article entitled "Emerging Business Realities." Here, the authors suggest that a competitive advantage can be increased by not only centralized planning but also by the rapid execution of these plans. The key to this rapid execution is the flexibility offered by a variety of organizational designs geared toward today's unstable business environment. We must be able to reconfigure resources as needed to meet customer demands.[16] Increased automation of many operations, particularly in the factory, can contribute to our competitive advantage; however, increased automation will aggravate unemployment. It will then become important to encourage the entrepreneurial spirit and make it easier for individuals to open new businesses to generate new jobs. See Chapter 2 for a discussion of entrepreneurship.

The North American Free Trade Agreement between Canada, the United States and Mexico will be a continuing subject of debate. For many small Canadian firms, NAFTA's predecessor—the Canada-U.S. Free Trade Agreement—opened up a huge new market in the United States. The addition of Mexico as a partner will ultimately create further opportunities for Canada. At the same time, Canadian businesses that have lived behind the protectionist wall (e.g., the wine and beer industry, textiles and shoes) will have to become more competitive and productive to survive.

NAFTA may ultimately be expanded to include all countries in Central and South America. Although it may take several decades, this trilateral agreement could be the forerunner of an American economic union, similar to what the European Union established in 1992. If we are to compete with other trade blocs, such as the EU and the remaining communist countries, a common market extending over the entire continent may eventually be a necessity.

The world is changing rapidly, as attested to by developments in Eastern Europe. As the former Soviet Union and other Eastern European countries move toward more-market-oriented economies, tremendous opportunities will develop for all developed industrial countries, including Canada. Developing nations will also look to improve their standard of living. They will insist that money be invested in machinery and equipment that will provide them with more goods and services, not new missiles and guns. A utopian view perhaps, but the world cannot remain an armed camp forever. Assisting the developing nations will be industrialized countries such as Canada, with their expertise in technology and business. It could be an exciting—and profitable—time for many businesspeople.

Another area in need of improvement is the relationship between business, labour and government. Although the European idea of worker representation might not be accepted by management in Canada today, social and economic developments could make better cooperation between business and labour a necessity. Even if collective bargaining remains the union's primary method of getting its share of the economic pie, some changes in the system will be required. Unions will have to adapt to the changing trends in Canadian society and to the changing face of the workplace.

First, strikes are an expensive luxury for our economy—they reduce total output and seldom allow the injured parties to recoup their losses. Although unions will retain the strike weapon, government may increase its use of back-to-work legislation, particularly in vital sectors of the economy. Eventually, continued government intervention in settling labour disputes is bound to lead to reform.

Second, both unions and management will be obliged to become more responsible toward society. Each side will have to open its books to the other, to allow the other side to determine for itself what can reasonably be expected. In cases where this approach still does not produce a settlement, unions may resort to the more sophisticated ways of pressuring the employer to concede, such as advertising, picketing and boycotts. Unions may also demand joint management of pension funds, which currently amount to more than $50 billion, and insist they not be invested in companies that condone anti-union practices or violate health and safety regulations. As the trend toward employer associations for management continues, bargaining will become industry-wide under government supervision. Unions may experience a significant drop in membership if economic conditions do not improve and union members begin to defect to non-union firms.

The Manager of the Future

The manager of the future will be a well-educated professional with a broad knowledge of psychology, sociology and economics. Highly developed conceptual skills will be required to analyze increasingly rapid changes in the environment and their effect on organizational plans and operations. Managers will have to be able to adjust quickly to change if they are to protect their organizations from loss and take advantage of new opportunities as they arise. Adequate time for decision making will be another luxury that few will be able to enjoy.

Moreover, although workers will be more affluent, many may still be required to perform monotonous jobs that offer little satisfaction for their higher-level needs. Managers will require strong communication skills that will enable them to listen to their employees and provide them with the necessary motivation. Depending on their level in the organizational hierarchy, some managers will have to deal with

< Managers of the future must be comfortable with rapid technological change

subordinate managers who are themselves dissatisfied, while others may be required to handle demands for collective bargaining from the lower levels of management.

Professional managers must be capable of working closely with a variety of groups in their own business organizations and in society at large. Since an increasing number of decisions will be made by workgroups and committees, managers must know how to conduct themselves with groups. The ability to cooperate will be essential for managers in their relations with those outside of the organization as well, whether they are consumers, government administrators, union leaders or politicians.

The use of committees for decision making may be one of the greatest problems facing managers in the future. For a committee to reach a consensus, a great deal of time is often required, yet in many cases the rapidly changing environment demands almost instantaneous action. Individuals flexible enough to listen to many competing views, yet able to obtain a consensus quickly and take appropriate action in a timely fashion, will be the most effective professional managers.

Canada's Charter of Rights and Freedoms, which came into effect April 17, 1982, will continue to influence current business practices, particularly those relating to employees. Although many practices have already been challenged in the courts, because the Charter has such broad implications, it will take many more years to determine the Charter's many ramifications for business. The future manager will have to be aware of these ramifications and work within the constraints of the Charter.

Managers must also have a global perspective as the Internet now has us irreversibly connected. What happens in a far off corner of the world may have important implications for their company's future. Several "pillars"" have been suggested in order for managers to succeed in today's world:

- Visioning—Refocus from short-term goals to rebuilding healthy organizations through work, wealth and well-being.

- Mapping—Shift our thinking to global dimensions.

- Journeying—Respect the past while moving to the future.

- Learning—Allow and encourage creative, expansive thinking.

- Mentoring—Inspire others to reach for the vision.

- Leading—Lead by also following, through the combined use of both the left and right hemispheres of the brain.

- Valuing—Reflect on our traditions and values to better understand our future global reality.[17]

Your Career in Business

Although you have many courses to complete before you graduate, assuming you are aiming for a business degree or diploma, it is not too early to think about your future career. In the remainder of this chapter, we review some of the advantages and disadvantages of going into business for yourself, and of joining a small or a large company. Then we look at the process of getting a job. This section is not meant to be an extensive treatise on career planning, resume writing or how to conduct yourself in an interview. It is simply meant to introduce you to the job search process. You are asked to give some thought to what you would like to do when you finish your course of study, as well as to what skills you have now and expect to have in the future. Finally, we provide tips and ideas that will help you in your job search.

When you graduate with your business degree or diploma, you can choose to go into business for yourself, or you can find a job with either a small company or a large company. Let us briefly review each of these business environments.

Going into Business for Yourself

Going into business for yourself means you are the boss. You do not have to answer to anyone else or live up to anyone else's expectations. Nevertheless, you must cater to customers and cope with the competition. There are also government regulations, which can be costly and time-consuming to deal with, not to mention frustrating. In terms of income, as a successful entrepreneur you can potentially make far more money than if you work for someone else.

On the other hand, running your own business is demanding. A business owner can seldom have a nine-to-five job. Long hours are normal, and if the business fails you could lose everything. Nevertheless, being in business can be exceptionally challenging and rewarding, and give the owner a good reputation in the community.

Before starting your own company, you must determine whether you have the knowledge and experience it takes to run a business. Another major consideration is the availability of financial resources. You may want to postpone starting your own business until you have gained some business experience in a small or large company.

Joining a Small Company

Students generally think of large companies when they look for a job, but a small company can provide many of the same advantages in terms of salary, insurance, pensions and other benefits. However, the pay scales may not go as high as those in larger companies.

A major advantage of joining a smaller company is that you feel nearer to the top because there are fewer levels of management. People also have a stronger sense of identity with the company because they have a better idea of the problems facing the firm as well as its successes.

Working in a small firm will probably give you more direct exposure to solving business problems and give you broader experience in a variety of fields. This is in contrast to a large company, where you are in a particular department, such as accounting or marketing, but interact little with other departments and get little chance to learn.

Another advantage of being in a smaller company is that there are fewer rules and restrictions, and fewer reports to make to superiors. Nevertheless, some rules and regulations must exist even in a small company.

Finally, a small company will not hire as many graduates; therefore, there will be less competition for the available jobs and for future promotion. On the other hand, there will also be fewer opportunities for promotions.

Joining a Large Company

Working for a large company has many advantages, including higher salary and benefits and more opportunities for promotion. Larger firms can also provide more job security than smaller ones, and can usually weather much more severe recessions without laying off employees. Another advantage is the ability to transfer to other departments and acquire experience in advertising, marketing, sales, production and so on. A job is more interesting when one can move from one department to another and learn new ways of doing things, or take advantage of training and development programs to further one's learning. Large companies also often provide their employees with free goods and services, discounts, specials, promotions, trips and so on, perks that smaller companies cannot provide. Last, but not least, there is generally more prestige attached to working for a large, well-known company.

There are also disadvantages, however. The size of the company makes it easy to get lost and forgotten among the hundreds, sometimes thousands, of employees. Climbing the corporate ladder may seem like a hopeless task. The feeling of insignificance one gets from making seemingly small decisions can be disheartening. Another potential source of frustration are the many rules and policies that must be followed.

Finally, large companies may require frequent moves around the country. Transfers may indicate a path to promotion, but the upheaval that accompanies them can be a source of stress.

Choosing a Career

In choosing a career, you must pay particular attention to yourself. What are your likes and dislikes? You must make sure that you match your aptitudes and skills with your interests; otherwise you will struggle in your job and not do well.

You should pick a company, large or small, where you can learn. This provides satisfaction and interest, and prevents you from becoming stale and set in your ways. You will also be ready either for new job opportunities when they come along or to establish your own business.

Having a good boss is another important factor, particularly to individuals who are new to the work world. A boss who is a good manager can teach you good management skills. He or she should be willing to help you become a good manager

Next Steps

www.nextsteps.org

and should take pride in seeing you develop. Guard against those who are incompetent, selfish and uninterested in their subordinates. Usually these individuals are interested only in furthering themselves by exploiting their subordinates, and will deny them the recognition to which they are entitled.

Finally, make sure you are in a career that is rewarding and gives you a feeling of accomplishment. If the paycheque is the only reward you get out of your job, it is time to look for something else.

Knowing What You Want to Do

How often do people graduate from a course of study or a program having little idea of what they really want to do? They wander aimlessly through college and university recruiting centres, hoping to get a job—any job.

Many graduates do find a job and eventually most settle into something that they like. However, finding a suitable job is so much easier if a few logical steps are followed and if the job seeker does some planning.

First, and perhaps most important, is to find out what you would like to do. What are your interests? If you want to excel at something, you have to be keenly interested in it. Unfortunately, what we would really like to do is often not immediately available to us, but if it is business-oriented, then perhaps through hard work we can eventually achieve it.

You should also look ahead to the future, perhaps 15 years down the road. How would you like to live at that time? What do you want to do then? What are some of the personal values that you hold? Perhaps most important of all, what do you really think you can accomplish?

Even if you have to accept a job that is not exactly in your field of interest, you can always look upon it as a learning experience. Make a change at a later time if you so desire, when you have gained some experience.

New graduates with very little work experience may discover that finding a job related to their area of study is a challenge

Finding Your Job: Beginning a Career Plan

As a graduate, especially one with very little work experience, finding work in a job related to your area of study is a challenge. There are a few things to remember.

First, as a new graduate, your job search should start when you begin the course of study. Perhaps now is the time to do so if you are reading this text for a course in your first year. Once you complete your program, the emphasis changes to self-assessment and the development of job leads.

Another thing to remember is that job search skills are not an innate talent. They are a combination of interpersonal and organizational skills that require a great deal of effort to develop.

The **job search process** shown in Figure 15.2 is a systematic method of finding a job. If this process is to be an effective tool, you should constantly update the various elements in it. Although you can deviate from this process if you wish, you will make very little progress unless you understand and are willing to work at all of the elements of your search. The skills that a job search requires should become integrated with your career, the process being part of career planning.

The Job Search Process

Figure 15.2 shows the job search process and its five major sections:

1. Pre-job search preparation

2. Developing job leads

3. Job search management

4. Interview management

5. Job maintenance

We will briefly discuss each of the sections to give you some idea of the process involved in getting a job.

1. Pre-Job Search Preparation

Few graduates can expect to have the perfect job waiting for them when they graduate. In most instances, it takes planning and considerable effort to contact potential employers. The following should be completed as part of the pre-job search preparation.

Self-Assessment This first step is to develop an indicator to show your potential employer what personal qualities you possess. As a recent graduate, you lack experience, but a potential employer knows that. You can overcome that deficiency by showing that you are positive in your outlook and have lots of energy and drive. That is how you will gain experience quickly and that is what your potential employer wants to see. Some positive action words are shown in Table 15.1 that you can use in your dealings with potential employers. Put them into your letters or into your résumé.

Skills Inventory During your time in school and the workplace you have developed many personal skills that could be real advantages to an employer. You should compile a list of these skills and select those that you want to highlight in a résumé or letter of employment. Table 15.2 provides a list of personal skills. Look through it and choose the ones that you think you have acquired.

CareerMosaic Canada

canada.careermosaic.com/

Job search process— a systematic method of finding a job.

15.2

Employment flow chart

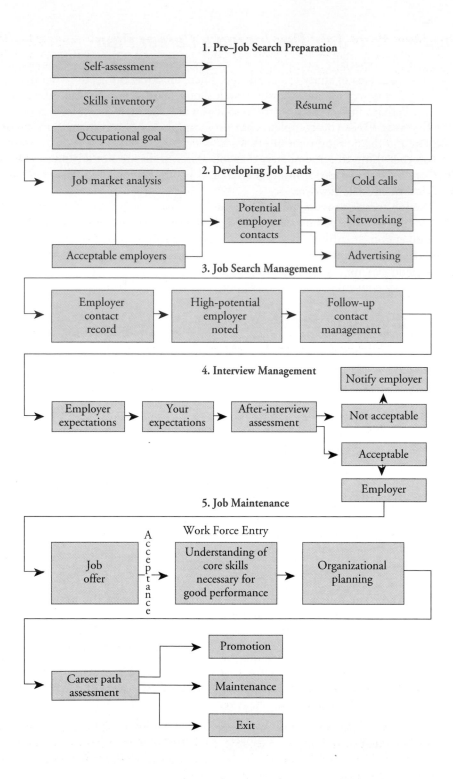

Occupational Goal It is difficult for a graduate to know what job to apply for. To find rewarding employment in your area of interest requires matching your skills and interests with the job titles used by employers for whom you would like to work. List those titles based on the information you have gained from potential employers and other sources.

The Résumé After completing the above steps, you should have enough information to put together one of your most valuable tools—your résumé. If you have a number of diverse occupational goals, you may need more than one résumé. Keep in mind, however, that you have time constraints. It may be impossible at this stage to conduct an effective multidirectional job search.

Figure 15.3 shows a sample, chronological résumé. This type of résumé is the one preferred by businesses employing recent graduates. There is a large degree of flexibility with this format, but keep in mind the following considerations in order to avoid giving an incorrect impression of yourself.

1. *Title page.* Optional; however, if you feel it provides the proper tone for your résumé, use it.

2. *Career objectives.* This is also optional but suggested for most résumés as it shows the potential employer that the applicant has thought through his or her goals and has matched them with the needs of the employer.

3. *Personal information.* This section follows career objectives and should provide the reader with basic personal information, such as your address.

4. *Education and knowledge.* Besides giving a history of your educational background, this section allows you to emphasize the relevant items from your skills inventory, experience and knowledge. This section is the place to pull it all together, especially as a lead-in to your employment history, if you have one.

5. *Employment history.* This section indicates where you have previously worked and acquired your listed skills. You should list and describe the most current job first and work backward. If you have not had any full-time jobs, list any part-time jobs you have had and their accompanying responsibilities.

6. *Scholarships and awards.* As a student, this is very important. If you have achieved anything that might set you apart as a high-quality student, the reader must know the details and when these achievements occurred.

7. *Affiliation.* Are you, or have you been, a member of any club, group or association? Any potential employer views this as an indication of the level of professionalism and commitment he or she can expect from the applicant.

8. *References.* Do not list them. Say that they are available on request and then have them ready for the interview. This allows you to select the references most appropriate for the potential employer.

9. *Introductory letter.* This letter must mention your present job or area of activity, field of interest, training and experience, knowledge of the company and the job desired. It should also emphasize that you are available for an interview with the employer and mention the attached resume.

Your résumé must make a good first impression on the person reading it. It must be well set up on the page, and your grammar and spelling must be impeccable. Read your résumé as if you were the employer. If you don't like what you see, change it until you are satisfied.

Using a word processor to develop a résumé is standard practice today. A word processor allows you to edit your résumé easily. If you want to make changes later, you can store the resume on disk and recall it when you need it. Similarly, you can store any letters you have written to various potential employers and recall them to alter the content as required for each application.

TABLE 15.1   **List of active words**

Competent	Profitable	Managed
Successful	Positive	Directed
Capable	Complete	Supervised
Resourceful	Investigated	Initiated
Qualified	Designed	Created
Versatile	Developed	Organized
Proficient	Maintained	Trained
Efficient	Built	Worked
Knowledgeable	Established	Led
Consistent	Communicated	Coordinated
Experienced	Processed	Analyzed
Productive	Participated	Improved
Effective	Sold	Repaired
Stable	Engineered	Employed
Well educated	Implemented	Expanded
Wide background	Controlled	Achieved
Equipped	Guided	Specialized
Accomplished	Administered	

TABLE 15.2   **List of personal skills**

Administering programs	Interviewing people
Advising people	Inventing new ideas
Analyzing data	Listening to others
Arranging social functions	Locating missing information
Assembling apparatus	Managing an organization
Auditing financial statements	Mediating between people
Budgeting expenses	Meeting the public
Calculating numerical data	Monitoring progress of others
Checking for accuracy	Motivating others
Classifying records	Negotiating contracts
Coaching individuals	Operating equipment
Collecting money	Organizing people and tasks
Compiling statistics	Persuading others
Confronting other people	Planning agendas
Constructing buildings	Planning organizational needs
Coordinating events	Preparing materials
Corresponding with others	Printing by hand
Counselling people	Problem solving
Creating new ideas	Programming computers

\>\>

Deciding uses of money	Promoting events
Delegating responsibility	Protecting property
Designing data systems	Raising funds
Dispensing information	Reading volumes of material
Displaying artistic ideas	Recording scientific data
Distributing products	Rehabilitating people
Dramatizing ideas or problems	Repairing mechanical devices
Editing publications	Reviewing programs
Enduring long hours	Running meetings
Entertaining people	Selling products
Estimating physical space	Serving individuals
Evaluating programs	Setting up demonstrations
Exhibiting plans	Sketching charts or diagrams
Finding information	Speaking in public
Handling complaints	Supervising others
Handling detailed work	Teaching classes
Inspecting physical objects	Updating files
Interpreting languages	Writing clear reports

Career Objective

To work in a company's information-processing department and eventually manage the department. To further educate myself in computers and business data processing as required.

FIGURE 15.3

A sample résumé

Personal Information

Name:	Linda Chan
Address:	222 Rosebank Street
	Lakeland, Ontario
Telephone number:	555-8888

Education and Training

Academic:	Grade 12 Matriculation
	Campbell College
	2712 King Street
	Towers, Prince Edward Island
	Business Management with major in Data Processing
	Inland College
	Winnipeg, Manitoba

Job Experience

May 1995 to present	Programmer
	Developed a customer appointment schedule for NU-Software. Worked mostly on my own. Occasional demonstrations required for customers. Salary: $37 500/year
July 1994 to April 1995	dBase programmerI was engaged in programming for a smal electronics company that was computerizing the parking industry. specific task was to develop report formats for the industry. Salary: $31 000/year
July 1993 to June 1994	Sales clerk
	Computer retail store. Sales of hardware and software. I was responsible for customer service and inventory control. Salary: $23 900/year

Scholarships and Awards:	Government Grant/Scholarship for both years at college. Elizabeth Henning Memorial Scholarship
Affiliations:	Member, Inland College Alumni Association
Other Activities:	Tennis, Skiing, Music
References:	Academic and work references available on request.

The Tailored Résumé

Think of your résumé as the first impression your reader gets of you. Don't use coloured paper, fancy type, graphics, pictures or quotations. Instead, make sure that every word is spelled correctly, and that you are using good grammar and punctuation.

Remember your resume has to accomplish two things. First, you must convey your qualifications. List your educational achievements, mentioning the most recent diploma or degree first. Similarly, under the title Work Experience, start your list with the most recent employer and then go backward in your employment history. As a student you may have limited job experience, so list any other community work or extracurricular activities.

Remember that such information as sex, race, disability and age is no longer required on a résumé. However, you may want to identify yourself as a member of a group (e.g., women, aboriginal peoples, the disabled, or some other minority), since complying with employment equity programs is of particular importance to some large employers and governments. When applying to smaller companies this may not be important.

Second, a résumé and covering letter should be *tailored to the job*. For example, if you are interested in a sales job, emphasize the marketing courses taken and grades received. List the additional training taken and the specific experience you have in that field. As a university graduate you may want to include letters of recommendation from a marketing professor and summer employer. In your covering letter, convey your interest in marketing and sales. Stress that you are interested in any entry-level job that would ultimately lead to the particular position you are interested in as a future career.

By tailoring your résumé you are not misrepresenting your qualifications. You are simply highlighting skills, aptitudes, interests, academic achievements and work experiences that you believe are important for the advertised job. Remember that you must stand out to the person looking through the résumés, who has no other information about you.

Résumé Checklist

1. *Have you described your major accomplishments in each position?* Instead of listing the responsibilities you were given, indicate what you have actually accomplished. For example, instead of saying, "Managed sales department of eight and was given profit and loss responsibility for overall department. Met all budgets," say "Led sales staff to five successive years of continuous sales growth. Developed new systems that improved department's profitability by $125 000 per year."

2. *Did you use action words when you described your accomplishments and work experience?* Some words convey an achievement-oriented attitude: Achieved, Coordinated, Directed, Introduced, Launched, Led, Produced, Sold. Start your sentences with these types of words. Use sparingly words such as Managed, Trained, Supervised, Oversaw and Performed. Although they give the impression that you are probably efficient, they do not imply great ambition. Words such as Liaised, Monitored, Researched should be avoided at all times. They tend to convey to the reader that you are not a go-getter, but instead tend toward too much deliberation and discussion.

3. *Did you show a steady progression in the amount of responsibility you were given in each position and the achievements you were able to accomplish in each job?* Instead of listing a steady stream of achievements in one area, use different positions to highlight accomplishments in different areas.

4. *Did you relate the information from your educational background to your work experience?* You must try to show that your education was a stepping stone to later career advancement. Indicate along with your degree or diploma any special studies you undertook.

5. *Did you include some of your personal interests?* A few short sentences describing your favourite sports, activities and hobbies will break the ice with your interviewer.

2. Developing Job Leads

You may have heard about the hidden job market. It simply means that about 80% of the jobs available are not advertised. You must go and find them. To do so, you must approach the job search systematically.

Job Market Analysis First you must decide what industries you want to work in, to ensure that you have not left a good potential job market out of your area of search.

Decision on Acceptable Employers Once you have decided on the industry, you must decide on the employers for whom you would like to work. This is also known as targeting. Out of the thousands of possible employers you can only talk to a few. Do not waste your time on mass mailouts. Use your time wisely. Research whom you want to work for and then put them on your contact list.

Making Contacts Now you are ready to take action. First, you should use all the personal contacts you have, an activity known as "networking." You may find them surprisingly willing to help. Second, do some "cold calls"—telephone contacts initiated by you. They are useful, though they require more research and time on your part in order to reach the person responsible for hiring you. Third, look at job advertisements. While these employers may ask for experience you do not have at the moment, they can be a source of employment later or may be able to refer you to other potential employers.

3. Job Search Management

Keep track of all the information you gather about employers. This allows you to compare information about employers and follow up on promising ones.

Employer Contact Record As soon as you finish a conversation, make notes of names and details of employment possibilities. This information is of critical importance to you.

High-Potential Employers While continuing to make new contacts, separate employers that promise a high probability of employment from those that do not.

Follow-up Contact Management As your job search matures, you should spend more and more time talking to those potential employers who show an interest in you, have a job you are interested in and, most important, have a reasonable opportunity for vacancy. Establish a mutually agreeable time and date for your next contact and follow through. This is an excellent way to demonstrate your organizational skills and motivation to the potential employer.

4. Interview Management

When you sit down with an employer, be organized: know the job and the company background, and be prepared to ask some questions. Be sure you understand the following:

Employer Expectations Whom does the employer see as the ideal person for the job?

Your Expectations Did the employer's statements about the job match what you expected to hear?

Post-interview Assessment Prepare a balance sheet of the positive and negative aspects of the job. You must decide whether you will accept the job should you receive an offer. If the position is not acceptable, notify the employer. There may be a job in the future, and, as a budding professional, you must demonstrate your skills to everyone with whom you come in contact. If the position is acceptable, notify the employer of your impressions of the position and thank him or her for the interview. How you conduct your post-interview follow-up can influence whether the interviewer will hire you.

5. Job Maintenance

Job maintenance is an ongoing activity once you are employed. Success on the job provides the basis for future promotion, either within the company or with another employer. If you are a recent graduate, your first job is critically important in that it allows you to demonstrate your skills and abilities. Job maintenance involves the following:

Understanding of Core Skills As your time on the job increases, you will develop a better understanding of the skills required to be successful in that particular job and in the company as a whole.

Organization and Planning How are you going to succeed and advance? Act on the knowledge you have of your job. If further study is needed, enroll in the necessary courses. If other direct knowledge of the company is needed, explore all means by

Tips on Interview Dress and Behaviour

If times are tough, then the prospects for an interview are as tough as shoe leather. In today's job market, interviews occur with the same frequency as job offers in better times.

Getting your foot in the door is a Herculean effort of countless career ads scrutinized and resumes sent. Then the telephone rings, and an interview is arranged, with its finality of reward or rejection.

Your best behaviour, best business clothes and best grooming are always recommended in an interview.

"Job seekers definitely need some help in physical presentation," says Michael Kordyback, Senior Vice-President of Strategy and Finance for Scott's Hospitality Inc., a diversified company with holdings in transportation, photography, hotels and restaurants. For Kordyback, there are still too many polyester shirts and sagging ankle socks around.

The key to physical presentation in an interview is conformity. This ensures that viewers are not distracted by the wearer's clothes or body.

For a man, a good physical impression is achieved with a well-pressed dark suit, white cotton shirt, subdued tie and polished shoes. A woman may wear any well-pressed, conservative skirt-and-jacket ensemble or dress.

For both sexes, leading edge haircuts or styles, unmanicured hands, an abundance of jewellery and strong cologne are inappropriate.

When the interviewer ushers you into the interview room, wait to be directed to a seat. Lower yourself gracefully into the chair—don't collapse into it. Keep your back straight and your arms still and relaxed throughout the interview.

Do not feel compelled to initiate the conversation. It is not your responsibility.

Many interviewers will present an agenda for the interview. This might be explained as beginning with a short overview by the interviewer of the job and company, followed by a discussion of your background and, finally, a more detailed exchange of information about the job. Also explained may be the interview stages after the first meeting.

If an agenda is presented, follow it. For example, do not break into the interviewer's overview with a comment about your background. Listen.

Do not take notes during the interview, since it is not conducive to rapport-building and can be interpreted as a sign of interpersonal weakness. If you are offered an annual report, tell the interviewer that you have already read it (if you did—which you should have), or thank the interviewer, say you'll read it in depth tonight and put it to one side.

If the hiring officer gives you a written job description during the interview, take a minute to read it carefully, and then refer to it as little as possible thereafter. Your attention should be focused on the interviewer.

Look at the hiring officer when you talk, and show your personality. Humour, enthusiasm, seriousness, concern and understanding are all appropriate emotions, as long as they are expressed in the proper context.

Work to create a balance in the conversation. At one end of the spectrum is a one-sided interrogation >>

of the job seeker; at the other is a one-sided interrogation of the interviewer. Neither results in a job offer.

If you find yourself talking, make sure you end with a question to the hiring officer. Seek information, get involved in what the officer is talking about, and a conversation will flow spontaneously.

Ask questions about the interviewer's background, tenure with the company, why he or she chose to work with this company. People like to talk about themselves, especially to someone who is interested.

Honesty and diplomacy are key tools of job seekers. If there is a problematic component in your job history, describe and explain it fully. Admit to mistakes grace

fully. You cannot change the past, but you have learned from it.

Be diplomatic about any wrongs suffered at the hands of previous employers. Interviewers can read between the lines without the help of an injustice clearly and aggrievedly spelled out.

In the experience of Andrew T Gratton, Director of Employment and Employee Relations with Sun Life Assurance Co. of Canada, many applicants try to cover up or quickly pass over a negative component of their career history.

"Termination is not viewed as a negative any more," Gratton says. "Employers recognize that a person can be a star in one organization and a bomb in another."

SOURCE: Katherine Gay, *The Financial Post* (June 29, 1992): 34.

---

which you might gain that knowledge.

Career Path Assessment Ultimately, you must decide whether you wish to remain in your present job or change careers. To avoid any negative experience on the job, ask yourself what your priorities are. Do not be surprised if your priorities have changed—if they have, it is up to you to adapt to the change.

Finding Your Job on the Internet

Many companies today advertise job postings on the internet either through their own home pages or using internet recruitment firms. For an example of job postings on a company home page try any major company you can think of and check out their home page. There is a very good chance the company will provide a link to employment opportunities. See www.telus.com or www.aircanada.com for examples.

Internet recruitment sites

www.monster.com
www.workopolis.com
www.careerpath.com

Chapter Summary

1. Forecasting and planning for the future is a major task of management, one that ensures the organization's achievement of its goals and objectives, even its survival. Accelerating changes in virtually all aspects of society, together with rapid technological development, make forecasting difficult. Nevertheless, business is sure to be affected by certain societal trends, including changes in population, age structure, lifestyle, economics and technology.

2. Changes will certainly continue to occur in the relationships between business and government, labour and society. The manager of the future will need to be highly educated, skilled in communication and willing to adapt to new situations

in order to effectively manage an organization subject to numerous outside pressures.

3. Choosing a business career is difficult. One of the most important tasks for potential business graduates is to determine their aptitudes and skills and match these with their interests. Opportunities for graduates exist in both large and small companies, although each has advantages and disadvantages. Starting one's own business is also an alternative. To ensure that the business will be successful, the graduate must obtain the business knowledge and management experience, which is best done by working for a number of years in one or more small or large firms.

4. To find that first job, a graduate should follow the job search process, which consists of five steps: pre-job search preparation, developing job leads, job search management, interview management and job maintenance. Students should begin the job search process when they begin their course of study, rather than wait until graduation. This will allow them to acquire a considerable amount of knowledge about various companies, and determine their own aptitudes and interests as they are progressing through their course of study. When the time comes to begin the actual job search, the graduate can concentrate on getting the right job with the right employer.

KEY TERMS

Demography .562   Lifestyle research 566   Job search process 575
Lifestyle 564

REVIEW QUESTIONS

1 What do we mean by "forecasting the future"?

2 Why is the world changing much more rapidly as time goes on?

3 What are the five major methods of predicting the future? Why should we not rely on only one method?

4 Why is lifestyle research becoming an important tool for business?

5 How will some of the changes in lifestyle affect business?

6 What will be the impact on business of anticipated population changes? Of changes in the age structure?

7 What is a key advantage of joining a small company? A large company?

8 Why should students begin the job search process when they first begin a program of study rather than wait until they graduate?

9 Briefly describe the key elements of the job search process.

10 Why is a résumé of critical importance? What are some key aspects of a good résumé?

DISCUSSION QUESTIONS

1 How will technological changes in computers and communications affect individuals? What are some of the business opportunities that may arise as a result of these changes?

2 How will private business be affected by a continued increase in expenditures by the public sector?

3 Write a scenario describing your view of Canada in the year 2030.

4 What major technological advances do you anticipate over the coming decades? How may they affect business and individuals?

5 How will the aging population present new benefits for business?

6 How may technological changes affect the jobs and careers of business graduates?

The Aging Nation

During the 1990s, many of the baby-boom generation—the group of people born between 1947 and 1966—have reached middle age. During this time, many have entered the senior ranks of business, government and other institutions. By 2011, the first baby boomers will become seniors, and by 2021 one out of every five Canadians will be 65 years of age and over.

The article in this chapter ("Demographics: How Does It Rate as a Forecasting Tool?") discussed the effect of the baby-boom generation on Canada's social and economic situation in the 1990s and beyond. Figure 15.1 superimposed the projected population in the year 2000 over the population in 1990 and indicated how the baby boomers will affect certain economic and social factors as they move through the age cycle. In contrast, the group of people born each year after 1966 is much smaller in numbers and will not face the same kinds of problems as they age.

Questions

1 With reference to the above-mentioned factors, discuss the pros and cons of retaining mandatory retirement.

2 Which industries might be most affected by the baby-boom population in the first decade of the 21st century?

3 What challenges might an aging population pose to Canada's social and economic institutions?

Making an Impact in Your First Job

Bryan acquired his first office job—analyzing purchase requisitions and developing procedures for capital acquisition—with a branch of the provincial government. He enjoyed his work and was anxious to do well. However, after only two months on the job he could not figure out why some members of the staff were exhibiting animosity toward him.

Because this office did not involve customer/client interaction, Bryan preferred to dress casually, even though his colleagues and supervisors wore business suits and ties. He took extended coffee breaks and lunch hours in order to interact with others in the office. He frequently spent considerable time on the phone with his girlfriend, who lived in another city. Bryan knew that these phone calls did not cost the office any additional expense because of the established telephone system in this branch of the government.

Bryan's work station was in an open area occupied by a number of other entry-level analysts, who sometimes found it difficult to concentrate on their work due to employee traffic through the area. In an attempt to reduce the through-traffic, Bryan, with the support of his supervisor, Mr. Azin, sent everyone in the office an electronic memo asking that employees not take the direct route past his desk to access a much-used filing cabinet.

The following day at a staff meeting, the branch director, Mr. Willingdon, made a derogatory comment (directed at Bryan) about traffic-flow instructions being sent around the office without his approval. The branch director had not discussed this issue with either Bryan or his supervisor prior to the staff meeting, and did not formally raise the issue as an agenda item.

Another supervisor, Ms. MacLeod (Mr. Azin's peer) told Bryan that he should in future approach her whenever such issues arose. She gave no explanation for her comment, and there was no indication of a change in reporting procedure for Bryan.

Some research into this government branch reveals that although Mr. Azin and Ms. MacLeod operate at the same level and report directly to Mr. Willingdon, Ms. MacLeod occupies a large office and has access to many of the resources she requests, while Mr. Azin shares office space with three other employees who report to another of his peers. Mr. Azin has advised the union of these inequities by lodging a formal complaint.

SOURCE: Written by Sandra Enns, Justice Institute of B.C. Reprinted by permission of the author.

Questions

1 What activities/events might have contributed to the attitude of staff members toward Bryan?

2 What can Bryan do to improve his image at the office in the short term? What can he do in the long term?

3 If you were the supervisor, how would you deal with this situation? How would you handle it if you were the branch director?

COMPREHENSIVE CASE 15-3

SOMERSET OPTICAL

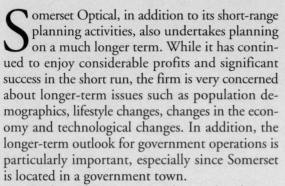

Somerset Optical, in addition to its short-range planning activities, also undertakes planning on a much longer term. While it has continued to enjoy considerable profits and significant success in the short run, the firm is very concerned about longer-term issues such as population demographics, lifestyle changes, changes in the economy and technological changes. In addition, the longer-term outlook for government operations is particularly important, especially since Somerset is located in a government town.

Fowler and Dewar are predicting that the eyewear industry should experience considerable growth in the long term as the aging baby boomers continue to need optical aids. In addition, it is expected that lifestyles will "slow down" and thus open the door for more intellectual pursuits. Somerset is predicting that new markets may become available for optically corrected computer screens as technology facilitates computer-based home banking, home education and home shopping.

On the other hand, technological advances in medicine could shut down the eyewear industry. If optical problems could be surgically corrected-permanently-the need for corrective lenses and eyewear would be eliminated.

Fowler and Dewar are nevertheless optimistic about the long-term prospects for the eyewear industry. In Dewar's words, "Business is about change. It is nothing more than an ongoing economic evolution. New technologies arrive that address old problems, but there are always new challenges on every horizon. As a company, we must focus on managing change in order to achieve a sustainable competitive advantage."

SOURCE: By David H. Jones-Delcourt. Reprinted by permission of the author.

Questions

1 Prepare an assessment of strengths, weaknesses, opportunities and threats for the eyewear industry in the future.

2 Do you agree with Dewar's view of business operations?

3 What other changes might technology necessitate in the eyewear industry?

VIDEO CASE—PART 5

CBC ⊛

NORTEL VS CISCO; EMG

In Part Five, we look at two videos. In the first segment, the heads of Nortel and Cisco discuss the future of their companies and how they stack up against each other. Both are vying for the position of primary player in the electronic transmission of data across networks.

In the second video segment, EMG, a government-supported entrepreneurial helper organization, is spotlighted. Here, entrepreneurs with sound ideas can learn about business management and receive help in raising money for manufacturing their products right on the premises. Individuals are thoroughly screened for suitability to entrepreneurship. But even with expert help, some don't make it.

SOURCE: Based on "Nortel vs Cisco," (January 1, 2000) "EMG," (January 28, 1990), *Venture* 733.

Questions

1 You are an engineer who could either work for Nortel or Cisco, or start your own business. What would you choose to do? Why?

2 By now, you should have a reasonable idea as to what it takes to be an entrepreneur. Do you think you would want to go into business for yourself? Why or why not? Do you have the qualities and perseverance that are required to be an entrepreneur?

Notes

Chapter 1: The Canadian Business System

1. "Calcutta: India's maligned metropolis," *National Geographic*, Vol. 143, No. 4 (April 1973): 534. See also "And if Mexico City seems bad…," *Time* (August 6, 1984): 26.
2. Robert L. Heilbroner, *The Making of Economic Society*, 6th ed. (Englewood Cliffs, N.J.: Prentice-Hall, 1980), chapters 3–4.
3. Ibid., p. 87.
4. D.G.Creighton, "The economic objectives of Confederation," in John J. Deutsch et al., eds., *The Canadian Economy: Selected Readings* (Toronto: MacMillan, 1962): 372-387.
5. "Report of the Royal Commission on Dominion–Provincial Relations" 1954, in ibid., pp. 420-24.
6. Lawrence LeDuc and J. Murray, "Survey finds public believes profits are excessive," *The Globe and Mail* (May 27, 1976): B4. Adapted from "World population, poor in abundance," *The Economist* (June 1, 1987): 51. Some statistics and figures have been updated for the seventh edition.

Chapter 2: Starting and Operating a Small Business

1. Industry Canada, *Small Business Quarterly*, Vol.1, No.1 (1999): 2–4.
2. Industry Canada, *Small Business Quarterly*, Winter(1999): 1-2.
3. Industry Canada, Small Business Quarterly, Vol. 1, No. 1 (1999): 5–6.
4. J. Watson and J. Everett, "Small business failure rates: Choice of definition and industry effects," *Journal of Small Business Management*, Vol. 34 No. 4 (October 1996): 45–62.
5. R. Lussier, "A startup business success versus failure prediction model for the retail industry," *The Mid-Atlantic Journal of Business*, Vol. 33, No. 1 (January 1995): 8–17
6. R. Lussier, "A nonfinancial business success versus failure prediction model for young firms," *Journal of Small Business Management*, Vol.33, No.1(January 1995): 8–17
7. S. Schiffman, "Venture capital is flowing to small business and still so many fail," *The American Salesman*, Vol.43, No. 12 (December 1998): 3–5
8. John Stanworth et al., "Franchise versus conventional small business failure rates in the U.S. and U.K.: More similarities than differences," *International Small Business Journal*, Vol. 16, No. 3 (April-June 1998): 56–69
9. Colin Languedoc, "Mismanagement main cause of failed fledgling ventures," *The Financial Post* (May 25, 1987): 18.
10. Op. cit.
11. G. Fenwick et al., "The determinants of franchisee performance: An empirical investigation", *International Small Business Journal*, Vol. 16, No. 4 (July-September 1998): 28–45

Chapter 3: Forms of Business Ownership

1. Michelle Gahagan, "Partnership agreement a definite must," *Vancouver Sun* (January 11, 1996): E3.
2. "Should you think Inc.," *The Financial Post Money Magazine* (December 1987): 57.
3. Rod McQueen, "The new world of corporate governance," *The Financial Post* (November 20,1993): S14; Rod McQueen, "Hard target," part two of a three-part series, *The Financial Post* (May 11, 1966): 6.
4. Amanda Lang, "Conglomerates dwindling," *The Financial Post* (November 23, 1996): 17.
5. Information from the Canadian Cooperative Association, http://coopcca.com.

Chapter 4: Management, Planning and Controlling

1. Robert L. Katz, "Skills of an effective administrator," *Harvard Business Review* (September-October 1974): 90–102.
2. T.A. Mahoney, T.H. Jerdee and S.J. Carroll, "The job(s) of management," *Industrial Relations*, Vol. 4 (February 1965): 97–110.
3. Henry Mintzberg, "The manager's job: folklore and fact," *Harvard Business Review* (July-August 1975): 46–61.
4. See Sumantra et al.," A new manifesto for management," *Sloan Management Review* (Spring 1999): 9–20.
5. See Robert Jamieson, "More than a railway," Financial Post 500 (Summer 1979): 80–89; Patrick Bloomfield, "New ethic pushing Canadian Pacific on track to profitability," Financial Post 500 (Summer 1988): 45; Canadian Pacific 1999 annual report. (http://www.cp.ca)
6. Source: Roy H. Blanchard, "How Wisconsin Central is practicing its mission statement," *Railway Age* (January 1999): 16–17.
7. N. Alperowicz, "Hickson moves into recovery mode," *Chemical Week*, Vol. 161, No. 15 (April 1999): 49–52.

Chapter 5: Organizing for Management

1. John R.P. French, Jr., and Bertram Raven, "The Bases of Social Power," in Darwin Cartwright and A.F. Zander, eds., *Group Dynamics: Research and Theory* (New York: Harper & Row, 1960).
2. Granville King III, "The implications of an organization's structure on whistleblowing," *Journal of Business Ethics*, Vol. 20, No. 4 (July 1999): 315–326.
3. C.M. Dickerson, "Virtual organizations: From dominance to

opportunism," *New Zealand Journal of Industrial Relations*, Vol. 23, No. 2 (June 1998): 35–46. See also J. Lipnack and J. Stamps, "Virtual teams: The new way to work," *Strategy and Leadership*, Vol. 27, No. 1 (January/February 1999): 14–19. See also P. Vice, "Going virtual," *Canadian Insurance*, Vol. 104, No. 2 (February 1999): 18–19.

4. P.M.J. Christie and R.R. Levary, "Virtual corporations: Recipe for success," *Industrial Management*, Vol. 40, No.4 (July/August 1998): 7–11.

Chapter 6: Managing People

1. Frederick W. Taylor, *The Principles of Scientific Management* (New York: Harper and Bros., 1916).
2. John Rowan, "Maslow amended," *The Journal of Humanistic Psychology*, Vol. 38, No.1 (Winter 1998): 81-92.
3. John Rowan, "Ascent and descent in Maslow's theory," *The Journal of Humanistic Psychology*, Vol. 39, No. 3(Summer 1999): 125–133.
4. Ron Zemke, "Maslow for a new millennium," *Training*, Vol. 35, No. 12 (December 1998): 54–58.
5. Frederick Herzberg, *Work and the Nature of Man* (Cleveland: World Publishing, 1966).
6. Douglas McGregor, *The Human Side of Enterprise* (New York: McGraw-Hill, 1960): 33–55.
7. Fred Patton, "Money talks when it comes to recognition," *Workforce*, Vol. 78, No. 5 (May 1999): 101-103.
8. Sally Trelford, "Choice rewards," *Marketing Week*, Vol. 22, No. 21 (June 24, 1999): 71-75.
9. See Chris Argyris, *Personality and Organization* (New York: Harper Brothers, 1957); *Interpersonal Competence and Organizational Effectiveness* (Homewood, Ill.. Dorsey Press, 1962); *Integrating the Individual and the Organization* (New York: John Wiley and Sons, Inc., 1964).
10. Robert Blake and Jane S. Mouton, *The Managerial Grid* (Houston. Gulf Publishing, 1964).
11. Robert Tannenbaum and Warren H. Schmidt, "How to choose a leadership pattern," *Harvard Business Review* (May-June 1973): 164.
12. Fred Fiedler, *A Theory of Leadership Effectiveness* (New York: McGraw-Hill, 1967).
13. See Robert J. House, "A path-goal theory of leadership effectiveness," *Administrative Science Quarterly*, Vol. 16, No. 5 (September 1971): 321-28.
14. Paul Hersey and Kenneth H. Blanchard, *Management and Organizational Behavior*, 3rd ed. (Englewood Cliffs, N.J.: Prentice-Hall, 1977): 165.
15. Peg Thoms and David Greenberger, " A test of vision training and potential antecedents to leaders' visioning ability", *Human Resource Development Quarterly*, Vol. 9, No. 1 (Spring 1998): 3–19.
16. Joey Goddings, "Study pins down leadership competencies," *Canadian HR Reporter* (September 6, 1999): 3.
17. William G. Ouchi, *Theory Z: How American Business Can Meet the Japanese Challenge* (Reading, Mass.: Addison-Wesley, 1981).
18. Wolfgang Lux, " Japanese management evolves again," *Management Review*, Vol. 86, No. 6 (June 1997): 36–39.
19. Max Messmer, "Improving your listening skills," *Strategic Finance*, Vol. 79, No. 9 (March 1998): 14–15.
20. Stephen Mulvany, "New you: Improving listening skills", *Journal of Property Management*, Vol. 63, No. 4 (July/August 1998): 20–21.
21. Paul Sanchez, "How to craft successful employee communication in the information age," *Communication World*, Vol. 16, No. 7 (August/September 1999): 9–15.
22. Kathy Byrd and Robert Gulbro, "E-mail and the organization of tomorrow," *Ivey Business Quarterly*, Vol. 63, No. 1 (Autumn 1998): 14–15.
23. Karen Escalera, "Pre-emptive ways to boost morale," *Nation's Business*, Vol. 86, No. 6 (June 1998): 12–13.
24. Josh Martin, "Building morale keeps employee spirits high in tough times," *HR Focus*, Vol. 76, No. 4 (April 1999): 9–10.
25. Marcia Stepanek, "How an intranet opened up the door to profit," *Business Week* (July 26, 1999): 32.
26. Paul Romani, "MBO by any other name is still MBO," *Supervision*, Vol. 58, No. 12 (December 1997): 6–8.

Chapter 7: Production and Operations Management

(No notes in Chapter 7)

Chapter 8: Marketing Management

1. AMA, Marketing Definitions (Chicago: American Marketing Association, 1960): 15.
2. G. Koprowski, "Marketers say 'information' has replaced brand loyalty," *Insight on the News*, Vol. 13, No. 47 (December 1997): 42–44.
3. B. Gralpois, "Fighting the illusion of brand loyalty," *Direct Marketing*, Vol. 61, No. 8 (December 1998). 62 65.
4. Ibid.
5. J. Masterton, "Autos running second in ad-spending race," *Mediaweek*, Vol. 9, No. 11 (March 15, 1999): 39.
6. K. Cottrill, "UPS's green packaging," *Traffic World*, Vol. 256, No. 10 (December 1998): 38.
7. J. Frock, "Disney tempts web visitors to buy," *Internetweek*, Vol. 707 (March 23, 1998): 19.
8. J. Brody, T. Burgess, and J.T. Horner, "In Net Advertising, the Customer is Still King," *Business Week*, No. 3606 (November 30, 1998): 10.
9. J. Cohen, "Internet gains strength as a marketing medium," *Retail Delivery News*, Vol.4, No. 22: 1.
10. G. Anthes, "Future.com," *Computerworld*, Vol. 33, No. 19 (May 10, 1999): 80–82.
11. A. Rosespan, "A direct marketing odyssey," *Direct Marketing*, Vol. 62, No. 3 (July 1999): 52–55.
12. Statistics Canada, "Major releases, retail trade," *The Daily* (April 22, 1999), pp. 1-19, Internet version.
13. Statistics Canada, *Canadian Economic Observer* (Ottawa: January 1997), Cat. no. 11-101-XPB.
14. Statistics Canada, "Major releases, retail trade," *The Daily* (April 22, 1999), pp. 1-19, Internet version.

Chapter 9: Accounting and Financial Management

(No notes in Chapter 9)

Chapter 10: Human Resource Management

1. M. Richtel, "Need for computer experts is making recruiters frantic," *New York Times* (November 18,1999): 1.
2. C. Fyock, "Recruiting today's elusive job candidate," *HR Focus* (June 1999): 7.
3. M. Bigelow, "Recruitment online: Reinventing the process," *Ohio CPA Journal*, Vol. 58, No. 3 (July-September 1999): 30.
4. Royal Bank web site at www.royalbank.com/english/hr/ee/index.html
5. Deborah Stokes, "Employers take defensive approach to hiring," *The Financial Post* (February 15, 1996): 19.
6. See Milkovich, Glueck, Barth, and McShane, *Canadian Personnel/Human Resource Management: A Diagnostic Approach* (Business Publications, Inc., 1988) for a discussion of personnel/human relations management and detailed discussions of the various personnel functions. This book also lists references about the studies conducted on interviewing.
7. "Hopeful signs on job training," editorial, *The Financial Post* (February 11, 1991); "Job training key to being competitive," *The Financial Post* (November 21, 1990).
8. B. Leonard, "Study examines keys to recruiting, retention", *HR Magazine*, Vol.44, No. 9 (September 1999): 32.
9. D. Knoke and I. Yoshito, "The gender gap in company job training," *Work and Occupations*, Vol. 25, No. 2 (May 1998): 141–167.
10. Ibid.
11. Madelaine Drohan, "CLC says business should fund training," *The Financial Post* (January 25, 1988): 5.
12. Shona McKay, "Getting even," *Canadian Business* (May 1988): 48–54.
13. Information obtained at web site of McCarthy Tetrault www.mccarthy.ca/mt-payea.html
14. Randall Scotland, *The Financial Post* (October 14, 1995): 19.
15. B. Jeffrey and G. Jelf, "The effects of gainsharing on grievance rates and absenteeism over time," *Journal of Labor Research*, Vol. 20, No. 1 (Winter 1999): 133–145.
16. Tessa Wilmot, "Crash sparks review of employee share plans," *The Financial Post* (November 9, 1987): 32.
17. Mark Witten, "Employees can be partners too," *Canadian Business* (November 1979): 86.
18. Nadine Winter, "Consultation is key in making incentive plans work," *The Financial Post* (July 19, 1995): 11.
19. Bill Davidson, "Silver lining to high cost of having employees," *Vancouver Sun* (January 20, 1997): D2.
20. Anonymous, "Asbestos illness skyrocket in plant workers," *OH & S Canada*, Vol. 14, No. 7 (December 1998): 14.
21. Anonymous, "Quarter of a million asbestos deaths predicted in next 35 years," *The Safety & Health Practitioner*, Vol. 17, No. 3 (March 1999): 4.

Chapter 11: Business and Labour

1. See John Crispo, *The Canadian Industrial Relations System* (Toronto: McGraw-Hill Ryerson, 1978), 220–29.
2. See David A. Peach and David Kuechle, *The Practice of Industrial Relations* (Toronto: McGraw-Hill Ryerson, 1975): chapter 2. See also Eugene Forsey, "History of the Labour Movement in Canada," in John V. Deutsch et al., eds., *The Canadian Economy: Selected Readings* (Toronto: Macmillan of Canada, 1962), 106–19.
3. John DeMont, "CLC seeking peace with teamsters," *The Financial Post* (January 18, 1988): 3.
4. See Peach and Kuechle, *The Practice of Industrial Relations*, Chapter 3.
5. Crispo, *The Canadian Industrial Relations System*, 52–55.
6. Roy La Berge, "Work stoppages and the problems of conflict duration," *The Labour Gazette* (November-December 1978): 498–500.
7. "Canada and Italy head strike table," *International Labour Organization (ILO) News* (December 12, 1977).
8. Robert Gibbens and Laura Fowlie, "New era of labour peace dawns," *The Financial Post* (May 8, 1993): 3.
9. "A union boss on the board," *Maclean's* (May 16, 1983): 34.
10. Colin Languedoc, "Informed workers linked to success," *The Financial Post* (June 1988).
11. Ibid.
12. Woodruff Timberman, "Good credibility is good management," *The Financial Post* (June 27, 1985): 37.
13. The Labour Gazette (November-December 1978): 492–93. See also James Bagnall, "Tough new era faces public-sector unions," *The Financial Post* (October 19, 1987): 3.

Chapter 12: Business and Government

1. Hawley Black, *Easy Money: Your Guide to Government Giveaways* (Toronto: Macmillan of Canada, 1989): 14–19.
2. Industry Canada: A Partnership to Serve You Better (Ottawa: Minister of Supply and Services Canada, 1994), cat. no. C21–221/1994.
3. Giles Gherson, "Competition law discord: business lobbies Tories to back off on reforms," *The Financial Post* (June 15, 1985): 1.
4. Adapted from Robert J. Bertram, "What does business want: competition legislation or government regulation?" *Canadian Business Review* (Winter 1977): 45–48.
5. For an overview of the National Transportation Legislation, 1986, consult *Freedom to Move: The Legislation*, published by Transport Canada (#TP 7749). Transport Canada has also published a series of pamphlets that cover all aspects of the new act.
6. D.K. Jackson, "Trucking faces up to challenge of deregulation," *The Financial Post* (November 8, 1990).
7. Linda Gregg Stulberg, "New rules, economy create rocky road for trucking industry," *The Financial Post* (February 19, 1991): 18.
8. Robert Sheppard, "$4.6 billion later, privatization gets tough,"

The Globe and Mail (August 15, 1988): B1; Richard Blackwell, "Air Canada welcomes freer hand at throttle," *The Financial Post* (April 16–18, 1988): 1; Mathew Horsman, "Innovation marks province's privatization spree," *The Financial Post* (June 22, 1987): S4.

9. Martin Bermingham, "Privatization: unions balk at it due to self-interest," *Canadian HR Reporter* (May 2, 1988): 7.

10. Bruce Cohen, "Defining tax freedom not so easy," *The Financial Post* (June 12, 1993): 14; Gillian Livingston, "Tax freedom day comes one day later this year," *The Financial Post* (June 25, 1996).

11. "Canadian tax rises heftiest among G7," *Vancouver Sun* (November 21, 1993).

12. Robert L. Perry, *Treadmill to Ruin* (Toronto: Maclean-Hunter, 1977): 61.

13. Philip Mathias, "Deeper in debt," *The Financial Post* (September 14–16, 1991): 1, 4; Geoffrey Scotton, "Truckers travelling rough road despite Ontario help to industry," *The Financial Post* (June 5, 1993): S21.

14. Speech in the House of Commons by Joe Clark, Leader of the Opposition (February 2, 1977).

15. Ibid.

16. "Erase the paper burden and the result will be more jobs," *The Vancouver Sun* (January 31, 1997): 10.

17. Peter Worthington, "Let's revolt against too much government," *The Financial Post* (June 12, 1991).

Chapter 13: International Business

1. David J. Freiman, *The Marketing Path to Global Profits* (New York: AMACOM, a division of the American Management Association, 1979): 41–42.

2. Eric Reguly, "New rules a boost for Canada," *The Financial Post* (December 16, 1993): 10.

3. Ibid.

4. *The Financial Post* (December 3, 1990): 34.

5. Ibid.

6. John Daly, *Maclean's* (October 8, 1990): 48.

7. Richard Lipsey, "Four questions for free trade critics," *The Financial Post* (November 9, 1987): 18.

8. See website http://www.mexicanshowroom.com/industry/Paginas/canTrade.html

9. Ibid.

10. "Canada able to elude U.S. guns," *The Financial Post* (November 18, 1993): 9.

11. See the APEC website, *http://www.sccp.org/about/menu.htm*

12. "Pacific partners," *Vancouver Sun* (July 13, 1993): Section D.

13. Jill Vardy, "Provincial barriers under siege," *The Financial Post* (August 6, 1993); David Bond, "Interprovincial barriers cost $7 billion a year," *Vancouver Sun* (July 25, 1996): C2; Neville Nankivell, "Don't lose internal trade momentum," *The Financial Post* (March 28, 1996): 17.

14. Lawrence G. Tapp, "Europe 1992: Canadians get ready!" *Business Quarterly* (Summer 1990): 10–12. See also Andrew Phillips, "A single market dream," *Maclean's* (January 18, 1993): 50.

15. Andrew Coyne, "Other nations play free trade, and win," *The Financial Post* (October 12, 1987): 38.

16. Fred Lebolt, "Panic missing as companies see C$ rise eat away profit," *The Financial Post* (March 21, 1988): 4.

17. Aron Gampel, "Rx for an ailing dollar," *The Financial Post* (June 15, 2000): p. C19.

18. Statistics Canada, "Foreign control of Canadian corporations declines," INFOMAT (Ottawa: January 15, 1988), Cat. No. 11–002E. See also Statistics Canada, 1984, Ottawa: The Minister of Supply and Services, Cat. No. 67–202, pp. 31–5; A. E. Sofarian, "Some myths about foreign business investment," in David K. Banner, ed., *Business and Society: Canadian Issues* (Toronto: McGraw-Hill Ryerson, 1979): 286–90.

19. Banner, *Business and Society*, 261.

20. Sofarian, "Some myths about foreign business investment."

21. John Van der Feyst, "Exodus! The flight of Canadian capital," *Canadian Business* (December 1976).

Chapter 14: Social Responsibility and Business

1. P. Verburg, "Take a hike, Sheila," *Canadian Business*, Vol. 71, No. 12 (July 31, 1998): 16–18.

2. M. Brown, "A green piece of the action," *Management Today* (May 1997): 84–88.

3. L. Phillips, "Green attitude," *American Demographics*, Vol. 21, No. 4 (April 1999): 46–47.

4. M. Vincent and S. Fick, "Out of the trash, into the blue box," *Canadian Geographic*, Vol. 119, No. 4 (May/June 1999): 64–65.

5. Anonymous, "Analyzing what goes into a landfill," *BioCycle*, Vol. 40, No. 9 (September 1999): 8.

6. S.K. Kirschner, "Landfill of the future," *Popular Science*, Vol. 252, No. 6 (June 1998): 24.

7. Anonymous, "Conference eyes sustainable development," *Oil & Gas Journal*, Vol. 97, No. 37 (September 1999): 40.

8. A. Roddick, *Body and Soul*, p. 17.

9. Ibid., p. 15.

10. C. Hartman and C. Beck-Dudley, "Marketing strategies and the search for virtue: A case analysis of the Body Shop," *Journal of Business Ethics*, Vol. 20, No. 3 (July 1999): 249–263.

11. A. Roddick, *Body and Soul*, p. 250.

12. Daniel Stoffman, "The principles of profit," *Canadian Business* (May 1991): 28–32.

13. Ibid.

Chapter 15: Business, the Future and Your Career

1. Alvin Toffler, *Future Shock* (New York: Bantam, 1970), 13–14.

2. Dennis L. Meadows, *The Limits to Growth* (New York: Universe Books, 1972).

3. Steven Mosher, "UN used 'Baby Six Billion' in anti-baby crusade," *Human Events*, Vol. 55, No. 39 (October 22, 1999): p. 4.

4. Dawn Stover, "Six billion and counting," *Popular Science*, Vol. 255, No. 4 (October 1999): 39.

5. David Foot and Daniel Scoffman, *Boom, Bust and Echo* (Toronto: Macfarlane Walter & Ross, 1996), pp. 223–224.

6. Richard Blackwell, "Full automation getting nearer as more plants go on-line," *The Financial Post*, Special Quarterly Report (June 29, 1985). This report provides many examples of computerization in factories, and also indicates where Canada stands in the manufacture and use of robots.

7. David Foot and Daniel Scoffman, *Boom, Bust and Echo* (Toronto: Macfarlane Walter & Ross, 1996), p. 24.

8. Margaret Munro, *Vancouver Sun* (May 1, 1993): Section B.

9. Anonymous, "The city in the global village," *Organization for Economic Cooperation and Development, The OECD Observer* (Summer 1999): 33–35.

10. Marion S. Matathia, "Lifestyles of the next millenium: 65 forecasts," *The Futurist*, Vol. 32, No. 5 (June/July 1998): 51–56.

11. Ibid.

12. Wynn Quon, "The Internet implosion," *The Financial Post*, January 27, 2000.

13. Industry Canada, Strategis, "Internet service providers in Canada: an economic analysis," (July 23 1998), p. 14.

14. Retail Council of Canada, "The future of Canadian retailing and 1998 state of the industry report." (1999).

15. George S. Day, "Managing marketing relationships," *Academy of Marketing Science,* Vol. 28, No. 1 (Winter 2000): 24–30.

16. D. Quinn et al., "Emerging business realities," *Journal of Management Consulting,* Vol.10, No. 4 (November 1999): 39–45.

17. Michael Cox, and Michael Rock, *The Seven Pillars of Visionary Leadership* (Toronto: Harcourt Brace & Company, 1997), p. xviii.

Index

Note: Boldface page numbers indicate definitions

A

Ability to pay
  wages and salaries by business, 387
Absolute advantage
  in trade, **484**
Accessory equipment, 281
Accountability, 170
  in delegation, 169
Accountants, 323
Account executive, **294**
Accounting, 323
  financial, 322
  management, 323
  process, 323
  statements, 323-30
  statements, examples, 325
Accounting statements, 322-30
  comparative analysis, 336
Accounting system, 323
Acquisition
  corporate, **93**
Action plans, 117, **126**
Activity ratios, 332
administrative decisions
  see programmed decisions, 115
Adverse effect, 375
Adverse intent, 375
Advertising, **293**-6
  account executive, 294
  agencies, **294**
  deceptive, 537
  dollars spent on various media, 295
  geographic selectivity, 294
  magazine categories, 293
  media, **294**
    characteristics, 294
  point-of-purchase, 297
  qualitative selectivity, 294
  specialty, 297
Advertising agencies, 294
Agency shop, 424
Aggregate planning, 247
Agreement on Internal Trade (AIT), **502**
Agricultural development incentives, 444
All Canadian Congress of Labour, 412

American Federation of Labour, 412
Analytic production process, **229**
Application
  for employment, 377
Appraisal by results, 396
Apprenticeship program, **383**
Arbitration, **420**
Articles of incorporation, 85
Asia Pacific Economic Cooperation (APEC), **499**-501
  processes & objectives, 500
Assembly production process, **230**
Assembly line, **225**
Assets, 324
Atlantic Canada Opportunities Agency, 443
Auditing, **130**
  external, **130**
  internal, **130**
Authority
  centralization vs decentralization, 173
  defined, 164
  formal, 114
  functional, 167-8
  line, 165-7
  line and staff, 167
  staff, 167
  types, 165-8
Authority relationships
  establishing, 163
Authorized shares, 345
Automation, **226**
  in production, 262
Autopact, 498
Average collection period, 333

B

Balance of payments, **510**
  For Canada, 512
Balance sheets, 323, 324
  examples, 326
Balance of trade, 487, **509**
Bank of Canada, **464**, 467, 474

effect on economy, 468
  services, 466
  web site, 469
Bank loans
  demand, 320
  line of credit, 320
  secured, 319
  unsecured, 321
Bank rate, **467**, 468
Bankruptcy, 329
  commercial, 77
Bargaining in good faith, **417**
Bargaining unit, **417**
Barriers to trade, 488-91
BC Tel, 454
Bearer bond, **343**
Bell Canada, 454
Bell Canada Enterprises, 95
Big box stores, 304
Bill of materials, **249**
Black Thursday, 17
Blanchard, Kenneth, 200
Board of directors, **89**
Bona-fide occupational qualifications, 375
Bonds, **343**
  bearer/registered, 343
  calling/converting, 345
  certificate, example of, 344
  comparing to stocks, 343
  interest, 343
  interest rate setting, 345
  maturity date of, 343
  principal, 343
Bonus, **388**
Bonus plans, 388
Bookkeeping, 323
Boycott
  primary, secondary, **423**
Brand, **286**
Branding, 286-7
Break-even analysis, **130**, 290, 340-2
Break-even analysis pricing, **290**
Break-even chart, 342
Budget, **123**, 128, 336
  capital, 338
  cash, 339
  direct labour, 338
  factory overhead, 338
  forecast, 336
  manufacturing, 338

operating expenditures, 338
  raw materials, 338
Budgetary control, 129-30
Budgeting
  benefits to organization, 340
  process, 336
  process, steps in, 337
  use of computer for, 135
Bureau of Consumer Affairs, 538
Business, **10**
  community, and, 538
  cycles, **10**
  employees, and responsibility, 536
  importance for study, 29-30
  social responsibility, 533-5
  Starting a business, 572
Business Development Bank (BDB) 446-7
  small business, 66
Business ethics, 532
Business organization, **9**
Business plan, **61**-4
  factors to address, 63
Buying
  marketing function, 274

C

CAD/CAM, **260**-62
CAM, 259
Canada
  trade liberalization, 492
Canada Business Service Centres, 505
Canada Customs and Revenue Agency, 56
Canada Employment and Immigration, 446
Canada Labour Code, 415, 416
Canada Pension Plan, 391
Canada Post, 479
Canada Small Business Financing Act, 66
Canada Transportation Act, **451**, 453

Canada - U.S. Auto Agreement, 488, **498**-99
Canada - U.S. Free Trade Agreement, (FTA) 442, **495**, 569
Canadian business system future of, 569
Canadian Center for Occupational Health and Safety, 394
Canadian Commercial Corporation (CCC), **507**
Canadian Cooperative Association, 98
Canadian economic development, 17-20
Canadian Federation of Labour, 412
Canadian foreign trade *see* trade
Canadian Human Rights Act (1977), **375**
Canadian Human Rights Commission, 375
Canadian Intellectual Property Office, 447
Canadian International Development Agency (CIDA), **507**
Canadian Labour Congress, 412, **413** structure, 414
Canadian labour market study, 381
Canadian labour movement, 409-13
Canadian Labour Union, 409
Canadian Pacific Inc., 95
Canadian Pacific Railway, 412, 440 mission, 119
Canadian Radio-Television and Telecommunications Commission CRTC **453**, 454, 452, 454
Canadian Transportation Agency, **451**
Capacity planning, **230**-1
Capital budget, 338 debt/equity, 343 factor of production, **6** operating, **64** raising for business, 65 start up, **64**
Capital account international trade, 510
Capital cost allowance, 326
Capital goods, **9, 281**
Capitalism, **12**-15 in Canada, 20-29 characteristics of, 20-21
Career development, **396**-7
Career plan

development of, 575
Carnet System, 508
Carson, Rachel, 538
Cartels, **490**
Cash, 329
Cash budget, 316, 339 example of, 317
Cash discounts, 318
Cash flow, 315
Cash reserves, **466**
Caveat emptor, 448
Centralization, **173** authority of, 173
Centralized buying, **301**
Certification, **417**
Chain of command, **171**
Changes economic, 567 lifestyle, 564-5, 566 population, 563 technological, 568
Channels of distribution, **298**-301
Charter of Rights and Freedoms, 571
Chief executive officer, **92**
CIM, 259
Classical theory of motivation, 187-8
Closed shop, **424**
Collateral, 319 accounts receivable, 320 inventories, 320 other property, 320
Collective agreement, **418** bargaining, **418**-19 adversarial nature of, 427
Combines Investigations Act, 448, **449**
Commission, **388**
Committees, **173**-5 productive meetings, 175
Common Market, **503**
Common shares *see* common stock
Common stock, **345**-6
Communication, 204-7 being understood, 208 listening skills required, 206 overcoming barriers to, 205-6 process, **204** using e-mail, 206-7
Communications small business, 58
Communism, **15**
Comparative advantage in trade, **484**
Compensating balance, 321
Compensation methods, 386-8 system, **384**

Compensatory method, **377**
Competition anti combines legislation, 448-9 characteristics of, 29 defined, **27** effective, **27** government regulation of, 448-50 monopolistic, 28 monopoly, 28 oligopoly, 28 perfect or pure, 27 responsible, **27** types, 27-8
Competition Act, **449**
Competition Tribunal, 449
Compulsory arbitration, **420, 428**
Computerized trading of stocks and bonds, 352
Computers and automation in production, 259 hardware, choice, 138 software, choice of, 138 use in business, 131-8 vendors, choice of, 138
Conceptual skills, **113**
Conciliation, **419**
Conciliation Act, 415
Conciliation and Labour Act, 415
Conglomerates, **95**
Congress of Industrial Organization, 412
Conservation energy, of, 544
Consignment, 318
Consumer goods, **9, 280** channels of distribution, 299-300
Consumer interest rates, **468**
Consumerism, 537
Consumer movement, **537**
Consumer price index (CPI), **470**
Consumer protection, 449-50
Consumers business' responsibility to, 537
Contingency Theory of Leadership, **199**
Control, **127** of foreign investment, 456 of public utilities, 454 of retailing, 449 techniques, 129-31 techniques, budgetary, 129-30 techniques, non-budgetary, 130-1 of transportation by government, 450-2

Control cycle, 129
Controlling, **111** financial operations, 322-40 management function, 111 money supply, 465-8
Control process, 127-9
Convenience goods, **280**
Convenience stores, 304
Cooperative defined, **97**
Cooperative College of Canada, 98
Cooperatives largest financial and non-financial, 98
Cooperative Union of Canada, 98
Coordination, **163**
Copyrights, 446
Corporate income taxes, **460**
Corporate raider, **93**
Corporate social responsibility, **531**
Corporation, **80** governance, 92 growth of, 93 organization of, 85, 88-93
Corporations advantages, 82 disadvantages, 83 horizontal integration, 95 largest in Canada, 94 private, **81** public, **82** types, 81 vertical integration, 95
Cost in break-even analysis, 290 pricing, **289**
Cost-of-living allowance COLA, **424**
Counselling Assistance to Small Enterprises (CASE), **447**
CPM chart, 257
Craft union, **409**
Credit unions, **97**-8
Critical path, **257**
Critical path method, 131, 256
Crown corporations, **454**, 455, 457
CRTC, 452, 454
Cultural barriers to trade, 489
Currency exchange, 510-13 exchange rates, **502** fluctuations Canadian dollar, 512-13, 514
Current account international trade, 510
Current assets, 324, 326
Current ratio, 331
Customary pricing, **291**

Custom production, **227**
Customs duties, **461**

D

Data, **132**
Data communications
   use of computer for, 137
Data management, 135
Debentures, **344**
Debt capital, **343**
Debt/equity ratio, 334
Debt financing
   compared to equity financing, 348
   small business, **65**
Debt ratio, 334
Decentralization, **173**
   authority of, 173
Deceptive advertising, 537
Decertification, **417**
Decision making, **115**
   management, 115
   non-programmed, **115**
   operating production, 237
   programmed decisions, **115**
Deficit spending, **20**
Defined benefit plan
   pension, 391
Defined contribution plan
   pension, 391
Delegation, **169**
   process, 168-71
Delphi method, 561
Demand
   and supply, 26
Demand forecasting, 237-8
Demand loans, 320
Democratic socialism, **15**
Demographics, 562-3
Demography, **562**
Demonstration, 297
Departmentation, **156**-63
   customer, 161
   functional, **158**
   process, 161
   product or geographic, **158**
   project and matrix, 159
   simple number, 161
   time, 161
Department of
   Communications, **452**
Department of Foreign Affairs
   and International Trade,
   485
Department stores, 303
Depreciation, 324
Depression
   as in business cycle, **11**
Deregulation, **452**
   airlines, 452
   of trucking, 452
Developing countries

business responsibility for,
   549
Differential piece rate system,
   188
Direct investment, **518**
Direct labour budget, 338
Discount stores, 304
Discrimination
   employment, 546
Dispute resolution, 493
Distribution
   physical, 305
Distribution planning, **245**-6
Dividend tax credit, 347
Dues check-off, **424**
Dumping, **491**
Duty Drawback Program, 508

E

Ecology, **539**
Economic barriers to trade,
   489
Economic changes, 567
Economic development
   government involvement,
   440-41
Economic development incentives
   federal, 442-5
Economic forecast, **11**
Economic management, **21**
Economics
   defined, **10**
Economic stability, 464
Economic system, **11**-15
   capitalism, 12-15
   socialism, 12-16
   variation of, 12
Economies of scale, **225**
Education
   business responsibility for,
   546
Effectiveness
   defined, **23**
Efficiency
   defined, **23**
Electronic shopping, 304
E-mail, **139**, 206-7
   for recruitment of
      employees, 374
Embargo, **491**
Employee
   benefits, **390**-4
      business' responsibility
         to, 536
   evaluation, 396
   cost of to business, 393,
      394
   employment insurance,
      392
   insurance plans, 391
   pension plans, 391

selection, 375
   process, 376-9
   stock ownership plans,
      389-90
   training, 381-4
      on-the-job, 382
      on-the-job, vestibule, 383
      supervisory, 384
Employer's associations, **423**
Employment
   discrimination, 375, 546
   interview, 378
   interview, conduct, 380
   insurance, **391**
   orientation, 379, 381
   reference checks, 378
   selection process, 377 - 379
   termination, 397-8
   testing, 378
Energy
   Conservation, 544
Entrepreneur
   factor of production, 7
Environmental
   audit, **549**, 551
   pollution, 538
Environmental Protection and
   Enhancement Act, 539
Equal pay for equal work, **385**
Equal pay for work of equal
   value, **385**
Equilibrium point, **26**
Equity
   capital, **343**
   financing
   small business, **64**
Ergonomics, **393**
Estate taxes, **460**
Esteem or ego needs, **190**
Ethical issues, **545**, 546
Ethics, **532**
   business, **532**
   study of, 547
European Community, 492
European Economic
   Community (EEC),
   503-4
European Free Trade
   Association (EFTA), **503**
European Union (EU), **504**
Excise taxes, **461**
Expense goods, **281**
Export Development
   Corporation (EDC), **507**
Export Financing Services,
   508
Exports, **484**
   Canada, 486-8
External auditing, 130
Extraction
   production process, 230
Extrinsic rewards, **209**, 210

F

Fabrication
   production process, **230**
Facility layout, 234
Factoring, 321
Factor of production, 5-7
Factory overhead budget, 338
Featherbedding, **425**
Federal Business Development
   Bank (FBDB), 446
Federal government deficits,
   470
Federal industrial
   development
   incentives, 442-44
Fiedler, Fred, 199, 201, 202
Fiedler's contingency theory of
   leadership, 199
Finance companies, 321-2
Financial
   accounting, 322
   analysis, 330-36
   budget, 339
   forecasting, 336
      flow in economy, 8
   leverage, **348**
   ratios, 334-5
   operations
      control of, 322-40
   securities
      see Securities,
   solvency, 314
   statements, 322-30
      pro-forma, 339
Financing, 314
   borrowing of funds, 316-22
   chartered banks, 319
   debt, 64
   department, 314
   equity, 64
   Federal government, 322
   chartered banks, 319
   finance companies, 321
   investors, 322
   long-term, 342-51
   marketing function, 274
   of new business, 96
   small business, 57
   small business, 41
   sources of, 65-6
Fiscal
   policy, **461**, 464
   program, **461**
Fixed
   assets, 324
   capital, 315
   costs, 290, 340
Flexible pricing, **291**
Floating currencies, **502**
Forecasting
   financial, 336
   sales, 336-8
Foreign control, 518
Foreign investment

abroad, 522
advantages, 520
Canada, 518-23
disadvantages, 521
problems for Canada, 521
Foreign Investment Review
Agency, 456
Foreign
licensing, **515**
marketing, **515**
ownership, **520**
Formal authority, 114
Formal organization
defined, 150
Form of business ownership,
75-84
choosing a form of, 96-7
Form utility, **273**
Forward buying, **241**
Franchise, **50**
Franchisee, **50**
Franchiser, **50**
Franchising, 50-4
advantages, 51
disadvantages, 51
Freedom
of choice, 20
of competition, 21
from government
interference, 21
Free trade
debate, 496
Friedman, Milton, 534
Functional authority, **167**
Functional departmentation,
158
Functions of management,
109-111
Future
prediction of, 560-1

G

Gantt chart, **130**, 251
General Agreement on Tariffs
and Trade GATT, 442,
483, 492, 527
General Motors, 534
General purpose machines,
234
General stores, 303
General Theory of
Employment, Interest
and Money, 19
Geographic departmentation,
158
Geographic selectivity
for advertising media, **294**
Gift taxes, 460
Goals, **118**
how to achieve, 120-23
Going-rate pricing, **291**

Goods
capital, 9, 281
Consumer, 280
consumer, 9, 280
expense, 281
Industrial, 281
shopping, 280
specialty, 280
Good and Services tax, **460**
Goods and Services tax, 462
Government
control of business, 447-58
debt, 470-72, 473
financing of, 458-61,
469-72
growth, 469, 469-76
industrial strategy, 475
involvement in economic
development, 440
ownership, 454-5
programs
regulation of small busi-
ness, 42
voluntary restraints, 548
regulation, 472-4
of business, 450
role in economic develop-
ment, 474-6
Great Depression, **17**
Great depression, 464, 469
Greenpeace Foundation, 181
Grievances, **421**
Gross
domestic product (GDP), **4**
national income (GNI), **4**
national product (GNP), **4**
profit, 327
profit margin ratio, 334

H

Hand-to-mouth buying, **241**
Harassment, 376
Hawthorne effect, **188**
Health and Safety, 394-5
Hersey, Paul, 201
Hierarchy of objectives, 121
Hiring
defensively, 377
Home
business, 54-60, **55**
shopping, 304
Horizontal integration, **95**
Hostile takeover, **93**
Hours of work, 424
Human resource
acquiring, 370, 373, 374
planning, 367-8
planning process, 368
recruiting, 373-5

Human Resource
Development Canada
(HRDC), 373, 415
Human resource
function, 365-7
management, **365**
Human rights legislation,
375-6
Human skills, **112**
Hygiene factors, **192**
Herzberg's theory of moti-
vation, 192

I

IBM, 534
Import quotas, **491**
Imports, **484**
Canada, 486-8
Income statement, 324, 327
comparative analysis, 334
example, 328
Income taxes, **459**, 462
Incorporation
how to, 84-5
name search, 85
requirements for, 88
Industrial Accident Prevention
Association, 395
Industrial Development Bank,
446
Industrial Disputes
Investigations Act, 415
Industrial
designs, 446
goods, **281**
channels of distribution,
300-1
parks, **232**
strategy, **475**
union, **409**
Industry Canada, **444**
Inflation
in Canada, 20
defined, **21**
Influence, **164**
Informal organization, 151
Information, **132**
gathering, marketing
function, 274
processing, 132
sharing
with unions, 429-30
system
management, 131
Injunction, **423**
Insider trading, 536
Insolvency, **77**
Installations, 281
Intellectual property, 493
Interest, **343**
Interest rates

consumer, 468
prime, 468
Internal auditing, 130
International Finance, 509-13
International Monetary Fund
(IMF), **501**
and world bank, 506
International trade
Agreements, 492-505
importance of, 483
International union, **413**
International trade
barriers, 488-91
Internet, **137**, 139
for recruitment of
employees, 374
stock trading, 354
using for job search, 583
Interview
dress tips, 582
management, Job leads
job leads, 581
Intranets, **134**
systems, 211
Intrinsic rewards, **209**
Inventory
carrying costs, **242**
control methods, 244
control system, 241-44
economic order quantity,
242-3
management, **238**-44
just in time, 250
use of computer for, 136
ordering cost, 242
physical count, 244
records file, **249**
turnover ratios, 332-3
Investing in stocks and bonds
reasons for, 355
Investment Canada, **456**
ISO standard, 128
Issued shares, **345**

J

Job
analysis, **368**
description, **369**, 371
results oriented, **369**-70
design, **236**
maintenance, 582
performance, 210
satisfaction, **193**
and Herzberg, 193
intrinsic, extrinsic rewards,
209
search management, 581
search preparation, 575
search process, 575
security
union contract, 425

shop, **227**
shop scheduling
production, 251
specification, **368**
example, 372
training programs
federal and provincial, 382
Just in time inventory management, 250

K

Keynes, John Maynard, **19**
Knights of Labour, 412

L

Labeling, **288**
Labour
aims of, 409
as factor of production, 6
disputes in Canada, 428
Labour Canada, 446
Labour, **6**
council, **413**
legislation
federal, provincial, 415-16
management
relations,427-9
relations board, **416**
union, 409
Laissez-faire, **14**
Land
as factor of production, **6**
Lans
computers, 133
Laws, 532
of society, **532**
Layoff, **397**
Leaders
criteria for choosing, 202-3
Leadership, **196**-204
continuum theory of, **198**
Fiedler's contingency theory, 199-200
managerial grid theory, 196-7
matching style to situation, 201
situational theory, 200-1
traits, **196**
visionary, 202
Leading, **110**
management function, 110
Lead time, **242**
Legal barriers to trade, 489
Letters Patent
incorporation method, **84**
Liabilities, 324
current, 326

long-term, 327
Liability
limited, 77, **82**
unlimited, 77
Lifestyle changes, **564**-5, 566
Lifestyle research, **566**
Limited liability, 82, 96
Line authority, **165**
Line of credit, 320
Line and staff
authority, **228**
organization, **167**
Liquidity ratios, 331-2
Load chart, **251**
Loading
production, **251**
Local union, **413**
Lockout, **423**
Long range planning, **117**
Low income cut off (LICO), 3

M

Machinery and equipment
plant layout requirements, 234
Mail order, 304
Mainframe computers, **133**
Maintenance
for production, 256
Make-or-buy decisions, **253**
Management, **108**
accounting, 323
aims of in labour relations, 408
by objectives, **211**-14
by objectives, benefits, problems, 213
decision making, 115
development, **383**
functions, **109**-111
hierarchy, **111**-12
human resources, 365
information system (MIS), **131**
interview by job seeker, 581
importance, 108-9
Japanese style, 203-4
levels, 111
middle, 112
operating or supervisory, **112**
philosophy, **548**, 549
process, 109
project in production, 256
roles, 108, 114
skills, 41, 112-13
small business, 96
small business, 41, 44-6
top, 112
Manager
future requirements, 570

Managerial grid, **197**
Manufacturer's agents, **301**
Manufacturing automation
protocol, **262**
Manufacturing budget, 338
Market
competition, and, 25
economy, 21
growth stage, 285
introductory stage, 284
maturity stage, 285
sales decline stage, 285
segmentation, **277**
Marketing, **273**
concept, 275
corporate securities, 350
four P's, 277, 278
functions, 273-4
importance of, 273
internet, use for, 294, 296
mix, **277**
and pricing, 288-91
and promotions, 292-8
Quebec market, 282-3
research, 275-6
small business, 44
strategy, 275-8
utilities, 273
Marketing era, **275**
Markets
consideration in plant
location, 231
consumer, 278-80
industrial, 278, 281
Market system, **25**
Mark-up pricing, **289**
Marxism-Leninism, **15**
Maslow, Abraham, 189-92
Mass
advertising, 292
production, **225**
Master
operating budget, 339
schedule, **248**
Material requirements
planning, **248**
Matrix
departmentation, 159
structure, **161**
Maturity date, **343**
Mayo, Elton, 188
MBO, 211-13
benefits of using, 213
problems with process, 213
process, 212
Merchandise trade balance, **510**
Mechanization, **226**
Mediation, **419**
Memorandum of association, 86
Mercedes-Benz, 293
Merger, **93**, 536
Merit, **383**

Use of in promotion, 397
Methods analysis, **237**
Microcomputers, 133
Microsoft Corporation, 133
Middle management, **112**
Minicomputers, **133**
Mintzberg, Henry, 114
Mission
organization, 119
Mitbestimmung, **428**
Mixed economy, **20**
Model building
future forecasting, 561
Monetary policy, **464**
Monopolistic competition, **28**
Monopoly, **28**
Monopsony, **28**
Moral code, **532**
Morale, **207**-11
factors of, 209
job satisfaction and, 209
Morals, 532
Motion studies, **237**
Motivation, **187**
classical theory of, **187**-8
Herzberg and Maslow
compared, 192
Herzberg's theory, 192-3
human relations theory, 188
Maslow's need hierarchy, 189-90
McGregor's theory X and Y, 194-6
money, and, 189, 193, 195
Motivators, **193**
Herzberg's theory of
motivation, 193
Motor Vehicle Transport Act, 452
Multinational Corporation
(MNC), 513-23
advantages, 516
characteristics, **515**
domestic vs international
corporate planning, 516
disadvantages, 516
evolution of, 515
management of, 515
Multinational trade communities, 502-5, 505
Multiple hurdles method, **377**

N

Nader, Ralph, 537
NAFTA
see North American Free
Trade Agreement
National Employment
Service, **392**
National Policy
objectives, **16**-17

National Transportation Act, 451
National Union, **413**
Natural resource development incentive, 444
Needs
Maslow's need hierarchy, 189-90
Net
profit, 328
profit margin ratio, 335
public debt, **470**
New Deal, **18**
New Democratic Party, 30
Non-budgetary methods of control, 130
Non-profit organization, **9**
Non-tariff barriers, **442**
North American Free Trade Agreement (NAFTA), 426, 442, **495**-7, 499, 569
key facts, 498
and Mexico, 495
Notice of office, 87

O

Objectives, **120**
hierarchy of, 121
Oligopoly, **28**
On-the-job training, **382**
Open
book credit, 318
market operations, **467**
shop, 424
Open skies agreement, **452**
Operating
expenditures budget, 338
management, 112
responsibility, **171**
Operations
management, 237
research, 226
Organization, **150**
charts, **150**, 152-3
formal, **150**
functional, 169
goals and objectives, 118
informal, **151**
line, 166
line and staff, 168
mission, **119**
purpose, **118**
virtual type, 177
Organizational
structure, **154**-5
building, 155
evolution of, 176
Organizing, **110**
function of management, 156

importance of, 151
management function, 110
and planning, 153-4
process, 156-7
Ouchi, William J., 203
Overhead, 340
Over-the-counter market, **353**-4
Ownership utility, **273**

P

Pacific Rim
trade, 501
Packaging, **287**
Partnerships
advantages, 79
agreement, importance of, 80
defined, **78**
disadvantages, 79-80
formation of, 78
kinds, 78
Parts, 281
Patents, 446
Path-goal theory of leadership, **200**
Pay equity, 385
in Ontario, Quebec, 386
Penetration pricing
pricing strategy, **289**
People-oriented leader, **196**
Per capita GNP, **4**
Perfect competition, **27**
Performance evaluation, **395**
Periodic inventory control, **244**
Perpetual inventory control, **244**
Personal
inspection, **130**
selling, 292, **296**-7
sales process, 297
Personnel planning, 368
Physical
distribution, **305**
inventory count, 244
Physiological needs, **189**
Picketing, **422**
Piecework incentive, **387**
Pirating
employees, 374
Place, 278
Place utility, **273**
Planning, **110**
and controlling, 127-31
elements of, 118-123
flexibility of, 116
for distribution, 245
and management, 115
management function, 110
need for, 116

and organizing, 153-4
production department, 229, 230-3
process, 123-7
strategic, 123-4
Plans
action, 126
policy, 122
procedure, 122
profit, 126
rules, 122
single-use, 120, 122-3
budget, 123
program, 122
project, 122
standing, 120, 123
strategic, 123
types, 117
Plant layout, **234**, 235
retail firms, 236
service firms, 236
types, 234
Plant location, 231-3
community factors, 231
industrial parks, 232-3
regional factors, 231-2
site-related factors, 231
Point-of-purchase advertising, **297**
Poison pill, **94**
Policy, **122**
Political barriers to trade, 490
Pollution
types, 544
Population changes, 563-4
Portfolio investment, **518**
Power, **164**
coercive, **164**
expert, **164**
legitimate, **164**
referent, **164**
reward, **164**
Power Corporation of Canada, 95
Preferred shares, **347**-8
Presentation
sales process, 297
Presentations
use of computer for, 136
President, **93**
Prevailing market prices, **291**
Prevailing wages, 387
Price, 278
Pricing
approaches, 289-91
based on
break-even analysis, 290
cost, 289
mark-up, 289
customary, 291
flexible, 291
going-rate, 291
list, 291
prevailing market, 291

product, 288-91
psychological, 291
strategies, 288-9
suggested, 291
Primary boycott, 423
Primary stakeholders, 535
Prime rate, **468**
Principal, **343**
Principal trading countries with Canada, 486
Private
placement, **351**
placement agencies, 374
property, 20
Privatization, **457**
Procedure, **122**
Process
controlling, 127-9
Process layout, **234**
Product, 278
brand, branding, 286-7
creation of, 283-8
development, **284**
distribution, 298-304
labeling, 288
life cycles, **284**-5
effect on firm, 285-6
line, **283**
mix, **283**
packaging, 287
planning in marketing, **283**-4
pricing, 288-91
safety, 537
Product departmentation, 158
Production, **224**
computer use in, 257-63
custom, 226
definition, 224, **5**
factors of, 5, 6-7
function, 224
loading, 251
machinery and equipment, 234, 236
maintenance, 256
mass, 225
operating decisions, 237-56
organization, 227-9
planning, 229
planning and control, 246-7
processes, **229**-30
scheduling, 249-51
sequencing, 251
and standard of living, 4
system, 224
Production
marketing era, 275
planning, 256-7
aggregate, 247-8
subsidies, 442
Productivity
and morale, 209
sharing, **388**

Product layout, 234
Product life cycle stages,
    284-5
Profit
    capital formation, and, 23
    and capitalism, 22-25
    contribution to society, as,
        23
    defined, **22**
    gross, 327
    importance of, 22
    incentive, as, 22
    maximization of, 25
    measure of effectiveness and
        efficiency, 23
    net, 328
    return to investors, as, 23
    view of by individuals, 24
Profitability ratio, 334
Profit
    plan, **126**
    sharing, **388**
    sharing plans
    how to set up, 389
Pro-forma financial
    statements, 339
Program, **122**
Program evaluation and
    review technique
    (PERT), **131**, 256
Program for Export Market
    Development (PEMD),
    508
Project, **122**
Project departmentation, 159
    management, **256**-7
    schedule example, **256**
    use of computer for, 136
    network, schedule, 256
Promissory notes, 318
Promotion, 278, **292**-8, 396
Promotional
    mix, **292**
Promotional Projects Program
    (PPP), 508
Property taxes, **460**
Prospectus, **89**
Provincial industrial incentive
    programs, 443
Proxy, **89**
Psychological pricing, **291**
Public issues, 535
Publicity, 292, **298**
Public utilities
    control of by government,
    454
Purchasing, **253**-4
Purchasing department, 242

Q

Qualitative selectivity
    for advertising media, **294**
Quality control, **254**-5
Quantity restrictions, **442**
Quick (acid test) ratio, 332

R

Rand formula, **424**
Ratification, **419**
Ratio analysis, **130**, 331-5
Raw materials, 281
    consideration in plant
        location, 231
Raw materials budget, 338
Recession
    as in business cycle, **10**
Recruiting, **373**
    using e-mail, 374
    web sites, 374
Recruitment
    media advertising, 374
Recycling, **541**
Redesigning work, **211**
Registered bond, **343**
Registration system
    incorporation method, **84**
Regulatory taxes, **461**
Remission of Duty Program,
    508
Reorder point, **242**
Responsibility
    operating, 171
    ultimate, 171
Resume, 579, 580
Retailers, **301**-4
    centralized buying, 301
    chain stores, 301, 302
    franchises, 303
    sales in Canada, 1999, 302
    types, 303-4
Retail franchises, **303**
Retailing
    changing concepts, 304
    control of by government,
        449-50
Retained earnings, 327
Retirement, **397**
    mandatory, 376
Return on investment, 335
Revenue Canada, 458
Revenue taxes, **459**-60
Risk-taking
    marketing function, 274
Robots, **262**
    in production, 259, 262-3
Rotating strike, **422**
Rule, **122**

S

Safety
    needs, **190**
    stock, **238**
Salary, **387**
Sales
    management, 297
Sales forecast
    example, 240
Sales-oriented marketing era,
    275
Sales
    promotion, 292, **297**-8
    taxes, **460**
Scenario
    future forecasting, 561
Schedule chart, **251**
Scheduling, **249**-52
Scientific management, **187**
Scrambled merchandising,
    304
Seat-of-the-pants technique
    future forecasting, 561
Secondary
    boycott, 423
    stakeholders, 535
Secretary
    of the board, **93**
Secured loan, 319
Securities
    how to choose for
        financing, 348-50
    marketing of, 350,
    markets, 351-4
Securities underwriter, **350**
Self-actualization needs, **190**
Selling
    marketing function, 274
Seniority, **396**
Separation
    from employer, **397**
Sequencing, **251**
Services trade balance, **510**
    international payments,
    510
Service businesses, **225**
Services, 281
Shareholders
    business' responsibility to,
    535
    common, **89**
Shareholders' equity, 324, 327
Shopping goods, **280**
Short
    range plans, 117
    term borrowing, 316-22
    term financing, 316
Single-use plans, **120**
Situational theory of leader-
    ship, **200**-1
Skills
    conceptual, 113
    human, 112

listening, 206
    management, 112-13
    technical, 112
Skimming the market
    pricing strategy, **288**
Small business, **39**
    avoiding failure, 46
    Buying a business, 48-50
    in Canada 38-41
    defined, 38-41
    failure, reasons for, 43
    failures, 40
    financing, 41, 64
    franchising, 50-4
    going into business, 46-66
    home business
    (see home business)
    insurance and security, 59
    problems of owners, 41-3
    strategic planning, 124
    successful operation, 44-6
Small Business Loans Act, 65
Social
    audit, **549**, 551
    barriers to trade, 489
Socialism, 12-15, **14**
Social
    issues, **535**
    needs, **190**
responsibility, 531
    and business, 533-5
    measuring, 551
Sole proprietorship
    advantages, 76
    defined, **75**
    disadvantages, 77
Span of control, **171**-3
Special Drawing Rights
    (SDRs), **503**
Special purpose machines,
    234
Specialty
    advertising, **297**
    goods, **280**
    stores, 304
Stability
    economic, **21**
Staffing
    management function, **110**
Stakeholders, **535**
    primary, secondary, **535**
Standardization, **226**
    marketing function, 274
Standard of living
    and production, **4**
    raising, 7
Stand-by fee, 321
Standing plans, **120**
Statement of changes in finan-
    cial position, 324,
    329-30
Statistical analysis
    use of computer for, 136
Statistics Canada, 446

Stock
  exchange, **352**
  broker, **352**
  market, 351-4
  trading
    on internet, 354
Storing
  marketing function, 274
Strategic
  management, 126
  planning, **117**, **123**-4
  small business, 124
Strategy, **120**
Strike, 421, **422**
  effectiveness of, 428
  government employees, 435
Suggested/list pricing, **291**
Supermarkets, 304
Suppliers
  purchasing for production,
    253
Supplies, 281
Supply
  and demand, 26
Sustainable development, **541**
Sustainable scenario, 561
Sympathy strike, **422**
Synthetic
  production process, 230

T

Tactical plans, **117**
Takeover, 536
Target market, **277**
Tariff, **441**, 461, 493
  barrier to trade, 441, **491**
Task-oriented leader, **196**
Taxation
  types of taxes, 458-61
Taxes
  corporate, 460
  estate, gift, 460
  goods and services, 460
  income, 459
  property, 460
  revenue, 459-60
  sales, 460
  and small business, 42
  value-added, 460
Tax freedom day, 458
Tax incentives, 464
Taylor, Frederick W, 188
Teamsters, 413
Technical skills, **112**

Technological changes, 568
Technology
  factor of production, **6**
Temporary adjustment assis-
    tance, **443**
Tender offer, **93**
Theory X and Theory Y, **194**
  McGregor's motivation
    theory, 194-6
Theory Z, **203**
  Japanese leadership style,
    203
Time
  draft, 318
  management, 135
  series analysis, 238
  study, **237**
  utility, **273**
Toffler, Alvin, 560
Top management, **112**
Toronto Dominion Bank, 98
Toronto Stock Exchange, 95
Toronto Trades Assembly, 409
Total quality management,
    128
Trade
  absolute, comparative ad-
    vantage, 484
  balance of, 509
  balance of payments, 510
  Canadian trade with other
    countries, 484-6
  commissioners, **505**
  commodity grouping, 485
Trade acceptance, 318
Trade barriers
  interprovincial, 503
Trade Commissioner Service
    (TCS), 508
Trade credit, 316, 318
  types, 318-19
Trade drafts, 318
Trademarks, 446
Trade offices
  regional, 508
Trade restrictions, 491
Trade shows, **298**
Trades and Labour Congress
    of Canada, 415
Trade Union Act, 415
Trading on the equity, 348
Transfer, **397**
Transportation
  control of by government,
    450-2
Transporting
  marketing function, 274

Treasurer, **93**
Trend analysis
  future forecasting, 561

U

Ultimate responsibility, **171**
Undercapitalization, **66**
Union, 409
  arbitration, 420
  boycott, 423
  collective bargaining,
    417-19
  conciliation, 419
  items for bargaining, 418
  ratification, 419
  craft, 409
  government employees and
    strike, 435
  grievance, 421
  industrial, 409
  international, 413
  local, 413
  mediation, 419
  membership distribution in
    industry, 410
  membership of selected
    unions, 410
  membership, 426
  movement, history, 409-13
  national, 413
  picketing, 422
  process, 416-21
  security, 423-4
  shop, **424**
  strike, 421, 422
Unions
  business relations with, 547
Union shop with preferential
    hiring, 424
United Auto Workers, 413
Universal product code, **244**
Unlimited liability, **77**
Utility
  marketing, **273**

V

Value added tax, **460**
Value analysis, **253**
Variable costs, 290, **340**
Vending machines, 304
Venture capitalists, **65**

Vertical integration, **95**
Vestibule training, **383**
Video disk player, 279-80,
    309
Virtual organization, 177
Visionary leadership, 202
Voluntary arbitration, **420**
Voluntary restraints
  acceptance of by business,
    548

W

Wage legislation, 387
Wages, **387**
  union negotiations, 424
Wage and Salary
    Administration, 384-94
Wages and salaries
  establishing levels, 384-5
War Measures Act, 415
Warranties
  for consumer products, 537
Western Economic
    Diversification, 443
Wheel of retailing, **304**
Whistle blowing, 170
White knight, **94**
Wholesalers, **300**-1
  merchant, **301**
Wide area networks, 134
Wildcat strike, **422**
Winnipeg general strike, 413
Word processing, 135
Workers' Compensation
    Board, 395
Working capital, 315
Work measurement, **237**
Workplace Hazardous
    Materials Information
    System, 395
Work system design, **236**
Work-to-rule, **422**
World Bank, 501
  and International
    Moneatary Fund, 506
World Trade Organization
    (WTO), 483, 493-4
World Wide Web, **139**

Photo Credits

Chapter 1
Page 3, SIPA Press/Pono Press; page 7, Gamma/Pono Press; page 7, Prentice Hall Archives; page 18, courtesy of The Scott Mission; page 25, Marco Shark.

Chapter 2
Pages 50 and 55, Bob Carroll.

Chapter 3
Page 76, Dick Hemingway.

Chapter 4
Page 111, PhotoDisc, page 132, Superstock; page 134, Superstock.

Chapter 5
Page 157, Al Harvey/The Slide Farm; page 174, PhotoDisc.

Chapter 6
Page 195, PhotoDisc.

Chapter 7
Page 227, Chrysler Corporation; page 233, courtesy of the city of Woodstock; pages 242 and 254, Upjohn Company of Canada; page 261, Stone.

Chapter 8
Page 275, PhotoDisc; page 279, The Canadian Press/AP Photo/Shizuo Kambayashi; page 293, courtesy of Microcell Solutions Inc.; page 298, The Canadian Press/AP Photo/Jerry Henkel; page 303, Bob Carroll.

Chapter 9
Page 354, Superstock.

Chapter 10
Page 382, Al Harvey/The Slide Farm.

Chapter 11
Page 422, The Canadian Press/Tannis Toohey.

Chapter 12
Page 447, Business Development Bank of Canada; page 465, Bank of Canada.

Chapter 13
Page 490, courtesy of Canadian Ports Corporation; page 501, courtesy of World Bank/Michele Iannacci; page 517, The Canadian Press.

Chapter 14
Page 540, Environment Canada.

Chapter 15
Page 566, Superstock; page 567, PhotoDisc; page 571, Stone; page 574, Superstock.